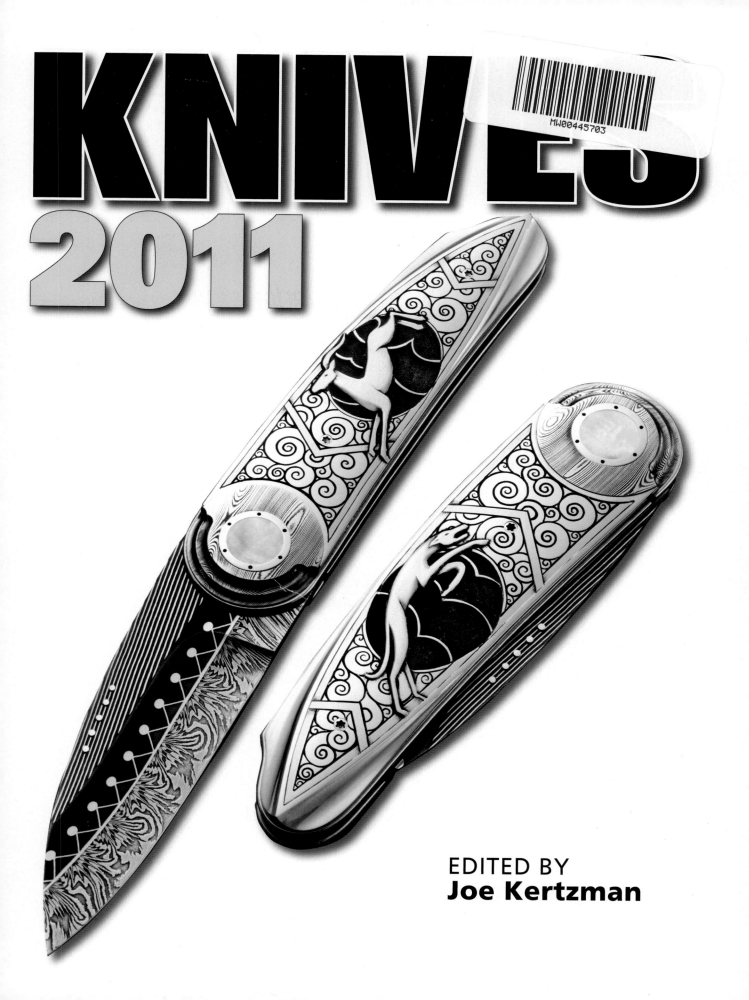

KNIVES
2011

EDITED BY
Joe Kertzman

MW00445703

Copyright ©2010 F+W Media, Inc.

All rights reserved. No portion of this publication may be reproduced or transmitted in any form or by any means, electronic or mechanical, including photocopy, recording, or any information storage and retrieval system, without permission in writing from the publisher, except by a reviewer who may quote brief passages in a critical article or review to be printed in a magazine or newspaper, or electronically transmitted on radio, television, or the Internet.

Published by

Krause Publications, a division of F+W Media, Inc.
700 East State Street • Iola, WI 54990-0001
715-445-2214 • 888-457-2873
www.krausebooks.com

To order books or other products call toll-free 1-800-258-0929
or visit us online at www.krausebooks.com or www.Shop.Collect.com

Cover photography by Kris Kandler

ISSN: 0277-0725

ISBN-13: 978-1-4402-1113-3
ISBN-10: 1-4402-1113-2

Cover Design by Kara Grundman
Designed by Kara Grundman
Edited by Corrina Peterson

Printed in the United States of America

Dedication and Acknowledgments

He's the point man in charge of sending out nomination forms to living BLADE Magazine Cutlery Hall-Of-Fame® members each year so they can nominate potential Hall-Of-Famers, and then he mails and collects ballots, tallying up the votes. Yet he is not a Hall-Of-Fame member. He deserves to be, but he'd be embarrassed by that.

Steve Shackleford began his career as a newspaper sports reporter after serving his country. To this day, he is a sports nut, lives and breathes Tennessee Volunteers football and basketball, can remember games from before most *Knives* readers were born and, rumor has it, bleeds bright orange when he accidentally cuts himself with his pocketknife. He was hired on as Associate Editor for *BLADE Magazine* nearly three decades ago, taking over complete editorial reigns after his boss, close friend and then-publisher, J. Bruce Voyles, sold the World's Number One Knife Publication to Krause Publications in the early 1990s.

Steve has been lead Editor of *BLADE* ever since. His editing skills are unmatched, his copy clean, attention to detail focused, and writing fun and conversational. Steve is as likeable when he writes as he is in person.

It's more than that, though. Steve knows and loves his subject. As the knife industry has embraced the man who, along with his wife, Susan, calls McDonald, Tennessee, home, Steve has learned to love the knife industry.

Steve also has a solid work ethic, gets behind knife causes, supports the efforts of Knife Rights, the American Knife & Tool Institute and other knife advocacy groups, and sheds a positive, concise, real and bright light on knives. His passion is the one thing that shows through it all. Though I only see Steve at the occasional knife show, usually the BLADE Show and SHOT Show, I work with him daily, communicating through email and over the phone. He taught me the ropes, guided me through knife terminology, supported me, accepted all my quirks, laughed alongside me, beat my brow when needed, raised an eyebrow when my humor was too weird, and put up with way too much nonsensical chatter.

Through it all, Steve never stopped teaching me about knives, about people, about life. He gave me historical perspective and made me aware of modern developments, helping me hone my editorial skills as he polished his. I treasure our friendship and dedicate this book, *Knives 2011*, to the best, nicest and funniest knife editor on the planet. Thanks, Steve.

Joe Kertzman

On the Cover

A sub-hilt fighter, dagger and a tactical folder embody dissimilar styles of knives, yet combine on the cover like a themed work of art. The lines have it, and without ever touching, they wrap around each other like the arms of a mother. At far left is the integral sub-hilt fighter, a collaborative effort between Burt Foster and David Broadwell. Based on Broadwell's own design, the knife features a 52100-and-416 laminated steel blade with a smoky temper line, a carved and textured damascus hilt and sub-hilt, and an exhibition Koa wood handle, also carved by Foster. The dagger in the middle, by none other than Bertie Rietveld, parades a pointed stainless steel pommel and S-shaped guard, each inlaid with 24k gold, anodized-titanium ferrules, a five-bar "Turkish-twist" damascus blade and an exhibition-grade lapis lazuli grip. A Stanhope lens with the maker's logo—a Rietveld trademark—lies at the base of the blade. Look to the right and there one finds Jeremy Marsh's "Assassin" locking-liner folder boasting a modified re-curved hawk-bill blade of CPM S30V stainless steel, a titanium frame and liners, the latter anodized blue, and a carbon fiber handle. So the question remains, of the three, which one has the hottest lines?

Contents

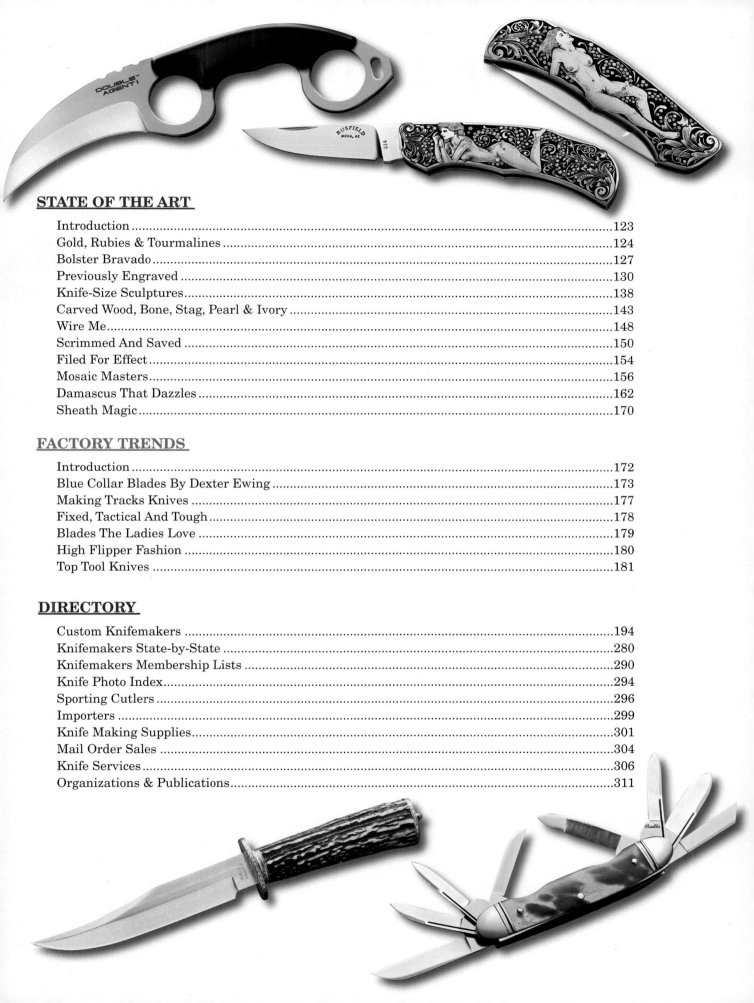

STATE OF THE ART

FACTORY TRENDS

DIRECTORY

Introduction

Trends in movies include stop movement animation, computer generated special effects, live action, and too often, little character or story development. Modeling and fashion trends involve Botox injections, facelifts, tummy tucks, breast enhancements and wrinkle removal. Musical movements integrate electronica, techno beat, breakbeat, down tempo, hip-hop, rap, and very few instruments anywhere in the "mix." How much "reality" TV have you watched lately?

Fake, fake, fake and more fake.

Such developments make knifemakers and knives seem all that much more real. Technical advancements in knives are palpable, measurable and dimensionally sound. Some knives are sculpted to fit the hand, others guarded to protect it. Many modern pieces are tactical or built for soldiers protecting our land, country, people and way of life. Hunters take blade bellies to breast briskets, and the wind whistles through the tree branches as they competently complete their work.

Mammoth molars make for nice grips. Coral is a colorful addition, and gold, rubies and tourmalines look so sexy inlaid into bolsters, handles, guards, spacers and spines. File work is always a fan favorite, and some knives have the ability to transport you across the globe to different lands, cultures, people and places. Damascus dazzles while mosaic damascus provides picture-perfect alloy alignment.

Like thoroughbred racehorses, the lineage of many knives and swords can be traced back to their roots, through time and history to original makers and methods of making. The country of origin is evident in some patterns, and obscure or hidden in others. There is exotic allure and mystery. Some are sinister, their bloody backgrounds barely hidden.

Hands have been laid on these knives, buffing cloths on blades, sanding compound, elbow grease, grinding wheels and belts. They've all touched the cold steel. Oil is applied. Their edges softened, corners rounded and points sharpened. Their tangs are tapered, pommels smoothed and grips molded. They've been worked, tested and hardened. The blades are quenched, polished and finished. They are meant for hard use.

Some say there is little new in knives, nothing, in fact, that can be called revolutionary. It's all been done. To them the time has passed. The past is the proudest, and the future unlikely, or at least uneventful. Nothing could be further from the truth. The evolution of knives is as evident as body styles in cars. Like autos, the knives have become sleeker, more aerodynamic, efficient and fast.

Automobiles, it seems, are also as real, palpable and penetrable as bladed objects. Many comparisons can be made, from safety in cars and knives, to efficiency of the cut and corner, to the lines, curves and body styles. Cars are mechanical creations much like knives are physical renderings. As enthusiasts often note, knives are aesthetic tools and functional art.

It's nice to live in the real world. No reality television shows here, no actors or sets, just knife junkies, basement shops, dirty machines, clean surfaces, hard work and American ingenuity. Knives may be getting facelifts, but there are no Botox injections, breastplate enhancements, electronic gadgetry or special effects. What you see is what you get, and what a refreshing change of pace that is.

From pages 8 to 56, *Knives 2011* readers are treated to feature stories covering one of the best wedges in the business, friction forging, "Swordplay Renaissance Style," the latest in cleaver offerings, "Scrimshaw That Drives Men Crazy" and villagers' blade art. Learn how one knife collector—Paul Lansingh—is giving back to the world of knives. Find out the answer to the question, "Why Do We Love Knives?" Follow author James Ayres and his wife, Mary Lou, on their quest to find carbon steel along cobblestone streets. In the "Factory Trends" section of the book, be treated to the newest in "Blue Collar Blades."

In between enjoy the latest Trends and State Of The Art in knives. It's a trip worth having, in the real world, among ordinary folks, current time and space. The pages are palpable, the text worth reading and the pictures worth a thousand words and more. Each bladed creation is a work of art in its own right, a credit to its maker and a far cry from the unrealities of the rest of the whacky world.

Joe Kertzman

2011 WOODEN SWORD AWARD

This is an extremely rich knife, one that has everything. Born into the privileged class of Bob Loveless-style boot dirks, the S.R. Johnson art knife is also integrally stunning. A close look at the mother-of-pearl handle inlays reveals impeccable fit, including thin red liners separating nacre from steel. Barry Lee Hands performed delicate 24k-gold inlay work, or gilded pearl, using a vine and leaf pattern that extends from the mother-of-pearl onto the engraved T-416 bolsters. The vine seemingly disappears down into the pearl before resurfacing onto the guard area.

Hands took his handiwork a step further and continued the pattern by burnishing the CPM 154CM blade. Even the pin heads are engraved in a floral motif, and the stainless steel bail features a gold leaf on one side and

Steven R. Johnson

golden hands on the other, the latter a play on Barry's name and a tribute to the skilled hands that work so wisely with the most precious of metals.

Called "La Daga de Oro de Princesa Dulcinea," Johnson's knife is a one-of-a-kind (as if there'd be another!) tribute to the fictional but legendary object of Don Quixote's love, The Princess Dulcinea. So, to Steve, Barry, Mr. Quixote and Princess Dulcinea, the *Knives* editor waves and presents the "2011 Wooden Sword Award" for which to fight windmills and all other moving obstacles.

Joe Kertzman

PointSeven photo

A Fondness For San Francisco Knives

Imagine well-heeled gamblers drawing these beautiful but deadly blades to settle disputes

By Roger Pinnock

Phil Lobred's name is one well known within the custom knife community. A lifelong collector and patron of custom knives, his impact upon the field has been as a significant as it has been positive. His commission of the truly spectacular King Tut dagger by the late Buster Warenski all but redefined the concept of what a true custom knife could be.

His bi-annual Art Knife Invitational, hosted every other year in San Diego, provides a unique opportunity for top collectors to view and acquire exceptional pieces that define the state of the art in custom knives. It also challenges an elite group of makers to fashion fine knives that reflect nothing less than the ultimate expression of their skill and creativity. Suffice it to say that Phil's enduring passion for the field of custom knives has already made a lasting difference.

The handle of Larry Fuegen's San Francisco knife is carved nickel damascus showcasing a carved orange-fossil-walrus-ivory flower with a gold center. The guard is carved 14k gold and sterling silver, and the handle wrap is 18-gauge, 14k yellow gold that is carved and engraved.
(PointSeven photo)

The great California gold rush of the late 1840s to early 1850s is also familiar to those steeped in the history of custom knives. A colorful period of American history, where vast fortunes could be made in a day, then lost just as swiftly at gaming tables at night, the gold rush never fails to capture the imagination. Of particular significance to the world of knives, however, is the fact that during the gold rush a group of San Francisco knifemakers with now-legendary names such as Michael Price, Hugh McConnell and Will & Finck, collectively gave birth to a new and uniquely American genre of elegant custom knives.

So how are these two topics related? Well, among Phil Lobred's diverse and impressive credentials lurks one of his perhaps lesser-known accomplishments: he just happens to be one of the top collectors of, and leading experts on, San Francisco knives. As such, he is well positioned to provide valuable insight into the times and the knives that combined to present what he has described as nothing less than the first American renaissance of custom knives.

The San Francisco knives, as they have now come to be known, were by no means simple or rudimentary tools. Rather,

In addition to perhaps the most significant knife of the modern handmade era—the King Tut Dagger—Buster Warenski also made high-end San Francisco art knife reproductions such as this gold-quartz-inlaid dagger with engraved gold handle wrap, guard, and silver sheath with engraved gold tip and throat.
(PointSeven photo)

they represented an extremely high level of craftsmanship often combined with heavy embellishment. The level of artistry put them out of the economic reach of the simple prospector, at least until his lucky strike.

Whiskey & Price Knives

As Phil relates, "There were many wealthy people in San Francisco in the 1850s due to the gold rush, not necessarily because they found gold but because of the population explosion. It was said back then that men loved 'fast horses, beautiful women, smooth whiskey and Michael Price Knives.' These fancy knives were part of their dress. Like a fine tie today, you were not dressed until you put your fancy knife on.

"These knives were small bowie-type blades or double edged, but usually of medium size. The handles were made of materials indigenous to the San Francisco area, such as marine ivory, abalone, mother-of-pearl, and gold and silver. Many ivory handles were carved, and many of these knives were engraved. Each knife could cost up to $250, so they were very expensive even back then."

Push daggers and gamblers dirks are among the more recognizable styles from this genre, and it's hard not to have romantic notions of well-heeled, ruthless gamblers drawing beautiful but deadly blades to settle heated disputes.

Phil suggests, however, that such notions might have less than solid grounding in the reality of times. "It would not seem reasonable that a wealthy person of that time went out expecting to get in a knife fight or use such a knife," he remarks. "They were usually worn so that they could be seen, sometimes in a sash or on a belt. Gamblers dirks and push daggers were probably more concealed and used once in a while."

The emergence of Phil's interest in the San Francisco knives coincided roughly with his move from Anchorage, Alaska, to San Diego in 1977. His interest would be significantly diverted for a period of time, however, when Phil came down with a serious case of "King Tut fever." His determined pursuit of that famous Warenski dagger project consumed much of his time and its funding mandated the sale of most of his collection.

Still, his fondness for San Francisco knives would be further fueled by Bernard Levine's excellent book *Knifemakers of Old San Francisco*. Phil's original idea was to have the most skilled modern makers of art knives reproduce the best antique examples, but his study of San Francisco knives inevitably led to a desire to acquire not only exquisite contemporary renderings, but some of the original antique knives as well.

Luck Be A Lady Knife

This proved to be quite a challenge. According to Phil, "There are probably less than 100 fine San Francisco antique knives known to exist." Images of needles in haystacks come to mind—these things definitely don't grow on trees. In fact, getting your hands on one today might require a dainty helping hand from the same source to which the hopeful prospector and risk-taking gambler so often turned: lady luck. Phil would count himself fortunate indeed to bask in the glow of her warm smile on at least one memorable occasion, and the tale must rank highly in the annals of vintage collector lore.

In 1992 Phil received a phone call from knifemaker and friend Ted Dowell. A machinist friend had been flipping through Ted's copy of *Knifemakers of Old San Francisco* when the gentleman muttered something to the effect of "I've got a knife that looks like that." Ted didn't give the comment much thought, but when the fellow said, "I've got a knife that looks like this one, too," he captured Ted's complete attention.

The machinist couldn't remember who made the knives, but promised to call Ted with the information later, which he did. And as it happened, one knife was a Michael Price ring dagger, and the other by Will & Finck. One can only begin to imagine the excitement at Phil's end of the line when Ted called with the news.

As Phil recounts: "Ted gave me the phone number and I called the machinist and made a deal. After the deal, the friend gave the knives to Ted who delivered them to me at the Solvang Knife Show. I called my friend William R. Williamson, who lived in Santa Barbara, and asked him to authenticate them for me. Williamson completely deflated me on the phone. He said that it would be almost impossible to

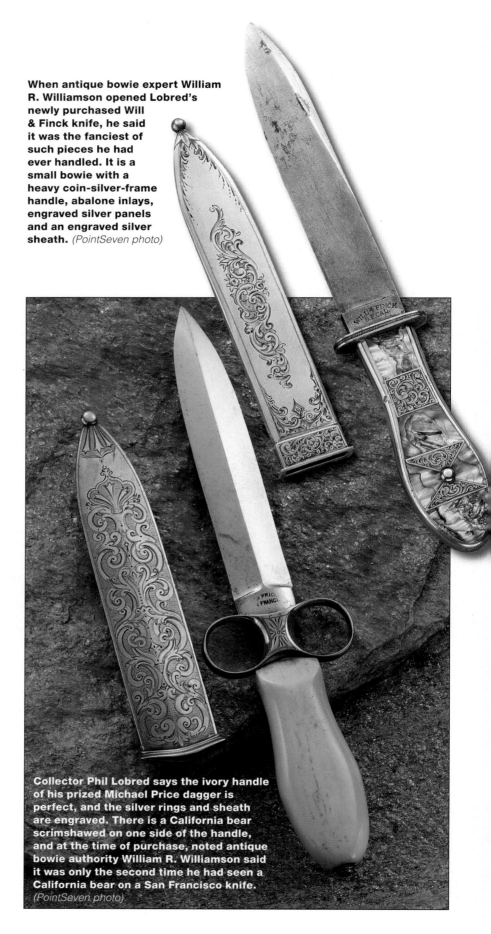

When antique bowie expert William R. Williamson opened Lobred's newly purchased Will & Finck knife, he said it was the fanciest of such pieces he had ever handled. It is a small bowie with a heavy coin-silver-frame handle, abalone inlays, engraved silver panels and an engraved silver sheath. *(PointSeven photo)*

Collector Phil Lobred says the ivory handle of his prized Michael Price dagger is perfect, and the silver rings and sheath are engraved. There is a California bear scrimshawed on one side of the handle, and at the time of purchase, noted antique bowie authority William R. Williamson said it was only the second time he had seen a California bear on a San Francisco knife. *(PointSeven photo)*

find two knives of this magnitude at the same time but he would drive to Solvang the next day and look at them. I was crushed.

"I could not sleep that night. Williamson came about noon the next day and we went to my room to see the knives. I remember when he took the first one out he was stunned. It was the Michael Price ring dagger. There are three or four Price ring daggers known but this one is the best. The ivory handle is perfect and the silver rings and sheath are engraved. It has a 6 ¼-inch blade, and there is a California bear scrimshawed on one side of the handle. Williamson said it was only the second time he had seen a California bear on a San Francisco knife.

"When he opened the Will & Finck he could not believe it either. He said it was the most fancy Will & Finck he had ever handled. It is a small bowie with a heavy coin-silver-frame handle, abalone inlays, engraved silver panels and an engraved silver sheath. It has a 6-inch blade. Needless to say I was thrilled with both knives and am very proud of these two knives today."

Knife Collecting Peak

Notwithstanding his acquisition of these and other exceptional vintage pieces, Phil still pursued contemporary renditions by some of today's most talented makers. The downside of the successful assembly of several such superb pieces, however, is perhaps reflected in the question that confronts the determined climber at the summit of the mountain: "Now what?"

As Phil describes, "I am very hard to please when it comes to contemporary San Francisco knives. I am somewhat jaded after all these years. It takes quite a knife to get me excited. The last piece that really excited me was my Larry Fuegen carved-damascus-handle knife. It was a completely contemporary idea inspired only by other Larry Fuegen pieces. I received the knife at the Santa Barbara show and I was very impressed by it. This knife stands out in my collection and is an outstanding piece of work. It is one of my favorites. I believe Larry Fuegen is as talented a maker as any working today, and this knife shows that talent."

An American Bladesmith Society master smith, Fuegen recalls that particular piece very well. As Larry recounts: "Phil placed an order and at the time he was interested in having a San Francisco knife with a gold quartz handle. We decided to do something a little different since I offer a lot of carving on the majority of my knives. We chose a carved damascus handle with a gold wrap. During the design process, Phil suggested adding some carved ivory into the handle and he lamented the fact that, years ago, you could find orange fossil walrus ivory. Today, it's almost impossible to find. Fortunately, I had several small pieces that I had been saving for the last 15 years and I offered them to Phil for this special project."

The details of the finished knife itself remain fresh in the maker's memory. "The blade is hand-forged 6-inch carbon steel and the overall length is 10.75 inches. The handle is carved nickel damascus showcasing a carved orange-fossil-walrus-ivory flower with a gold center," Fuegen details. "The guard is carved 14k gold and sterling silver, and the handle wrap is 18-gauge, 14k yellow gold that is carved and engraved.

"The engraving I chose to do is an older, more bold style of engraving. The knife also had a custom sheath with sterling silver fittings, carved damascus, walrus ivory overlays, and 14k-gold accents. A black calfskin overlay covered the body of the sheath. In designing this knife, I maintained certain elements of the classic San Francisco knives, while creating a unique look for Phil that was different from pieces he had in his collection. My shop is limited to very basic tools, so the majority of the work was accomplished by hand. By using these simple hand tools, I was able to achieve a more organic look and feel."

Phil believes that a significant measure of the success of the designs crafted by this small group of San Francisco makers rests upon the fact that they are still being emulated to this day. "These knife styles still fascinate collectors today," he says. "The best of the contemporary San Francisco knives are very involved, highly decorated or engraved, and usually come with the traditional high price. Most high-end collectors have at least one or two San Francisco style knives in their collection. I suppose I am one of the few that has specialized in them for so many years."

The end result of his specialization over such a lengthy period of time is a collection that stands apart as a preservation—and celebration—of a unique and vibrant chapter in history of American knifemaking.

Besh Wedge In The Business

Multiple knife companies adopt the broad, piercing point of the double-chisel-ground Besh Wedge

By Michael Janich

In describing a knife—any knife—a defining characteristic is the blade shape. Descriptions like "drop point," "clip point," and "dagger" conjure up vivid images of certain knife styles. Similarly, our first glimpse of a knife is typically followed by a mental classification that might include a bowie, trailing point, or another knife style, based primarily on blade shape.

Given the long history of the knife and the many well-established blade styles in existence, developing a truly new blade design is a difficult task. Doing it successfully and making a significant mark on the knife industry is even more difficult and a true landmark event in the history of edged tools. Sure, a "recurved drop-point" sounds cool and innovative, until you put it next to a kukri that was made before the knifemaker was born and realize that it's been done.

Contrast that with Lynn Thompson's Cold Steel Tanto and you get a very different story.

SOG Specialty Knives has also embraced the Besh Wedge, exploring its potential as a wharncliffe-style blade. Shown are three prototypes that reflect SOG's approach.

Boker adapted the Besh Wedge to the classic Applegate-Fairbairn Dagger design to create a new classic. The knife is shown here with Col. Rex Applegate's "Fitz Special"—a .45 revolver customized by J.H. Fitzgerald and carried by the Colonel as his personal sidearm in World War II.

There were plenty of traditional Japanese tantos around before the 1980s, but adapting a sword point to a tanto-length blade was an innovation that established the Americanized tanto as a recognized modern blade pattern. Something truly new is something *really* special.

That's why, when an energetic custom knifemaker named Brent Beshara promised to show me a totally new blade profile back in 2002, I was skeptical. I've been around knives all my life and have a solid understanding of knife history and blade styles. Would it be a variation on an established theme? Sure. Would it be totally new and never seen before? I didn't think so. Well, I was wrong.

What Beshara showed me was what is now officially known as "The Besh Wedge®." To understand what it is and where it came from, you need to understand Beshara—or as he is more commonly known, "Besh."

Beshara is a former clearance diver for the Canadian military, an expert in Explosive Ordnance Disposal (EOD), and a veteran of Joint Task Force 2 (JTF-2), Canada's most elite military special operations and counterterrorist

unit. Add to that the fact that he is a lifelong martial artist with extensive experience in a number of reality-based combat arts and you begin to understand that he has an exceptional insight into the tools of warfare.

During his 24 years of military service and worldwide travel with the Canadian forces, Besh saw many knives in use in the field. He also noted that some of the most iconic knives—traditional military daggers—tended to perform the worst. In fact, a disturbing number of daggers that he saw in use by military forces suffered from broken tips due to the inherent weakness created when the double-edged, diamond-shaped cross section of the blade is ground to a sharp point.

Heart & Soul Man

Never content to accept second best, Besh began analyzing knife design with the goal of developing a dagger that possessed all the attributes of a traditional design, yet had a point that was practically unbreakable. While the average person might be content to sketch his ideas or maybe carve a wooden model, Besh puts his heart and soul into everything he does. To develop his knife design, he needed to possess knifemaking skills. He befriended renowned custom knifemaker, American Blade-smith Society master smith and fellow Canadian Wally Hayes, and began an intensive knife-making apprenticeship under Wally.

Once he had developed the requisite skills, Besh began expressing his own ideas on knife design by building custom pieces under the business name of Besh Knives. He also continued to experiment with unconventional grinds, setting a goal of creating the ultimate military dagger.

One day, he was partway through the grinding process of a traditional dagger when he had an epiphany. Rather than the orthodox double bevel of a dagger, Besh began experimenting with two diagonally-opposed chisel-ground edges to provide superior strength. He then merged the two edges, not at a fragile needle-point, but at a broad third cutting edge. The result was a *triple-edged* blade design with a cutting tip not unlike a wood chisel.

Besh immediately heat-treated the blade and set about testing its performance. He discovered that the wide, sharp tip penetrated extremely well and the wedge created by the twin chisel grinds provided exceptional strength.

The body of the blade also retained its full thickness, while the zero-ground chisel bevels integrated a superior balance of strength and cutting power. The Besh Wedge had been born.

Although Besh was convinced

TOPS Knives' inaugural Besh Wedge design is the GTG-1 (Good to Go-1) fixed blade. In this stout design a chisel-ground primary edge and a sharpened false edge meet at an angled Besh Wedge point.

Buck Knives offers three Besh Wedge models: the Bravo, the Bravo Rescue and the fixed-blade Nighthawk Bravo. The company's version of the Besh Wedge features a high, primary chisel grind for improved cutting performance.

The XSF-1 was one of Brent Beshara's initial—and most popular—expressions of the Besh Wedge concept. The custom versions of the knife (left and middle) inspired the BlackHawk/Masters of Defense commercial versions, which were produced in both A-2 tool steel and 6AL/4V titanium (right).

The Mil-Tac CS-1BW combat and survival knife combines concealed-tang construction, a long, primary cutting edge, and a sharpened false edge to yield a formidable Besh Wedge blade.

that he was onto something extraordinary, his military experience had taught him that theory only goes so far. To truly validate the Besh Wedge, it needed to be tested by experienced operators under realistic field conditions. To do this, he first refined the concept into a purpose-designed military dagger, which he christened the XSF-1.

This full-tang, wasp-waisted design featured his unique interpretation of a coffin handle and an integral double guard. Its name also had dual symbolism: it

represented his status as "ex-Special Forces" ("XSF") and, when pronounced quickly, became the "excessive one"—an appropriate moniker for a radically different design.

Custom versions of the XSF-1 went into service with elite operators in Iraq and Afghanistan and quickly established themselves as robust, reliable, high-performance knives. They also validated the Besh Wedge blade profile as a quantum leap over the traditional military dagger.

In 2004, I joined BlackHawk

Products Group as director of product development. Since my job was to drive the development of new and unique designs for the tactical market, the XSF-1 and the revolutionary Besh Wedge concept seemed a perfect fit. To be sure, I first personally tested and validated the design using a custom-built ballistic pendulum. Comparing the performance of the Besh Wedge against traditional daggers, tantos, bowies and other conventional blade profiles, I confirmed that it provided a superior combination of strength and penetration.

With the support of Jim Ray, then brand manager and founder of the Masters of Defense knife company, BlackHawk developed American-made production versions of the XSF-1. These included a tungsten-DLC-coated steel version machined from A2 tool steel, and a non-magnetic version fashioned from solid 6AL-4V titanium. Although produced in limited numbers, both were well received and many of them found their way into the kits of elite military and law enforcement operators.

Wedge Expressionism

By the time the XSF-1 began earning an enviable reputation in the tactical industry, Beshara was already deep into the development of other expressions of the Besh Wedge concept. Although he was convinced that the point design was clearly among the strongest ever produced, he realized that the use of chisel grinds and a dagger profile limited the edge geometry and cutting ability of the blade.

He began experimenting with all possible variations of the Besh Wedge concept, focusing on changing the relative widths of the bevels and the angle of the cutting edge at the tip. He later devised a method to add secondary grinds to the primary bevels of blades to create a Besh Wedge point and extreme tip strength while maintaining superior edge geometry and cutting performance.

The result was an entire family of blade geometry that shared all the salient features of the Besh Wedge, yet provided a full range of other performance characteristics that could be tuned to the mission of a specific knife design. The Besh Wedge had truly achieved status as a revolutionary development in the knife industry.

Although BlackHawk had produced two Beshara neck knife designs in addition to the XSF-1, knives were only a small part of the overall business. Beshara understood that the Besh Wedge had industry-wide potential and was committed to spreading the word beyond a few specialized projects. With BlackHawk's blessing, he set out to educate the rest of the knife industry concerning the advantages of his revolutionary design. With a roll of hand-ground wooden blade samples under his arm and the energy and determination of 100 men, he made the rounds at the SHOT Show and the BLADE Show.

He met with major and minor knife companies alike, explaining the evolution of the Besh Wedge concept and demonstrating its broad application to all aspects of knife design. While most custom knifemakers would be fortunate to land a contract for one design collaboration with a knife company, as of late 2009, Beshara had contracted with many manufac-

BlackHawk's versions of the Besh Wedge included two concealable neck knife designs—the XSF Punch Dagger and the XSF Micro.

turers eager to produce versions of his unique blade geometry. If that success rate doesn't confirm that the Besh Wedge is in fact a landmark development in the history of edged weapons and tools, I don't know what does.

The increasing popularity of the Besh Wedge has also motivated a number of custom makers to incorporate it into their designs. Always supportive of fellow knifemakers, Beshara typically allows them to employ the Besh Wedge design on their knives free of charge. However, since the original concept was clearly his, and since the term "Besh Wedge" is formally trademarked in his name, he asks that all makers and manufacturers respect his innovation by referring to the grind by its proper name and referencing the formal trademark.

Wedged Favorites

To date, my favorite expressions of the Besh Wedge—besides

the original XSF-1 design—are the Buck Bravo and its variant the Bravo Rescue, the TOPS Good to Go-1 (GTG-1) fixed blade, and Boker's Besh Wedge version of the legendary Applegate-Fairbairn Combat Dagger.

The Buck Bravo is a single-edged, locking-liner folder that takes the Besh Wedge concept to its logical extreme as a high-performance cutting tool. By extending one of the chisel-ground blade bevels nearly the full width of the blade, it achieves very acute edge geometry for cutting performance.

The short bevel on the opposite side of the blade is actually an unsharpened swedge, while the third cutting edge is a single-bevel chisel grind that creates the distal cutting edge and point of the knife. This highly unusual blade grind faithfully expresses all the core elements of the Besh Wedge while yielding a blade that cuts aggressively.

The TOPS GTG-1 takes a

similar approach, but with some subtle differences that produce a distinctly different blade. The primary edge bevel is a shorter chisel grind, and the back bevel is also chisel ground to a sharp edge. They are connected by a third cutting edge that intersects the two to produce an offset angle that yields a sharp, leading point rather than the full-width cutting point of a symmetrical dagger. The result is a distinctive fusion of strength, penetration, and cutting performance.

Having had the tremendous honor of working directly with the late Col. Rex Applegate during the last years of his life, I have a special affinity for all his work. As such, I regard the Applegate-Fairbairn dagger as one of the most evolved and near-perfect combat dagger designs ever produced. At the same time, I know that the Colonel never stopped learning and remained open to new ideas until the very end. As such, I'm confident that he would have considered Boker's Besh Wedge version of his iconic design a valid evolution of a combat-proven pattern.

The Boker design incorporates second-generation Besh Wedge design concepts, using secondary bevels on the *same* side as the primary chisel-ground blade bevels to achieve a third edge at the point and continuous cutting edges along both sides of the blade. Combining the strength of the Besh-style point with the double-edged cutting power of the Applegate-Fairbairn design may very well redefine the ultimate combat dagger.

Although we may never know exactly what Jim Bowie's original "Bowie Knife" looked like, the many variations of the Bowie style are collectively regarded among the most iconic designs in knife history. In the same vein, I am confident that the Besh Wedge has already carved out a well-deserved spot in the evolution of edged weapons. And like the clip-point, Mexican, Searles and Sheffield patterns of the bowie, its current and future variations will ultimately be just as institutionally recognized and respected.

Something truly new is something really special. Beshara's revolutionary Besh Wedge is one of the few knives to come along in recent years and qualify on both counts.

Master Cutlery has adopted the Besh Wedge in a big way, offering a number of beefy folder designs intended for the tactical market.

Master Cutlery is also manufacturing unique tactical fixed-blade variants of the Besh Wedge that combine acute edge geometry for cutting power with the strength of the Besh Wedge point.

Leave It to Cleaver

Put the chop back on the block—the butcher block—and swing low sweet weary-not

By Roderick T. Halvorsen

Saw this. Saw that. See chopper left behind.

Saw it down. Saw it up. The saw's the best you'll find!

This little rhyme, of course, is aimed at the timber industry where the chainsaw has almost totally replaced the axe, but these same words can be said to be the mantra of meat cutters throughout the modern world.

When it comes to heavy butcher work, saws rule.

The saw most commonly used in homes, hunt camps and non-commercial locations, where wild game or livestock is butchered, is the bow style with hacksaw-like replaceable blades. Such saws are common in commercial locales also but there the power-driven band saw has made short shrift of many chores that, in pre-electric days, were handled with a heavy blade, usually a cleaver. And in the field, some fellows have even resorted to using chainsaws lubed with vegetable oil for splitting the carcasses of heavy game such as elk and moose.

No longer does the heavy cleaver possess a place near home, hearth and the game pole. Seldom is the sound of the heavy "chop!" heard near a chilled carcass and a cutting block. Rarely can the arms of the butcher be seen above the heads of gathered customers as, rising and falling, he makes the big meat small, and the small smaller.

Today the whine and buzz of the saw is followed by the almost imperceptible "swish" of the light boning knives. The cleaver seems mostly relegated to hanging as a decoration on the walls of smoke-filled steak houses, or found rusting in the junk piles of the pawnshops across town.

For years we have used saws and bolo knives—multipurpose, heavy field knives—for butchering and even some kitchen chores, relying mostly on the former to separate the quarters or other heavy parts of game and to butcher stock before the lighter

Sheep shoulder can be converted into nice steaks using a heavy meat cleaver.

The author pitted his handmade cleaver and a field bolo against each other, as well as against heavy bone and thick meat. The bolo edge chipped, but the cleaver proved no worse for wear.

knives come into play. I am nigh embarrassed to say I have never even owned a heavy cleaver!

And then some time ago it dawned on me, first as a question: "Are the days of the heavy cleaver actually over, replaced by the buzz of the power band saw?" Should a delectable lamb "chop" no longer be referred to as such, but rather as a lamb "buzz?" A lamb "buzz" with mint sauce washed down with a glass of fine Pinot Noir?

Good heavens, no.

Pride of the Butcher

A tool that for so many centuries was the centerpiece of the butcher shop seems to deserve

better. Or so I thought, and so, eventually, I found.

The "finding" started with a perusal of the Internet where I searched for a true, heavy cleaver. I wasn't looking for the typical type of stainless, flexi-blade job that masquerades as a cleaver on abrasive TV ads these days, but a real, live massive chopper that would fit right in at home in the typical meat market of many a yesteryear. It would have to be the kind heard hard at work thumping away six or eight storefronts down from the butcher's place.

My Internet search was mostly unsuccessful. And thus, as necessity is the mother of invention, my

almost cantankerous, historical curiosity sent me to the metal mess in my shop corner, that pile of chainsaw and log processor bars and other sundry steel bits and pieces I use from time to time to convert into something useful for around the ranch.

Etched in my mind were the pictures I'd seen of decades-gone-by shops with varieties of the heavy blades hanging on the wall or being wielded by bushy-mustachioed fellows sporting forearms thick as double-stacked 2x4s. The cleaver in my mind would not flex, bend or spring against the resistance of bone or meat, whether chilled or thawed. My mental model was, and became, an almost 4-pound, dead-lead-heavy cleaver of bull-femur-breaking potential.

Rooting through the piles of antique chainsaw and log processor bars, I found a nice, wide straight one, and a neat piece of walnut for the handle scales, and went to work.

The design of a cleaver demands first a definition of what it is going to cut. Butcher knives are for meat, fat and sinew. The heavy cleaver needs to face up to all of those plus hard, edge-breaking bone. It is the bone part that separates the TV cleavers with their spatula-like blades from the real deals of the old-time chop shops. For my cleaver I used a log processor bar that was a full ¼-inch thick. Some of the old-timers' cleavers I've handled were even thicker than this, but the processor bar provided complete stiffness, and in light of the final weight of the tool, is probably about perfect.

The general shape of the tool I left to metal smiths of millennia gone by. This is one tool I had no desire to personalize. I wanted mine to look right at home in the butcher shop where my then-teenage father swept floors and stocked shelves back in the 1930s.

Blade lengths on traditional meat cleavers vary. No doubt about that. Some two-handed models I've seen run over a foot long. Others hover in the 8-inch range. For mine, after much mental gymnastics, I settled on a hair over 11 inches. Width was dictated by the bar itself, but at 3 ½ inches was just what I wanted anyway, the combination of all dimensions giving the heretofore-mentioned final weight of just about 4 pounds. This is a really massive knife, its handling reminding me a bit of the old World War II-era Medical Corps bolos.

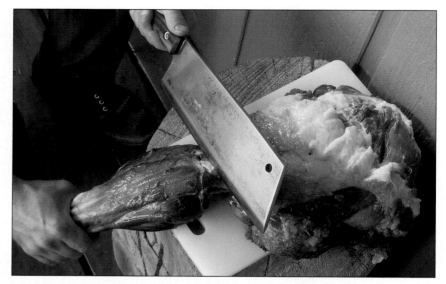

Dividing up a bear shank was no problem with the heavy cleaver.

Log processors and chainsaw bars make for excellent heavy knife blades. The author used the log processor steel for his cleaver blade.

The author says this is exactly where a cleaver belongs when not in use—hanging from a nail in the pantry, or even on the kitchen wall.

Massive bone is a grueling test for any heavy knife.

Splitting an elk carcass can be accomplished with a saw or, in this case, a meat cleaver.

Heave the Cleave

Making such a massive thing work safely demands a good handle, and mine has it. For strength I used a traditional full tang and gave the grip a width of 1 1/8 inches and a thickness of 1 inch. Length of the handle is an ample 6 inches, allowing a hand-and-a-half grip when necessary, and for the work this tool is subjected to, sometimes it's necessary.

Grip scales were bonded to the tang with JB Weld and finally secured with three deep-set iron rivets, the countersinking providing aggressive friction for a safe grip when the handle is slick with blood and fat. The finish was simple; the handle was submerged in linseed oil overnight. After each use it is rubbed liberally with olive oil, continuing on up the blade, as well, to protect it from corrosion while the big thing is hanging on the nail in the pantry.

Heat treatment of a cleaver is something to ponder, as is the angle of the edge grind. Today's mass- and custom-produced, deservedly-acclaimed knives of all sorts often feature very high levels of hardness. Such hardness levels seem to work well when faced with cutting chores, but when a knife is to be used almost exclusively for heavy chopping, high hardness can set a blade up for chipping and cracking. My chopper would be subjected to a steady diet of what can only be called abuse, and using the scrap steels at hand, my technique was performed accordingly.

During the hardening process, I found that due to the

mass of the blade, my normal oil quench would not produce the pre-temper hardness I wanted, and I had to switch to a water quench instead. Tempering was performed in my old kitchen oven I had installed in my shop years ago. Initial tempering was done at 400 degrees for 1 ½ hours, and then I applied a differential flame tempering that left the tang springy, the spine soft, and the cutting edge about 55 Rc on the Rockwell Hardness scale.

Sharpening can be accomplished with a new, hard and sharp file, but mostly, I've used stones for rough work, and I apply the blade to sharpening steel constantly. Frequent use of a steel markedly prolongs the useful life of the edge between working it with a stone.

In providing for good cutting properties without any chipping or denting of the edge, the grind angle took care of the rest. I confess that in making knives, I use maximum intuition and minimum deduction. That means I make by feel. Over the years I've developed ingrained ideas about what looks right for the intended job at hand, and in so grinding the edge on my cleaver, I relied heavily on this experience.

Using neither hatchet nor machete grind, suffice it to say that the edge approximates the convex *cannel grind* and is similar to the edges on the aforementioned USMC bolos. This edge is far steeper than that I use on a felling axe.

The final buffing leaves the edge hair popping sharp, but with a mass of metal on either side of the fine edge, thus preventing any chipping or rolling of the edge. And none has occurred in spite of now-extensive use

against heavy bone of all sorts of critters, including heavy bones from sheep, steer, bear and elk. The edge on a cleaver must do two things very well—cut and protect itself. One quick experiment was all I needed to prove the success of the end product.

Bolo vs. Cleaver

My cleaver and one of my fine-edged, chisel-ground field bolos were matched against heavy bone and thick meat. The bolo suffered a chipped and damaged edge. The cleaver remained undaunted, ready for more. Fortunately, since I made it, I can fix it, and the bolo is back to work in its own right, edge reground and razor sharp. The cleaver needed no repair.

The long axis of the cleaver edge was provided with a very slight curve, nearly level, but not quite, allowing the slightest ability to rock the edge over meat or sinew left hanging on after a heavy chop. This curve is not pronounced, so that many cuts can be fully made with one strike of the blade. Handle placement on a traditional cleaver keeps the knuckles off the chopping block.

Two lanyard holes were part of my design. One is located in the grip and one in the traditional spot on the blade. Did I say lanyard holes? No, nail holes. Everyone knows true cleavers are stored hanging on a nail on the wall!!

The saw gets very little use now, as most all livestock I process gets cut into roasts. If I want steaks, I thaw the roasts and out comes the cleaver! Lamb shoulder roasts are easily turned into steaks, and the whole butchering process of medium game, like deer and bear, as well as home butcher stock like pork

and lamb, has become a breeze, as is carcass splitting and other heavy work. What is a messy and oft times difficult job—sawing small cuts and chops out of floppy, thawed joints—is now done as I prepare for dinner itself!

There is no doubt, however, that a relatively high degree of skill is needed to make efficient use of the heavy cleaver. Making presentable cuts and chops is more difficult than it looks, and there is, naturally, some danger in using such a heavy tool. I use heavy bolos and parang-type knives constantly in my work, but for those to whom the "heavy knife culture" is foreign, getting the hang of a cleaver might take some time.

A heavy, stout, chopping block of some kind is a must. I can imagine how easy it would be to ruin an expensive kitchen counter in the process of putting together a single meal of lamb chop delicacies. I nearly did it! For my use, I cut a heavy pine stump, and using my chainsaw decorated the front of it with my ranch brand. It now sits on the kitchen deck, an end-table server of sorts that is easily accessed whenever the cleaver is called up for service.

I can't remember when I've worked on any knife project that made me feel dumber about past, missed opportunities. Since adopting the big cleaver, I do not know how I got along without it.

The heavy cleaver is an ancient, heretofore common, now almost extinct blade that is so practical it deserves more recognition. So if you want a bone-smashing, meat-chopping, carcass-splitting do-all, get yourself a real-deal heavy cleaver and give your saws a rest.

Trip The Knife Fantastic

Mainly because they like knives, the author and his wife seek carbon steel along cobblestone streets

By James Morgan Ayres

The only question remaining was which knives we should pack. New regulations on international travel pop up like gophers in a cabbage patch and I didn't want our entire armory and tool kit to be confiscated by an overzealous TSA or customs agent. I considered taking a TOPS Steel Eagle. You just never know when you might need a tactical edge. On the other hand, this wasn't supposed to be a survivalist excursion. I reached a quick decision, tossed some steel into our bags and ran for the airport.

The flight was a misery. After planes, trains, buses and a taxi we arrived at the chateau deep in the French countryside at 22:00 local time. The taxi driver, a tough looking Turk, found the place after much asking for directions and wandering around on night roads. The gates swung open, we drove up the winding driveway and the driver said "O la la."

O la la, indeed. The grounds and building were lighted and the deserted chateau was spectacular. The driver dumped our bags and departed. We then discovered that none of the codes given us by the head of security worked. Nor did the keys fit the locks. I was to rendezvous here with associates before going to another country far to the East on business. The others weren't scheduled to arrive for two days. We were marooned in the courtyard with about 416 pounds of rolling luggage.

Mary Lou (ML), loving wife, loyal and long-suffering companion of a hundred journeys, suggested pitching our emergency tarp and sleeping on the grass. ML is very adaptable. But I had no interest in sleeping outside. This was a chateau. Chateaus have wine cellars, right? We *would* get in. After a half hour of messing around with the security system, I said, "Forget about it. I'll just burgle the joint."

I wished I had packed the TOPS Steel Eagle, a knife perfectly suited to ripping open doors. My methods tend to be direct. Lacking a Steel Eagle, subtlety might be required.

Deploying my favorite Swiss Army Knife, a Rucksack, the one with a locking main blade, saw and basic tools, I fumbled around for 10 minutes poking at tumblers. I decided I would have to

In desperation the author jimmied the door of his friends' French chateau using a Spyderco Street Beat.

After spotting the storefront window of the Armurier Sipps, the author and his wife had the pleasure of meeting Vincent Gattu, who showed them a horn-handle hunting knife, among many other fine forged specimens. *(ML Ayres photo)*

go with what I know and revert to more direct action. But I couldn't bear to break one of the stained glass windows. It was time for a fixed blade. Although I had not brought the Steel Eagle I did have a Spyderco Street Beat.

Fred Perrin, French knife designer, martial artist and veteran of Special Operations, designed the Street Beat for Spyderco. The slick little fixed blade looks like a polite picnic knife and will slice your baguette and spread your Brie without anyone raising an eyebrow.

It is also strong enough to punch through a plaster wall with no damage to the knife. I tried it a few years ago for a field review. With its smooth, flat grind and reserve of strength I was sure

the Street Beat could stand up to hacking through the two-inch thick iron-bound oak door. As a significant plus, the Street Beat has a nicely contoured handle, which makes it comfortable for extended work periods, even when cutting seasoned oak.

Breaching Of Fortress

ML, always the grown-up, reminded me that this was not an enemy fortress I was proposing to assault but the property of friends. Exercising appropriate caution and concern for the carved wooden door I jimmied the lock with the Spyderco Street Beat and the portal popped open.

Of course the silent alarm portion of the security system worked flawlessly. The rapid response

team charged in, all of them dressed in black with flashlights that looked like Star Wars light sabers in hand. They were sweating profusely and obviously ready to do battle with housebreakers. I was relieved to note that their handguns were holstered.

"*Bon soir*," I said, "would you like a glass of wine?" By then I had found the wine cabinet. The guards refused a glass of the disappointing and somewhat sour Sancerre. After lecturing us on the hazards of the area, bands of roving burglars, armed bandits, werewolves, etc., the boys in black shook hands with ML and me and departed.

We wandered through corridors and up and down stairways. Finally finding our bedroom,

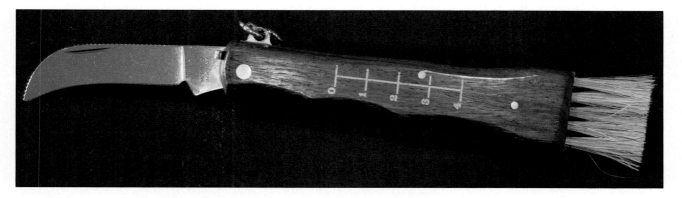

The brush on a French truffle (a mushroom considered a delicacy) knife is used to brush dirt off the fungus without breaking the delicate and prized model. The ruler ensures only legal-size mushrooms are harvested. *(ML Ayres photo)*

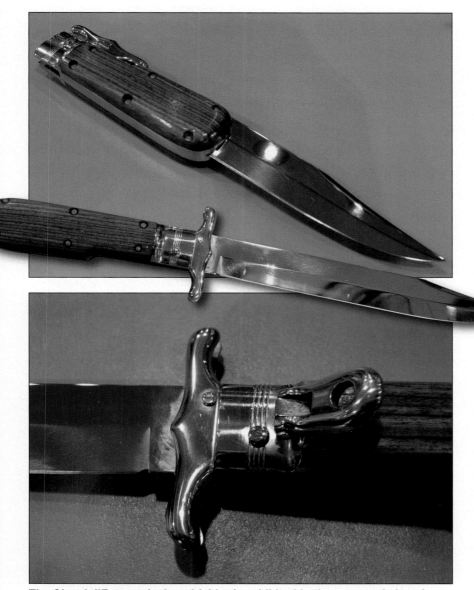

The Girard d'Estang-designed folder is exhibited in the open and closed (with the blade still protruding from the handle, but shorter) positions. Such a knife can be, and is, used to dispatch wild boar. *(ML Ayres photos)*

we stepped in and dropped our overnight bags. We were tired. There was nothing to be done but take a shower and go to bed. At least the sheets were clean.

Two hours later a rooster awakened me. We had business in town—knife business.

One of my favorite activities in a new city is to seek out the local knife shops, mainly because I just plain like knives. In most European cities you can find military surplus stores near the central train or bus station. Strasbourg is no exception. We found one of the stores, a French chain operation, around the corner from the regional bus station. In glass cases there were a Benchmade Ruckus, a Spyderco Endura, a SOG folder, and that old soldier—a Ka-Bar.

In tourist shops surrounding the cathedral we found plenty of standard Opinels, the traditional French twist-lock folder with wooden handle and carbon steel blade, and many SAKs, all good knives but nothing exceptional. We walked the streets for hours. Finally, footsore from cobblestones, at number 12 rue du

22 Novembre I spotted a store window with a huge rack of antlers surrounded by knives.

There were stag-handle fixed blades, horn-handle folders from the famed workshop of Mongin, and graceful Laguioles. The sign announced that this was Armurerie Sipp. Later I understood it to be the shop of M. Jean-Jacques Sipp, renowned gun maker to heads of state. But for the moment it was knives I was seeking.

Mushroom Mincer

As I entered the door I noticed an Opinel with a curved blade and a brush attached to the butt. This, I thought, must be a French truffle knife. Truffles, first cousins to mushrooms, are a prized and highly valued delicacy that grow underground in France and Italy. Everything associated with them, locations where they grow, methods of finding and taking them, is shrouded in secrecy, understandably since they sell for about $3,000 U.S. dollars a pound.

I had read of a special knife used to unearth and cut truffles without damaging the connecting network that spreads for many meters underground. The truffle knife was said to have a brush on its handle, used to carefully brush away the clinging earth without damaging the valuable fungus.

Inside the shop, Vincent Gattu, an employee and knowledgeable aficionado of the blade, explained that Armurerie Sipp

When she travels, the author's wife, Mary Lou, carries a Spyderco Street Beat (right) and her ever-present Cricket folder. *(ML Ayres photo)*

made and sold only fine guns for hunting, and therefore for a knife to be offered in the shop it must be suitable for hunting, and in accordance with the fine guns offered, esthetically pleasing.

Vincent introduced us to M. Sipp, who graciously allowed us the run of his shop and Vincent's full attention. Over the next couple of hours drawers were opened, and special treasures revealed. There were at least two dozen Mongins, many in patterns I had never before seen, and I've been buying Mongins for 30 years.

Forged Scandinavian knives, hammer marks still visible on the blades, were available from a selection of custom makers, along with sturdy, wide-blade skinners and thin daggers used for the *coup de grace.* M. Sipp displayed a Laguiole that had been forged from parts of a surplus supersonic Concorde jetliner, along with the blueprints and a certification that all materials had been drawn from the engines or airframe of the famous plane.

"A most unusual hunting knife," I said.

Vincent shrugged and smiled,

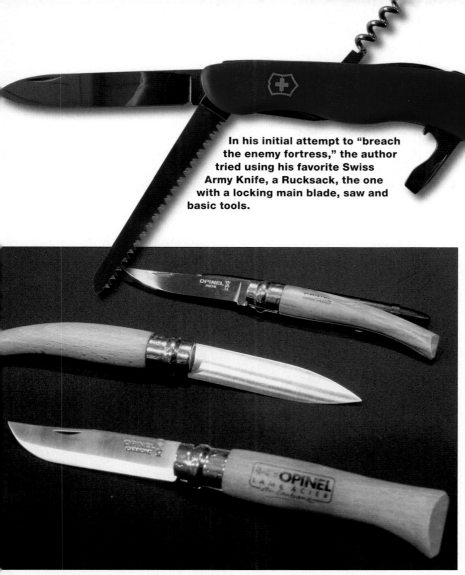

In his initial attempt to "breach the enemy fortress," the author tried using his favorite Swiss Army Knife, a Rucksack, the one with a locking main blade, saw and basic tools.

A standard Opinel is shown with two new models. *(ML Ayres photo)*

"It *could* be used for hunting."

"What about that knife?" I asked, pointing to the Opinel with the brush on the handle. "Is that knife for hunting truffles?"

"Ah, no. A truffle knife is much different. This is for the chasseur—hunter of mushrooms."

Vincent then brought out a true truffle knife. The distinction was undoubtedly clear to the discerning eye, but not mine. The truffle knife's blade curved more tightly and was shorter. It also had a ruler for measuring on the handle so the truffle hunter could be sure he was taking only those of legal length.

Wild Boar Blade

Vincent then showed me a folding knife with a long blade extending beyond the handle when closed. First designed by the Comte Girard du Estang in the 19th century, these knives were meant for self-defense and for hunting wild boar, not just for dressing out the game, for actually dispatching the animal.

I had seen this style of knife before in Thiers, the famed knifemaking town in the central mountains of France, and had talked with hunters who went forth with nothing more than spears and knives such as this in search of the wild boar of the region. I agreed that this was in fact a true hunting knife, and the men who used them true hunters.

While we talked I noticed an Opinel on the counter that had been modified—the blade and handle re-profiled and a name burned into the Beechwood handle. Modifying Opinels is popular among Opinel enthusiasts, including myself. If forced to do so I could get along fine with just one folder, the Opinel. Although it cannot match modern tactical folders for strength, the Opinel's carbon-steel blade takes a fierce edge, its twist lock is secure, and the blade can be opened with one hand.

On my Opinels, I always sand the handles and soak them in linseed oil for a few days. This stabilizes the wood and prevents it from swelling when wet. Vincent had done the same with his Opinel after reshaping the blade and handle, both of which can be easily done with hand tools, all in all a triumph of low technology. Seeing that I was a fellow Opinalist, Vincent brought out a new model, an Opinel with a corkscrew set into the side of the handle, surely the quintessential French knife.

It was a pleasant afternoon, spent with fine knives and finer people. Everyone at Armurerie Sipp was knowledgeable and courteous and gave freely of their time. Vincent also gave me a handbill advertising a custom knife show to be held in two weeks' time. As much as I wanted to attend the show we could not. We had to return to the chateau and prepare for the rendezvous with my associates tomorrow. Our brief holiday was over.

Scrim That Drives Men Crazy!

The scrimshaw of Dr. Peter Jensen seduces you into spending more time with the knives

By Don Guild

The first time my eyes fixed on Dr. Peter Jensen's scrimshaw, magnetism grabbed me like iron filings drawn to a magnet. Scrumptious. Absolutely sensational! Is it okay to keep staring at this semi-erotic art? Will the wading beauty turn around and give back a "Whatcha look'n' at, Pop?"

Ultimately, the intellectual part of me takes over, and I ask myself, "What elements enable this conglomeration of incised, colored dots to come together and create such impact? Of what significance is the snake tattoo on this beautiful young body? Could she be Eve? And is she wading into a tranquil sea where the tide's rising?"

Four years ago, I received an email order from Jensen who said he wanted a knife with a white ivory handle on which to inscribe his scrimshaw. A short while later, he ordered a Joe Kious knife for the same purpose. I mentioned I'd like to see a sample of his work, and shortly thereafter a picture of this wading nymph showed up. I wondered how a doctor found time to do scrimshaw …

The year of 1939 was not too gentle a time in Germany as World War II was starting, nevertheless little Peter arrived. Six years later he'd survived the war, and he was recognized as having outstanding artistic talents for a six-year-old. After completing high school, he went on to medical school and trained as a surgeon, remaining in that profession until he retired in 2005. And by this time he'd had seven years of experience plying the art of scrimshaw.

Jensen told me why scrimshaw appealed to him. "I first came in contact with the custom knife scene in 1998 when I saw Jim Weyer's book *Knives: Points of Interest*. The pictures of Rick Field's fantastic scrimshaw fascinated me," he says. "He could scrim an impressing and realistic color picture of a salmon-fishing grizzly bear on the tiny scale of a folder, and you could even see that the bear's coat was wet! This was inspiring. I attempted to study scrimshaw in order to learn how to do it. Then I found a copy of Bob Engnath's *Second Scrimshaw Connection*, and I could start."

He went on to say, "The practical advice in the book was very helpful. The results of my first attempt were satisfying. This was the perfect creative activity for me. I did one sample in black and white, and one in color, and began at once to scrim knives. You can learn perfectly 'by doing' if you take a needle and make your stitches."

History's earliest example of scrimshaw dates to 1817. The

When the author saw Dr. Peter Jensen's scrimshaw of a tattooed woman wading in the water on the bark-mammoth-ivory handle of a Richard Zirbes integral hunter, he was at first smitten. The author then turned inquisitive as to how the scrim was achieved, who the woman was, and why the subject matter was chosen in the first place.

great American whaling days were in full force, and the life of a seaman provided many leisure hours to burn, especially a whaler's, as he did not work at night. Sailors used a sail-mending needle to puncture or scratch various whale teeth, bones and baleen. Once the pattern was done in a manner that penetrated the surface, a pigment of lamp black or candle black was rubbed into the incisions and the excess wiped off. Voila, a black etching on a white field. Scrimshaw is considered by some to be the only art form originated in America, a true American folk art. A number of scrimshaw artists use dental tools and colored pigments.

Jensen said, "When I began to scrimshaw, I had the goal of achieving the best technique, so from step to step I chose more difficult themes and worked at first with a magnifying glass, and later with a stereo microscope at a magnification of 20X, in order to be able to scrim tiny details. Looking through the scope, the area you want to fill with stitches is 20 times larger than the real scrimshaw, and this takes time to learn.

"All my scrimshaw is done by hand," Jensen adds, "without using a machine; the only tools are simple needles of various dimensions. Looking through the magnifying glass you can see at once, after coloring it, your result. Then you understand how deep and how often you have to stitch and what needs to change in your technique. You are forced to imagine what you want to see as the result. Doing scrim in color is another time-consuming factor."

Dr. Peter Jensen has this to say about the Moby Dick scene he scrimshawed on the hippo-ivory handle and sheath of the Arpad Bojtos knife: "This subject goes back to the roots—scrimshaw made by the whalers of the 19th century. The front side shows the ramming and sinking of the whaler *Essex* by a huge sperm whale. On the sheath is the drama's finale, the lancing of the harpooned and exhausted whale."

"I'm pleased with the swimming lady and her erotic dream, because this scrimshaw was rather difficult to realize," admits Dr. Peter Jensen. He created the scene on the elephant-ivory handle of a Siegfried Rinkes knife that also includes a satin-finished Damasteel blade.

And in Jensen's opinion, "The pictures of females I use for my scrimshaw are real eye-catchers, and they are not discriminating. They show free women with power. They are powerful because they are able to force up the testosterone level, even of the most intelligent men so that they are only capable to do foolish things. Already during antiquity men went to war for decades for the sole purpose of winning back one lady."

Lori Ristinen, one of the day's most accomplished scrimshanders, commented on Jensen, "I got to know his scrimshaw from a book I have, *Contemporary Scrimshaw* by Eva Halat (originally in German). He was one of the scrimshanders in the book that really stood out to me. He has a unique style. I think he does a really nice job fitting the subject he scrims onto the shape of the knife handle. In other words his scrimshaw complements

A Princely Sum

Soon after I became aware of Jensen's work, a prince living in Riyadh, who had bought several knives from me, wrote that he'd like a large auto with ivory scales made by the Rhode Island knifemaker, Stephen Olszewski, and he wanted it scrimmed with the woman's picture he'd sent along. After I provided the prince with samples of some good scrimshaw artists, he chose Jensen as the one he thought best portrayed a woman's body. A price of $8,000 was agreed on for the scrim work.

So Olszewski crafted a 12-inch auto and shipped its two, white, mammoth-ivory scales off to Jensen in Germany. The prince was delighted with the contrasting juxtaposition of feminine art with the large, macho, automatic knife.

Scrimshaw artist Dr. Peter Jensen says the human face, especially that of Indian chiefs, is a great theme, because it can tell stories of pride, daring, cruelty, resignation and despair. To this end, he succeeded, enlivening the bark-mammoth-ivory handle of a Friedrich Schneider Damasteel hunter.

the art of the knife rather than competing with it. Another aspect of his art that I like is his ability to scrim the human form."

I asked Jensen about his technique, and he said, "When I use a very detailed picture with the dimension of 10 x 15 inches for making a scrimshaw, it thrills me that the finished scrimshaw shows exactly the same details on an area that's only as large as a thumb."

And what knife best represents Jensen's ideal? "I'm most pleased with the Moby Dick

Fellow scrimshaw artist Lori Ristinen commented that Dr. Peter Jensen does a nice job fitting the subject he scrims onto the shape of the knife handle, noting that she also admires his ability to scrim the human form. Both were accomplished on a Wolfgang Dell Damasteel hunter.

When Dr. Peter Jensen first saw the scrimshaw work of Rick Fields, he says he was impressed by the way Fields could scrim a salmon-fishing grizzly bear on the tiny scale of a folder, and you could even see that the bear's coat was wet. Now Jensen has reached that point, as evidenced by his work on a Jockl Greiss piece with a clip-point Jerry Rados damascus blade.

knife, because this subject goes back to the roots—scrimshaw made by the whalers of the 19th century. But it's no copy of these old works; it is a whaling scene portrayed with the optical aid of a microscope, but done with the same simple tool—a needle."

Jensen's Moby Dick knife joins three distant artisans—Herman Melville, the novelist from America, Arpad Bojtos, the knifemaker from Slovak Republic, and Jensen, the scrimshander from Germany. An explosive story evolves.

Jensen continued, "See the Bojtos knife with the whaling scenes. It shows the destiny of the whaler 'Essex' after be-ing rammed by a huge sperm whale bull, as well as scenes of 'Moby Dick.' To make the four scrimshaws of this knife I needed several months for the investigation of the theme and 1,300 hours for the work."

Mowed Down By Moby

Though the appeal of scrimshaw varies among knife collectors, the art enchants longtime collector Walter Hoffman. He says, "That Moby Dick knife knocked me right off my chair the first time I saw it. I love scrim; it adds another dimension to a knife. It's best on hunting and fighter knives. Good scrim can make a knife. I have over 20 knives with scrim, and I look at them all the time."

"Naturally," Jensen said, "it is possible to decorate each knife handle with the head of a wolf or a tiger, but this soon becomes boring. When a powerful animal is used, the scene should inspire your fantasy, and the animal should have eye contact with the onlooker. The human face, especially that of Indian chiefs, is a great theme, because it can tell stories of pride, daring, cruelty, resignation and despair."

Scrimshaw requires perseverance, and he added, "Scrimshaw is a fantastic creative activity. You need only a needle, color and an optical aid (magnifying glass).

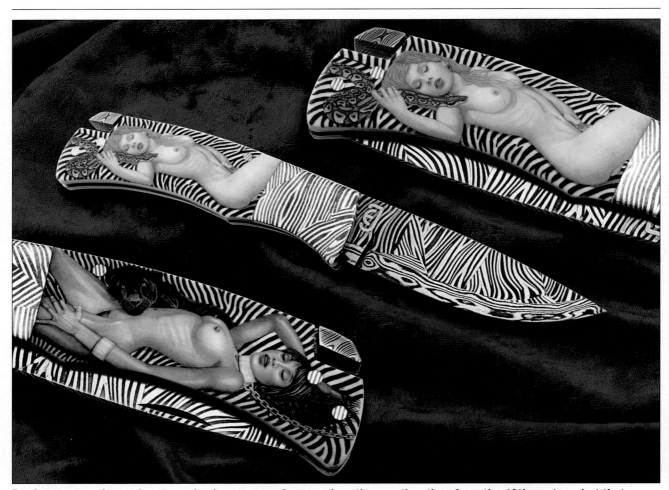

Dr. Jensen says he prefers to scrimshaw women from modern times rather than from the 19th century, but that they must show mystery and intrigue. He also insists that they are powerful in their ability to turn men into fools. Johannes Ebner built the mosaic-damascus tab-lock folder.

An animal should have eye contact with the onlooker, says scrimshaw artist Dr. Peter Jensen. The mammoth-ivory handle of Andre Thorburn's Damasteel folder makes other scrimshanders green with envy.

You get some basic advice from a book, and the rest is learned 'by doing,' a perfect method for an autodidact. But you must have one virtue: patience. For achieving top results, a little bit [of] drawing talent is helpful. Finding the right motif for the scrimshaw is much more difficult.

"The shape of the knife and the handle forces you mostly to be content with a small and unfavorable area, and the design of the knife is an essential point for the choice of the motif," Jensen explains. "The best material to work on is undoubtedly elephant ivory, because this is the best ground for the effect of colors. It is more difficult to work on dark bark ivory or black water buffalo horn, because you then have to use covering colors (colors mixed with white), and you cannot wipe away the color surplus. Besides the stitching, you have to do a miniature painting."

Jensen produces some of the most artful and entrancing scrim on the planet. Along with the Moby Dick knife, he said, "I'm pleased with the swimming lady and her erotic dream, because this scrimshaw was rather difficult to realize. A knife at first is a tool, but it also signalizes danger, and I believe this makes a great part of the knife's fascination. The scrimshaw on the knife handle should reflect such danger, even if it is an erotic subject."

And where is the doctor on eroticism? "Naturally it is possible to scrim a beautiful woman copied from the hand of a painter in the Victorian era, for example J. W. Waterhouse. This would be pretty scrimshaw, but these are women of the 19th century. I prefer to use pictures of women from our time period, but they must have mystery. Scrimshaw should embellish the knife, but for me it's often a little bit more. It's an eye-catcher—it seduces you to have a closer look and to spend time for it.

"To reach this goal, I have to note a couple rules:

1. The scrimshaw motif has to be a 'knockout theme,' like eroticism, [a] powerful animal or a dangerous situation; and

2. The performance should be plastic, three-dimensional, almost looking like a sculpture.

"I have no real secrets. Scrimshaw is an art. It's like in my former profession as a surgeon—you must have the absolute desire to reach your goal, and you have to work extremely clear and correct," Jensen instructs. "Then you get it.

"I admired the beauty and artistry of the works of the knifemakers, but above all I was searching for an inspiring canvas for my scrimshaw, so I purchased only knives with an ivory or horn handle. I admit this is no cheap way of getting a canvas, but a very special way to build a knife-collection," Jensen surmises.

Gratification and satisfaction are key elements with Jensen, and his take on it is, "What makes the scrimshander happy? When the onlooker takes the knife, then sits down, takes the magnifying glass and looks for a while. This spectator understands him."

He concludes, "I began to collect custom knives under the precipice that all my knives should get a small part of myself—the scrimshander. Seen from this angle, knives for me mainly are my canvas. But naturally I also admire the beauty and artistry of the works of the knifemakers and master smiths. At the moment half of my knives have got 'a part of myself,' and I hope God will give me the time to do the rest."

Feel The Frictional Heat

Friction Forging™ involves pressure, a pin, rotational movement, frictional heat and no quenching

By Durwood Hollis

Traditionally, forging has been characterized by four elements—heat (forge), pressure (hammer), cooling (quench) and the resultant plastic deformation of steel. The knifemaker repeatedly heating and hammering steel into a desired blade form is the image most associated with such a characterization. However, there's a new process that has expanded the parameters of the traditional understanding of forging.

Nearly 10 years ago, Charles Allen, owner of Knives of Alaska, joined forces with Drs. Carl Sorenson and Tracy Nelson, both metallurgists and materials experts, as well as chaired professors at Brigham Young University, in Provo, Utah. The trio's initiative was to develop a new forging methodology. The ultimate goal was to achieve an ultra-fine steel grain structure, allowing for enhanced hardness without brittleness, differential heat treatment to withstand user abuse, and a corrosion-proof edge zone (to eliminate corrosive edge dulling).

Sorenson and Nelson had extensive experience in the field of "Friction Stir Processing" of hard metals, a process used in the petroleum and space industries to fuse metals without the addition of external welding material.

Combing this knowledge with Allen's production-knife manufacturing experience, the men were able to adapt the Friction Stir process to knife blade production. And after more than five years of development and testing, "Friction Forging" joined other blade production processes (hammer forging, drop forging and roll forging) as a legitimate forging technology.

Friction Forging is accomplished by plunging a rotating Polycrystalline Cubic Boron Nitride (PCBN) pin into a blade blank, under pressure, thereby creating frictional heat. When the pin is fully engaged, it slowly traverses the length of the eventual edge zone. As the pin moves, it deforms the micro-granular steel matrix, leaving in its wake a transformed granular structure. During the process the actual size of the steel grain in the edge zone is reduced from .5

Available individually or in a two-knife set, the Pinnacle I (top) and Pinnacle II feature Friction Forged D2 tool steel blades, and handles (shown here in presentation-grade desert ironwood) that fit nicely in the palm of the hand.
(Durwood Hollis image)

microns to an extremely fine .05 microns, eliminating any need for further stabilization by subsequent cryogenic treatment.

Due to the fact that the heat generated during the rotational movement of the pin is completely localized, the newly transformed grain structure, produced as a result of the process, is instantly stabilized by heat dissipation into the surrounding steel. Unlike traditional quenching methods, the instantaneous heat transfer actually serves as a quench.

While a number of steels were used during the development stage, the best results were seen with D2 tool steel. The D2 blade blank is initially heat treated to a Rockwell hardness 42-44 Rc, which provides a tough "spring steel" blade body. And after Friction Forging, the edge zone of the blade blank reaches a hard 65-68 Rc. In simple terms, a Friction Forged edge is harder without the usual accompanying blade brittleness. When a hard edge is combined with a less hard, tough blade body through differential heat treatment, the result is optimal performance and extended edge retention.

Furthermore, during Friction Forging some of the chromium content (D2 tool steel is composed of 12 percent chromium) of the steel is freed from the chromium carbides and "frozen" into the surrounding ferrite. The result is the production of a totally stainless edge zone, which is unaffected by environmental invectives.

Test of Steel

Once the development team had all the bugs worked out of the Friction Forging process, something that took many months to accomplish, objective testing was undertaken. A number of blades,

Friction Forging is a highly technical methodology. To accomplish the actual forging process, a blade blank is clamped into a computer-controlled mill, which is closely monitored by the operator. *(Durwood Hollis image)*

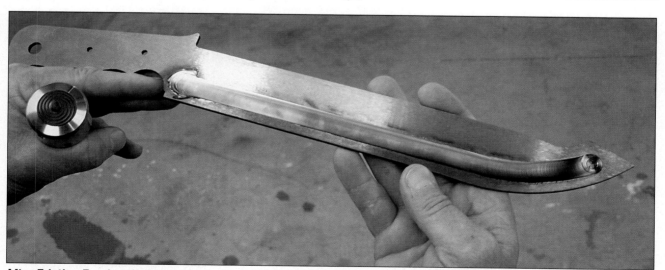

After Friction Forging the blade blank, the processed edge zone is clearly delineated by the discoloration resulting from rotational heat. *(Durwood Hollis image)*

New Friction Forged Knives

Currently there are five fixed-blade Friction Forged knives (including a tactical model) and six lock-blade models in the Diamond-Blade line. Prices start at $299.99 each, and vary according to model and choice of handle material. Handle choices include presentation-grade desert ironwood, Micarta®, Texillum™, ram's horn and stag. DiamondBlade Friction Forged knives are only available direct from the factory. For more information, go to www.diamond-bladeknives.com.

including those of 440C, ATS-34, 154CM, AUS-6, CPM S90V and CPM S30V steels, were tested along with a Friction Forged blade. Each of the test blades was identical in size, shape and edge geometry. Furthermore, with the exception of the Friction Forged test blade, each was properly heat-treated and cryogenically quenched to obtain an optimal hardness of 59-61 Rc. Testing of sharpness and edge retention were undertaken.

A Razor Edge Sharpness Test machine, manufactured by the Cutlery & Allied Trade Research Association (CATRA), was employed to measure the force needed to cut into silicone test media. And an Edge Retention Test machine was used to record the number of cuts each blade made on ¾-inch manila rope before edge sharpness failed.

Knife performance tests, such as chopping through wood and slicing a free-hanging rope typically involve both the knife and the tester's ability to use the knife. Therefore, any objective comparison not only must include identical blade geometry, but also the elimination of any human factors.

The Razor Edge Sharpness test and the Edge Retention test were conducted with a hands-off approach. Testing was done without any human involvement other then simply turning on the test machines. Without exception, the performance of the Friction Forged blade in both tests exceeded all other test blades by a wide margin.

More compact than their fixed-blade cousins, the Monarch, with black-carbon-fiber handle scales and pocket clip, and Summit folders feature Friction Forged blades. *(Durwood Hollis image)*

Several field tests involving a number of prominent outdoor writers were conducted at Tejon Ranch, in California. The object of these tests was for each of the writers to use a Friction Forged knife during the course of their pursuit of wild pigs. Anyone who has ever hunted wild boars knows that the grit embedded in their hides, along with their wire-like hair, can quickly erode the edge of any blade. In my own experience, I've never found a blade steel that could handle more than a couple of wild hogs without some attention given to edge maintenance.

After two days of hunting and numerous pigs taken, including several big boars, all of the writers (me included) had more than one opportunity to use a Friction Forged knife. Not one of writers had to tune-up the edge of their knife. Without exception, everybody involved in the field test had glowing reports. "The knife was scary sharp," said one writer. "I field-dressed two big boars and my knife was still shaving sharp," said another. At the conclusion of the hunt, every single knife that had been used was functionally sharp, with many still razor-sharp.

While that initial experience was impressive, for me the real test of the new technology came later in the year during a hunt for coastal brown bear in Southeast Alaska. With Allen as my guide (Charles is not only the owner of Knives of Alaska and a senior partner in DiamondBlade L.L.C., but also a registered Alaskan guide and a licensed bush pilot), we were in place at dawn on opening day of bear season. It didn't take too

The latest addition to the DiamondBlade Friction Forged line of lock-blade folders is the compact Viper. The upswept blade pattern has enough point to be useful as an edged field-dressing tool, while the belly is just the ticket for hide removal. *(Durwood Hollis image)*

Author Durwood Hollis used a DiamondBlade Summit fixed blade to skin an Alaskan coastal brown bear. The entire procedure was accomplished without any sharpening effort. *(Durwood Hollis image)*

long to spot a bear. In fact, we located four bears, one of which was a truly a trophy animal.

Bear Crossing

Quickly we moved into position, and as luck would have it, the largest bear crossed right in front us. Charles managed to stop the animal in its tracks with a loud wail from a varmint call. When everything came together, I squeezed the trigger and the hunt was over. "Now the real Friction Forged field test begins," Charles said.

Over the course of nearly eight hours, we skinned the bear from claws to fangs, including fleshing and detailed trophy work, without ever sharpening our knives. Considering that the animal's hide was embedded with coarse sand, I was astonished that edge integrity wasn't adversely affected. Afterwards, we cleaned the blades and amazingly both knives were able to shave hair from our arms. That's peerless performance in my book.

While there have been many unique and outstanding advances in the world of cutlery, most have centered on mechanical functioning, like various blade-locking mechanisms, knife components, new blade steels, thermoplastic handle material or enhanced heat-treatment and quenching using computer-controlled furnaces and cryogenic treatment. Friction forging is one of only a few new processes, with powder-metallurgical steel being another, that deals directly with the micro-structure of the blade steel itself, imparting desirable characteristics unobtainable through most other forging or heat-treatment processes.

In actual field use, Friction Forged knives have proven over and over again that they outperform others, including some hand-forged and production-made knives. While no steel known to man can remain sharp forever, Friction Forging has raised the sharpness and edge retention bar to new heights.

Some may argue that Friction Forging is not actually forging, since there isn't a forge, a hammer or an external quench utilized, and it is true that the process isn't traditional by any stretch of the imagination. Nevertheless, the properties of the blade steel are still transformed by heat, pressure and quenching. And by so doing, the work of Allen, Sorenson and Nelson has expanded the parameters of the traditional understanding of forging.

Giving Back to the World Of Knives

Paul Lansingh shares a treasure trove of history and tradition from 65 years of collecting knives

By Mike Haskew

Knives have become more than a hobby for Paul Lansingh. Through 65 years as a collector and knife enthusiast, his role has evolved from that of casual interest to one of a volunteer historian, caretaker and curator.

At 71, Lansingh still owns the two-blade, slip-joint folder he was given as a six-year-old boy. Today, he hesitates to even estimate the number of knives in his possession, and to call his custom knife holdings a "collection" is a classic understatement.

"That first knife was given to me by a neighbor," says the Ford Motor Co. retiree who worked in 25 jobs, in six cities, at 13 of the giant automaker's office buildings. "I collected baseball cards, marbles, comic books, yo-yos, plus knives and letter openers from around the world. The more I learned about knives

the more the knife became my main interest and I dropped the other childhood things; however, I added many other collections, from cameras, to ethnic art, to mid-century modern furniture, to the Apollo 11 Mission [collectibles]. And I just completed a Christian art collection and display called '65 Events in the Life of Jesus' that includes 45 two- and three-dimensional media forms collected from 26 countries."

Paul has a family history in fine art, design and architecture. He likes sole-authorship and one-of-a-kind items made by true craftsmen. "I have won several marksmanship awards,

Among the Paul Lansingh collection is the first tanto ever displayed at the Knifemakers' Guild Show, this one by BLADE Magazine Cutlery Hall-Of-Famer® Jimmy Lile. It features an ivory handle, nickel silver fittings, a tiger-maple sheath, a "take-apart" feature with a stainless steel pin, and is signed on the blade under the handle in Japanese tradition. *(Point Seven Photo)*

but I would rather collect knives than guns because guns are machine made in factories that have no face," Lansingh says. He appreciates personal bench-made craftsmanship, innovative blade shapes, and the hand embellishments that are applied to upscale knives (carving, engraving, scrimshaw, checkering, inlays, etc.).

For Lansingh, through the years, knives have continued to be his main collecting passion, and he has amassed more than just a large number of them. In fact, his holdings could be divided into dozens of collecting subcategories, each of which stands up in its own right. For example, he owns a knife made by each of the presidents, vice presidents, and secretary-treasurers in the history of the Knifemakers' Guild.

For 25 years, noted collector Don Henderson presented the W.W. Cronk Award for the Best Knife at the annual Guild Show. While he does not own each specific award-winning knife, Paul has a representative knife from each award winner, all of which he displayed at the 2009 Guild Show held in Louisville, Ky.

He's collected a knife made by each custom maker who has been inducted into the BLADE Magazine Cutlery Hall Of Fame®. And commemorating the 34-year history of the Guild's Red Watson Memorial Friendship Award, he has managed to gather and display upscale knives from each of the winners, most of which he already owned before they won the award.

Titled "Hunter and the Hunted," the first knife Arpad Bojtos sold in the United States is fully carved on the handle, guard, blade and sheath with two sides of the story. On one side, a lioness awaits her prey and then attacks a zebra while the male lion stands guard. On the other side, native hunters stalk the lioness with the mail lion protecting his mate. When the hunters get too close, the male lion attacks. *(Point Seven Photo)*

Paul has collected knives from every maker who is a member of the American Bladesmith Society (ABS) Hall of Fame, from every ABS chairman, the three knife-making founding fathers of the ABS, and a damascus knife from each of the first 13 makers to become ABS master smiths. He has 60 knives made by 34 present and former members of the Art Knife Invitational. And yes, the list of such collecting categories goes on, and on.

Pre-War Knife Pioneers

"I started learning about 20th-century custom knives in America and separated them into two categories," remembers Lansingh. "There are the older knives by makers who started making knives in the 'vintage year' of 1902 [William Scagel, Earnest Warther and H.H. Buck], and they are the oldest three in the collection of those who I consider to be the top 10 custom makers from 1900 to 1938. I call this group the 'pre-war knife pioneers,' and some of the knives are crude by today's standards, but the makers' names are recognized."

He also possesses a vast number of knives from the post-World War II era and has further divided his 35 collecting categories by maker, type of knife and period. Some of the other eras and styles in which he concentrates his collecting efforts range from ancient times and pieces to San Francisco-style knives, to integrals, doctor's knives, and international hand-made knives from the ethnic tribes of Africa, the Lapland people of Finland, the Northwest Tlinget Indians, and the native Alaskan cultures, such as the Inuit tribes.

"In the 1970s, I started collecting contemporary knives and buying from Nate Posner at the San Francisco Gun Exchange," says Lansingh. "I became interested in San Francisco knives after buying the book *Knifemakers of Old San Francisco* by Bernard R. Levine. Of all the older knives made in the United States, there are two stand-out categories. There are the mid-19th-century San Francisco bowies, dirks, push daggers and such, which could be considered the first real 'art knives' made in the U.S.

"In my personal opinion, the antique bowie knife is the other American knife of real historical importance. If you are a collector, those two categories would be the heart of any American historical knife collection," Lansingh surmises.

His collecting journey is similar to that of others in that he joined several knife clubs, bought knife books, and attended gun and knife shows. However, the similarity ends with his visit to the Guild Show in the 1970s, when it was still held in Kansas City.

"That was my first show," he recalls, "and I saw more wonder-

Paul Lansingh commissioned Gary Barnes (one of the first knifemakers to receive his ABS master smith stamp in 1983) to make "The Wizard" art knife. The wizard is a gold-plated casting with flowing robes made from walrus ivory and abalone. The wizard holds a 14k-gold rod with a genuine diamond at the end, and touches his wand to the steel, which, in turn, magically starts turning into precious damascus. (Point Seven Photo)

ful custom knives that day than I had seen in my entire life. I also started meeting some of the people who were featured in the articles I had read. That was one of the most significant events for me. I went from looking at 15 custom knives to looking at more than 1,000 custom knives, half of which I wanted to buy. So, that was my first exposure to a large number of custom knives and their makers."

After the premature passing of Dr. Jack R. Holifield in 1977, a landmark auction of his knife collection was held in April 1978 by Sotheby Parke Bernet that established the custom knife as a legitimate part of the art world.

"Holifield was considered the premiere knife collector in the country for many years," Paul comments, "and he had the largest custom knife collection around.

At the time he died, he was actually a major promoter of the 'art knife.' He would challenge a custom maker, 'I'll buy whatever you make if you will make me the best knife that you can conceive,' and money was no object. Jack had become kind of a patron to custom knifemakers, and I was able to acquire several of these 'Holifield challenge' knives through the auction."

A Eureka Moment

Another significant thing that Holifield did was to display his knives for public viewing at the Guild Show. Certainly, this contributed to the growing popularity of custom knives. Lansingh borrowed that idea and built on it in the years to come. In Knoxville, Tenn., Paul attended the banquet at the annual BLADE Show. As he thumbed through the program, he experienced one of those "eureka" moments.

Walter Erickson built the rare malachite-handle izmail knife in a Balisong™ configuration. In traditional Jewish circumcision, a rabbi uses an izmail knife on the eighth day of a baby boy's life. It even comes with an interchangeable spare blade to make sure the rabbi has a sharp edge at all times. *(Point Seven Photo)*

"I was reading the names of the people who were in the Hall Of Fame, and I noticed that I already had a knife from every person who was actually a knife-maker," he smiled. "I mentioned it and was later asked to bring the collection to the BLADE Show the next year."

Lansingh did some research and then wrote a little history about each knife in his Hall Of Fame collection so that anyone could read about the maker, his specialties, and the knife that was on display. "Up to that time, I suppose, I was more of an accumulator than a true collector. I'm not an accumulator anymore. I used to collect beautiful knives, buying what I liked. Then, I decided that there were so many knives in the world that I should have several meaningful collections and not just a large 'accumulation.' So, it was when I was displaying the Hall Of Fame collection I had an epiphany that this was indeed something more meaningful than just having a bunch of pretty knives."

Gradually, his focus evolved from collecting knives to collecting people and their work. With such a perspective, it becomes readily apparent that he has succeeded in moving beyond the knife itself and into the realm of real living, recording and preserving the stories behind the knives, and offering a glimpse into the character and quality of the people who made them.

In all his vast experience, Paul relates that it truly is the connection between the people, their knives, and those who appreciate the talent, which has fueled his passion. "There is historical purpose here," he reasons. "It isn't necessarily the knife, but the maker. In most cases, the knives are one-of-a-kind or have historical significance, but in all cases the person I am displaying performed some significant function in custom knives.

"Besides, after collecting for 65 years you don't want to just put the knives in a walk-in safe. In the tradition of Jack Holifield and Joe Drouin, you want to 'give something back' to the world of knives and share your knives with the public," he says. Over the years Lansingh has displayed 12 different collections at the Guild Show and the BLADE Show, and he has committed to the Guild to bring a new display each of the next five years.

Another twist on his public displays is the grouping of several modern knives along with an example of the same design or style that may have been made 200 or more years ago. Paul calls this display, which also includes a narrative description of the knives being viewed, a "juxtaposition." It is, in truth, a blending of the old and the new, in recognition of the common thread that runs throughout.

One of Lansingh's most vivid memories is that of his first visit to the shop of knifemaker D.E. "Ed" Henry, who Nate Posner said was making the finest bowie knives in the nation. "He was a very controversial person," Paul commented, "and if you wanted to visit him, he would interview you for a half hour on the phone and decide if you were worthy of his time. As it turned out, most people never were allowed to visit his backwoods property, let alone his shop. I think I passed the interview because I knew something about his passion: Collins machetes.

I may be the only person who ever went to D.E. Henry's as his first visit to a knifemaker's shop!"

For a man who has collected knives for more than six decades, lived in seven states, visited 44 countries on five continents, and received the 2004 Nate Posner Award for "Outstanding Service in the Promotion of Handcrafted Cutlery," as voted by the Knifemakers'

W.W. Cronk Award-winner Doug Casteel fashioned a one-of-a-kind folder with a Mike Norris damascus blade and handle, a cutout in the blade, extensive filework, and a window in the handle highlighting the colorful black-lip mother-of-pearl inlays. *(Point Seven Photo)*

One of only three Canadians to have his ABS master smith stamp, Christoph Deringer forged the integral fighter with a fileworked blade, Spanish notch, sculpted rosewood handle, and sculpted steel collar and pommel. The integral steel tang runs horizontally through the handle. *(Point Seven Photo)*

Steve R. Johnson's sub-hilt fighter (top) features sheep-horn handle scales and extensive 18K gold-highlighted engraving by Ron Skaggs. D.E. Kressler is one of Europe's finest makers. His damascus fighter (center) sports a buffalo-horn handle and fine detail engraving. Master smith Jerry Fisk forged two patterns of damascus for a 21st-century version of a San Francisco bowie (bottom), also featuring an ivory handle, and engraving on the guard, collar and pins. *(Point Seven Photo)*

Guild Board of Directors, it would seem that there are few worlds left to conquer. Today, Lansingh continues filling in the blanks. As individuals are elected to a hall of fame or assume a leadership role in a custom knife organization, it is a safe bet that he will add to the number of knives he owns on a continuing basis.

When Lansingh speaks to knife clubs or at show seminars, he is often asked about opportunities to build collections. His response is to find something with a theme, such as "top female makers" or "top makers from a certain state or country." As an example, he has his own collection of those who he considers the top 10 knifemakers from Canada.

In the end, the number of knives and their values individually or as a collection are quite secondary. Lansingh sees value in the journey, value in the story, value in the heritage, and above all, value in the people.

Part of his sense of purpose, satisfaction and service has been realized through his love of the custom knife, and his legacy will last. There may be no better illustration of the true essence of collecting.

Swordplay Renaissance Style

The element of play, whether with swords, knives or period costumes, lends allure to Renaissance Faires

By Jordan Clary

If you've ever felt like you were born in the wrong century, that you'd rather be jousting or folk dancing to the twang of lutes, you can travel through time. And you can do it without getting lice in your hair or encountering bad sewage. Renaissance Faires, which first came into existence sometime after World War II and blossomed during the 1960s, continue to proliferate today.

Brawny men in tights and buxom women in flowing skirts and tight bodices stroll along grassy paths greeting each other as "m'lady" or "sir." Spontaneity and improvisation are part of what draws people to these Faires.

Attendees come from all walks of life, some for relaxation and others as an escape. "Some simply like the dress-up concept," says Ronald Cleveland, organizer of the Seattle Renaissance Faire (www.washingtonrenfaire.com). "But most just want good, clean family entertainment, and we surely provide that."

Renaissance Faires happen all over the country, from coast to coast. Each has its own flavor, its own personality. "People are searching for who they are," says Cleveland. "We are a nation with very little past or long history."

Swords are an integral part of Renaissance Faires, and the

This close-up view of a knight in full armor gives a good feel for the burden such warriors bore.

A fight broke out at a Society For Creative Anachronism event. *(photo courtesy of Kelli Thompson)*

Dusk descends on the Faire. *(photo courtesy of Kelli Thompson, a.k.a. Esmerelda of the Lake, www.esmeraldaofthelakes.com)*

people who take part in the swordplay, whether as organizers or as participants, take them seriously. One doesn't need to look far to understand why the lure of the ancient sword is so powerful. Old manuscripts are full of stories of mystical swords inscribed with runes that could defeat enemies and make men quail just at the sight of them. In the Old English elegy, *Beowulf*, the hero receives a powerful sword named Hrunting that he uses to defeat the monster, Grendel. The Scandinavian classic, *Poems of the Elder Edda*, contains numerous accounts of serpents and giants felled by mighty warriors.

Many people yearn for a time when magic still ruled the lives of men and women. All of this and more are recreated in the contemporary world of Renaissance Faires.

Renaissance is a term used loosely. While many Faires are set up as villages during the reign of Queen Elizabeth and the height of the European Renaissance of the 1500s, others have an earlier, medieval flair and are recreated from circa-1000 A.D. to the 1400s. Still others embrace the golden age of pirates on the high seas, around the end of the 17th century. Though the time span may be broad, one thing they all share is a love of close combat through the use of swords or sticks.

While most Faires include loose interpretations of history, others try to stay true to historical events of a particular time period. Brian Caton of Neville Companye (www.nevillecompanye.com), a group of actors who portray the military unit of Sir Richard Neville, Earl of Warwick, says that he and the other members of Neville Companye research the period extensively. The period his group chose is the era of the War of the Roses, a series of civil wars that took place between 1455-1487 for the throne of England.

"We aren't actors," Caton says. "We're re-enactors. Everything we do is ad-libbed. Although the knights and other members of the Companye each portray a certain character—a character that has to be based, however loosely, on history—we don't have lines to repeat.

Although costumes and props can be bought or rented at Faires, many take pride in making their own equipment and clothing.

War In The Woods

The element of play is a large part of the lure of Renaissance Faires. Cleveland says as a child in Scotland, he and his friends played war in the woods "with real swords and somehow none of us were injured." However, while most of his friends lost interest in swordplay as they got older, he "fell in love with it." He's continued for more than 50 years and says the Faires are a great "release and escape from the mundane life."

Custom knifemakers are frequent participants at Renaissance Faires, usually hammering and forging blades in a fashion typical of the age. Others, however, take a more eclectic approach. Jon Schulps, a custom knifemaker who has been a regular at the southern California Renaissance Faire since 1968, always "throws a bit of his

own self and style into it, even if it's a period piece," according to his apprentice, Jason McPherson.

The dueling and battles are focal points for many players, and the preparation for these events goes on long before the actual re-enactments take place. Steaphen Fick, author of *Reclaiming the Blade* and *The Beginners Guide to the Long Sword*, teaches sword enthusiasts fencing techniques

at the school he founded, Davenriche European Martial Arts School in Santa Clara, Calif. Like Caton, Fick researches extensively to perfect his instruction. Although, he has created his own methodology, it's loosely based on medieval manuscripts and a thorough study of art books from the period.

"With art you can see both the clothing and the musculature,

Brian Caton plays the role of a circa-mid-1400s knight. Caton is with the Neville Company, a group of actors who portray the military unit of Sir Richard Neville, Earl of Warwick.

Tents stand and flags wave at the village erected in anticipation of a fun-filled event. *(photo courtesy of Kelli Thompson, a.k.a. Esmerelda of the Lake, www.esmeraldaofthelakes.com)*

the way the body moves and where the balance is," Fick says. He adds that clothing can tell a lot about the way a person fights. "Different clothes offer or restrict different kinds of movement. In Eastern martial arts, the fighters wear big billowy pants where you can't see the feet. But in European medieval fighting, the sign of a gentleman was a well-turned calf. If you want to show off your calf, you can't hide your feet. This makes for two different styles of fighting."

While Fick finds studying fashion helpful in developing ancient sword techniques, he also says that he's trying to enlighten people that practicing ancient sword fighting is more than dress up. "People see dress up and they think role playing. They don't take it as seriously," he notes.

"Your techniques are the icing on the cake. But you also need to learn the underlying principles," he says. "If I want to grasp the greater whole, I need to comprehend what makes things work. I need to understand the principles. Technique is a great way to learn, but once you get it down, you have to move past that. Why do we do things? How does geometry play into it? You need to learn sociology, history and geometry. All of this plays into sword fighting."

Not all Renaissance enthusiasts are interested in recreating actual historical scenes. The Society for Creative Anachronism (SCA) makes up another component of the reenactment scene. Unlike Renaissance Faires, SCA is not-for-profit. They also base their events on an earlier period than the Renaissance.

Fantasy Aficionados

SCA began in Berkeley, Calif., in 1966, when a group of writers, historians, and science fiction and fantasy aficionados threw a tournament. They had so much fun that they decided to hold a second one in a larger setting in a local park.

Today SCA has 19 "Kingdoms in the Known Worlde," and over 60,000 people participate in events each year. "People like fantasy and they like acting out fantasy. You get a chance to explore it on a deep level. You become completely immersed in this whole culture," says Aurelia de Montfort, media contact for the West Kingdom.

"Organizing nearly 500 volunteers and vendors in and of itself is a major accomplishment," says Cleveland. "Sometimes it truly feels as though we're herding cats."

The rewards, however, are clearly worth it for both organizers and attendees. Where else can one learn how to make beeswax candles, spin and weave, participate in medieval folk dancing, or take place in a major battle in full armor all in one place? "It is a difficult undertaking with great financial risks, but the reward of seeing thousands of happy people enjoying the fruits of our labor makes it worthwhile," Cleveland says.

Today, Renaissance Faires take place in virtually every state in the country, and in many foreign countries. You can find groups on social media networks like Facebook, My Space and Twitter. If you have a longing for the distant past, there is likely a Faire that will meet your needs. "This is the best hobby in the world," says de Montefort. "I've learned so many wonderful things. You never get bored."

Why Do We Love Knives?

A simple answer to the million-dollar question remains elusive, but is well worth seeking

By Wm. Hovey Smith

When viewing knives as utilitarian tools only, then besides being useful their appeal remains somewhat of a mystery. One point in their favor is that, if well made, they're likely to last several lifetimes. Then the question becomes, if we already own a dozen knives why would we want more, especially if each one outlives our children and even grandchildren? Why do we love knives so much?

Knives tug at deep, inner emotions, compelling us to buy the edged beauties. Those who search for only one reason find themselves reaching for a very slippery fish. No sooner do we nail down a particular reason to own a knife, we see another piece and are compelled to buy it for a completely different reason.

All of the knives showcased herein caught my eye at the 2009 BLADE Show in Atlanta. Among the hundreds of exhibitors and thousands of knives, there's no doubt that other attendees would have made different choices.

Knife Design

It could be argued that knife design is the first thing that attracts a potential customer to a blade. A collector may be looking for a particular model to fill a gap in his collection. A hunter might take a liking to the shape of a blade, or how easily

it can be carried in the field. A serviceman may be searching for a lightweight knife that is easily accessed while he or she is weighed down with 80 pounds of battle gear. There is no best knife design just as there are no ideal car models.

What appeals to me are ethnic designs developed over

thousands of years. My preference is for unadorned, traditional working pieces that were actually worn and used. In modern knives I am often attracted to makers who mix ethnic traditions with pleasing designs.

The first knives that grabbed my attention at the show were those of E. Jay Hendrickson of

The author suggests that a beautiful blade, such as the fileworked and etched damascus piece with discernable brown hues forged by knifemaker Herbert Derr, is motivation enough to buy a new knife.

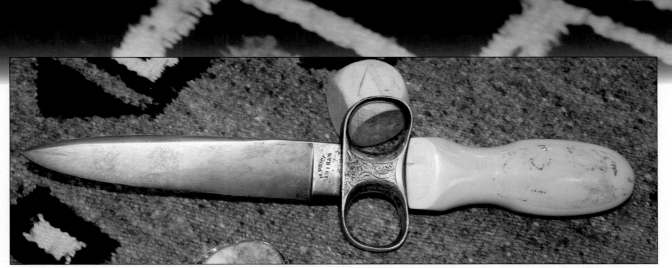

Historical significance is a draw for knife enthusiasts, with this original Michael Price ring dagger being no exception. It showcases an ivory handle with faded scrimshaw of a hunter shooting a California bear.

Frederick, Md. He sold his first knife in 1974 and eventually rose to the level of an American Bladesmith Society (ABS) master smith. He worked with Bill Moran, who he credits with strongly influencing his future output of over 2,000 knives.

One of Hendrickson's pieces incorporates a mix of Scandinavian and Persian design influences. Being of Nordic descent, Hendrickson fashioned a sheath to incorporate a bone tip, a natural extension and evolution of the all-horn sheaths used by the Lapps. The Persian-influenced handle combined with a damascus blade and upswept tip proved an interesting style to Hendrickson. He learned silver-wire inlay from Moran. The open scroll design of the wire inlay is more a reflection of Hendrickson's own interpretation than that of outside influences.

He said that he strives to "create something that 'grabs' the viewer." Hendrickson explains, "A potential buyer likely doesn't know why he likes a knife so much, but he does."

Back To The Blade

Damascus blades have obvious eye appeal enhanced through etching. Herbert K. Derr of St. Albans, W. Va., forged O-1 and L6 steels with nickel to create a 2,700-layer damascus blade. The brown hues of the hand-finished and heat-blued blade are complemented by a stabilized box-elder-burl spacer, a gemsbok horn handle, and nickel-silver end caps and bolster, all of which lead the eye immediately back to the blade.

The leather sheath appears banded, the illusive result of ostrich-leg leather inlay. With this knife, the blade is undoubtedly the most eye-catching element, as every part of the knife accentuates it.

Derr forges his own damascus using a 50-pound mechanical power hammer and a 42-ton hydraulic press that he built himself.

Utilitarian Edge

Few knives are more utilitarian than the A.G. Russell Fruit Testing Knife. The ATS-34 stainless steel blade resists the corrosive effects of acidic fruits, rates 59-61 Rc on the Rockwell Hardness scale, and does not dull easily. The 4.5-inch spay blade is lengthy enough to slice melon, while the entire knife weighs a

slight 2 ounces, and is flat enough to carry in a pants pocket.

Historical Aspect

Countless knives have turned up in interesting places during interesting times, and few are more fascinating than those made in San Francisco during the California gold rush. Few miners made their fortunes during the gold rush, and in fact many more folks became wealthy selling goods to miners, catering to their needs and by speculating in real estate.

One of the city's most famous knifemaking sons, Michael Price, fashioned high-end knives often fitted with walrus-ivory grips and engraved fittings, such as an original Price piece offered for sale by Jason Baldwin of Chicago. Price's knives are highly desirable, and the best known examples have recently sold for over $100,000.

The piece Baldwin exhibited at the BLADE Show falls into the realm of Price's mid-range knives. It features an unusual double-ring guard, and showcases an ivory handle with faded scrimshaw of a hunter shooting a California bear. Baldwin, who collects and trades American fighting knives and relics, said this is only one of three "M. Price"-marked knives known to exist.

Before the advent of conceal-able pistols and metal cartridges, having a good knife was vitally important in the saloons and gambling halls of San Francisco during the mid-1800s. From all appearances the knife was often carried, and could very well have visited the goldmines and the streets of San Francisco.

Soul Of A Knife

Douglas Noren, an ABS master smith from Spring Lake, Minn., puts a tremendous amount of time and mental energy into his knives. One recent project was a Victorian-era Scottish officer's dagger with sheath and box that would be an outstanding knife even if exhibited in the fanciest showroom in London. This is a remarkable achievement for a person who did not start making knives until he was 56 years old. Throughout his life as a furniture maker he remained a meticulous craftsman who felt that every part of a piece of furniture needed to be finished, even parts that no one would ever see.

On a trip to Edinburgh, Scot-land, Noren purchased a period officer's dagger in the original wooden box, and decided that he wanted to fashion an even finer example. Instead of the silver grip of the original dagger, he opted for an ebony handle carved in a Celtic knot pattern and studded with ivory, choosing to forge an 11.5-inch damascus blade for the piece.

"I did the knife in stages over more than six months. The blade was forged first. Then I started working on the hilt. I carved a model first to make sure I had the design right before I started working on the final version," Noren relates.

"I had to lay out the precise positioning of the ivory pins and fit them. The hilt was drilled for the screw-threaded tang and then fixed with a hand-forged nut, just like the originals," he says. "I made a wooden copy of the blade and used this to stretch the leather for the sheath. The silver fittings on the sheath are attached just as in the original with a cross-pin."

"Every knife I make is like climbing a mountain." Noren says. "Sometimes the trip to the top is easy, and at other times it is a real struggle." The struggle lent "soul" to the knife.

Knife Value

There are two aspects to the value of a knife, the first having to do with its usefulness, and the second with how much money someone is willing to pay for the piece. Some established U.S. knife companies, like W.R. Case & Sons Cutlery Co., are known not only for catering to collectors, but also for building pieces worth collecting. As with any desirable collectable, the value of the knife depends on its craftsmanship, quality, condition and rarity.

A blade smith's soul seems to be transferred into his knives, says the author. Knifemaker Doug Noren fashioned a reproduction of a Victorian-era Scottish officer's dagger, complete with an ebony handle carved in a Celtic knot pattern and studded with ivory, and an 11.5-inch damascus blade.

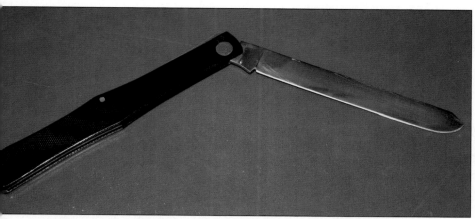

There aren't many knives more utilitarian and task oriented than that of the A.G. Russell Fruit Knife designed for slicing fruit and melon.

If knife design factors into the desire to buy a knife, then E. Jay Hendrickson might be selling a few of his pieces that incorporate a mix of Scandinavian and Persian influences.

Each year Case launches limited-production runs of several knife patterns designed to appeal to collectors, while simultaneously being attractive and usable knives to sell to the world at large. For the most part these are traditional slip-join pocketknives. Most collectors focus on a particular style, handle material or time period. According to Case's John Sullivan, collectors will often spot variations in tang stamp markings or handle, blade or bolster materials that will enhance the value of one knife over another made during the same period.

At the BLADE Show the W.R. Case & Sons booth on one side of the hall included an exhibit of new knives that were mostly priced under the $100 apiece, while on the other side of the room was a dealer selling old Case folders marked at thousands of dollars each. Visitors on both sides of the room were valuing the knives and making decisions whether to buy, trade or hold their commodity stock of knives. If this sounds rather like the stock market, that is an apt analogy.

What Is A Knive's Appeal?

The causes vary for having an insatiable appetite for knives. You might have a particular reason, like wanting to collect examples of your grandfather's handmade knives. The reasons why I think knives appeal to us include design, blade, utility, history, soul and value. Whatever draws enthusiasts and collectors there is an undeniable connection between those who love knives and those who make them, and a fascination with the incredible artistry, utility and craftsmanship of edged objects.

Discover Classic Villager's Blade Art

Goloks, parangs and klewangs are machetes steeped in Southeast Asian history and tradition

By Keith Spencer

Machete is the universally recognized name describing large and frequently heavy knives, primarily used in Latin American countries as agricultural tools and sometimes weapons.

While in operation from 1845-1965, Collins & Co. manufactured a wide range of practical machetes under the Legitimus brand, and the patterns are well documented in the book *Collins Machetes & Bowies 1845-1965*

authored by D.E. Henry. An English machete manufacturer, Ralph Martindale & Co. Ltd., established in 1874, continues to produce an extensive range of Crocodile brand machetes, said to be, according to the Martindale

The selection of five 150-250-year-old Javanese goloks features a variety of original forge-patterned pamors and customary furnishings, some of which have been restored or replaced. Pamor refers to whitish striations seen in the dark patina of the blades, deriving from laminations of nickel iron, often of meteoric origin. The origin of traditional villager's knives can be traced to what is referred to as the "10-40 Window"—north of Australia between 10 degrees south and 40 degrees north of the equator.

A Klewang-inspired English Martindale brand 4-01 British Army issue Jungle Knife gets top billing, with an equally impressive modern-made Indonesian villager's klewang with buffalo horn handle below it.

catalog, "outstandingly well-balanced tools to meet the arduous demands of rural farmers throughout the tropical regions of the world."

In the process of developing their respective lines of machetes, Collins & Co. and Martindale & Co. Ltd. popularized a number of blade shapes and dimensions peculiar to indigenous users in various regions around the world.

Machetes, not too far removed in terms of shape and size from swords, understandably have been, like knives, utilized as weapons of war and human conflict over the years. In a life-threatening situation, frantic people grab whatever is on hand to use as a weapon for offense or defense. Where masses of people are employed in predominantly rural regions, user-friendly blades remain nearby, designed as edged tools and adopted as weapons.

Collins and Martindale produced certain machetes specifically for self-defense in tropical environments, with the dual purpose of cutting vegetation when necessary. The companies transformed tried-and-true practical knife concepts into formidable edged weapons in the hands of trained soldiers engaged in close-quarters combat.

Of the military patterns recorded under the two best-known machete manufacturers, it's clear that three styles can clearly be identified as inspired by Southeast Asian villager's blades. They are the Collins pattern 1253 USA Paratroop Machete (WWII era) *parang*, the Martindale pattern 2-01 British Army (WWII era) *golok*, and Martindale pattern 4-01 British Army Jungle Knife (modern era) *klewang*.

Parang, Golok and Klewang

To simplify the identification and classification of popular blade shapes for Western readers, Indonesian names of villager blades have been applied, mainly parang, golok and klewang.

The parang-inspired Collins pattern 1253 Paratroop Machete, made for Cruver Mfg. Co., is surrounded by intrigue that spawned folklore. Amid the mist and mirrors that swirled around the American OSS (Office of Strategic Services), with its clandestine procedures and designs of specialized hardware, emerged the rare "OSS Machete."

We know that Collins produced the pattern 1253 Paratroop Machete on order number E64760, according to blueprints submitted by the Cruver Mfg. Co. Three variations were made, Types 1, 2 and 3, with different blade tips. Type 1 with a long leather scabbard appears in this article. Whilst there has been much speculation to do with its origin and efficiency as a jungle knife, the following is most likely closest to the truth.

Prior to the Spanish-American War that, in 1898, saw the Philippines ceded to the United States, Filipinos repeatedly tried to revolt against the Spaniards. After the execution of Filipino national hero Jose Rizel, co-founder of a Filipino movement called

At top is a modern Javanese golok with buffalo horn handle and traditional wooden scabbard. Below it rests a British Army-type golok with canvas scabbard and sharpening stone produced at Lithgow Small Arms Factory in Australia.

"the Propagandists," Andres Bonifacio founded a secret brotherhood named "the Katipuneros" in 1892. Bonifacio's objective was the complete separation from Spain of Filipino people by way of revolution.

To accomplish this, Bonifacio marshaled about a quarter of a million Filipinos trained in the techniques of *eskrima*, the classical martial art of sword and dagger fighting. Bonifacio gathered his followers for a secret meeting in Balintawak to affirm that they'd fight to the death, and so began the Philippine Revolution of 1896. The big blade, or sword, that was adopted during the Revolution measured up to 30 inches long and was named after the meeting place—Balintawak. Andres preferred a shorter, more stylish version with a 22-inch blade, and to this day it is known as the Bonifacio pattern.

OSS Machete Origin

The American-made OSS/ Paratroop Machete bears an incredible likeness to the Bonifacio/ Philippine Revolution knife and features design characteristics of traditional Southeast-Asian-made bladeware. Specifically it resembles the *piso sanalenggam* of Sumatra, widely considered throughout the Archipelago as being in the same genre as the parang.

According to D.E. Henry, Filipino-American Army troops in training at Fort Ord, California, used the pattern 1253 Paratroop Machete as an infiltration device during the invasion of the Philippines. Japan occupied the Philippines from 1941 until Gen. Douglas MacArthur liberated the island in 1945.

Harking back to the Martindale models, the 2-01 Golok was fashioned during WWII by the English firm Martin Davis and

To maximize cutting efficiency and minimize fatigue on machetes with angled-down handles, firmly grip each handle with forefinger, and thumb and loosely grip with three remaining fingers. Cock the hand back at the wrist for forward and backward, upward and downward slashes. In a relaxed fashion, sweep and direct the working part of the blade to the point of focus. At the moment of impact un-cock the wrist and snap the three fingers firmly around the handle.

The rare Collins brand USA-made OSS Machete with leather scabbard is held over an original-style but modern-made Filipino Balintawak, and the shorter, better-known Bonifacio village bladeware.

A modern-made golok with buffalo horn handle is pictured above an ancient golok with forge-welded blade bearing exquisite pamor.

Left to right are a SICUT brand parang with an 18-inch blade, a golok featuring a 14-inch blade, and a Klewang with a 12-inch blade. Manufactured at Bandung in Central Java, the knives come with traditional wooden scabbards and canvas belt sheaths.

Lithgow Small Arms Factory in Australia. It is the only Western-made machete referred to by the Southeast Asian knife name that gave rise to its adaptation for military use—golok (of Java).

The Martindale 4-01 Jungle Knife appears to have been made in the vein of the broad klewang, a villager's knife favored throughout the Indonesian Archipelago, mainly on the island of Sumatra. Although practical to use, the Western renditions of klewang and golok fall short of the original villager's versions, because they lack the angled-down grip that facilitates a particular gripping technique for maximizing cutting efficiency.

Two things in particular contribute to the functional reliability of Southeast Asian bladeware—the technical characteristics of shape, style and balance, and the acquired technique of using them.

Village Knife Culture

Given my Western upbringing, it took quite a while to sort out samples, sift through information and gain an Eastern understanding of a village knife culture that stretches back in Java, for instance, to the Mataram Kingdom of 732.

There have been two Mataram Kingdoms in Javanese history. The first existed from 732-870 and was based upon the Hindu-Sjiwaistic religion. The ancestors of the Sultans of Yogyakarta and Surakarta ruled the second, based on the Islamic religion, from 1582-1755. In 1755 the original kingdom was halved and ruled under two sultans, Hamengku Buwono I of Yogyakarta (sometimes still called Mataram), and Sunan Pakubuwono III of Surakarta.

Buwono is recorded as a versatile personality, a knight and expert in government, warfare, art and culture, economy, religion and psychology. He fought the Dutch from 1749 until 1755, and is recognized in Dutch history as a worthy opponent who defeated them in many battles. Buwono is especially remembered for winning the battle at the Bogowonto River, west of Yogyakarta. The Dutch made a treaty in 1755, a part of which saw Buwono installed as the first Sultan in the Kraton at Yogyakarta, such was their respect for Buwono's capacity to lead and manage his people.

Against this 1,200-year-old background of agriculture and conflict, a wide variety of uniquely styled bladeware has evolved, which Albert Van Zonneveld succinctly sums up in his book *Traditional Weapons of the Indonesian Archipelago*:

"Almost no other area in the world has produced such a varied arsenal of traditional weapons as the Indonesian Archipelago. Laden with symbolism and blessed with divine power, the keris especially has achieved great fame. However, this vast region has brought forth numerous other functional and ritual weapons. Through the centuries an almost endless quantity of weapons and other implements of war have been produced by people and groups living all over the archipelago."

Keris aside, for it has evolved into more of a spiritual symbol rather than a practical implement, villager's knives of the "10-40 Window" can be broadly categorized under the terminology of golok, parang and klewang.

Western-friendly, fully functional renditions of each are featured here under the brand of SICUT. Produced by skilled village craftsmen at Bandung in Central Java for global distribution by Matrose Agencies (www.knivesaustralia.com.au), the SICUT handmade edged tools faithfully integrate the essential characteristics of ancient forge-made blade technology. Other modern-made artifacts with buffalo horn handles appearing in this article are distributed by Valiant Trading of Australia (www.valiantco.com).

A selection of superbly fashioned, centuries-old, hand-forged damascene golok blades emanating from the Indonesian Archipelago is also featured. Surviving blade artistry—that's what it's all about. The crafted accoutrements—handles and scabbards—can be replaced over and over, but the legacy of traditional villager's blade art lives on, indelibly etched into the Southeast Asian psyche.

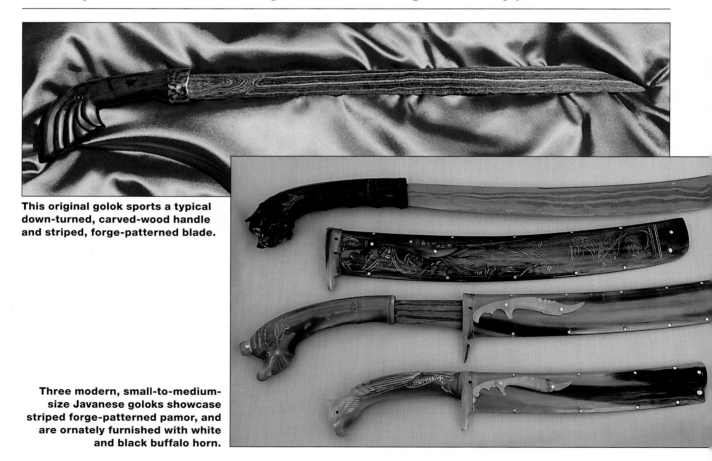

This original golok sports a typical down-turned, carved-wood handle and striped, forge-patterned blade.

Three modern, small-to-medium-size Javanese goloks showcase striped forge-patterned pamor, and are ornately furnished with white and black buffalo horn.

Trends

Coral. That was the answer—coral. We were wondering what the next hot handle material would be, and figured, no matter what it was, it couldn't get any more exotic than other knife grips to come along in recent years. Think about it, knifemakers have gone from the good old days of bone, stag and stone to ancient mammoth tooth, spalted maple, camel leg and mastodon ivory. In between, wily knifemakers employed, and continue to use, Micarta®, carbon fiber, Timascus™ and G-10. Now we have coral, and it's as stunning as the Great Barrier Reef.

The Blade Builders Union (don't you think knifemakers should unionize just to revolt?) has gravitated toward abalone and black-lip pearl for a natural touch. And who knew there were more varieties of grip-sufficient wood grains than trees in our own Sequoia National Park?

This year a few creative blade builders set their sites on knives featuring "take down construction," just like guns that can be disassembled and reassembled. Now the coral comes off the handle and can be put back on again. If that wasn't enough, double-guard daggers, chute knives, slip joints, fighters, swords and bowies continue their popularity contest.

As a good coworker and friend of mine is fond of saying, "It's never boring," and why should it be? Knifemaking is a handcraft, and one of the most beautiful art forms in the world. With art comes creativity, and knifemakers are one of the most creative, trendsetting bunches to ever hand rub a blade. Let's enjoy the fruits of their labor. The next hot handle material is just around the next reef.

Around The World In Eight Blades

If you've ever watched the opening ceremonies of the Olympics and seen athletes enter the arena, proudly representing their countries, carrying and waving their national flags, smiling, gesturing, awestruck and humbled, you realize how much alike we all are, and what a small world with many cultural and ethnic differences it is in which we live. How beautiful is that?!

The more I travel to other countries, the more I realize that everything I read, heard and thought I knew about them was wrong or misleading, that the only way to understand a people and a place is to visit. Or, as Shirley MacLaine once said, "The more I traveled, the more I realized that fear makes strangers of people who should be friends." The more I travel, the more I realize there are more right ways to live and correct cultural heritages than wrong ones. Ours is not the only way of doing things, and sometimes it's not even the most logical way.

You can't really travel around the world in eight blades, but what the exotic edged objects on this and the facing page represent are styles of people, interpretations of similar tools and weapons, cultural identities and deep-rooted heritage. The differences are great, but the similarities far outweigh the departures, and taking them as a whole, an open-minded individual realizes how very much the same they are.

▼ **FRED OTT:** Literally a big-game hunter or guide in India, the meaning of the name "Shikari" can be translated to the knife at hand, a 13.75-inch, hand-forged, clay-tempered 1086 carbon-steel piece with a wrought-iron and copper blade collar, and a carved reindeer antler handle. *(BladeGallery.com photo)*

▶ **RICHARD VAN DIJK:** The proud Gurkha soldiers from Nepal carried kukris, this being a slim damascus example with an ebony handle and a sterling silver bolster.

◀ **PEKKA TUOMINEN:** Traditional Finnish or Scandinavian belt knives, two puukkos are done up in Silversteel blades, brass mountings and birch-bark handles.

TERRY RODGERS: Tlingit daggers originated in the northern reaches of Alaska, where they are thought to have been sacrificial daggers, thus the broad 5160 blade, "Y" pommel, and leather-wrapped handle of this integral interpretation. *(Ward photo)*

T.C. ROBERTS: The damascus Scottish dirk showcases a Roman-knot-work-style, carved blackwood handle, some nice pique work, a crown-like damascus pommel and precious gemstone inlays. *(Ward photo)*

ALLEN NEWBERRY: Naval forces traveling the world have carried cutlasses, but few as handsome as the 1095-bladed beauty quenched with a copper etch and married with a stabilized-cherry-burl handle. *(Ward photo)*

E. JAY HENDRICKSON: A large Persian Jambiya is sent to market in a foot-long, swooping blade and wire-inlaid curly-maple grip. *(SharpByCoop.com photo)*

BILL BURKE: The Japanese-style W2 Hira Zukuri tanto sports a cocobolo handle and Shakudo (gold and copper) blade collar. *(PointSeven photo)*

Out Of The Chute Knives

▶ **THAD BUCHANAN:** In the realm of the parachute knives Bob Loveless designed, this piece comes with a 4 5/8-inch CPM 154 blade, a stainless steel guard and stag handle. *(Custom Knife Gallery of Colorado photo)*

◀ **DENNIS FRIEDLY:** Not only did Bob Loveless design and popularize chute knives, but he can be credited for bringing ATS-34 stainless steel, like the blade on this piece, into the United States. Bruce Shaw engraved the stainless guard. *(Buddy Thomason photo)*

◀ **CHARLES VESTAL:** The traditionally styled chute knife, complete with swedge along the blade spine, is done up in CPM 154 steel, a stainless guard and amber-stag grip. *(SharpByCoop.com photo)*

◀ **S.R. JOHNSON:** The oversize Bob Loveless-style 154CM chute knife stretches 11 inches overall. *(PointSeven photo)*

◀ **ROBERT PARKER:** Mammoth tooth and engraving liven up an ATS-34 chute knife. Dave Lark engraved and gold inlaid the piece, and Paul Bos is credited for the heat treating. *(SharpByCoop.com photo)*

Try These Tactics

It seems like decades ago that tactical folders came into vogue. They were deemed trendy, diving headlong toward a short existence, extinction really, soon to be retired like other trends in knives, for instance turn-ring folders, gravity knives, belt buckle knives, projectile blades or swing-guard folders.

The tactical folder, and tactical fixed blade for that matter, was handsome and romantic, yet doomed, or as Elton John sang about Marilyn Monroe, "Your candle burned out long before your legend ever did." Or did it? Is that flame extinguished? Not by a long shot. Just like the 9-11 terrorists failed miserably in snuffing out the Statue of Liberty torch, as well as the American spirit that goes along with it, tactical folders and fixed blades are as hot as subway tracks during a weekday commute. And they embody that American spirit.

Such embodiment includes evolution of a form. The tactical folder began as a folding knife with a pocket clip. Some had thumb studs, holes in the blades or discs for one-hand opening. Others were locking-liner folders in the spirit of Michael Walker. A few were lock backs, and still more relied on springs to hold the fast-opening blades in their handle halves.

Then a man named Ken Onion came along and popularized the assisted-opening folder. Another fashioned "flipper" extensions from blade tangs that assisted in opening blades and seconded as guards with the blades fully open. Then the gods of blade grinding started getting creative, and pretty soon we had gorgeously ground, textured, grooved and sculpted tactical folders that looked like alien edges.

Where are tactical folders headed? Only the future will tell, and as Elton also sings, "You can't plant me in your penthouse. I'm goin' back to my plough, back to the howlin' old owl in the woods, huntin' the hornyback toad. Oh I've finally decided my future lies beyond the yellow brick road."

▼ **SAL MANARO:** Amenities of the CPM 154 folder include a full swedge along the blade spine, dovetailed titanium bolsters, carbon fiber handle scales and a three-piece pocket clip that will hold a lanyard. (SharpByCoop. com photo)

◄ **PAUL FOX:** Sorry for the play on your name, Paul, but folders like this titanium-laden piece with 3.8-inch blade will literally outfox you. Look where the thumb stud landed.

◄ **BRENT BESHARA and WALLY HAYES:** The "Besh Wedge" includes two chisel grinds, one on each side of the blade that combine to create a triangular tip when viewed point on, as well as a double edge. Hayes incorporates the Besh Wedge into his damascus fixed blade with carbon fiber handle scales. (PointSeven photo)

▶ **MIKKEL WILLUMSEN:** Bright orange and black crackle their way along the grip of the recurved fixed blade.

▼ **KEITH OUYE:** Keith did the groovy grinding of the ATS-34 blade, while Bruce Shaw engraved the stainless handle scales to vie for attention. *(SharpByCoop.com photo)*

▼ **SCOT MATSUOKA:** The tanto tactical folder is hollow-ground, curvaceous and cool. *(SharpByCoop.com photo)*

◀ **MICHAEL BURCH:** Here's a dress tactical folder, the "Impetus," done in "trashcan" damascus, and we all love trash. Other features include a carbon fiber grip with mother-of-pearl inlays, a titanium frame and the IKBS system for smooth flipping, and we all love flips. *(SharpByCoop.com photo)*

◀ **DAVID MOSIER:** The tip-up titanium pocket clip secures the satin-finished CPM 154 blade, thick titanium liners and carbon fiber handle in your jeans or trousers for safe keeping and eventual flipping.

▶ **JENS ANSO:** A bore beetle couldn't have made the black-and-orange G-10 handle any groovier, nor could a crane have whooped up such a curvaceous RWL-34 blade. *(SharpByCoop.com photo)*

▶ **JEREMY MARSH:** Marsh's mantra: carve it, differentially anodize it, bead blast it, grind it and rub it to a 600-grit finish. *(SharpByCoop.com photo)*

◀ **NORMAN SANDOW:** Both edges of the ATS-34 locking-liner folder can be sharpened because the blade folds completely into the ivory handle.

▶ **TIM GALYEAN:** Make room for the "Monster Moab," a work of geometric art that involves a non-traditional tanto tip, flipper mechanism, and a titanium and carbon fiber handle. It even sports a damascus pivot cap. *(Mitch Lum photo)*

◀ **ROSS MITSUYUKI:** As clean as a flipper folder gets, Ross's S30V and green-and-black G-10 tactical piece is one smooth operator.

▶ **CHERUSKER MESSER** and **BRAM FRANK:** Bram's design influence on the file-worked AUS-8 tactical fixed blade is unmistakable. Pressure and indexing points meet blade point. *(PointSeven photo)*

◀ **REESE WEILAND and LOUIS KRUDO:** Louis designed one karambit for money, two for show and three to get ready. They all go. *(PointSeven photo)*

◀ **DON HANSON III:** Things to notice on the "Monster Clack" might include that deep, recurved W2 blade with wavy temper line, the "Monster" mosaic-damascus bolsters, anodized titanium pocket clip and liners, and perhaps the "old ivory Micarta" handle scales. *(SharpByCoop.com photo)*

▶ **ALLEN ELISHEWITZ:** Ruby ball bearings pretty up the carbon fiber handle of the otherwise stealth flipper folder with Mike Norris damascus blade and pronounced flipper mechanism.

◀ **JIM BURKE:** The "Burke Villain" involves a multi-ground CPM 154 blade and hand-jigged green Micarta handle scales. The bolsters are of the Chad Nichols stainless damascus variety. *(SharpByCoop.com photo)*

SHANE SIBERT: The CPM S30V, titanium and G-10 "Mini Pocket Rocket" will put you into orbit. *(BladeGallery.com photo)*

WALLY HAYES: Eastern influence includes a stingray-skin handle, distinct temper line, bamboo pocket clip motif, and a leaf-shaped 1084 blade. *(PointSeven photo)*

DANIEL STUCKY: Stabilized juniper burl rarely makes its way onto a steel and titanium tactical folder, but perhaps it should more often. *(BladeGallery.com photo)*

BRIAN TIGHE: Call it "groovitational pull," if you will, the attraction to the flipper folders is undeniable. *(PointSeven photo)*

R.J. MARTIN: It took two tactics to fit in all the innovations Martin wanted to include in his CNC-machined carbon fiber, titanium and steel flipper folders. *(SharpByCoop.com photo)*

Coral Arrangement

▶ **PETER MARTIN:** Like water lily leaves floating in a steely-blue pond, the damascus flows from the fossil coral. More amenities include a tangerine-garnet-inlaid 14k-gold thumb stud, and file-worked and anodized titanium liners. *(Cory Martin Imaging)*

◀ **ROBERT MERZ:** Shell-sculpted bolsters sandwich a coral handle and lead to a folding Devin Thomas damascus dagger blade. *(Ward photo)*

▼ **MARK NEVLING:** Mosaic damascus can do so much, including the seeming continuation of the fossil coral pattern.

◀ **RAYMOND SMITH:** The "brain coral" of the granddaddy Barlow is dyed black to better blend with the damascus steel.

▶ **DICK FAUST:** "Fossil brain coral" sure looks smart on a 154CM drop-point hunter.

Take-Down Construction

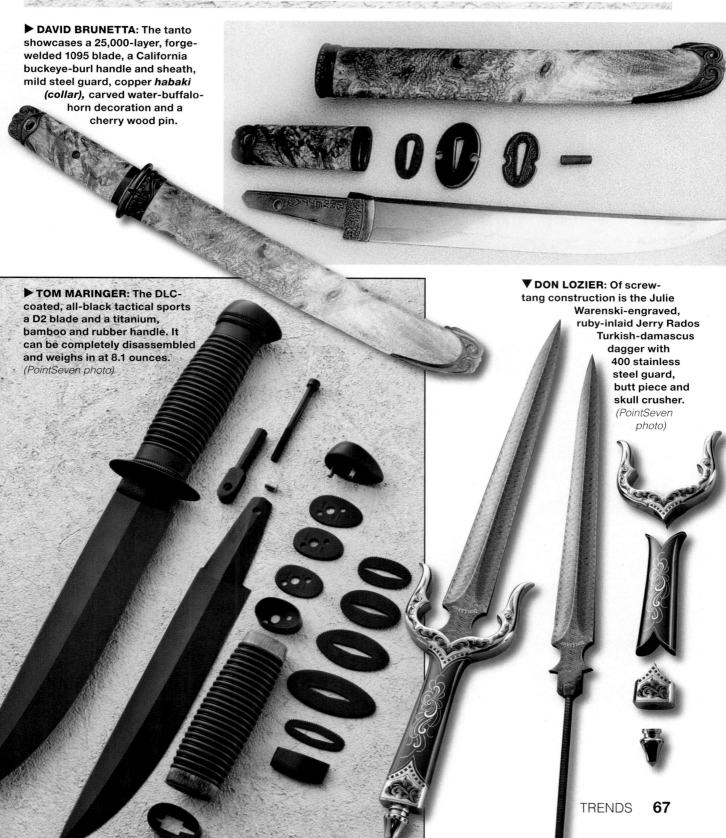

▶ **DAVID BRUNETTA:** The tanto showcases a 25,000-layer, forge-welded 1095 blade, a California buckeye-burl handle and sheath, mild steel guard, copper *habaki (collar),* carved water-buffalo-horn decoration and a cherry wood pin.

▶ **TOM MARINGER:** The DLC-coated, all-black tactical sports a D2 blade and a titanium, bamboo and rubber handle. It can be completely disassembled and weighs in at 8.1 ounces. *(PointSeven photo)*

▼ **DON LOZIER:** Of screw-tang construction is the Julie Warenski-engraved, ruby-inlaid Jerry Rados Turkish-damascus dagger with 400 stainless steel guard, butt piece and skull crusher. *(PointSeven photo)*

Happy Hunting Grinds

▶ **JOHN PERRY:** Rounding the linen-Micarta® handle of the 154CM semi skinner became an obsession that yielded a prized possession. Even the guard is smooth and seamless. *(Buddy Thomason photo)*

▶ **THOMAS HASLINGER:** Between the San Mai damascus blade with an O-1 core, and the spalted-maple handle, this one just screams classic hunting knife for discriminating tastes.

◀ **ART SUMMERS:** Elk, oosic, and black and red spacers take turns on the stacked handle of a damascus trailing point hunter.

▲ **MARK KNAPP:** Nature never made knife handle material this hot, and the damascus blades aren't bad, either. *(SharpByCoop.com photo)*

◀ **GUY HIELSCHER:** Get a hold of the giraffe bone handle and don't let go until the damascus blade has skinned ye another one. *(Buddy Thomason photo)*

▶ **JACK JONES:** The drop-point blade and stag handle are done in a classic design, complete with finger notches on the blade spine. *(PointSeven photo)*

◀ **ALBERT TRUJILLO:** Sambar stag, file work and damascus never looked so nice. *(PointSeven photo)*

◀ **R.B. MCDONALD:** If the ironwood and 5160 aren't hunt worthy, nothing is. *(Ward photo)*

▲ **ROB HUDSON:** The clean lines of the "Presentation Hunter" stretch from the CPM 154 CM trailing-point blade to the fossilized walrus ivory grip, buffalo horn spacers, and stainless guard and pommel.

▶ **JOHN BARTLOW:** A Green River blade and a drop-point caper are paired in ATS-34 and ivory. *(PointSeven photo)*

▶ **HENRY TORRES:** Curly maple sends shock waves down the 52100 blade and curls the pommel just so. *(Buddy Thomason photo)*

◀ **PETER CROWL:** Just because a drop-point hunter in 1080 steel and stag is a classic design doesn't mean it's easy to execute, especially this neatly and cleanly. *(Hoffman photo)*

▶ **MICHAEL MCCLURE:** Mammoth ivory and the slender build of the 5160 blade make the bird-and-trout knife nice to look at. *(BladeGallery.com photo)*

▲ S.R. JOHNSON: Proving himself capable of a pristine caper, Johnson used ATS-34 blade steel, stainless fittings and a mother-of-pearl handle.

◄ DICK FAUST: Dick put a sub-hilt on a 154CM hunter, planting desert ironwood between guard and sub-guard, and Sambar stag at the handle end.

► ALAN WARREN: The sweet utility skinner is sent hunting in satin-finished ATS-34 blade steel, a nickel-silver guard, and an African blackwood handle with pre-ban ivory spacers. *(BladeGallery.com photo)*

► ROB HUDSON: Maple and Amboyna burl are the beginning and middle of a CPM 154 trailing-point hunter. *(PointSeven photo)*

▼ JERRY JOHNSON: Handy to hold and use is the stag-handle hunter with plenty of finger choil.

▶ **MICHAEL SPANGLER:** The wide CPM 154 blade gets a good handful of cocobolo to counterbalance it. *(SharpByCoop.com photo)*

◀ **JERRY MCCLURE:** Giraffe bone brings color to the damascus hunter that only horsehair could emulate. *(Ward photo)*

◀ **J.W. RANDALL:** A bold radial-pattern-damascus blade coaxes a sheep-horn handle and nickel silver guard to fall in line.

◀ **C.R. MILES JR.:** Quite a few makers get their starts by fashioning blades from files. This maker made it to the finish line and beyond fashioning a hot drop-point hunter from a file, the blade heat treated and tempered to 58-60RC, and adding brass furniture and a curly maple handle. *(Hoffman photo)*

▲ **MARK NEVLING:** Between the "Morse-code"-pattern damascus blade and California buckeye burl handle, all the i's are dotted.

▶ **LARRY LITTLE:** Crown stag and fiber spacers lead to a nickel silver guard and file-worked skinner blade.

▶ **BEN MIDGLEY:** The full-tang, file-worked, drop-point 154CM blade is almost leaf shaped, and stemmed in highly figured sheep horn. *(PointSeven photo)*

▶ **BILL WIGGINS:** Lightning struck across the 1095-and-416 blade of the ironwood-handle hunter. *(PointSeven photo)*

◀ **JERRY MOEN:** Everything from the engraved guard and pins to the signature on the CPM 154 blade and smooth ivory grip come together for the hunt. *(PointSeven photo)*

▼ **ANDERS HOGSTROM:** The "Mid-Game Hunter" wanders the woods in Conny Persson random-pattern damascus, copper fittings and a fossil-walrus-ivory handle.

▶ **AARON WILBURN:** The character and markings of snakewood make for a fierce hunter, particularly in conjunction with a hand-forged 52100 blade that's fang sharp. *(BladeGallery.com photo)*

▶ **JENS JORGEN SCHIERMER:** The simplicity and workmanship of the RWL-34 blade and green-canvas-Micarta® grip give the drop-point hunter a clean look and feel. *(BladeGallery.com photo)*

◀ **RON NEWTON:** Tracks lead across the 5160 blade of the "Treed Raccoon" hunter, and the coon can be seen hiding in its carved-stag home. *(Ward photo)*

◀ **EDDIE STALCUP:** Trace a line along the bottom of the jigged-bone grip, stainless steel bolsters and CPM 154 blade, and it's a wavy ride indeed. *(Balance Digital image)*

◀ **JONATHAN WICK:** Brass that resembles a bullet casing, only prettier, acts as a Shibuichi frame, collar and guard, anchoring mesquite-burl handle slabs and an S160 drop-point blade. *(Balance Digital image)*

◀ **TRAVIS WUERTZ:** Easy to catch and release is the rounded desert ironwood handle and oval guard of the 200-layer damascus hunter. *(Balance Digital image)*

◀ **RANDY GOLDEN:** The hunter with the false top edge is done up in a 4.75-inch 154CM blade, a dropped Sambar stag handle and a stainless guard, butt cap and spacer. *(Bill Ingalls photo)*

Mammoth Undertakings

► LOYD MCCONNELL: Dimpled bark mammoth ivory allows the bolsters and blade of the "Cowden" model to shine.

◄ SERGIO RAMONDETTI: All a hunter needs is some RWL 34 steel, a stainless guard, mosaic pins and mammoth-ivory handle scales.

▲ STEVE CULVER: Culver's locking-liner folder parades a palpable mammoth-ivory grip, damascus dagger blade and blue-anodized titanium liners.

► TIM BRITTON: Like a teardrop, the mammoth-ivory inches its way down into a BG-42 blade with elongated pull.

► STEVE HILL: Meet the "Ragin' Cajun" automatic knife featuring a 3.5-inch damascus blade, muddy-colored ivory grip, "swamp creatures" gator-style-engraved rocker button and "water moccasin" file-worked spine. *(PointSeven photo)*

► RON NEWTON: Whether it's the "West Texas Wind" damascus blade, the carved-damascus guard or the mammoth-ivory grip that starts your engines, the spark has been introduced. *(Ward photo)*

◀ **DON HANSON:** The master smith makes one up in mosaic damascus, titanium and some of the bluest mammoth ivory this side of the Pleistocene Era. *(SharpByCoop.com photo)*

◀ **KEVIN CASEY:** Highly figured mammoth ivory makes its home along Gibeon meteorite bolsters, titanium liners, a damascus blade and jade-inlaid thumb stud. *(SharpByCoop.com photo)*

▶ **TERRY VANDEVENTER:** The mammoth ivory crackles and pops in all the right places, butted up against a sculpted damascus guard and a mosaic-damascus English bowie blade. *(Ward photo)*

▲ **NORMAN SANDOW:** Mammoth tooth and damascus are a match made in heaven, then transported to an ATS-34 locking-liner folder with a tiger-eye-inlaid thumb stud.

▼ **MICHAEL TYRE:** It's unusual to see mammoth ivory so dark and green, or damascus steel so black and beautiful. *(BladeGallery.com photo)*

▼ **R.F. DODD:** The assisted-opening damascus blade pops out of the black-mammoth-ivory grip faster than a mastodon could chew a leafy stalk.

◄ **KYLE ROYER:** Not only is the mammoth ivory as blue as the heavens above, but if the collector of the fine knife wants, he can take down, or take apart, the heavenly "Explosion"-damascus fixed blade, starting with the clam-shell and ring guards, and shapely pommel. *(SharpByCoop.com photo)*

◄ **HARVEY DEAN:** Pretty patterns include that of the feather-damascus blade, mammoth-ivory grip and bolster engraving by Steve Dunn. *(PointSeven photo)*

► **BRUCE BUMP:** Clay coating and differential tempering is what it took to make the W2 blade look that way, and years of deterioration to make the mammoth ivory become so appealing. Tom Ferry blessed us with the bolster engraving, and it comes with a Paul Long cross-draw sheath. *(PointSeven photo)*

► **PAUL PANAK:** So many amenities on the switchblades, and so little time, but they include Turkish-twist-damascus blades and bolsters forged by Jerry Rados, wooly-mammoth-ivory handles and square auto buttons. *(SharpByCoop.com photo)*

Black Lips Pink Grips

The pearl actually pinks, purples, blues, greens, reds and gold-hues grips. The multi-colored black-lip mother-of-pearl is considered by many to be of the prettiest knife handle materials, compared to such classics as elephant ivory, white mother-of-pearl, gold-lip mother-of-pearl, exotic wood, camel bone, wooly mammoth tusk, mammoth tooth and ancient walrus ivory. The way the green and pink combine in black-lip pearl is a color combination most painters would aspire to achieve.

The translucency adds to the inherent beauty and intrinsic value. Collectors of fine art, whether it's knives, sculptures or sculpted knives, recognize a perfect form or shape. Like gemologists, knife collectors scrutinize clarity, color and quality. All can be found in the lacquered nacre, the pearl of wisdom, mother of all mollusks, the shocking shell.

While loose lips sink ships, black-lip pearl has made many seasoned sea captains part their lips in delight. It's truly a treasure trove, some-thing that is inherently beautiful, polishes up like fine silver and sparkles in the sun. Inlay a knife handle with black-lip mother-of-pearl, and you're likely to not only pink the grip but also grease the palm and sweeten the deal.

▶ **GAIL LUNN:** Between the "dragonskin"-damascus and black-lip-pearl scales, the folder comes alive, further aided by texturing, and gold and precious stone accents.
(SharpByCoop.com photo)

◀ **KEN STEIGERWALT:** The 18k-gold pins, inlays and button add yet another art element to the carved, black-lip-pearl-inlaid folder with Doug Ponzio Turkish-damascus blade and bolsters.
(SharpByCoop.com photo)

◀ **JOSH SMITH:** White and black-lip mother-of-pearl share double billing on a blued-damascus art folder that looks like it will take wing and fly away at any moment. *(PointSeven photo)*

► HOWARD HITCHMOUGH: Black-lip pearl looks perfectly palpable on the Damasteel and blued steel folder. *(PointSeven photo)*

◄ LARRY NEWTON: The gold-inlaid, small, symmetrical dagger showcases Devin Thomas raindrop-pattern damascus, file-worked titanium liners, and carved and stippled premium black-lip pearl. *(PointSeven photo)*

▲ CLIFF PARKER: The sea theme includes black-lip pearl and swirling oceanic images within the blade steel. *(PointSeven photo)*

◄ LEE FERGUSON: Golden rays arch toward precious stone inlays on the damascus bolsters, and black-lip mother-of-pearl pretties up the handle half. *(Ward photo)*

◄ RUSS SUTTON: Purple, pink, blue, green, gold and brown emit and radiate from the handle inlay of a Jere Davidson-engraved stainless steel lock-back folder. *(PointSeven photo)*

Legendary Lineage

GEOFF KEYES: The "come-hither" carved guard, shapely walrus ivory handle and damascus blade make for a fashionable ensemble ala a Michael Price San Francisco dirk. *(Mitch Lum photo)*

TOM FERRY: By the time Tom forged the W2 blade, carved the stainless guard and engraved the nickel silver handle, he truly had left his heart in San Francisco. *(Mitch Lum photo)*

LIN RHEA: The Bill Bagwell-style bowie parades a 5160 blade, stainless guard and stag grip. *(Ward photo)*

BILL HERNDON: He may have copied a J.A. Henckels late 1800s bowie, but done up this well in an engraved guard, and finely fit and finished damascus blade and stag grip, it's more of a compliment.

CURT ERICKSON: Legendary lineage comes California style, including a heat-blued handle that's gold inlaid and engraved by Julie Warenski, and a 440C blade. *(PointSeven photo)*

▼ **E. JAY HENDRICKSON:** Exuding tradition is a "Nanook High Clip Hunter" that features a 5160 blade, a silver-wire and scroll-inlaid curly maple handle, Sambar stag butt, and a stainless steel guard. *(Buddy Thomason photo)*

▼ **KEN DURHAM:** A reproduction of an 1831 Henry Schively bowie is presented in a checkered African blackwood handle, sterling silver mounts, a clay-tempered steel blade and a nickel silver sheath engraved by Billy Bates. *(SharpByCoop.com photo)*

▶ **DENNIS FRIEDLY:** If you can get past the Robert Eggerling damascus blade, Gil Rudolph engraving and sculpted fossil walrus ivory handle, its early American heritage reveals itself. *(PointSeven photo)*

▶ **STEVEN RAPP:** Borrowing from Sheffield and California, the maker had a lot to work with using stag, 440C and his own advanced skills. *(PointSeven photo)*

▶ **CHARLES VESTAL:** The ripped and ribbed CPM-154 blade and hunky ironwood-burl handle of the Loveless-style boot knife make for a foxy model. *(SharpByCoop.com photo)*

◀ **ROY THOMPSON:** The reproduction of a William Scagel piece remains true to materials used by the Michigan master, including elk horn, brass and carbon steel. *(Buddy Thomason photo)*

▶ **RON LAKE:** Since Ron actually is the legendary lineage of his own tab-lock, inter-frame folders, we'll give him all the credit for the barrel-damascus, gold, tortoise and walnut-color-Bakelite™ grip, as well as the unblemished blade and frame. *(PointSeven photo)*

▶ **JON CHRISTENSEN:** The coffin-shaped, fossil-walrus-ivory and mosaic-damascus grip gets along good with the "perspective-boxes"-pattern mosaic damascus blade of the San Francisco-style knife. *(Mitch Lum photo)*

▶ **S.R. JOHNSON:** In the realm of a Loveless-style "Wilderness" model is a mammoth-ivory and CPM 154CM piece that slides neatly into a Zac Buchanan leather sheath. *(PointSeven photo)*

▶ **TIM HANCOCK:** Gold and ivory get double takes on a California gold rush dagger, as does the silver frame engraved by Bruce Christensen. *(PointSeven photo)*

Pathfinders

▼ DANIEL WINKLER: Designed with utility in mind is the "Lost Lake Camp Knife," forged of high-carbon steel, and featuring an elk-antler handle and a rawhide-covered sheath by Karen Shook, the latter decorated with glass beads, tin cones and horse hair.

▲ TODD BEGG: Brown-green Micarta® steadies a wicked, re-curved, 10-inch A2 steel blade. Notice the groovy camouflage-pattern sheath. *(PointSeven photo)*

▶ TAD LYNCH: Meet the "Turkey Mt. Chopper," a burly brute with a full 9-inch 1095 blade and a wavy temper line. *(Ward photo)*

▶ DAN FARR: The camp knife of CruForge V steel dons a handle with two sheets of carbon fiber laminated between three slabs of black walnut burl (see inset at bottom). *(SharpByCoop.)*

▶ DOUG CAMPBELL: Spotless 52100 steel is secured to ironwood with six pins, and butts up against a nice nickel silver guard. *(SharpByCoop. com photo)*

Impacting Molars

▶ **MIKE TURNER:** The character of the mammoth tooth holds its own against the "W's"-pattern damascus blade. Paul Long fashioned a leather sheath for the pretty piece. *(Barbara Phelps photo)*

▶ **PETE TRUNCALI:** The mammoth-molar handle scales are no less impacting than the stainless-damascus blade and bolsters. *(PointSeven photo)*

◀ **LARRY PRIDGEN:** As if the "wasp nest" damascus blade and bolsters didn't create enough buzz, mammoth tooth handle scales and file-worked liners add sting to the piece. *(PointSeven photo)*

▼ **SHANE ATWOOD:** Mammoth tusk and tooth make up the bolsters and handle of the hunter in Devin Thomas damascus. The fine knife also features mosaic pins and pearl inlays. *(BladeGallery.com photo)*

▶ **STEPHEN MACKRILL:** Nickel silver bolsters separate the hippo-tooth and mammoth-ivory handle from the damascus dagger blade. It comes with a pigskin sheath with a nickel silver head and tail (or tip and throat). *(PointSeven photo)*

R.J. MARTIN: For the "Dress Overkill" number, Martin assembles a cast of damascus, titanium, mammoth tooth and mammoth ivory. And for his next act … (SharpByCoop.com photo)

KEVIN CASEY: Knock-out punches include blue mammoth tooth handle scales, Casey's own leaf-pattern damascus blade steel, Gibeon meteorite bolsters, file-worked titanium liners and a blue lapis thumb stud. (SharpByCoop.com photo)

GAYLE BRADLEY: Take what looks like a standard slip-joint folder, file work the liners, add a unique locking mechanism and inlay it with mammoth tooth, and the ordinary just became extraordinary. (Ward photo)

ROBERT NELSON PARKER: Mammoth tooth and Dave Lark's engraved bolsters and pins enliven an ATS-34 fixed blade fighter. Paul Bos heat treated the blade. (SharpByCoop.com photo)

MARK KNAPP: Musk ox, mammoth ivory and mammoth tooth mix it up on the grip of a fixed-blade hunter, also outfitted with Mike Norris "hornets nest"-pattern stainless damascus. (SharpByCoop.com photo)

Great Grains

▶ **ERIK FRITZ:** Cocobolo gets all chocolaty on a sweet personal carry knife. *(PointSeven photo)*

▶ **SCOTT SLOBODIAN:** The appropriately named "Dark Forest" ken dagger is done up in clay-tempered 1050 high-carbon steel, an Amboyna burl grip and scabbard, and silver fittings.

◀ **JASON HOWELL:** The droplet-like damascus patterning of the blade and bolsters blends into the stabilized Nuguni wood grip. Check out the matching thong fob. *(PointSeven photo)*

◀ **GARTH HINDMARCH:** Wander through the wood grains of maple burl, stopping to rest on the mosaic pin heads of the 440C hunter.

▲ **GEORGE COUSINO:** Great wood grains share the limelight with vine file work and clean execution.

▶ **HARVEY KING:** A classically designed drop-point hunter is outfitted in box elder burl and D2 blade steel. *(Ward photo)*

◀ **DAN DICK:** The bulbous black-ash-burl grip is grab worthy, indeed.

▲ **S.R. JOHNSON:** The "Wilderness"-style fighter ala Bob Loveless benefits from a spalted hackberry handle, a CPM 154 blade and stainless steel fittings. *(Peterson Studios photo)*

◀ **STEVE VANDERKOLFF:** The medieval dagger adds Jerusalem olive wood to the mix of exotic knife handle materials, and is particularly pretty with a damascus ferrule, butt cap and blade. *(SharpByCoop.com photo)*

▶ **DOUG CAMPBELL:** Snakewood holds a place of honor on a lengthy 1084 bowie. *(PointSeven photo)*

▶ **AARON WILBURN:** Lacewood leaves its legacy on a hand-forged, triple-quenched and double-tempered 52100 hunter. The brass and black-fiber spacers allow the handle to breathe when adjusting to changes in temperature and humidity. *(BladeGallery.com photo)*

▼ **KEVIN CASEY:** Neither an emerald-inlaid thumb stud nor a damascus blade and bolsters could upstage the Tasmanian eucalyptus burl grip. *(SharpByCoop.com photo)*

◀ **DANIEL CHINNOCK:** Mother-of-pearl inlays embellish a snakewood grip in spades, strategically placed near a Chad Nichols damascus blade and bolsters, and tiger eye-inlaid thumb stud. *(SharpByCoop.com photo)*

▼ **ED CAFFREY:** Highly figured Afzelia lay wood keeps step with a twist-pattern damascus blade and carved nickel-silver guard. *(BladeGallery.com photo)*

▶ **BILL WIGGINS:** Ringed Gidgee wood will forever be ingrained in the psych of a flat-ground camp knife. *(SharpByCoop.com photo)*

▶ **MICHAEL BURCH:** The forged *hamon*, or temper line, of the 1095 blade is the perfect segue into the dark grains of spalted maple. *(SharpByCoop.com photo)*

▶ **CAL GANSHORN:** Stabilized buckeye burl and ladder-pattern damascus run circles around the hunter.

▲ **ROB HUDSON:** Stacking box elder and red maple burl is akin to alternating flapjacks and syrup.

◀▲ **MIKE MOONEY:** The set includes boning, chef and paring knives in satin-finished CPM S30V steel, stabilized spalted Makore wood handles and mosaic pins.

◀ **MICHAEL RADER:** Curly Koa wood and box elder burl join forces for the grip of a differentially-heat-treated 52100 Santoku chef's knife. *(BladeGallery.com photo)*

◀ **RON RICHERSON:** The damascus skinner is green behind the guard thanks to stabilized spalted maple. Sherry Lott inlaid the leather sheath with fish skin to further the effect. *(Cory Martin Imaging)*

◀ **RAY KIRK:** California buckeye burl befits a fine 52100 folder. *(Ward photo)*

▶ **LYNN MAXFIELD:** The full, hidden tang of the 154CM "Cougar" model stretches beneath the curly maple and Bubinga wood grip.

▶ **MIKE TAMBOLI:** The colorized maple burl makes a perfect backdrop for a horse menuki (handle charm), and complements the copper habaki (blade collar) and 1060 tanto blade. *(Ward photo)*

◀ **MIKE RUTH:** Watch that desert ironwood and damascus bowie dance. *(Ward photo)*

▶ **JAMES R. COOK:** Counting the rings of the white-oak grip will help the proud owner of the 5160 "Musso Bowie" wile away the evening hours. *(Ward photo)*

◀ **KEITH BAGLEY:** Stabilized buckeye burl brings the woods to the hunter. *(Ward photo)*

◀ **FOREST "BUTCH" SHEELY:** A 5160 bowie is cloaked in curly maple for a fair occasion. *(PointSeven photo)*

▼ **MACE VITALE:** "Blister-curl maple" won't put any blisters on the palm of the lucky knife user. Check out the simple but elegant silver wire inlay. *(SharpByCoop.com photo)*

▶ **ROBERT BEATY:** The swayback skinner benefits from vine file work, a brass guard, turquoise spacers and a stabilized-buckeye-burl handle. *(BladeGallery.com photo)*

▶ **ROSS MITSUYUKI:**
Curly Hawaiian Koa wood left its leaves on the bolster of a CPM 154 flipper folder.

▶ **ARMIN DRUMM:**
The feather damascus forged from O1, nickel and 1085 tool steel brushes lightly against the O1 ferrule and guard, and the straight grains of a rosewood grip.

▶ **CHUCK SCHUETTE:** Highly figured olivewood and 52100 steel make the oyster knife a beautiful and mollusk-ular piece. *(SharpByCoop. com photo)*

▶ **BILL POST:**
The gunstock-shaped wooden grip doesn't just lumber along, but gets right to the 5160 point. *(Ward photo)*

◀ **FRED OTT:** The bone spacer and bronze ferrule provide a nice respite from the active patterns of ironwood burl and double-ladder-pattern damascus. *(Buddy Thomason photo)*

► **BILL BUXTON:** Wouldn't it be nice if it were as easy as gettin' ye some ringed Gidgee and makin' yer-self a mosaic-damascus hunter? *(Ward photo)*

▼ **MICHAEL O'MACHEARLEY:** Ironwood and spalted maple collectively bulge out the handle of a 5160 fighter with brass guard.

◄ **EDMUND DAVIDSON:** The design from Henry Diller is done up integrally in A2 tool steel and some of the most colorful stabilized box elder to bow before the emperor. *(PointSeven photo)*

▼ **DICK FAUST:** Box elder burl gives a 154CM notchback hunter a smoky blue and brown hue.

► **TOM LEWIS:** Segments of maple wood and ebony were carefully inlaid into the grip of an ATS-34 hunter.

Double-Guard Daggers

If you are a movie buff, you probably remember the "double-dog dare" in A Christmas Story. There was no greater challenge than the double-dog dare, and if you found yourself on the receiving end of the ultimate ultimatum, there was only one thing a respectable 1940s-era adolescent boy could do—accept the dare. Turn it down, and there'd be no showing your face around friends for an eternity. A kid could get his tongue stuck on a flagpole in the middle of winter for accepting a double-dog dare.

Double-guard daggers have a few things in common with the double-dog dare. There's no walking away from a double-guard dagger, at least not one as beautifully crafted as the stickers on this and the following page. There is no greater challenge than making a double-guard dagger. And if you walk away from one, there's no showing your face around fellow collectors for an eternity.

Seriously, the style is classic, the lines flowing, edges tapering, each point remains perfect and the handles are hard not to like. In between remain guards, throats, spacers and a lot of handiwork. Unlike the knives they create, makers of daggers are unguarded. They put it all out there in shape, form and fashion. These are the knives the politically correct take to task, they shun as too dangerous, weapons even, and evil.

But nothing so splendid can be condemned. Doubled-dog dares don't claim to aid in the betterment of society, yet 1940s youth wouldn't have been the same without them. Double-guard daggers are no different. Like them or not, they're a permanent and pleasurable part of the knife fabric.

◄ **JIMMY CHIN:** The twisted-silver-wire-inlaid, fluted blackwood handle is protected from the "Christmas tree"-mosaic-damascus blade by a clam-shell guard. *(Ward photo)*

◄ **WOLFGANG LOERCHNER:** The hand-carved damascus dagger takes an organic shape that a tropical plant would envy. *(SharpByCoop.com photo)*

▲ **DAN WESTLIND:** The maker allowed the pattern of the damascus to speak through the form of the double-guard dagger, which features a blued, twisted-wire-inlaid ironwood handle. *(BladeGallery.com photo)*

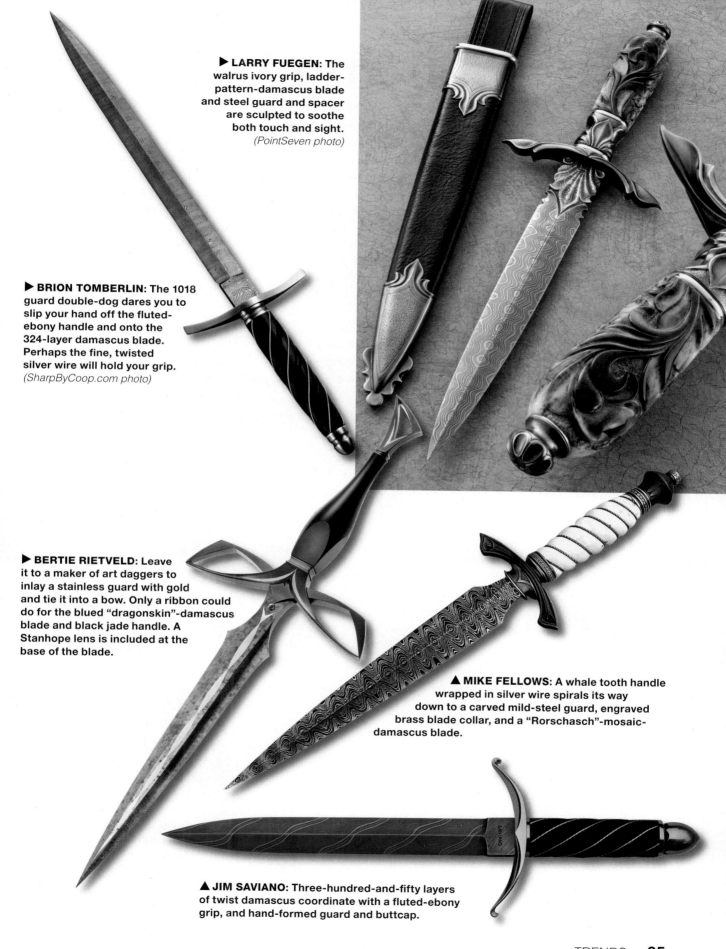

► **LARRY FUEGEN:** The walrus ivory grip, ladder-pattern-damascus blade and steel guard and spacer are sculpted to soothe both touch and sight. *(PointSeven photo)*

► **BRION TOMBERLIN:** The 1018 guard double-dog dares you to slip your hand off the fluted-ebony handle and onto the 324-layer damascus blade. Perhaps the fine, twisted silver wire will hold your grip. *(SharpByCoop.com photo)*

► **BERTIE RIETVELD:** Leave it to a maker of art daggers to inlay a stainless guard with gold and tie it into a bow. Only a ribbon could do for the blued "dragonskin"-damascus blade and black jade handle. A Stanhope lens is included at the base of the blade.

▲ **MIKE FELLOWS:** A whale tooth handle wrapped in silver wire spirals its way down to a carved mild-steel guard, engraved brass blade collar, and a "Rorschasch"-mosaic-damascus blade.

▲ **JIM SAVIANO:** Three-hundred-and-fifty layers of twist damascus coordinate with a fluted-ebony grip, and hand-formed guard and buttcap.

Elite Fighting Unit

You've seen the soldiers, hair cut close, bristle straight, in rounded, even form, shining scalp. Even the cheekbones of military men are chiseled, leading to square jaws and broad shoulders. Their waists narrow, and want not. Chests bulge, and ripple from muscles within. Arrows are not straight enough to compare to how stiff they stand, at attention, in honor, glory, and keeping with sacrifice. Boots shine, pants are pleated, and swords, guns and insignia sparkle.

Those are the living fighters. What about the inanimate objects that also do warfare? Fighting knives remain an elite unit with forms no less sculpted. Blades start thin, taper narrow and end in perfect points. Guards are deliberate and forceful, handles sleek and rounded, swedges along blade spines soft yet effective. The steel shines or dulls depending on duty, and the tangs are full, not weak or worthless.

As much as we like to view knives as tools, not weapons, craft, not destructive,

and art, not ugly, the bowies, fighters, daggers and swords of the world stand united. They remain true to the cause, one of historic significance, bravery and fortitude. Nothing, inanimate or living, dare ask them to compromise their ideals, question their motives or dishonor them in any way, shape or form.

▶ **HENRY TORRES:** The master smith uses no unnecessary embellishment, but performs the fighter in 52100 steel, 416 stainless and beautiful blackwood. (SharpByCoop.com photo)

▲ **STEVE JOHNSON:** Ribbed fighters are so soothing to the eye, their hollow-ground blades piercing the perception, bowing to neither desert ironwood grips nor stainless steel guards. (SharpByCoop.com photo)

◀ **DON HANSON:** "Painted Fighter" is an appropriate moniker, telling of the fossil walrus ivory grip and W2 blade with distinct and nervous temper line. (SharpByCoop.com photo)

▶ **BILL BUXTON:** Follow the fighting temper line to damascus guard and blackwood grip. *(Ward photo)*

◀ **DAN PIERGALLINI:** Getting into the mind of Sergio Franco, who designed the knife, is an exercise of humility and futility, yet the sub-hilt fighter takes such a splendid form, decked out in 440C, zebrawood, mammoth bark ivory and nickel silver. *(SharpByCoop.com photo)*

◀ **WALTER BREND:** The colonel of fighters, a force to be reckoned with, built a re-curved, hollow-ground hunk in 154CM steel, stainless guard and black-Micarta® grip. *(SharpByCoop.com photo)*

▼ **DAVID BROADWELL:** A presentation "MLR Sub-Hilt Fighter" sports an 8.5-inch CPM 154 stainless blade, and a handle of ironwood burl. *(SharpByCoop.com photo)*

▲ **JASON KNIGHT:** Indeed damascus makes for a good fighting knife, in a flat, convex edge, and attached to a stainless guard with ironwood grip. *(SharpByCoop.com photo)*

▶ **MICHAEL RUTH:** May the "Tombstone Fighter" with 8.5-inch damascus blade, oosic handle and bowtie-shaped guard rest in complete peace. *(Ward photo)*

▶ **JIM HAMMOND:** Let's see—a hollow ground, re-curved CPM-3V blade, full and tapered tang, sculpted black/green linen-Micarta® handle and modular, handmade leather sheath. The country is in good hands. *(SharpByCoop.com photo)*

◀ **SHAWN MCINTYRE:** Let the box elder burl lead you to the stainless guard and well-planned damascus patterning. *(SharpByCoop.com photo)*

◀ **BILL LUCKETT:** Don't let the "DeathStalker" sub-hilt fighter scare you. The CPM 154 stainless blade with wicked pommel and black, brass and stainless spacers is held in check by a stabilized burl wood grip.

▼ **PETER DEL RASO:** Hidden tangs, flat-ground, satin-finished CPM S30V blades, and G-10 and black-linen-Micarta® handles make up a pair of ferocious fighters.

▶ **RICK BARRETT:** "Desert Camouflage Micarta®" is a stupendous choice for a Karambit-style ring fighter in mostly damascus steel. *(Cory Martin Imaging)*

◀ **JIMMY CHIN:** In ironwood and O1 comes a fierce fighter with a winsome demeanor. *(Ward photo)*

◀ **STEVE LIKARICH:** Never has a "New York Special" looked so special, or clean in CPM154 steel, ivory and beryllium copper. *(Buddy Thomason photo)*

▲ **DAVID SLOAN:** The fighter is small, but the W2, wrought iron and curly maple make for an elite fighting unit. *(SharpByCoop.com photo)*

▶ **MACE VITALE:** If a five-layer San Mai blade with wicked temper line doesn't slay ya, perhaps the Sambar stag grip will knock you flat. *(SharpByCoop.com photo)*

Abalone Inlays

Some things in nature simply cannot be duplicated no matter how hard the desktop designers try, regardless of what computer programs the illustrators use, and despite who digitally enhances a photograph or painting. Abalone is one of those anomalies that can't be copied. It's like the ink that doesn't show up on photocopier paper. It's there in real life, but when you try to transfer it, reality becomes blurred.

It's not that abalone is magical; it's just illusive. If the U.S. Treasury could figure out a way to make abalone $100 bills, forgers would be out of business, not to mention that Ben Franklin would look a lot better with an abalone complexion.

The material is a natural wonder, born as a marine mollusk with an oval or semi-spiral shell that is perforated near the edge and lined with mother-of-pearl. There's another suggestion for the Treasury Department—line Ben Franklins with mother-of-pearl.

The colors of the sea are reflected in abalone, like mountains in the glassy surface of a freshwater lake. But dropping a pebble on abalone won't make it ripple, or the reflection disappear. The sea is immortalized in the mollusk shell, and when polished up, it seems all that much more alive. It is smooth to the touch, soothing to the eye, stable enough to inlay into steel, and like snowflakes or fingerprints, it's unable to be duplicated, ever, no matter the designer, programmer, illustrator, enhancer or even forger.

◀ **MICHAEL PELLEGRIN:** The pointed and shapely lock-back folder, designed by Scott Allred and given a Chuck Hawes damascus blade, is inlaid with a drop of abalone so soft, the pattern pops! *(PointSeven photo)*

◀ **CHESTER DARCY:** The tight, feathery pattern of the damascus gives abalone room to swirl and whirl. *(PointSeven photo)*

◀ **BUTCH BALL:** Abalone anchored by blued Chad Nichols and Larry Donnelly damascus is like an oil painting framed in a vase. It's a spine-release automatic with a 4-inch hollow-ground blade, by the way. *(SharpByCoop.com photo)*

▶ **NORMAN SANDOW:** The ATS-34 locking-liner folder was treated to heat-colored-damascus bolsters, jeweled-titanium liners and abalone overlays.

◀ **RON BEST:** The dress locking-liner folder dons a Mike Norris stainless damascus blade and a lustrous abalone inlay. *(SharpByCoop.com photo)*

▲ **JERALD NICKELS:** Abalone adds allure to a CPM 154CM saddle-horn trapper. *(Ward photo)*

▶ **RICHARD WHEELER:** When Richard saw the abalone, mother-of-pearl and black-lip pearl, he thought of a butterfly wing, and what a vision, inlaid in ironwood and placed next to steel. *(BladeGallery.com photo)*

All Points West

Westerns never go out of style, as evidenced by recent movies like 3:10 To Yuma, Unforgiven, The Assassination of Jesse James by the Coward Robert Ford, The Proposition, and HBO TV's Deadwood. Similarly, the lure of the Old West is permanently ingrained in the American psyche, as well as in the fantasies, daydreams and historical perspectives of people living in other countries and continents.

As Ian van Reenen Jr., a knifemaker from Africa who now resides in Texas, recently wrote, "Amongst the cattle and the dust, amongst the Indians and the mines, the American identity was forged in the West.

Like hard rock made into steel, the American West was the place where a man could be his own man, a place where he could find his true place in the world. The West was a place that needed to be overcome, that needed to be conquered; nothing good is ever gained for free, every inch of land was battled with blood and sweat.

"Every knifemaker knows that the art of knifemaking is not much different," Ian continued. "Hours and hours are spent hunching over machines, grinding away errors and creating new, sustaining form."

When Ian left South Africa in 2001 to move to Texas, he knew that he immigrated to a place that not only required endurance, but also guts. He came from a continent that was in turmoil, and much like Texas, an environment that never took kindly to weakness, but where a man can come into his own.

All points West.

◀ **HARVEY DEAN:** The sterling silver star and pins gussy up the clean Texas bowie with a 1084 blade. *(PointSeven photo)*

▶ **RON NEWTON:** Texas is well represented on the "Alamo Trapper," which showcases a 3-inch ladder-pattern-damascus blade and bolsters, an amber-stag handle and a viewing lens, or Stanhope lens, at the butt of the grip that reveals a picture of the Alamo. Neat stuff. *(Ward photo)*

▶ **ROBERT SMITH:** The cowboy-boot-shaped ivory, ironwood and nickel silver handle boasts one sharp damascus spur. *(Ward photo)*

▶ **JERRY JOHNSON:** Knives like the crown-stag-handle damascus fighter helped win the West. The turquoise spacer and grab-worthy guard are nice touches.

▼ **COLLABORATIVE KNIFE:** The Devin Thomas ladder-pattern damascus blade points West, thanks to hand cutting and hollow grinding by Wilde Bill Cody, and heat treating by Paul Bos. David Yellowhorse designed, textured and accented the nickel silver, black jet, white turquoise and fire opal handle. *(PointSeven photo)*

▲ **J. NEILSON:** The coyote jawbone bites into your grip while you skin the rest of the howling beast using the 30-layer damascus blade. John Cohea fashioned the rawhide, trade bead, horsehair, bronze and bear-claw sheath. *(Ward photo)*

◀ **JERRY VAN EIZENGA:** Green jigged bone was a smart choice for the boot knife that also features a 6.75-inch "W's"-pattern damascus blade, mosaic pins and fine file work. *(Ward photo)*

◀ **GLEN KOLAJCZYK:** The "Spoontoon Tomahawk" showcases a well-patterned and shaped damascus bowl and head, a tiger-maple haft, brass pins, turquoise accents, red beads, an eagle claw and horsehair accents. *(Cory Martin Imaging)*

Slip-Joint Ventures

▶ **DAN BURKE:** Fluting pearl was a tiny part of he venture, while fashioning the implements, finishing them, and making them work smoothly remained the brunt of the load.
(PointSeven photo)

◀ **C. GRAY TAYLOR:** Four colors of 14k gold make up the liners, sculpted bolsters and inlays, with shading of the gold flowers done by Tim George, not to mention the antique-tortoise-shell handle slabs and dozen working implements. Words cannot describe ...
(PointSeven photo)

◀ **MICHAEL VAGNINO:** Damascus, 24k gold, antique tortoise shell and W2 blade steel hold court on a Schatt & Morgan gunstock-pattern slip joint.
(PointSeven photo)

▲ **IAN VAN REENEN:** Gentlemen's pocketknives don't get much finer than the hollow-ground, hand-polished, Roman knot file-worked, mammoth-ivory-handle ATS-34 wharncliffe pattern.

▶ **RAYMOND L. SMITH:** File-worked ATS-34 and mammoth ivory is the winning combination of a Barlow-pattern folder.

▶ **GRACE HORNE:** Using RWL-34 blade steel and a silver enamel, Grace created a "Shadow Of Opportunity" folder that's opportunistic. *(PointSeven photo)*

◀ **JOHN PERRY:** Parading mother-of-pearl and twist damascus before a review board, the congress is now in session. *(PointSeven photo)*

◀ **JERRY VAN EIZENGA:** Many are the slip joints in O1 tool steel and stag, but few look like this, and that's saying a lot. *(Ward photo)*

◀ **CALVIN ROBINSON:** A pretty pair of slip joints includes one in a Sambar stag handle, and one in jigged chocolate paper Micarta®, both with 2.75-inch D2 blades and stainless steel bolsters. *(PointSeven photo)*

▲ **RICHARD ROGERS:** A surgeon's folder includes six ATS-34 implements, four additional, removable tools, an antique-tortoise-shell handle and a nice figure, even before surgery. *(SharpByCoop.com photo)*

Slip-Joint Ventures

▶ **KIRBY LAMBERT:** Who says a straight razor can't double as a one-hand folder, or feature a hollow-ground Devin Thomas damascus blade, Thuya burl handle and titanium liners? *(SharpByCoop.com photo)*

◀ **MIKE ZSCHERNY:** Green bone gets jiggy on a CPM 154CM dogleg jackknife. *(SharpByCoop.com photo)*

▶ **TY MONTELL:** Ice-checked mastodon ivory crackles along the grip of the two-blade trapper in Devin Thomas "matrix"-pattern stainless damascus, and titanium bolsters and liners. *(Ward photo)*

▶ **T.R. OVEREYNDER:** Rose gold and pearl are best friends who like to double with a couple blades they met. *(PointSeven photo)*

◀ **JOEL CHAMBLIN:** The translucency of antique tortoise shell is in direct contrast to the steely exterior of eight CPM 154 blades. *(Buddy Thomason photo)*

► **TAKESHI MATSUSAKI:** You could fix about anything with the 20-plus ATS-34 tools and blades, perhaps even perform surgery, all while holding the stag grip. *(PointSeven photo)*

► **KAJ EMBRETSEN:** Shape shifting takes place among shimmering damascus, highly figured stag, a comely corkscrew and small foil cutting blade. *(PointSeven photo)*

◄ **BILL RUPLE:** Slinky is the sowbelly split-back whittler in a Sambar stag body and CPM 154 blades. *(SharpByCoop.com photo)*

◄ **JERRY HALFRICH:** There's nary a square corner on the "Rounder" in CPM 154CM steel, amber stag, a stainless shield, and integral bolsters and liners. *(SharpByCoop.com photo)*

◄ **STEVE DUNN:** Bow tie shields and scroll engraving fancy up a pair of CPM 154CM slip joints. *(SharpByCoop.com photo)*

◀ **PETER MARTIN:** The knightly 376-layer damascus folder is fetching in gold-lip pearl and gold-plated screws. *(Cory Martin Imaging)*

▶ **RYUICHI KAWAMURA:** All four ATS-34 appendages are unfolded to show off the form, each splayed out from a stag grip with acorn shield. *(PointSeven photo)*

▲ **AL WARREN:** The trapper in S30V and amber stag will cut itself out of any snag or snare. *(Ward photo)*

▶ **GARY HEADRICK:** A subtle, carved gold screw head lays flush against pure ivory, offset by a damascus blade and two other gold pins planted at opposite ends of the grip.

◀ **ENRIQUE PENA:** Any hunter worth his salt would proudly put to use the two-blade folder in Remington jigged bone and stainless steel. *(Balance Digital photo)*

▶ **STEVE SCHWARZER:** Seldom does one see hand-forged, clay tempered 1095 blades on a saddle horn trapper of Tony Bose's design, and with a giraffe-bone handle, it's one of a kind. *(PointSeven photo)*

▶ **TIM BRITTON:** The jack with the sweet sway back is the beneficiary of amber stag, BG-42 blade steel and nickel silver bolsters. *(SharpByCoop.com photo)*

◀ **BILL KENNEDY JR.:** Make mine a Utica jigged-bone pocketknife with a stainless blade and bolsters. *(Ward photo)*

◀ **HARVEY DEAN:** The "W's"-pattern damascus blade of the California jackknife, together with the engraved bolsters, put to rest for good the notion that stripes and checks don't go together. *(Buddy Thomason photo)*

▶ **YOSHIO SAKAUCHI:** At 1.25 inches overall, the pearl-handle multi-blade would make a nice addition to anyone's collection of miniature knives. *(PointSeven photo)*

Sworded Affairs

Now these are big drinks of water, long reaches, tall and lean, really stretched out. The long blades aren't only impressive in size, but they also bespeak tradition, war, history and handcraft, a skill passed down from generation to generation, and in Japan's case, from maser sword smith to apprentice through thousands of years.

The amazing thing is that modern American blade smiths and their brethren across the far reaches of the universe—in European and Scandinavian countries, South America, Canada, Africa and elsewhere—fashion swords as skillfully and of similar or higher quality as early Japanese masters. The materials have progressed and working conditions have gotten better, but it's the passion and dedication that have raised the bar on contemporary sword making.

A story passed onto me by knifemaker Wayne Goddard involves a class he taught on forging steel. As the students started heating and hammering their billets, one student began with a larger billet than the others and started stretching the steel in all kinds of wild and imaginative directions. The student was Mardi Meshejian, and Wayne said he looked at Mardi and said, "Go boy, keep it up. Stretch that blade out." That's the passion of modern blade smiths who desire to overbuild, study, test and rebuild. It's what sword making is all about, and everyone benefits from such "sworded affairs."

▶ **VINCE EVANS:** A sterling example of an early Anglo-Saxon sword showcases a 28.5-inch, six-bar, composite-damascus blade, a fossil-walrus-ivory hilt, and antiqued bronze and silver mounts. *(PointSeven photo)*

▶ **MARDI MESHEJIAN:** The convex-ground 1080-and-15N20 damascus blade is hand carved along the length of the spine up to the heat-colored copper and titanium guard, and fossil-walrus-ivory hilt. *(SharpByCoop.com photo)*

◀ **STEVE SCHWARZER:** The double-edge 1086 V sword features a full-length central groove, leather-wrapped ray-skin hilt and a wood scabbard. *(PointSeven photo)*

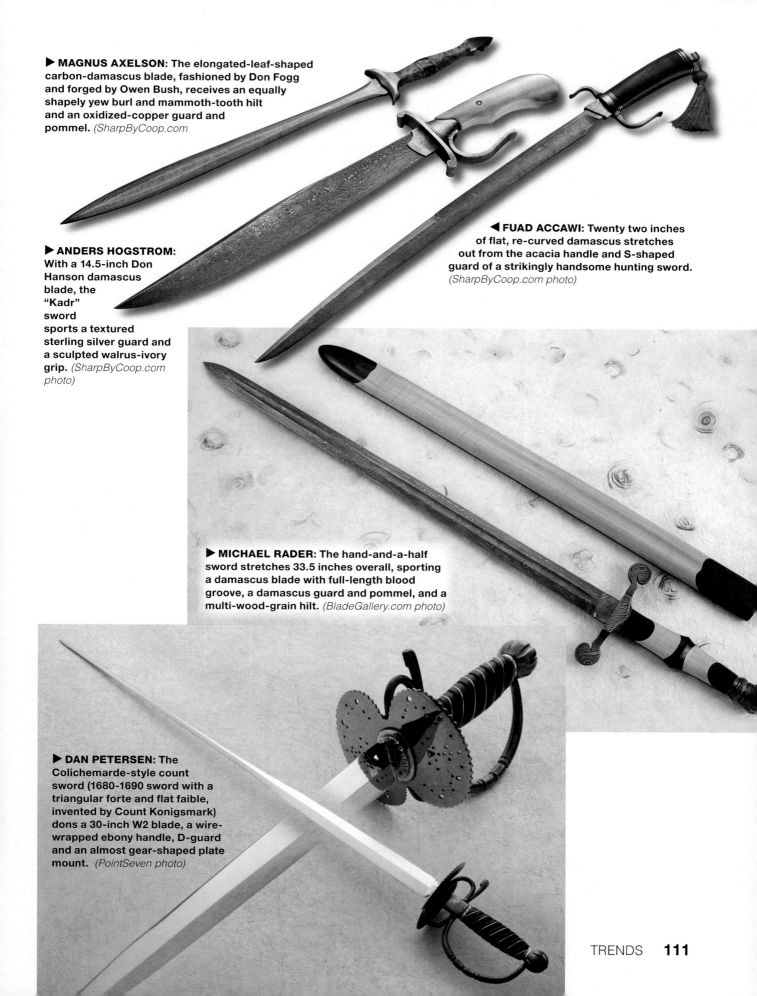

▶ **MAGNUS AXELSON:** The elongated-leaf-shaped carbon-damascus blade, fashioned by Don Fogg and forged by Owen Bush, receives an equally shapely yew burl and mammoth-tooth hilt and an oxidized-copper guard and pommel. *(SharpByCoop.com)*

▶ **ANDERS HOGSTROM:** With a 14.5-inch Don Hanson damascus blade, the "Kadr" sword sports a textured sterling silver guard and a sculpted walrus-ivory grip. *(SharpByCoop.com photo)*

◀ **FUAD ACCAWI:** Twenty two inches of flat, re-curved damascus stretches out from the acacia handle and S-shaped guard of a strikingly handsome hunting sword. *(SharpByCoop.com photo)*

▶ **MICHAEL RADER:** The hand-and-a-half sword stretches 33.5 inches overall, sporting a damascus blade with full-length blood groove, a damascus guard and pommel, and a multi-wood-grain hilt. *(BladeGallery.com photo)*

▶ **DAN PETERSEN:** The Colichemarde-style count sword (1680-1690 sword with a triangular forte and flat faible, invented by Count Konigsmark) dons a 30-inch W2 blade, a wire-wrapped ebony handle, D-guard and an almost gear-shaped plate mount. *(PointSeven photo)*

Stagmascus

It shouldn't be surprising that knifemakers have seen fit to marry stag with damascus. One is a solid, the other a stripe. You cannot wear stripes with checks any sooner than you can stripes with polka dots, or stripes with stripes (you'd look like an inmate, or a candy striper at best), but you can certainly wear stripes with solids. In fact, you can *only* wear stripes with solids. Nothing else coordinates.

Stag is a solid, and damascus usually includes some sort of stripes, or lines, weather controlled, smooth, swooping lines, static ebbing and flowing lines, or wild, electric lines (not the kind that power houses.) And damascus has character. If a knifemaker chooses the right slab of stag, whether

crown stag or a mid-section, it is knobby, colorful, gnarly and groovy all at the same time. Add that to a prettily patterned damascus blade, and a fine knife starts to take shape.

Fine knives are the ultimate goal, those that look good and cut like no others. The art of making knives combines a good eye with craftsmanship and ability. Matching materials up is only part of it, lining them up, fitting them, finishing them, honing the steel, polishing the metal, sanding out the rough spots, rounding the corners and pinning every-

thing down are other steps in the knifemaking process.

Stagmascus, or the combination of stag and damascus, is a solid (and striped) starting point. The rest is up to the imagination and ability of the knifemaker. It shouldn't be surprising that knifemakers combine stag and damascus. They've already learned to blend tools and aesthetics, time and energy, work and fun, a hobby and a profession.

◄**AARON WILBURN:** Stag antler is separated from a forged-to-shape damascus blade by alternating red-fiber and brass spacers. *(BladeGallery.com photo)*

►**JERRY VAN EIZENGA:** A coffin handle of stag leads to a 9-inch, ladder-pattern damascus blade with a swooping swedge grind. *(PointSeven photo)*

◄**ARTHUR LYNN:** A stag grip and 1084-and-15N20-damascus blade are the solid and stripes of the fine fighter. *(Buddy Thomason photo)*

▶ **DAVID LISCH:** The stag bowie sports a 9-inch 1084-and-15N20 damascus blade, carved guard and a wrought-iron bolster. *(Mitch Lum photo)*

▲ **STEVE DUNN:** The stag and damascus fighter is done up Dunn style, in a flat grind, engraved 416 stainless steel guard, clean lines, and impeccable fit and finish. *(SharpByCoop.com photo)*

▶ **BOB CROWDER:** The multi-ground, re-curved, dipping damascus blade makes up the cutting end of the business, while the stag grip and blued 1018, copper and damascus guard handle the rest. *(SharpByCoop.com photo)*

▲ **CHESTER DARCEY:** Nice, knobby Sambar stag is paired up with the maker's own damascus for a couple of hunky hunting knives. *(PointSeven photo)*

◀ **TERRY VANDEVENTER:** Make mine a mosaic-damascus and stag bowie, please, with a Turkish-twist damascus guard and silicon-bronze spacer. *(SharpByCoop.com photo)*

Micro Chips

Considering the amount of handwork, fit and finish, making of mechanisms, inlay and embellishment that goes into each miniature knife, it wouldn't be surprising if the bite-size blades could be plugged into computers for storing information. But, alas, the "micro chip" in the headline is a play on words for the tiny little chippers that could cut through tree limbs given enough time and effort.

And it would be easier to make the miniatures if the knifemakers' fingers and thumbs were tiny digits like the numbers on a computer screen. Then reality rears her ugly head again, and we realize it's not the knifemakers who are height challenged, but the blades, grips, guards and bolsters. If the springs, spacers and choils were pre-fabricated in scale sizes, then it would be a breeze to assemble the microscopic choppers. Yet that doesn't seem to be the case. Each part is handmade by normal sized men.

So it wasn't a simple matter of making a knife. The diminutive dicers were worked on under microscopes, loupes and headlamps. Tiny parts meant tiny tolerances, fits and finishes. And rue the day that a knifemaker drops one of the microscopic parts, and then spends the rest of his waking hours scouring the shop floor for a peewee pin. Fashioning these micro chips was no easy task, which makes the craftsmanship more enviable, the attention to detail essential and the finished products undeniably endearing.

▲ **C. GRAY TAYLOR:** Done in antique tortoise shell and CPM 154 steel, the sleeveboard miniature stretches a mere 1 3/16 inches overall. *(PointSeven photo)*

◄ **TY MONTELL:** The miniature trapper comes in a 1-inch ATS-34 blade, a bit of black-lip pearl and 410 stainless steel bolsters. *(Buddy Thomason photo)*

▲ **MICHAEL WALKER:** While the "Tiny Zipper" is not meant to hold up small pants, the miniature zipped blade in Damasteel, accented by blue and gold, would excel at cutting a thread from a nice pair of slacks. *(PointSeven photo)*

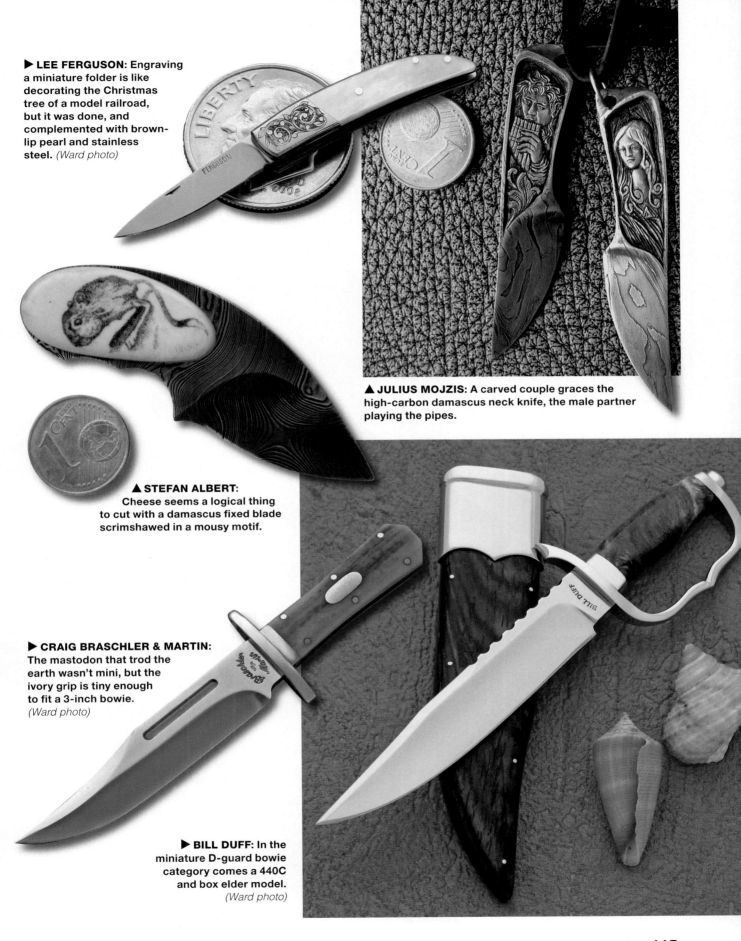

► **LEE FERGUSON:** Engraving a miniature folder is like decorating the Christmas tree of a model railroad, but it was done, and complemented with brown-lip pearl and stainless steel. *(Ward photo)*

▲ **JULIUS MOJZIS:** A carved couple graces the high-carbon damascus neck knife, the male partner playing the pipes.

▲ **STEFAN ALBERT:** Cheese seems a logical thing to cut with a damascus fixed blade scrimshawed in a mousy motif.

► **CRAIG BRASCHLER & MARTIN:** The mastodon that trod the earth wasn't mini, but the ivory grip is tiny enough to fit a 3-inch bowie. *(Ward photo)*

► **BILL DUFF:** In the miniature D-guard bowie category comes a 440C and box elder model. *(Ward photo)*

Back-You-Down Bowies

◄ **JERRY MCCLURE:** The material-rich bowie camp knife flaunts a cracked-ice-damascus blade, mokumé guard, sea-cow-bone spacer and walrus-ivory grip. *(Buddy Thomason image)*

◄ **DON NORRIS:** While the deceased knifemaker will forever be sadly missed, the carved and sculpted eagle-head damascus bowie will be around for generations to come. *(Balance Digital photo)*

► **J.W. RANDALL:** Soldier straight is the "Ranger Bowie" in premium stag, nickel silver and 1095 blade steel.

◄ **BILL DUFF:** The maker blends ebony, stag, anodized titanium and file-worked stainless steel into a blindingly beautiful bowie. *(Ward photo)*

◄ **MICHAEL MOONEY:** A little African blackwood, a stretch of ATS-34 stainless steel, a gifted knifemaker and some stamina can go a long way. *(Balance Digital image)*

▶ **PAUL HAPPY:** Curly maple and 5160 steel allow the bowie shape to speak for itself. *(Ward photo)*

▶ **JAMES BATSON:** Even Edwin Forrest would admire the checkered rosewood, German silver and full-tang 9260 blade. *(Ward photo)*

▶ **JIMMY CHIN and RON NEWTON:** Images within the damascus are in clever contrast to the stainless guard and dog-bone-style blackwood handle. *(Ward photo)*

▲ **HERMAN SCHNEIDER:** The single-clip, convex blade is as tasty as single-malt Scotch, and almost as deadly. Hold onto the African blackwood grip.

▲ **STEVE CULVER:** Damascus ripples along the blade of the dog-bone bowie, creating a Spanish knot in its wake, and leading to an ivory handle with domed pins and shield. *(Ward photo)*

Back-You-Down Bowies

▶ **BILL COFFEY:** Jim Whitehead's engraving lent a good deal of class to a stag-handle CPM 154 bowie with titanium spacers and skull crusher pommel. *(Duane Weikum photo)*

▶ **BRION TOMBERLIN:** The smooth African blackwood handle called for an S-guard to separate it from the damascus blade. *(Ward photo)*

◀ **JACK A. FULLER:** Imagery in the blade is always so mesmerizing, with only a camel bone handle, silver pins and stainless steel fittings to jolt us back to reality.

▶ **TIM HANCOCK:** All of the damascus parts, including the clam-shell pommel are from the same billet of "4th Of July" damascus, and the mammoth ivory from one beautiful beast. *(PointSeven photo)*

◀ **JOHN PERRY:** The Sambar stag "carver" handle dips one way, the mild-steel S-guard both ways, and the 5160 blade quite another. *(Buddy Thomason photo)*

▲ **RONALD WELLING:** Stacked spacers prove to be a sweet spot between stag and steel. *(Ward photo)*

▲ **KEVIN EVANS:** The bowie set goes from large to small, but all in 5160 steel, African blackwood and turquoise. *(Ward photo)*

▶ **MIKE WILLIAMS:** It's natural to palm the rounded grip, turning the knife around in your hand to admire the damascus blade, guard and full-length tang. *(PointSeven photo)*

▶ **HARVEY DEAN:** The engraved "El Diablo" in stag and 1084 steel *es muy delicioso*. *(Buddy Thomason photo)*

◀ **TERRY VANDEVENTER:** The back-you-down bowie does it in stag and 8.5 inches of dizzying damascus. *(Ward photo)*

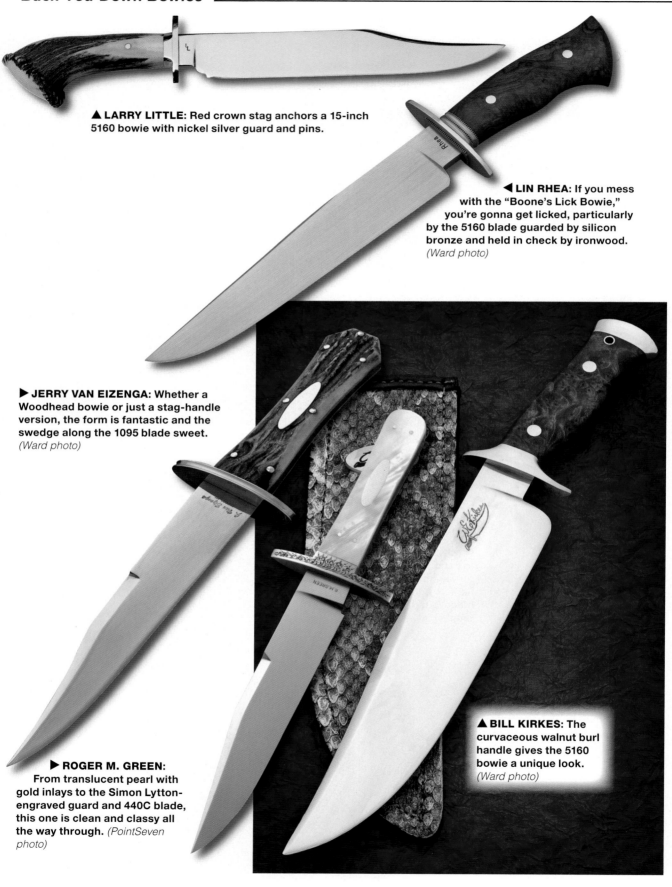

▲ **LARRY LITTLE:** Red crown stag anchors a 15-inch 5160 bowie with nickel silver guard and pins.

◀ **LIN RHEA:** If you mess with the "Boone's Lick Bowie," you're gonna get licked, particularly by the 5160 blade guarded by silicon bronze and held in check by ironwood. *(Ward photo)*

▶ **JERRY VAN EIZENGA:** Whether a Woodhead bowie or just a stag-handle version, the form is fantastic and the swedge along the 1095 blade sweet. *(Ward photo)*

▶ **ROGER M. GREEN:** From translucent pearl with gold inlays to the Simon Lytton-engraved guard and 440C blade, this one is clean and classy all the way through. *(PointSeven photo)*

▲ **BILL KIRKES:** The curvaceous walnut burl handle gives the 5160 bowie a unique look. *(Ward photo)*

▶ **CLAUDE MONTJOY:** The big, brutal bowie slays 'em with ATS-34, stag and style. *(SharpByCoop.com photo)*

▲ **E. JAY HENDRICKSON:** The classic clip-point, coffin-handle bowie is enshrined in 5160 blade steel, carved nickel silver, ivory and silver-wire-inlaid curly maple. *(Buddy Thomason image)*

▲ **RALPH RICHARDS:** Bouncing along the damascus pattern lands you on an amboyna burl handle that's just as active. *(Ward photo)*

▲ **JOHN WHITE:** Clamshell carving is the only embellishment an ivory-handle 5160 bowie needed. *(Ward photo)*

▲ **MIKE RUTH:** A silicon bronze spacer blends the color of stag with the glint of 5160 steel. *(Ward photo)*

▼**GARTH HINDMARCH:** Stabilized giraffe bone and nickel silver do their best to balance the 9.5-inch 440 blade.

◄**RUSS ANDREWS II:** It's all about the movement—the random-pattern and two-bar-twist damascus, and wavy walnut grains. *(SharpByCoop.com photo)*

►**CHARLES STOUT:** Popcorn stag and buttery sweet damascus make their theatrical debut. *(Ward photo)*

▲**SHAWN MCINTYRE:** The spear-point 52100 bowie is less clip point and more to the point. *(SharpByCoop.com photo)*

▼**DON HANSON III:** The "Pirate Bowie," garbed in fossil walrus ivory and a W2 blade with a wicked temper, would overthrow seasoned sailors. *(SharpByCoop.com photo)*

STATE OF THE ART

Virtuosos are those musical geniuses so schooled, naturally talented and versatile, they can pick up one of several instruments, whether in the strings, brass, percussion or woodwinds section, and play sweet melodies, beautiful music, soothing tunes. They have so much untapped talent, and can easily call it to action at will. Theirs is a lucky lot in life.

There are virtuosos in the world of knives, too. Knifemakers have been overheard saying they took classes to engrave handles, blades and bolsters because they wanted to do so themselves rather than rely on other artists in the field. There are blade smiths—steel wrestlers, really—who forge pattern-welded steel, create mosaic-damascus patterns, and then doff the goggles and leather aprons for loupes, needles and ink, all employed to scrimshaw ivory. Such instinctual tradesmen carve wood and sculpt steel with equal aplomb. They inlay silver wire into wood grips as easily as they facet precious gems, tan and tool leather, or file-work blade spines.

These are creative cutlers, those whose tasteful embellishments speak volumes. Like writers of books, mural painters and sidewalk chalk artists, they hold their pallets before them, using art to make a statement and create a mood. It's the state of art in knives, and it is held in virtuous hands.

Gold, Rubies & Tourmalines

▶ **HARUMI HIRAYAMA:** Pink tourmaline stones and 18k-gold pins highlight the amber handle and drive home the 440C blade. *(Tomo Hasegawa photo)*

◀ **TOM FERRY:** The 24k-gold-inlaid dragon crouches among dark, brownish damascus, surrounded by classic, exotic engraving. *(Mitch Lum photo)*

◀ **REINHARD TSCHAGER:** In the jewel knife category is a full integral inter-frame folder inlaid with gold, engraved by Valerio Peli and outfitted with a gold chain and pendant.

▼ **JOE KIOUS:** The "Medium Persian" in golden Ron Skaggs engraving is larger than life, including the 3.75-inch Mike Norris stainless damascus blade and random file work. *(SharpByCoop.com photo)*

◀ **ARPAD BOJTOS:** Lay, lady, lay. Lay across my big damascus bed. Her hair, the sun and stars are gold, and she's in the company of walrus tusk, buffalo horn, titanium and steel. Mike Norris did the damascus honors. *(PointSeven photo)*

▼ **HOWARD HITCHMOUGH:** Golden, lazing, floating sea otters are compliments of Lisa Tomlin, surrounded by a sea of engraving, black-lip pearl and Damasteel damascus.

◄ **JURGEN STEINAU:** The solid 18k-gold inter-frame folder parades gold accents, and pearl and semi-precious-stone inlays. *(Francesco Pachi photo)*

► **WARREN OSBORNE:** Tim George's gold inlay work frames black-lip mother-of-pearl and Mike Norris Damasteel. *(PointSeven photo)*

▲ **OWEN WOOD:** The knifemaker's dramatic damascus fuses with other steel and gets the gold treatment through Tim George's Art Deco inlay and engraving. Black-lip pearl plants itself on the bolster. *(PointSeven photo)*

► **CURT ERICKSON:** Lab rubies, gold inlays and Julie Warenski engraving accent a 440C art dagger with a white-marble handle. *(PointSeven photo)*

◄ JACK LEVIN: The gold mask and sun of the "Blue Devil" decorate a folding dagger that integrates hand carving, high-profile machining, forging, engraving, jewelry casting, heat treating and bluing, not to mention a folding shield that pops up automatically when the blade is unfolded.

◄ DON LOZIER: As if damascus, silver and gold weren't enough, matched rubies embellish the Persian fixed blade. (PointSeven photo)

▼ ZAZA REVISHVILI: The red stones are head turners, as are the damascus and filigree. (PointSeven photo)

◄ RICK EATON: Rick's been doing this so long, you tend to forget that it's not easy for him to inlay and engrave gold cheetahs into the jungle-like settings of damascus folding daggers. (PointSeven photo)

► GAIL LUNN: Twisted gold wire is woven into the Robert Eggerling damascus blade and handle, accompanied by 20 rubies in the grip, back bar, frame and thumb stud. (PointSeven photo)

Bolster Bravado

The middleman. An axis. The center, core, heart and anchor. It's what holds the other pieces together. Bolsters of folders cover the pivots. It's the area of the knife that determines how much friction is felt during opening and closing of the blades. It's where the pins are, the washers, the bushings.

The outer bolsters are just a pretty covering for all the action that happens underneath. So why not make the bolsters just that—pretty? So goes the reasoning of some reasonable makers of fine knives, and that's just what they did. Knifemakers are paying attention to the centerpieces of folding knives and some fixed blades, the bolsters. Think of it as adding a chrome air filter or exhaust manifold to a classic hotrod. It just pretties up the

place a bit, and we all know that finery makes for increased knife sales.

Sound the bolster alarm. Bring some bravado to the go-between of blades and handles. Here's where creativity is really tried. Handles can be carved, sculpted, engraved, scrimshawed, grooved and otherwise textured. Blades are forged, heat-treated, tempered, laminated and pattern welded. But what about the middleman, the axis, center, core,

heart, soul and anchor? What embellishments befit he? All of the aforementioned arrive in bolster land, and some not heretofore seen in these knife parts.

◀ **DON VOGT:** Just like the blade before them, the bolsters of the latch-release auto are hand-carved Devin Thomas damascus, in this case with gold flower-pedal-like embellishments that drip nectar onto honed steel and complement a carved mother-of-pearl grip.

▶ **MIKE TYRE:** A star burst all over the Larry Donnelly damascus bolsters, sending orbital shapes down the Chris Marks mosaic-damascus blade. A peridot thumb stud and mammoth-ivory grip complete the piece. *(PointSeven photo)*

▶ **JAY FISHER:** The Atlantisite and Tasmania gemstone handle is given sweet "bunches of grapes" bolster treatment.

▶ **JON CHRISTENSEN:** Feather and leaf damascus sprout from the vase-shaped handle of the "Bouquet Folder." *(PointSeven photo)*

◀ **DAN CHINNOCK:** Between the black of the Larry Donnelly damascus blade and the brown of the mammoth-ivory grip is the blue of the bolsters, also from Donnelly. Gold highlights and an emerald-inlaid thumb stud add further hues. *(PointSeven photo)*

▲ **JOHNNY STOUT:** Golden flowers flavor the blue Chad Nichols mosaic-damascus bolsters and find comfort in the steely shade of a Hiro-Hito damascus blade. Fossil walrus ivory plants itself on the grip. *(Ward photo)*

▲ **BUZZ BEZUIDENHOUT:** The knife known as "Stacey" flaunts orange Ettore Gianferrari nickel-damascus bolsters, a Bertie Rietveld ladder-pattern damascus blade and a translucent pearl posterior.

▲ **PETER MARTIN:** Tightly patterned mosaic-damascus bolsters offset the bold imagery of the blade and combo black-and-yellow pearly grip. The 14k-gold thumb stud is inlaid with a tangerine garnet. *(Cory Martin Imaging)*

▶ **ANDERS HEDLUND:** Forged by Johan Gustavsson, the leaf-pattern, mosaic-damascus bolsters and mosaic-damascus blade bookend mammoth ivory that's carved to reveal mother-of-pearl underlay and gold-dot inlay.

▶ **JERRY MCCLURE:** Dark-brown Chris Marks "T-pattern"-damascus bolsters accentuate a walrus-ivory handle and a 30-bar twist-Damasteel blade.

◀ **JEREMY MARSH:** Three-color Mike Sakmar mokumé bolsters sweeten up the "Assassin" tactical folder, which also features a Mike Norris damascus blade, 3-D mokumé thumb stud and a carbon-fiber grip. *(SharpByCoop.com photo)*

◀ **FRED OTT:** A sculpted nickel silver collar and ferrule bring a carved oosic handle and twist-damascus blade together for a steel summit. *(BladeGallery.com photo)*

▶ **BILL POST:** The Corian handle comes with granite-like bolsters and a shapely D2 blade. *(Ward photo)*

▶ **R.B. JOHNSON:** Mosaic damascus bolsters transition a Devin Thomas damascus blade into a tortoise-shell handle. A tiger-eye thumb stud and gold leaf scales contribute to the effect.

Previously Engraved

It must be like a hibernating bear awakening from a long winter slumber. When an engraver emerges from behind the headlamp and loop, the magnifying glass and overhead light, to peer out at his surroundings, it has to feel as though he's been in another dimension for the past several hours of his existence.

In a way, the act of engraving does occur on another dimension, multiple dimensional planes, and to understand them all, one must immerse his or herself in the work, the tedious yet addictive practice of giving dimension to a flat surface. It is the act of enlivening steel, surface carving with a sharpened instrument. Adorning molecular alloys requires not only a steady hand, clear mind and total concentration, but also the creative ability to live among layers, carve away media, navigate depth and dance in the shadows.

Some engravers reside in black-and-white worlds while others thrive in brilliant dreamscapes. Engraving can be as subtle as scrollwork or as sensory as bustling marketplaces in populated urban centers. Knights on white horses save princesses trapped in castles, and mythological creatures breathe fiery life into alien lands. Such is the subject matter of the men holding gravers, summoning steel shavings and willing carbon masses into enlightened etchings.

They immerse themselves in otherworldly realms and give us the engravings we've come to enjoy and appreciate beyond the ordinary existence of knives unembellished. Don't wake the slumbering bears.

▼ KEN HURST: The bronze bolsters of Kevin Casey's dress locking-liner folder made for dynamic engraving surfaces, blended colorfully with a mammoth-ivory grip, a tiger-eye-inlaid thumb stud, file work and a damascus blade that dips in all the right places. *(SharpByCoop.com photo)*

▲ SIMON LYTTON: The elongated handle of Eugene Shadley's two-blade quill knife lent itself beautifully to scroll and flower engraving. *(SharpByCoop.com photo)*

◄ TIM GEORGE: Knifemaker Howard Hitchmough outfitted the folding dagger with a white mother-of-pearl handle, all the better to draw attention toward the gold-laden bolster engraving. *(PointSeven photo)*

► **JOHN W. SMITH:** Black-lip pearl and white mother-of-pearl are the sun rays that sprouted the leaf engraving of the locking-liner folder. *(PointSeven photo)*

▼ **C.J. CAI:** Jack Busfield's dress slip-joint folder is completely undressed and steamy as molten gold. *(SharpByCoop.com photo)*

◄ **KEN HURST:** The guard, frame and pommel of Greg Shahan's fixed-blade fighter are milled from a single billet of 1018 steel, and otherwise engraved to perfection. *(SharpByCoop. com photo)*

◄ **JERE DAVIDSON:** While it was Ronald Best who fashioned the upswept, Persian-style integral fighter, he stopped short of embellishment, allowing the engraver to work the steel, and Faustina Mead to scrimshaw a steed-riding, sword-wielding woman in ivory. *(PointSeven photo)*

◄ **C.J. CAI:** Under the turtle-shell handle inlays of Joe Kious's damascus auto dagger swim sharks and sea turtles, and engraved on its bolsters are mermaids and an Orpheus-like mythical man. *(SharpByCoop.com photo)*

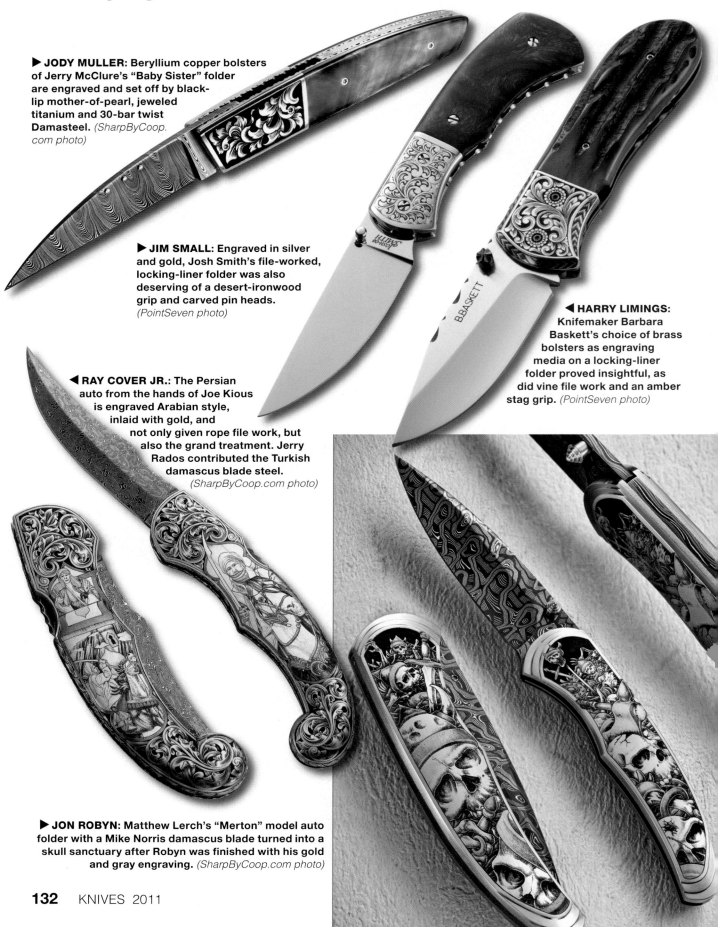

▶ **JODY MULLER:** Beryllium copper bolsters of Jerry McClure's "Baby Sister" folder are engraved and set off by black-lip mother-of-pearl, jeweled titanium and 30-bar twist Damasteel. *(SharpByCoop.com photo)*

▶ **JIM SMALL:** Engraved in silver and gold, Josh Smith's file-worked, locking-liner folder was also deserving of a desert-ironwood grip and carved pin heads. *(PointSeven photo)*

◀ **RAY COVER JR.:** The Persian auto from the hands of Joe Kious is engraved Arabian style, inlaid with gold, and not only given rope file work, but also the grand treatment. Jerry Rados contributed the Turkish damascus blade steel. *(SharpByCoop.com photo)*

◀ **HARRY LIMINGS:** Knifemaker Barbara Baskett's choice of brass bolsters as engraving media on a locking-liner folder proved insightful, as did vine file work and an amber stag grip. *(PointSeven photo)*

▶ **JON ROBYN:** Matthew Lerch's "Merton" model auto folder with a Mike Norris damascus blade turned into a skull sanctuary after Robyn was finished with his gold and gray engraving. *(SharpByCoop.com photo)*

► **ALVIN CHEWIWI:** The bolsters of a mammoth-ivory-handle Don Hethcoat locking-liner damascus folder were scrolled and buffaloed.

▼ **RICHARD and ANNETTE WRIGHT:** The carved and color-anodized bolsters and back bar of the ambidextrous bolster-release switchblade brighten up the Jerry Rados damascus blade and mother-of-pearl handle slabs.

► **RON SKAGGS:** What a wedding gift: Herman Schneider built this foot-long ring dagger in 1978, and recently bought it back from a dealer or collector and presented it to his grandson as a wedding gift. *(PointSeven photo)*

◄ **GAIL LUNN:** Most knifemakers would have been satisfied with the green tint of the pearl handle, but Gail engraved the "Flower Girl" folder, outfitted it with a damascus blade, and inlaid the file-worked spine with more of the pearl. *(Terrill Hoffman photo)*

◄ **RICHARD ZIRBES:** The knifemaker had nacre for the handle and a knack for engraving.

STATE OF THE ART **133**

► **BARBARA SLOBODIAN:** A damascus blade by Bill Burke and a knife by Scott Slobodian, including silver work and musk-ox-horn handle, are met head on by Barbara's born-to-be-blue engraving. *(SharpByCoop.com photo)*

► **GIL RUDOLPH:** Dennis Friedly's shapely fixed blade with a fossil-walrus-ivory handle is the beneficiary of big horn sheep and wild cat imagery, as well as a few strands of gold. *(PointSeven photo)*

▲ **TIM ADLAM:** The handle and sheath of the traditional Kirpan fashioned by Jot Singh Khalsa are pearl inlaid and engraved, while the damascus blade is of the Devin Thomas kind. *(SharpByCoop.com photo)*

◄ **JULIUS MOJZIS:** Shields, scrolls, symbols, quill, parchment and a topless scribe are all subjects of the bolster engraving on an ebony-handle dagger.

▲ **KIRBY BLETCHER:** The patterns of Larry Donnelly damascus, box elder burl and bolster scroll engraving move about the lock-back folder like desert-dwelling fire ants. *(Ward photo)*

► **SHAUN and SHARLA HANSEN:** Spear-wielding gods and girls with golden hair dare tread on the damascus folding dagger. *(PointSeven photo)*

JON ROBYN: A Warren Osborne folder benefits from color depictions of James Dean in character from the films *Rebel Without A Cause and Giant.* *(PointSeven photo)*

► **BILL MAINS:** In the style of Bill Scagel comes a Ronald Welling knife that would stun even Scagel, and includes a mammoth-ivory grip and two gorgeously engraved blades. *(Ward photo)*

◄ **TIM GEORGE:** The gold-inlaid and engraved jumping marlin and scroll take up residence on a Warren Osborne mid-lock folder. *(PointSeven photo)*

▲ **MARCELLO PEDINI:** A cobra readies itself to strike out at anyone who comes before Peter Del Raso's Warenski-style hunter, complete with a full, tapered tang, ATS-34 blade and ivory handle scales.

▶ **JON ROBYN:** Gold and red dinosaurs duke it out on the engraved bolsters of Tom Overeynder's "dino-bone-handle" folding dagger. The blade is of chevron explosion-pattern damascus that will never go extinct. *(SharpByCoop. com photo)*

◀ **LEE GRIFFITHS:** The tang of John Young's ATS-34 hunter tapers to the butt, and is covered by big-horn-sheep handle slabs and engraving of the sheepish one himself. *(SharpByCoop.com photo)*

▼▶ **C.J. CAI:** Even the pocket clip of Keith Ouye's "Aka Fuji" folder is engraved Bushiido style, and the titanium handle is a haven for exoticism. *(PointSeven photo)*

▶ **TIM ADLAM and JIM SMALL:** The late Frank Centofante built lock-back folders so beautifully it took two engravers to embellish them. *(PointSeven photo)*

▶ **JODY MULLER:** Southeast Asia is well represented on the bolsters of a mammoth-ivory-handle damascus folder. *(SharpByCoop.com photo)*

▶ **AAD VAN RYSWYK:** Scrollwork and damascus dutifully and beautifully do folder duty.

◀ **TOM FERRY:** The "Koi Tanto" is named for gold-scaled fish everywhere that swim in damascus seas. *(PointSeven photo)*

▶ **JACK LEVIN:** Metalwork techniques practiced on the "Mysteria" folder include hand carving, precision machining, forging, engraving, jewelry casting, heat treatment and bluing. The scene is after a Pieter Bruegel painting, and the folding shield pops up automatically when the blade is unfolded. *(Francesco Pachi photo)*

◀ **DES HORN:** With a texture similar to coral or shell, the hand-carved stainless steel bolsters are butted up against black-lip pearl on one end and droplet-like damascus on the other. *(Francesco Pachi photo)*

◀ **RICK EATON:** A sole-authored piece, the mosaic-damascus fixed blade showcases a mammoth-ivory handle and flare-cut engraving of the "bank note Arabesque" style. *(PointSeven photo)*

▲ **JULIE WARENSKI:** The damascus, carved-amber, and engraved and gold-inlaid Curt Erickson dagger sends less-experienced knifemakers and embellishers back to their drawing boards. *(PointSeven photo)*

Knife-Size Sculptures

The type of person who chooses steel to be his or her sculpting medium is safely described as rough and tumble, or edgy, determined, tough and tenacious. There are not many things in the world harder than steel. It's not exactly malleable. You can't sand away steel. Well, you can, but it is called filing, and you might as well be softening marble.

Few sculptors of life-size steel ever seem to live in the suburbs, but imagine if they did. You walk out your door to get the newspaper wearing your favorite fuzzy slippers and bathrobe, and the guy next door is cutting sheet metal with a handheld circular saw, or hidden behind a welding mask with sparks flying, swinging a sledgehammer to pound steel, power sanding it and making it shine. While the average suburbanite talks to the neighbor over the fence, hot metal is bent with steel bars and tongs two doors down. A bigger than life steel Teddy Roosevelt, astride horse of course, overlooks the neighborhood in one corner of the guy's yard, and a 30-foot statue of Nero dwarfs the garage at the end of his driveway.

It takes a certain type of person to sculpt, and for steel to be the material of choice makes the artist that much more eclectic. Thank goodness for the varied human race, for diversity. Because otherwise, we wouldn't have such gorgeous sculpted steel displays, and the world would be a few folks short in the rough and tumble area, the tough and tenacious, the determined and edgy.

▶ **WOLFGANG LOERCHNER:** The hand-carved "Wings" folder is all sculpted, smooth and sexy. *(SharpByCoop.com photo)*

◀ **PHILIP BOOTH:** The front-engine slingshot dragster reunites switchblades and hotrods as only a skilled steel sculptor could. *(PointSeven photo)*

▲ **OLEG ALEXANDER:** Casting sterling silver into a bear takes a steady hand, one that also honed the damascus blade and sanded the ebony wood. *(SharpByCoop.com photo)*

▶ **DONALD BELL:** Silver and gold, pierced over brown-lip pearl, grips not only the Chris Marks carved damascus blade, but all who enter into its fray. *(SharpByCoop.com photo)*

▶ **ARPAD BOJTOS:** In antler and steel are Hercules and the "stag," or deer creature of which the muscular man is astride. *(PointSeven photo)*

▼ **MICHAEL WALKER:** A bit more subtle than some of the other steel sculptures, the "Big Wheel Chomper" in stainless damascus, titanium, gold and mokumé is no less impressive. *(PointSeven photo)*

▶ **JULIUS MOJZIS:** "The Bear Hunter" in Ladislav Lasky damascus and African hardwood depicts one up the tree and the other considering the climb.

▶ **MATTHEW LERCH:** Armed with Damasteel, gold, Mike Norris stainless damascus and Paua-shell inlays, Lerch sculpted it all into a shapely dagger. *(SharpByCoop.com photo)*

▲ **J.D. SMITH and JOSEPH SHNAYDER:** Carver Joseph Shnayder fashioned a sterling silver, gold, diamond and ruby panther to reign over damascus and African blackwood. *(SharpByCoop.com photo)*

▶ **JEFFREY CORNWELL:** The Robert Eggerling random-pattern steel snakes its way around. *(SharpByCoop.com photo)*

▶ **STEPHEN OLSZEWSKI:** Hidden-screw construction was a good choice for the stainless girl with bronze hair, as to not blemish the smooth form, and gracefully transition her into a Robert Eggerling damascus blade.

◀ **RICHARD VAN DIJK:** A sculpted licking-flame-like, twist-damascus blade is pointy sharp and held back only by deer antler and coined bronze.

▶ **WADE COLTER:** The man face in 15N20-and-1084 damascus sports opal eyes and ebony hair. *(PointSeven photo)*

▶ **WILLIAM TUCH:** The hand-carved, all-steel lock-back folder is grooved and curved in all the right places. *(PointSeven photo)*

◀ **THOMAS HASLINGER:** The edgy display includes 10.2 ounces of cast and engraved gold, a fully fluted damascus grip, mother-of-pearl inlays and a ladder-pattern damascus blade. *(PointSeven photo)*

► **SHANE TAYLOR:** Carved and sculpted steel branches its way across the handle of the mosaic-damascus folder, one that exudes precious stone inlays and attention to detail. *(PointSeven photo)*

▲ **ROBERT KOVACIK:** The file-worked Damasteel hunter is blessed with a little good buck.

▼ **MARDI MESHEJIAN:** The fluted, or quilt-twisted ebony handle was feeling good about itself until it happened upon the sculpted blade and was brought back down to earth. *(SharpByCoop.com photo)*

◄ **GUSTAVO T. CECCHINI:** Some folks grind blades on the wild side, achieving tactical toughness in an RWL-34 steel package. *(SharpByCoop.com photo)*

▲ **ROGER BERGH:** Integrally sculpted steel forms a C-guard fixed blade with ring pommel and mammoth-ivory inserts.

▶ **PAUL COOPER:** The knife sports a wavy Keris-style blade, carved ferrule and dropped wood grip. *(PointSeven photo)*

▼ **DANIEL STEPHAN:** Hafted spear in O1 steel, ebony and copper, a blade that is carved so cleverly, and titanium that hues the crowd. *(PointSeven photo)*

◀ **GARRI DADYAN:** A sterling example of repousse metal work, the "Silver Serpent" is inlaid with faceted peridot and rubies, and wags a Hank Knickmeyer mosaic-damascus tail. *(BladeGallery.com photo)*

▶ **CHARLES ROULIN:** When the pierced blade is folded into the sculpted handle, there are a few more trees on the savannah where elephants and gazelle take refuge.

▶ **ZAZA REVISHVILI:** Known for more than filigree, Zaza also bends a wicked Doug Ponzio damascus blade and creates grab-worthy guards and precious stone inlays. *(PointSeven photo)*

Carved Wood, Bone, Stag, Pearl and Ivory

What won't knifemakers carve? Well that's what knives are for, aren't they, carving? It's no wonder so many modern knives are chiseled like professional bodybuilders. They used to call it whittling when Grandpa was a youngster. He'd set (not sit) on the front porch wiling away the hours whittling foot soldiers and carousel horses from birch wood. His dad would chew tobacco in time to the crunch of wood beneath the pocketknife blade. And Granny's knitting needles would never stop clackin'. Those were the days.

Today, knifemakers carve the knives and not so much whittle with them. Although some still do. It seems time passes so quickly, especially fast when knife artisans get lost in the folds of the knife handles they carve. Exotic wood, ancient ivory and mother-of-pearl make for nice carving media, as do bone and stag. They all seem to take soothing shapes when whittled … 'er … carved just so. Or is it the skill of the carver?

The combination of the perfect cutting medium and a trained eye results in some of the most dramatic shapes and forms to ever grace knives. Carving is yet one more embellishment that crafty knife crafters have come up with in recent times.

Fleur-de-lis decoration meets up with eagle heads, grizzly bear, gargoyles and grapevines. Knifemakers mimic nature, architecture and sculpture, among other outside influences, when choosing subjects wisely. One only wishes that foot soldiers and carousel horses would make a comeback.

◄ **ANDERS HEDLUND:** John Davis and Mattias Styrefors contributed the "grape wine"-mosaic-damascus bolsters and twist-damascus blade, but it was Anders who checkered the black-lip pearl and secured it with 24k-gold pins.

▲ **ROBERT MERZ:** Ivory made wavy, bolsters made bold and a serpentine damascus blade from the hands of Devin Thomas all help define the 1850s-style folding boot knife. *(Ward photo)*

► **JONATHAN P. WICK:** When you can make mammoth ivory do that, then the damascus tanto blade, and 14k-gold and diamond inlays are not beyond your abilities. *(PointSeven photo)*

◄ **JERRY VAN EIZENGA:** Carved ivory is a suitable mate for the W's-pattern damascus blade of the California bowie denomination. *(PointSeven photo)*

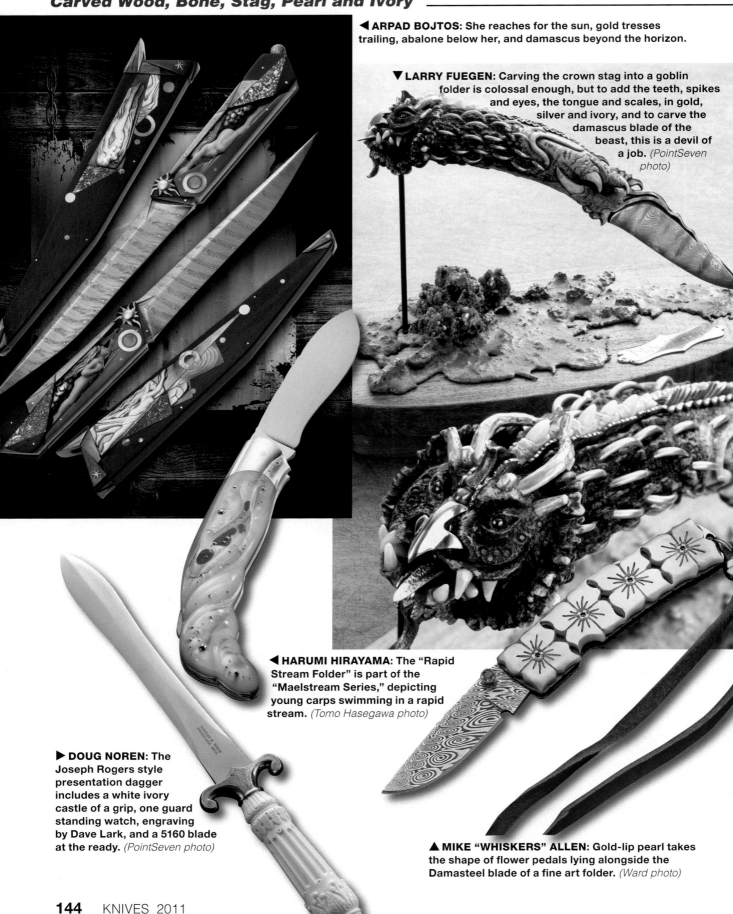

◀ **ARPAD BOJTOS:** She reaches for the sun, gold tresses trailing, abalone below her, and damascus beyond the horizon.

▼ **LARRY FUEGEN:** Carving the crown stag into a goblin folder is colossal enough, but to add the teeth, spikes and eyes, the tongue and scales, in gold, silver and ivory, and to carve the damascus blade of the beast, this is a devil of a job. *(PointSeven photo)*

◀ **HARUMI HIRAYAMA:** The "Rapid Stream Folder" is part of the "Maelstream Series," depicting young carps swimming in a rapid stream. *(Tomo Hasegawa photo)*

▶ **DOUG NOREN:** The Joseph Rogers style presentation dagger includes a white ivory castle of a grip, one guard standing watch, engraving by Dave Lark, and a 5160 blade at the ready. *(PointSeven photo)*

▲ **MIKE "WHISKERS" ALLEN:** Gold-lip pearl takes the shape of flower pedals lying alongside the Damasteel blade of a fine art folder. *(Ward photo)*

◀ **SHIGENO and SIMON LYTTON:** The carved ivory grips crown the finely fit and finished fixed blades, complete with sterling silver sheaths gorgeously engraved by Lytton himself. *(PointSeven photo)*

▶ **LOWELL BRAY:** The warrior is crowned by stag, presented with an eagle feather and protected by the blade. *(PointSeven photo)*

◀ **JOHN W. SMITH:** A seven-point diamond thumb stud will help you rotate the hot-blued damascus blade out of the checkered black-lip-pearl grip so you can admire the 24k-gold embellishments of the **dagger.** *(Buddy Thomason photo)*

▶ **C. GRAY TAYLOR:** Golden flowers take root on the pearl grip, capped by carved gold bolsters, and sprouting eight sharp CPM 154 **blades.** *(PointSeven photo)*

▼ **VLADIMIR PULIS:** The animals of the Brazilian rainforest awake in the Buxus wood and stretch their tired limbs, looking over the mosaic-damascus edge.

▶ **JULIUS MOJZIS:** Weasels wander all around the mammoth-ivory and Amboyna burl handle of a carved Ladislav Lasky damascus blade.

▲ **BILL HERNDON:** The carved ivory grapevines grow among cocobolo and pommel wood, and cover the random-pattern-damascus ladies dagger.

▼ **ROBERT KOVACIK:** Snails suckle berries in the wilds where this hunter gathers.

▲ **DAVID BRUNETTA:** The basket and pommel are carved mild steel with 24k-gold and fine-silver-wire inlays, the hilt of the carved mountain mahogany variety, and the blade forged down to 33 layers of four-bar Turkish twist damascus. It awakens the senses and dazzles the crowd.

DONALD VOGT: "Good" and "Evil" folders, the "Evil" being a latch-release automatic, feature, among other amenities, hand-carved Devin Thomas damascus blades, carved pearl handles, file-worked titanium liners, carved damascus bolsters, carved damascus spines and file-worked 14k-gold bails. Other than that, they're plain janes.

JESSE DAVIS: This bird is made up of carved stag headed in one direction and a Chad Nichols damascus blade pointed the other way. D.R. Good conducted the carving duties. *(Ward photo)*

KAJ EMBRETSEN: The pure white of the carved ivory stands in contrast to the Damascus blade patern, complementing the rope file work of the spine and benefiting from a gold bail and pins. *(PointSeven photo)*

CHARLIE and HARRY MATHEWS: Upon scrolling through the sambar stag, the brother knifemakers fancied up a drop-point hunter of the Chad Nichols damascus kind. *(SharpByCoop.com photo)*

GARY ROOT: The carved rattlesnake head of stag is complemented by engraved rattlers on the underside of a bronze guard and a Raymond Rybar damascus blade. *(SharpByCoop. com photo)*

Wire Me

Maybe the inspiration more than a century ago was a barbed wire strand embedded in a decaying fence post on a ranch in Montana. It could have been a wooden clothespin with wire spring, or a wood bobbin wrapped in wiry thread. Whatever gave knifemakers the idea to inlay gold, silver and nickel silver wire into wood knife handles, or to twist and wrap wire around the burly grips, it was a stroke of genius.

The art of inlaying is more difficult than first meets the eye, mainly because mistakes leave deep grooves in polished grips, but also taking into consideration that maintaining smooth, rounded, non jagged or ragged lines, particularly with scroll inlays, is an art form in and of itself. Similar to scrimshaw, the difference between a skilled artist who practices wire inlay and a novice becomes apparent to the trained eye. A talented scrimshaw artist makes people and animals seem real and alive. Non-professional scrimshanders often leave the faces of man and beast out of proportion, shallow or hollow.

Wire inlay and wrap is either perfectly executed or flawed. There are few in betweens. Talented craftsmen achieved the wire-inlaid and wrapped knife handles on this and the following page. It is an honor to parade the embellished grips before appreciative eyes, those who imagine early attempts at mimicking fence posts embedded with barbed strands, or wooden bobbins with wiry wraps.

▶ **E. JAY HENDRICKSON:** Eleven and three-eighths inches of bowie blade are followed in suit by a silver-wire-inlaid curly maple handle and sheath, the latter, in this case, portraying the "Dead Man's Hand" of aces and eights. *(PointSeven photo)*

▼▲ **LIN RHEA:** Fluted blackwood covered in silver wire spirals into a damascus guard and dagger blade. *(Ward photo)*

◀ **W.F. MORAN:** The late Bill Moran wanted folks to know it was his 50th year of knifemaking, so he told them so on the wood spacer between sectioned crown stag. *(PointSeven photo)*

► **MARK MCCOUN:** Walnut burl gets a wire twist on a file-worked Edwards damascus drop-point hunter.

▼ **BILL HERNDON:** Twisted wire crosses over itself, the ebony handle and the Red Mountain jade beads of a triangular-bladed, left-hand dagger.

▲ **BILL JOHNSON:** A classic dagger with pointed pommel parades a George Wirth damascus blade and a fluted snakewood handle with twisted silver wire accents. *(Cory Martin Imaging)*

◄ **FRED OTT:** The "Cache La Poudre Camp Knife" showcases some of the fanciest wire inlay this Knives editor has ever laid eyes on, all over a tiger-maple grip, and complemented by a ladder-pattern-damascus blade. *(Buddy Thomason photo)*

► **A.G. BARNES:** The Green Beret and dagger, and "De Oppresso Liber," are powerful reminders of those who served and continue to serve selflessly and fight honorably. *(PointSeven photo)*

Scrimmed And Saved

◀ **SHARON BURGER:** The checkered and piqued handle of the Jerry Corbit folding dagger is the beneficiary of color leopard and leopard-eyes scrimshaw on mammoth-ivory inserts.

◀ **FAUSTINA MEAD:** Bear scrimshaw highlights a Ron Best 440C fixed blade all framed out in Jere Davidson engraving. *(PointSeven photo)*

▶ **SHARON BURGER:** What a sheath, with color scrimshaw of Atlas on buffalo horn, in which to slide the Stephen Mackrill dagger, also featuring a buffalo horn grip. *(PointSeven photo)*

▲ **GARY "GARBO" WILLIAMS:** Whether viewing the water-buffalo or elephant side of the Gene Baskett folder, each is equally appealing, as is the Devin Thomas damascus. *(PointSeven photo)*

KATHERINE PLUMER: Antique elephant ivory was the medium of choice for color zebra scrimshaw on a Don Cowles knife that also dons a Delbert Ealy damascus blade. *(SharpByCoop.com photo)*

MARY BAILEY: Sea turtles swim in ivory oceans, all within the confines of Boyd Ashworth "Turtle" folders. *(PointSeven photo)*

SANDRA BRADY: With lions wandering the plains, all is well on the mammoth-ivory grip of a Mike Tamboli damascus folder. Fain damascus bolsters, a ruby-inlaid thumb stud and gold pins help highlight the piece. *(PointSeven photo)*

LINDA KARST STONE: A "Seminole Chief Set" of Leon Treiber lock-back folders features Terry Theis bolster engraving, and color scrimshaw of Chiefs Tuko-See Mathla, Osceola and Billy Bow Legs. *(Ward photo)*

STEFAN ALBERT: An expressive tribal girl graces the grip of a drop-point, re-curved hunter that is also embellished with the king of the jungle in high relief engraving.

TOM HIGH: Scrimshaw of a Native American in Tom's Kiowa tribe highlights the ATS-34 hunter that also showcases a brass guard with engraved elk track, a bison-horn spacer and sheep-horn butt cap.

LINDA KARST STONE: Alaskan scenery gives the Loveless-style Edmund Davidson integral-sub-hilt fighter a tranquil feel. *(PointSeven photo)*

GARY "GARBO" WILLIAMS: True Vikings, like he on the fossil-walrus-ivory handle of a Gene Baskett dagger, do more than protect Brett Favre. *(PointSeven photo)*

RICHARD ZIRBES: Of the gorgeous female nude variety is an ATS-34 integral in mammoth ivory and gold inserts.

LORI RISTINEN: The "I Frame. I Saw. I Conk 'Em." Three Stooges bowie, made by Steve Hill, features scrimshaw on fossil-walrus ivory and a "maidenhair"-damascus blade. *(SharpByCoop.com photo)*

ANDREA PULISOVA: Whimsical Oriental renderings on deer bone make for a fetching Vladimir Pulis damascus fixed blade.

DR. H.P. JENSEN: The buffalo hunt is presented in living color on the elephant ivory handle of a Siegfried Rinkes Damasteel fixed blade.

FAUSTINA MEAD: The tiger scrimshaw roars volumes on a Larry Lunn folder that includes Robert Eggerling San Mai damascus, a mammoth-ivory grip, a ruby-inlaid thumb stud and 18k-gold screws. *(SharpByCoop.com photo)*

GARY "GARBO" WILLIAMS: The Kit Carson dress tactical folder was professionally pirated. *(SharpByCoop.com photo)*

MIRELLA PACHI: The cat prowls in tall grasses, forever immortalized in the mammoth-ivory grip of a Sergio Ramondetti mosaic-damascus folder. *(Francesco Pachi photo)*

RONI DIETRICH: Chief Sitting Bull is the scrimmed subject of a Howard Hitchmough walrus-ivory-handle bowie in Devin Thomas stainless damascus.

Filed For Effect

▶ **YASUTAKA WADA:** The combination of a grooved and sculpted snakewood and whale-tooth handle, and the filed stainless steel blade, makes for a dramatic effect.

▶ **LARRY FUEGEN:** The carved sterling silver handle wrap, like plant buds parting leaves along every inch of the grip, is complemented by a carved walrus ivory handle, a carved-damascus guard and a ladder-pattern damascus blade. *(PointSeven photo)*

▼ **IAN VAN REENAN:** Roman knot file work is one more gentlemanly element on a hand-polished ATS-34 gentleman's slip joint with a mother-of-pearl handle.

◀ **RICK DUNKERLEY:** Call it coined, sculpted, file-worked or shaped, the handle frame surrounding blued damascus is blown out, that's for sure. *(PointSeven photo)*

◀ **ROBERT ROSSDEUTSCHER:** The file-worked hunting knife in 1095 high-carbon steel and a snakewood handle takes a whimsical form that would make a seasoned blade smith smile.

▶ **DAN PIERGALLINI:** The maker says his shapely fixed blade featuring a Jerry Rados damascus blade, an ivory handle and nickel-silver fittings is "filed a bunch."

► **STEVE SCHWARZER:** What seems like multiple strands of rope-like file work along the back spacer continues down the damascus blade spine on toward the tip. *(PointSeven photo)*

► **LARRY HOSTETLER:** As if the re-curved Alabama Damascus blade wasn't fierce enough, the maker extensively file-worked the spine, and gave the knife a damascus finger guard, a red spacer, stag-horn handle and damascus butt plate. *(PointSeven photo)*

◄ **GEORGE TROUT:** An integral 440C fixed blade sports a snakewood grip, and file work to boot. *(PointSeven photo)*

► **COLTEN TIPPETS:** Filed like a file is the blade of a Sambar-stag-handle beauty in a brass guard engraved by Bruce Shaw, and a mammoth-ivory spacer. *(PointSeven photo)*

▼ **RON NEWTON:** The tire-tread-like filing of the damascus handle, complete with black-lip-pearl inlays, hugs the hand, while the lengthy damascus blade bites into its cutting medium. *(Ward photo)*

◄ **AAD VAN RYSWYK:** File work along the mosaic-damascus blade and back spacer lends one more art element to a gorgeous wood-handle locking-liner folder.

Mosaic Masters

A couple of scenes come to mind. The first is a bird's-eye view of a family gathered around a kitchen table on a rainy day. They're not eating, but hunched over, heads nearly touching from opposite sides of the table. So engrossed in their project, they're blissfully unaware of any watchers over. The 2,000-piece puzzle is coming together, through no small effort of their own, as they scan tiny parts of pictures, studying their shapes, projecting perfect fits between several pieces.

The second scene is of a man wearing kneepads, crouched awkwardly in a small bathroom, planting tile after tile in perfect squares, using plastic spacers to ensure equal spacing and grouting in between them. It is tedious, time-consuming work, but the result is a sparkling mosaic, and a tread-worthy tiled toilet. But don't let the landscaped loo fool you, mosaic Grecian foyers and alfresco patios precede it.

The art of mosaic making is not founded in knifemaking or blade forging, but no finer artisans ever took up the craft. And it could be argued that forging steel into picturesque knife blades is an equal undertaking to tiling mausoleums and mosques, and certainly greater than piecing puzzles together. One thing is for certain, after blade smiths complete mosaic-damascus masterpieces they never look at tiled lavatory floors the same way again.

▶ **ANDERS HOGSTROM:** The spine-tingling "Backbone Bowie" is pieced together with a Johan Gustafsson mosaic-damascus blade, sterling silver guard and walrus-ivory handle. *(SharpByCoop.com photo)*

◀ **DON HANSON:** Like displaying a Warhol and Picasso side-by-side, Hanson's own mosaic damascus is matched with mammoth ivory. *(Ward photo)*

▶ **COLLABORTIVE KNIFE:** Dave Lisch did the mosaic damascus honors, while Jon Christensen forged and ground the blade, Tom Ferry engraved the guard and pommel, and Michael Rader fashioned the redwood and maple handle. *(Mitch Lum photo)*

▲ **DAVID STEIER:** White lines between the squares of Robert Eggerling mosaic damascus are the express lanes to mother-of-pearl and ruby inlays. *(SharpByCoop.com photo)*

► **REINHARD TSCHAGER:** Damascus patterning repeats itself but never becomes redundant, while carved gold and amber stag complement the steel. *(Francesco Pachi photo)*

◄ **STEVE MYERS:** Webbed and blued Doug Ponzio bolsters spider their way into a damascus folding dagger blade and ironwood grip. *(PointSeven photo)*

▲ **GARY HOUSE:** Employing O1, 15N20 and 4600E steels, Gary creates his "Bathroom Man" mosaic damascus, showing us what the steel looks like before the blades and bolsters are built. *(PointSeven photo)*

◄ **JON CHRISTENSEN:** The downy damascus blade and bolsters lie feathery light against a mammoth-ivory grip. *(Mitch Lum photo)*

► **MIKE ZIMA:** Squares of high-contrast stainless damascus are the building blocks of the "Sonora" button-lock auto that also features a mother-of-pearl grip and button.

RALPH TURNBULL: Turnbull allows Chris Marks to take a turn at forging the mosaic-damascus bolsters for a pair of fancy autos, these with stag and abalone handle scales.

STEVEN KELLY: Equipped with Chad Nichols mosaic damascus, Kelly set about fashioning a blued locking-liner folder, complete with titanium frame and ruby-inlaid thumb stud. *(SharpByCoop.com photo)*

RAY RYBAR: Cowboy boots, buffalo and pistols litter the steel of the "Last Man Standing Ranch" knife, the one with the crown stag grip, engraving, file work and Western flair. *(PointSeven photo)*

ROBERT FLYNT: Struck from mosaic-damascus steel are a blued blade and bolsters that cut right through the fat and to the meat of the matter.

▶ ANDERS HEDLUND: Ribbons of mosaic damascus wend their way along the blade and bolsters of the "Nordic Dragon," into the reindeer horn handle engraved by Jonny Walker Nilsson. *(PointSeven photo)*

◀ HANK KNICKMEYER: Hank captured the "Martyrdom of St. Joan" and "Whores Burning in Hell" within the confines of a San Mai mosaic-damascus blade. *(PointSeven photo)*

◀ BILL BUXTON: Call it a star fighter if you will, but the blackwood and mosaic-damascus piece is too pretty to pair off against just any enemy. *(Ward photo)*

◀ JOHN DAVIS: Mosaic and mammoth make for fine locking-liner bedfellows. *(BladeGallery.com photo)*

▶ FRANK NIRO: The heat-colored Rob Calcinore multi-bar mosaic damascus is as hard to make as it sounds, but orchestrated beautifully on an art folder with blue-wooly-mammoth-ivory handle scales, heat-colored Seymchan meteorite bolsters, and a ruby-inlaid thumb stud and back spacer. *(Custom Knife Gallery of Colorado photo)*

◀ **SHANE TAYLOR:** Swooping along the re-curved blade and crown-stag handle are bats that only a vampire could love. *(PointSeven photo)*

◀ **CLIFF PARKER:** The bark of the walrus, or the walrus-ivory handle for that matter, is not as bad as the bite of the picturesque blade. *(PointSeven photo)*

◀ **J.W. RANDALL:** A vest bowie benefits from a radial-pattern mosaic damascus blade, a damascus ferrule and butt cap, heat-colored stainless steel guard, spacers and finial, and a natural grip.

▶ **R.J. MARTIN:** The "One-Hand Shuffle" mosaic damascus was forged by Cliff Parker, using both hands, and married to the walrus-ivory handle and titanium bolsters of the "Overkill" flipper folder. *(SharpByCoop.com photo)*

▲ **BILL COFFEY:** The knifemaker reveals the color of cut through mosaic damascus and black-lip pearl. *(Buddy Thomason photo)*

▶ **JOSH SMITH:** Josh forged the mosaic damascus, and carved it into flames that lick antique tortoise shell. *(PointSeven photo)*

▲ **JOE OLSON:** There are no handle screws on the folder to interrupt the fantastic enameled Oriental scene, and few knife blades as fun as the "guitar" damascus piece. *(SharpByCoop.com photo)*

▲ **PHILIP BOOTH:** If the Bob Eggerling mosaic-damascus blade doesn't start your engines, perhaps the carved ivory interior, aluminum wheels, gear shifter, steering wheel, three deuces or spark-plug thumb opener will fire your cylinders. *(PointSeven photo)*

◀▼ **AAD VAN RYSWYK:** Tiles of mosaic damascus are tempered by the antique tortoise shell grip, gold bail and file work.

◀ **PETER MARTIN:** What would a tactical folder be without skulls and fire emblazoned across a Doug Ponzio damascus blade and bolsters, titanium liners and carbon-fiber handle scales? *(Cory Martin Imaging)*

Damascus That Dazzles

▶ **HARVEY DEAN:** The feather damascus tickles the edge, flying in formation with an ancient ivory grip, and Steve Dunn gold-inlaid and engraved bolsters. *(PointSeven photo)*

▼ **RODRIGO SFREDDO:** The damascus pattern and wood grain work well together. *(SharpByCoop.com photo)*

▼ **R.B. JOHNSON:** The dot matrix of Devin Thomas damascus synchronizes well with the stingray-skin handle scales, the pattern broken only by Joel Davis mosaic-damascus bolsters.

◀ **FRED OTT:** Multiple bars of damascus follow the curve of a hunter dressed in an ironwood, spalted maple and sea-cow-bone handle. *(BladeGallery.com photo)*

▶ **DAVE LISCH:** A ribbon of white stretches across the feather-pattern damascus blade of the "Artifact Fighter," named for it's artifact-ivory grip. *(BladeGallery.com photo)*

RON NEWTON: The "West Texas Wind" damascus blows across the blade, a sheriff's star is planted in the ferrule, and the state of Texas graces the butt of the bowie. *(Ward photo)*

J.W. RANDALL: Damascus delivers punch to a stag-handle hunter.

KEVIN CASEY: Few folks know that the quill of a feather turns into the rachis, or vein, but Kevin shows you just where that is, bringing it in line with a meteorite bolsters and mammoth ivory grip. *(SharpByCoop.com photo)*

CLIFF PARKER: The fossil walrus ivory grip generated enough static electricity for the bolsters and blade. *(PointSeven photo)*

ANDERS HOGSTROM: Something dramatic like a Kaj Embretsen damascus dagger blade was needed to compete with the smoky amber handle.

▶ **RUSS ANDREWS:** Ladder-pattern damascus really does climb up the blade and onto the stabilized-Amboyna-burl handle. *(Buddy Thomason photo)*

◀ **JERRY FISK:** A clamshell guard, engraving, gold inlay and 10 inches of powerfully patterned damascus embellish an ivory-handle bowie. *(Ward photo)*

▲ **JAMES HARRISON:** The Mike Norris stainless damascus blade and frame get the point across.

▶ **KEVIN LESSWING:** Eighteen hundred layers of ladder-pattern damascus are anchored by giraffe bone and mastodon ivory. *(PointSeven photo)*

▲ **JOHN WHITE:** The stag-handled "Cowboy Bowie" blade is as spirited as a young stallion. *(Ward photo)*

▶ **DON MAXWELL:** The gent's folder looks smart in heat-colored Chris Marks damascus and gold-lip mother-of-pearl.

▼ **JEFF HARKINS:** Engraved art deco motifs from the Chrysler building transition into the Mountain Forge damascus dagger blade.

◀ **ALLEN ELISHEWITZ:** The "Kopis" flipper folder sports a Mike Norris damascus blade that does flips all along the edge and toward the ivory handle scales and skull-crusher pommel.

◀ **J. NEILSON:** With a damascus blade forged from 52100 canister steel, and a stabilized cherry handle, the looking is as fun as the cutting.

▶ **RALPH TURNBULL:** Heavenly heat coloring hues a dramatic Chris Marks damascus blade and bolsters, color coordinating with a red-jigged-bone grip and ruby-inlaid thumb stud

▶ **RAYMOND L. SMITH:** Harley-Davidson motorcycle timing chain makes for choice damascus blade stock.

◀ **TODD KOPP:** The Brad Vice ladder-pattern-damascus blade flows into the double-pointed guard, file-worked spacers and ebony handle. *(Custom Knife Gallery Of Colorado photo)*

▼ **MICHAEL MCCLURE:** The rings of the wooly mammoth molar are emulated by the pattern of the damascus bowie blade. *(BladeGallery.com photo)*

▶ **EMIL BUCHARSKY:** Amonite inlays break up the otherwise all-damascus and stainless steel, sculpted one-hand folder. *(BladeGallery.com photo)*

◀ **RICK DUNKERLEY:** The blades and bolsters of the knives are matching niter-blued "Santa Ana Wind" damascus, and the handles, from top to bottom, fossil mammoth ivory, tortoise shell and black-lip mother-of-pearl. *(BladeGallery.com photo)*

MARVIN SOLOMON: Maple and damascus are the sticky and sweet of a 15-inch bowie. *(Ward photo)*

DAN CHINNOCK: The choice of "snakeskin" damascus was spot on for a locking-liner folder with mammoth-ivory grip. *(Ward photo)*

KYLE ROYER: The fine "Feathered Fighter" in damascus and desert ironwood flies like a butterfly and stings like a bee. *(Ward photo)*

MARK NEVLING: "Kaleidoscope" damascus is a clearly focused pattern, and maple burl grains are equally easy on the eyes.

JIM SAVIANO: Three hundred and fifteen layers of damascus pinstripe the blade, while the redwood handle accessorizes the piece nicely.

◄ MIKE FELLOWS: The "ripple-twist"-damascus bolsters and seven-bar composite-damascus blade capture the character of the elephant bark ivory.

► LARRY PRIDGEN: It's not so obvious where the box elder burl ends and the Alabama Damascus begins. *(PointSeven photo)*

◄ BERTIE RIETVELD: A swath of color cuts across the "dragonskin"-damascus blade, tapering into a textured comet tail that starts with the Stanhope lens and ends at a gold starburst hovering over a milky mammoth-ivory grip.

▲ CORRIE SCHOEMAN: Whether the Ettoré Gianferrari damascus pattern reveals faces, cells, internal organs or just an illusion is up to the lucky owner of the mammoth-ivory handle "Illusion" folder.

▲ REINHARD TSCHAGER: The pattern of the Johannes Ebner damascus blade is like a thousand connected rainbows ending at a pot of engraved gold.

▼ JOHN WHITE: The waves of the sea and the grains of the sand-colored elephant-ivory handle are captured on the damascus "Shell Guard Bowie." *(Ward photo)*

◄ BILL BAGWELL: An emerald eye looks over the blackwood body of a damascus "Vidalia Maiden" bowie. *(PointSeven photo)*

► GARY MULKEY: Damascus reverberates continuously from the blade into a steel guard and fossil-walrus-ivory grip. *(Ward photo)*

► RICHARD S. WRIGHT: A bowie and ambidextrous bolster-release switchblade are dressed in Jerry Rados "Turkish-twist" damascus, carved sterling silver, gold and Sambar stag.

◄ SERGIO RAMONDETTI: Pools of damascus form on the blades and bolsters of a pair of fossil-walrus-ivory-handle folding knives, one a "Roteor" spin-opening model, and the second a locking-liner folder. *(Francesco Pachi photo)*

Sheath Magic

JOT SINGH KHALSA: The maker of the Devin Thomas stainless damascus Kirpan wanted to keep it safe in a Pietersite *(South African mineral)* sheath that matches its grip. *(SharpByCoop.com photo)*

LARRY PARSONS: Larry fashioned a carved, inlaid, overlaid and tooled leather sheath for the Brion Tomberlin fixed blade. *(PointSeven photo)*

BOB SCHRAP: A cowhide scabbard-style sheath comes with a framed alligator panel that makes an attractive background for a silver Concho.

JAMES RODEBAUGH: The "Deadwood Bowie" sports a 7.75-inch damascus blade, an ivory handle, and an inlaid leather sheath featuring a Silver Eagle dollar coin overlay. *(PointSeven photo)*

DAVID BRUNETTA: What chef wouldn't love to keep this ATS-34 knife in the kitchen, complete with a Bubinga-wood sheath and carved motif featuring an ebony-eyed frog on a flower?

KAREN SHOOK: Daniel Winkler crafted the hunter in a "firestorm"-damascus blade, buffalo-horn handle, forged finger pad and curl, while Karen fashioned a rawhide-covered sheath for the piece, with woven-porcupine-quill medicine wheel, and hand-cut fringe and thongs decorated with glass beads, tin cones and horsehair.

ED BRANDSEY: The bowie of Alabama Damascus, stag, pipestone and ironwood makes its home in a fringed buckskin sheath embellished with an eagle feather burned into its front side and a cut-out Silver Eagle dollar. (Ward photo)

RON NEWTON: Some lucky fixed blade inherits a hand-stitched and inlaid leather sheath with frog button. (Ward photo)

RANDY GOLDEN: The cowhide sheath with tooling showcases an ostrich-skin inlay and medallion. (Bill Ingalls photo)

CRAIG BRASCHLER & MARTIN: The engraved throat and tip of the leather-wrapped sheath complement the guard engraving of the Chad Nichols damascus bowie with ironwood grip. (Ward photo)

FACTORY TRENDS

The knife industry has overcome some high hurdles and obstacles over the past year, including an encroachment on Americans' knife rights by U.S. Customs. Inexplicably, in 2009, Customs began seizing shipments of one-hand, spring-assisted folding knives being sent from overseas manufacturing plants to American knife companies, and classifying the knives as switchblades. The knife industry turned to the American Knife & Tool Institute and to KnifeRights.org to help lobby Congressional leaders to add language to the antiquated Federal Switchblade Law that would differentiate between push-button switchblades and spring-assisted, one-hand-opening knives. The knife industry claimed a major victory when the new language went into law in late 2009. Such knives as the flipper folders in "High Flipper Fashion" on page 182 were saved from being banned, as were many folders that can be opened with one hand.

Soon after the victory, in late 2009 and early 2011, New Hampshire State Rep. Jenn Coffey submitted a Knife Rights Bill that passed the full New Hampshire House of Representatives (400 Legislators). The Bill is a straight repeal of New Hampshire's antiquated "switchblade, dirk, dagger and stiletto" law. Coffey is also an EMT who could use automatic folders that open with one hand to help cut accident victims from seatbelts and generally save lives. But she cannot legally carry such knives. The bill was set to go to the Senate as of the printing of *Knives 2011.* No wallflower is Coffey, but even she'd take a liking to the "Blades The Ladies Love" knives on page 180, as well as the "Fixed, Tactical & Tough" knives on page 178.

Some industries excel under the heat of pressure, and the knife industry is one of them, pulling together with innovative designs, such as the "Making Tracks Knives" and those of "Discreet Collaborations" on pages 177 and 184, respectively. The Factory Trends are fresh and new, and the American knife industry is alive and well. Enjoy.

Blue Collar Blades

Not only is there a place for hard-working knives in the industry, it remains a place of honor

Text and photos by Dexter Ewing

Men and women working in the blue collar trades know a thing or two about owning quality edged tools, and the valuable service they provide. Plumbers, mechanics, farmers, electricians, construction workers and landscapers, skilled craftsmen and hard workers alike, rely on edges that cut. The value of a good knife is the same for them as for collectors of fine art knives.

Fortunately for the tradesmen—the ladies and gentlemen who remain the backbone of America—quality, hard working and affordable knives are available. Such knives in today's world tend to combine style, utility, and affordable cost all rolled into one package, equating to

a life of long, enjoyable service. Featured herein are some of the finest examples of "blue color blades" currently available on the marketplace.

Benchmade's Griptilian series has been a steady seller for the company since its introduction in the early 2000s. The Griptilian combines the company's high-grade materials with the exclusive and patented Axis Lock™ blade lock. Including Noryl™ GTX polymer handle scales, the Griptilian is lightweight but tough at the same time.

In 2009, the company unveiled yet another version of the Griptilian, the model 551H2O. Based off of the large Griptilian model 551, the main difference is blade steel. Benchmade employs

X15-T.N stainless steel, which boasts higher corrosion resistance than the 154CM stainless of previous Griptilian patterns.

Martin Mills, manufacturing engineer for Benchmade Knife Co., says, "It has the capability to resist rust in harsh environments and maintain a sharp edge." How exactly does it work? "What the X15 T.N steel offers are lower levels of carbon replaced with nitrogen," begins Mills. "This ends up providing more corrosion resistance with the same high level of hardness."

He goes on to explain that X15-T.N is more corrosion resistant than 440C stainless steel, yet reaches 58 Rc on the Rockwell Hardness scale. "When it comes to blade steel, more carbon gives you higher hardness. Yet, this decreases the corrosion resistance in the steel," Mills details. By adding nitrogen in place of carbon, the steel retains hardness with increased stainless steel qualities.

The 551H2O also sports an orange Noryl GTX molded handle, making it easy to spot when accidentally dropped on the ground or laid down in an area where lighting is minimal. A checkered handle provides a nice grip, and the combination of a rust-resistant X15-T.N blade, orange handle and a pocket clip that can be switched from one side of the handle to the other makes the 551H2O Griptilian a

The newest member of the Benchmade Griptilian family—the 551H20—sports an X-15 T.N stainless steel blade and an orange, molded-Noryl GTX handle.

great choice for hard, ambidextrous use.

The Axis lock makes it truly a safe, ambidextrous knife, holding the blade bank-vault tight in the open position. Closing the folder involves pulling back on one of the lock release buttons, and gliding the blade smoothly and effortlessly into the handle. The Benchmade 551H2O Griptilian is available now from retailers with a 3.4-inch blade in either a plain or partially serrated edge. The manufacturer's suggested retail price (MSRP) is $120.

Razzle-Dazzle Razel

Columbia River Knife & Tool (CRKT) has a rather unique offering to tradesmen in a multi-function knife known as the Razel. Designed by custom knifemakers Jon and Josh Graham, the Razel is part knife, part chisel and part scraper. The blades are squared off and beveled, much like sharpened chisels, with razor-sharp cutting edges.

The black-and-gray Micarta® handles of the fixed-blade and folding Razels combine a nice comfortable grip with good looks. The series is available in two sizes of folders and three sizes of fixed blades. Regardless of varying knife tastes, there is a CRKT Razel for everyone.

Though the appearance of the Razel is a bit disarming for knife enthusiasts at first blush, compared to their edged counterparts the knives exude high utility value. The Stubby Pocket Razel is the smallest fixed blade version of the bunch, measuring 4 inches overall.

"I've carried the Stubby Razel [model 2011] in my front pocket just like I've carried a folding

Columbia River Knife & Tool teamed with Jon and Josh Graham to bring out the unique Razel series of folders and fixed blades. The Ringed Razel has a finger ring in the end of the handle where the user can insert his or her pinky finger for added grip security.

knife," says Doug Flagg, vice president of sales and marketing for CRKT. "The Kydex® sheath fits nicely in the front pocket and the clip keeps the sheath in place so that when you need the knife, you just pull it out of the sheath and it's ready to go."

With a blade of 9Cr18MoV—the China-made equivalent of 440C stainless—the Stubby Pocket Razel offers toughness needed to withstand heavy use whether cutting or scraping with the squared-off tip. "The chisel end of the Razel saved me a trip to the tool box when I needed something to scrape gaskets with," Flagg says. "As a weekend garage mechanic, the Razel has been invaluable."

The Ringed Razel is the middle size of the three fixed blades, with an overall length of 5 inches. Also fashioned from 9Cr18MoV stainless, it features a large finger ring incorporated into the handle. "This knife will not fall out of your hands even when you are doing chores in cold, wet weather," Flagg offers. The user can pass their pinky through

the finger ring when gripping the knife, so if the knife slips, it swings down from the little finger. Additionally, "The Micarta handle offers hand purchase in all conditions," Flagg points out.

The Folding Razel has the same advantages of a knife, chisel and scraper that the fixed blades offer except in a much more pocket-friendly version. Like any modern, single-blade folder, the Folding Razel sports a sturdy pocket clip and ambidextrous thumb studs, allowing it to be carried in the pocket for ultimate portability and ease of opening.

The handle of the Folding Razel is contoured for a comfortable grip, and the Stubby Folding Razel showcases a ram-horn handle. As interesting as its name suggests, the Stubby Folding Razel dons a 2-inch blade handy enough to tackle most cutting chores expected of a pocketknife. "The Stubby Folding Razel has become an essential tool that I carry every day," Flagg confirms. "The sturdy frame lock gives me confidence this knife will hold up to any chore."

Brawny Blade

Anchoring the large end of the Razel family is the big and brawny Razel SS7, a camp-knife-sized behemoth that is literally sharp all the way around. It showcases a plain-edge main blade, edged blade tip, and a run of serrations along the blade spine that make quick work of rope and cardboard.

Leatherman's Super Tool 300 features replaceable wire cutter inserts, a beefy lock mechanism for the fold out tools, and easily accessible plain and serrated blades.

A 7 ¼-inch blade helps make the SS7 an ideal multi-function cutting and chopping tool for any camping trip. The knife also sports a Kydex sheath with a quick-release belt fastener. For more information on the Razel series, visit http://www.crkt.com/.

Leatherman is a recognized name in knives specifically built for the blue-collar workforce. The originator of the genre, Leatherman multi-tools can be found on the belts of tradesmen in all specialty fields. The company's multi-tools are handy, and usually feature full-size pliers, wire cutters, screwdrivers, files, saws, reams, bottle and can openers, and punches. It's like toting a toolbox in the pocket.

In 2009, Leatherman unveiled its newest heavy-duty multi-tool in the form of the Super Tool 300, the third generation of the Super Tool. "The new Super Tool 300 has more than 10 years of compiled customer feedback and engineering expertise in every feature," says Juli Warner, corporate communications specialist for Leatherman Tool Group. "Each one is designed to address the user who demands strength, quick access to tools, and comfort for tough jobs," she stresses.

An improved feature of the Super Tool 300 is the removable and re-sharpen-able wire cutter inserts. Warner points out they are made of premium 154CM steel, the same steel found in high-end production and custom knives, and selected due to its wear resistance in hard-use applications.

"By optimizing the heat treatment process and replacing the standard stainless steel with premium 154CM, the wire cutters hold an edge three times as long for maximum durability," Warner

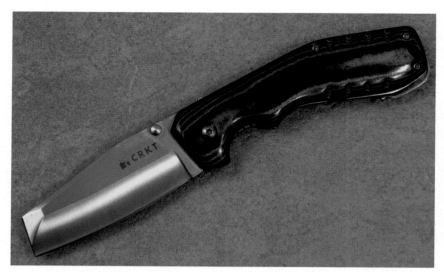

The Folding Razel offers all of the handy advantages of the fixed-blade Razel but in a more pocket-friendly folder format.

points out. Other innovations include what she calls "edge safety clumping" of the foldout tools. "Clumping" was first introduced on the original Super Tool. Grab one of the tools and all of them come out for easy tool selection.

In regards to the ST300, Warner explains what she means by "edge safety clumping." "If you pull on either of the two knife blades, it will be the only implement that comes out of the handle," she begins. "Conversely if you pull on any of the other tools, the sharp-edged ones stay put." Other notable enhancements on the ST300 are the hollow-ground, plain-edge blade, screwdrivers in the most popular sizes used by tradesmen, and handles with contoured edges for grip comfort. Cutouts in the sides of the handles allow easy access of the tool's knife blades, even with gloved hands. The Super Tool 300 is available now from favorite retailers, and each tool is backed by Leatherman's 25-year warranty. Learn more about the Super Tool 300 at http://www.leatherman.com.

Employable Folder

The "Needs Work" by Kershaw Knives needs very little work, but an introduction is in order. A funny name for a knife, the Needs Work folder is purpose-built as a working folder, and includes a straight, plain-edge, modified-wharncliffe blade, and a comfortable, ergonomic handle.

Thomas Welk, director of sales and marketing for Kershaw, says, "The Needs Work is really a nice total package, as it has performance, a contemporary presence, is value priced, and is put together right here in the USA."

The 3-inch blade is hollow ground for a razor sharp cutting edge. Sandvik 14C28N stainless steel gives a great performance for the price point. Welk notes, "We like the steel for this specific project, as it works well with both thin and thick edge geometry. The Rockwell hardness of our 14C28N runs 58-60, which will bring balance with edge retention and sharpening."

In addition, Welk points out that the straight-line edge makes sharpening easier, and it is a bit easier to keep sharp than other blade shapes, especially for the novice knife user. Polyamide thermoplastic handle scales were chosen for cost and comfort, while the edges of the scales are rounded for a comfortable grip.

"The Polyamide scales were patterned in a way to create a modern appeal, and it kept the pricing to a minimum," Welk says. This is durable material, and according to Welk, it shows little wear over time. Thus a great choice for a hard working knife! One also notices that when the Needs Work is opened, there is an angled appearance to the knife.

"The offset handle aids in leverage when cutting, and gives your fingers clearance when finishing certain tasks," says Welk. In addition to all these features, the Needs Work also sports the Speed Safe™ assisted opener to promote quick and easy blade opening with one hand. The assisted opener deploys the blade only after its movement has been initiated by applying moderate pressure to the exposed flipper on the blade tang. With a suggested retail price of just $54.95, the Kershaw model 1820 Needs Work folder makes for an affordable, great work knife available to folks who use a blade on a daily basis.

There are many value-priced knives available to those employed in one of the specialty trades. Knives with suggested retail prices of $100 or less fit into such a category, and most major manufacturers today offer knives that fit the budget for the blue-collar worker. The toughest part is deciding which one to ultimately purchase.

Making Tracks Knives

◄ Designed by Randall King, the Meyerco Tsavo Neck Knife offers lion's paw prints in the handle in tandem with a 3 1/8-inch blade based on the shape of a lion's claw.

► Outdoor Edge tries a different track tack with the Dark Timber Combo. It has the tracks, a deer in this case, on the ricasso instead of the handle.

▲ The Buck Knives Stockman Elk Hoof three-blade folder boasts an elk-antler handle with elk hooves laser etched into it.

▲ Spyderco's Ocelot features a G-10 handle machined with the paw prints of an Ocelot.

▲ Man's best friend is the subject of a series of Chris Reeve Sebenza Doggy Knives available from Plaza Cutlery. The titanium handles are etched and anodized with paw prints.

Fixed, Tactical And Tough

◄ SOG Specialty Knives offers the FX-10 Fixation Dagger in a 8Cr13MoV stainless steel double-edge, semi-serrated, spear-point blade and a wrap-around, checkered Kraton grip.

► Curtis Lovito and Mark Carey collaborated on the design of the Spartan Blades Ares with a blade tip in line with the hand for balance, even though it retains an upward cutting edge.

◄ The black texture-powder-coated 1095 blade of the RAT Cutlery RC-6 is complemented by gray, removable linen-Micarta® handle scales.

◄ Benchmade's 147BK NIM Cub II features a matte-black154CM stainless steel blade with an integral finger guard and EDM texture-finished Noryl™ GTX handle slabs.

◄ Ethan Becker designed the Ka-Bar BK-7 Combat Utility Knife to have a clip-point 1095 high-carbon blade and a black Grivory™ reinforced-nylon handle.

▲ Bill Harsey is credited with designing the Chris Reeve Knives Pacific in a semi-serrated, clip-point CPM S30V stainless steel blade and a grooved, sandblasted canvas Micarta grip.

▼ The Allen Elishewitz-designed Columbia River Knife & Tool F.T.W.S. (For Those Who Served) is a modified spear point with a chisel-ground chopping edge along the blade spine.

◄ Part of the Boker Plus line, the William C. "Bill" Johnson-designed 02B0161 440C re-curved, satin-finished bowie comes in a handsome black-and-green linen-Micarta handle.

▲ The only serrated sheepsfoot rescue knife in the genre, Spyderco offers the Jumpmaster with a hollow-ground H-1 blade and a bi-directionally textured fiberglass-reinforced nylon handle.

Blades The Ladies Love

◄ Part of the sales proceeds of the Victorinox Classic Swiss Army Knife in translucent pink goes toward breast cancer research.

► The Spyderco Laydbug in an H-1 blade sports the only purple handle of the bunch.

◄ Juli Warner of Leatherman says the SquirtS4 is a great way to introduce women to the practicality of multi-tools.

High Flipper Fashion

▶ The dual guard of the Boker Applegate folding dagger doubles as a flipper to open the 3 7/8-inch bead-blasted blade of CPM S60V stainless steel.

◀ SureFire's Edge flipper folder sports a 3.88-inch 154CM blade in a modified spear point, a hard-anodized 7075 aluminum handle, and hexagonal holes in the blade and grip that work as a wrench for 7/16-, 3/8-, 5/16- and 1/2-inch nuts.

▲ Flipper folders come in all shapes and forms, as evidenced by the Columbia River Knife & Tool Tuition (top), Kershaw Hawk R.A.M. (middle) and SOG Twitch XL.

Top Tool Knives

◀ **Wenger's Alinghi Yachtsman SUI1 Swiss Army Knife** includes a marlinspike, ruler, cap lifter, screwdrivers, partially serrated blade, needle nose pliers with wire cutter and other tools one might need on the yacht.

◀ **The SOG PowerLock** multi-tool incorporates a pliers/gripper, hard wire cutter, crimper, double-toothed wood saw, partially serrated blade, scissors, a three-sided file and more.

▶ **Leatherman reintroduces the Super Tool 300** with upgraded features, including bigger, beefier needle-nose and regular pliers incorporating 154CM removable wire cutters, hollow-ground 420HC clip and sheepsfoot blades, electrical crimper, screwdrivers, a wood and metal file, saw and other implements.

▶ **The Victorinox Cyber Tool 34** has large and small blades, a corkscrew, can opener with small screwdriver, wire stripper, a bit wrench, 5-millimeter hex socket and more.

KNIVES MARKETPLACE

INTERESTING PRODUCT NEWS FOR BOTH THE CUTLER AND THE KNIFE ENTHUSIAST

The companies and individuals represented on the following pages will be happy to provide additional information — feel free to contact them.

TRUE NORTH KNIVES

TNK®

PURVEYOR NEIL H. OSTROFF

WWW.TRUENORTHKNIVES.COM

info@TrueNorthKnives.com
Tel: 514.748.9985   Toll Free: 866.748.9985   Fax: 514.748.6312
P.O. Box 176, Westmount Station, Montreal, Quebec, Canada H3Z 2T2

A.G. Russell KNIVES

SUMMER SPECIAL 2010
A. G. Russell Field Knife 2 - Bull Strong and Boar Tough (page 37)

Don't Forget!
A.G. Russell's Knife Event
Friday, July 30 - Sunday, August 1
John Q. Hammons Convention Center
Rogers, Arkansas

knifeevent.com for more info
and to pre-purchase tickets,
or call us at 800-255-9034

For your free catalog
call 479.571.6161 Dept #KA11

©Copyright 2011, A.G. Russell Knives, Inc.

A.G. Russell KNIVES
Shop Online at **agrussell.com**

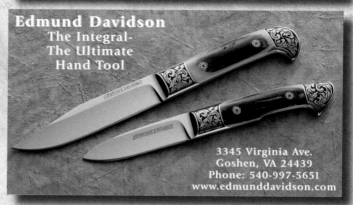

Edmund Davidson
The Integral-
The Ultimate
Hand Tool

3345 Virginia Ave.
Goshen, VA 24439
Phone: 540-997-5651
www.edmunddavidson.com

TIM ADLAM Engraving

1705 WITZEL AVE.
OSHKOSH, WI 54902
(920) 235-4589

WWW.ADLAMENGRAVING.COM

Beckwith's Blades

The right knife... at the right price... for the work you do!!!

 **AL MAR KNIVES**

 Adventure Medical Kits

 BENCHMADE KNIFE COMPANY

 DMT

 **COLUMBIA RIVER KNIFE & TOOL**

 ASP

 **EMERSON** KNIVES INC.

 HANWEI

 **KA-BAR** Knives, Inc.

 kershaw

 **Lone Wolf Knives**

 MERCWORX

 **LANSKY** SHARPENERS

 PRO-TECH USA

 **SOG.** Creators of Extraordinary Tools & Blades

 Spyderco. **VICTORINOX**

 MICROTECH

 WB

Smith&Wesson®

 ZT ZERO TOLERANCE KNIVES

www.beckwithsblades.com
713-935-0886 - 10801 Hammerly Blvd., #240, Houston, TX 77043

a.k.a. "The Gunny"
R. Lee Ermey, USMC Veteran,
TV Show Host, Film Star

WORTHY OF BEING CARRIED ON ANY FRONT IN THE WORLD... EVEN YOUR OWN BACKYARD.

The PowerAssist takes multi-tools to the next level. It's earned the right to be called Gunny Approved™. With patented technology, such as SOG's Assisted Fast Opening Action, and Compound Leverage, it packs what no other multi-tool does. The PowerAssist comes with over a dozen components that you can depend on in any situation. That's just one of the many reasons why R. Lee Ermey has carried SOG Knives and Tools around for over 10 years.

GUNNY APPROVED

SOG.
Specialty Knives & Tools

www.sogknives.com | 888-SOG-BEST

For Sale

The Much-Anticipated Book on the Life of Bill Scagel by Jim Lucie

The authoritative book about **Bill Scagel** covering his life as well as approx. 100 photos of knives and other items that he made, his property and family.

- Hard-bound, high-quality, cloth-covered book with gold imprinting and a separate dust jacket (above).
- **Printed in the United States of America.**
- $125, includes shipping media mail in the contl. U.S.

Send full payment (and 6% sales tax if shipped to Michigan) to

Sandi Doctor, 65 N. Crooked Lake Dr., Kalamazoo, MI 49009
Email: sdoctor@lvmcapital.com ■ Phone: 269-720-1454

WWW.BLADEGALLERY.COM

The Online Source for Fine Custom Knives

BladeGallery.com

BG

Fine Knives

Santa Ana with Tortoise Shell
by Rick Dunkerley, M.S.

Commander by Emerson Knives

BC BLADE CONNECTION

WWW.BLADECONNECTION.COM

Practical & Tactical ~ The Best of Handmade and Production for Daily Carry

Chef's Knife by Azai & O'Malley

Spicy Tighe by Brian Tighe

The Epicurean Edge

The Knife that Makes the Meal ~ Cutlery for the Discerning Chef

WWW.EPICUREANEDGE.COM

"Get the best deals on exclusive knives."

KnifeBroker.com

The Premier Online Auction of Knives and Accessories

Volume Discounts

Buyer Rewards

Free Auction Listings

Charity Auctions

Knife News

Knife Give Aways

KnifeBroker.com
**is the only choice for
buying and selling knives**

Join Now!

www.KnifeBroker.com

Photo by Daniel Martin

Miss KnifeBroker, *Laurie Hart*

BRIAN TIGHE

TIGHE KNIFE DESIGN

#4

905.892.2734 • www.briantighe.com

New Graham Knives

www.newgraham.com

Al Mar	Blade-Tech	Emerson Knives	Master of Defense	TOPS
Benchmade	Boker	Fallkniven	Microtech	Victorinox
Benchmade H&K	Bradley Cutlery	Gerber	Ontario	Vtech
Benchmade NRA Knives	Buck	Ka-Bar	Randall Made Knives	William Henry
Beretta	Byrd	Kershaw	Shun Kitchen Knives	Custom Knives
Blackhawk Blades	Case	Leatherman	Spyderco	**And More!**
Blackjack	Case Select	Lone Wolf	SOG	

New Graham Knives is part of New Graham Pharmacy Est. in 1935. We offer a large selection of production knives by the best names in the knife world. Along with great prices we provide exceptional customer service in the style of the old corner drug stores of days gone by.

New Graham Knives offers over 70 different brands and all are in stock ready for shipping at the time of your order, or come by the store and spend the day browsing.

Along with the drug store and knife store offerings we also feature the "Last Fountain" where you can take a break from shopping and have a good old fashion fountain soda and your favorite food.

Mcusta Damascus

Shun/Ken Onion

Kershaw Leek Damascus

Zero Tolerance

Proud Sponsor of The Blade Show

Case/Tony Bose Cotton Sampler

New Graham Knives

www.newgraham.com

Visit us online 24 hours a day at:
WWW.NEWGRAHAM.COM
Call us toll free during business hours
1.866.333.4445
Visit us at:
560 VIRGINIA AVE.
BLUEFIELD, VIRGINIA 24605

YOU'VE GOT THE VISION

Masecraft Supply Co. offers the world's largest selection of natural and synthetic materials for knife handles, gun grips, pens, musical instrument inlays, pool cue inlays and endless other creative applications. Several of these materials are exclusive to us.

Our customers include some of the largest and well known major manufacturers and artisans in the world.

Our selection of natural material includes Pearl white Mother of Pearl, Black Lip Pearl, Gold Lip Pearl, Paua, Green Abalone and many types of Laminated Pearl Veneers (LVS) plus custom shell inlays, India Stag, Bone, Horn and Exotic Woods.

Our decorative synthetic materials include Alternative Ivory and many other decorative Polyester and Acrylic materials in sheet, rod and bar form. We also offer a full line of Reconstituted Stone slabs and blocks. There are literally hundreds of colors and patterns available to choose from. We are adding new products every year. We also offer a wide variety of Rigid Composite Laminates in Canvas, Linen and Paper Micarta, G-10's and Carbon Fiber.

Masecraft Supply Co. specializes in large manufacture orders and the individual needs of artisans and hobbyist alike.

WE'VE GOT YOUR MATERIALS

Please visit our
E-commerce store
www.masecraftsupply.com
for full product selection
with pictures

MASECRAFT SUPPLY COMPANY

Call us today for a free catalog
1-800-682-5489

BUSSE COMBAT

Team Gemini

© 2010 Busse Knife Company. All rights reserved.

WHERE KNIFE COLLECTORS **CONNECT** WITH KNIFEMAKERS

The Knife Showcase at **BladeMag.com** is the premier site for knife-collecting. Chat with knifemakers, visit their blogs, find other collectors, or buy knives. Whatever it is that you love about knife-collecting, you'll find it in the Knife Showcase.

JOIN US TODAY.
click on Knife Showcase at www.BladeMag.com

BLADE

KNIFEMAKERS: INTERESTED IN SHOWCASING YOUR PRODUCT? CALL 888.457.2873

for the peak of sharpness on all your knife blades

LANSKY®
SHARPENERS

Lansky has been the world leader in knife and tool sharpening since 1979. We are the originators of the easy, foolproof Controlled-Angle Sharpening System, the home of the famous Crock Stick® sharpeners, and we offer the largest selection of pocket-sized ceramic, diamond, natural Arkansas and tungsten-carbide sharpeners.

Visit our online catalog of over 70 knife and tool sharpeners:

www.lansky.com

O Box 50830, Dept. K11, Henderson, NV 89016 • Phone: 716-877-7511 • Email: info@lansky.com

More Titles Worth Wielding!

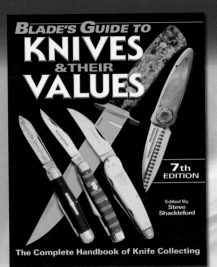

BLADE'S GUIDE TO KNIVES & THEIR VALUES

7th EDITION

Edited By Steve Shackleford

The Complete Handbook of Knife Collecting

Covers most all knives made around the world, mostly from the 19th century through to the present, with up-to-date values, 2,000+ photos, and feature articles covering trends in the industry. Plus, detailed histories of knife companies, and contact information.
*Softcover • 8-1/4 x 10-7/8 • 576 pages
2,000 b&w photos*
Item# Z5054 • $29.99

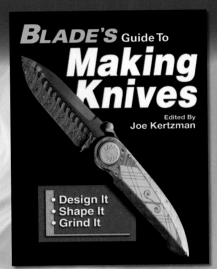

BLADE'S Guide To Making Knives

Edited By Joe Kertzman

• Design It
• Shape It
• Grind It

Gain professional technique tips and instruction for grinding blades, crafting hunting knives, forging pattern-welded steel into intricate designs, making folding knives, and fashioning the important bolster between knife and blade.
*Softcover • 8-1/4 x 10-7/8 • 160 pages
250 color photos*
Item# BGKFM • $24.99

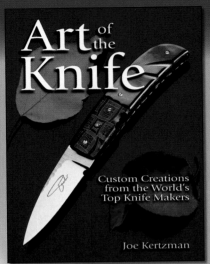

Art of the Knife

Custom Creations from the World's Top Knife Makers

Joe Kertzman

Explore the creativity and craftsmanship of knifemaking in 350 brilliant color photos of highly engraved folders, engraved fixed blades, wire-wrapped knifes and more, with a basic explanation of materials.
*Hardcover • 8-1/4 x 10-7/8 • 256 pages
350 color photos*
Item# Z0733 • $35.00

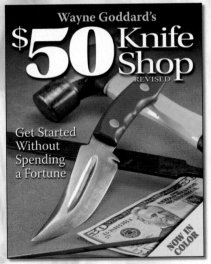

Wayne Goddard's $50 Knife Shop REVISED

Get Started Without Spending a Fortune

NOW IN COLOR

Explore Wayne Goddard's trusted techniques through detailed instructions, demonstrated in 250 color photos and outlined in cost-saving hints for building your own workshop.
*Softcover • 8-1/4 x 10-7/8 • 160 pages
250 color photos*
Item# WGBWR • $19.99

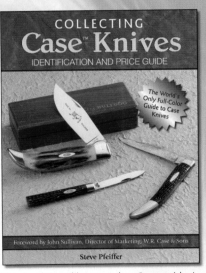

COLLECTING Case™ Knives

IDENTIFICATION AND PRICE GUIDE

The World's Only Full-Color Guide to Case Knives

Foreword by John Sullivan, Director of Marketing, W.R. Case & Sons

Steve Pfeiffer

This book is unlike any other Case guide. In addition to company history, it features 800 color photographs of Case knives, and listings of the most popular Case knives, with tang stamp, blade and shield data, plus current values.
*Softcover • 8-1/4 x 10-7/8 • 304 pages
750+ color photos*
Item# Z4387 • $29.99

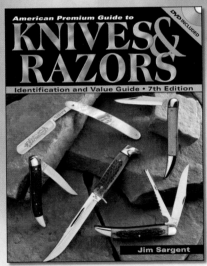

American Premium Guide to KNIVES & RAZORS

DVD INCLUDED

Identification and Value Guide • 7th Edition

Jim Sargent

Features current values and identification for thousands of Case, Crandall, Queen and Schatt & Morgan pocket knives, sheath knives and straight razors, as well as company histories. Plus, you'll discover a stunning color photo section.
*Softcover • 8-1/2 x 11 • 504 pages
2,500+ b&w photos • 32-page color section*
Item# Z2189 • $27.99

Order directly from the publisher at **www.krausebooks.com**

Krause Publications, Offer **KNBA**
P.O. Box 5009
Iola, WI 54945-5009
www.krausebooks.com

Call **800-258-0929** M-F 8 a.m. - 5 p.m. to order direct from the publisher, or shop booksellers nationwide.
Please reference offer **KNBA** with all direct-to-publisher orders

News to Forge Ahead in Your Hobby at www.blademag.com

DIRECTORY

A

ABEGG, ARNIE,
5992 Kenwick Cr, Huntington Beach, CA 92648, Phone: 714-848-5697

ABERNATHY, PAUL J,
3033 Park St., Eureka, CA 95501, Phone: 707-442-3593
Specialties: Period pieces and traditional straight knives of his design and in standard patterns. **Patterns:** Miniature daggers, fighters and swords. **Technical:** Forges and files SS, brass and sterling silver. **Prices:** $100 to $250; some to $500. **Remarks:** Part-time maker. Doing business as Abernathy's Miniatures. **Mark:** Stylized initials.

ACCAWI, FUAD,
131 Bethel Rd, Clinton, TN 37716, Phone: 865-414-4836, gaccawi@comcast.net; Web: www.acremetalworks.com
Specialties: I create one of a kind pieces from small working knives to performance blades and swords. **Patterns:** Styles include, and not limited to hunters, Bowies, daggers, swords, folders and camp knives. **Technical:** I forge primarily 5160, produces own Damascus and does own heat treating. **Prices:** $150 to $3000. **Remarks:** I am a full-time bladesmith. I enjoy producing Persian and historically influenced work. **Mark:** My mark is an eight sided Middle Eastern star with initials in the center.

ACKERSON, ROBIN E,
119 W Smith St, Buchanan, MI 49107, Phone: 616-695-2911

ADAMS, JIM,
322 Parkway Dr., Scottsville, KY 42164, Phone: 270-622-8776, jim@blacktoeknives.com
Specialties: Fixed blades in classic design. **Patterns:** Hunters, fighters, and Bowies. **Technical:** Grinds Damascus, O1, others as requested. **Prices:** Starting at $150. **Remarks:** Full-time maker. **Mark:** J. Adams, Scottsville, KY.

ADAMS, LES,
6413 NW 200 St, Hialeah, FL 33015, Phone: 305-625-1699
Specialties: Working straight knives of his design. **Patterns:** Fighters, tactical folders, law enforcing autos. **Technical:** Grinds ATS-34, 440C and D2. **Prices:** $100 to $500. **Remarks:** Part-time maker; first knife sold in 1989. **Mark:** First initial, last name, Custom Knives.

ADAMS, WILLIAM D,
PO Box 439, Burton, TX 77835, Phone: 713-855-5643, Fax: 713-855-5638
Specialties: Hunter scalpels and utility knives of his design. **Patterns:** Hunters and utility/camp knives. **Technical:** Grinds 1095, 440C and 440V. Uses stabilized wood and other stabilized materials. **Prices:** $100 to $200. **Remarks:** Part-time maker; first knife sold in 1994. **Mark:** Last name in script.

ADDISON, KYLE A,
588 Atkins Trail, Hazel, KY 42049-8629, Phone: 270-492-8120, kylest2@yahoo.com
Specialties: Hand forged blades including Bowies, fighters and hunters. **Patterns:** Custom leather sheaths. **Technical:** Forges 5160, 1084, and his own Damascus. **Prices:** $175 to $1500. **Remarks:** Part-time maker, first knife sold in 1996. ABS member. **Mark:** First and middle initial, last name under "Trident" with knife and hammer.

ADKINS, LARRY,
10714 East County Rd. 100S, Indianapolis, IN 46231, Phone: 317-838-7292
Specialties: Single blade slip joint folders. Bear Jaw Damascus hunters, Bowies, and fighters. Handles from stag, ossic, pearl, bone, mastodon-mammoth elephant. **Technical:** Forges own Damascus and all high carbon steels. Grinds 5160, 52100, 1095, O1 and L6. **Prices:** $150 and up. **Remarks:** Part-time maker, first knife sold in 2001. **Mark:** L. Adkins.

ADKINS, RICHARD L,
138 California Ct, Mission Viejo, CA 92692-4079

AIDA, YOSHIHITO,
26-7 Narimasu 2-chome, Itabashi-ku, Tokyo 175-0094, JAPAN, Phone: 81-3-3939-0052, Fax: 81-3-3939-0058
Specialties: High-tech working straight knives and folders of his design. **Patterns:** Bowies, lockbacks, hunters, fighters, fishing knives, boots. **Technical:** Grinds CV-134, ATS-34; buys Damascus; works in traditional Japanese fashion for some handles and sheaths. **Prices:** $700 to $1200; some higher. **Remarks:** Full-time maker; first knife sold in 1978. **Mark:** Initial logo and Riverside West.

ALBERICCI, EMILIO,
19 Via Masone, 24100, Bergamo, ITALY, Phone: 01139-35-215120
Specialties: Folders and Bowies. **Patterns:** Collector knives. **Technical:** Uses stock removal with extreme accuracy; offers exotic and high-tech materials. **Prices:** Not currently selling. **Remarks:** Part-time maker. **Mark:** None.

ALBERT, STEFAN,
U Lucenecka 434/4, Filakovo 98604, SLOVAK REPUBLIC, albert@albertknives.com Web: www.albertknives.com
Specialties: Art Knives, Miniatures, Scrimshaw, Bulino. **Prices:** From USD $500 to USD $25000. **Mark:** Albert

ALCORN, DOUGLAS A.,
14687 Fordney Rd., Chesaning, MI 48616, Phone: 989-845-6712, fortalcornknives@centurytel.net
Specialties: Gentleman style and presentation knives. **Patterns:** Hunters, miniatures, and military type fixed blade knives and axes. **Technical:** Blades are stock removal and forged using best quality stainless, carbon, and damascus steels. Handle materials are burls, ivory, pearl, leather and other exotics. **Prices:** $300 and up. **Motto:** Simple, Rugged, Elegant, Hand-crafted **Remarks:** Knife maker since 1989 and full time since 1999, Knife Makers Guild (voting member), member of the Bladesmith Society. **Mark:** D.A. Alcorn (Loveless style mark), Maker, Chesaning, MI.

ALDERMAN, ROBERT,
2655 Jewel Lake Rd., Sagle, ID 83860, Phone: 208-263-5996
Specialties: Classic and traditional working straight knives in standard patterns or to customer specs and his design; period pieces. **Patterns:** Bowies, fighters, hunters and utility/camp knives. **Technical:** Casts, forges and grinds 1084; forges and grinds L6 and O1. Prefers an old appearance. **Prices:** $100 to $350; some to $700. **Remarks:** Full-time maker; first knife sold in 1975. Doing business as Trackers Forge. Knife-making school. Two-week course for beginners; covers forging, stock removal, hardening, tempering, case making. All materials supplied; $1250. **Mark:** Deer track.

ALDRETE, BOB,
PO Box 1471, Lomita, CA 90717, Phone: 310-326-3041

ALEXANDER, DARREL,
Box 381, Ten Sleep, WY 82442, Phone: 307-366-2699, dalexwyo@tctwest.net
Specialties: Traditional working straight knives. **Patterns:** Hunters, boots and fishing knives. **Technical:** Grinds D2, 440C, ATS-34 and 154CM. **Prices:** $75 to $120; some to $250. **Remarks:** Full-time maker; first knife sold in 1983. **Mark:** Name, city, state.

ALEXANDER, EUGENE,
Box 540, Ganado, TX 77962-0540, Phone: 512-771-3727

ALEXANDER, OLEG, Cossack Blades,
15460 Stapleton Way, Wellington, FL 33414, Phone: 443-676-6111, Web: www.cossackblades.com
Technical: All knives are made from hand-forged Damascus (3-4 types of steel are used to create the Damascus) and have a HRC of 60-62. Handle materials are all natural, including various types of wood, horn, bone and leather. Embellishments include the use of precious metals and stones, including gold, silver, diamonds, rubies, sapphires and other unique materials. All knives include hand-made leather sheaths, and some models include wooden presentation boxes and display stands. **Prices:** $395 to over $10,000, depending on design and materials used. **Remarks:** Full-time maker, first knife sold in 1993. **Mark:** Rectangle enclosing a stylized Cyrillic letter "O" overlapping a stylized Cyrillic "K."

ALLEN, MIKE "WHISKERS",
12745 Fontenot Acres Rd, Malakoff, TX 75148, Phone: 903-489-1026, whiskersknives@aol.com; Web: www.whiskersknives.com
Specialties: Working and collector-quality lockbacks, liner locks and automatic folders to customer specs. **Patterns:** Folders only. **Technical:** Grinds Damascus, 440C and ATS-34, engraves. **Prices:** $200 and up. **Remarks:** Full-time maker; first knife sold in 1984. **Mark:** Whiskers and date.

ALLRED, BRUCE F,
1764 N. Alder, Layton, UT 84041, Phone: 801-825-4612, allredbf@msn.com
Specialties: Custom hunting and utility knives. **Patterns:** Custom designs that include a unique grind line, thumb and mosaic pins. **Technical:** ATS-34, 154CM and 440C. **Remarks:** The handle material includes but not limited to Micarta (in various colors), natural woods and reconstituted stone.

ALLRED, ELVAN,
31 Spring Terrace Court, St. Charles, MO 63303, Phone: 636-936-8871, allredknives@yahoo.com; Web: www.allredcustomknives.com
Specialties: Innovative sculpted folding knives designed by Elvan's son Scott that are mostly one of a kind. **Patterns:** Mostly folders but some high-end straight knives. **Technical:** ATS-34 SS, 440C SS, stainless Damascus, S30V, 154cm; inlays are mostly natural materials such as pearl, coral, ivory, jade, lapis, and other precious stone. **Prices:** $500 to $4000, some higher. **Remarks:** Started making knives in the shop of Dr. Fred Carter in the early 1990s. Full-time maker since 2006, first knife sold in 1993. Take some orders but work mainly on one-of-a-kind art knives. **Mark:** Small oval with signature Eallred in the center and handmade above.

ALVERSON, TIM (R.V.),
622 Homestead St., Moscow, ID 83843, Phone: 208-874-2277, alvie35@yahoo.com Web: cwknives.blogspot.com
Specialties: Fancy working knives to customer specs; other types on request. **Patterns:** Bowies, daggers, folders and miniatures. **Technical:** Grinds 440C, ATS-34; buys some Damascus. **Prices:** Start at $100. **Remarks:** Full-time maker; first knife sold in 1981. **Mark:** R.V.A. around rosebud.

AMERI, MAURO,
Via Riaello No. 20, Trensasco St Olcese, 16010 Genova, ITALY, Phone: 010-8357077
Specialties: Working and using knives of his design. **Patterns:** Hunters, Bowies and utility/camp knives. **Technical:** Grinds 440C, ATS-34 and 154CM. Handles in wood or Micarta; offers sheaths. **Prices:** $200 to $1200.

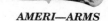

Remarks: Spare-time maker; first knife sold in 1982. **Mark:** Last name, city.

AMMONS, DAVID C,
6225 N. Tucson Mtn. Dr, Tucson, AZ 85743, Phone: 520-307-3585
Specialties: Will build to suit. **Patterns:** Yours or his. **Prices:** $250 to $2000. **Mark:** AMMONS.

AMOUREUX, A W,
PO Box 776, Northport, WA 99157, Phone: 509-732-6292
Specialties: Heavy-duty working straight knives. **Patterns:** Bowies, fighters, camp knives and hunters for world-wide use. **Technical:** Grinds 440C, ATS-34 and 154CM. **Prices:** $80 to $2000. **Remarks:** Full-time maker; first knife sold in 1974. **Mark:** ALSTAR.

ANDERS, DAVID,
157 Barnes Dr, Center Ridge, AR 72027, Phone: 501-893-2294
Specialties: Working straight knives of his design. **Patterns:** Bowies, fighters and hunters. **Technical:** Forges 5160, 1080 and Damascus. **Prices:** $225 to $3200. **Remarks:** Part-time maker; first knife sold in 1988. Doing business as Anders Knives. **Mark:** Last name/MS.

ANDERS, JEROME,
14560 SW 37th St, Miramar, FL 33027, Phone: 305-613-2990, web:www.andersknives.com
Specialties: Case handles and pin work. **Patterns:** Layered and mosiac steel. **Prices:** $275 and up. **Remarks:** All his knives are truly one-of-a-kind. **Mark:** J. Anders in half moon.

ANDERSEN, HENRIK LEFOLII,
Jagtvej 8, Groenholt, 3480, Fredensborg, DENMARK, Phone: 0011-45-48483026
Specialties: Hunters and matched pairs for the serious hunter. **Technical:** Grinds A2; uses materials native to Scandinavia. **Prices:** Start at $250. **Remarks:** Part-time maker; first knife sold in 1985. **Mark:** Initials with arrow.

ANDERSON, GARY D,
2816 Reservoir Rd, Spring Grove, PA 17362-9802, Phone: 717-229-2665
Specialties: From working knives to collectors quality blades, some folders. **Patterns:** Traditional and classic designs; customer patterns welcome. **Technical:** Forges Damascus carbon and stainless steels. Offers silver inlay, mokume, filework, checkering. **Prices:** $250 and up. **Remarks:** Part-time maker; first knife sold in 1985. Some engraving, scrimshaw and stone work. **Mark:** GAND, MS.

ANDERSON, MARK ALAN,
1176 Poplar St, Denver, CO 80220, mcantdrive95@comcast.net; Web: www.malancustomknives.com
Specialties: Stilettos. Automatics of several varieties and release mechanisms. **Patterns:** Drop point hunters, sub hilt fighters & drop point camp knives. **Technical:** Almost all my blades are hollow ground. **Prices:** $200 to $1800. **Remarks:** Focusing on fixed blade hunting, skinning & fighting knives now. **Mark:** Dragon head.

ANDERSON, MEL,
29505 P 50 Rd, Hotchkiss, CO 81419-8203, Phone: 970-872-4882, Fax: 970-872-4882, artnedge1@wmconnect.com
Specialties: Full-size, miniature and one-of-a-kind straight knives and folders of his design. **Patterns:** Tantos, Bowies, daggers, fighters, hunters and pressure folders. **Technical:** Grinds 440C, 5160, D2, 1095. **Prices:** Start at $145. **Remarks:** Knifemaker and sculptor, full-time maker; first knife sold in 1987. **Mark:** Scratchy Hand.

ANDERSON, TOM,
955 Canal Rd. Extd., Manchester, PA 17345, Phone: 717-266-6475, andersontech1@comcast.net Web: artistryintitanium.com

ANDREWS, ERIC,
132 Halbert Street, Grand Ledge, MI 48837, Phone: 517-627-7304
Specialties: Traditional working and using straight knives of his design. **Patterns:** Full-tang hunters, skinners and utility knives. **Technical:** Forges carbon steel; heat-treats. All knives come with sheath; most handles are of wood. **Prices:** $80 to $160. **Remarks:** Part-time maker; first knife sold in 1990. Doing business as The Tinkers Bench.

ANDREWS, RUSS,
PO Box 7732, Sugar Creek, MO 64054, Phone: 816-252-3344, russandrews@sbcglobal.net; Web:wwwrussandrewsknives.com
Specialties: Hand forged bowies & hunters. **Mark:** E. R. Andrews II. ERAII.

ANGELL, JON,
22516 East C R1474, Hawthorne, FL 32640, Phone: 352-475-5380, syrjon@aol.com

ANKROM, W.E.,
14 Marquette Dr, Cody, WY 82414, Phone: 307-587-3017, Fax: 307-587-3017, weankrom@hotmail.com
Specialties: Best quality folding knives of his design. Bowies, fighters, chute knives, boots and hunters. **Patterns:** Lock backs, liner locks, single high art. **Technical:** ATS-34 commercial Damascus, CPM 154 steel. **Prices:** $500 and up. **Remarks:** Full-time maker; first knife sold in 1975. **Mark:** Name or name, city, state.

ANSO, JENS,
GL. Skanderborgvej, 116, 8472 Sporup, DENMARK, Phone: 45 86968826, info@ansoknives.com; Web: www.ansoknives.com
Specialties: Working knives of his own design. **Patterns:** Balisongs, swords, folders, drop-points, sheepsfoots, hawkbill, tanto, recurve. **Technical:** Grinds RWL-34 Damasteel S30V, CPM 154CM. Handrubbed or beadblasted finish. **Price:** $400 to $1200, some up to $3500. **Remarks:** Full-time maker since January 2002. First knife sold 1997. Doing business as ANSOKNIVES. **Mark:** ANSO and/or ANSO with logo.

ANTONIO JR., WILLIAM J,
6 Michigan State Dr, Newark, DE 19713-1161, Phone: 302-368-8211, antonioknives@aol.com
Specialties: Fancy working straight knives of his design. **Patterns:** Hunting, survival and fishing knives. **Technical:** Grinds D2, 440C and 154CM; offers stainless Damascus. **Prices:** $125 to $395; some to $900. **Remarks:** Part-time maker; first knife sold in 1978. **Mark:** Last name.

APELT, STACY E,
8076 Moose Ave, Norfolk, VA 23518, Phone: 757-583-5872, sapelt@cox.net
Specialties: Exotic wood and burls, ivories, Bowies, custom made knives to order. **Patterns:** Bowies, hunters, fillet, professional cutlery and Japanese style blades and swords. **Technical:** Hand forging, stock removal, scrimshaw, carbon, stainless and Damascus steels. **Prices:** $65 to $5000. **Remarks:** Professional Goldsmith. **Mark:** Stacy E. Apelt - Norfolk VA.

APPLEBY, ROBERT,
746 Municipal Rd, Shickshinny, PA 18655, Phone: 570-864-0879, applebyknives@yahoo.com; Web: www.applebyknives.com
Specialties: Working using straight knives and folders of his own and popular and historical designs. **Patterns:** Variety of straight knives and folders. **Technical:** Hand forged or grinds O1, 1084, 5160, 440C, ATS-34, commercial Damascus, makes own sheaths. **Prices:** Starting at $75. **Remarks:** Part-time maker, first knife sold in 1995. **Mark:** APPLEBY over SHICKSHINNY, PA.

APPLETON, RON,
315 Glenn St, Bluff Dale, TX 76433, Phone: 254-728-3039, ron@helovesher.com; Web: http://community.webshots.com/user/angelic574
Specialties: One-of-a-kind folding knives. **Patterns:** Unique folding multi-locks and high-tech patterns. **Technical:** All parts machined, D2, S7, 416, 440C, 6A14V et.al. **Prices:** Start at $9500. **Remarks:** Spare-time maker; first knife sold in 1996. **Mark:** Initials with anvil or initials within arrowhead, signed and dated.

ARBUCKLE, JAMES M,
114 Jonathan Jct, Yorktown, VA 23693, Phone: 757-867-9578, a_r_bukckle@hotmail.com
Specialties: One-of-a-kind of his design; working knives. **Patterns:** Mostly chef's knives and hunters. **Technical:** Forged and stock removal blades using exotic hardwoods, natural materials, Micarta and stabilized woods. Forge 5160, 1084 and O1; stock remove D2, ATS-34, 440C. Makes own pattern welded steel. **Prices:** $175 to $900. **Remarks:** Forge, grind, heat-treat, finish and embellish all knives himself. Does own leatherwork. Part-time maker. ABS Journeyman smith 2007; ASM member. **Mark:** J. Arbuckle or Arbuckle with maker below it.

ARCHER, RAY AND TERRI,
4207 South 28 St., Omaha, NE 68107, Phone: 402-505-3084, archerrt@cox.net
Specialties: Back to basics high finish working knives and upscale. **Patterns:** Hunters/skinners, camping. **Technical:** Flat grinds ATS-34, 440C, S30V. Buys Damascus. **Price:** $100 to $500, some higher. **Remarks:** Full time maker. Make own sheaths; first knife sold 1994. Member of PKA & OK CA (Oregon Knife Collector Assoc.). **Mark:** Last name over city and state.

ARDWIN, COREY,
4700 North Cedar, North Little Rock, AR 72116, Phone: 501-791-0301, Fax: 501-791-2974, Boog@hotmail.com

ARM-KO KNIVES,
PO Box 76280, Marble Ray 4035 KZN, SOUTH AFRICA, Phone: 27 31 5771451, arm-koknives.co.za; Web: www.arm-koknives.co.za
Specialties: They will make what your fastidious taste desires. Be it cool collector or tenacious tactical with handles of mother-of-pearl, fossil & local ivories. Exotic dye/stabilized burls, giraffe bone, horns, carbon fiber, g10, and titanium etc. **Technical:** Via stock removal, grinding Damasteel, carbon & mosaic. Damascus, ATS-34, N690, 440A, 440B, 12C27, RWL34 and high carbon EN 8, 5160 all heat treated in house. **Prices:** From $200 and up. **Remarks:** Father a part-time maker for well over 10 years and member of Knifemakers Guild in SA. Son full-time maker over 3 years. **Mark:** Logo of initials A R M and H A R M "Edged Tools."

ARMS, ERIC,
11153 7 Mile Road, Tustin, MI 49688, Phone: 231-829-3726, ericarms@netonecom.net
Specialties: Working hunters, high performance straight knives. **Patterns:** Variety of hunters, scagel style, Ed Fowler design and drop point. **Technical:** Forge 52100, 5160, 1084 hand grind, heat treat, natural handle, stag horn, elk, big horn, flat grind, convex, all leather sheath work. **Prices:** Starting at $150 **Remarks:** Part-time maker **Mark:** Eric Arms

ARNOLD—BANKS

ARNOLD, JOE,
47 Patience Cres, London, Ont., CANADA N6E 2K7, Phone: 519-686-2623
Specialties: Traditional working and using straight knives of his design and to customer specs. **Patterns:** Fighters, hunters and Bowies. **Technical:** Grinds 440C, ATS-34 and 5160. **Prices:** $75 to $500; some to $2500. **Remarks:** Part-time maker; first knife sold in 1988. **Mark:** Last name, country.

ARROWOOD, DALE,
556 Lassetter Rd, Sharpsburg, GA 30277, Phone: 404-253-9672
Specialties: Fancy and traditional straight knives of his design and to customer specs. **Patterns:** Bowies, fighters and hunters. **Technical:** Grinds ATS-34 and 440C; forges high-carbon steel. Engraves and scrimshaws. **Prices:** $125 to $200; some to $245. **Remarks:** Part-time maker; first knife sold in 1989. **Mark:** Anvil with an arrow through it; Old English "Arrowood Knives."

ASHBY, DOUGLAS,
10123 Deermont, Dallas, TX 75243, Phone: 972-238-7531
Specialties: Traditional and fancy straight knives of his design or to customer specs. **Patterns:** Hunters, fighters and utility/camp knives. **Technical:** Grinds ATS-34 and commercial Damascus. **Prices:** $75 to $200; some to $500. **Remarks:** Part-time maker; first knife sold in 1990. **Mark:** Name, city.

ASHWORTH, BOYD,
1510 Bullard Place, Powder Springs, GA 30127, Phone: 770-422-9826, boydashworth@comcast.net; Web: www.boydashworthknives.com
Specialties: Turtle folders. Fancy Damascus locking folders. **Patterns:** Fighters, hunters and gents. **Technical:** Forges own Damascus; offers filework; uses exotic handle materials. **Prices:** $500 to $2500. **Remarks:** Part-time maker; first knife sold in 1993. **Mark:** Last name.

ATHEY, STEVE,
3153 Danube Way, Riverside, CA 92503, Phone: 951-850-8612, stevelonnie@yahoo.com
Specialties: Stock removal. **Patterns:** Hunters & Bowies. **Prices:** $100 to $500. **Remarks:** Part-time maker. **Mark:** Last name with number on blade.

ATKINSON, DICK,
General Delivery, Wausau, FL 32463, Phone: 850-638-8524
Specialties: Working straight knives and folders of his design; some fancy. **Patterns:** Hunters, fighters, boots; locking folders in interframes. **Technical:** Grinds A2, 440C and 154CM. Likes filework. **Prices:** $85 to $300; some exceptional knives. **Remarks:** Full-time maker; first knife sold in 1977. **Mark:** Name, city, state.

AYARRAGARAY, CRISTIAN L.,
Buenos Aires 250, (3100) Parana-Entre Rios, ARGENTINA, Phone: 043-231753
Specialties: Traditional working straight knives of his design. **Patterns:** Fishing and hunting knives. **Technical:** Grinds and forges carbon steel. Uses native Argentine woods and deer antler. **Prices:** $150 to $250; some to $400. **Remarks:** Full-time maker; first knife sold in 1980. **Mark:** Last name, signature.

B

BAARTMAN, GEORGE,
PO Box 1116, Bela-Bela 0480, Limpopo, SOUTH AFRICA, Phone: 27 14 736 4036, Fax: 086 636 3408, thabathipa@gmail.com
Specialties: Fancy and working LinerLock® folders of own design and to customers specs. Specialize in pattern filework on liners. **Patterns:** LinerLock® folders. **Technical:** Grinds 12C27, ATS-34, and Damascus, prefer working with stainless damasteel. Hollow grinds to hand-rubbed and polished satin finish. Enjoys working with mammoth, warthog tusk and pearls. **Prices:** Folders from $380 to $1000. **Remarks:** Part-time maker. Member of the Knifemakers Guild of South Africa since 1993. **Mark:** BAARTMAN.

BACHE-WIIG, TOM,
N-5966, Eivindvik, NORWAY, Phone: 475-778-4290, Fax: 475-778-1099, tom.bache-wiig@enivest.net; Web: tombachewiig.com
Specialties: High-art and working knives of his design. **Patterns:** Hunters, utility knives, hatchets, axes and art knives. **Technical:** Grinds Uddeholm Elmax, powder metallurgy tool stainless steel. Handles made of rear burls of Nordic woods stabilized with vacuum/high-pressure technique. **Prices:** $430 to $900; some to $2300. **Remarks:** Part-time maker; first knife sold 1988. **Mark:** Etched name and eagle head.

BACON, DAVID R.,
906 136th St E, Bradenton, FL 34202-9694, Phone: 813-996-4289

BAGLEY, R. KEITH,
OLD PINE FORGE, 4415 Hope Acres Dr, White Plains, MD 20695, Phone: 301-932-0990, oldpineforge@hotmail.com
Specialties: Hand-made Damascus hunters, skinners, Bowies. **Technical:** Use ATS-34, 5160, O1, 1085, 1095. **Patterns:** Ladder-wave lightning bolt. **Price:** $275 to 750. **Remarks:** Farrier for 25 years, blacksmith for 25 years, knifemaker for 10 years. **Mark:** KB inside horseshoe and anvil.

BAILEY, I.R.,
Lamorna Cottage, Common End, Colkirk, ENGLAND NR 21 7JD, Phone: 01-328-856-183, irbailey1975@tiscali.co.uk
Specialties: Hunters, utilities, Bowies, camp knives, fighters. Mainly influenced by Moran, Loveless and Lile. **Technical:** Primarily stock removal using flat ground 1095, 1075, and 80CrV2. Occasionally forges including own basic Damascus. Uses both native and exotic hardwoods, stag, Leather, Micarta and other synthetic handle materials, with brass or 301 stainless fittings. Does some filework and leather tooling. Does own heat treating. **Remarks:** Part-time maker since 2005. All knives and sheaths are sole authorship. **Mark:** Last name stamped.

BAILEY, JOSEPH D.,
3213 Jonesboro Dr, Nashville, TN 37214, Phone: 615-889-3172, jbknfemkr@aol.com
Specialties: Working and using straight knives; collector pieces. **Patterns:** Bowies, hunters, tactical, folders. **Technical:** 440C, ATS-34, Damascus and wire Damascus. Offers scrimshaw. **Prices:** $85 to $1200. **Remarks:** Part-time maker; first knife sold in 1988. **Mark:** Joseph D Bailey Nashville Tennessee.

BAILEY, RYAN,
4185 S. St. Rt. 605, Galena, OH 43021, Phone: 740-965-9970, dr@darrelralph.com; Web: www.darrelralph.com
Specialties: Fancy, high-art, high-tech, collectible straight knives and folders of his design and to customer specs; unique mechanisms, some disassemble. **Patterns:** Daggers, fighters and swords. **Technical:** Does own Damascus and forging from high-carbon. Embellishes with file work and gold work. **Prices:** $200 to $2500. **Remarks:** Full-time maker; first knife sold in 1999. Doing business as Briar Knives. **Mark:** RLB.

BAKER, HERB,
14104 NC 87 N, Eden, NC 27288, Phone: 336-627-0338

BAKER, RAY,
PO Box 303, Sapulpa, OK 74067, Phone: 918-224-8013
Specialties: High-tech working straight knives. **Patterns:** Hunters, fighters, Bowies, skinners and boots of his design and to customer specs. **Technical:** Grinds 440C, 1095 spring steel or customer request; heat-treats. Custom-made scabbards for any knife. **Prices:** $125 to $500; some to $1000. **Remarks:** Full-time maker; first knife sold in 1981. **Mark:** First initial, last name.

BAKER, WILD BILL,
Box 361, Boiceville, NY 12412, Phone: 914-657-8646
Specialties: Primitive knives, buckskinners. **Patterns:** Skinners, camp knives and Bowies. **Technical:** Works with L6, files and rasps. **Prices:** $100 to $350. **Remarks:** Part-time maker; first knife sold in 1989. **Mark:** Wild Bill Baker, Oak Leaf Forge, or both.

BALBACH, MARKUS,
Heinrich - Worner - Str 3, 35789 Weilmunster-Laubuseschbach/Ts., GERMANY 06475-8911, Fax: 912986, Web: www.schmiede-balbach.de
Specialties: High-art knives and working/using straight knives and folders of his design and to customer specs. **Patterns:** Hunters and daggers. **Technical:** Stainless steel, one of Germany's greatest Smithies. Supplier for the forges of Solingen. **Remarks:** Full-time maker; first knife sold in 1984. Doing business as Schmiedewerkstatte M. Balbach. **Mark:** Initials stamped inside the handle.

BALL, BUTCH,
2161 Reedsville Rd., Floyd, VA 24091, Phone: 540-392-3485, ballknives@yahoo.com
Ball Custom Knives

BALL, KEN,
127 Sundown Manor, Mooresville, IN 46158, Phone: 317-834-4803
Specialties: Classic working/using straight knives of his design and to customer specs. **Patterns:** Hunters and utility/camp knives. **Technical:** Flat-grinds ATS-34. Offers filework. **Prices:** $150 to $400. **Remarks:** Part-time maker; first knife sold in 1994. Doing business as Ball Custom Knives. **Mark:** Last name.

BALLESTRA, SANTINO,
via D. Tempesta 11/17, 18039 Ventimiglia (IM), ITALY 0184-215228, ladasin@libero.it
Specialties: Using and collecting straight knives. **Patterns:** Hunting, fighting, skinners, Bowies, medieval daggers and knives. **Technical:** Forges ATS-34, D2, O2, and his own Damascus. Uses ivory and silver. **Prices:** $500 to $2000; some higher. **Remarks:** Full-time maker; first knife sold in 1979. **Mark:** First initial, last name.

BALLEW, DALE,
PO Box 1277, Bowling Green, VA 22427, Phone: 804-633-5701
Specialties: Miniatures only to customer specs. **Patterns:** Bowies, daggers and fighters. **Technical:** Files 440C stainless; uses ivory, abalone, exotic woods and some precious stones. **Prices:** $100 to $800. **Remarks:** Part-time maker; first knife sold in 1988. **Mark:** Initials and last name.

BANKS, DAVID L.,
99 Blackfoot Ave, Riverton, WY 82501, Phone: 307-856-3154/Cell: 307-851-5599
Specialties: Heavy-duty working straight knives. **Patterns:** Hunters, Bowies and camp knives. **Technical:** Forges Damascus 1084-15N20, L6-W1 pure nickel, 5160, 52100 and his own Damascus; differential heat treat and tempers. Handles made of horn, antlers and exotic wood. Hand-stitched harness leather sheaths. **Prices:** $300 to $2000. **Remarks:** Part-time maker. **Mark:** Banks Blackfoot forged Dave Banks and initials connected.

BARBARA BASKETT CUSTOM KNIVES,
427 Sutzer Ck Rd, Eastview, KY 42732, Phone: 270-862-5019, baskettknives@windstream; Web: www.geocities.com/baskettknives
  Specialties: Fancy working knives and fantasy pieces, often set up in desk stands. **Patterns:** Fighters, Bowies and survival knives; locking folders and traditional styles. Cutting competition knives. **Technical:** Liner locks. Grinds O1, 440C, S30V, power CPM 154, CPM 4 buys Damascus. Filework provided on most knives. **Prices:** Start at $250 and up. **Remarks:** Part-time maker; first knife sold in 1980. **Mark:** B. Baskett.

BARDSLEY, NORMAN P.,
197 Cottage St, Pawtucket, RI 02860, Phone: 401-725-9132, norman.bardsley@verizon.net
  Specialties: Working and fantasy knives. **Patterns:** Fighters, boots, fantasy, renaissance and native American in upscale and presentation fashion. **Technical:** Grinds all steels and Damascus. Uses exotic hides for sheaths. **Prices:** $100 to $15,000. **Remarks:** Full-time maker. **Mark:** Last name in script with logo.

BAREFOOT, JOE W.,
1654 Honey Hill, Wilmington, NC 28442, Phone: 910-641-1143
  Specialties: Working straight knives of his design. **Patterns:** Hunters, fighters and boots; tantos and survival knives. **Technical:** Grinds D2, 440C and ATS-34. Mirror finishes. Uses ivory and stag on customer request only. **Prices:** $50 to $160; some to $500. **Remarks:** Part-time maker; first knife sold in 1980. **Mark:** Bare footprint.

BARKER, REGGIE,
603 S Park Dr, Springhill, LA 71075, Phone: 318-539-2958, wrbarker@cmaaccess.com; Web: www.reggiebarkerknives.com
  Specialties: Camp knives and hatchets. **Patterns:** Bowie, skinning, hunting, camping, fighters, kitchen or customer design. **Technical:** Forges carbon steel and own pattern welded steels. **Prices:** $225 to $2000. **Remarks:** Full-time maker. Winner of 1999 and 2000 Spring Hammering Cutting contest. Winner of Best Value of Show 2001; Arkansas Knife Show and Journeyman Smith. Border Guard Forge. **Mark:** Barker JS.

BARKER, ROBERT G.,
2311 Branch Rd, Bishop, GA 30621, Phone: 706-769-7827
  Specialties: Traditional working/using straight knives of his design. **Patterns:** Bowies, hunters and utility knives, ABS Journeyman Smith. **Technical:** Hand forged carbon and Damascus. Forges to shape high-carbon 5160, cable and chain. Differentially heat-treats. **Prices:** $200 to $500; some to $1000. **Remarks:** Spare-time maker; first knife sold in 1987. **Mark:** BARKER/J.S.

BARKER, STUART,
14 Belvoir Close, Oadby, Leicester, England LE2 4SG, Phone: +447887585411, sc_barker@hotmail.com
  Specialties: Fixed blade working knives of his design. **Patterns:** Kitchen, hunter, utility/camp knives. **Technical:** Grinds O1, Rw134 & Damasteel, hand rubbed or shot blast finishes. **Prices:** $150 - $500 **Remarks:** Part-time maker, first knife sold 2006. **Mark:** Last initial

BARKES, TERRY,
14844 N. Bluff Rd., Edinburgh, IN 46124, Phone: 812-526-6390, knifenpocket@sbcglobal.net; Web:http:// my.hsonline.net/wizard/TerryBarkesKnives.htm
  Specialties: Traditional working straight knives of his designs. **Patterns:** Drop point hunters, boot knives, skinning, fighter, utility, all purpose, camp, and grill knives. **Technical:** Grinds 1095 - 1084 - 52100 - 01, Hollow grinds and flat grinds. Hand rubbed finish from 400 to 2000 grit or High polish buff. Hard edge and soft back, heat treat by maker. Likes File work, natural handle material, bone, stag, water buffalo horn, wildbeast bone, ironwood. **Prices:** $200 and up **Remarks:** Full-time maker, first knifge sold in 2005. Doing business as Barkes Knife Shop. **Marks:** Barkes - USA, Barkes Double Arrow - USA

BARLOW, JANA POIRIER,
3820 Borland Cir, Anchorage, AK 99517, Phone: 907-243-4581

BARNES, AUBREY G.,
11341 Rock Hill Rd, Hagerstown, MD 21740, Phone: 301-223-4587, a.barnes@myactv.net
  Specialties: Classic Moran style reproductions and using knives of his own design. **Patterns:** Bowies, hunters, fighters, daggers and utility/camping knives. **Technical:** Forges 5160, 1085, L6 and Damascus, Silver wire inlays. **Prices:** $500 to $5000. **Remarks:** Full-time maker; first knife sold in 1992. Doing business as Falling Waters Forge. **Mark:** First and middle initials, last name, M.S.

BARNES, GARY L.,
Box 138, New Windsor, MD 21776-0138, Phone: 410-635-6243, Fax: 410-635-6243, mail@glbarnes.com; Web: www.glbarnes.com or www.barnespneumatic.com
  Specialties: Ornate button lock Damascus folders. **Patterns:** Barnes original. **Technical:** Forges own Damascus. **Prices:** Average $2500. **Remarks:** ABS Master Smith since 1983. **Mark:** Hand engraved logo of letter B pierced by dagger.

BARNES, GREGORY,
266 W Calaveras St, Altadena, CA 91001, Phone: 626-398-0053, snake@annex.com

BARNES, JACK,
PO Box 1315, Whitefish, MT 59937-1315, Phone: 406-862-6078

BARNES, JIM,
PO Box 50, Christoval, TX 76935, Phone: 325-896-7819
  Specialties: Traditional and working straight and folder knives of all designs. Standard or customer request specialties. **Technical:** Grinds ATS-34, 440C, and D2 heat treats. All folders have filework. **Prices:** Start at $175 for straight and start at $275 for folders. **Remarks:** Full-time maker first knife sold in 1984. DBA Jim Barnes Custom Knives **Mark:** Logo with Name City and State

BARNES, MARLEN R.,
904 Crestview Dr S, Atlanta, TX 75551-1854, Phone: 903-796-3668, MRBlives@worldnet.att.net
  Specialties: Hammer forges random and mosaic Damascus. **Patterns:** Hatchets, straight and folding knives. **Technical:** Hammer forges carbon steel using 5160, 1084 and 52100 with 15N20 and 203E nickel. **Prices:** $150 and up. **Remarks:** Part-time maker; first knife sold 1999. **Mark:** Script M.R.B., other side J.S.

BARNES, WENDELL,
PO Box 272, Clinton, MT 59825, Phone: 406-825-0908
  Specialties: Working straight knives. **Patterns:** Hunters, folders, neck knives. **Technical:** Grinds 440C, ATS-34, D2 and Damascus. **Prices:** Start at $75. **Remarks:** Spare-time maker; first knife sold in 1996. **Mark:** First initial and last name around broken heart.

BARNES, WILLIAM,
591 Barnes Rd, Wallingford, CT 06492-1805, Phone: 860-349-0443

BARNES JR., CECIL C.,
141 Barnes Dr, Center Ridge, AR 72027, Phone: 501-893-2267

BARNETT, BRUCE,
PO Box 447, Mundaring 6073, Western Australia, Phone: 61-8-92955502, bruce@barnettcustomknives.com; web: www.barnettcustomknives.com
  Specialties: Most types of fixed blades, folders, carving sets. **Patterns:** Hunters, Bowies, Camp Knives, Fighters, Lockback and Slipjoint Folders. **Prices:** $175 up **Remarks:** Part time maker. Member Australian Knifemakers Guild and American Bladesmith Society. **Mark:** Barnett

BARNETT, VAN,
BARNETT INT'L INC, 1135 Terminal Way Ste #209, Reno, NV 89502, Phone: 304-727-5512, artknife@suddenlink.net; Web: www.VanBarnett.com
  Specialties: Collector grade one-of-a-kind / embellished high art daggers and art folders. **Patterns:** Art daggers and folders. **Technical:** Forges and grinds own Damascus. **Prices:** Upscale. **Remarks:** Designs and makes one-of-a-kind highly embellished art knives using high karat gold, diamonds and other gemstones, pearls, stone and fossil ivories, carved steel guards and blades, all knives are carved and or engraved, does own engraving, carving and other embellishments, sole authorship; full-time maker since 1981. Does one high art collaboration a year with Dellana. Member of ABS. Member Art Knife Invitational Group (AKI) **Mark:** V. H. Barnett or Van Barnett in script.

BARR, A.T.,
153 Madonna Dr, Nicholasville, KY 40356, Phone: 859-887-5400, Web: www.customknives.com
  Specialties: Fine gent's user and collector grade LinerLock® folders and sheath knives. **Patterns:** LinerLock® folders and sheath knives. **Technical:** Flat grinds S30V, ATS-34, D2 commercial Damascus; all knives have a hand rubbed satin finish. Does all leather work. **Prices:** Start at $250 for folders and $200 for sheath knives. **Remarks:** Full-time maker, first knife sold in 1979. Knifemakers' Guild voting member. "Don't you buy no ugly knife." **Mark:** Full name.

BARR, JUDSON C.,
1905 Pickwick Circle, Irving, TX 75060, Phone: 972-790-7195, judsonbarrknives@yahoo.com
  Specialties: Bowies. **Patterns:** Sheffield and Early American. **Technical:** Forged carbon steel and Damascus. Also stock removal. **Remarks:** Journeyman member of ABS. **Mark:** Barr.

BARRETT, CECIL TERRY,
2514 Linda Lane, Colorado Springs, CO 80909, Phone: 719-473-8325
  Specialties: Working and using straight knives and folders of his design, to customer specs and in standard patterns. **Patterns:** Bowies, hunters, kitchen knives, locking folders and slip-joint folders. **Technical:** Grinds 440C, D2 and ATS-34. Wood and leather sheaths. **Prices:** $65 to $500; some to $750. **Remarks:** Full-time maker. **Mark:** Stamped middle name.

BARRETT, RICK L. (TOSHI HISA),
18943 CR 18, Goshen, IN 46528, Phone: 574-533-4297, barrettrick@hotmail.com
  Specialties: Japanese-style blades from sushi knives to katana and fantasy pieces. **Patterns:** Swords, axes, spears/lances, hunter and utility knives. **Technical:** Forges and grinds Damascus and carbon steels, occasionally uses stainless. **Prices:** $250 to $4000+. **Remarks:** Full-time bladesmith, jeweler. **Mark:** Japanese mei on Japanese pieces and stylized initials.

BARRON, BRIAN,
123 12th Ave, San Mateo, CA 94402, Phone: 650-341-2683
Specialties: Traditional straight knives. **Patterns:** Daggers, hunters and swords. **Technical:** Grinds 440C, ATS-34 and 1095. Sculpts bolsters using an S-curve. **Prices:** $130 to $270; some to $1500. **Remarks:** Part-time maker; first knife sold in 1993. **Mark:** Diamond Drag "Barron."

BARRY, SCOTT,
Box 354, Laramie, WY 82073, Phone: 307-721-8038, scottyb@uwyo.edu
Specialties: Currently producing mostly folders, also make fixed blade hunters & fillet knives. **Technical:** Steels used are 440/C, ATS/34, 154/CM, S30V, Damasteel & Mike Norris stainless Damascus. **Prices:** Range from $300 $1000. **Remarks:** Part-time maker. First knife sold in 1972. **Mark:** DSBarry, etched on blade.

BARRY III, JAMES J.,
115 Flagler Promenade No., West Palm Beach, FL 33405, Phone: 561-832-4197
Specialties: High-art working straight knives of his design also high art tomahawks. **Patterns:** Hunters, daggers and fishing knives. **Technical:** Grinds 440C only. Prefers exotic materials for handles. Most knives embellished with filework, carving and scrimshaw. Many pieces designed to stand unassisted. **Prices:** $500 to $10,000. **Remarks:** Part-time maker; first knife sold in 1975. Guild member (Knifemakers) since 1991. **Mark:** Branded initials as a J and B together.

BARTH, J.D.,
101 4th St, PO Box 186, Alberton, MT 59820, Phone: 406-722-4557, mtdeerhunter@blackfoot.net; Web: www.jdbarthcustomknives.com
Specialties: Working and fancy straight knives of his design. LinerLock® folders, stainless and Damascus, fully file worked, nitre bluing. **Technical:** Grinds ATS-34, 440-C, stainless and carbon Damascus. Uses variety of natural handle materials and Micarta. Likes dovetailed bolsters. Filework on most knives, full and tapered tangs. Makes custom fit sheaths for each knife. **Mark:** Name over maker, city and state.

BARTLOW, JOHN,
5078 Coffeen Ave, Sheridan, WY 82801, Phone: 307 673-4941, bartlow@bresnan.net
Specialties: Working hunters, greenriver skinners, classic capers and bird & trouts. **Technical:** ATS-34, CPM154, Damascus available on all linerlocks. **Prices:** Full-time maker, guild member from 1988. **Mark:** Bartlow, Sheridan WYO.

BARTRUG, HUGH E.,
2701 34th St N #142, St. Petersburg, FL 33713, Phone: 813-323-1136
Specialties: Inlaid straight knives and exotic folders; high-art knives and period pieces. **Patterns:** Hunters, Bowies and daggers; traditional patterns. **Technical:** Diffuses mokume. Forges 100 percent nickel, wrought iron, mosaic Damascus, shokeedo and O1 tool steel; grinds. **Prices:** $210 to $2500; some to $5000. **Remarks:** Retired maker; first knife sold in 1980. **Mark:** Ashley Forge or name.

BASKETT, BARBARA,
Custom Knives, 427 Sutzer Ck Rd, Eastview, KY 42732, Phone: 270-862-5019, baskettknives@windstream.net
Specialities: Hunters and LinerLocks. **Technical:** 440-C, CPM 154, S30V. **Prices:** $250 and up. **Mark:** B. Baskett.

BASKETT, LEE GENE,
427 Sutzer Ck. Rd., Eastview, KY 42732, Phone: 270-862-5019, Fax: Cell: 270-766-8724, baskettknives@hotmail.com Web: www.baskettknives.com
Specialties: Fancy working knives and fancy art pieces, often set up in fancy desk stands.
Patterns: Fighters, Bowies, and Surival Knives; lockback folders and liner locks along with traditional styles. Cutting competition knives.
Technical: Grinds O1, 440-c, S30V, power CPM154, CPM 4, D2, buys Damascus. Filework provided on most knives.
Prices: $250 and up.
Remarks: Part-time maker, first knife sold in 1980.
Mark: Baskett

BASSETT, DAVID J.,
P.O. Box 69-102, Glendene, Auckland 0645, NEW ZEALAND, Phone: 64 9 818 9083, Fax: 64 9 818 9013, david@customknifemaking.co.nz; Web:www.customknifemaking.co.nz
Specialties: Working/using knives. **Patterns:** Hunters, fighters, boot, skinners, tanto. **Technical:** Grinds 440C, 12C27, D2 and some Damascus via stock removal method. **Prices:** $150 to $500. **Remarks:** Part-time maker, first knife sold in 2006. Also carries range of natural and synthetic handle material, pin stock etc. for sale. **Mark:** Name over country in semi-circular design.

BATLEY, MARK S.,
PO Box 217, Wake, VA 23176, Phone: 804 776-7794

BATSON, JAMES,
176 Brentwood Lane, Madison, AL 35758
Specialties: Forged Damascus blades and fittings in collectible period pieces. **Patterns:** Integral art knives, Bowies, folders, American-styled blades and miniatures. **Technical:** Forges carbon steel and his Damascus. **Prices:** $150 to $1800; some to $4500. **Remarks:** Semi retired full-time maker; first knife sold in 1978. **Mark:** Name, bladesmith with horse's head.

BATSON, RICHARD G.,
6591 Waterford Rd, Rixeyville, VA 22737, Phone: 540-937-2318
Specialties: Military, utility and fighting knives in working and presentation grade. **Patterns:** Daggers, combat and utility knives. **Technical:** Grinds O1, 1095 and 440C. Etches and scrimshaws; offers polished, Parkerized finishes. **Prices:** $350 to $1500. **Remarks:** Semi-retired, limit production. First knife sold in 1958. **Mark:** Bat in circle, hand-signed and serial numbered.

BATTS, KEITH,
450 Manning Rd, Hooks, TX 75561, Phone: 903-277-8466, kbatts@valornet.com
Specialties: Working straight knives of his design or to customer specs. **Patterns:** Bowies, hunters, skinners, camp knives and others. **Technical:** Forges 5160 and his Damascus; offers filework. **Prices:** $245 to $895. **Remarks:** Part-time maker; first knife sold in 1988. **Mark:** Last name.

BAUCHOP, ROBERT,
PO Box 330, Munster, Kwazulu-Natal 4278, SOUTH AFRICA, Phone: +27 39 3192449
Specialties: Fantasy knives; working and using knives of his design and to customer specs. **Patterns:** Hunters, swords, utility/camp knives, diver's knives and large swords. **Technical:** Grinds Sandvick 12C27, D2, 440C. Uses South African hardwoods red ivory, wild olive, African blackwood, etc. on handles. **Prices:** $200 to $800; some to $2000. **Remarks:** Full-time maker; first knife sold in 1986. Doing business as Bauchop Custom Knives and Swords. **Mark:** Viking helmet with Bauchop (bow and chopper) crest.

BAUMGARDNER, ED,
PO Box 81, Glendale, KY 42740, Phone: 502-435-2675
Specialties: Working fixed blades, some folders. **Patterns:** Drop point and clip point hunters, fighters, small Bowies, traditional slip joint folders, lockbacks, Liner locks and art folders with gold & gemstone inlays. **Technical:** Grinds O1, 154CM, ATS-34, and Damascus likes using natural handle materials. **Prices:** $100 to $2000. **Remarks:** Part-time maker, first knife sold in 2001. **Mark:** Last name.

BAXTER, DALE,
291 County Rd 547, Trinity, AL 35673, Phone: 256-355-3626, dale@baxterknives.com
Specialties: Bowies, fighters, and hunters. **Patterns:** No patterns: all unique true customs. **Technical:** Hand forge and hand finish. Steels: 1095 and L6 for carbon blades, 1095/L6 for Damascus. **Remarks:** Full-time bladesmith and sold first knife in 1998. **Mark:** Dale Baxter (script) and J.S. on reverse.

BEAM, JOHN R.,
1310 Foothills Rd, Kalispell, MT 59901, Phone: 406-755-2593
Specialties: Classic, high-art and working straight knives of his design. **Patterns:** Bowies and hunters. **Technical:** Grinds 440C Damascus and scrap. **Prices:** $175 to $600; some to $3000. **Remarks:** Part-time maker; first knife sold in 1950. Doing business as Beam's Knives. **Mark:** Beam's Knives.

BEASLEY, GENEO,
PO Box 339, Wadsworth, NV 89442, Phone: 775-575-2584

BEATTY, GORDON H.,
121 Petty Rd, Seneca, SC 29672, Phone: 864-882-6278
Specialties: Working straight knives, some fancy. **Patterns:** Traditional patterns, mini-skinners and letter openers. **Technical:** Grinds 440C, D2 and ATS-34; makes knives one-at-a-time. **Prices:** $75 to $450. **Remarks:** Part-time maker; first knife sold in 1982. **Mark:** Name.

BEATY, ROBERT B.,
CUTLER, 1995 Big Flat Rd, Missoula, MT 59804, Phone: 406-549-1818
Specialties: Plain and fancy working knives and collector pieces; will accept custom orders. **Patterns:** Hunters, Bowies, utility, kitchen and camp knives; locking folders. **Technical:** Grinds D-2, ATS-34, Dendritie D-2, makes all tool steel Damascus, forges 1095, 5160, 52100. **Prices:** $150 to $600, some to $1100. **Remarks:** Full-time maker; first knife sold 1995. **Mark:** Stainless: First name, middle initial, last name, city and state. Carbon: Last name stamped on Ricasso.

BEAUCHAMP, GAETAN,
125 de la Rivire, Stoneham, PQ, CANADA G3C 0P6, Phone: 418-848-1914, Fax: 418-848-6859, knives@gbeauchamp.ca; Web: www.gbeauchamp.ca
Specialties: Working knives and folders of his design and to customer specs. **Patterns:** Hunters, fighters, fantasy knives. **Technical:** Grinds ATS-34, 440C, Damascus. Scrimshaws on ivory; specializes in buffalo horn and black backgrounds. Offers a variety of handle materials. **Prices:** Start at $250. **Remarks:** Full-time maker; first knife sold in 1992. **Mark:** Signature etched on blade.

BECKER, FRANZ,
AM Kreuzberg 2, 84533, Marktl/Inn, GERMANY 08678-8020
Specialties: Stainless steel knives in working sizes. **Patterns:** Semi- and full-integral knives; interframe folders. **Technical:** Grinds stainless steels; likes natural handle materials. **Prices:** $200 to $2000. **Mark:** Name, country.

BEERS, RAY,
8 Manorbrook Rd, Monkton, MD 21111, Phone: Summer 410-472-2229

BEERS, RAY,
2501 Lakefront Dr, Lake Wales, FL 33898, Phone: Winter 863-696-3036, rbknives@copper.net

BEETS, MARTY,
390 N 5th Ave, Williams Lake, BC, CANADA V2G 2G4, Phone: 250-392-7199
Specialties: Working and collectable straight knives of his own design. **Patterns:** Hunter, skinners, Bowies and utility knives. **Technical:** Grinds 440C-does all his own work including heat treating. Uses a variety of handle material specializing in exotic hardwoods, antler and horn. **Price:** $125 to $400. **Remarks:** Wife, Sandy does handmade/hand stitched sheaths. First knife sold in 1988. Business name Beets Handmade Knives.

BEGG, TODD M.,
420 169 St S, Spanaway, WA 98387, Phone: 253-531-2113, web:www.beggknives.com
Specialties: Hand rubbed satin finished 440c stainless steel. Mirror polished 426 stainless steel. Stabilized mardrone wood.

BEHNKE, WILLIAM,
8478 Dell Rd, Kingsley, MI 49649, Phone: 231-263-7447, bill@billbehnkeknives.com Web: www.billbehnkeknives.com
Specialties: Hunters, belt knives, folders, hatchets and tomahawks. **Patterns:** Traditional styling in moderate-sized straight and folding knives. **Technical:** Forges own Damascus, W-2 and CRU Forge V. **Prices:** $150 to $2000. **Remarks:** Part-time maker. **Mark:** Bill Behnke Knives.

BELL, DON,
Box 98, Lincoln, MT 59639, Phone: 406-362-3208, dlb@linctel.net
Patterns: Folders, hunters and custom orders. **Technical:** Carbon steel 52100, 5160, 1095, 1084. Making own Damascus. Flat grinds. Natural handle material including fossil. ivory, pearl, & ironwork. **Remarks:** Full-time maker. First knife sold in 1999. **Mark:** Last name.

BELL, DONALD,
2 Division St, Bedford, Nova Scotia, CANADA B4A 1Y8, Phone: 902-835-2623, donbell@accesswave.ca; Web: www.bellknives.com
Specialties: Fancy knives: carved and pierced folders of his own design. **Patterns:** Locking folders, pendant knives, jewelry knives. **Technical:** Grinds Damascus, pierces and carves blades. **Prices:** $500 to $2000, some to $3000. **Remarks:** Spare-time maker; first knife sold in 1993. **Mark:** Bell symbol with first initial inside.

BELL, MICHAEL,
88321 N Bank Lane, Coquille, OR 97423, Phone: 541-396-3605, michael@dragonflyforge.com; Web: www. Dragonflyforge.com
Specialties: Full line of combat quality Japanese swords. **Patterns:** Traditional tanto to katana. **Technical:** Handmade steel and welded cable. **Prices:** Swords from bare blades to complete high art $1500 to $28,000. **Remarks:** Studied with Japanese master Nakajima Muneyoshi. Instruction in sword crafts. Working in partnership with son, Gabriel. **Mark:** Dragonfly in shield or tombo kunimitsu.

BELL, TONY,
PO Box 24, Woodland, AL 36280, Phone: 256-449-2655, tbell905@aol.com
Specialties: Hand forged period knives and tomahawks. Art knives and knives made for everyday use. **Technical:** Makes own Damascus. Forges 1095, 5160,1080,L6 steels. Does own heat treating. **Prices:** $75-$1200. **Remarks:** Full time maker. **Mark:** Bell symbol with initial T in the middle.

BENDIK, JOHN,
7076 Fitch Rd, Olmsted Falls, OH 44138

BENJAMIN JR., GEORGE,
3001 Foxy Ln, Kissimmee, FL 34746, Phone: 407-846-7259
Specialties: Fighters in various styles to include Persian, Moro and military. **Patterns:** Daggers, skinners and one-of-a-kind grinds. **Technical:** Forges O1, D2, A2, 5160 and Damascus. Favors Pakkawood, Micarta, and mirror or Parkerized finishes. Makes unique para-military leather sheaths. **Prices:** $150 to $600; some to $1200. **Remarks:** Doing business as The Leather Box. **Mark:** Southern Pride Knives.

BENNETT, BRETT C,
4717 Sullivan St, Cheyenne, WY 82009, Phone: 307-220-3919, brett@bennettknives.com; Web: www.bennettknives.com
Specialties: Hand-rubbed finish on all blades. **Patterns:** Most fixed blade patterns. **Technical:** ATS-34, D-2, 1084/15N20 Damascus, 1084 forged. **Prices:** $100 and up. **Mark:** "B.C. Bennett" in script or "Bennett" stamped in script.

BENNETT, GLEN C,
5821 S Stewart Blvd, Tucson, AZ 85706

BENNETT, PETER,
PO Box 143, Engadine N.S.W. 2233, AUSTRALIA, Phone: 02-520-4975 (home), Fax: 02-528-8219 (work)
Specialties: Fancy and embellished working and using straight knives to customer specs and in standard patterns. **Patterns:** Fighters, hunters, bird/trout and fillet knives. **Technical:** Grinds 440C, ATS-34 and Damascus. Uses rare Australian desert timbers for handles. **Prices:** $90 to $500; some to $1500. **Remarks:** Full-time maker; first knife sold in 1985. **Mark:** First and middle initials, last name; country.

BENNICA, CHARLES,
11 Chemin du Salet, 34190 Moules et Baucels, FRANCE, Phone: +33 4 67 73 42 40, cbennica@bennica-knives.com; Web: www.bennica-knives.com
Specialties: Fixed blades and folding knives; the latter with slick closing mechanisms with push buttons to unlock blades. Unique handle shapes, signature to the maker. **Technical:** 416 stainless steel frames for folders and ATS-34 blades. Also specializes in Damascus.

BENSON, DON,
2505 Jackson St #112, Escalon, CA 95320, Phone: 209-838-7921
Specialties: Working straight knives of his design. **Patterns:** Axes, Bowies, tantos and hunters. **Technical:** Grinds 440C. **Prices:** $100 to $150; some to $400. **Remarks:** Spare-time maker; first knife sold in 1980. **Mark:** Name.

BENTLEY, C L,
2405 Hilltop Dr, Albany, GA 31707, Phone: 912-432-6656

BER, DAVE,
656 Miller Rd, San Juan Island, WA 98250, Phone: 206-378-7230
Specialties: Working straight and folding knives for the sportsman; welcomes customer designs. **Patterns:** Hunters, skinners, Bowies, kitchen and fishing knives. **Technical:** Forges and grinds saw blade steel, wire Damascus, O1, L6, 5160 and 440C. **Prices:** $100 to $300; some to $500. **Remarks:** Full-time maker; first knife sold in 1985. **Mark:** Last name.

BERG, LOTHAR,
37 Hillcrest Ln, Kitchener ON, CANADA NZK 1S9, Phone: 519-745-3260; 519-745-3260

BERGER, MAX A.,
5716 John Richard Ct, Carmichael, CA 95608, Phone: 916-972-9229, bergerknives@aol.com
Specialties: Fantasy and working/using straight knives of his design. **Patterns:** Fighters, hunters and utility/camp knives. **Technical:** Grinds ATS-34 and 440C. Offers fileworks and combinations of mirror polish and satin finish blades. **Prices:** $200 to $600; some to $2500. **Remarks:** Part-time maker; first knife sold in 1992. **Mark:** Last name.

BERGH, ROGER,
Dalkarlsa 291, 91598 Bygdea, SWEDEN, Phone: 469-343-0061, knivroger@hotmail.com; Web: www.rogerbergh.com
Specialties: Collectible all-purpose straight-blade knives. Damascus steel blades, carving and artistic design knives are heavily influenced by nature and have an organic hand crafted feel.

BERGLIN, BRUCE D,
17441 Lake Terrace Place, Mount Vernon, WA 98274, Phone: 360-422-8603, bruce@berglins.com
Specialties: Working and using fixed blades and folders of his own design. **Patterns:** Hunters, boots, bowies, utility, liner locks and slip joints some with vintage finish. **Technical:** Forges carbon steel, grinds carbon steel. Prefers natural handle material. **Prices:** Start at $300. **Remarks:** Part-time maker since 1998. **Mark:** First initial, middle initial and last name, surrounded with an oval.

BERTOLAMI, JUAN CARLOS,
Av San Juan 575, Neuquen, ARGENTINA 8300, fliabertolami@infovia.com.ar
Specialties: Hunting and country labor knives. All of them unique high quality pieces and supplies collectors too. **Technical:** Austrian stainless steel and elephant, hippopotamus and orca ivory, as well as ebony and other fine woods for the handles.

BERTUZZI, ETTORE,
Via Partigiani 3, 24068 Seriate (Bergamo), ITALY, Phone: 035-294262, Fax: 035-294262
Specialties: Classic straight knives and folders of his design, to customer specs and in standard patterns. **Patterns:** Bowies, hunters and locking folders. **Technical:** Grinds ATS-34, D3, D2 and various Damascus. **Prices:** $300 to $500. **Remarks:** Part-time maker; first knife sold in 1993. **Mark:** Name etched on ricasso.

BESEDICK, FRANK E,
195 Stillwagon Rd, Ruffsdale, PA 15679, Phone: 724-696-3312, bxtr.bez3@verizon.net
Specialties: Traditional working and using straight knives of his design. **Patterns:** Hunters, utility/camp knives and miniatures; buckskinner blades and tomahawks. **Technical:** Forges and grinds 5160, O1 and Damascus. Offers filework and scrimshaw. **Prices:** $75 to $300; some to $750. **Remarks:** Part-time maker; first knife sold in 1990. **Mark:** Name or initials.

BESHARA, BRENT (BESH),
207 Cedar St, PO Box 1046, Stayner, Ont., CANADA L0M 1S0, Phone: 705-428-3152, beshknives@sympatico.ca; Web: www.beshknives.com
Specialties: Tactical fighting fixed knives. **Patterns:** Tantos, fighters, neck and custom designs. **Technical:** Grinds 0-1, L6 and stainless upon request. Offers Kydex sheaths, does own Paragon heat treating. **Prices:** Start at $150. **Remarks:** Inventor of Besh wedge™. Part-time maker. Active serving military bomb disposal driver. **Mark:** "BESH" stamped.

BEST, RON,
1489 Adams Lane, Stokes, NC 27884, Phone: 252-714-1264, ronbestknives@msn.com; Web: www.ronbestknives.com
Specialties: All integral fixed blades, interframe. **Patterns:** Bowies, hunters, fighters, fantasy, daggers & swords. **Technical:** Grinds 440C, D-2 and ATS-34. **Prices:** $600 to $8000.

BETANCOURT, ANTONIO L.,
5718 Beefwood Ct., St. Louis, MO 63129, Phone: 314-306-1869, bet2001@charter.net
Specialties: One-of-a-kind fixed blades and art knives. **Patterns:** Hunters and Bowies with embellished handles. **Technical:** Uses cast sterling silver and lapidary with fine gemstones, fossil ivory, and scrimshaw. Grinds Damascus and 440C. **Prices:** $100 to $800. **Remarks:** Part-time maker, first knife sold in 1974. **Mark:** Initials in cursive.

BEUKES, TINUS,
83 Henry St, Risiville, Vereeniging 1939, SOUTH AFRICA, Phone: 27 16 423 2053
Specialties: Working straight knives. **Patterns:** Hunters, skinners and kitchen knives. **Technical:** Grinds D2, 440C and chain, cable and stainless Damascus. **Prices:** $80 to $180. **Remarks:** Part-time maker; first knife sold in 1993. **Mark:** Full name, city, logo.

BEVERLY II, LARRY H,
PO Box 741, Spotsylvania, VA 22553, Phone: 540-898-3951
Specialties: Working straight knives, slip-joints and liner locks. Welcomes customer designs. **Patterns:** Bowies, hunters, guard less fighters and miniatures. **Technical:** Grinds 440C, A2 and O1. **Prices:** $125 to $1000. **Remarks:** Part-time maker; first knife sold in 1986. **Mark:** Initials or last name in script.

BEZUIDENHOUT, BUZZ,
PO BOX 28284, Malvern, KZN, SOUTH AFRICA 4055, Phone: 031-4632827, Fax: 031-4632827, buzzbee@mweb.co.za
Specialties: Working and Fancy Folders, my or customer design. **Patterns:** Boots, hunters, kitchen knives and utility/camp knives. **Technical:** Use 12-C-27 + stainless damascus, some carbon damascus. Uses local hardwoods, horn: kudu, impala, buffalo, giraffe bone and ivory for handles. **Prices:** $250 to upscale. **Remarks:** Part-time maker; first knife sold in 1985. Member S.A. Knife Makers Guild **Mark:** First name with a bee emblem.

BIGGERS, GARY,
VENTURA KNIVES, 1278 Colina Vista, Ventura, CA 93003, Phone: 805-658-6610, Fax: 805-658-6610
Specialties: Fixed blade knives of his design. **Patterns:** Hunters, boots/fighters, Bowies and utility knives. **Technical:** Grinds ATS-34, O1 and commercial Damascus. **Prices:** $150 to $550. **Remarks:** Part-time maker: first knife sold in 1996. Doing business as Ventura Knives. **Mark:** First and last name, city and state.

BILLGREN, PER,
Stallgatan 9, S815 76 Soderfors, SWEDEN, Phone: +46 293 30600, Fax: +46 293 30124, mail@damasteel.se Web:www.damasteel.se
Specialties: Damasteel, stainless Damascus steels. **Patterns:** Bluetongue, Heimskringla, Muhammad's ladder, Rose, Twist, Odin's eye, Vinland, Hakkapelliitta. **Technical:** Modern Damascus steel made by patented powder metallurgy method. **Prices:** $80 to $180. **Remarks:** Damasteel is available through distributors around the globe.

BIRDWELL, IRA LEE,
PO Box 1448, Congress, AZ 85332, Phone: 928-925-3258, heli.ira@gmail.com
Specialties: Special orders. **Mark:** Engraved signature.

BIRNBAUM, EDWIN,
9715 Hamocks Blvd I 206, Miami, FL 33196

BISH, HAL,
9347 Sweetbriar Trace, Jonesboro, GA 30236, Phone: 770-477-2422, halbish@hp.com

BISHER, WILLIAM (BILL),
1015 Beck Road, Denton, NC 27239, Phone: 336-859-4686, blackturtleforge@wildblue.net; Web: www.blackturtleforge.com
Specialties: Period pieces, also contemporary belt knives, friction folders. **Patterns:** Own design, hunters, camp/utility, Bowies, belt axes, neck knives, carving sets. **Technical:** Forges straight high carbon steels, and own Damascus, grinds ATS34 and 154CM. Uses natural handle materials (wood, bone, staghorn), micarta and stabilized wood. **Prices:** Starting at $75 - $2500. **Remarks:** President North Carolina Custom Knifemakers Guild, member ABS, Full-time maker as of 2007, first knife made 1989, all work in house, blades and sheaths **Mark:** Last name under crown and turtle

BIZZELL, ROBERT,
145 Missoula Ave, Butte, MT 59701, Phone: 406-782-4403, patternweld@yahoo.com
Specialties: Damascus Bowies. **Patterns:** Composite, mosaic and traditional. **Technical:** Fixed blades & LinerLock® folders. **Prices:** Fixed blades start at $275. Folders start at $500. **Remarks:** Currently not taking orders. **Mark:** Hand signed.

BLACK, EARL,
3466 South, 700 East, Salt Lake City, UT 84106, Phone: 801-466-8395
Specialties: High-art straight knives and folders; period pieces. **Patterns:** Boots, Bowies and daggers; lockers and gents. **Technical:** Grinds 440C and 154CM. Buys some Damascus. Scrimshaws and engraves. **Prices:** $200 to $1800; some to $2500 and higher. **Remarks:** Full-time maker; first knife sold in 1980. **Mark:** Name, city, state.

BLACK, SCOTT,
27100 Leetown Rd, Picayune, MS 39466, Phone: 601-799-5939, copperheadforge@telepak.net
Specialties: Friction folders; fighters. **Patterns:** Bowies, fighters, hunters, smoke hawks, friction folders, daggers. **Technical:** All forged, all work done by him, own hand-stitched leather work; own heat-treating. **Prices:** $100 to $2200. **Remarks:** ABS Journeyman Smith. Cabel / Damascus/ High Carbone. **Mark:** Hot Mark - Copperhead Snake.

BLACK, SCOTT,
570 Malcom Rd, Covington, GA 30209
Specialties: Working/using folders of his design. **Patterns:** Daggers, hunters, utility/camp knives and friction folders. **Technical:** Forges pattern welded, cable, 1095, O1 and 5160. **Prices:** $100 to $500. **Remarks:** Part-time maker; first knife sold in 1992. Doing business as Copperhead Forge. **Mark:** Hot mark on blade, copperhead snake.

BLACK, TOM,
921 Grecian NW, Albuquerque, NM 87107, Phone: 505-344-2549, blackknives@comcast.net
Specialties: Working knives to fancy straight knives of his design. **Patterns:** Drop-point skinners, folders, using knives, Bowies and daggers. **Technical:** Grinds 440C, 154CM, ATS-34, A2, D2 and Damascus. Offers engraving and scrimshaw. **Prices:** $250 and up; some over $8500. **Remarks:** Full-time maker; first knife sold in 1970. **Mark:** Name, city.

BLACKWELL, ZANE,
PO BOX 234, Eden, TX 76837, Phone: 325-869-8821, blackwellknives@hotmail.com
Specialties: Hunters and slipjoint folders. **Patterns:** Drop point fixed-blade hunter and classic slipjoint patterns. **Prices:** Hunters start at $200, folders at $250. **Mark:** Name and Eden, Texas.

BLACKWOOD, NEIL,
7032 Willow Run, Lakeland, FL 33813, Phone: 863-701-0126, neil@blackwoodknives.com; Web: www.blackwoodknives.com
Specialties: Fixed blades and folders. **Technical:** Blade steels D2 Talonite, Stellite, CPM S30V and RWL 34. Handle materials: G-10 carbon fiber and Micarta in the synthetics: giraffe bone and exotic woods on the natural side. **Remarks:** Makes everything from the frames to the stop pins, pivot pins: everything but the stainless screws; one factory/custom collaboration (the Hybrid Hunter) with Outdoor Edge is in place and negotiations are under way for one with Benchmade.

BLANCHARD, G R (GARY),
1208 Ariell Lea, Sevierville, TN 37862, Phone: 865-908-7466, Fax: 865-908-7466, blanchardscutlery@yahoo.com; Web: www.blanchardscutlery.com
Specialties: Fancy folders with patented button blade release and high-art straight knives of his design. **Patterns:** Boots, daggers and locking folders. **Technical:** Grinds 440C and ATS-34 and Damascus. Engraves his knives. **Prices:** $1500 to $18,000 or more. **Remarks:** Full-time maker; first knife sold in 1989. **Mark:** First and middle initials, last name or last name only.

BLAUM, ROY,
319 N Columbia St, Covington, LA 70433, Phone: 985-893-1060
Specialties: Working straight knives and folders of his design; lightweight easy-open folders. **Patterns:** Hunters, boots, fishing and woodcarving/whittling knives. **Technical:** Grinds A2, D2, O1, 154CM and ATS-34. Offers leatherwork. **Prices:** $40 to $800; some higher. **Remarks:** Full-time maker; first knife sold in 1976. **Mark:** Engraved signature or etched logo.

BLOODWORTH CUSTOM KNIVES,
3502 W. Angelica Dr., Meridian, ID 83646, Phone: 208-888-7778
Patterns: Working straight knives, hunters, skinners, bowies, utility knives of his designs or customer specs. Scagel knives. Period knives and traditional frontier knives and sheaths. **Technical:** Grinds D2, ATS34, 154CM, 5160, 01, Damascus, Heat treats, natural and composite handle materials. **Prices:** $185.00 to $1,500. **Remarks:** Roger Smith knife maker. Full-time maker; first knife sold in 1978 **Mark:** Sword over BLOODWORTH.

BLOOMER, ALAN T,
PO Box 154, 116 E 6th St, Maquon, IL 61458, Phone: 309-875-3583, alant.bloomer@winco.net
Specialties: Folders & straight knives & custom pen maker. **Patterns:** All kinds. **Technical:** Does own heat treating. **Prices:** $400 to $1000. **Remarks:** Part-time maker. No orders. **Mark:** Stamp Bloomer.

BLUM, CHUCK,
743 S Brea Blvd #10, Brea, CA 92621, Phone: 714-529-0484
Specialties: Art and investment daggers and Bowies. **Technical:** Flat-grinds; hollow-grinds 440C, ATS-34 on working knives. **Prices:** $125 to $8500. **Remarks:** Part-time maker; first knife sold in 1985. **Mark:** First and middle initials and last name with sailboat logo.

BLUM, KENNETH,
1729 Burleson, Brenham, TX 77833, Phone: 979-836-9577
Specialties: Traditional working straight knives of his design. **Patterns:** Camp knives, hunters and Bowies. **Technical:** Forges 5160; grinds 440C and D2. Uses exotic woods and Micarta for handles. **Prices:** $150 to $300. **Remarks:** Part-time maker; first knife sold in 1978. **Mark:** Last name on ricasso.

BOARDMAN, GUY,
39 Mountain Ridge R, New Germany 3619, SOUTH AFRICA, Phone: 031-726-921
Specialties: American and South African-styles. **Patterns:** Bowies, American and South African hunters, plus more. **Technical:** Grinds Bohler steels, some ATS-34. **Prices:** $100 to $600. **Remarks:** Part-time maker; first knife sold in 1986. **Mark:** Name, city, country.

BOCHMAN, BRUCE,
183 Howard Place, Grants Pass, OR 97526, Phone: 541-471-1985, 183bab@echoweb.net
Specialties: Hunting, fishing, bird and tactical knives. **Patterns:** Hunters, fishing and bird knives. **Technical:** ATS34, 154CM, mirror or satin finish. **Prices:** $250 to $350; some to $750. **Remarks:** Part-time maker; first knife sold in 1977. **Mark:** Hand made by B. Bochman.

BODEN, HARRY,
Via Gellia Mill, Bonsall Matlock, Derbyshire DE4 2AJ, ENGLAND, Phone: 0629-825176
Specialties: Traditional working straight knives and folders of his design. **Patterns:** Hunters, locking folders and utility/camp knives. **Technical:** Grinds Sandvik 12C27, D2 and O1. **Prices:** £70 to £150; some to £300. **Remarks:** Full-time maker; first knife sold in 1986. **Mark:** Full name.

BODNER, GERALD "JERRY",
4102 Spyglass Ct, Louisville, KY 40229, Phone: 502-968-5946
Specialties: Fantasy straight knives in standard patterns. **Patterns:** Bowies, fighters, hunters and micro-miniature knives. **Technical:** Grinds Damascus, 440C and D2. Offers filework. **Prices:** $35 to $180. **Remarks:** Part-time maker; first knife sold in 1993. **Mark:** Last name in script and JAB in oval above knives.

BODOLAY, ANTAL,
Rua Wilson Soares Fernandes #31, Planalto, Belo Horizonte MG-31730-700, BRAZIL, Phone: 031-494-1885
Specialties: Working folders and fixed blades of his design or to customer specs; some art daggers and period pieces. **Patterns:** Daggers, hunters, locking folders, utility knives and Khukris. **Technical:** Grinds D6, high-carbon steels and 420 stainless. Forges files on request. **Prices:** $30 to $350. **Remarks:** Full-time maker; first knife sold in 1965. **Mark:** Last name in script.

BOEHLKE, GUENTER,
Parkstrasse 2, 56412 Grossholbach, GERMANY 2602-5440, Boehlke-Messer@t-online.de; Web: www.boehlke-messer.de
Specialties: Classic working/using straight knives of his design. **Patterns:** Hunters, utility/camp knives and ancient remakes. **Technical:** Grinds Damascus, CPM-T-440V and 440C. Inlays gemstones and ivory. **Prices:** $220 to $700; some to $2000. **Remarks:** Spare-time maker; first knife sold in 1985. **Mark:** Name, address and bow and arrow.

BOGUSZEWSKI, PHIL,
PO Box 99329, Lakewood, WA 98499, Phone: 253-581-7096, knives01@aol.com
Specialties: Working folders—some fancy—mostly of his design. **Patterns:** Folders, slip-joints and lockers; also makes anodized titanium frame folders. **Technical:** Grinds BG42 and Damascus; offers filework. **Prices:** $550 to $3000. **Remarks:** Full-time maker; first knife sold in 1979. **Mark:** Name, city and state.

BOJTOS, ARPAD,
Dobsinskeho 10, 98403 Lucenec, SLOVAKIA, Phone: 00421-47 4333512, botjos@stonline.sk; Web: www.arpadbojtos.sk
Specialties: Art knives. **Patterns:** Daggers, fighters and hunters. **Technical:** Grinds ATS-34. Carves on steel, handle materials and sheaths. **Prices:** $5000 to $10,000; some over. **Remarks:** Full-time maker; first knife sold in 1990. **Mark:** AB.

BOLEWARE, DAVID,
PO Box 96, Carson, MS 39427, Phone: 601-943-5372
Specialties: Traditional and working/using straight knives of his design, to customer specs and in standard patterns. **Patterns:** Bowies, hunters and utility/camp knives. **Technical:** Grinds ATS-34, 440C and Damascus. **Prices:** $85 to $350; some to $600. **Remarks:** Part-time maker; first knife sold in 1989. **Mark:** First and last name, city, state.

BOLEY, JAMIE,
PO Box 477, Parker, SD 57053, Phone: 605-297-0014, jamie@polarbearforge.com
Specialties: Working knives and historical influenced reproductions. **Patterns:** Hunters, skinners, scramasaxes, and others. **Technical:** Forges 5160, O1, L6, 52100, W1, W2 makes own Damascus. **Prices:** Starts at $125. **Remarks:** Part-time maker. **Mark:** Polar bear paw print with name on the left side and Polar Bear Forge on the right.

BONASSI, FRANCO,
Via Nicoletta 4, Pordenone 33170, ITALY, Phone: 0434-550821, frank.bonassi@alice.it
Specialties: Fancy and working one-of-a-kind folder knives of his design. **Patterns:** Folders, linerlocks and back locks. **Technical:** Grinds CPM, ATS-34, 154CM and commercial Damascus. Uses only titanium foreguards and pommels. **Prices:** Start at $350. **Remarks:** Spare-time maker; first knife sold in 1988. Has made cutlery for several celebrities; Gen. Schwarzkopf, Fuzzy Zoeller, etc. **Mark:** FRANK.

BOOCO, GORDON,
175 Ash St, PO Box 174, Hayden, CO 81639, Phone: 970-276-3195
Specialties: Fancy working straight knives of his design and to customer specs. **Patterns:** Hunters and Bowies. **Technical:** Grinds 440C, D2 and A2. Heat-treats. **Prices:** $150 to $350; some $600 and higher. **Remarks:** Part-time maker; first knife sold in 1984. **Mark:** Last name with push dagger artwork.

BOOS, RALPH,
6018-37A Avenue NW, Edmonton, Alberta, CANADA T6L 1H4, Phone: 780-463-7094
Specialties: Classic, fancy and fantasy miniature knives and swords of his design or to customer specs. **Patterns:** Bowies, daggers and swords. **Technical:** Hand files O1, stainless and Damascus. Engraves and carves. Does heat bluing and acid etching. **Prices:** $125 to $350; some to $1000. **Remarks:** Part-time maker; first knife sold in 1982. **Mark:** First initials back to back.

BOOTH, PHILIP W,
301 S Jeffery Ave, Ithaca, MI 48847, Phone: 989-875-2844, Web: wwwphilipbooth.com
Specialties: Folding knives of his design using various mechanisms. **Patterns:** "Minnow" folding knives, a series of small folding knives started in 1996 and changing yearly. One of a kind hot-rod car themed folding knives. **Technical:** Grinds ATS-34, 1095 and commercial Damascus. Offers gun blue finishes and file work. **Prices:** $200 and up. **Remarks:** Part-time maker, first knife sold in 1991. **Mark:** Last name or name with city and map logo.

BORGER, WOLF,
Benzstrasse 8, 76676 Graben-Neudorf, GERMANY, Phone: 07255-72303, Fax: 07255-72304, wolf@messerschmied.de; Web: www.messerschmied.de
Specialties: High-tech working and using straight knives and folders, many with corkscrews or other tools, of his design. **Patterns:** Hunters, Bowies and folders with various locking systems. **Technical:** Grinds 440C, ATS-34 and CPM. Uses stainless Damascus. **Prices:** $250 to $900; some to $1500. **Remarks:** Full-time maker; first knife sold in 1975. **Mark:** Howling wolf and name; first name on Damascus blades.

BOSE, REESE,
PO Box 61, Shelburn, IN 47879, Phone: 812-397-5114
Specialties: Traditional working and using knives in standard patterns and multi-blade folders. **Patterns:** Multi-blade slip-joints. **Technical:** ATS-34, D2 and CPM 440V. **Prices:** $275 to $1500. **Remarks:** Full-time maker; first knife sold in 1992. Photos by Jack Busfield. **Mark:** R. Bose.

BOSE, TONY,
7252 N. County Rd, 300 E., Shelburn, IN 47879-9778, Phone: 812-397-5114
Specialties: Traditional working and using knives in standard patterns; multi-blade folders. **Patterns:** Multi-blade slip-joints. **Technical:** Grinds commercial Damascus, ATS-34 and D2. **Prices:** $400 to $1200. **Remarks:** Full-time maker; first knife sold in 1972. **Mark:** First initial, last name, city, state.

BOSSAERTS, CARL,
Rua Albert Einstein 906, 14051-110, Ribeirao Preto, S.P., BRAZIL, Phone: 016 633 7063
Specialties: Working and using straight knives of his design, to customer specs and in standard patterns. **Patterns:** Hunters, fighters and utility/camp knives. **Technical:** Grinds ATS-34, 440V and 440C; does filework. **Prices:** 60 to $400. **Remarks:** Part-time maker; first knife sold in 1992. **Mark:** Initials joined together.

BOST, ROGER E,
30511 Cartier Dr, Palos Verdes, CA 90275-5629, Phone: 310- 541-6833, rogerbost@cox.net
Specialties: Hunters, fighters, boot, utility. **Patterns:** Loveless-style. **Technical:** ATS-34, 60-61RC, stock removal and forge. **Prices:** $300 and up. **Remarks:** First knife sold in 1990. Cal. Knifemakers Assn., ABS. **Mark:** Diamond with initials inside and Palos Verdes California around outside.

BOSWORTH, DEAN,
329 Mahogany Dr, Key Largo, FL 33037, Phone: 305-451-1564, DLBOZ@bellsouth.net
Specialties: Free hand hollow ground working knives with hand rubbed satin finish, filework and inlays. **Patterns:** Bird and Trout, hunters, skinners, fillet, Bowies, miniatures. **Technical:** Using 440C, ATS-34, D2, Meier Damascus, custom wet formed sheaths. **Prices:** $250 and up. **Remarks:** Part-time maker; first knife made in 1985. Member Florida Knifemakers Assoc. **Mark:** BOZ stamped in block letters.

BOURBEAU, JEAN YVES,
15 Rue Remillard, Notre Dame, Ile Perrot, Quebec, CANADA J7V 8M9, Phone: 514-453-1069
Specialties: Fancy/embellished and fantasy folders of his design. **Patterns:** Bowies, fighters and locking folders. **Technical:** Grinds 440C, ATS-34 and Damascus. Carves precious wood for handles. **Prices:** $150 to $1000. **Remarks:** Part-time maker; first knife sold in 1994. **Mark:** Interlaced initials.

BOWLES, CHRIS,
PO Box 985, Reform, AL 35481, Phone: 205-375-6162
Specialties: Working/using straight knives, and period pieces. **Patterns:** Utility, tactical, hunting, neck knives, machetes, and swords. **Grinds:** 0-1, 154 cm, BG-42, 440V. **Prices:** $50 to $400 some higher. **Remarks:** Full-time maker. **Mark:** Bowles stamped or Bowles etched in script.

BOXER, BO,
LEGEND FORGE, 6477 Hwy 93 S #134, Whitefish, MT 59937, Phone: 505-799-0173, legendforge@aol.com; Web: www.legendforgesknives.com
Specialties: Handmade hunting knives, Damascus hunters. Most are antler handled. Also, hand forged Damascus steel. **Patterns:** Hunters and Bowies. **Prices:** $125 to $2500 on some very exceptional Damascus knives. **Remarks:** Makes his own custom leather sheath stamped with maker stamp. His knives are used by the outdoorsman of the Smoky Mountains, North Carolina, and the Rockies of Montana and New Mexico. Spends one-half of the year in Montana and the other part of the year in Taos, New Mexico. **Mark:** The name "Legend Forge" hand engraved on every blade.

BOYD, FRANCIS,
1811 Prince St, Berkeley, CA 94703, Phone: 510-841-7210
Specialties: Folders and kitchen knives, Japanese swords. **Patterns:** Push-button sturdy locking folders; San Francisco-style chef's knives. **Technical:** Forges and grinds; mostly uses high-carbon steels. **Prices:** Moderate to heavy. **Remarks:** Designer. **Mark:** Name.

BOYE, DAVID,
PO Box 1238, Dolan Springs, AZ 86441, Phone: 800-853-1617, Fax: 928-767-4273, boye@cltlink.net; Web: www.boyeknives.com
Specialties: Folders and Boye Basics. Forerunner in the use of dendritic steel and dendritic cobalt for blades. **Patterns:** Lockback folders and fixed blade sheath knives in cobalt. **Technical:** Casts blades in cobalt. **Prices:** From $129 to $360. **Remarks:** Part-time maker; author of *Step-by-Step Knifemaking*. **Mark:** Name.

BOYER, MARK,
10515 Woodinville Dr #17, Bothell, WA 98011, Phone: 206-487-9370, boyerbl@mail.eskimo.com
Specialties: High-tech and working/using straight knives of his design. **Patterns:** Fighters and utility/camp knives. **Technical:** Grinds 1095 and D2. Offers Kydex sheaths; heat-treats. **Prices:** $45 to $120. **Remarks:** Part-time maker; first knife sold in 1994. Doing business as Boyer Blades. **Mark:** Eagle holding two swords with name.

BOYES, TOM,
731 Jean Ct, Addison, WI 53002, Phone: 262-391-2172
Specialties: Hunters, working knives. **Technical:** Grinds ATS-34, 440C, O1 tool steel and Damascus. **Prices:** $60 to $1000. **Remarks:** First knife sold in 1998. Doing business as R. Boyes Knives.

BOYSEN, RAYMOND A,
125 E St Patrick, Rapid Ciy, SD 57701, Phone: 605-341-7752
Specialties: Hunters and Bowies. **Technical:** High performance blades forged from 52100 and 5160. **Prices:** $200 and up. **Remarks:** American Bladesmith Society Journeyman Smith. Part-time bladesmith. **Mark:** BOYSEN.

BRACK, DOUGLAS D,
1591 Los Angeles Ave #8, Ventura, CA 93004, Phone: 805-659-1505
Specialties: Fighters, daggers, boots, Bowies. **Patterns:** One of a kind. **Technical:** Grinds 440-ATS, own Damascus. **Prices:** $300 to $3000. **Remarks:** Full-time maker; first knife sold in 1984. **Mark:** tat.

BRADBURN, GARY,
BRADBURN CUSTOM CUTLERY, 1714 Park Place, Wichita, KS 67203, Phone: 316-640-5684, gary@bradburnknives.com; Web:www.bradburnknives.com
Specialties: Specialize in clay-tempered Japanese-style knives and swords. **Patterns:** Also Bowies and fighters. **Technical:** Forge and/or grind carbon steel only. **Prices:** $150 to $1200. **Mark:** Initials GB stylized to look like Japanese character.

BRADFORD, GARRICK,
582 Guelph St, Kitchener ON, CANADA N2H-5Y4, Phone: 519-576-9863

BRADLEY, DENNIS,
178 Bradley Acres Rd, Blairsville, GA 30512, Phone: 706-745-4364
Specialties: Working straight knives and folders, some high-art. **Patterns:** Hunters, boots and daggers; slip-joints and two-blades. **Technical:** Grinds ATS-34, D2, 440C and commercial Damascus. **Prices:** $100 to $500; some to $2000. **Remarks:** Part-time maker; first knife sold in 1973. **Mark:** BRADLEY KNIVES in double heart logo.

BRADLEY, JOHN,
PO Box 33, Pomona Park, FL 32181, Phone: 386-649-4739, johnbradleyknives@yahoo.com
Specialties: Fixed-blade using and art knives; primitive folders. **Patterns:** Skinners, Bowies, camp knives and primitive knives. **Technical:** Forged and ground 52100, 1095, O1 and Damascus. **Prices:** $250 to $2000. **Remarks:** Full-time maker; first knife sold in 1988. **Mark:** Last name.

BRADSHAW, BAILEY,
PO Box 564, Diana, TX 75640, Phone: 903-968-2029, bailey@bradshawcutlery.com
Specialties: Traditional folders and contemporary front lock folders. **Patterns:** Single or multi-blade folders, Bowies. **Technical:** Grind CPM 3V, CPM 440V, CPM 420V, Forge Damascus, 52100. **Prices:** $250 to $3000. **Remarks:** Engraves, carves and does sterling silver sheaths. **Mark:** Tori arch over initials back to back.

BRANDON, MATTHEW,
4435 Meade St, Denver, CO 80211, Phone: 303-458-0786, mtbrandon@hotmail.com
Specialties: Hunters, skinners, full-tang Bowies. **Prices:** $150 to $1000. **Remarks:** Satisfaction or full refund. **Mark:** MTB.

BRANDSEY, EDWARD P,
4441 Hawkridge Ct, Janesville, WI 53546, Phone: 608-868-9010, ebrandsey@centurytel.net
Patterns: Large bowies, hunters, neck knives and buckskinner-styles. Native American influence on some. An occasional tanto, art piece. Does own scrimshaw. See Egnath's second book. Now making locking liner folders. **Technical:** ATS-34, CPM154, 440-C, 0-1, and some Damascus. Paul Bos treating past 20 years. **Prices:** $250 to $600; some to $3000. **Remarks:** Full-time maker. First knife sold in 1973. **Mark:** Initials connected - registered Wisc. Trademark since March 1983.

BRANDT, MARTIN W,
833 Kelly Blvd, Springfield, OR 97477, Phone: 541-747-5422, oubob747@aol.com

BRANTON, ROBERT,
4976 Seewee Rd, Awendaw, SC 29429, Phone: 843-928-3624
Specialties: Working straight knives of his design or to customer specs; throwing knives. **Patterns:** Hunters, fighters and some miniatures. **Technical:** Grinds ATS-34, A2 and 1050; forges 5160, O1. Offers hollow- or convex-grinds. **Prices:** $25 to $400. **Remarks:** Part-time maker; first knife sold in 1985. Doing business as Pro-Flyte, Inc. **Mark:** Last name; or first and last name, city, state.

BRASCHLER, CRAIG W.,
HC4 Box 667, Doniphan, MO 63935, Phone: 573-996-5058
Specialties: Art knives, Bowies, utility hunters, slip joints, miniatures, engraving. **Technical:** Flat grinds. Does own selective heat treating. Does own engraving. **Prices:** Starting at $200. **Remarks:** Full-time maker since 2003. **Mark:** Braschler over Martin Oval stamped.

BRATCHER, BRETT,
11816 County Rd 302, Plantersville, TX 77363, Phone: 936-894-3788, Fax: (936) 894-3790, brett_bratcher@msn.com
Specialties: Hunting and skinning knives. **Patterns:** Clip and drop point. Hand forged. **Technical:** Material 5160, D2, 1095 and Damascus. **Price:** $200 to $500. **Mark:** Bratcher.

BRAY JR., W LOWELL,
6931 Manor Beach Rd, New Port Richey, FL 34652, Phone: 727-846-0830, brayknives@aol.com
Specialties: Traditional working and using straight knives and folders of his design. **Patterns:** Hunters, fighters and utility knives. **Technical:** Grinds 440C and ATS-34; forges 52100 and Damascus. **Prices:** $125 to $800. **Remarks:** Spare-time maker; first knife sold in 1992. **Mark:** Lowell Bray Knives in shield or Bray Primative in shield.

BREED, KIM,
733 Jace Dr, Clarksville, TN 37040, Phone: 931-645-9171, sfbreed@yahoo.com
Specialties: High end through working folders and straight knives. **Patterns:** Hunters, fighters, daggers, Bowies. His design or customers. Likes one-of-a-kind designs. **Technical:** Makes own Mosiac and regular Damascus, but will use stainless steels. Offers filework and sculpted material. **Prices:** $150 to $2000. **Remarks:** Full-time maker. First knife sold in 1990. **Mark:** Last name.

BREND, WALTER,
353 Co Rd 1373, Vinemont, AL 35179, Phone: 256-739-1987, walterbrend@hotmail.com
Specialties: Tactical-style knives, fighters, automatics. **Technical:** Grinds D-Z and 440C blade steels, 154CM steel. **Prices:** Micarta handles, titanium handles.

BRENNAN, JUDSON,
PO Box 1165, Delta Junction, AK 99737, Phone: 907-895-5153, Fax: 907-895-5404
Specialties: Period pieces. **Patterns:** All kinds of Bowies, rifle knives, daggers. **Technical:** Forges miscellaneous steels. **Prices:** Upscale, good value. **Remarks:** Muzzle-loading gunsmith; first knife sold in 1978. **Mark:** Name.

BRESHEARS, CLINT,
1261 Keats, Manhattan Beach, CA 90266, Phone: 310-372-0739, Fax: 310-372-0739, breshears1@verizon.net; Web: www.clintknives.com
Specialties: Working straight knives and folders. **Patterns:** Hunters, Bowies and survival knives. Folders are mostly hunters. **Technical:** Grinds 440C, 154CM and ATS-34; prefers mirror finishes. **Prices:** $125 to $750; some to $1800. **Remarks:** Part-time maker; first knife sold in 1978. **Mark:** First name.

BREUER, LONNIE,
PO Box 877384, Wasilla, AK 99687-7384
Specialties: Fancy working straight knives. **Patterns:** Hunters, camp knives and axes, folders and Bowies. **Technical:** Grinds 440C, AEB-L and D2; likes wire inlay, scrimshaw, decorative filing. **Prices:** $60 to $150; some to $300. **Remarks:** Part-time maker; first knife sold in 1977. **Mark:** Signature.

BRITTON, TIM,
PO Box 71, Bethania, NC 27010, Phone: 366-923-2062, timbritton@yahoo.com; Web: www.timbritton.com
Specialties: Small and simple working knives, sgian dubhs, slip joint folders and special tactical designs. **Technical:** Forges and grinds stainless steel. **Prices:** $165 to ???. **Remarks:** Veteran knifemaker. **Mark:** Etched signature.

BROADWELL, DAVID,
PO Box 4314, Wichita Falls, TX 76308, Phone: 940-692-1727, Fax: 940-692-4003, david@broadwell.com; Web: www.david.broadwell.com
Specialties: Sculpted high-art straight and folding knives. **Patterns:** Daggers, sub-hilted fighters, folders, sculpted art knives and some Bowies. **Technical:** Grinds mostly Damascus; carves; prefers natural handle materials, including stone. Some embellishment. **Prices:** $350 to $3000; some higher. **Remarks:** Full-time maker; first knife sold in 1982. **Mark:** Stylized emblem bisecting "B"/with last name below.

BROCK, KENNETH L,
PO Box 375, 207 N Skinner Rd, Allenspark, CO 80510, Phone: 303-747-2547, brockknives@nedernet.net
Specialties: Custom designs, full-tang working knives and button lock folders of his design. **Patterns:** Hunters, miniatures and minis. **Technical:** Flat-grinds D2 and 440C; makes own sheaths; heat-treats. **Prices:** $75 to $800. **Remarks:** Full-time maker; first knife sold in 1978. **Mark:** Last name, city, state and serial number.

BRODZIAK, DAVID,
27 Stewart St, Albany, Western Australia, AUSTRALIA 6330, Phone: 61 8 9841 3314, Fax: 61898115065, brodziakomninet.net.au; Web: www.brodziakcustomknives.com

BROMLEY, PETER,
BROMLEY KNIVES, 1408 S Bettman, Spokane, WA 99212, Phone: 509-534-4235, Fax: 509-536-2666
Specialties: Period Bowies, folder, hunting knives; all sizes and shapes. **Patterns:** Bowies, boot knives, hunters, utility, folder, working knives. **Technical:** High-carbon steel (1084, 1095 and 5160). Stock removal and forge. **Prices:** $85 to $750. **Remarks:** Almost full-time, first knife sold in 1987. A.B.S. Journeyman Smith. **Mark:** Bromley, Spokane, WA.

BROOKER, DENNIS,
55858 260th Ave., Chariton, IA 50049, Phone: 641-862-3263, dbrooker@dbrooker.com Web: www.dbrooker.com
Specialties: Fancy straight knives and folders of his design. Obsidian and glass knives. **Patterns:** Hunters, folders and boots. **Technical:** Forges and grinds. Full-time engraver and designer; instruction available. **Prices:** Moderate to upscale. **Remarks:** Part-time maker. Takes no orders; sells only completed work. **Mark:** Name.

BROOKS, BUZZ,
2345 Yosemite Dr, Los Angles, CA 90041, Phone: 323-256-2892

BROOKS, MICHAEL,
2811 64th St, Lubbock, TX 79413, Phone: 806-799-3088, chiang@nts-online.net
Specialties: Working straight knives of his design or to customer specs. **Patterns:** Martial art, Bowies, hunters, and fighters. **Technical:** Grinds 440C, D2 and ATS-34; offers wide variety of handle materials. **Prices:** $75 & up. **Remarks:** Part-time maker; first knife sold in 1985. **Mark:** Initials.

BROOKS, STEVE R,
1610 Dunn Ave, Walkerville, MT 59701, Phone: 406-782-5114, Fax: 406-782-5114, steve@brooksmoulds.com; Web: brooksmoulds.com
Specialties: Working straight knives and folders; period pieces. **Patterns:** Hunters, Bowies and camp knives; folding lockers; axes, tomahawks and buckskinner knives; swords and stilettos. **Technical:** Damascus and mosaic Damascus. Some knives come embellished. **Prices:** $400 to $2000. **Remarks:** Full-time maker; first knife sold in 1982. **Mark:** Lazy initials.

BROOME, THOMAS A,
1212 E. Aliak Ave, Kenai, AK 99611-8205, Phone: 907-283-9128, tomlei@ptialaska.ent; Web: www.alaskanknives.com
Specialties: Working hunters and folders **Patterns:** Traditional and custom orders. **Technical:** Grinds ATS-34, BG-42, CPM-S30V. **Prices:** $175 to $350. **Remarks:** Full-time maker; first knife sold in 1979. Doing business as Thom's Custom Knives, Alaskan Man O; Steel Knives. **Mark:** Full name, city, state.

BROTHERS, DENNIS L.,
, Oneonta, AL 35121, Phone: 205-466-5193, www.brothersblades.com
Specialties: Fixed blade hunting/working knives of maker's deigns. Works with customer designed specifications. **Patterns:** Hunters, camp knives, kitchen/utility, bird, and trout. Standard patterns and customer designed. **Technical:** Stock removal. Works with stainless and tool steels. SS cryo-treatment. Hollow and flat grinds. **Prices:** $100 - $300. **Remarks:** Sole authorship knives and customer leather sheaths. Part-time maker. **Mark:** "D.L. Brothers, 4B, Oneonta, AL" on obverse side of blade.

BROTHERS, ROBERT L,
989 Philpott Rd, Colville, WA 99114, Phone: 509-684-8922
Specialties: Traditional working and using straight knives and folders of his design and to customer specs. **Patterns:** Bowies, fighters and hunters.

Technical: Grinds D2; forges Damascus. Makes own Damascus from saw steel wire rope and chain; part-time goldsmith and stone-setter. **Prices:** $100 to $400; some higher. **Remarks:** Part-time maker; first knife sold in 1986. **Mark:** Initials and year made.

BROWER, MAX,
2016 Story St, Boone, IA 50036, Phone: 515-432-2938, mbrower@mchsi.com
Specialties: Working/using straight knives. **Patterns:** Bowies, hunters and boots. **Technical:** Grinds 440C and ATS-34. **Prices:** Start at $150. **Remarks:** Spare-time maker; first knife sold in 1981. **Mark:** Last name.

BROWN, DENNIS G,
1633 N 197th Pl, Shoreline, WA 98133, Phone: 206-542-3997, denjilbro@msn.com

BROWN, HAROLD E,
3654 NW Hwy 72, Arcadia, FL 34266, Phone: 863-494-7514, brknives@strato.net
Specialties: Fancy and exotic working knives. **Patterns:** Folders, slip-lock, locking several kinds. **Technical:** Grinds D2 and ATS-34. Embellishment available. **Prices:** $175 to $1000. **Remarks:** Part-time maker; first knife sold in 1976. **Mark:** Name and city with logo.

BROWN, JIM,
1097 Fernleigh Cove, Little Rock, AR 72210

BROWN, ROB E,
PO Box 15107, Emerald Hill 6011, Port Elizabeth, SOUTH AFRICA, Phone: 27-41-3661086, Fax: 27-41-4511731, rbknives@global.co.za
Specialties: Contemporary-designed straight knives and period pieces. **Patterns:** Utility knives, hunters, boots, fighters and daggers. **Technical:** Grinds 440C, D2, ATS-34 and commercial Damascus. Knives mostly mirror finished; African handle materials. **Prices:** $100 to $1500. **Remarks:** Full-time maker; first knife sold in 1985. **Mark:** Name and country.

BROWNE, RICK,
980 West 13th St, Upland, CA 91786, Phone: 909-985-1728
Specialties: Sheffield pattern pocket knives. **Patterns:** Hunters, fighters and daggers. No heavy-duty knives. **Technical:** Grinds ATS-34. **Prices:** Start at $450. **Remarks:** Part-time maker; first knife sold in 1975. **Mark:** R.E. Browne, Upland, CA.

BROWNING, STEVEN W,
3400 Harrison Rd, Benton, AR 72015, Phone: 501-316-2450

BRUCE, RICHARD L.,
13174 Surcease Mine Road, Yankee Hill, CA 95965, Phone: 530-532-0880, Richardkarenbruce@yahoo.com
RL Bruce Custom Knives

BRUNCKHORST, LYLE,
COUNTRY VILLAGE, 23706 7th Ave SE Ste B, Bothell, WA 98021, Phone: 425-402-3484, bronks@bronksknifeworks.com; Web: www.bronksknifeworks.com
Specialties: Forges own Damascus with 1084 and 15N20, forges 5160, 52100. Grinds CPM 154 CM, ATS-34, S30V. Hosts Biannual Northwest School of Knifemaking and Northwest Hammer In. Offers online and in-house sharpening services and knife sharpeners. Maker of the Double L Hoofknife. Traditional working and using knives, the new patent pending Xross-Bar Lock folders, tomahawks and irridescent RR spike knives. **Patterns:** Damascus Bowies, hunters, locking folders and featuring the ultra strong locking tactical folding knives. **Prices:** $185 to $1500; some to $3750. **Remarks:** Full-time maker; first knife made in 1976. **Mark:** Bucking horse or bronk.

BRUNER JR., FRED BRUNER BLADES,
E10910W Hilldale Dr, Fall Creek, WI 54742, Phone: 715-877-2496, brunerblades@msn.com
Specialties: Pipe tomahawks, swords, makes his own. **Patterns:** Drop point hunters. **Prices:** $65 to $1500. **Remarks:** Voting member of the Knifemakers Guild. **Mark:** Fred Bruner.

BRUNETTA, DAVID,
PO Box 4972, Laguna Beach, CA 92652, Phone: 949-497-9857, lethalsculpture@cox.net Web: www.sculpturesbydavid.com
Specialties: Straights, folders and art knives. **Patterns:** Bowies, camp/hunting, folders, fighters. **Technical:** Grinds ATS-34, D2, BG42. forges O1, 52100, 5160, 1095, makes own Damascus. **Prices:** $300 to $9000. **Mark:** Circle DB logo with last name straight or curved.

BRYAN, TOM,
14822 S Gilbert Rd, Gilbert, AZ 85296, Phone: 480-812-8529
Specialties: Straight and folding knives. **Patterns:** Drop-point hunter fighters. **Technical:** ATS-34, 154CM, 440C and A2. **Prices:** $150 to $800. **Remarks:** Part-time maker; sold first knife in 1994. DBA as T. Bryan Knives. **Mark:** T. Bryan.

BUCHANAN, THAD,
THAD BUCHANAN CUSTOM KNIVES, 915 NW Perennial Way, Prineville, OR 97754, Phone: 541-416-2556, knives@crestviewcable.com; Web: www.buchananblades.com
Specialties: Fixed blades. **Patterns:** Various hunters, trout, bird, utility, boots & fighters, including most Loveless patterns. **Technical:** Stock removal, high polish, variety handle materials. **Prices:** $450 to $2000. **Remarks:** 2005 and 2008 Blade Magazine handmade award for hunter/utility. 2006 Blade West best fixed blade award; 2008 Blade West best hunter/utility. **Mark:** Thad Buchanan Oregon USA.

custom knifemakers

BUCHMAN, BILL,
63312 South Rd, Bend, OR 97701-9027, Phone: 541-382-8851
Specialties: Leather cutting knives for saddle makers and leather crafters. **Patterns:** Many. **Technical:** Sandkik-Swedish carbon steel. **Prices:** Varies: $35 to $130. **Remarks:** Full-time maker; first knife sold in 1982. **Mark:** BB & # of knife on large knives - no mark on small knives.

BUCHNER, BILL,
PO Box 73, Idleyld Park, OR, 97447, Phone: 541-498-2247, blazinhammer@ earthlink.net; Web: www.home.earthlin.net/~blazinghammer
Specialties: Working straight knives, kitchen knives and high-art knives of his design. **Technical:** Uses W1, L6 and his own Damascus. Invented "spectrum metal" for letter openers, folder handles and jewelry. Likes sculpturing and carving in Damascus. **Prices:** $40 to $3000; some higher. **Remarks:** Full-time maker; first knife sold in 1978. **Mark:** Signature.

BUCKBEE, DONALD M,
243 South Jackson Trail, Grayling, MI 49738, Phone: 517-348-1386
Specialties: Working straight knives, some fancy, in standard patterns; concentrating on kitchen knives. **Patterns:** Kitchen knives, hunters, Bowies. **Technical:** Grinds D2, 440C, ATS-34. Makes ultra-lights in hunter patterns. **Prices:** $100 to $250; some to $350. **Remarks:** Part-time maker; first knife sold in 1984. **Mark:** Antlered bee—a buck bee.

BUCKNER, JIMMIE H,
PO Box 162, Putney, GA 31782, Phone: 229-436-4182
Specialties: Camp knives, Bowies (one-of-a-kind), liner-lock folders, tomahawks, camp axes, neck knives for law enforcement and hide-out knives for body guards and professional people. **Patterns:** Hunters, camp knives, Bowies. **Technical:** Forges 1084, 5160 and Damascus (own), own heat treats. **Prices:** $195 to $795 and up. **Remarks:** Full-time maker; first knife sold in 1980, ABS Master Smith. **Mark:** Name over spade.

BUDELL, MICHAEL,
1100-A South Market St, Brenham, TX 77833, Phone: 979-836-0098
Specialties: Slip Joint Folders. **Technical:** Grinds 01, 440C. File work springs, blades and liners. Natural material scales giraffe, mastadon ivory, elephant ivory, and jigged bone. **Prices:** $175 - $350. **Remarks:** Part-time maker; first knife sold 2006. **Mark:** XA

BUEBENDORF, ROBERT E,
108 Lazybrooke Rd, Monroe, CT 06468, Phone: 203-452-1769
Specialties: Traditional and fancy straight knives of his design. **Patterns:** Hand-makes and embellishes belt buckle knives. **Technical:** Forges and grinds 440C, O1, W2, 1095, his own Damascus and 154CM. **Prices:** $200 to $500. **Remarks:** Full-time maker; first knife sold in 1978. **Mark:** First and middle initials, last name and MAKER.

BULLARD, RANDALL,
7 Mesa Dr., Canyon, TX 79015, Phone: 806-655-0590
Specialties: Working/using straight knives and folders of his design or to customer specs. **Patterns:** Hunters, locking folders and slip-joint folders. **Technical:** Grinds O1, ATS-34 and 440C. Does file work. **Prices:** $125 to $300; some to $500. **Remarks:** Part-time maker; first knife sold in 1993. Doing business as Bullard Custom Knives. **Mark:** First and middle initials, last name, maker, city and state.

BULLARD, TOM,
117 MC 8068, Flippin, AR 72634, Phone: 870-453-3421, tbullard@southshore. com; Web: www.southshore.com/~tombullard
Specialties: Traditional folders and hunters. **Patterns:** Bowies, hunters, single and 2-blade trappers, lockback folders. **Technical:** Grinds 440-C, ATS-34, 0-1, commercial Damascus. **Prices:** $150 and up. **Remarks:** Offers filework and engraving by Norvell Foster and Terry Thies. Does not make screw-together knives. **Mark:** T Bullard.

BUMP, BRUCE D.,
1103 Rex Ln, Walla Walla, WA 99362, Phone: 509 522-2219, bruceandkaye@ charter.net; Web: www.brucebumpknives.com
Specialties: Complete range of knives from field grade to "one-of-a-kind" cut and shoots. **Patterns:** Black Powder pistol/folders, "Brutus" axe/gun, shooting swords, slipjoint folders. **Technical:** Dual threat weapons of his own design inspired from early centuries. **Prices:** $250 to $20,000. **Remarks:** Full-time maker ABS mastersmith 2003. **Mark:** Bruce D. Bump, Bruce D Bump Custom Walla Walla WA.

BURDEN, JAMES,
405 Kelly St, Burkburnett, TX 76354

BURGER, FRED,
Box 436, Munster 4278, Kwa-Zulu Natal, SOUTH AFRICA, Phone: 27 39 3192316, info@swordcane.com; Web: www.swordcane.com
Specialties: Sword canes, folders, and fixed blades. **Patterns:** 440C and carbon steel blades. **Technical:** Double hollow ground and Poniard-style blades. **Prices:** $300 to $3000. **Remarks:** Full-time maker with son, Barry, since 1987. Member South African Guild. **Mark:** Last name in oval pierced by a dagger.

BURGER, PON,
12 Glenwood Ave, Woodlands, Bulawayo, ZIMBABWE 75514
Specialties: Collector's items. **Patterns:** Fighters, locking folders of traditional styles, buckles. **Technical:** Scrimshaws 440C blade. Uses polished buffalo horn with brass fittings. Cased in buffalo hide book. **Prices:** $450 to $1100. **Remarks:** Full-time maker; first knife sold in 1973. Doing business as Burger Products. **Mark:** Spirit of Africa.

BURGER, TIAAN,
69 Annie Botha Ave, Riviera, Pretoria, South Africa, tiaan_burger@hotmail. com
Specialties: Sliplock and multi-blade folder. **Technical:** High carbon or stainless with African handle materials **Remarks:** Occasional fixed blade knives.

BURKE, BILL,
12 Chapman Lane, Boise, ID 83716, Phone: 208-336-3792, billburke@ bladegallery.com
Specialties: Hand-forged working knives. **Patterns:** Fowler pronghorn, clip point and drop point hunters. **Technical:** Forges 52100 and 5160. Makes own Damascus from 15N20 and 1084. **Prices:** $450 and up. **Remarks:** Dedicated to fixed-blade high-performance knives. ABS Journeyman. Also makes "Ed Fowler" miniatures. **Mark:** Initials connected.

BURKE, DAN,
22001 Ole Barn Rd, Edmond, OK 73003, Phone: 405-341-3406, Fax: 405-340-3333, burkeknives@aol.com
Specialties: Slip joint folders. **Patterns:** Traditional folders. **Technical:** Grinds D2 and BG-42. Prefers natural handle materials; heat-treats. **Prices:** $440 to $1900. **Remarks:** Full-time maker; first knife sold in 1976. **Mark:** First initial and last name.

BURNLEY, LUCAS,
1005 La Font Rd. SW, Albuquerque, NM 87105, Phone: 505-265-4297, burnleyknives@comcast.net
Specialties: Contemporary tactical fixed blade, and folder designs, some art knives. **Patterns:** Hybrids, neo Japanese, defensive, utility and field knives. **Technical:** Grinds CPM154, A2, D2, BG42, Stainless Damascus as well as titanium and aerospace composites. **Prices:** Most models $150 - $1000. Some specialty pieces higher. **Remarks:** Full-time maker, first knife sold in 2003. **Mark:** Last name, Burnley Knives, or Burnley Design.

BURRIS, PATRICK R,
11078 Crystal Lynn Ct, Jacksonville, FL 32226, Phone: 904-757-3938, keenedge@comcast.net
Specialties: Traditional straight knives. **Patterns:** Hunters, Bowies, locking liner folders. **Technical:** Flat grinds CPM stainless and Damascus. **Remarks:** Offers filework, embellishment, exotic materials and Damascus **Mark:** Last name in script.

BURROWS, CHUCK,
WILD ROSE TRADING CO, 289 La Posta Canyon Rd, Durango, CO 81303, Phone: 970-259-8396, chuck@wrtcleather.com; Web: www.wrtcleather. com
Specialties: Presentation knives, hawks, and sheaths based on the styles of the American frontier incorporating carving, beadwork, rawhide, braintan, and other period correct materials. Also makes other period style knives such as Scottish Dirks and Moorish jambiyahs. **Patterns:** Bowies, Dags, tomahawks, war clubs, and all other 18th and 19th century frontier style edged weapons and tools. **Technical:** Carbon steel only: 5160, 1080/1084, 1095, O1, Damascus-Our Frontier Shear Steel, plus other styles available on request. Forged knives, hawks, etc. are made in collaborations with bladesmiths. Gib Guignard (under the name of Cactus Rose) and Mark Williams (under the name UB Forged). Blades are usually forge finished and all items are given an aged period look. **Prices:** $500 plus. **Remarks:** Full-time maker, first knife sold in 1973. 40+ years experience working leather. **Mark:** A lazy eight or lazy eight with a capital T at the center. On leather either the lazy eight with T or a WRTC makers stamp.

BURROWS, STEPHEN R,
1020 Osage St, Humboldt, KS 66748, Phone: 816-921-1573
Specialties: Fantasy straight knives of his design, to customer specs and in standard patterns; period pieces. **Patterns:** Fantasy, bird and trout knives, daggers, fighters and hunters. **Technical:** Forges 5160 and 1095 high-carbon steel, O1 and his Damascus. Offers lost wax casting in bronze or silver of cross guards and pommels. **Prices:** $65 to $600; some to $2000. **Remarks:** Full-time maker; first knife sold in 1983. Doing business as Gypsy Silk. **Mark:** Etched name.

BUSCH, STEVE,
1989 Old Town Loop, Oakland, OR 97462, Phone: 541-459-2833, steve@ buschcustomknives.com; Web: wwwbuschcustomknives.blademakers. com
Specialties: D/A automatic right and left handed, folders, fixed blade working mainly in Damascus file work, functional art knives, nitrate bluing, heat bluing most all scale materials. **Prices:** $150 to $2000. **Remarks:** Trained under Vallotton family 3 1/2 years on own since 2002. **Mark:** Signature and date of completion on all knives.

BUSFIELD, JOHN,
153 Devonshire Circle, Roanoke Rapids, NC 27870, Phone: 252-537-3949, Fax: 252-537-8704, busfield@charter.net; Web: www.busfieldknives.com
Specialties: Investor-grade folders; high-grade working straight knives. **Patterns:** Original price-style and trailing-point interframe and sculpted-frame folders, drop-point hunters and semi-skinners. **Technical:** Grinds 154CM and ATS-34. Offers interframes, gold frames and inlays; uses jade, agate and lapis. **Prices:** $275 to $2000. **Remarks:** Full-time maker; first knife sold in 1979. **Mark:** Last name and address.

BUSSE, JERRY,
11651 Co Rd 12, Wauseon, OH 43567, Phone: 419-923-6471
Specialties: Working straight knives. **Patterns:** Heavy combat knives and camp knives. **Technical:** Grinds D2, A2, INFI. **Prices:** $1100 to $3500. **Remarks:** Full-time maker; first knife sold in 1983. **Mark:** Last name in logo.

BUTLER, BART,
822 Seventh St, Ramona, CA 92065, Phone: 760-789-6431

BUTLER, JOHN,
777 Tyre Rd, Havana, FL 32333, Phone: 850-539-5742
Specialties: Hunters, Bowies, period. **Technical:** Damascus, 52100, 5160, L6 steels. **Prices:** $80 and up. **Remarks:** Making knives since 1986. Journeyman (ABS). **Mark:** JB.

BUTLER, JOHN R,
20162 6th Ave N E, Shoreline, WA 98155, Phone: 206-362-3847, rjjjrb@sprynet.com

BUXTON, BILL,
155 Oak Bend Rd, Kaiser, MO 65047, Phone: 573-348-3577, camper@yhti.net; Web: www.billbuxtonknives.com
Specialties: Forged fancy and working straight knives and folders. Mostly one-of-a-kind pieces. **Patterns:** Fighters, daggers, Bowies, hunters, linerlock folders, axes and tomahawks. **Technical:** Forges 52100, 0-1, 1080. Makes own Damascus (mosaic and random patterns) from 1080, 1095, 15n20, and powdered metals 1084 and 4800a. Offers sterling silver inlay, n/s pin patterning and pewter pouring on axe and hawk handles. **Prices:** $300 to $1500. **Remarks:** Full-time maker, sold first knife in 1998. **Mark:** First and last name.

BYBEE, BARRY J,
795 Lock Rd. E, Cadiz, KY 42211-8615
Specialties: Working straight knives of his design. **Patterns:** Hunters, fighters, boot knives, tantos and Bowies. **Technical:** Grinds ATS-34, 440C. Likes stag and Micarta for handle materials. **Prices:** $125 to $200; some to $1000. **Remarks:** Part-time maker; first knife sold in 1968. **Mark:** Arrowhead logo with name, city and state.

BYRD, WESLEY L,
189 Countryside Dr, Evensville, TN 37332, Phone: 423-775-3826, w.l.byrd@worldnet.att.net
Specialties: Hunters, fighters, Bowies, dirks, sgian dubh, utility, and camp knives. **Patterns:** Wire rope, random patterns. Twists, W's, Ladder, Kite Tail. **Technical:** Uses 52100, 1084, 5160, L6, and 15n20. **Prices:** Starting at $180. **Remarks:** Prefer to work with customer for their design preferences. ABS Journeyman Smith. **Mark:** BYRD, WB <X.

C

CABE, JERRY (BUDDY),
62 McClaren Ln, Hattieville, AR 72063, Phone: 501-354-3581

CABRERA, SERGIO B,
24500 Broad Ave, Wilmington, CA 90744

CAFFREY, EDWARD J,
2608 Central Ave West, Great Falls, MT 59404, Phone: 406-727-9102, caffreyknives@gmail.com; Web: www.caffreyknives.net
Specialties: One-of-a-kind using and collector quality pieces. Will accept some customer designs. **Patterns:** Bowies, folders, hunters, fighters, camp/utility, tomahawks and hatchets. **Technical:** Forges all types of Damascus, specializing in Mosaic Damascus, 52100, 5160, 1084 and most other commonly forged steels. **Prices:** Starting at $185; typical hunters start at $400; collector pieces can range into the thousands. **Remarks:** Offers one-on-one basic and advanced bladesmithing classes. ABS Mastersmith. Full-time maker. **Mark:** Stamped last name and MS on straight knives. Etched last name with MS on folders.

CALDWELL, BILL,
255 Rebecca, West Monroe, LA 71292, Phone: 318-323-3025
Specialties: Straight knives and folders with machined bolsters and liners. **Patterns:** Fighters, Bowies, survival knives, tomahawks, razors and push knives. **Technical:** Owns and operates a very large, well-equipped blacksmith and bladesmith shop with six large forges and eight power hammers. **Prices:** $400 to $3500; some to $10,000. **Remarks:** Full-time maker and self-styled blacksmith; first knife sold in 1962. **Mark:** Wild Bill and Sons.

CALLAHAN, F TERRY,
PO Box 880, Boerne, TX 78006, Phone: 830-981-8274, Fax: 830-981-8279, ftclaw@gvtc.com
Specialties: Custom hand-forged edged knives, collectible and functional. **Patterns:** Bowies, folders, daggers, hunters & camp knives . **Technical:** Forges 5160, 1095 and his own Damascus. Offers filework and handmade sheaths. **Prices:** $125 to $2000. **Remarks:** First knife sold in 1990. ABS/Journeyman Bladesmith. **Mark:** Initials inside a keystone symbol.

CALVERT JR., ROBERT W (BOB),
911 Julia, Rayville, LA 71269, Phone: 318-728-4113, Fax: (318) 728-0000, rcalvert1@gmail.com
Specialties: Using and hunting knives; your design or his. Since 1990. **Patterns:** Forges own Damascus; all patterns. **Technical:** 5160, D2, 52100, 1084. Prefers natural handle material. **Prices:** $250 and up. **Remarks:** TOMB Member, ABS. Journeyman Smith. Board of directors-ABS. **Mark:** Calvert (Block) J S.

CAMERER, CRAIG,
3766 Rockbridge Rd, Chesterfield, IL 62630, Phone: 618-753-2147, craig@camererknives.com; Web: www.camererknives.com
Specialties: Everyday carry knives, hunters and Bowies. **Patterns:** D-guard, historical recreations and fighters. **Technical:** Most of his knives are forged to shape. **Prices:** $100 and up. **Remarks:** Member of the ABS and PKA. Journeymen Smith ABS.

CAMERON, RON G,
PO Box 183, Logandale, NV 89021, Phone: 702-398-3356, rntcameron@mvdsl.com
Specialties: Fancy and embellished working/using straight knives and folders of his design. **Patterns:** Bowies, hunters and utility/camp knives. **Technical:** Grinds ATS-34, AEB-L and Devin Thomas Damascus or own Damascus from 1084 and 15N20. Does filework, fancy pins, mokume fittings. Uses exotic hardwoods, stag and Micarta for handles. Pearl & mammoth ivory. **Prices:** $175 to $850 some to $1000. **Remarks:** Part-time maker; first knife sold in 1994. Doing business as Cameron Handmade Knives. **Mark:** Last name, town, state or last name.

CAMERON HOUSE,
2001 Delaney Rd Se, Salem, OR 97306, Phone: 503-585-3286
Specialties: Working straight knives. **Patterns:** Hunters, Bowies, fighters. **Technical:** Grinds ATS-34, 530V, 154CM. **Remarks:** Part-time maker, first knife sold in 1993. **Prices:** $150 and up. **Mark:** HOUSE.

CAMPBELL, DICK,
196 Graham Rd, Colville, WA 99114, Phone: 509-684-6080, dicksknives@aol.com
Specialties: Working straight knives, folders & period pieces. **Patterns:** Hunters, fighters, boots: 19th century Bowies, Japanese swords and daggers. **Technical:** Grinds 440C, 154CM. **Prices:** $200 to $2500. **Remarks:** Full-time maker. First knife sold in 1975. **Mark:** Name.

CAMPBELL, DOUG,
46 W Boulder Rd., McLeod, MT 59052, Phone: 406-222-8153, dkcampbl@yahoo.com
Specialties: Sole authorship of most any fixed blade knife. **Patterns:** Capers, hunters, camp knives, bowies, fighters. **Technical:** Forged from 1084, 5160, 52100, and self forged pattern-welded Damascus. **Prices:** $150-$750. **Remarks:** Part-time knifesmith. Built first knife in 1987, tried to make every knife since better than the one before. Pursuing ABS JS stamp. **Mark:** Grizzly track surrounded by a C.

CAMPOS, IVAN,
R.XI de Agosto 107, Tatui, SP, BRAZIL 18270-000, Phone: 00-55-15-2518092, Fax: 00-55-15-2594368, ivan@ivancampos.com; Web: www.ivancompos.com
Specialties: Brazilian handmade and antique knives.

CANDRELLA, JOE,
1219 Barness Dr, Warminster, PA 18974, Phone: 215-675-0143
Specialties: Working straight knives, some fancy. **Patterns:** Daggers, boots, Bowies. **Technical:** Grinds 440C and 154CM. **Prices:** $100 to $200; some to $1000. **Remarks:** Part-time maker; first knife sold in 1985. Does business as Franjo. **Mark:** FRANJO with knife as J.

CANNADY, DANIEL L,
Box 301, 358 Parkwood Terrace, Allendale, SC 29810, Phone: 803-584-2813, Fax: 803-584-2813
Specialties: Working straight knives and folders in standard patterns. **Patterns:** Drop-point hunters, Bowies, skinners, fishing knives with concave grind, steak knives and kitchen cutlery. **Technical:** Grinds D2, 440C and ATS-34. **Prices:** $65 to $325; some to $1000. **Remarks:** Full-time maker; first knife sold in 1980. **Mark:** Last name above Allendale, S.C.

CANOY, ANDREW B,
3420 Fruchey Ranch Rd, Hubbard Lake, MI 49747, Phone: 810-266-6039, canoy1@shianet.org

CANTER, RONALD E,
96 Bon Air Circle, Jackson, TN 38305, Phone: 731-668-1780, canterr@charter.net
Specialties: Traditional working knives to customer specs. **Patterns:** Beavertail skinners, Bowies, hand axes and folding lockers. **Technical:** Grinds 440C, Micarta & deer antler. **Prices:** $75 and up. **Remarks:** Spare-time maker; first knife sold in 1973. **Mark:** Three last initials intertwined.

CANTRELL, KITTY D,
19720 Hwy 78, Ramona, CA 92076, Phone: 760-788-8304

CAPDEPON, RANDY,
553 Joli Rd, Carencro, LA 70520, Phone: 318-896-4113, Fax: 318-896-8753
Specialties: Straight knives and folders of his design. **Patterns:** Hunters and locking folders. **Technical:** Grinds ATS-34, 440C and D2. **Prices:** $200 to $600. **Remarks:** Part-time maker; first knife made in 1992. Doing business as Capdepon Knives. **Mark:** Last name.

CAPDEPON, ROBERT,
829 Vatican Rd, Carencro, LA 70520, Phone: 337-896-8753, Fax: 318-896-8753
Specialties: Traditional straight knives and folders of his design. **Patterns:** Boots, hunters and locking folders. **Technical:** Grinds ATS-34, 440C and D2. Hand-rubbed finish on blades. Likes natural horn materials for handles, including ivory. Offers engraving. **Prices:** $250 to $750. **Remarks:** Full-time maker; first knife made in 1992. **Mark:** Last name.

CAREY, PETER,
P.O. Box 4712, Lago Vista, TX 78645, Phone: 512-358-4839, Web: www.careyblade.com
Specialties: Tactical folders, Every Day Carry to presentation grade. Working straight knives, hunters, and tactical. **Patterns:** High-tech patterns of his own design, Linerlocks, Framelocks, Flippers. **Technical:** Hollow grings CPM154, S30V, 154cm, stainless Damascus, Talonite, Stellite. Uses titanium, carbon fiber, G10, and select natural handle materials. **Prices:** Starting at $400. **Remarks:** Full-time maker, first knife sold in 2002. **Mark:** Last name in diamond.

CARLISLE, JEFF,
PO Box 282 12753 Hwy 200, Simms, MT 59477, Phone: 406-264-5693

CARLSON, KELLY,
54 S Holt Hill, Antrim, NH 03440, Phone: 603-588-2765, kellycarlson@tds.net; Web: www.carlsonknives.com
Specialties: Unique folders of maker's own design. **Patterns:** One-of-a-kind, artistic folders, mostly of liner-lock design, along with interpretations of traditional designs. **Technical:** Grinds and heat treats S30V, D2, ATS-34, stainless and carbon Damascus steels. Prefers hand sanded finishes and natural ivories and pearls, in conjunction with decorative accents obtained from mosaic Damascus, Damascus and various exotic materials. **Prices:** $400 to $4000. **Remarks:** Full-time maker as of 2002, first knife sold in 1975. New mechanism designs include assisted openers, top locks, and galvanic slipjoints powered by neodymium magnets, patent pending. **Mark:** "Carlson," usually inside backspacer.

CAROLINA CUSTOM KNIVES, SEE TOMMY MCNABB,

CARPENTER, RONALD W,
Rt. 4 Box 323, Jasper, TX 75951, Phone: 409-384-4087

CARR, JOSEPH E.,
W183 N8974 Maryhill Drive, Menomonee Falls, WI 53051, Phone: 920-625-3607, carsmith1@SBCGlobal.net; Web: Hembrook3607@charter.net
Specialties: JC knives. **Patterns:** Hunters, Bowies, fighting knives, every day carries. **Technical:** Grinds ATS-34 and Damascus. **Prices:** $200 to $750. **Remarks:** Full-time maker for 2 years, being taught by Ron Hembrook.

CARR, TIM,
3660 Pillon Rd, Muskegon, MI 49445, Phone: 231-766-3582, tim@blackbearforgemi.com Web:www.blackbearforgemi.com
Specialties: Hunters, camp knives. **Patterns:** His or yours. **Technical:** Hand forges 5160, 52100 and Damascus. **Prices:** $125 to $700. **Remarks:** Part-time maker. **Mark:** The letter combined from maker's initials TRC.

CARRILLO, DWAINE,
C/O AIRKAT KNIVES, 1021 SW 15th St, Moore, OK 73160, Phone: 405-503-5879, Web: www.airkatknives.com

CARROLL, CHAD,
12182 McClelland, Grant, MI 49327, Phone: 231-834-9183, CHAD724@msn.com
Specialties: Hunters, Bowies, folders, swords, tomahawks. **Patterns:** Fixed blades, folders. **Prices:** $100 to $2000. **Remarks:** ABS Journeyman May 2002. **Mark:** A backwards C next to a forward C, maker's initials.

CARSON, HAROLD J "KIT",
1076 Brizendine Lane, Vine Grove, KY 40175, Phone: 270 877-6300, Fax: 270 877 6338, KCKnives@bbtel.com; Web: www.kitcarsonknives.com/album
Specialties: Military fixed blades and folders; art pieces. **Patterns:** Fighters, D handles, daggers, combat folders and Crosslock-styles, tactical folders, tactical fixed blades. **Technical:** Grinds Stellite 6K, Talonite, CPM steels, Damascus. **Prices:** $400 to $750; some to $5000. **Remarks:** Full-time maker; first knife sold in 1973. **Mark:** Name stamped or engraved.

CARTER, FRED,
5219 Deer Creek Rd, Wichita Falls, TX 76302, Phone: 904-723-4020
Specialties: High-art investor-class straight knives; some working hunters and fighters. **Patterns:** Classic daggers, Bowies; interframe, stainless and blued steel folders with gold inlay. **Technical:** Grinds a variety of steels. Uses no glue or solder. Engraves and inlays. **Prices:** Generally upscale. **Remarks:** Full-time maker. **Mark:** Signature in oval logo.

CARTER, MURRAY M,
PO Box 307, Vernonia, OR 97064, Phone: 503-429-0447, murray@cartercutlery.com; Web:www.cartercutlery.com
Specialties: Traditional Japanese cutlery, utilizing San soh ko (three layer) or Kata-ha (two layer) blade construction. Laminated neck knives, traditional Japanese etc. **Patterns:** Works from over 200 standard Japanese and North American designs. **Technical:** Hot forges and cold forges Hitachi white steel #1, Hitachi blue super steel exclusively. **Prices:** $800 to $10,000. **Remarks:** Owns and operates North America's most exclusive traditional Japanese bladesmithing school; web site available at which viewers can subscribe to 10 free knife sharpening and maintenance reports. **Mark:** Name in cursive, often appearing with Japanese characters. **Other:** Very interestng and informative monthly newsletter.

CASEY, KEVIN,
10583 N. 42nd St., Hickory Corners, MI 49060, Phone: 269-719-7412, kevincasey@tds.net; Web: www.kevincaseycustomknives.com
Specialties: Fixed blades and folders. **Patterns:** Liner lock folders and feather Damascus pattern, mammoth ivory. **Technical:** Forges Damascus and carbon steels. **Prices:** Starting at $500 - $2500. **Remarks:** Member ABS, Knifemakers Guild, Custom Knifemakers Collectors Association.

CASHEN, KEVIN R,
5615 Tyler St, Hubbardston, MI 48845, Phone: 989-981-6780, kevin@cashenblades.com; Web: www.cashenblades.com
Specialties: Working straight knives, high art pattern welded swords, traditional renaissance and ethnic pieces. **Patterns:** Hunters, Bowies, utility knives, swords, daggers. **Technical:** Forges 1095, 1084 and his own O1/L6 Damascus. **Prices:** $100 to $4000+. **Remarks:** Full-time maker; first knife sold in 1985. Doing business as Matherton Forge. **Mark:** Black letter Old English initials and Master Smith stamp.

CASTEEL, DIANNA,
PO Box 63, Monteagle, TN 37356, Phone: 931-212-4341, ddcasteel@charter.net; Web: www.casteelcustomknives.com
Specialties: Small, delicate daggers and miniatures; most knives one-of-a-kind. **Patterns:** Daggers, boot knives, fighters and miniatures. **Technical:** Grinds 440C. Offers stainless Damascus. **Prices:** Start at $350; miniatures start at $250. **Remarks:** Full-time maker. **Mark:** Di in script.

CASTEEL, DOUGLAS,
PO Box 63, Monteagle, TN 37356, Phone: 931-212-4341, Fax: 931-723-1856, ddcasteel@charter.net; Web: www.casteelcustomknives.com
Specialties: One-of-a-kind collector-class period pieces. **Patterns:** Daggers, Bowies, swords and folders. **Technical:** Grinds 440C. Offers gold and silver castings.Offers stainless Damascus **Prices:** Upscale. **Remarks:** Full-time maker; first knife sold in 1982. **Mark:** Last name.

CASTELLUCIO, RICH,
220 Stairs Rd, Amsterdam, NY 12010, Phone: 518-843-5540, rcastellucio@nycap.rr.com
Patterns: Bowies, push daggers, and fantasy knives. **Technical:** Uses ATS-34, 440C, 154CM. I use stabilized wood, bone for the handles. Guards are made of copper, brass, stainless, nickle, and mokume.

CASTON, DARRIEL,
3725 Duran Circle, Sacramento, CA 95821, Phone: 916-359-0613, dcaston@surewest.net
Specialties: Investment grade jade handle folders of his design and gentleman folders. **Patterns:** Folders: slipjoints and lockback. Will be making linerlocks in the near future. **Technical:** Small gentleman folders for office and desk warriors. Grinds ATS-34, 154CM, S30V and Damascus. **Prices:** $250 to $900. **Remarks:** Part-time maker; won best new maker at first show in Sept 2004. **Mark:** Etched rocket ship with "Darriel Caston" or just "Caston" on inside spring on Damascus and engraved knives.

CASWELL, JOE,
173 S Ventu Park Rd, Newbury, CA 91320, Phone: 805-499-0707, Web:www.caswellknives.com
Specialties: Historic pattern welded knives and swords, hand forged. Also high precision folding and fixed blade "gentleman" and "tactical" knives of his design, period firearms. Inventor of the "In-Line" retractable pocket clip for folding knives. **Patterns:**Hunters, tactical/utility, fighters, bowies, daggers, pattern welded medieval swords, precision folders. **Technical:** Forges own Damascus especially historic forms. Sometimes uses modern stainless steels and Damascus of other makers. Makes some pieces entirely by hand, others using the latest CNC techniques and by hand. Makes sheaths too.**Prices:**$100-$5,500. **Remarks:**Full time makers since 1995. Making mostly historic recreations for exclusive clientele. Recently moving into folding knives and 'modern' designs. **Mark:**CASWELL or CASWELL USA Accompanied by a mounted knight logo.

CATOE, DAVID R,
4024 Heutte Dr, Norfolk, VA 23518, Phone: 757-480-3191
Technical: Does own forging, Damascus and heat treatments. **Price:** $200 to $500; some higher. **Remarks:** Part-time maker; trained by Dan Maragni 1985-1988; first knife sold 1989. **Mark:** Leaf of a camellia.

CAWTHORNE, CHRISTOPHER A,
PO Box 604, Wrangell, AK 99929, Phone: 661-902-3724, chriscawthorne@hotmail.com
Specialties: High-carbon steel, cable wire rope, silver wire inlay. **Patterns:** Forge welded Damascus and wire rope, random pattern. **Technical:** Hand forged, 50 lb. little giant power hammer, W-2, 0-1, L6, 1095. **Prices:** $650 to $2500. **Remarks:** School ABS 1985 w/Bill Moran, hand forged, heat treat. **Mark:** Cawthorne, forged in stamp.

CEPRANO, PETER J.,
213 Townsend Brooke Rd., Auburn, ME 04210, Phone: 207-786-5322, bpknives@gmail.com
Specialties: Traditional working/using straight knives; tactical/defense straight knives. Own designs or to a customer's specs. **Patterns:** Hunters, skinners, utility, Bowies, fighters, camp and survival, neck knives. **Technical:** Forges 1095, 5160, W2, 52100 and old files; grinds CPM154cm, ATS-34, 440C, D2, CPMs30v, Damascus from other makes and other tool steels. Hand-sewn and tooled leather and Kydex sheaths. **Prices:** Starting at $125.

Remarks: Full-time maker, first knife sold in 2001. Doing business as Big Pete Knives. **Mark:** Bold BPK over small BigPeteKnivesUSA.

CHAFFEE, JEFF L,
14314 N. Washington St, PO Box 1, Morris, IN 47033, Phone: 812-212-6188
Specialties: Fancy working and utility folders and straight knives. **Patterns:** Fighters, dagger, hunter and locking folders. **Technical:** Grinds commercial Damascus, 440C, ATS-34, D2 and O1. Prefers natural handle materials. **Prices:** $350 to $2000. **Remarks:** Part-time maker; first knife sold in 1988. **Mark:** Last name.

CHAMBERLAIN, CHARLES R,
PO Box 156, Barren Springs, VA 24313-0156, Phone: 703-381-5137

CHAMBERLAIN, JON A,
15 S. Lombard, E. Wenatchee, WA 98802, Phone: 509-884-6591
Specialties: Working and kitchen knives to customer specs; exotics on special order. **Patterns:** Over 100 patterns in stock. **Technical:** Prefers ATS-34, D2, L6 and Damascus. **Prices:** Start at $50. **Remarks:** First knife sold in 1986. Doing business as Johnny Custom Knifemakers. **Mark:** Name in oval with city and state enclosing.

CHAMBERLIN, JOHN A,
11535 Our Rd., Anchorage, AK 99516, Phone: 907-346-1524, Fax: 907-562-4583
Specialties: Art and working knives. **Patterns:** Daggers and hunters; some folders. **Technical:** Grinds ATS-34, 440C, A2, D2 and Damascus. Uses Alaskan handle materials such as oosic, jade, whale jawbone, fossil ivory. **Prices:** Start at $150. **Remarks:** Does own heat treating and cryogenic deep freeze. Full-time maker; first knife sold in 1984. **Mark:** Name over English shield and dagger.

CHAMBLIN, JOEL,
960 New Hebron Church Rd, Concord, GA 30206, Phone: 678-588-6769, chamblinknives@yahoo.com Web: chamblinknives.com
Specialties: Fancy and working folders. **Patterns:** Fancy locking folders, traditional, multi-blades and utility. **Technical:** Uses ATS-34, 440C, and commercial Damascus. Offers filework. **Prices:** Start at $400. **Remarks:** Full-time maker; first knife sold in 1989. **Mark:** Last name.

CHAMPION, ROBERT,
7001 Red Rock Rd., Amarillo, TX 79118, Phone: 806-622-3970
Specialties: Traditional working straight knives. **Patterns:** Hunters, skinners, camp knives, Bowies, daggers. **Technical:** Grinds 440C and D2. **Prices:** $100 to $600. **Remarks:** Part-time maker; first knife sold in 1979. Stream-line hunters. **Mark:** Last name with dagger logo, city and state.

CHAPO, WILLIAM G,
45 Wildridge Rd, Wilton, CT 06897, Phone: 203-544-9424
Specialties: Classic straight knives and folders of his design and to customer specs; period pieces. **Patterns:** Boots, Bowies and locking folders. **Technical:** Forges stainless Damascus. Offers filework. **Prices:** $750 and up. **Remarks:** Full-time maker; first knife sold in 1989. **Mark:** First and middle initials, last name, city, state.

CHARD, GORDON R,
104 S. Holiday Lane, Iola, KS 66749, Phone: 620-365-2311, Fax: 620-365-2311, gchard@cox.net
Specialties: High tech folding knives in one-of-a-kind styles. **Patterns:** Liner locking folders of own design. Also fixed blade Art Knives. **Technical:** Clean work with attention to fit and finish. Blade steel mostly ATS-34 and 154CM, some CPM440V Vaso Wear and Damascus. **Prices:** $150 to $2500. **Remarks:** First knife sold in 1983. **Mark:** Name, city and state surrounded by wheat on each side.

CHASE, ALEX,
208 E. Pennsylvania Ave., DeLand, FL 32724, Phone: 386-734-9918, chase8578@bellsouth.net
Specialties: Historical steels, classic and traditional straight knives of his design and to customer specs. **Patterns:** Art, fighters, hunters and Japanese style. **Technical:** Forges O1-L6 Damascus, meteoric Damascus, 52100, 5160; uses fossil walrus and mastodon ivory etc. **Prices:** $150 to $1000; some to $3500. **Remarks:** Full-time maker; Guild member since 1996. Doing business as Confederate Forge. **Mark:** Stylized initials-A.C.

CHASE, JOHN E,
217 Walnut, Aledo, TX 76008, Phone: 817-441-8331, jchaseknives@sbcglobal.net
Specialties: Straight high-tech working knives in standard patterns or to customer specs. **Patterns:** Hunters, fighters, daggers and Bowies. **Technical:** Grinds D2, O1, 440C; offers mostly satin finishes. **Prices:** Start at $265. **Remarks:** Part-time maker; first knife sold in 1974. **Mark:** Last name in logo.

CHAUVIN, JOHN,
200 Anna St, Scott, LA 70583, Phone: 337-237-6138, Fax: 337-230-7980
Specialties: Traditional working and using straight knives of his design, to customer specs and in standard patterns. **Patterns:** Bowies, fighters, and hunters. **Technical:** Grinds ATS-34, 440C and O1 high-carbon. Paul Bos heat treating. Uses ivory, stag, oosic and stabilized Louisiana swamp maple for handle materials. Makes sheaths using alligator and ostrich. **Prices:** $200 and up. Bowies start at $500. **Remarks:** Part-time maker; first knife sold in 1995. **Mark:** Full name, city, state.

CHAUZY, ALAIN,
1 Rue de Paris, 21140 Seur-en-Auxios, FRANCE, Phone: 03-80-97-03-30, Fax: 03-80-97-34-14
Specialties: Fixed blades, folders, hunters, Bowies-scagel-style. **Technical:** Forged blades only. Steels used XC65, 07C, and own Damascus. **Prices:** Contact maker for quote. **Remarks:** Part-time maker. **Mark:** Number 2 crossed by an arrow and name.

CHEATHAM, BILL,
PO Box 636, Laveen, AZ 85339, Phone: 602-237-2786, blademan76@aol.com
Specialties: Working straight knives and folders. **Patterns:** Hunters, fighters, boots and axes; locking folders. **Technical:** Grinds 440C. **Prices:** $150 to $350; exceptional knives to $600. **Remarks:** Full-time maker; first knife sold in 1976. **Mark:** Name, city, state.

CHERRY, FRANK J,
3412 Tiley N.E., Albuquerque, NM 87110, Phone: 505-883-8643

CHEW, LARRY,
515 Cleveland Rd Unit A-9, Granbury, TX 76049, Phone: 817-573-8035, chewman@swbell.net; Web: www.voodooinside.com
Specialties: High-tech folding knives. **Patterns:** Double action automatic and manual folding patterns of his design. **Technical:** CAD designed folders utilizing roller bearing pivot design known as "VooDoo." Double action automatic folders with a variety of obvious and disguised release mechanisms, some with lock-outs. **Prices:** Manual folders start at $475, double action autos start at $750. **Remarks:** Made and sold first knife in 1988, first folder in 1989. Full-time maker since 1997. **Mark:** Name and location etched in blade, Damascus autos marked on spring inside frame. Earliest knives stamped LC.

CHINNOCK, DANIEL T.,
380 River Ridge Dr., Union, MO 63084, Phone: 314-276-6936, Web: www.DanChinnock.com; email: Sueanddanc@cs.com
Specialties: One of a kind folders in Damascus and Mammoth Ivory. Performs intricate pearl inlays into snake wood and giraffe bone. Makes matchingt ivory pistol grips for colt 1911's and Colt SAA. **Patterns:** New folder designs each year, thin ground and delicate gentleman's folders, large "hunting" folders in stainless Damascus and CPM154. Several standard models carried by Internet dealers. **Prices:** $500-$1500 **Remarks:** Full-time maker in 2005 and a voting member of the Knifemakers Guild. Performs intricate file work on all areas of knife. **Mark:** Signature on inside of backbar, starting in 2009 blades are stamped with a large "C" and "Dan" buried inside the "C".

CHOATE, MILTON,
1665 W. County 17-1/2, Somerton, AZ 85350, Phone: 928-627-7251, mccustom@juno.com
Specialties: Classic working and using straight knives of his design, to customer specs and in standard patterns. **Patterns:** Bowies, hunters and utility/camp knives. **Technical:** Grinds 440C; grinds and forges 1095 and 5160. Does filework on top and guards on request. **Prices:** $200 to $800. **Remarks:** Full-time maker, first knife made in 1990. All knives come with handmade sheaths by Judy Choate. **Mark:** Knives marked "Choate."

CHRISTENSEN, JON P,
516 Blue Grouse, Stevensville, MT 59870, Phone: 406-697-8377, jpcknives@gmail.com; Web: www.jonchristensenknives.com
Specialties: Hunting/utility knives, folders, art knives. **Patterns:** Mosaic damascus **Technical:** Sole authorship, forges 01, 1084, 52100, 5160, Damascus from 1084/15N20. **Prices:** $220 and up. **Remarks:** ABS Mastersmith, first knife sold in 1999. **Mark:** First and middle initial surrounded by last initial.

CHURCHMAN, T W (TIM),
475 Saddle Horn Drive, Bandera, TX 78003, Phone: 830-796-8350
Specialties: Fancy and traditional straight knives. Bird/trout knives of his design and to customer specs. **Patterns:** Bird/trout knives, Bowies, daggers, fighters, boot knives, some miniatures. **Technical:** Grinds 440C, D2 and 154CM. Offers stainless fittings, fancy filework, exotic and stabilized woods and hand sewed lined sheaths. Also flower pins as a style. **Prices:** $80 to $650; some to $1500. **Remarks:** Part-time maker; first knife made in 1981 after reading *KNIVES '81*." Doing business as "Custom Knives Churchman Made." **Mark:** "Churchman Made" over Texas Logo "Bandera, Texas" under.

CLAIBORNE, JEFF,
1470 Roberts Rd, Franklin, IN 46131, Phone: 317-736-7443, jeff@claiborneknives.com; Web: www.claiborneknives.com
Specialties: Multi blade slip joint folders. All one-of-a-kind by hand, no jigs or fixtures, swords, straight knives, period pieces, camp knives, hunters, fighters, ethnic swords all periods. Handle: uses stag, pearl, oosic, bone ivory, mastadon-mammoth, elephant or exotic woods. **Technical:** Forges high-carbon steel, makes Damascus, forges cable grinds, O1, 1095, 5160, 52100, L6. **Prices:** $250 and up. **Remarks:** Part-time maker; first knife sold in 1989. **Mark:** Stylized initials in an oval.

CLAIBORNE, RON,
2918 Ellistown Rd, Knox, TN 37924, Phone: 615-524-2054, Bowie@icy.net
Specialties: Multi-blade slip joints, swords, straight knives. **Patterns:** Hunters, daggers, folders. **Technical:** Forges Damascus: mosaic, powder

mosaic. Prefers bone and natural handle materials; some exotic woods. **Prices:** $125 to $2500. **Remarks:** Part-time maker; first knife sold in 1979. Doing business as Thunder Mountain Forge Claiborne Knives. **Mark:** Claiborne.

CLARK, D E (LUCKY),
413 Lyman Lane, Johnstown, PA 15909-1409
Specialties: Working straight knives and folders to customer specs. **Patterns:** Customer designs. **Technical:** Grinds D2, 440C, 154CM. **Prices:** $100 to $200; some higher. **Remarks:** Part-time maker; first knife sold in 1975. **Mark:** Name on one side; "Lucky" on other.

CLARK, HOWARD F,
115 35th Pl, Runnells, IA 50237, Phone: 515-966-2126, howard@mvforge.com; Web: mvforge.com
Specialties: Currently Japanese-style swords. **Patterns:** Katana. **Technical:** Forges L6 and 1086. **Prices:** $1200 to 5000. **Remarks:** Full-time maker; first knife sold in 1979. Doing business as Morgan Valley Forge. **Prior Mark:** Block letters and serial number on folders; anvil/initials logo on straight knives. **Current Mark:** Two character kanji "Big Ear."

CLARK, NATE,
604 Baird Dr, Yoncalla, OR 97499, nateclarkknives@hotmail.com; Web: www.nateclarkknives.com
Specialties: Automatics (push button and hidden release) ATS-34 mirror polish or satin finish, Damascus, pearl, ivory, abalone, woods, bone, Micarta, G-10, filework and carving and sheath knives. **Prices:** $100 to $2500. **Remarks:** Full-time knifemaker since 1996. **Mark:** Nate Clark on spring, spacer or blade.

CLARK, R W,
R.W. CLARK CUSTOM KNIVES, 17602 W. Eugene Terrace, Surprise, AZ 85388-5047, Phone: 909-279-3494, info@rwclarkknives.com
Specialties: Military field knives and Asian hybrids. Hand carved leather sheaths. **Patterns:** Fixed blade hunters, field utility and military. Also presentation and collector grade knives. **Technical:** First maker to use liquid metals LM1 material in knives. Other materials include S30V, O1, stainless and carbon Damascus. **Prices:** $75 to $2000. Average price $300. **Remarks:** Started knifemaking in 1990, full-time in 2000. **Mark:** R.W. Clark, Custom, Corona, CA in standard football shape. Also uses three Japanese characters, spelling Clark, on Asian Hybrids.

CLAY, WAYNE,
Box 125B, Pelham, TN 37366, Phone: 931-467-3472, Fax: 931-467-3076
Specialties: Working straight knives and folders in standard patterns. **Patterns:** Hunters and kitchen knives; gents and hunter patterns. **Technical:** Grinds ATS-34. **Prices:** $125 to $500; some to $1000. **Remarks:** Full-time maker; first knife sold in 1978. **Mark:** Name.

CLINCO, MARCUS,
821 Appelby Street, Venice, CA 90291, Phone: 818-610-9640, marcus@clincoknives.com
Specialties: I make mostly fixed blade knives with an emphasis on everyday working and tactical models. Most of my knives are stock removal with the exception of my sole authored damascus blades. I have several integral models including a one piece tactical model named the viper. **Technical:** Most working knife models in ATS 34. Integrals in O-1, D-2 and 440 C. Damascus in 1080 and 15 N 20. Large camp and Bowie models in 5160 and D-2. Handle materials used include micarta, stabilized wood, G-10 and occasionally stag and ivory. **Prices:** $200 - $600.

COATS, KEN,
317 5th Ave, Stevens Point, WI 54481, Phone: 715-544-0115, kandk_c@charter.net
Specialties: Does own jigged bone scales **Patterns:** Traditional slip joints - shadow patterns **Technical:** ATS-34 Blades and springs. Milled frames. Grinds ATS-34, 440C. Stainless blades and backsprings. Does all own heat treating and freeze cycle. Blades are drawn to 60RC. Nickel silver or brass bolsters on folders are soldered, neutralized and pinned. Handles are jigged bone, hardwoods antler, and Micarta. Cuts and jigs own bone, usually shades of brown or green. **Prices:** $300 and up

COCKERHAM, LLOYD,
1717 Carolyn Ave, Denham Springs, IA 70726, Phone: 225-665-1565

COFFEY, BILL,
68 Joshua Ave, Clovis, CA 93611, Phone: 559-299-4259
Specialties: Working and fancy straight knives and folders of his design. **Patterns:** Hunters, fighters, utility, LinerLock® folders and fantasy knives. **Technical:** Grinds 440C, ATS-34, A-Z and commercial Damascus. **Prices:** $250 to $1000; some to $2500. **Remarks:** Full-time maker. First knife sold in 1993. **Mark:** First and last name, city, state.

COFFMAN, DANNY,
541 Angel Dr S, Jacksonville, AL 36265-5787, Phone: 256-435-1619
Specialties: Straight knives and folders of his design. Now making liner locks for $650 to $1200 with natural handles and contrasting Damascus blades and bolsters. **Patterns:** Hunters, locking and slip-joint folders. **Technical:** Grinds Damascus, 440C and D2. Offers filework and engraving. **Prices:** $100 to $400; some to $800. **Remarks:** Spare-time maker; first knife sold in 1992. Doing business as Customs by Coffman. **Mark:** Last name stamped or engraved.

COHEA, JOHN M,
114 Rogers Dr., Nettleton, MS 38855, Phone: 662-322-5916, jhncohea@hotmail.com Web: http://jmcknives.blademakers.com
Specialties: Frontier style knives, hawks, and leather. **Patterns:** Bowies, hunters, patch/neck knives, tomahawks, and friction folders. **Technical:** Makes both forged and stock removal knives using high carbon steels and damascus. Uses natural handle materials that include antler, bone, ivory, horn, and figured hardwoods. Also makes rawhide covered sheaths that include fringe, tacks, antique trade beads, and other period correct materials. **Prices:** $100 - $1500, some higher. **Remarks:** Part-time maker, first knife sold in 1999. **Mark:** COHEA stamped on riccasso.

COHEN, N J (NORM),
2408 Sugarcone Rd, Baltimore, MD 21209, Phone: 410-484-3841, NJC528@verizon.net; Web:www.njcknives.com
Specialties: Working class knives. **Patterns:** Hunters, skinners, bird knives, push daggers, boots, kitchen and practical customer designs. **Technical:** Stock removal 440C, ATS-34. Uses Micarta, Corian. Some woods in handles. **Prices:** $50 to $250. **Remarks:** Part-time maker; first knife sold in 1982. **Mark:** NJC engraved.

COHEN, TERRY A,
PO Box 406, Laytonville, CA 95454
Specialties: Working straight knives and folders. **Patterns:** Bowies to boot knives and locking folders; mini-boot knives. **Technical:** Grinds stainless; hand rubs; tries for good balance. **Prices:** $85 to $150; some to $325. **Remarks:** Part-time maker; first knife sold in 1983. **Mark:** TERRY KNIVES, city and state.

COIL, JIMMIE J,
2936 Asbury Pl, Owensboro, KY 42303, Phone: 270-684-7827
Specialties: Traditional working and straight knives of his design. **Patterns:** Hunters, Bowies and fighters. **Technical:** Grinds 440C, ATS-34 and D2. Blades are flat-ground with brush finish; most have tapered tang. Offers filework. **Prices:** $65 to $250; some to $750. **Remarks:** Spare-time maker; first knife sold in 1974. **Mark:** Name.

COLE, DAVE,
620 Poinsetta Dr, Satellite Beach, FL 32937, Phone: 321-773-1687, Web: http://dcknivesandleather.blademakers.com
Specialties: Fixed blades and friction folders of his design or customers. **Patterns:** Utility, hunters, and Bowies. **Technical:** Grinds O1, 1095. 440C stainless Damascus; prefers natural handle materials, handmade sheaths. **Prices:** $100 and up. **Remarks:** Part-time maker, custom sheath services for others; first knife sold in 1991. **Mark:** D Cole.

COLE, JAMES M,
505 Stonewood Blvd, Bartonville, TX 76226, Phone: 817-430-0302, dogcole@swbell.net

COLE, WELBORN I,
365 Crystal Ct, Athens, GA 30606, Phone: 404-261-3977
Specialties: Traditional straight knives of his design. **Patterns:** Hunters. **Technical:** Grinds 440C, ATS-34 and D2. Good wood scales. **Prices:** NA. **Remarks:** Full-time maker; first knife sold in 1983. **Mark:** Script initials.

COLEMAN, JOHN A,
732 S. Bonita Way, Citrus Heights, CA 95610-3003, Phone: 916-335-1568
Specialties: Traditional working straight knives of his design or yours. **Patterns:** Plain to fancy file back working knives hunters, bird, trout, camp knives, skinners. Trout knives miniatures of Bowies and cappers. **Technical:** Grinds 440C, ATS-34, 145CM and D2. Exotic woods bone, antler and some ivory. **Prices:** $80 to $200, some to $450. **Remarks:** Part-time maker. First knife sold in 1989. Doing business as Slim's Custom Knives. Enjoys making knives to your specs; all knives come with handmade sheath by Slim's Leather. **Mark:** Cowboy setting on log whittling Slim's Custom Knives above cowboy and name and state under cowboy.

COLLINS, LYNN M,
138 Berkley Dr, Elyria, OH 44035, Phone: 440-366-7101
Specialties: Working straight knives. **Patterns:** Field knives, boots and fighters. **Technical:** Grinds D2, 154CM and 440C. **Prices:** Start at $150. **Remarks:** Spare-time maker; first knife sold in 1980. **Mark:** Initials, asterisks.

COLTER, WADE,
PO Box 2340, Colstrip, MT 59323, Phone: 406-748-4573
Specialties: Fancy and embellished straight knives, folders and swords of his design; historical and period pieces. **Patterns:** Bowies, swords and folders. **Technical:** Hand forges 52100 ball bearing steel and L6, 1090, cable and chain Damascus from 5N20 and 1084. Carves and makes sheaths. **Prices:** $250 to $3500. **Remarks:** Part-time maker; first knife sold in 1990. Doing business as "Colter's Hell" Forge. **Mark:** Initials on left side ricasso.

CONKLIN, GEORGE L,
Box 902, Ft. Benton, MT 59442, Phone: 406-622-3268, Fax: 406-622-3410, 7bbgrus@3rivers.net
Specialties: Designer and manufacturer of the "Brisket Breaker." **Patterns:** Hunters, utility/camp knives and hatchets. **Technical:** Grinds 440C, ATS-34, D2, 1095, 154CM and 5160. Offers some forging and heat-treats for others. Offers some jewelling. **Prices:** $65 to $200; some to $1000. **Remarks:** Full-time maker. Doing business as Rocky Mountain Knives. **Mark:** Last name in script.

CONLEY, BOB,
1013 Creasy Rd, Jonesboro, TN 37659, Phone: 423-753-3302
Specialties: Working straight knives and folders. **Patterns:** Lockers, two-blades, gents, hunters, traditional-styles, straight hunters. **Technical:** Grinds 440C, 154CM and ATS-34. Engraves. **Prices:** $250 to $450; some to $600. **Remarks:** Full-time maker; first knife sold in 1979. **Mark:** Full name, city, state.

CONN JR., C T,
206 Highland Ave, Attalla, AL 35954, Phone: 205-538-7688
Specialties: Working folders, some fancy. **Patterns:** Full range of folding knives. **Technical:** Grinds O2, 440C and 154CM. **Prices:** $125 to $300; some to $600. **Remarks:** Part-time maker; first knife sold in 1982. **Mark:** Name.

CONNOLLY, JAMES,
2486 Oro-Quincy Hwy, Oroville, CA 95966, Phone: 530-534-5363, rjconnolly@sbcglobal.net
Specialties: Classic working and using knives of his design. **Patterns:** Boots, Bowies, daggers and swords. **Technical:** Grinds ATS-34, BG42, A2, O1. **Prices:** $100 to $500; some to $1500. **Remarks:** Part-time maker; first knife sold in 1980. Doing business as Gold Rush Designs. **Mark:** First initial, last name, Handmade.

CONNOR, JOHN W,
PO Box 12981, Odessa, TX 79768-2981, Phone: 915-362-6901

CONNOR, MICHAEL,
Box 502, Winters, TX 79567, Phone: 915-754-5602
Specialties: Straight knives, period pieces, some folders. **Patterns:** Hunters to camp knives to traditional locking folders to Bowies. **Technical:** Forges 5160, O1, 1084 steels and his own Damascus. **Prices:** Moderate to upscale. **Remarks:** Spare-time maker; first knife sold in 1974. ABS Master Smith 1983. **Mark:** Last name, M.S.

CONTI, JEFFREY D,
21104 75th St E, Bonney Lake, WA 98390, Phone: 253-447-4660, Fax: 253-512-8629
Specialties: Working straight knives. **Patterns:** Fighters and survival knives; hunters, camp knives and fishing knives. **Technical:** Grinds D2, 154CM and O1. Engraves. **Prices:** Start at $80. **Remarks:** Part-time maker; first knife sold in 1980. Does own heat treating. **Mark:** Initials, year, steel type, name and number of knife.

CONWAY, JOHN,
13301 100th Place NE, Kirkland, WA 98034, Phone: 425-823-2821, jcknives@verizon.net
Specialties: Folders; working and Damascus. Straight knives, camp, utility and fighting knives. **Patterns:** LinerLock® folders of own design. Hidden tang straight knives of own design. **Technical:** Flat grinds forged carbon steels and own Damascus steel, including mosaic. **Prices:** $300 to $850. **Remarks:** Part-time maker since 1999. **Mark:** Oval with stylized initials J C inset.

COOGAN, ROBERT,
1560 Craft Center Dr, Smithville, TN 37166, Phone: 615-597-6801, http://iweb.tntech.edu/rcoogan/
Specialties: One-of-a-kind knives. **Patterns:** Unique items like ulu-style Appalachian herb knives. **Technical:** Forges; his Damascus is made from nickel steel and W1. **Prices:** Start at $100. **Remarks:** Part-time maker; first knife sold in 1979. **Mark:** Initials or last name in script.

COOK, JAMES R,
455 Anderson Rd, Nashville, AR 71852, Phone: 870 845 5173, jr@jrcookknives.com; Web: www.jrcookknives.com
Specialties: Working straight knives and folders of his design or to customer specs. **Patterns:** Bowies, hunters and camp knives. **Technical:** Forges 1084 and high-carbon Damascus. **Prices:** $195 to $5500. **Remarks:** Full-time maker; first knife sold in 1986. **Mark:** First and middle initials, last name.

COOK, LOUISE,
475 Robinson Ln, Ozark, IL 62972, Phone: 618-777-2932
Specialties: Working and using straight knives of her design and to customer specs; period pieces. **Patterns:** Bowies, hunters and utility/camp knives. **Technical:** Forges 5160. Filework; pin work; silver wire inlay. **Prices:** Start at $50/inch. **Remarks:** Part-time maker; first knife sold in 1990. Doing business as Panther Creek Forge. **Mark:** First name and Journeyman stamp on one side; panther head on the other.

COOK, MIKE,
475 Robinson Ln, Ozark, IL 62972, Phone: 618-777-2932
Specialties: Traditional working and using straight knives of his design and to customer specs. **Patterns:** Bowies, hunters and utility/camp knives. **Technical:** Forges 5160. Filework; pin work. **Prices:** Start at $50/inch. **Remarks:** Spare-time maker; first knife sold in 1991. **Mark:** First initial, last name and Journeyman stamp on one side; panther head on the other.

COOK, MIKE A,
10927 Shilton Rd, Portland, MI 48875, Phone: 517-242-1352, macook@hughes.net Web: www.artofishi.com
Specialties: Fancy/embellished and period pieces of his design. **Patterns:** Daggers, fighters and hunters. **Technical:** Stone bladed knives in agate, obsidian and jasper. Scrimshaws; opal inlays. **Prices:** $60 to $300; some to $800. **Remarks:** Part-time maker; first knife sold in 1988. Doing business as Art of Ishi. **Mark:** Initials and year.

COOMBS JR., LAMONT,
546 State Rt 46, Bucksport, ME 04416, Phone: 207-469-3057, Fax: 207-469-3057, theknifemaker@hotmail.com; Web: www.knivesby.com/coomb-knives.html
Specialties: Classic fancy and embellished straight knives; traditional working and using straight knives. Knives of his design and to customer specs. **Patterns:** Hunters, folders and utility/camp knives. **Technical:** Hollow- and flat-grinds ATS-34, 440C, A2, D2 and O1; grinds Damascus from other makers. **Prices:** $100 to $500; some to $3500. **Remarks:** Full-time maker; first knife sold in 1988. **Mark:** Last name on banner, handmade underneath.

COON, RAYMOND C,
21135 S.E. Tillstrom Rd, Gresham, OR 97080, Phone: 503-658-2252, Raymond@damascusknife.com; Web: Damascusknife.com
Specialties: Working straight knives in standard patterns. **Patterns:** Hunters, Bowies, daggers, boots and axes. **Technical:** Forges high-carbon steel and Damascus or 97089. **Prices:** Start at $235. **Remarks:** Full-time maker; does own leatherwork, makes own Damascus, daggers; first knife sold in 1995. **Mark:** First initial, last name.

COPELAND, THOM,
171 Country Line Rd S, Nashville, AR 71852, tcope@cswnet.com
Specialties: Hand forged fixed blades; hunters, Bowies and camp knives. **Remarks:** Member of ABS and AKA (Arkansas Knifemakers Association). **Mark:** Copeland.

COPPINS, DANIEL,
7303 Sherrard Rd, Cambridge, OH 43725, Phone: 740-439-4199
Specialties: Grinds 440 C, D-2. Antler handles. **Patterns:** Drop point hunters, fighters, Bowies, bird and trout daggers. **Prices:** $40 to $800. **Remarks:** Sold first knife in 2002. **Mark:** DC.

CORBY, HAROLD,
218 Brandonwood Dr, Johnson City, TN 37604, Phone: 423-926-9781
Specialties: Large fighters and Bowies; self-protection knives; art knives. Along with art knives and combat knives, Corby now has a all new automatic MO.PB1, also side lock MO LL-1 with titanium liners G-10 handles. **Patterns:** Sub-hilt fighters and hunters. **Technical:** Grinds 154CM, ATS-34 and 440C. **Prices:** $200 to $6000. **Remarks:** Full-time maker; first knife sold in 1969. Doing business as Knives by Corby. **Mark:** Last name.

CORDOVA, JOSEPH G,
PO Box 977, Peralta, NM 87042, Phone: 505-869-3912, kcordova@rt66.com
Specialties: One-of-a-kind designs, some to customer specs. **Patterns:** Fighter called the 'Gladiator', hunters, boots and cutlery. **Technical:** Forges 1095, 5160; grinds ATS-34, 440C and 154CM. **Prices:** Moderate to upscale. **Remarks:** Full-time maker; first knife sold in 1953. Past chairman of American Bladesmith Society. **Mark:** Cordova made.

CORKUM, STEVE,
34 Basehoar School Rd, Littlestown, PA 17340, Phone: 717-359-9563, sco7129849@aol.com; Web: www.hawknives.com

COSTA, SCOTT,
409 Coventry Rd, Spicewood, TX 78669, Phone: 830-693-3431
Specialties: Working straight knives. **Patterns:** Hunters, skinners, axes, trophy sets, custom boxed steak sets, carving sets and bar sets. **Technical:** Grinds D2, ATS-34, 440 and Damascus. Heat-treats. **Prices:** $225 to $2000. **Remarks:** Full-time maker; first knife sold in 1985. **Mark:** Initials connected.

COTTRILL, JAMES I,
1776 Ransburg Ave, Columbus, OH 43223, Phone: 614-274-0020
Specialties: Working straight knives of his design. **Patterns:** Caters to the boating and hunting crowd; cutlery. **Technical:** Grinds O1, D2 and 440C. Likes filework. **Prices:** $95 to $250; some to $500. **Remarks:** Full-time maker; first knife sold in 1977. **Mark:** Name, city, state, in oval logo.

COURTNEY, ELDON,
2718 Bullinger, Wichita, KS 67204, Phone: 316-838-4053
Specialties: Working straight knives of his design. **Patterns:** Hunters, fighters and one-of-a-kinds. **Technical:** Grinds and tempers L6, 440C and spring steel. **Prices:** $100 to $500; some to $1500. **Remarks:** Full-time maker; first knife sold in 1977. **Mark:** Full name, city and state.

COURTOIS, BRYAN,
3 Lawn Ave, Saco, ME 04072, Phone: 207-282-3977, bryancourtois@verizon.net; Web: http://mysite.verizon.net/vzeui2z01
Specialties: Working straight knives; prefers customer designs, no standard patterns. **Patterns:** Functional hunters; everyday knives. **Technical:** Grinds 440C or customer request. Hollow-grinds with a variety of finishes. Specializes in granite handles and custom skeleton knives. **Prices:** Start at $75. **Remarks:** Part-time maker; first knife sold in 1988. Doing business as Castle Knives. **Mark:** A rook chess piece machined into blade using electrical discharge process.

COUSINO, GEORGE,
7818 Norfolk, Onsted, MI 49265, Phone: 517-467-4911, cousinoknives@yahoo.com; Web: www.cousinoknives.com
Specialties: Hunters, Bowies using knives. **Patterns:** Hunters, Bowies, buckskinners, folders and daggers. **Technical:** Grinds 440C. **Prices:** $95 to $300. **Remarks:** Part-time maker; first knife sold in 1981. **Mark:** Last name.

COVER, RAYMOND A,
1206 N Third St, Festus, MO 63028-1628, Phone: 636-937-5955
Specialties: High-tech working straight knives and folders in standard patterns. **Patterns:** Slip joint folders, two-bladed folders. **Technical:** Grinds D2, and ATS-34. **Prices:** $165 to $250; some to $400. **Remarks:** Part-time maker; first knife sold in 1974. **Mark:** Name.

COWLES, DON,
1026 Lawndale Dr, Royal Oak, MI 48067, Phone: 248-541-4619, don@cowlesknives.com; Web: www.cowlesknives.com
Specialties: Straight, non-folding pocket knives of his design. **Patterns:** Gentlemen's pocket knives. **Technical:** Grinds CPM154, S30V, Damascus, Talonite. Engraves; pearl inlays in some handles. **Prices:** Start at $300. **Remarks:** Full-time maker; first knife sold in 1994. **Mark:** Full name with oak leaf.

COX, COLIN J,
107 N. Oxford Dr, Raymore, MO 64083, Phone: 816-322-1977, colin4knives@aol.com; Web: www.colincoxknives.com
Specialties: Working straight knives and folders of his design; period pieces. **Patterns:** Hunters, fighters and survival knives. Folders, two-blades, gents and hunters. **Technical:** Grinds D2, 440C, 154CM and ATS-34. **Prices:** $125 to $750; some to $4000. **Remarks:** Full-time maker; first knife sold in 1981. **Mark:** Full name, city and state.

COX, LARRY,
701 W. 13th St, Murfreesboro, AR 71958, Phone: 870-258-2429, Fax: Cell: 870-557-8062
Patterns: Hunters, camp knives, Bowies, and skinners. **Technical:** Forges carbon steel 1084, 1080, 15N29, 5160 and Damascus. Forges own pattern welded Damascus as well as doing own heat treat. **Prices:** $150 and up. **Remarks:** Sole ownership; knives and sheaths. Part-time maker; first knife sold in 2007. Member ABS and Arkansas Knifemakers Association. **Mark:** COX.

COX, SAM,
1756 Love Springs Rd, Gaffney, SC 29341, mail@samcox.us; Web: www.samcox.us
Remarks: Started making knives in 1981 for another maker. 1st knife sold under own name in 1983. Full-time maker 1985-2009. Retired in 2010. Now part time. **Mark:** Different logo each year.

CRAIG, ROGER L,
2617 SW Seabrook Ave, Topeka, KS 66614, Phone: 785-249-4109
Specialties: Working and camp knives, some fantasy; all his design. **Patterns:** Fighters, hunter. **Technical:** Grinds 1095 and 5160. Most knives have file work. **Prices:** $50 to $250. **Remarks:** Part-time maker; first knife sold in 1991. Doing business as Craig Knives. **Mark:** Last name-Craig.

CRAIN, JACK W,
PO Box 212, Granbury, TX 76048, jack@jackcrainknives.com Web: www.jackcrainknives.com
Specialties: Fantasy and period knives; combat and survival knives. **Patterns:** One-of-a-kind art or fantasy daggers, swords and Bowies; survival knives. **Technical:** Forges Damascus; grinds stainless steel. Carves. **Prices:** $350 to $2500; some to $20,000. **Remarks:** Full-time maker; first knife sold in 1969. Designer and maker of the knives seen in the films *Dracula 2000*, *Executive Decision*, *Demolition Man*, *Predator I* and *II*, *Commando*, *Die Hard I* and *II*, *Road House*, *Ford Fairlane* and *Action Jackson*, and television shows *War of the Worlds*, *Air Wolf*, *Kung Fu: The Legend Cont.* and *Tales of the Crypt*. **Mark:** Stylized crane.

CRAMER, BRENT,
PO BOX 99, Wheatland, IN 47597, Phone: 812-881-9961, Bdcramer@juno.com Web: BDCramerKnives.com
Specialties: Traditional and custom working and using knives. **Patterns:** Traditional single blade slip-joint folders and standard fixed blades. **Technical:** Stock removal only. Pivot bushing construction on folders. Steel: D-2, 154 CM, ATS-34, CPM-D2, CPM-154CM, O-1, 52100, A-2. All steels heat treated in shop with LN Cryo. Handle Material: Stag, Bone, Wood, Ivory, and Micarta. **Prices:** $150 - $550. **Remarks:** Part-time maker. First fixed blade sold in 2003. First folder sold in 2007. **Mark:** BDC and B.D.Cramer.

CRAWFORD, PAT AND WES,
205 N. Center, West Memphis, AR 72301, Phone: 870-732-2452, patcrawford1@earthlink.com; Web: www.crawfordknives.com
Specialties: Stainless steel Damascus. High-tech working self-defense and combat types and folders. **Patterns:** Tactical-more fancy knives now. **Technical:** Grinds S30V. **Prices:** $400 to $2000. **Remarks:** Full-time maker; first knife sold in 1973. **Mark:** Last name.

CRAWLEY, BRUCE R,
16 Binbrook Dr, Croydon 3136 Victoria, AUSTRALIA
Specialties: Folders. **Patterns:** Hunters, lockback folders and Bowies. **Technical:** Grinds 440C, ATS-34 and commercial Damascus. Offers filework and mirror polish. **Prices:** $160 to $3500. **Remarks:** Part-time maker; first knife sold in 1990. **Mark:** Initials.

CRENSHAW, AL,
Rt 1 Box 717, Eufaula, OK 74432, Phone: 918-452-2128
Specialties: Folders of his design and in standard patterns. **Patterns:** Hunters, locking folders, slip-joint folders, multi blade folders. **Technical:** Grinds 440C, D2 and ATS-34. Does filework on back springs and blades; offers scrimshaw on some handles. **Prices:** $150 to $300; some higher. **Remarks:** Full-time maker; first knife sold in 1981. Doing business as A. Crenshaw Knives. **Mark:** First initial, last name, Lake Eufaula, state stamped; first initial last name in rainbow; Lake Eufaula across bottom with Okla. in middle.

CRIST, ZOE,
HC82 BOX 217A, Marlinton, WV 24954, Phone: 304-799-6782, zoe@zoecristknives.com Web: www.zoecristknives.com
Specialties: Mosaic and classic pattern Damascus. Custom Damascus and traditional Damascus working and art knives. Also makes Mokume. Works to customer specs. **Patterns:** All Damascus hunters, bowies, fighters, neck, boot, and high-end art knives. **Technical:** Makes all his own Damascus Steel from 1095, L6, 15n20. Forges all knives, heat treats, filework, differential heat treating. **Prices:** $150 - $2500. **Remarks:** Full-time maker, has been making knives since 1988, went full-time 2009. Also makes own leather sheaths. **Mark:** Small "z" with long tail on left side of blade at ricaso.

CROCKFORD, JACK,
1859 Harts Mill Rd, Chamblee, GA 30341, Phone: 770-457-4680
Specialties: Lockback folders. **Patterns:** Hunters, fishing and camp knives, traditional folders. **Technical:** Grinds A2, D2, ATS-34 and 440C. Engraves and scrimshaws. **Prices:** Start at $175. **Remarks:** Part-time maker; first knife sold in 1975. **Mark:** Name.

CROSS, ROBERT,
RMB 200B, Manilla Rd, Tamworth 2340, NSW, AUSTRALIA, Phone: 067-618385

CROWDER, ROBERT,
Box 1374, Thompson Falls, MT 59873, Phone: 406-827-4754
Specialties: Traditional working knives to customer specs. **Patterns:** Hunters, Bowies, fighters and fillets. **Technical:** Grinds ATS-34, 154CM, 440C, Vascowear and commercial Damascus. **Prices:** $225 to $500; some to $2500. **Remarks:** Full-time maker; first knife sold in 1985. **Mark:** R Crowder signature & Montana.

CROWELL, JAMES L,
PO Box 822, 676 Newnata Cutoff, Mtn. View, AR 72560, Phone: 870-746-4215, crowellknives@yahoo.com
Specialties: Bowie knives; fighters and working knives. **Patterns:** Hunters, fighters, Bowies, daggers and folders. Period pieces: War hammers, Japanese and European. **Technical:** Forges 10 series carbon steels as well as O1, L6 and his own Damascus. **Prices:** $425 to $4500; some to $7500. **Remarks:** Full-time maker; first knife sold in 1980. Earned ABS Master Bladesmith in 1986. **Mark:** A shooting star.

CROWL, PETER,
5786 County Road 10, Waterloo, IN 46793, Phone: 260-488-2532, pete@petecrowlknives.com; Web: www.petecrowlknives.com
Specialties: Bowie, hunters. **Technical:** Forges 5160, 1080, W2, 52100. **Prices:** $200 and up. **Remarks:** ABS Journeyman smith. **Mark:** Last name in script.

CROWNER, JEFF,
1565 Samuel Drive, Cottage Grove, OR 97424, Phone: 541-201-3182, Fax: 541-579-3762
Specialties: Custom knife maker. I make some of the following: wilderness survival blades, martial art weapons, hunting blades. **Technical:** I differentially heat treat every knife. I use various steels like 5160, L-6, Cable Damascus, 52100, 6150, and some stainless types. I use the following for handle materials: TeroTuf by Columbia Industrial products and exotic hardwoods and horn. I make my own custom sheaths as well with either kydex or leather.

CROWTHERS, MARK F,
PO Box 4641, Rolling Bay, WA 98061-0641, Phone: 206-842-7501

CUCCHIARA, MATT,
387 W. Hagler, Fresno, CA 93711, Phone: 559-917-2328, matt@cucchiaraknives.com Web: www.cucchiaraknives.com
Specialties: I make large and small, plain or hand carved Ti handled Tactical framelock folders. All decoration and carving work done by maker. Also known for my hand carved Ti pocket clips. **Prices:** Start at around $400 and go as high as $1500 or so.

CULPEPPER, JOHN,
2102 Spencer Ave, Monroe, LA 71201, Phone: 318-323-3636
Specialties: Working straight knives. **Patterns:** Hunters, Bowies and camp knives in heavy-duty patterns. **Technical:** Grinds O1, D2 and 440C; hollow-grinds. **Prices:** $75 to $200; some to $300. **Remarks:** Part-time maker; first knife sold in 1970. Doing business as Pepper Knives. **Mark:** Pepper.

CULVER, STEVE,
5682 94th St, Meriden, KS 66512, Phone: 866-505-0146, Web: www.culverart.com
Specialties: Edged tools and weapons, collectible and functional. **Patterns:** Bowies, daggers, swords, hunters, folders and edged tools. **Technical:** Forges carbon steels and his own pattern welded steels. **Prices:** $350 to $2500; some to $5000. **Remarks:** Full-time maker; first knife sold in 1989. **Mark:** Last name, M. S.

CUMMING, BOB,

CUMMING KNIVES, 35 Manana Dr, Cedar Crest, NM 87008, Phone: 505-286-0509, cumming@comcast.net; Web: www.cummingknives.com

Specialties: One-of-a-kind exhibition grade custom Bowie knives, exhibition grade and working hunters, bird & trout knives, salt and fresh water fillet knives. Low country oyster knives, custom tanto's plains Indian style sheaths & custom leather, all types of exotic handle materials, scrimshaw and engraving. Added folders in 2006. Custom oyster knives. **Prices:** $95 to $3500 and up. **Remarks:** Mentored by the late Jim Nolen, sold first knife in 1978 in Denmark. Retired U.S. Foreign Service Officer. Member NCCKG. **Mark:** Stylized CUMMING.

CURTISS, STEVE L,

PO Box 448, Eureka, MT 59914, Phone: 406-889-5510, Fax: 406-889-5510, slc@bladerigger.com; Web: http://www.bladerigger.com

Specialties: True custom and semi-custom production (SCP), specialized concealment blades; advanced sheaths and tailored body harnessing systems. **Patterns:** Tactical/personal defense fighters, swords, utility and custom patterns. **Technical:** Grinds A2 and Talonite®; heat-treats. Sheaths: Kydex or Kydex-lined leather laminated or Kydex-lined with Rigger Coat™. Exotic materials available. **Prices:** $50 to $10,000. **Remarks:** Full-time maker. Doing business as Blade Rigger L.L.C. Martial artist and unique defense industry tools and equipment. **Mark:** For true custom: Initials and for SCP: Blade Rigger.

CUTE, THOMAS,

State Rt 90-7071, Cortland, NY 13045, Phone: 607-749-4055

Specialties: Working straight knives. **Patterns:** Hunters, Bowies and fighters. **Technical:** Grinds O1, 440C and ATS-34. **Prices:** $100 to $1000. **Remarks:** Full-time maker; first knife sold in 1974. **Mark:** Full name.

D

DAILEY, G E,

577 Lincoln St, Seekonk, MA 02771, Phone: 508-336-5088, gedailey@msn.com; Web: www.gedailey.com

Specialties: One-of-a-kind exotic designed edged weapons. **Patterns:** Folders, daggers and swords. **Technical:** Reforges and grinds Damascus; prefers hollow-grinding. Engraves, carves, offers filework and sets stones and uses exotic gems and gold. **Prices:** Start at $1100. **Remarks:** Full-time maker. First knife sold in 1982. **Mark:** Last name or stylized initialed logo.

DAKE, C M,

19759 Chef Menteur Hwy, New Orleans, LA 70129-9602, Phone: 504-254-0357, Fax: 504-254-9501

Specialties: Fancy working folders. **Patterns:** Front-lock lockbacks, button-lock folders. **Technical:** Grinds ATS-34 and Damascus. **Prices:** $500 to $2500; some higher. **Remarks:** Full-time maker; first knife sold in 1988. Doing business as Bayou Custom Cutlery. **Mark:** Last name.

DAKE, MARY H,

Rt 5 Box 287A, New Orleans, LA 70129, Phone: 504-254-0357

DALLYN, KELLY,

14695 Deerridge Dr SE, Calgary, AB, CANADA T2J 6A8, Phone: 403-475-3056, kdallyn@machinexrs.com

Specialties: Kitchen and hunters

DAMASTEEL STAINLESS DAMASCUS,

3052 Isim Rd., Norman, OK 73026, Phone: 888-804-0683; 405-321-3614, damascus@newmex.com; Web: www.ssdamacus.com

Patterns: Rose, Odin's eye, 5, 20, 30 twists Hakkapelitta, TNT, and infinity

DAMLOVAC, SAVA,

10292 Bradbury Dr, Indianapolis, IN 46231, Phone: 317-839-4952

Specialties: Period pieces, fantasy, Viking, Moran type all Damascus daggers. **Patterns:** Bowies, fighters, daggers, Persian-style knives. **Technical:** Uses own Damascus, some stainless, mostly hand forges. **Prices:** $150 to $2500; some higher. **Remarks:** Full-time maker; first knife sold in 1993. Specialty, Bill Moran all Damascus dagger sets, in Moran-style wood case. **Mark:** "Sava" stamped in Damascus or etched in stainless.

D'ANDREA, JOHN,

8517 N Linwood Loop, Citrus Springs, FL 34433-5045, Phone: 352-489-2803, jpda@optonline.net

Specialties: Fancy working straight knives and folders with filework and distinctive leatherwork. **Patterns:** Hunters, fighters, daggers, folders and an occasional sword. **Technical:** Grinds ATS-34, 154CM, 440C and D2. **Prices:** $180 to $600; some to $1000. **Remarks:** Part-time maker; first knife sold in 1986. **Mark:** First name, last initial imposed on samurai sword.

D'ANGELO, LAURENCE,

14703 NE 17th Ave, Vancouver, WA 98686, Phone: 360-573-0546

Specialties: Straight knives of his design. **Patterns:** Bowies, hunters and locking folders. **Technical:** Grinds D2, ATS-34 and 440C. Hand makes all sheaths. **Prices:** $100 to $200. **Remarks:** Full-time maker; first knife sold in 1987. **Mark:** Football logo—first and middle initials, last name, city, state, Maker.

DANIEL, TRAVIS E,

1655 Carrow Rd, Chocowinity, NC 27817, Phone: 252-940-0807, tedsknives@mail.com

Specialties: Traditional working straight knives of his design or to customer specs. **Patterns:** Hunters, fighters and utility/camp knives. **Technical:**

Grinds ATS-34, 440-C, 154CM, forges his own Damascus. Stock removal. **Prices:** $90 to $1200. **Remarks:** Full-time maker; first knife sold in 1976. **Mark:** TED.

DANIELS, ALEX,

1416 County Rd 415, Town Creek, AL 35672, Phone: 256-685-0943, akdknives@hughes.net

Specialties: Working and using straight knives and folders; period pieces, reproduction Bowies. **Patterns:** Mostly reproduction Bowies but offers full line of knives. **Technical:** BG-42, 440C, 1095, 52100 forged blades. **Prices:** $350 to $2500. **Remarks:** Full-time maker; first knife sold in 1963. **Mark:** First and middle initials, last name, city and state.

DANNEMANN, RANDY,

RIM RANCH, 27752 P25 Rd, Hotchkiss, CO 81419

Specialties: Classic pattern working hunters, skinners, bird, trout, kitchen & utility knives. **Technical:** Grinds 440C, 154CM, & D2 steel, in house heat treating and cryogenic enhancement. Most are full tapered tang with finger guard and working satin finish. Custom fitted leather sheath for every hunting style knife, both serialized. Uses imported hardwoods, stag, or Micarta for handles. **Prices:** $140 to $240 some higher. **Remarks:** First knife sold 1974. **Mark:** R. Dannemann Colorado or stamped Dannemann.

DARBY, DAVID T,

30652 S 533 Rd, Cookson, OK 74427, Phone: 918-457-4868, knfmkr@fullnet.net

Specialties: Forged blades only, all styles. **Prices:** $350 and up. **Remarks:** ABS Journeyman Smith. **Mark:** Stylized quillion dagger incorporates last name (Darby).

DARBY, JED,

7878 E Co Rd 50 N, Greensburg, IN 47240, Phone: 812-663-2696

Specialties: Traditional working/using straight knives of his design and to customer specs. **Patterns:** Bowies, hunters and utility/camp knives. **Technical:** Grinds 440C, ATS-34 and Damascus. **Prices:** $70 to $550; some to $1000. **Remarks:** Full-time maker; first knife sold in 1992. Doing business as Darby Knives. **Mark:** Last name and year.

DARBY, RICK,

71 Nestingrock Ln, Levittown, PA 19054

Specialties: Working straight knives. **Patterns:** Boots, fighters and hunters with mirror finish. **Technical:** Grinds 440C and CPM440V. **Prices:** $125 to $300. **Remarks:** Part-time maker; first knife sold in 1974. **Mark:** First and middle initials, last name.

DARCEY, CHESTER L,

1608 Dominik Dr, College Station, TX 77840, Phone: 979-696-1656, DarceyKnives@yahoo.com

Specialties: Lockback, LinerLock® and scale release folders. **Patterns:** Bowies, hunters and utilities. **Technical:** Stock removal on carbon and stainless steels, forge own Damascus. **Prices:** $200 to $1000. **Remarks:** Part-time maker, first knife sold in 1999. **Mark:** Last name in script.

DARK, ROBERT,

2218 Huntington Court, Oxford, AL 36203, Phone: 256-831-4645, dark@darkknives.com; Web: www.darkknives.com

Specialties: Fixed blade working knives of maker's designs. Works with customer designed specifications. **Patterns:** Hunters, Bowies, camp knives, kitchen/utility, bird and trout. Standard patterns and customer designed. **Technical:** Forged and stock removal. Works with high carbon, stainless and Damascus steels. Hollow and flat grinds. **Prices:** $175 to $750. **Remarks:** Sole authorship knives and custom leather sheaths. Full-time maker. **Mark:** "R Dark" on left side of blade.

DARPINIAN, DAVE,

12484 S Greenwood St, Olathe, KS 66062, Phone: 913-244-7114, darpo1956@yahoo.com

Specialties: Working knives and fancy pieces to customer specs. **Patterns:** Full range of straight knives including art daggers and short swords. **Technical:** Art grinds ATS-34, 440C, 154 CM, 5160, 1095. **Prices:** $300 to $1000. **Remarks:** First knife sold in 1986, part-time maker. **Mark:** Last name.

DAVIDSON, EDMUND,

3345 Virginia Ave, Goshen, VA 24439, Phone: 540-997-5651, Web: www.edmunddavidson.com

Specialties: High class art integrals. **Patterns:** Many hunters and art models. **Technical:** CPM 154-CM. **Prices:** $100 to infinity. **Remarks:** Full-time maker; first knife sold in 1986. **Mark:** Name in deer head or custom logos.

DAVIDSON, LARRY,

14249 River Rd., New Braunfels, TX 78132, Phone: 830-214-5144, lazza@davidsonknives.com; Web: www.davidsonknives.com

DAVIS, BARRY L,

4262 US 20, Castleton, NY 12033, Phone: 518-477-5036, daviscustomknives@yahoo.com

Specialties: Collector grade Damascus folders. Traditional designs with focus on turn-of-the-century techniques employed. Sole authorship. Forges own Damascus, does all carving, filework, gold work and piquet. Uses only natural handle material. Enjoys doing multi-blade as well as single blade folders and daggers. **Prices:** Prices range from $2000 to $7000. **Remarks:** First knife sold in 1980.

DAVIS, CHARLIE,
ANZA KNIVES, PO Box 710806, Santee, CA 92072, Phone: 619-561-9445, Fax: 619-390-6283, sales@anzaknives.com; Web: www.anzaknives.com
Specialties: Fancy and embellished working straight knives of his design. Patterns: Hunters, camp and utility knives. Technical: Grinds high-carbon files. Prices: $20 to $185, custom depends. Remarks: Full-time maker; first knife sold in 1980. Now offers custom. Mark: ANZA U.S.A.

DAVIS, DON,
8415 Coyote Run, Loveland, CO 80537-9665, Phone: 970-669-9016, Fax: 970-669-8072
Specialties: Working straight knives in standard patterns or to customer specs. Patterns: Hunters, utility knives, skinners and survival knives. Technical: Grinds 440C, ATS-34. Prices: $75 to $250. Remarks: Full-time maker; first knife sold in 1985. Mark: Signature, city and state.

DAVIS, JESSE W,
7398A Hwy 3, Sarah, MS 38665, Phone: 662-382-7332, janddvais1@earthlink.net
Specialties: Working straight knives and boots in standard patterns and to customer specs. Patterns: Boot knives, daggers, fighters, subhilts & Bowies. Technical: Grinds A2, D2, 440C and commercial Damascus. Prices: $125 to $1000. Remarks: Full-time maker; first knife sold in 1977. Former member Knifemakers Guild (in good standing). Mark: Name or initials.

DAVIS, JOEL,
74538 165th, Albert Lea, MN 56007, Phone: 507-377-0808, joelknives@yahoo.com
Specialties: Complete sole authorship presentation grade highly complex pattern-welded mosaic Damascus blade and bolster stock. Patterns: To date Joel has executed over 900 different mosaic Damascus patterns in the past four years. Anything conceived by maker's imagination. Technical: Uses various heat colorable "high vibrancy" steels, nickel 200 and some powdered metal for bolster stock only. Uses 1095, 1075 and 15N20. High carbon steels for cutting edge blade stock only. Prices: 15 to $50 per square inch and up depending on complexity of pattern. Remarks: Full-time mosaic Damascus metal smith focusing strictly on never-before-seen mosaic patterns. Most of maker's work is used for art knives ranging between $1500 to $4500.

DAVIS, JOHN,
235 Lampe Rd, Selah, WA 98942, Phone: 509-697-3845, 509-945-4570
Specialties: Damascus and mosaic Damascus, working knives, working folders, art knives and art folders. Technical: Some ATS-34 and stainless Damascus. Embellishes with fancy stabilized wood, mammoth and walrus ivory. Prices: Start at $150. Remarks: Part-time maker; first knife sold in 1996. Mark: Name city and state on Damascus stamp initials; name inside back RFR.

DAVIS, STEVE,
3370 Chatsworth Way, Powder Springs, GA 30127, Phone: 770-427-5740, bsdavis@bellsouth.net
Specialties: Gents and ladies folders. Patterns: Straight knives, slip-joint folders, locking-liner folders. Technical: Grinds ATS-34 forges own Damascus. Offers filework; prefers hand-rubbed finishes and natural handle materials. Uses pearl, ivory, stag and exotic woods. Prices: $250 to $800; some to $1500. Remarks: Full-time maker; first knife sold in 1988. Doing business as Custom Knives by Steve Davis. Mark: Name engraved on blade.

DAVIS, TERRY,
Box 111, Sumpter, OR 97877, Phone: 541-894-2307
Specialties: Traditional and contemporary folders. Patterns: Multi-blade folders, whittlers and interframe multiblades; sunfish patterns. Technical: Flat-grinds ATS-34. Prices: $400 to $1000; some higher. Remarks: Full-time maker; first knife sold in 1985. Mark: Name in logo.

DAVIS, VERNON M,
2020 Behrens Circle, Waco, TX 76705, Phone: 254-799-7671
Specialties: Presentation-grade straight knives. Patterns: Bowies, daggers, boots, fighters, hunters and utility knives. Technical: Hollow-grinds 440C, ATS-34 and D2. Grinds an aesthetic grind line near choil. Prices: $125 to $550; some to $5000. Remarks: Part-time maker; first knife sold in 1980. Mark: Last name and city inside outline of state.

DAVIS, W C,
1955 S 1251 Rd, El Dorado Springs, MO 64744, Phone: 417-876-1259
Specialties: Fancy working straight knives and folders. Patterns: Folding lockers and slip-joints; straight hunters, fighters and Bowies. Technical: Grinds A2, ATS-34, 154, CPM T490V and CPM 530V. Prices: $100 to $300; some to $1000. Remarks: Full-time maker; first knife sold in 1972. Mark: Name.

DAVIS JR., JIM,
5129 Ridge St, Zephyrhills, FL 33541, Phone: 813-779-9213 813-469-4241 Cell, jimdavisknives@aol.com
Specialties: Presentation-grade fixed blade knives w/composite hidden tang handles. Employs a variety of ancient and contemporary ivories. Patterns: One-of-a-kind gents, personal, and executive knives and hunters w/unique cam-lock pouch sheaths and display stands. Technical: Flat grinds ATS-34 and stainless Damascus w/most work by hand w/assorted files. Prices: $300 and up. Remarks: Full-time maker, first knives sold in 2000. Mark: Signature w/printed name over "HANDCRAFTED."

DAVISON, TODD A.,
415 So. Reed, Lyons, KS 67554, Phone: 620-894-0402, todd@tadscustomknives.com; Web: www.tadscustomknives.com
Specialties: Making working/using and collector folders of his design. All knives are truly made one of a kind. Each knife has a serial number inside the liner. Patterns: Single and double blade traditional slip-joint pocket knives. Technical: Free hand hollow ground blades, hand finished. Using only the very best materials possible. Holding the highest standards to fit & finish and detail. Does his own heat treating. ATS34 and D2 steel. Prices: $450 to $900, some higher. Remarks: Full time maker, first knife sold in 1981. Mark: T.A. DAVISON stamped.

DAWKINS, DUDLEY L,
221 NW Broadmoor Ave., Topeka, KS 66606-1254, Phone: 785-235-0468, dawkind@sbcglobal.net
Specialties: Stylized old or "Dawkins Forged" with anvil in center. New tang stamps. Patterns: Straight knives. Technical: Mostly carbon steel; some Damascus-all knives forged. Prices: $175 and up. Remarks: All knives supplied with wood-lined sheaths. Also make custom wood-lined sheaths $55 and up. ABS Member, sole authorship. Mark: Stylized "DLD or Dawkins Forged with anvil in center.

DAWSON, BARRY,
10A Town Plaza Suite 303, Durango, CO 81301, lindad@northlink.com; Web: www.knives.com
Specialties: Samurai swords, combat knives, collector daggers, tactical, folding and hunting knives. Patterns: Offers over 60 different models. Technical: Grinds 440C, ATS-34, own heat-treatment. Prices: $75 to $1500; some to $5000. Remarks: Full-time maker; first knife sold in 1975. Mark: Last name, USA in print or last name in script.

DAWSON, LYNN,
7760 E Hwy 69 #C-5 157, Prescott Valley, AZ 86314, Phone: 928-713-7548/928/713/8493, Fax: 928-772-1729, lynnknives@commspeed.net; Web: www.lynnknives.com
Specialties: Swords, hunters, utility, and art pieces. Patterns: Over 25 patterns to choose from. Technical: Grinds 440C, ATS-34, own heat treating. Prices: $80 to $1000. Remarks: Custom work and her own designs. Mark: The name "Lynn" in print or script.

DE MARIA JR., ANGELO,
12 Boronda Rd, Carmel Valley, CA 93924, Phone: 831-659-3381, Fax: 831-659-1315, angelodemaria1@mac.com
Specialties: Damascus, fixed and folders, sheaths. Patterns: Mosaic and random. Technical: Forging 5160, 1084 and 15N20. Prices: $200+. Remarks: Part-time maker. Mark: Angelo de Maria Carmel Valley, CA etch or AdM stamp.

DEAN, HARVEY J,
3266 CR 232, Rockdale, TX 76567, Phone: 512-446-3111, Fax: 512-446-5060, dean@tex1.net; Web: www.harveydean.com
Specialties: Collectible, functional knives. Patterns: Bowies, hunters, folders, daggers, swords, battle axes, camp and combat knives. Technical: Forges 1095, O1 and his Damascus. Prices: $350 to $10,000. Remarks: Full-time maker; first knife sold in 1981. Mark: Last name and MS.

DEBRAGA, JOSE C,
1341 9e Rue, Trois Rivieres, Quebec, CANADA G8Y 2Z2, Phone: 418-948-0105, Fax: 819-840-5864, josecdebragaglovetrotter.net; Web: www.geocities.com/josedebraga
Specialties: Art knives, fantasy pieces and working knives of his design or to customer specs. Patterns: Knives with sculptured or carved handles, from miniatures to full-size working knives. Technical: Grinds and hand-files 440C and ATS-34. A variety of steels and handle materials available. Offers lost wax casting. Prices: Start at $300. Remarks: Full-time maker; wax modeler, sculptor and knifemaker; first knife sold in 1984. Mark: Initials in stylized script and serial number.

DEBRAGA, JOVAN,
141 Notre Dame des Victoir, Quebec, CANADA G2G 1J3, Phone: 418-997-0819/418-877-1915, jovancdebraga@msn.com
Specialties: Art knives, fantasy pieces and working knives of his design or to customer specs. Patterns: Knives with sculptured or carved handles, from miniatures to full-sized working knives. Technical: Grinds and hand-files 440C, and ATS-34. A variety of steels and handle materials available. Prices: Start at $300. Remarks: Full time maker. Sculptor and knifemaker. First knife sold in 2003. Mark: Initials in stylized script and serial number.

DEL RASO, PETER,
28 Mayfield Dr, Mt. Waverly, Victoria, 3149, AUSTRALIA, Phone: 61398060644, delraso@optusnet.com.au
Specialties: Fixed blades, some folders, art knives. Patterns: Daggers, Bowies, tactical, boot, personal and working knives. Technical: Grinds ATS-34, commercial Damascus and any other type of steel on request. Prices: $100 to $1500. Remarks: Part-time maker, first show in 1993. Mark: Maker's surname stamped.

DELAROSA, JIM,
2116 N Pontiac Dr, Janesville, WI 53545, Phone: 608-754-1719, d-knife@hotmail.com
Specialties: Working straight knives and folders of his design or customer specs. Patterns: Hunters, skinners, fillets, utility and locking folders. Tech-

nical: Grinds ATS-34, 440-C, D2, O1 and commercial Damascus. **Prices:** $75 to $450; some higher. **Remarks:** Part-time maker. **Mark:** First and last name.

DELL, WOLFGANG,
Am Alten Berg 9, D-73277 Owen-Teck, GERMANY, Phone: 49-7021-81802, wolfgang@dell-knives.de; Web: www.dell-knives.de
Specialties: Fancy high-art straight of his design and to customer specs. **Patterns:** Fighters, hunters, Bowies and utility/camp knives. **Technical:** Grinds ATS-34, RWL-34, Elmax, Damascus (Fritz Schneider). Offers high gloss finish and engraving. **Prices:** $500 to $1000; some to $1600. **Remarks:** Full-time maker; first knife sold in 1992. **Mark:** Hopi hand of peace.

DELLANA,
STARLANI INT'L INC, 1135 Terminal Way Ste #209, Reno, NV 89502, Phone: 304-727-5512, dellana@dellana.cc; Web: www.dellana.cc
Specialties: Collector grade fancy/embellished high art folders and art daggers. **Patterns:** Locking folders and art daggers. **Technical:** Forges her own Damascus and W-2. Engraves, does stone setting, filework, carving and gold/platinum fabrication. Prefers exotic, high karat gold, platinum, silver, gemstone and mother-of-pearl handle materials. **Price:** Upscale. **Remarks:** Sole authorship, full-time maker, first knife sold in 1994. Also does one high art collaboration a year with Van Barnett. **Member:** Art Knife Invitational and ABS. **Mark:** First name.

DELONG, DICK,
17561 E. Ohio Circle, Aurora, CO 80017, Phone: 303-745-2652
Specialties: Fancy working knives and fantasy pieces. **Patterns:** Hunters and small skinners. **Technical:** Grinds and files O1, D2, 440C and Damascus. Offers cocobolo and Osage orange for handles. **Prices:** Start at $50. **Remarks:** Part-time maker. Member of Art Knife Invitational. Voting member of Knifemakers Guild. Member of ABS. **Mark:** Last name; some unmarked.

DEMENT, LARRY,
PO Box 1807, Prince Fredrick, MD 20678, Phone: 410-586-9011
Specialties: Fixed blades. **Technical:** Forged and stock removal. **Prices:** $75 to $200. **Remarks:** Affordable, good feelin', quality knives. Part-time maker.

DEMPSEY, DAVID,
1644 Bass Rd, Apt 2202, Macon, GA 31210, Phone: 229-244-9101, dempsey@dempseyknives.com; Web: www.dempseyknives.com
Specialties: Tactical, utility, working, classic straight knives. **Patterns:** Fighters, tantos, hunters, neck, utility or customer design. **Technical:** Grinds carbon steel and stainless including S30V (differential heat treatment), stainless steel. **Prices:** Start at $150 for neck knives. **Remarks:** Full-time maker. First knife sold 1998. **Mark:** First and last name over knives.

DEMPSEY, GORDON S,
PO Box 7497, N. Kenai, AK 99635, Phone: 907-776-8425
Specialties: Working straight knives. **Patterns:** Pattern welded Damascus and carbon steel blades. **Technical:** Pattern welded Damascus and carbon steel. **Prices:** $80 to $250. **Remarks:** Part-time maker; first knife sold in 1974. **Mark:** None.

DENNEHY, DAN,
PO Box 470, Del Norte, CO 81132, Phone: 719-657-2545
Specialties: Working knives, fighting and military knives, throwing knives. **Patterns:** Full range of straight knives, tomahawks, buckle knives. **Technical:** Forges and grinds A2, O1 and D2. **Prices:** $200 to $500. **Remarks:** Full-time maker; first knife sold in 1942. Latest inductee into cutlery hall of fame, #44 **Mark:** First name and last initial, city, state and shamrock.

DENNEHY, JOHN D,
8463 Woodlands Way, Wellington, CO 80549, Phone: 970-568-3697, jd@thewildirishrose.com
Technical: 440C, & O1, heat treats own blades, part-time maker, first knife sold in 1989. **Patterns:** Small hunting to presentation Bowies, leatherworks round and head knives. **Prices:** $200 and up. **Remarks:** Custom sheath maker, sheath making seminars at the Blade Show.

DENNING, GENO,
CAVEMAN ENGINEERING, 135 Allenvalley Rd, Gaston, SC 29053, Phone: 803-794-6067, cden101656@aol.com; Web: www.cavemanengineering.com
Specialties: Mirror finish. **Patterns:** Hunters, fighters, folders. **Technical:** ATS-34, 440V, S-30-V D2. **Prices:** $100 and up. **Remarks:** Full-time maker since 1996. Sole income since 1999. Instructor at Montgomery Community College (Grinding Blades). A director of SCAK: South Carolina Association of Knifemakers. **Mark:** Troy NC.

DERESPINA, RICHARD,
Willow Grove, PA, Phone: 917-843-7627
Specialties: Custom fixed blades and folders, Kris and Karambit. **Technical:** I use the stock removal method. Steels I use are S30V, 154CM, D2, 440C, BG42. Handles made of G10 particularly Micarta, etc. **Prices:** $150 to $550 depending on model. **Remarks:** Full-time maker. **Mark:** My etched logos are two, my last name and Brooklyn NY mark as well as the Star/Yin Yang logo. The star being both representative of various angles of attack common in combat as well as being three triangles, each points to levels of metaphysical understanding. The Yin and Yang have my company initials on each side D & K. Yin and Yang shows the ever present physics of life.

DERINGER, CHRISTOPH,
625 Chemin Lower, Cookshire, Quebec, CANADA J0B 1M0, Phone: 819-345-4260, cdsab@sympatico.ca
Specialties: Traditional working/using straight knives and folders of his design and to customer specs. **Patterns:** Boots, hunters, folders, art knives, kitchen knives and utility/camp knives. **Technical:** Forges 5160, O1 and Damascus. Offers a variety of filework. **Prices:** Start at $250. **Remarks:** Full-time maker; first knife sold in 1989. **Mark:** Last name stamped/engraved.

DERR, HERBERT,
413 Woodland Dr, St. Albans, WV 25177, Phone: 304-727-3866
Specialties: Damascus one-of-a-kind knives, carbon steels also. **Patterns:** Birdseye, ladder back, mosaics. **Technical:** All styles functional as well as artistically pleasing. **Prices:** $90 to $175 carbon, Damascus $250 to $800. **Remarks:** All Damascus made by maker. **Mark:** H.K. Derr.

DESAULNIERS, ALAIN,
100 Pope Street, Cookshire, Quebec, Canada J0B 1M0, pinklaperez@sympatico.ca Web: www.desoknives.com
Specialties: Mostly Loveless style knives. **Patterns:** Double grind fighters, hunters, daggers, etc. **Technical:** Stock removal, ATS-34, CPM. High-polished blades, tapered tangs, high-quality handles. **Remarks:** Full-time. Collaboration with John Young. **Prices:** $425 and up. **Mark:** Name and city in logo.

DETMER, PHILLIP,
14140 Bluff Rd, Breese, IL 62230, Phone: 618-526-4834, jpdetmer@att.net
Specialties: Working knives. **Patterns:** Bowies, daggers and hunters. **Technical:** Grinds ATS-34 and D2. **Prices:** $60 to $400. **Remarks:** Part-time maker; first knife sold in 1977. **Mark:** Last name with dagger.

DEUBEL, CHESTER J.,
6211 N. Van Ark Rd., Tucson, AZ 85743, Phone: 520-444-5246, cjdeubel@yahoo.com; Web: www.cjdeubel.com
Specialties: Fancy working straight knives and folders of his or customer design, with intricate filework. **Patterns:** Fighters, Bowies, daggers, hunters, camp knives, and cowboy. **Technical:** Flat guard, hollow grind, antiqued, all types Damascus, 154cpm Stainsteel, high carbon steel, 440c Stainsteel. **Prices:** From $250 to $3500. **Remarks:** Started making part-time in 1980; went to full-time in 2000. Don Patch is my engraver. **Mark:** C.J. Deubel.

DI MARZO, RICHARD,
1417 10th St S, Birmingham, AL 35205, Phone: 205-252-3331
Specialties: Handle artist. Scrimshaw carvings.

DICK, DAN,
P.O. Box 2303, Hutchinson, KS 67504-2303, Phone: 620-669-6805, Dan@DanDickKnives.com; Web: www.dandickknives.com
Specialties: Traditional working/using fixed bladed knives of maker's design. **Patterns:** Hunters, Skinners, Utility, Kitchen, Tactical, Bowies. **Technical:** Stock removal maker using D2, forges his own Damascus and is dabbling in forging knives. Prefers natural handle materials such as: exotic and fancy burl woods and some horn. Makes his own leather sheaths, many with tooling, also makes sheaths from Kydex for his tacticals. **Prices:** $80 and up. **Remarks:** Part-time maker since 2006. **Marks:** Dan Dick using one big D for beginning of first and last name, with first name over last name outlined by the shape Kansas.

DICKERSON, GAVIN,
PO Box 7672, Petit 1512, SOUTH AFRICA, Phone: +27 011-965-0988, Fax: +27 011-965-0988
Specialties: Straight knives of his design or to customer specs. **Patterns:** Hunters, skinners, fighters and Bowies. **Technical:** Hollow-grinds D2, 440C, ATS-34, 12C27 and Damascus upon request. Prefers natural handle materials; offers synthetic handle materials. **Prices:** $190 to $2500. **Remarks:** Part-time maker; first knife sold in 1982. **Mark:** Name in full.

DICKERSON, GORDON S,
47 S Maple St, New Augusta, MS 38462, Phone: 931-796-1187
Specialties: Traditional working straight knives; Civil War era period pieces. **Patterns:** Bowies, hunters, tactical, camp/utility knives; some folders. **Technical:** Forges carbon steel; pattern welded and cable Damascus. **Prices:** $150 to $500; some to $3000. ABS member. **Mark:** Last name.

DICKISON, SCOTT S,
179 Taylor Rd, Fisher Circle, Portsmouth, RI 02871, Phone: 401-847-7398, squared22@cox .net; Web: http://members.cox.net/squared22
Specialties: Working and using straight knives and locking folders of his design and automatics. **Patterns:** Trout knives, fishing and hunting knives. **Technical:** Forges and grinds commercial Damascus and D2, O1. Uses natural handle materials. **Prices:** $400 to $750; some higher. **Remarks:** Part-time maker; first knife sold in 1989. **Mark:** Stylized initials.

DICRISTOFANO, ANTHONY P,
PO Box 2369, Northlake, IL 60164, Phone: 847-845-9598, sukemitsu@sbcglobal.net Web: www.namahagesword.com
Specialties: Japanese-style swords. **Patterns:** Katana, Wakizashi, Otanto, Kozuka. **Technical:** Tradition and some modern steels. All clay tempered and traditionally hand polished using Japanese wet stones. **Remarks:** Part-time maker. **Prices:** Varied, available on request. **Mark:** Blade tang signed in "SUKEMITSU."

DIETZ, HOWARD,
421 Range Rd, New Braunfels, TX 78132, Phone: 830-885-4662
Specialties: Lock-back folders, working straight knives. **Patterns:** Folding hunters, high-grade pocket knives. ATS-34, 440C, CPM 440V, D2 and stainless Damascus. **Prices:** $300 to $1000. **Remarks:** Full-time gun and knifemaker; first knife sold in 1995. **Mark:** Name, city, and state.

DIETZEL, BILL,
PO Box 1613, Middleburg, FL 32068, Phone: 904-282-1091
Specialties: Forged straight knives and folders. **Patterns:** His interpretations. **Technical:** Forges his Damascus and other steels. **Prices:** Middle ranges. **Remarks:** Likes natural materials; uses titanium in folder liners. Master Smith (1997). **Mark:** Name.

DIGANGI, JOSEPH M,
Box 950, Santa Cruz, NM 87567, Phone: 505-753-6414, Fax: 505-753-8144, Web: www.digangidesigns.com
Specialties: Kitchen and table cutlery. **Patterns:** French chef's knives, carving sets, steak knife sets, some camp knives and hunters. Holds patents and trademarks for "System II" kitchen cutlery set. **Technical:** Grinds ATS-34. **Prices:** $150 to $595; some to $1200. **Remarks:** Full-time maker; first knife sold in 1983. **Mark:** DiGangi Designs.

DILL, DAVE,
7404 NW 30th St, Bethany, OK 73008, Phone: 405-789-0750
Specialties: Folders of his design. **Patterns:** Various patterns. **Technical:** Hand-grinds 440C, ATS-34. Offers engraving and filework on all folders. **Prices:** Starting at $450. **Remarks:** Full-time maker; first knife sold in 1987. **Mark:** First initial, last name.

DILL, ROBERT,
1812 Van Buren, Loveland, CO 80538, Phone: 970-667-5144, Fax: 970-667-5144, dillcustomknives@msn.com
Specialties: Fancy and working knives of his design. **Patterns:** Hunters, Bowies and fighters. **Technical:** Grinds 440C and D2. **Prices:** $100 to $800. **Remarks:** Full-time maker; first knife sold in 1984. **Mark:** Logo stamped into blade.

DILLUVIO, FRANK J,
13611 Murthum, Warren, MI 48088, Phone: 586-294-5280, frankscustomknives@hotmail.com; Web: www.fdilluviocustomknives.com
Specialties: Traditional working straight knives. **Patterns:** Hunters, Bowies, fishing knives, sub-hilts, LinerLock® folders and miniatures. **Technical:** Grinds D2, 440C, CPM; works for precision fits—no solder. **Prices:** $95 to $450; some to $800. **Remarks:** Full-time maker; first knife sold in 1984. **Mark:** Name and state.

DION, GREG,
3032 S Jackson St, Oxnard, CA 93033, Phone: 805-483-1781
Specialties: Working straight knives, some fancy. Welcomes special orders. **Patterns:** Hunters, fighters, camp knives, Bowies and tantos. **Technical:** Grinds ATS-34, 154CM and 440C. **Prices:** $85 to $300; some to $600. **Remarks:** Part-time maker; first knife sold in 1985. **Mark:** Name.

DIOTTE, JEFF,
DIOTTE KNIVES, 159 Laurier Dr, LaSalle Ontario, CANADA N9J 1L4, Phone: 519-978-2764

DIPPOLD, AL,
90 Damascus Ln, Perryville, MO 63775, Phone: 573-547-1119, adippold@midwest.net
Specialties: Fancy one-of-a-kind locking folders. **Patterns:** Locking folders. **Technical:** Forges and grinds mosaic and pattern welded Damascus. Offers filework on all folders. **Prices:** $500 to $3500; some higher. **Remarks:** Full-time maker; first knife sold in 1980. **Mark:** Last name in logo inside of liner.

DISKIN, MATT,
PO Box 653, Freeland, WA 98249, Phone: 360-730-0451
Specialties: Damascus autos. **Patterns:** Dirks and daggers. **Technical:** Forges mosaic Damascus using 15N20, 1084, 02, 06, L6; pure nickel. **Prices:** Start at $500. Remarks; Full-time maker. **Mark:** Last name.

DIXON JR., IRA E,
PO Box 2581, Ventura, CA 93002-2581, irasknives@yahoo.com
Specialties: Utilitarian straight knives of his design. **Patterns:** Camp, hunters, fighters, utility knives and art knives. **Technical:** Grinds CPM, S30V, 1095, Damascus and D2. **Prices:** $200 to $1500. **Remarks:** Part-time maker; first knife sold in 1993. **Mark:** First name, Handmade.

DODD, ROBERT F,
4340 E Canyon Dr, Camp Verde, AZ 86322, Phone: 928-567-3333, rfdknives@commspeed.net; Web: www.rfdoddknives.com
Specialties: Folders, fixed blade hunter/skinners, Bowies, daggers. **Patterns:** Drop point. **Technical:** ATS-34 and Damascus. **Prices:** $250 and up. **Remarks:** Hand tooled leather sheaths. **Mark:** R. F. Dodd, Camp Verde AZ.

DOGGETT, BOB,
1310 Vinetree Rd, Brandon, FL 33510, Phone: 813-205-5503, dogman@tampabay.rr.com; Web: www.doggettcustomknives.com
Specialties: Clean, functional working knives. **Patterns:** Classic-styled hunter, fighter and utility fixed blades; liner locking folders. **Technical:** Uses stainless steel and commercial Damascus, 416 stainless for bolsters

and hardware, hand-rubbed satin finish, top quality handle materials and titanium liners on folders. **Prices:** Start at $175. **Remarks:** Part-time maker. **Mark:** Last name.

DOIRON, DONALD,
6 Chemin Petit Lac des Ced, Messines, PQ, CANADA JOX-2JO, Phone: 819-465-2489

DOMINY, CHUCK,
PO Box 593, Colleyville, TX 76034, Phone: 817-498-4527
Specialties: Titanium LinerLock® folders. **Patterns:** Hunters, utility/camp knives and LinerLock® folders. **Technical:** Grinds 440C and ATS-34. **Prices:** $250 to $3000. **Remarks:** Full-time maker; first knife sold in 1976. **Mark:** Last name.

DOOLITTLE, MIKE,
13 Denise Ct, Novato, CA 94947, Phone: 415-897-3246
Specialties: Working straight knives in standard patterns. **Patterns:** Hunters and fishing knives. **Technical:** Grinds 440C, 154CM and ATS-34. **Prices:** $125 to $200; some to $750. **Remarks:** Part-time maker; first knife sold in 1981. **Mark:** Name, city and state.

DORNELES, LUCIANO OLIVERIRA,
Rua 15 De Novembro 2222, Nova Petropolis, RS, BRAZIL 95150-000, Phone: 011-55-54-303-303-90, tchebufalo@hotmail.com
Specialties: Traditional "true" Brazilian-style working knives and to customer specs. **Patterns:** Brazilian hunters, utility and camp knives, Bowies, Dirk. A master at the making of the true "Faca Campeira Gaucha," the true camp knife of the famous Brazilian Gauchos. A Dorneles knife is 100 percent hand-forged with sledge hammers only. Can make spectacular Damascus hunters/daggers. **Technical:** Forges only 52100 and his own Damascus, can put silver wire inlay on customer design handles on special orders; uses only natural handle materials. **Prices:** $250 to $1000. **Mark:** Symbol with L. Dorneles.

DOTSON, TRACY,
1280 Hwy C-4A, Baker, FL 32531, Phone: 850-537-2407
Specialties: Folding fighters and small folders. **Patterns:** LinerLock® and lockback folders. **Technical:** Hollow-grinds ATS-34 and commercial Damascus. **Prices:** Start at $250. **Remarks:** Part-time maker; first knife sold in 1995. **Mark:** Last name.

DOUCETTE, R,
CUSTOM KNIVES, 112 Memorial Dr, Brantford, Ont., CANADA N3R 5S3, Phone: 519-756-9040, randy@randydoucetteknives.com; Web: www.randydoucetteknives.com
Specialties: Filework, tactical designs, multiple grinds. **Patterns:** Tactical folders, fancy folders, daggers, tantos, karambits. **Technical:** All knives are handmade. The only outsourcing is heat treatment. **Prices:** $500 to $2,500. **Remarks:** Full-time knifemaker; 2-year waiting list. **Mark:** R. Doucette

DOUGLAS, JOHN J,
506 Powell Rd, Lynch Station, VA 24571, Phone: 804-369-7196
Specialties: Fancy and traditional straight knives and folders of his design and to customer specs. **Patterns:** Locking folders, swords and sgian dubhs. **Technical:** Grinds 440C stainless, ATS-34 stainless and customer's choice. Offers newly designed non-pivot uni-lock folders. Prefers highly polished finish. **Prices:** $160 to $1400. **Remarks:** Full-time maker; first knife sold in 1975. Doing business as Douglas Keltic. **Mark:** Stylized initial. Folders are numbered; customs are dated.

DOURSIN, GERARD,
Chemin des Croutoules, F 84210, Pernes les Fontaines, FRANCE
Specialties: Period pieces. **Patterns:** Liner locks and daggers. **Technical:** Forges mosaic Damascus. **Prices:** $600 to $4000. **Remarks:** First knife sold in 1983. **Mark:** First initial, last name and I stop the lion.

DOUSSOT, LAURENT,
1008 Montarville, St. Bruno, Quebec, CANADA J3V 3T1, Phone: 450-441-3298, doussot@skalja.com; Web: www.skalja.com, www.doussot-knives.com
Specialties: Fancy and embellished folders and fantasy knives. **Patterns:** Fighters and locking folders. **Technical:** Grinds ATS-34 and commercial Damascus. Scale carvings on all knives; most bolsters are carved titanium. **Prices:** $350 to $3000. **Remarks:** Part-time maker; first knife was sold in 1992. **Mark:** Stylized initials inside circle.

DOWELL, T M,
139 NW St Helen's Pl, Bend, OR 97701, Phone: 541-382-8924, Fax: 541-382-8924, tmdknives@webtv.net
Specialties: Integral construction in hunting knives. **Patterns:** Limited to featherweights, lightweights, integral hilt and caps. **Technical:** Grinds D-2, BG-42 and Vasco wear. **Prices:** $275 and up. **Remarks:** Full-time maker; first knife sold in 1967. **Mark:** Initials logo.

DOWNIE, JAMES T,
10076 Estate Dr, Port Franks, Ont., CANADA NOM 2LO, Phone: 519-243-1488, Web: www.ckg.org (click on members page)
Specialties: Serviceable straight knives and folders; period pieces. **Patterns:** Hunters, Bowies, camp knives, fillet and miniatures. **Technical:** Grinds D2, 440C and ATS-34, Damasteel, stainless steel Damascus. **Prices:** $100 to $500; some higher. **Remarks:** Full-time maker, first knife sold in 1978. **Mark:** Signature of first and middle initials, last name.

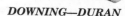

DOWNING, LARRY,
12268 Hwy 181N, Bremen, KY 42325, Phone: 270-525-3523, larrydowning@bellsouth.net; Web: www.downingcustomknives.com
Specialties: Working straight knives and folders. **Patterns:** From mini-knives to daggers, folding lockers to interframes. **Technical:** Forges and grinds 154CM, ATS-34 and his own Damascus. **Prices:** $195 to $950; some higher. **Remarks:** Part-time maker; first knife sold in 1979. **Mark:** Name in arrowhead.

DOWNING, TOM,
2675 12th St, Cuyahoga Falls, OH 44223, Phone: 330-923-7464
Specialties: Working straight knives; period pieces. **Patterns:** Hunters, fighters and tantos. **Technical:** Grinds 440C, ATs-34 and CPM-T-440V. Prefers natural handle materials. **Prices:** $150 to $900, some to $1500. **Remarks:** Part-time maker; first knife sold in 1979. **Mark:** First and middle initials, last name.

DOWNS, JAMES F,
2247 Summit View Rd, Powell, OH 43065, Phone: 614-766-5350, jfdowns1@yahoo.com
Specialties: Working straight knives of his design or to customer specs. **Patterns:** Folders, Bowies, boot, hunters, utility. **Technical:** Grinds 440C and other steels. Prefers mastodon ivory, all pearls, stabilized wood and elephant ivory. **Prices:** $75 to $1200. **Remarks:** Full-time maker; first knife sold in 1980. **Mark:** Last name.

DOX, JAN,
Zwanebloemlaan 27, B 2900 Schoten, BELGIUM, Phone: 32 3 658 77 43, jan.dox@scarlet.be
Specialties: Working/using knives, from kitchen to battlefield. **Patterns:** Own designs, some based on traditional ethnic patterns (Scots, Celtic, Scandinavian and Japanese) or to customer specs. **Technical:** Grinds D2/A2 and stainless, forges carbon steels, convex edges. Handles: Wrapped in modern or traditional patterns, resin impregnated if desired. Natural or synthetic materials, some carved. **Prices:** $50 and up. **Remarks:** Spare-time maker, first knife sold 2001. **Mark:** Name or stylized initials.

DOZIER, BOB,
PO Box 1941, Springdale, AR 72765, Phone: 888-823-0023/479-756-0023, Fax: 479-756-9139, info@dozierknives.com; Web www.dozierknives.com
Specialties: Using knives (fixed blades and folders). **Patterns:** Some fine collector-grade knives. **Technical:** Uses D2. Prefers Micarta handle material. **Prices:** Using knives $195 to $700. **Remarks:** Full-time maker; first knife sold in 1965. No longer doing semi-handmade line. **Mark:** State, made, last name in a circle (for fixed blades); Last name with arrow through 'D' and year over name (for folders).

DRAPER, AUDRA,
#10 Creek Dr, Riverton, WY 82501, Phone: 307-856-6807 or 307-851-0426 cell, adraper@wyoming.com; Web: www.draperknives.com
Specialties: One-of-a-kind straight and folding knives. Also pendants, earring and bracelets of Damascus. **Patterns:** Design custom knives, using, Bowies, and minis. **Technical:** Forge Damascus; heat-treats all knives. **Prices:** Vary depending on item. **Remarks:** Full-time maker; master bladesmith in the ABS. Member of the PKA; first knife sold in 1995. **Mark:** Audra.

DRAPER, MIKE,
#10 Creek Dr, Riverton, WY 82501, Phone: 307-856-6807, adraper@wyoming.com
Specialties: Mainly folding knives in tactical fashion, occasonal fixed blade. **Patterns:** Hunters, Bowies and camp knives, tactical survival. **Technical:** Grinds S30V stainless steel. **Prices:** Starting at $250+. **Remarks:** Full-time maker; first knife sold in 1996. **Mark:** Initials M.J.D. or name, city and state.

DREW, GERALD,
213 Hawk Ridge Dr, Mill Spring, NC 28756, Phone: 828-713-4762
Specialties: Blade ATS-34 blades. Straight knives. **Patterns:** Hunters, camp knives, some Bowies and tactical. **Technical:** ATS-34 preferred. **Price:** $65 to $400. **Mark:** GL DREW.

DRISCOLL, MARK,
4115 Avoyer Pl, La Mesa, CA 91941, Phone: 619-670-0695
Specialties: High-art, period pieces and working/using knives of his design or to customer specs; some fancy. **Patterns:** Swords, Bowies, fighters, daggers, hunters and primitive (mountain man-styles). **Technical:** Forges 52100, 5160, O1, L6, 1095, and maker his own Damascus and mokume; also does multiple quench heat treating. Uses exotic hardwoods, ivory and horn, offers fancy file work, carving, scrimshaws. **Prices:** $150 to $550; some to $1500. **Remarks:** Part-time maker; first knife sold in 1986. Doing business as Mountain Man Knives. **Mark:** Double "M."

DROST, JASON D,
Rt 2 Box 49, French Creek, WV 26218, Phone: 304-472-7901
Specialties: Working/using straight knives of his design. **Patterns:** Hunters and utility/camp knives. **Technical:** Grinds 154CM and D2. **Prices:** $125 to $5000. **Remarks:** Spare-time maker; first knife sold in 1995. **Mark:** First and middle initials, last name, maker, city and state.

DROST, MICHAEL B,
Rt 2 Box 49, French Creek, WV 26218, Phone: 304-472-7901
Specialties: Working/using straight knives and folders of all designs. **Patterns:** Hunters, locking folders and utility/camp knives. **Technical:** Grinds ATS-34, D2 and CPM-T-440V. Offers dove-tailed bolsters and spacers, filework and scrimshaw. **Prices:** $125 to $400; some to $740. **Remarks:** Full-time maker; first knife sold in 1990. Doing business as Drost Custom Knives. **Mark:** Name, city and state.

DRUMM, ARMIN,
Lichtensteinstrasse 33, D-89160 Dornstadt, GERMANY, Phone: 49-163-632-2842, armin@drumm-knives.de; Web: www.drumm-knives.de
Specialties: One-of-a-kind forged and Damascus fixed blade knives and folders. **Patterns:** Classic Bowie knives, daggers, fighters, hunters, folders, swords. **Technical:** Forges own Damascus and carbon steels, filework, carved handles. **Prices:** $250 to $800, some higher. **Remarks:** First knife sold in 2001, member of the German Knifemakers Guild. **Mark:** First initial, last name.

DUFF, BILL,
2801 Ash St, Poteau, OK 74953, Phone: 918-647-4458
Specialties: Straight knives and folders, some fancy. **Patterns:** Hunters, folders and miniatures. **Technical:** Grinds 440-C and commercial Damascus. **Prices:** $200 to $1000 some higher. **Remarks:** First knife some in 1976. **Mark:** Bill Duff.

DUFOUR, ARTHUR J,
8120 De Armoun Rd, Anchorage, AK 99516, Phone: 907-345-1701
Specialties: Working straight knives from standard patterns. **Patterns:** Hunters, Bowies, camp and fishing knives—grinded thin and pointed. **Technical:** Grinds 440C, ATS-34, AEB-L. Tempers 57-58R; hollow-grinds. **Prices:** $135; some to $250. **Remarks:** Part-time maker; first knife sold in 1970. **Mark:** Prospector logo.

DUGDALE, DANIEL J.,
11 Eleanor Road, Walpole, MA 02081, Phone: 508-668-3528, dlpdugdale@comcast.net
Specialties: Button-lock and straight knives of his design. **Patterns:** Utilities, hunters, skinners, and tactical. **Technical:** Falt grinds D-2 and 440C, aluminum handles with anodized finishes. **Prices:** $150 to $500. **Remarks:** Part-time maker since 1977. **Mark:** Deer track with last name, town and state.

DUGGER, DAVE,
2504 West 51, Westwood, KS 66205, Phone: 913-831-2382
Specialties: Working straight knives; fantasy pieces. **Patterns:** Hunters, boots and daggers in one-of-a-kind styles. **Technical:** Grinds D2, 440C and 154CM. **Prices:** $75 to $350; some to $1200. **Remarks:** Part-time maker; first knife sold in 1979. Not currently accepting orders. Doing business as Dog Knives. **Mark:** DOG.

DUNCAN, RON,
1432 County Road 1635, Cairo, MO 65239, Phone: 660-263-8949, www.duncanmadeknives.com
Remarks: Duncan Made Knives

DUNKERLEY, RICK,
PO Box 601, Lincoln, MT 59639, Phone: 406-210-4101, rick@dunkerleyhandmadeknives.com Web: www.dunkerleyknives.com
Specialties: Mosaic Damascus folders and carbon steel utility knives. **Patterns:** One-of-a-kind folders, standard hunters and utility designs. **Technical:** Forges 52100, Damascus and mosaic Damascus. Prefers natural handle materials. **Prices:** $200 and up. **Remarks:** Full-time maker; first knife sold in 1984, ABS Master Smith. Doing business as Dunkerley Custom Knives. Dunkerley handmade knives, sole authorship. **Mark:** Dunkerley, MS.

DUNN, CHARLES K,
17740 GA Hwy 116, Shiloh, GA 31826, Phone: 706-846-2666
Specialties: Fancy and working straight knives and folders of his design and to customer specs. **Patterns:** Bowies, hunters and locking folders. **Technical:** Grinds 440C and ATS-34. Engraves; filework offered. **Prices:** $75 to $300. **Remarks:** Part-time maker; first knife sold in 1988. **Mark:** First initial, last name, city, state.

DUNN, STEVE,
376 Biggerstaff Rd, Smiths Grove, KY 42171, Phone: 270-563-9830, dunndeal@verizon.net; Web: www.stevedunnknives.com
Specialties: Working and using straight knives of his design; period pieces. Also offer engraving & gold inlays. **Patterns:** Hunters, skinners, Bowies, fighters, camp knives, folders, swords and battle axes. **Technical:** Forges own Damascus, 1075, 15N20, 52100, 1084, L6. **Prices:** Moderate to upscale. **Remarks:** Full-time maker; first knife sold in 1990. **Mark:** Last name and MS.

DURAN, JERRY T,
PO Box 80692, Albuquerque, NM 87198-0692, Phone: 505-873-4676, jtdknives@hotmail.com; Web: www.kmg.org/jtdknives
Specialties: Tactical folders, Bowies, fighters, liner locks, autopsy and hunters. **Patterns:** Folders, Bowies, hunters and tactical knives. **Technical:** Forges own Damascus and forges carbon steel. **Prices:** Moderate to upscale. **Remarks:** Full-time maker; first knife sold in 1978. **Mark:** Initials in elk rack logo.

custom knifemakers

DURHAM, KENNETH,
BUZZARD ROOST FORGE, 10495 White Pike, Cherokee, AL 35616, Phone: 256-359-4287, www.home.hiwaay.net/~jamesd/
   Specialties: Bowies, dirks, hunters. **Patterns:** Traditional patterns. **Technical:** Forges 1095, 5160, 52100 and makes own Damascus. **Prices:** $85 to $1600. **Remarks:** Began making knives about 1995. Received Journeyman stamp 1999. Got Master Smith stamp in 2004. **Mark:** Bull's head with Ken Durham above and Cherokee AL below.

DURIO, FRED,
144 Gulino St, Opelousas, LA 70570, Phone: 337-948-4831/cell 337-351-2652, fdurio@yahoo.com
   Specialties: Folders. **Patterns:** Liner locks; plain and fancy. **Technical:** Makes own Damascus. **Prices:** Moderate to upscale. **Remarks:** Full-time maker. **Mark:** Last name-Durio.

DUVALL, FRED,
10715 Hwy 190, Benton, AR 72015, Phone: 501-778-9360
   Specialties: Working straight knives and folders. **Patterns:** Locking folders, slip joints, hunters, fighters and Bowies. **Technical:** Grinds D2 and CPM440V; forges 5160. **Prices:** $100 to $400; some to $800. **Remarks:** Part-time maker; first knife sold in 1973. **Mark:** Last name.

DWYER, DUANE,
120 N. Pacific St., L7, San Marcos, CA 92069, Phone: 760-471-8275, striderknives@aol.com Web: www.striderknives.com
   Specialties: Primarily tactical. **Patterns:** Fixed and folders. **Technical:** Primarily stock removal specializing in highly technical materials. **Prices:** $100 and up, based on the obvious variables. **Remarks:** Full-time maker since 1996.

DYER, DAVID,
4531 Hunters Glen, Granbury, TX 76048, Phone: 817-573-1198
   Specialties: Working skinners and early period knives. **Patterns:** Customer designs, his own patterns. **Technical:** Coal forged blades; 5160 and 52100 steels. Grinds D2, 1095, L6. **Prices:** $150 for neck knives and small (3" to 3-1/2"). To $600 for large blades and specialty blades. **Mark:** Last name DYER electro etched.

DYESS, EDDIE,
1005 Hamilton, Roswell, NM 88201, Phone: 505-623-5599, eddyess@msn.com
   Specialties: Working and using straight knives in standard patterns. **Patterns:** Hunters and fighters. **Technical:** Grinds 440C, 154CM and D2 on request. **Prices:** $150 to $300, some higher. **Remarks:** Spare-time maker; first knife sold in 1980. **Mark:** Last name.

DYRNOE, PER,
Sydskraenten 10, Tulstrup, DK 3400 Hilleroed, DENMARK, Phone: +45 42287041
   Specialties: Hand-crafted knives with zirconia ceramic blades. **Patterns:** Hunters, skinners, Norwegian-style tolle knives, most in animal-like ergonomic shapes. **Technical:** Handles of exotic hardwood, horn, fossil ivory, etc. Norwegian-style sheaths. **Prices:** Start at $500. **Remarks:** Part-time maker in cooperation with Hans J. Henriksen; first knife sold in 1993. **Mark:** Initial logo.

E

EAKER, ALLEN L,
416 Clinton Ave Dept KI, Paris, IL 61944, Phone: 217-466-5160
   Specialties: Traditional straight knives and folders of his design. **Patterns:** Hunters, locking folders and slip-joint folders. **Technical:** Grinds 440C; inlays. **Prices:** $125 to $325; some to $500. **Remarks:** Spare-time maker; first knife sold in 1994. **Mark:** Initials in tankard logo stamped on tang, serial number on back side.

EALY, DELBERT,
PO Box 121, Indian River, MI 49749, Phone: 231-238-4705

EATON, FRANK L JR,
41 Vista Woods Rd, Stafford, VA 22556, Phone: 540-657-6160, FEton2@aol.com
   Specialties: Full tang/hidden tang fixed working and art knives of his own design. **Patterns:** Hunters, skinners, fighters, Bowies, tacticals and daggers. **Technical:** Stock removal maker, prefer using natural materials. **Prices:** $175 to $400. **Remarks:** Part-time maker - Active Duty Airborn Ranger-Making 4 years. **Mark:** Name over 75th Ranger Regimental Crest.

EATON, RICK,
313 Dailey Rd, Broadview, MT 59015, Phone: 406-667-2405, rick@eatonknives.com; Web: www.eatonknives.com
   Specialties: Interframe folders and one-hand-opening side locks. **Patterns:** Bowies, daggers, fighters and folders. **Technical:** Grinds 154CM, ATS-34, 440C and other maker's Damascus. Offers high-quality hand engraving, Bulino and gold inlay. **Prices:** Upscale. **Remarks:** Full-time maker; first knife sold in 1982. **Mark:** Full name or full name and address.

EBISU, HIDESAKU,
3-39-7 Koi Osako Nishi Ku, Hiroshima City, JAPAN 733 0816

ECHOLS, ROGER,
46 Channing Rd, Nashville, AR 71852-8588, Phone: 870-451-9089, blademanechols@aol.com
   Specialties: Liner locks, auto-scale release, lock backs. **Patterns:** His or

yours. **Technical:** Autos. **Prices:** $500 to $1700. **Remarks:** Likes to use pearl, ivory and Damascus the most. Made first knife in 1984. Part-time maker; tool and die maker by trade. **Mark:** Name.

EDDY, HUGH E,
211 E Oak St, Caldwell, ID 83605, Phone: 208-459-0536

EDEN, THOMAS,
PO Box 57, Cranbury, NJ 08512, Phone: 609-371-0774, njirrigation@msn.com
   Specialties: Chef's knives. **Patterns:** Fixed blade, working patterns, hand forged. **Technical:** Damascus. **Remarks:** ABS Smith. **Mark:** Eden (script).

EDGE, TOMMY,
1244 County Road 157, Cash, AR 72421, Phone: 501-477-5210, tedge@tex.net
   Specialties: Fancy/embellished working knives of his design. **Patterns:** Bowies, hunters and utility/camping knives. **Technical:** Grinds 440C, ATS-34 and D2. Makes own cable Damascus. **Prices:** $70 to $250; some to $1500. **Remarks:** Part-time maker; first knife sold in 1973. **Mark:** Stamped first initial, last name and stenciled name, city and state in oval shape.

EDMONDS, WARRICK,
Adelaide Hills, South Australia, Phone: 61-8-83900339, warrick@riflebirdknives.com Web: www.riflebirdknives.com
   Specialties: Fixed blade knives with select and highly figured exotic or unique Australian wood handles. Themed collectors knives to individually designed working knives from Damascus, RWL34, 440C or high carbon steels. **Patterns:** Hunters, utilities and workshop knives, cooks knives with a Deco to Modern flavour. Hand sewn individual leather sheaths. **Technical:** Stock removal using only steel from well known and reliable sources. **Prices:** $250Aust to $1000Aust. **Remarks:** Part-time maker since 2004. **Mark:** Name stamped into sheath.

EDWARDS, FAIN E,
PO Box 280, Topton, NC 28781, Phone: 828-321-3127

EDWARDS, MITCH,
303 New Salem Rd, Glasgow, KY 42141, Phone: 270-404-0758 / 270-404-0758, medwards@glasgow-ky.com; Web: www.traditionalknives.com
   Specialties: Period pieces. **Patterns:** Neck knives, camp, rifleman and Bowie knives. **Technical:** All hand forged, forges own Damascus O1, 1084, 1095, L6, 15N20. **Prices:** $200 to $1000. **Remarks:** Journeyman Smith. **Mark:** Broken heart.

EHRENBERGER, DANIEL ROBERT,
1213 S Washington St, Mexico, MO 65265, Phone: 573-633-2010
   Specialties: Affordable working/using straight knives of his design and to custom specs. Patterns: 10" western Bowie, fighters, hunting and skinning knives. **Technical:** Forges 1085, 1095, his own Damascus and cable Damascus. **Prices:** $80 to $500. **Remarks:** Full-time maker, first knife sold 1994. **Mark:** Ehrenberger JS.

EKLUND, MAIHKEL,
Fone Stam V9, S-820 41 Farila, SWEDEN, info@art-knives.com; Web: www.art-knives.com
   Specialties: Collector-grade working straight knives. **Patterns:** Hunters, Bowies and fighters. **Technical:** Grinds ATS-34, Uddeholm and Dama steel. Engraves and scrimshaws. **Prices:** $200 to $2000. **Remarks:** Full-time maker; first knife sold in 1983. **Mark:** Initials or name.

ELDER JR., PERRY B,
1321 Garrettsburg Rd, Clarksville, TN 37042-2516, Phone: 931-647-9416, pbebje@bellsouth.net
   Specialties: Hunters, combat Bowies bird and trout. **Technical:** High-carbon steel and Damascus blades. **Prices:** $350 and up depending on blade desired. **Mark:** ELDER.

ELDRIDGE, ALLAN,
7731 Four Winds Dr, Ft. Worth, TX 76133, Phone: 817-370-7778
   Specialties: Fancy classic straight knives in standard patterns. **Patterns:** Hunters, Bowies, fighters, folders and miniatures. **Technical:** Grinds O1 and Damascus. Engraves silver-wire inlays, pearl inlays, scrimshaws and offers filework. **Prices:** $50 to $500; some to $1200. **Remarks:** Spare-time maker; first knife sold in 1965. **Mark:** Initials.

ELISHEWITZ, ALLEN,
3960 Lariat Ridge, New Braunfels, TX 78132, Phone: 830-899-5356, allen@elishewitzknives.com; Web: elishewitzknives.com
   Specialties: Collectible high-tech working straight knives and folders of his design. **Patterns:** Working, utility and tactical knives. **Technical:** Designs and uses innovative locking mechanisms. All designs drafted and field-tested. **Prices:** $600 to $1000. **Remarks:** Full-time maker; first knife sold in 1989. **Mark:** Gold medallion inlaid in blade.

ELLEFSON, JOEL,
PO Box 1016, 310 S 1st St, Manhattan, MT 59741, Phone: 406-284-3111
   Specialties: Working straight knives, fancy daggers and one-of-a-kinds. **Patterns:** Hunters, daggers and some folders. **Technical:** Grinds A2, 440C and ATS-34. Makes own mokume in bronze, brass, silver and shibuishi; makes brass/steel blades. **Prices:** $100 to $500; some to $2000. **Remarks:** Part-time maker; first knife sold in 1978. **Mark:** Stylized last initial.

ELLERBE, W B,
3871 Osceola Rd, Geneva, FL 32732, Phone: 407-349-5818
Specialties: Period and primitive knives and sheaths. **Patterns:** Bowies to patch knives, some tomahawks. **Technical:** Grinds Sheffield O1 and files. **Prices:** Start at $35. **Remarks:** Full-time maker; first knife sold in 1971. Doing business as Cypress Bend Custom Knives. **Mark:** Last name or initials.

ELLIOTT, JERRY,
4507 Kanawha Ave, Charleston, WV 25304, Phone: 304-925-5045, elliottknives@verizon.net
Specialties: Classic and traditional straight knives and folders of his design and to customer specs. **Patterns:** Hunters, locking folders and Bowies. **Technical:** Grinds ATS-34, 154CM, O1, D2 and T-440-V. All guards silver-soldered; bolsters are pinned on straight knives, spot-welded on folders. **Prices:** $80 to $265; some to $1000. **Remarks:** Full-time maker; first knife sold in 1972. **Mark:** First and middle initials, last name, knife maker, city, state.

ELLIS, DAVE/ABS MASTERSMITH,
380 South Melrose Dr #407, Vista, CA 92081, Phone: 760-643-4032 Eves: 760-945-7177, www.exquisiteknives.com
Specialties: Bowies, utility and combat knives. **Patterns:** Using knives to art quality pieces. **Technical:** Forges 5160, L6, 52100, cable and his own Damascus steels. **Prices:** $300 to $4000. **Remarks:** Part-time maker. California's first ABS Master Smith. **Mark:** Dagger-Rose with name and M.S. mark.

ELLIS, WILLIAM DEAN,
2767 Edgar Ave, Sanger, CA 93657, Phone: 559-314-4459, urleebird@comcast.net; Web: www.billysblades.com
Specialties: Classic and fancy knives of his design. **Patterns:** Boots, fighters and utility knives. **Technical:** Grinds ATS-34, D2 and Damascus. Offers tapered tangs and six patterns of filework; tooled multi-colored sheaths. **Prices:** $250 to $1500 **Remarks:** Part-time maker; first knife sold in 1991. Doing business as Billy's Blades. Also make shave-ready straight razors for actual use. **Mark:** "B" in a five-point star next to "Billy," city and state within a rounded-corner rectangle.

ELLIS, WILLY B,
4941 Cardinal Trail, Palm Harbor, FL 34683, Phone: 727-942-6420, Web: www.willyb.com
Specialties: One-of-a-kind high art and fantasy knives of his design. Occasional customs full size and miniatures. **Patterns:** Bowies, fighters, hunters and others. **Technical:** Grinds 440C, ATS-34, 1095, carbon Damascus, ivory bone, stone and metal carving. **Prices:** $175 to $15,000. **Remarks:** Full-time maker, first knife made in 1973. Member Knifemakers Guild. Jewel setting inlays. **Mark:** Willy B. or WB'S C etched or carved.

ELROD, ROGER R,
58 Dale Ave, Enterprise, AL 36330, Phone: 334-347-1863

EMBRETSEN, KAJ,
FALUVAGEN 67, S-82830 Edsbyn, SWEDEN, Phone: 46-271-21057, Fax: 46-271-22961, kay.embretsen@telia.com Web:www.embretsenknives.com
Specialties: Damascus folding knives. **Patterns:** Uses mammoth ivory and some pearl. **Technical:** Uses own Damascus steel. **Remarks:** Full time since 1983. **Prices:** $2500 to $8000. **Mark:** Name inside the folder.

EMERSON, ERNEST R,
PO Box 4180, Torrance, CA 90510-4180, Phone: 310-212-7455, info@emersonknives.com; Web: www.emersonknives.com
Specialties: High-tech folders and combat fighters. **Patterns:** Fighters, LinerLock® combat folders and SPECWAR combat knives. **Technical:** Grinds 154CM and Damascus. Makes folders with titanium fittings, liners and locks. Chisel grind specialist. **Prices:** $550 to $850; some to $10,000. **Remarks:** Full-time maker; first knife sold in 1983. **Mark:** Last name and Specwar knives.

ENCE, JIM,
145 S 200 East, Richfield, UT 84701, Phone: 435-896-6206
Specialties: High-art period pieces (spec in California knives) art knives. **Patterns:** Art, boot knives, fighters, Bowies and occasional folders. **Technical:** Grinds 440C for polish and beauty boys; makes own Damascus. **Prices:** Upscale. **Remarks:** Full-time maker; first knife sold in 1977. Does own engraving, gold work and stone work. Guild member since 1977. Founding member of the AKI. **Mark:** Ence, usually engraved.

ENGLAND, VIRGIL,
1340 Birchwood St, Anchorage, AK 99508, Phone: 907-274-9494, WEB:www.virgilengland.com
Specialties: Edged weapons and equipage, one-of-a-kind only. **Patterns:** Axes, swords, lances and body armor. **Technical:** Forges and grinds as pieces dictate. Offers stainless and Damascus. **Prices:** Upscale. **Remarks:** A veteran knifemaker. No commissions. **Mark:** Stylized initials.

ENGLE, WILLIAM,
16608 Oak Ridge Rd, Boonville, MO 65233, Phone: 816-882-6277
Specialties: Traditional working and using straight knives of his design. **Patterns:** Hunters, Bowies and fighters. **Technical:** Grinds 440C, ATS-34 and 154 CM. **Prices:** $250 to $500; some higher. **Remarks:** Part-time maker; first knife sold in 1982. All knives come with certificate of authenticity. **Mark:** Last name in block lettering.

ENGLEBRETSON, GEORGE,
1209 NW 49th St, Oklahoma City, OK 73118, Phone: 405-840-4784
Specialties: Working straight knives. **Technical:** Grinds A2, D2, 440C and ATS-34. **Prices:** Start at $150. **Remarks:** Full-time maker; first knife sold in 1967. **Mark:** "By George," name and city.

ENGLISH, JIM,
14586 Olive Vista Dr, Jamul, CA 91935, Phone: 619-669-0833
Specialties: Traditional working straight knives to customer specs. **Patterns:** Hunters, Bowies, fighters, tantos, daggers, boot and utility/camp knives. **Technical:** Grinds 440C, ATS-34, commercial Damascus and customer choice. **Prices:** $130 to $350. **Remarks:** Part-time maker; first knife sold in 1985. In addition to custom line, also does business as Mountain Home Knives. **Mark:** Double "A," Double "J" logo.

ENGLISH, JIM,
14586 Olive Vista Dr., Jamul, CA 91935, Phone: 619-669-0833
Specialties: High-quality working straight knives. **Patterns:** Hunters, fighters, skinners, tantos, utility and fillet knives, Bowies and *san-mai* Damascus Bowies. **Technical:** Hollow-grind 440C by hand. Feature linen Micarta handles, nickel-silver handle bolts and handmade sheaths. **Prices:** $65 to $270. **Remarks:** Company name is Mountain Home Knives. **Mark:** Mountain Home Knives.

ENNIS, RAY,
1220S 775E, Ogden, UT 84404, Phone: 800-410-7603, Fax: 501-621-2683, nifmakr@hotmail.com; Web:www.ennis-entrekusa.com

ENOS III, THOMAS M,
12302 State Rd 535, Orlando, FL 32836, Phone: 407-239-6205, tmenos3@att.net
Specialties: Heavy-duty working straight knives; unusual designs. **Patterns:** Swords, machetes, daggers, skinners, filleting, period pieces. **Technical:** Grinds 440C, D2, 154CM. **Prices:** $75 to $1500. **Remarks:** Full-time maker; first knife sold in 1972. No longer accepting custom requests. Will be making his own designs. Send SASE for listing of items for sale. **Mark:** Name in knife logo and year, type of steel and serial number.

ENTIN, ROBERT,
127 Pembroke St 1, Boston, MA 02118

EPTING, RICHARD,
4021 Cody Dr, College Station, TX 77845, Phone: 979-690-6496, rgeknives@hotmail.com; Web: www.eptingknives.com
Specialties: Folders and working straight knives. **Patterns:** Hunters, Bowies, and locking folders. **Technical:** Forges high-carbon steel and his own Damascus. **Prices:** $200 to $800; some to $1800. **Remarks:** Part-time maker, first knife sold 1996. **Mark:** Name in arch logo.

ERICKSON, L.M.,
1379 Black Mountain Cir, Ogden, UT 84404, Phone: 801-737-1930
Specialties: Straight knives; period pieces. **Patterns:** Bowies, fighters, boots and hunters. **Technical:** Grinds 440C, 154CM and commercial Damascus. **Prices:** $200 to $900; some to $5000. **Remarks:** Part-time maker; first knife sold in 1981. **Mark:** Name, city, state.

ERICKSON, WALTER E.,
22280 Shelton Tr, Atlanta, MI 49709, Phone: 989-785-5262, wberic@racc2000.com
Specialties: Unusual survival knives and high-tech working knives. **Patterns:** Butterflies, hunters, tantos. **Technical:** Grinds ATS-34 or customer choice. **Prices:** $150 to $500; some to $1500. **Remarks:** Full-time maker; first knife sold in 1981. **Mark:** Using pantograph with assorted fonts (no longer stamping).

ERIKSEN, JAMES THORLIEF,
dba VIKING KNIVES, 3830 Dividend Dr, Garland, TX 75042, Phone: 972-494-3667, Fax: 972-235-4932, VikingKnives@aol.com
Specialties: Heavy-duty working and using straight knives and folders utilizing traditional, Viking original and customer specification patterns. Some high-tech and fancy/embellished knives available. **Patterns:** Bowies, hunters, skinners, boot and belt knives, utility/camp knives, fighters, daggers, locking folders, slip-joint folders and kitchen knives. **Technical:** Hollow-grinds 440C, D2, ASP-23, ATS-34, 154CM, Vascowear. **Prices:** $150 to $300; some to $600. **Remarks:** Full-time maker; first knife sold in 1985. Doing business as Viking Knives. For a color catalog showing 50 different models, mail $5 to above address. **Mark:** VIKING or VIKING USA for export.

ERNEST, PHIL (PJ),
PO Box 5240, Whittier, CA 90607-5240, Phone: 562-556-2324, hugger883562@yahoo.com; Web:www.ernestcustomknives.com
Specialties: Fixed blades. **Patterns:** Wide range. Many original as well as hunters, camp, fighters, daggers, bowies and tactical. Specialzin in Wharncliff's of all sizes. **Technical:** Grinds commercial Damascus, Mosaid Damascus. ATS-34, and 440C. Full Tangs with bolsters. Handle material includes all types of exotic hardwood, abalone, peal mammoth tooth, mammoth ivory, Damascus steel and Mosaic Damascus. **Remarks:** Full time maker. First knife sold in 1999. **Prices:** $200 to $1800. Some to $2500. **Mark:** Owl logo with PJ Ernest Whittier CA or PJ Ernest.

ESSEGIAN, RICHARD,
7387 E Tulare St, Fresno, CA 93727, Phone: 309-255-5950
Specialties: Fancy working knives of his design; art knives. **Patterns:** Bowies and some small hunters. **Technical:** Grinds A2, D2, 440C and 154CM. Engraves and inlays. **Prices:** Start at $600. **Remarks:** Part-time maker; first knife sold in 1986. **Mark:** Last name, city and state.

ETZLER, JOHN,
11200 N Island, Grafton, OH 44044, Phone: 440-748-2460, jetzler@bright.net; Web: members.tripod.com/~etzlerknives/
Specialties: High-art and fantasy straight knives and folders of his design and to customer specs. **Patterns:** Folders, daggers, fighters, utility knives. **Technical:** Forges and grinds nickel Damascus and tool steel; grinds stainless steels. Prefers exotic, natural materials. **Prices:** $250 to $1200; some to $6500. **Remarks:** Full-time maker; first knife sold in 1992. **Mark:** Name or initials.

EVANS, BRUCE A,
409 CR 1371, Booneville, MS 38829, Phone: 662-720-0193, beknives@avsia.com; Web: www.bruceevans.homestead.com/open.html
Specialties: Forges blades. **Patterns:** Hunters, Bowies, or will work with customer. **Technical:** 5160, cable Damascus, pattern welded Damascus. **Prices:** $200 and up. **Mark:** Bruce A. Evans Same with JS on reverse of blade.

EVANS, CARLTON,
PO Box 72, Fort Davis, TX 79734, Phone: 817-886-9231, carlton@carltonevans.com; Web: www.evanshandmadeknives.com
Specialties: High end folders and fixed blades. **Technical:** Uses the stock removal methods. The materials used are of the highest quality. **Remarks:** Full-time knifemaker, voting member of Knifemakers Guild, member of the Texas Knifemakers and Collectors Association.

EVANS, RONALD B,
209 Hoffer St, Middleton, PA 17057-2723, Phone: 717-944-5464

EVANS, VINCENT K AND GRACE,
HC 1 Box 5275, Keaau, HI 96749-9517, Phone: 808-966-8978, evansvk@gmail.com Web: www.picturetrail.com/vevans
Specialties: Period pieces; swords. **Patterns:** Scottish, Viking, central Asian. **Technical:** Forges 5160 and his own Damascus. **Prices:** $700 to $4000; some to $8000. **Remarks:** Full-time maker; first knife sold in 1983. **Mark:** Last initial with fish logo.

EWING, JOHN H,
3276 Dutch Valley Rd, Clinton, TN 37716, Phone: 865-457-5757, johnja@comcast.net
Specialties: Working straight knives, hunters, camp knives. **Patterns:** Hunters. **Technical:** Grinds 440-D2. Forges 5160, 1095 prefers forging. **Prices:** $150 to $2000. **Remarks:** Part-time maker; first knife sold in 1985. **Mark:** First initial, last name, some embellishing done on knives.

F

FANT JR., GEORGE,
1983 CR 3214, Atlanta, TX 75551-6515, Phone: (903) 846-2938

FARID R, MEHR,
8 Sidney Close, Tunbridge Wells, Kent, ENGLAND TN2 5QQ, Phone: 011-44-1892 520345, farid@faridknives.com; Web: www.faridknives.com
Specialties: Hollow handle survival knives. High tech folders. **Patterns:** Flat grind blades & chisel ground LinerLock® folders. **Technical:** Grinds 440C, CPMT-440V, CPM-420V, CPM-15V, CPM5125V, and T-1 high speed steel. **Prices:** $550 to $5000. **Remarks:** Full-time maker; first knife sold in 1991. **Mark:** First name stamped.

FARR, DAN,
285 Glen Ellyn Way, Rochester, NY 14618, Phone: 585-721-1388
Specialties: Hunting, camping, fighting and utility. **Patterns:** Fixed blades. **Technical:** Forged or stock removal. **Prices:** $150 to $750.

FASSIO, MELVIN G,
420 Tyler Way, Lolo, MT 59847, Phone: 406-273-9143
Specialties: Working folders to customer specs. **Patterns:** Locking folders, hunters and traditional-style knives. **Technical:** Grinds 440C. **Prices:** $125 to $350. **Remarks:** Part-time maker; first knife sold in 1975. **Mark:** Name and city, dove logo.

FAUCHEAUX, HOWARD J,
PO Box 206, Loreauville, LA 70552, Phone: 318-229-6467
Specialties: Working straight knives and folders; period pieces. Also a hatchet with capping knife in the handle. **Patterns:** Traditional locking folders, hunters, fighters and Bowies. **Technical:** Forges W2, 1095 and his own Damascus; stock removal D2. **Prices:** Start at $200. **Remarks:** Full-time maker; first knife sold in 1969. **Mark:** Last name.

FAUST, DICK,
624 Kings Hwy N, Rochester, NY 14617, Phone: 585-544-1948, dickfaustknives@mac.com
Specialties: High-performance working straight knives. **Patterns:** Hunters and utility/camp knives. **Technical:** Hollow grinds 154CM full tang. Exotic woods, stag and Micarta handles. Provides a custom leather sheath with each knife. **Prices:** From $200 to $600, some higher. **Remarks:** Full-time maker. **Mark:** Signature.

FAUST, JOACHIM,
Kirchgasse 10, 95497 Goldkronach, GERMANY

FECAS, STEPHEN J,
1312 Shadow Lane, Anderson, SC 29625, Phone: 864-287-4834, Fax: 864-287-4834
Specialties: Front release lock backs, liner locks. Folders only. **Patterns:** Gents folders. **Technical:** Grinds ATS-34, Damascus-Ivories and pearl handles. **Prices:** $650 to $1200. **Remarks:** Full-time maker since 1980. First knife sold in 1977. All knives hand finished to 1500 grit. **Mark:** Last name signature.

FELIX, ALEXANDER,
PO Box 4036, Torrance, CA 90510, Phone: 310-320-1836, sgiandubh@dslextreme.com
Specialties: Straight working knives, fancy ethnic designs. **Patterns:** Hunters, Bowies, daggers, period pieces. **Technical:** Forges carbon steel and Damascus; forged stainless and titanium jewelry, gold and silver casting. **Prices:** $110 and up. **Remarks:** Jeweler, ABS Journeyman Smith. **Mark:** Last name.

FELLOWS, MIKE,
PO Box 162, Mosselbay 6500, SOUTH AFRICA, Phone: 27 82 960 3868, karatshin@gmail.com
Specialties: Miniatures, art knives and folders with occasionally hunters and skinners. **Patterns:** Own designs. **Technical:** Uses own Damascus. **Prices:** Upon request. **Remarks:** Use only indigenous materials. Exotic hard woods, horn & ivory. Does all own embellishments. **Mark:** "SHIN" letter from Hebrew alphabet over Hebrew word "Karat." **Other:** Member of knifemakers guild of Southern Africa.

FERGUSON, JIM,
32131 Via Bande, Temecula, CA 92592, Phone: 325-245-7106, Web: www.jimfergusonknives.com
Specialties: Nickel Damascus, Bowies, daggers, push blades. **Patterns:** All styles. **Technical:** Forges Damascus and sells in U.S. and Canada. **Prices:** $350 to $600, some to $1000. **Remarks:** 1200 sq. ft. commercial shop, 75 ton press. Has made over 11,000 lbs of Damascus. **Mark:** Jim Ferguson over push blade. Also make swords, battle axes and utilities.

FERGUSON, JIM,
PO Box 301, San Angelo, TX 76902, Phone: 915-651-6656
Patterns: Working belt knives, hunters, Bowies and some folders. **Technical:** Grinds ATS-34, D2 and Vascowear. Flat-grinds hunting knives. **Prices:** $200 to $600; some to $1000. **Remarks:** Full-time maker; first knife sold in 1987. **Mark:** First and middle initials, last name.

FERGUSON, LEE,
1993 Madison 7580, Hindsville, AR 72738, Phone: 479-443-0084, info@fergusonknives.com; Web: www.fergusonknives.com
Specialties: Straight working knives and folders, some fancy. **Patterns:** Hunters, daggers, swords, locking folders and slip-joints. **Technical:** Grinds D2, 440C and ATS-34; heat-treats. **Prices:** $50 to $600; some to $4000. **Remarks:** Full-time maker; first knife sold in 1977. **Mark:** Full name.

FERGUSON, LINDA,
1993 Madison 7580, Hindsville, AR 72738, Phone: 479-443-0084, info@fergusonknives.com; Web: www.fergusonknives.com
Specialties: Mini knives. **Patterns:** Daggers & hunters. **Technical:** Hollow ground, stainless steel or Damascus. **Prices:** $65 to $250. **Remarks:** 2004 member Knifemakers Guild, Miniature Knifemakers Society. **Mark:** LF inside a Roman numeral 2.

FERRARA, THOMAS,
122 Madison Dr, Naples, FL 33942, Phone: 813-597-3363, Fax: 813-597-3363
Specialties: High-art, traditional and working straight knives and folders of all designs. **Patterns:** Boots, Bowies, daggers, fighters and hunters. **Technical:** Grinds 440C, D2 and ATS-34; heat-treats. **Prices:** $100 to $700; some to $1300. **Remarks:** Part-time maker; first knife sold in 1983. **Mark:** Last name.

FERRIER, GREGORY K,
3119 Simpson Dr, Rapid City, SD 57702, Phone: 605-342-9280

FERRIS, BILL,
186 Thornton Dr, Palm Beach Garden, FL 33418

FERRY, TOM,
16005 SE 322nd St, Auburn, WA 98092, Phone: 253-939-4468, tomferryknives@Q.com; Web: tomferryknives.com
Specialties: Presentation grade knives. **Patterns:** Folders and fixed blades. **Technical:** Specialize in Damascus and engraving. **Prices:** $500 and up. **Remarks:** DBA: Soos Creek Ironworks. ABS Master Smith. **Mark:** Combined T and F in a circle and/or last name.

FILIPPOU, IOANNIS-MINAS,
7 Krinis Str Nea Smyrni, Athens 17122, GREECE, Phone: (1) 935-2093

FINCH, RICKY D,
2446 Hwy. 191, West Liberty, KY 41472, Phone: 606-743-7151, finchknives@mrtc.com; Web: www.finchknives.com
Specialties: Traditional working/using straight knives of his design or to customer spec. **Patterns:** Hunters, skinners and utility/camp knives.

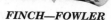

LinerLock® of his design. **Technical:** Grinds 440C, ATS-34 and CPM154, hand rubbed stain finish, use Micarta, stabilized wood, natural and exotic. **Prices:** $85 to $225. **Remarks:** Part-time maker, first knife made 1994. Doing business as Finch Knives. **Mark:** Last name inside outline of state of Kentucky.

FIORINI, BILL,
703 W. North St., Grayville, IL 62844, Phone: 618-375-7191, smallflowerlonchura@yahoo.com
Specialties: Fancy working knives. **Patterns:** Hunters, boots, Japanese-style knives and kitchen/utility knives and folders. **Technical:** Forges own Damascus, mosaic and mokune-gane. **Prices:** Full range. **Remarks:** Full-time metal smith researching pattern materials. **Mark:** Orchid crest with name KOKA in Japanese.

FISHER, JAY,
1405 Edwards, Clovis, NM 88101, Phone: 575-763-2268, jayfisher@jayfisher. com Web: www.JayFisher.com
Specialties: High-art, working and collector's knives of his design and client's designs. Military working and commemoratives. **Patterns:** Hunters, daggers, folding knives, museum pieces and high-art sculptures. **Technical:** Grinds 440C, ATS-34, O1and D2. Prolific maker of stone-handled knives and swords. **Prices:** $400 to $50,000; some higher. **Remarks:** Full-time maker; first knife sold in 1980. High resolution etching, computer and manual engraving. **Mark:** Signature "JaFisher"

FISHER, THEO (TED),
8115 Modoc Lane, Montague, CA 96064, Phone: 916-459-3804
Specialties: Moderately priced working knives in carbon steel. **Patterns:** Hunters, fighters, kitchen and buckskinner knives, Damascus miniatures. **Technical:** Grinds ATS-34, L6 and 440C. **Prices:** $65 to $165; exceptional knives to $300. **Remarks:** First knife sold in 1981. **Mark:** Name in banner logo.

FISK, JERRY,
10095 Hwy 278 W, Nashville, AR 71852, Phone: 870-845-4456, jerry@fisk-knives.com; Web: wwwfisk-knives.com
Specialties: Edged weapons, collectible and functional. **Patterns:** Bowies, daggers, swords, hunters, camp knives and others. **Technical:** Forges carbon steels and his own pattern welded steels. **Prices:** $250 to $15,000. **Remarks:** National living treasure. **Mark:** Name, MS.

FISTER, JIM,
PO Box 307, Simpsonville, KY 40067
Specialties: One-of-a-kind collectibles and period pieces. **Patterns:** Bowies, camp knives, hunters, buckskinners, and daggers. **Technical:** Forges, 1085, 5160, 52100, his own Damascus, pattern and turkish. **Prices:** $150 to $2500. **Remarks:** Part-time maker; first knife sold in 1982. **Mark:** Name and MS.

FITCH, JOHN S,
45 Halbrook Rd, Clinton, AR 72031-8910, Phone: 501-893-2020

FITZGERALD, DENNIS M,
4219 Alverado Dr, Fort Wayne, IN 46816-2847, Phone: 219-447-1081
Specialties: One-of-a-kind collectibles and period pieces. **Patterns:** Skinners, fighters, camp and utility knives; period pieces. **Technical:** Forges 1085, 1095, L6, 5160, 52100, his own pattern and Turkish Damascus. **Prices:** $100 to $500. **Remarks:** Part-time maker; first knife sold in 1985. Doing business as The Ringing Circle. **Mark:** Name and circle logo.

FLINT, ROBERT,
2902 Aspen, Anchorage, AK 99517, Phone: 907-243-6706
Specialties: Working straight knives and folders. **Patterns:** Utility, hunters, fighters and gents. **Technical:** Grinds ATS-34, BG-42, D2 and Damascus. **Prices:** $150 and up. **Remarks:** Part-time maker, first knife sold in 1998. **Mark:** Last name; stylized initials.

FLOURNOY, JOE,
5750 Lisbon Rd, El Dorado, AR 71730, Phone: 870-863-7208, flournoy@ipa. net
Specialties: Working straight knives and folders. **Patterns:** Hunters, Bowies, camp knives, folders and daggers. **Technical:** Forges only high-carbon steel, steel cable and his own Damascus. **Prices:** $350 Plus. **Remarks:** First knife sold in 1977. **Mark:** Last name and MS in script.

FLYNT, ROBERT G,
15173 Christy Lane, Gulfport, MS 39503, Phone: 228-265-0410, flyntstoneknives@bellsouth.net Web: www.flyntstoneknifeworks.com
Specialties:
All types of fixed blades: Drop point, clip point, trailing point, bull nose hunters, tactical, fighters and Bowies. Folders I've made include liner lock, slip joint and lock back styles.
Technical: Using 154 cm, cpm154, ats34, 440c, cpm3v and 52100 steel, most of my blades are made by stock removal, hollow and flat grind methods. I do forge some cable Damascus and use numerous types of Damascus that is purchased in billets from various makers. All file work and bluing is done by me.
I have made handles from a variety of wood, bone and horn materials, including some with wire inlay and other embellishments.
Most knives are sold with custom fit leather sheaves most include exotic skin inlay when appropriate.
Prices: $150 and up depending on embellishments on blade and sheath.

Remarks: Full time maker. First knife made in 1966.
Mark: Last name in cursive letters or a knife striking a flint stone.

FOGARIZZU, BOITEDDU,
via Crispi 6, 07016 Pattada, ITALY
Specialties: Traditional Italian straight knives and folders. **Patterns:** Collectible folders. **Technical:** forges and grinds 12C27, ATS-34 and his Damascus. **Prices:** $200 to $3000. **Remarks:** Full-time maker; first knife sold in 1958. **Mark:** Full name and registered logo.

FOGG, DON,
40 Alma Rd, Jasper, AL 35501-8813, Phone: 205-483-0822, dfogg@ dfoggknives.com; Web: www.dfoggknives.com
Specialties: Swords, daggers, Bowies and hunting knives. **Patterns:** Collectible folders. **Technical:** Hand-forged high-carbon and Damascus steel. **Prices:** $200 to $5000. **Remarks:** Full-time maker; first knife sold in 1976. **Mark:** 24K gold cherry blossom.

FONTENOT, GERALD J,
901 Maple Ave, Mamou, LA 70554, Phone: 318-468-3180

FORREST, BRIAN,
FORREST KNIVES, PO Box 203, Descanso, CA 91916, Phone: 619-445-6343, forrestknives@hotmail.com; Web: www.forrestknives.com
Specialties: Forged tomahawks, working knives, big Bowies. **Patterns:** Traditional and extra large Bowies. **Technical:** Hollow grinds: 440C, 1095, S160 Damascus. **Prices:** $125 and up. **Remarks:** Member of California Knifemakers Association. Full-time maker. First knife sold in 1971. **Mark:** Forrest USA/Tomahawks marked FF (Forrest Forge).

FORTHOFER, PETE,
5535 Hwy 93S, Whitefish, MT 59937, Phone: 406-862-2674
Specialties: Interframes with checkered wood inlays; working straight knives. **Patterns:** Interframe folders and traditional-style knives; hunters, fighters and Bowies. **Technical:** Grinds D2, 440C, 154CM and ATS-34. **Prices:** $350 to $2500; some to $1500. **Remarks:** Part-time maker; full-time gunsmith. First knife sold in 1979. **Mark:** Name and logo.

FORTUNE PRODUCTS, INC.,
205 Hickory Creek Rd, Marble Falls, TX 78654, Phone: 830-693-6111, Fax: 830-693-6394, Web: www.accusharp.com
Specialties: Knife sharpeners.

FOSTER, AL,
118 Woodway Dr, Magnolia, TX 77355, Phone: 936-372-9297
Specialties: Straight knives and folders. **Patterns:** Hunting, fishing, folders and Bowies. **Technical:** Grinds 440-C, ATS-34 and D2. **Prices:** $100 to $1000. **Remarks:** Full-time maker; first knife sold in 1981. **Mark:** Scorpion logo and name.

FOSTER, BURT,
23697 Archery Range Rd, Bristol, VA 24202, Phone: 276-669-0121, burt@ burtfoster.com; Web: www.burtfoster.com
Specialties: Working straight knives, laminated blades, and some art knives of his design. **Patterns:** Bowies, hunters, daggers. **Technical:** Forges 52100, W-2 and makes own Damascus. Does own heat treating. **Remarks:** ABS MasterSmith. Full-time maker, believes in sole authorship. **Mark:** Signed "BF" initials.

FOSTER, NORVELL C,
7945 Youngsford Rd, Marion, TX 78124-1713, Phone: 830-914-2078
Specialties: Engraving; ivory handle carving. **Patterns:** American-large and small scroll-oak leaf and acorns. **Prices:** $25 to $400. **Remarks:** Have been engraving since 1957. **Mark:** N.C. Foster - Marion - Tex and current year.

FOSTER, R L (BOB),
745 Glendale Blvd, Mansfield, OH 44907, Phone: 419-756-6294

FOSTER, RONNIE E,
95 Riverview Rd., Morrilton, AR 72110, Phone: 501-354-5389
Specialties: Working, using knives, some period pieces, work with customer specs. **Patterns:** Hunters, fighters, Bowies, liner-lock folders, camp knives. **Technical:** Forge-5160, 1084, O1, 15N20-makes own Damascus. **Prices:** $200 (start). **Remarks:** Part-time maker. First knife sold 1994. **Mark:** Ronnie Foster MS.

FOSTER, TIMOTHY L,
723 Sweet Gum Acres Rd, El Dorado, AR 71730, Phone: 870-863-6188

FOWLER, CHARLES R,
226 National Forest Rd 48, Ft McCoy, FL 32134-9624, Phone: 904-467-3215

FOWLER, ED A.,
Willow Bow Ranch, PO Box 1519, Riverton, WY 82501, Phone: 307-856-9815
Specialties: High-performance working and using straight knives. **Patterns:** Hunter, camp, bird, and trout knives and Bowies. New model, the gentleman's Pronghorn. **Technical:** Low temperature forged 52100 from virgin 5-1/2 round bars, multiple quench heat treating, engraves all knives, all handles domestic sheep horn processed and aged at least 5 years. Makes heavy duty hand-stitched waxed harness leather pouch type sheaths. **Prices:** $800 to $7000. **Remarks:** Full-time maker. First knife sold in 1962. **Mark:** Initials connected.

FOWLER, JERRY,
610 FM 1660 N, Hutto, TX 78634, Phone: 512-846-2860, fowler@inetport.com
Specialties: Using straight knives of his design. **Patterns:** A variety of hunting and camp knives, combat knives. Custom designs considered. **Technical:** Forges 5160, his own Damascus and cable Damascus. Makes sheaths. Prefers natural handle materials. **Prices:** Start at $150. **Remarks:** Part-time maker; first knife sold in 1986. Doing business as Fowler Forge Knife Works. **Mark:** First initial, last name, date and J.S.

FOX, PAUL,
4721 Rock Barn Rd, Claremont, NC 28610, Phone: 828-459-2000, jessepfox@gmail.com
Specialties: Unique locking mechanisms. **Patterns:** Pen knives, one-of-a-kind tactical knives. **Technical:** All locking mechanisms are his. **Prices:** $350 and up. **Remarks:** First knife sold in 1976. Guild member since 1977. **Mark:** Fox, P Fox, Paul Fox. Cuts out all parts of knives in shop.

FRALEY, D B,
1355 Fairbanks Ct, Dixon, CA 95620, Phone: 707-678-0393, dbtfnives@sbcglobal.net; Web:www.dbfraleyknives.com
Specialties Usable gentleman's fixed blades and folders. **Patterns:** Foure folders in four different sizes in liner lock and frame lock. **Technical:** Grinds CPMS30V, 154, 6K stellite. **Prices:** $250 and up. **Remarks:** Part time maker. First knife sold in 1990. **Mark:** First and middle initials, last name over a buffalo.

FRAMSKI, WALTER P,
24 Rek Ln, Prospect, CT 06712, Phone: 203-758-5634

FRANCE, DAN,
Box 218, Cawood, KY 40815, Phone: 606-573-6104
Specialties: Traditional working and using straight knives of his design. **Patterns:** Hunters, Bowies and utility/camp knives. **Technical:** Forges and grinds O1, 5160 and L6. **Prices:** $35 to $125; some to $350. **Remarks:** Spare-time maker; first knife sold in 1985. **Mark:** First name.

FRANCIS, JOHN D,
FRANCIS KNIVES, 18 Miami St., Ft. Loramie, OH 45845, Phone: 937-295-3941, jdfrancis@roadrunner.com
Specialties: Utility and hunting-style fixed bladed knives of 440 C and ATS-34 steel; Micarta, exotic woods, and other types of handle materials. **Prices:** $90 to $150 range. **Remarks:** Exceptional quality and value at factory prices. **Mark:** Francis-Ft. Loramie, OH stamped on tang.

FRANK, HEINRICH H,
1147 SW Bryson St, Dallas, OR 97338, Phone: 503-831-1489, Fax: 503-831-1489
Specialties: High-art investor-class folders, handmade and engraved. **Patterns:** Folding daggers, hunter-size folders and gents. **Technical:** Grinds 07 and O1. **Prices:** $4800 to $16,000. **Remarks:** Full-time maker; first knife sold in 1965. Doing business as H.H. Frank Knives. **Mark:** Name, address and date.

FRANKLIN, MIKE,
9878 Big Run Rd, Aberdeen, OH 45101, Phone: 937-549-2598, Web: www.mikefranklinknives.com, hawgcustomknives.com
Specialties: High-tech tactical folders. **Patterns:** Tactical folders. **Technical:** Grinds CPM-T-440V, 440-C, ATS-34; titanium liners and bolsters; carbon fiber scales. Uses radical grinds and severe serrations. **Prices:** $100 to $1000. **Remarks:** Full-time maker; first knife sold in 1969. All knives made one at a time, 100% by the maker. **Mark:** Stylized boar with HAWG.

FRAPS, JOHN R,
3810 Wyandotte Tr, Indianpolis, IN 46240-3422, Phone: 317-849-9419, Fax: 317-842-2224, jfraps@att.net; Web: www.frapsknives.com
Specialties: Working and collector grade LinerLock® and slip joint folders. **Patterns:** One-of-a kind linerlocks and traditional slip joints. **Technical:** Flat and hollow grinds ATS-34, Damascus, Talonite, CPM S30V, 154Cm, Stellite 6K; hand rubbed or mirror finish. **Prices:** $200 to $1500, some higher. **Remarks:** Voting member of the Knifemaker's Guild; Full-time maker; first knife sold in 1997. **Mark:** Cougar Creek Knives and/or name.

FRAZIER, RON,
2107 Urbine Rd, Powhatan, VA 23139, Phone: 804-794-8561
Specialties: Classy working knives of his design; some high-art straight knives. **Patterns:** Wide assortment of straight knives, including miniatures and push knives. **Technical:** Grinds 440C; offers satin, mirror or sand finishes. **Prices:** $85 to $700; some to $3000. **Remarks:** Full-time maker; first knife sold in 1976. **Mark:** Name in arch logo.

FRED, REED WYLE,
3149 X S, Sacramento, CA 95817, Phone: 916-739-0237
Specialties: Working using straight knives of his design. **Patterns:** Hunting and camp knives. **Technical:** Forges any 10 series, old files and carbon steels. Offers initialing upon request; prefers natural handle materials. **Prices:** $30 to $300. **Remarks:** Part-time maker; first knife sold in 1994. Doing business as R.W. Fred Knifemaker. **Mark:** Engraved first and last initials.

FREDERICK, AARON,
459 Brooks Ln, West Liberty, KY 41472-8961, Phone: 606-7432015, aaronf@mrtc.com; Web: www.frederickknives.com
Specialties: Makes most types of knives, but as for now specializes in the Damascus folder. Does all own Damascus and forging of the steel. Also prefers natural handle material such as ivory and pearl. Prefers 14k gold screws in most of the knives he do. Also offer several types of file work on blades, spacers, and liners. Has just recently started doing carving and can do a limited amount of engraving.

FREER, RALPH,
114 12th St, Seal Beach, CA 90740, Phone: 562-493-4925, Fax: same, ralphfreer@adelphia.net
Specialties: Exotic folders, liner locks, folding daggers, fixed blades. **Patters:** All original. **Technical:** Lots of Damascus, ivory, pearl, jeweled, thumb studs, carving ATS-34, 420V, 530V. **Prices:** $400 to $2500 and up. **Mark:** Freer in German-style text, also Freer shield.

FREILING, ALBERT J,
3700 Niner Rd, Finksburg, MD 21048, Phone: 301-795-2880
Specialties: Working straight knives and folders; some period pieces. **Patterns:** Boots, Bowies, survival knives and tomahawks in 4130 and 440C; some locking folders and interframes; ball-bearing folders. **Technical:** Grinds O1, 440C and 154CM. **Prices:** $100 to $300; some to $500. **Remarks:** Part-time maker; first knife sold in 1966. **Mark:** Initials connected.

FREY JR., W FREDERICK,
305 Walnut St, Milton, PA 17847, Phone: 570-742-9576, wffrey@ptd.net
Specialties: Working straight knives and folders, some fancy. **Patterns:** Wide range miniatures, boot knives and lock back folders. **Technical:** Grinds A2, O1 and D2; vaseo wear, cru-wear and CPM S60V and CPM S90V. **Prices:** $100 to $250; some to $1200. **Remarks:** Spare-time maker; first knife sold in 1983. All knives include quality hand stitched sheaths. **Mark:** Last name in script.

FRIEDLY, DENNIS E,
12 Cottontail Ln E, Cody, WY 82414, Phone: 307-527-6811, friedly_knives@hotmail.com
Specialties: Fancy working straight knives and daggers, lock back folders and liner locks. Also embellished bowies. **Patterns:** Hunters, fighters, short swords, minis and miniatures; new line of full-tang hunters/boots. **Technical:** Grinds 440C, commercial Damascus, mosaic Damascus and ATS-34 blades; prefers hidden tangs and full tangs. Both flat and hollow grinds. **Prices:** $350 to $2500. Some to $10,000. **Remarks:** Full-time maker; first knife sold in 1972. **Mark:** D.E. Friedly-Cody, WY. Friedly Knives

FRIGAULT, RICK,
3584 Rapidsview Dr, Niagara Falls, Ont., CANADA L2G 6C4, Phone: 905-295-6695, rfrigualt@cogeco.ca; Web: www.rfrigaultknives.ca
Specialties: Fixed blades. **Patterns:** Hunting, tactical and large Bowies. **Technical:** Grinds ATS-34, 440-C, D-2, CPMS30V, CPMS60V, CPMS90V, BG42 and Damascus. Use G-10, Micarta, ivory, antler, ironwood and other stabilized woods for carbon fiber handle material. Makes leather sheaths by hand. Tactical blades include a Concealex sheath made by "On Scene Tactical." **Remarks:** Sold first knife in 1997. Member of Canadian Knifemakers Guild. **Mark:** RFRIGAULT.

FRITZ, ERIK L,
837 River St Box 1203, Forsyth, MT 59327, Phone: 406-351-1101, tacmedic45@yahoo.com
Specialties: Forges carbon steel 1084, 5160, 52100 and Damascus. **Patterns:** Hunters, camp knives, bowies and folders as well as forged tactical. **Technical:** Forges own Mosaic and pattern welded Damascus as well as doing own heat treat. **Prices:** A$200 and up. **Remarks:** Sole authorship knives and sheaths. Part time maker first knife sold in 2004. ABS member. **Mark:** E. Fritz in arc on left side ricasso.

FRITZ, JESSE,
900 S. 13th St, Slaton, TX 79364, Phone: 806-828-5083
Specialties: Working and using straight knives in standard patterns. **Patterns:** Hunters, utility/camp knives and skinners with gut hook, Bowie knives, kitchen carving sets by request. **Technical:** Grinds 440C, O1 and 1095. Uses 1095 steel. Fline-napped steel design, blued blades, filework and machine jewelling. Inlays handles with turquoise, coral and mother-of-pearl. Makes sheaths. **Prices:** $85 to $275; some to $500. **Mark:** Last name only (FRITZ).

FRIZZELL, TED,
14056 Low Gap Rd, West Fork, AR 72774, Phone: 501-839-2516, mmhwaxes@aol.com Web: www.mineralmountain.com
Specialties: Swords, axes and self-defense weapons. **Patterns:** Small skeleton knives to large swords. **Technical:** Grinds 5160 almost exclusively—1/4" to 1/2"— bars some O1 and A2 on request. All knives come with Kydex sheaths. **Prices:** $45 to $1200. **Remarks:** Full-time maker; first knife sold in 1984. Doing business as Mineral Mountain Hatchet Works. Wholesale orders welcome. **Mark:** A circle with line in the middle; MM and HW within the circle.

FRONEFIELD, DANIEL,
20270 Warriors Path, Peyton, CO 80831, Phone: 719-749-0226, dfronfld@hiwaay.net
Specialties: Fixed and folding knives featuring meteorites and other exotic

materials. **Patterns:** San-mai Damascus, custom Damascus. **Prices:** $500 to $3000.

FROST, DEWAYNE,
1016 Van Buren Rd, Barnesville, GA 30204, Phone: 770-358-1426, lbrtyhill@ aol.com
    Specialties: Working straight knives and period knives. **Patterns:** Hunters, Bowies and utility knives. **Technical:** Forges own Damascus, cable, etc. as well as stock removal. **Prices:** $150 to $500. **Remarks:** Part-time maker ABS Journeyman Smith. **Mark:** Liberty Hill Forge Dewayne Frost w/liberty bell.

FRUHMANN, LUDWIG,
Stegerwaldstr 8, 84489 Burghausen, GERMANY
    Specialties: High-tech and working straight knives of his design. **Patterns:** Hunters, fighters and boots. **Technical:** Grinds ATS-34, CPM-T-440V and Schneider Damascus. Prefers natural handle materials. **Prices:** $200 to $1500. **Remarks:** Spare-time maker; first knife sold in 1990. **Mark:** First initial and last name.

FUEGEN, LARRY,
617 N Coulter Circle, Prescott, AZ 86303, Phone: 928-776-8777, fuegen@ cableone.net; Web: www.larryfuegen.com
    Specialties: High-art folders and classic and working straight knives. **Patterns:** Forged scroll folders, lockback folders and classic straight knives. **Technical:** Forges 5160, 1095 and his own Damascus. Works in exotic leather; offers elaborate filework and carving; likes natural handle materials, now offers own engraving. **Prices:** $600 to $12,000. **Remarks:** Full-time maker; first knife sold in 1975. Sole authorship on all knives. ABS Mastersmith. **Mark:** Initials connected.

FUJIKAWA, SHUN,
Sawa 1157 Kaizuka, Osaka 597 0062, JAPAN, Phone: 81-724-23-4032, Fax: 81-726-23-9229
    Specialties: Folders of his design and to customer specs. **Patterns:** Locking folders. **Technical:** Grinds his own steel. **Prices:** $450 to $2500; some to $3000. **Remarks:** Part-time maker.

FUJISAKA, STANLEY,
45-004 Holowai St, Kaneohe, HI 96744, Phone: 808-247-0017, s.fuj@earthlink. net
    Specialties: Fancy working straight knives and folders. **Patterns:** Hunters, boots, personal knives, daggers, collectible art knives. **Technical:** Grinds 440C, 154CM and ATS-34; clean lines, inlays. **Prices:** $400 to $2000; some to $6000. **Remarks:** Full-time maker; first knife sold in 1984. **Mark:** Name, city, state.

FUKUTA, TAK,
38-Umeagae-cho, Seki-City, Gifu-Pref, JAPAN, Phone: 0575-22-0264
    Specialties: Bench-made fancy straight knives and folders. **Patterns:** Sheffield-type folders, Bowies and fighters. **Technical:** Grinds commercial Damascus. **Prices:** Start at $300. **Remarks:** Full-time maker. **Mark:** Name in knife logo.

FULLER, BRUCE A,
1305 Airhart Dr, Baytown, TX 77520, Phone: 281-427-1848, fullcoforg@aol. com
    Specialties: One-of-a-kind working/using straight knives and folders of his designs. **Patterns:** Bowies, hunters, folders, and utility/camp knives. **Technical:** Forges high-carbon steel and his own Damascus. Prefers El Solo Mesquite and natural materials. Offers filework. **Prices:** $200 to $500; some to $1800. **Remarks:** Spare-time maker; first knife sold in 1991. Doing business as Fullco Forge. **Mark:** Fullco, M.S.

FULLER, JACK A,
7103 Stretch Ct, New Market, MD 21774, Phone: 301-798-0119
    Specialties: Straight working knives of his design and to customer specs. **Patterns:** Fighters, camp knives, hunters, tomahawks and art knives. **Technical:** Forges 5160, O1, W2 and his own Damascus. Does silver wire inlay and own leather work, wood lined sheaths for big camp knives. **Prices:** $400 and up. **Remarks:** Part-time maker. Master Smith in ABS; first knife sold in 1979. **Mark:** Fuller's Forge, MS.

FULTON, MICKEY,
406 S Shasta St, Willows, CA 95988, Phone: 530-934-5780
    Specialties: Working straight knives and folders of his design. **Patterns:** Hunters, Bowies, lockback folders and steak knife sets. **Technical:** Hand-filed, sanded, buffed ATS-34, 440C and A2. **Prices:** $65 to $600; some to $1200. **Remarks:** Full-time maker; first knife sold in 1979. **Mark:** Signature.

G

GADBERRY, EMMET,
82 Purple Plum Dr, Hattieville, AR 72063, Phone: 501-354-4842

GADDY, GARY LEE,
205 Ridgewood Lane, Washington, NC 27889, Phone: 252-946-4359
    Specialties: Working/using straight knives of his design; period pieces. **Patterns:** Bowies, hunters, utility/camp knives. **Technical:** Grinds ATS-34, O1; forges 1095. **Prices:** $100 to $225; some to $400. **Remarks:** Spare-time maker; first knife sold in 1991. **Mark:** Quarter moon logo.

GAETA, ANGELO,
R. Saldanha Marinho, 1295 Centro Jau, SP-17201-310, BRAZIL, Phone: 0146-224543, Fax: 0146-224543
    Specialties: Straight using knives to customer specs. **Patterns:** Hunters, fighting, daggers, belt push dagger. **Technical:** Grinds D6, ATS-34 and 440C stainless. Titanium nitride golden finish upon request. **Prices:** $60 to $300. **Remarks:** Full-time maker; first knife sold in 1992. **Mark:** First initial, last name.

GAETA, ROBERTO,
Rua Mandissununga 41, Sao Paulo, BRAZIL 05619-010, Phone: 11-37684626, karlaseno@uol.com.br
    Specialties: Wide range of using knives. **Patterns:** Brazilian and North American hunting and fighting knives. **Technical:** Grinds stainless steel; likes natural handle materials. **Prices:** $500 to $800. **Remarks:** Full-time maker; first knife sold in 1979. **Mark:** BOB'G.

GAINES, BUDDY,
GAINES KNIVES, 155 Red Hill Rd., Commerce, GA 30530, Web: www. gainesknives.com
    Specialties: Collectible and working folders and straight knives. **Patterns:** Folders, hunters, Bowies, tactical knives. **Technical:** Forges own Damascus, grinds ATS-34, D2, commercial Damascus. Prefers mother-of-pearl and stag. **Prices:** Start at $200. **Remarks:** Part-time maker, sold first knife in 1985. **Mark:** Last name.

GAINEY, HAL,
904 Bucklevel Rd, Greenwood, SC 29649, Phone: 864-223-0225, Web: www. scak.org
    Specialties: Traditional working and using straight knives and folders. **Patterns:** Hunters, slip-joint folders and utility/camp knives. **Technical:** Hollow-grinds ATS-34 and D2; makes sheaths. **Prices:** $95 to $145; some to $500. **Remarks:** Full-time maker; first knife sold in 1975. **Mark:** Eagle head and last name.

GALLAGHER, BARRY,
135 Park St, Lewistown, MT 59457, Phone: 406-538-7056, Web: www. gallagherknives.com
    Specialties: One-of-a-kind Damascus folders. **Patterns:** Folders, utility to high art, some straight knives, hunter, Bowies, and art pieces. **Technical:** Forges own mosaic Damascus and carbon steel, some stainless. **Prices:** $400 to $5000+. **Remarks:** Full-time maker; first knife sold in 1993. Doing business as Gallagher Custom Knives. **Mark:** Last name.

GAMBLE, FRANK,
4676 Commercial St SE #26, Salem, OR 97302, Phone: 503-581-7993, gamble6831@comcast.net
    Specialties: Fantasy and high-art straight knives and folders of his design. **Patterns:** Daggers, fighters, hunters and special locking folders. **Technical:** Grinds 440C and ATS-34; forges Damascus. Inlays; offers jewelling. Prices $150 to $10,000. **Remarks:** Full-time maker; first knife sold in 1976. **Mark:** First initial, last name.

GAMBLE, ROGER,
18515 N.W. 28th Pl., Newberry, FL 32669, rlgamble2@netzero.net
    Specialties: Traditional working/using straight knives and folders of his design. **Patterns:** Liner locks and hunters. **Technical:** Grinds ATS-34 and Damascus. **Prices:** $150 to $2000. **Remarks:** Part-time maker; first knife sold in 1982. Doing business as Gamble Knives. **Mark:** First name in a fan of cards over last name.

GANN, TOMMY,
2876 State Hwy. 198, Canton, TX 75103, Phone: 903-848-9375
    Specialties: Art and working straight knives of my design or customer preferences/design. **Patterns:** Bowie, fighters, hunters, daggers. **Technical:** Forges Damascus 52100 and grinds ATS-34 and D2. **Prices:** $200 to $2500. **Remarks:** Full-time knifemaker, first knife sold in 2002. ABS journey bladesmith. **Mark:** TGANN.

GANSHORN, CAL,
123 Rogers Rd., Regina, Saskatchewan, CANADA S4S 6T7, Phone: 306-584-0524
    Specialties: Working and fancy fixed blade knives. **Patterns:** Bowies, hunters, daggers, and filleting. **Technical:** Makes own forged Damascus billets, ATS, salt heat treating, and custom forges and burners. **Prices:** $250 to $1500. **Remarks:** Part-time maker. **Mark:** Last name etched in ricasso area.

GARCIA, MARIO EIRAS,
R. Edmundo Scanapieco, 300 Caxingui, Sao Paulo SP-05516-070, BRAZIL, Fax: 11-37214528
    Specialties: Fantasy knives of his design; one-of-a-kind only. **Patterns:** Fighters, daggers, boots and two-bladed knives. **Technical:** Forges car leaf springs. Uses only natural handle material. **Prices:** $100 to $200. **Remarks:** Part-time maker; first knife sold in 1976. **Mark:** Two "B"s, one opposite the other.

GARNER, LARRY W,
13069 FM 14, Tyler, TX 75706, Phone: 903-597-6045, lwgarner@classicnet. net
    Specialties: Fixed blade hunters and Bowies. **Patterns:** His designs or yours. **Technical:** Hand forges 5160. **Prices:** $200 to $500. **Remarks:** Apprentice bladesmith. **Mark:** Last name.

GARVOCK, MARK W,
RR 1, Balderson, Ont., CANADA K1G 1A0, Phone: 613-833-2545, Fax: 613-833-2208, garvock@travel-net.com
Specialties: Hunters, Bowies, Japanese, daggers and swords. **Patterns:** Cable Damascus, random pattern welded or to suit. **Technical:** Forged blades; hi-carbon. **Prices:** $250 to $900. **Remarks:** CKG member and ABS member. Shipping and taxes extra. **Mark:** Big G with M in middle.

GAUDETTE, LINDEN L,
5 Hitchcock Rd, Wilbraham, MA 01095, Phone: 413-596-4896
Specialties: Traditional working knives in standard patterns. **Patterns:** Broad-bladed hunters, Bowies and camp knives; wood carver knives; locking folders. **Technical:** Grinds ATS-34, 440C and 154CM. **Prices:** $150 to $400; some higher. **Remarks:** Full-time maker; first knife sold in 1975. **Mark:** Last name in Gothic logo; used to be initials in circle.

GEDRAITIS, CHARLES J,
GEDRAITIS HAND CRAFTED KNIVES, 444 Shrewsbury St, Holden, MA 01520, Phone: 508-963-1861, knifemaker_1999@yahoo.com; Web: www.gedraitisknives.com
Specialties: One-of-a-kind folders & automatics of his own design. **Patterns:** One-of-a-kind. **Technical:** Forges to shape mostly stock removal. **Prices:** $300 to $2500. **Remarks:** Full-time maker. **Mark:** 3 scallop shells with an initial inside each one: CJG.

GEISLER, GARY R,
PO Box 294, Clarksville, OH 45113, Phone: 937-383-4055, ggeisler@in-touch.net
Specialties: Period Bowies and such; flat ground. **Patterns:** Working knives usually modeled close after an existing antique. **Technical:** Flat grinds 440C, A2 and ATS-34. **Prices:** $300 and up. **Remarks:** Part-time maker; first knife sold in 1982. **Mark:** G.R. Geisler Maker; usually in script on reverse side because maker is left-handed.

GENSKE, JAY,
283 Doty St, Fond du Lac, WI 54935, Phone: 920-921-8019/Cell Phone 920-579-0144, jaygenske@hotmail.com
Specialties: Working/using knives and period pieces of his design and to customer specs. **Patterns:** Bowies, fighters, hunters. **Technical:** Grinds ATS-34 and 440C, O1 and 1095 forges and grinds Damascus and 1095. Offers custom-tooled sheaths, scabbards and hand carved handles. **Prices:** $95 to $500; some to $1000. **Remarks:** Full-time maker; first knife sold in 1985. Doing business as Genske Knives. **Mark:** Stamped or engraved last name.

GEORGE, HARRY,
3137 Old Camp Long Rd, Aiken, SC 29805, Phone: 803-649-1963, hdkkgeorge@scescape.net
Specialties: Working straight knives of his design or to customer specs. **Patterns:** Hunters, skinners and utility knives. **Technical:** Grinds ATS-34. Prefers natural handle materials, hollow-grinds and mirror finishes. **Prices:** Start at $70. **Remarks:** Part-time maker; first knife sold in 1985. Trained under George Herron. Member SCAK. Member Knifemakers Guild. **Mark:** Name, city, state.

GEORGE, LES,
6521 Fenwick Dr., Corpus Christi, TX 78414, Phone: 361-288-9777, les@georgeknives.com; Web: www.georgeknives.com
Specialties: Tactical frame locks and fixed blades. **Patterns:** Folders, balisongs, and fixed blades. **Technical:** CPM154, S30V, Chad Nichols Damascus. **Prices:** $200 to $800. **Remarks:** Full-time maker, first knife sold in 1992. Doing business as www.georgeknives.com. **Mark:** Last name over logo.

GEORGE, TOM,
550 Aldbury Dr, Henderson, NV 89014, tagmaker@aol.com
Specialties: Working straight knives, display knives, custom meat cleavers, and folders of his design. **Patterns:** Hunters, Bowies, daggers, buckskinners, swords and folders. **Technical:** Uses D2, 440C, ATS-34 and 154CM. **Prices:** $500 to $13,500. **Remarks:** Custom orders not accepted "at this time". Full-time maker. First knife 1982; first 350 knives were numbered; after that no numbers. Almost all his knives today are Bowies and swords. Creator and maker of the "Past Glories" series of knives. **Mark:** Tom George maker.

GEPNER, DON,
2615 E Tecumseh, Norman, OK 73071, Phone: 405-364-2750
Specialties: Traditional working and using straight knives of his design. **Patterns:** Bowies and daggers. **Technical:** Forges his Damascus, 1095 and 5160. **Prices:** $100 to $400; some to $1000. **Remarks:** Spare-time maker; first knife sold in 1991. Has been forging since 1954; first edged weapon made at 9 years old. **Mark:** Last initial.

GERNER, THOMAS,
PO Box 301 Walpole, Western Australia, AUSTRALIA 6398, gerner@bordernet.com.au; Web: www.deepriverforge.com
Specialties: Forged working knives; plain steel and pattern welded. **Patterns:** Tries most patterns heard or read about. **Technical:** 5160, L6, O1, 52100 steels; Australian hardwood handles. **Prices:** $220 and up. **Remarks:** Achieved ABS Master Smith rating in 2001. **Mark:** Like a standing arrow and a leaning cross, T.G. in the Runic (Viking) alphabet.

GEVEDON, HANNERS (HANK),
1410 John Cash Rd, Crab Orchard, KY 40419-9770
Specialties: Traditional working and using straight knives. **Patterns:** Hunters, swords, utility and camp knives. **Technical:** Forges and grinds his own Damascus, 5160 and L6. Cast aluminum handles. **Prices:** $50 to $250; some to $400. **Remarks:** Part-time maker; first knife sold in 1983. **Mark:** Initials and LBF tang stamp.

GIAGU, SALVATORE AND DEROMA MARIA ROSARIA,
Via V Emanuele 64, 07016 Pattada (SS), ITALY, Phone: 079-755918, Fax: 079-755918, coltelligiagu@jumpy.it
Specialties: Using and collecting traditional and new folders from Sardegna. **Patterns:** Folding, hunting, utility, skinners and kitchen knives. **Technical:** Forges ATS-34, 440, D2 and Damascus. **Prices:** $200 to $2000; some higher. **Mark:** First initial, last name and name of town and muflon's head.

GIBERT, PEDRO,
Los Alamos 410, 8370 San Martin de los Andes Neuquen, ARGENTINA, Phone: 054-2972-410868, rosademayo@infovia.com.ar
Specialties: Hand forges: Stock removal and integral. High quality artistic knives of his design and to customer specifications. **Patterns:** Country (Argentine gaucho-style), knives, folders, Bowies, daggers, hunters. Others upon request. **Technical:** Blade: Bohler k110 Austrian steel (high resistance to waste). Handles: (Natural materials) ivory elephant, killer whale, hippo, walrus tooth, deer antler, goat, ram, buffalo horn, bone, rhea, sheep, cow, exotic woods (South America native woods) hand carved and engraved guards and blades. Stainless steel guards, finely polished: semi-matte or shiny finish. Sheaths: Raw or tanned leather, hand-stitched; rawhide or cotton yarn embroidered. Box: One wood piece, hand carved. Wooden hinges and locks. **Prices:** $600 and up. **Remarks:** Full-time maker. Made first knife in 1987. **Mark:** Only a rose logo. Buyers initials upon request.

GIBO, GEORGE,
PO Box 4304, Hilo, HI 96720, Phone: 808-987-7002, geogibo@interpac.net
Specialties: Straight knives and folders. **Patterns:** Hunters, bird and trout, utility, gentlemen and tactical folders. **Technical:** Grinds ATS-34, BG-42, Talonite, Stainless Steel Damascus. **Prices:** $250 to $1000. **Remarks:** Spare-time maker; first knife sold in 1995. **Mark:** Name, city and state around Hawaiian "Shaka" sign.

GIBSON SR., JAMES HOOT,
90 Park Place Ave., Bunnell, FL 32110, Phone: 386-437-4383, hootsknives.aol.com
Specialties: Bowies, folders, daggers, and hunters. **Patterns:** Most all. **Technical:** ATS-440C hand cut and grind. Also traditional old fashioned folders. **Prices:** $250 to $3000. **Remarks:** 100 percent handmade. **Mark:** Hoot.

GILBERT, CHANTAL,
291 Rue Christophe-Colomb est #105, Quebec City Quebec, CANADA G1K 3T1, Phone: 418-525-6961, Fax: 418-525-4666, gilbertc@medion.qc.ca; Web: www.chantalgilbert.com
Specialties: Straight art knives that may resemble creatures, often with wings, shells and antennae, always with a beak of some sort, fixed blades in a feminine style. **Technical:** ATS-34 and Damascus. Handle materials usually silver that she forms to shape via special molds and a press; ebony and fossil ivory. **Prices:** Range from $500 to $4000. **Remarks:** Often embellishes her art knives with rubies, meteorite, 18k gold and similar elements.

GILBREATH, RANDALL,
55 Crauswell Rd, Dora, AL 35062, Phone: 205-648-3902
Specialties: Damascus folders and fighters. **Patterns:** Folders and fixed blades. **Technical:** Forges Damascus and high-carbon; stock removal stainless steel. **Prices:** $300 to $1500. **Remarks:** Full-time maker; first knife sold in 1979. **Mark:** Name in ribbon.

GILJEVIC, BRANKO,
35 Hayley Crescent, Queanbeyan 2620, N.S.W., AUSTRALIA 0262977613
Specialties: Classic working straight knives and folders of his design. **Patterns:** Hunters, Bowies, skinners and locking folders. **Technical:** Grinds 440C. Offers acid etching, scrimshaw and leather carving. **Prices:** $150 to $1500. **Remarks:** Part-time maker; first knife sold in 1987. Doing business as Sambar Custom Knives. **Mark:** Company name in logo.

GIRAFFEBONE INC.,
3052 Isim Road, Norman, OK 73026, Phone: 888-804-0683; 405-321-3614, sandy@giraffebone.com; Web: www.giraffebone.com
Specialties: Giraffebone, horns, African hardwoods, and mosaic Damascus

GIRTNER, JOE,
409 Catalpa Ave, Brea, CA 92821, Phone: 714-529-2388, conceptsinknives@aol.com
Specialties: Art knives and miniatures. **Patterns:** Mainly Damascus (some carved). **Technical:** Many techniques and materials combined. Wood carving knives and tools, hunters, custom orders. **Prices:** $55 to $3000. **Mark:** Name.

GITTINGER, RAYMOND,
6940 S Rt 100, Tiffin, OH 44883, Phone: 419-397-2517

GLOVER, RON,
100 West Church St., Mason, OH 45040, Phone: 513-404-7107, r.glover@zoomtown.com
Specialties: High-tech working straight knives and folders. **Patterns:** Hunters to Bowies; some interchangeable blade models; unique locking mechanisms. **Technical:** Grinds 440C, 154CM; buys Damascus. **Prices:** $70 to $500; some to $800. **Remarks:** Part-time maker; first knife sold in 1981. **Mark:** Name in script.

GLOVER, WARREN D,
dba BUBBA KNIVES, PO Box 475, Cleveland, GA 30528, Phone: 706-865-3998, Fax: 706-348-7176, warren@bubbaknives.net; Web: www.bubbaknives.net
Specialties: Traditional and custom working and using straight knives of his design and to customer request. **Patterns:** Hunters, skinners, bird and fish, utility and kitchen knives. **Technical:** Grinds 440, ATS-34 and stainless steel Damascus. **Prices:** $75 to $400 and up. **Remarks:** Full-time maker; sold first knife in 1995. **Mark:** Bubba, year, name, state.

GODDARD, WAYNE,
473 Durham Ave, Eugene, OR 97404, Phone: 541-689-8098, wgoddard44@comcast.net
Specialties: Working/using straight knives and folders. **Patterns:** Hunters and folders. **Technical:** Works exclusively with wire Damascus and his own-pattern welded material. **Prices:** $250 to $4000. **Remarks:** Full-time maker; first knife sold in 1963. **Mark:** Blocked initials on forged blades; regular capital initials on stock removal.

GODLESKY, BRUCE F.,
1002 School Rd., Apollo, PA 15613, Phone: 724-840-5786, brucegodlesky@yahoo.com; Web: www.birdforge.com
Specialties: Working/using straight knives and tomahawks, mostly forged. **Patterns:** Hunters, birds and trout, fighters and tomahawks. **Technical:** Most forged, some stock removal. Carbon steel only. 5160, O-1, W2, 10xx series. Makes own Damascus and welded cable. **Prices:** Starting at $75. **Mark:** BIRDOG FORGE.

GOERS, BRUCE,
3423 Royal Ct S, Lakeland, FL 33813, Phone: 941-646-0984
Specialties: Fancy working and using straight knives of his design and to customer specs. **Patterns:** Hunters, fighters, Bowies and fantasy knives. **Technical:** Grinds ATS-34, some Damascus. **Prices:** $195 to $600; some to $1300. **Remarks:** Part-time maker; first knife sold in 1990. Doing business as Vulture Cutlery. **Mark:** Buzzard with initials.

GOFOURTH, JIM,
3776 Aliso Cyn Rd, Santa Paula, CA 93060, Phone: 805-659-3814
Specialties: Period pieces and working knives. **Patterns:** Bowies, locking folders, patent lockers and others. **Technical:** Grinds A2 and 154CM. **Prices:** Moderate. **Remarks:** Spare-time maker. **Mark:** Initials interconnected.

GOLDBERG, DAVID,
321 Morris Rd, Ft Washington, PA 19034, Phone: 215-654-7117, david@goldmountainforge.com; Web: www.goldmountainforge.com
Specialties: Japanese-style designs, will work with special themes in Japanese genre. **Patterns:** Kozuka, Tanto, Wakazashi, Katana, Tachi, Sword canes, Yari and Naginata. **Technical:** Forges his own Damascus and makes his own handmade tamehagane steel from straw ash, iron, carbon and clay. Uses traditional materials, carves fittings handles and cases. Hardens all blades in traditional Japanese clay differential technique. **Remarks:** Full-time maker; first knife sold in 1987. Japanese swordsmanship teacher (jaido) and Japanese self-defense teach (aikido). **Mark:** Name (kinzan) in Japanese Kanji on Tang under handle.

GOLDEN, RANDY,
6492 Eastwood Glen Dr, Montgomery, AL 36117, Phone: 334-271-6429, rgolden1@mindspring.com
Specialties: Collectable quality hand rubbed finish, hunter, camp, Bowie straight knives, custom leather sheaths with exotic skin inlays and tooling. **Technical:** Stock removal ATS-34, CPM154, S30V and BG-42. Natural handle materials primarily stag and ivory. **Prices:** $500 to $1500. **Remarks:** Full-time maker, member Knifemakers Guild, first knife sold in 2000. **Mark:** R. R. Golden Montgomery, AL.

GOLTZ, WARREN L,
802 4th Ave E, Ada, MN 56510, Phone: 218-784-7721, sspexp@loretel.net
Specialties: Fancy working knives in standard patterns. **Patterns:** Hunters, Bowies and camp knives. **Technical:** Grinds 440C and ATS-34. **Prices:** $120 to $595; some to $950. **Remarks:** Part-time maker; first knife sold in 1984. **Mark:** Last name.

GONZALEZ, LEONARDO WILLIAMS,
Ituzaingo 473, Maldonado, CP 20000, URUGUAY, Phone: 598 4222 1617, Fax: 598 4222 1617, willyknives@hotmail.com
Specialties: Classic high-art and fantasy straight knives; traditional working and using knives of his design, in standard patterns or to customer specs. **Patterns:** Hunters, Bowies, daggers, fighters, boots, swords and utility/camp knives. **Technical:** Forges and grinds high-carbon and stainless Bohler steels. **Prices:** $100 to $2500. **Remarks:** Full-time maker; first knife sold in 1985. **Mark:** Willy, whale, R.O.U.

GOO, TAI,
5920 W Windy Lou Ln, Tucson, AZ 85742, Phone: 520-744-9777, taigoo@msn.com; Web: www.taigoo.com
Specialties: High art, neo-tribal, bush and fantasy. **Technical:** Hand forges, does own heat treating, makes own Damascus. **Prices:** $150 to $500 some to $10,000. **Remarks:** Full-time maker; first knife sold in 1978. **Mark:** Chiseled signature.

GOOD, D.R.,
D.R. Good Custom Knives and Weaponry, 6125 W. 100 S., Tipton, IN 46072, Phone: 765-963-6971, drntammigood@bluemarble.net
Specialties: Working knives, own design, Scagel style, "critter" knives, carved handles. **Patterns:** Bowies, large and small, neck knives and miniatures. Offers carved handles, snake heads, eagles, wolves, bear, skulls. **Technical:** Damascus, some stelite, 6K, pearl, ivory, moose. **Prices:** $150 - $1500. **Remarks:** Full-time maker. First knife was Bowie made from a 2-1/2 truck bumper in military. **Mark:** D.R. Good in oval and for minis, DR with a buffalo skull.

GOODE, BEAR,
PO Box 6474, Navajo Dam, NM 87419, Phone: 505-632-8184
Specialties: Working/using knives of his design and in standard patterns. **Patterns:** Bowies, hunters and utility/camp knives. **Technical:** Grinds 440C, ATS-34, 154-CM; forges and grinds 1095, 5160 and other steels on request; uses Damascus. **Prices:** $60 to $225; some to $500 and up. **Remarks:** Part-time maker; first knife sold in 1993. Doing business as Bear Knives. **Mark:** First and last name with a three-toed paw print.

GOODE, BRIAN,
203 Gordon Ave, Shelby, NC 28152, Phone: 704-434-6496, web:www.bgoodeknives.com
Specialties: Flat ground working knives with etched/antique or brushed finish. **Patterns:** Field, camp, hunters, skinners, survival, kitchen, maker's design or yours. Currently full tang only with supplied leather sheath. **Technical:** 0-1, D2 and other ground flat stock. Stock removal and differential heat treat preferred. Etched antique/etched satin working finish preferred. Micarta and hardwoods for strength. **Prices:** $150 to $700. **Remarks:** Part-time maker and full-time knife lover. First knife sold in 2004. **Mark:** B. Goode with NC separated by a feather.

GORDON, LARRY B,
23555 Newell Cir W, Farmington Hills, MI 48336, Phone: 248-477-5483, lbgordon1@aol.com
Specialties: Folders, small fixed blades. New design rotating scale release automatic. **Patterns:** Rotating handle locker. Ambidextrous fire (R&L) **Prices:** $450 minimum. **Remarks:** High line materials preferred. **Mark:** Gordon.

GORENFLO, JAMES T (JT),
9145 Sullivan Rd, Baton Rouge, LA 70818, Phone: 225-261-5868
Specialties: Traditional working and using straight knives of his design. **Patterns:** Bowies, hunters and utility/camp knives. **Technical:** Forges 5160, 1095, 52100 and his own Damascus. **Prices:** Start at $200. **Remarks:** Part-time maker; first knife sold in 1992. **Mark:** Last name or initials, J.S. on reverse.

GOSSMAN, SCOTT,
PO Box 815, Forest Hill, MD 21050, Phone: 410-452-8456, scott@gossmanknives.com Web:www. gossmanknives.com
Specialties: Heavy duty knives for big game hunting and survival. **Patterns:** Drop point spear point hunters. Large camp/survival knives. **Technical:** Grinds D-2, A2, O1 and 57 convex grinds and edges. **Price:** $100 to $350 some higher. **Remarks:** Full time maker does business as Gossman Knives. **Mark:** Gossman and steel type.

GOTTAGE, DANTE,
43227 Brooks Dr, Clinton Twp., MI 48038-5323, Phone: 810-286-7275
Specialties: Working knives of his design or to customer specs. **Patterns:** Large and small skinners, fighters, Bowies and fillet knives. **Technical:** Grinds O1, 440C and 154CM and ATS-34. **Prices:** $150 to $600. **Remarks:** Part-time maker; first knife sold in 1975. **Mark:** Full name in script letters.

GOTTAGE, JUDY,
43227 Brooks Dr, Clinton Twp., MI 48038-5323, Phone: 586-286-7275, jgottage@remaxmetropolitan.com
Specialties: Custom folders of her design or to customer specs. **Patterns:** Interframes or integral. **Technical:** Stock removal. **Prices:** $300 to $3000. **Remarks:** Full-time maker; first knife sold in 1980. **Mark:** Full name, maker in script.

GOTTSCHALK, GREGORY J,
12 First St. (Ft. Pitt), Carnegie, PA 15106, Phone: 412-279-6692
Specialties: Fancy working straight knives and folders to customer specs. **Patterns:** Hunters to tantos, locking folders to minis. **Technical:** Grinds 440C, 154CM, ATS-34. Now making own Damascus. Most knives have mirror finishes. **Prices:** Start at $150. **Remarks:** Part-time maker; first knife sold in 1977. **Mark:** Full name in crescent.

GOUKER, GARY B,
PO Box 955, Sitka, AK 99835, Phone: 907-747-3476
Specialties: Hunting knives for hard use. **Patterns:** Skinners, semi-skinners, and such. **Technical:** Likes natural materials, inlays, stainless steel. **Prices:** Moderate. **Remarks:** New Alaskan maker. **Mark:** Name.

GRAHAM, GORDON,
3145 CR 4008, New Boston, TX 75570, Phone: 903-293-2610, Web: www.grahamknives.com
Prices: $325 to $850. **Mark:** Graham.

GRANGER, PAUL J,
704 13th Ct. SW, Largo, FL 33770-4471, grangerknives@hotmail.com
Specialties: Working straight knives of his own design and a few folders. **Patterns:** 2.75" to 4" work knives, skinners, tactical knives and Bowies from 5"-9." **Technical:** Forges 52100 and 5160 and his own carbon steel Damascus. Offers filework. **Prices:** $95 to $400. **Remarks:** Part-time maker since 1997. Sold first knife in 1997. Doing business as Granger Knives and Pale Horse Fighters. Member of ABS and OBG. **Mark:** "Granger" or "Palehorse Fighters."

GRAVELINE, PASCAL AND ISABELLE,
38, Rue de Kerbrezillic, 29350 Moelan-sur-Mer, FRANCE, Phone: 33 2 98 39 73 33, atelier.graveline@wanadoo.fr; Web: www.graveline-couteliers.com
Specialties: French replicas from the 17th, 18th and 19th centuries. **Patterns:** Traditional folders and multi-blade pocket knives; traveling knives, fruit knives and fork sets; puzzle knives and friend's knives; rivet less knives. **Technical:** Grind 12C27, ATS-34, Damascus and carbon steel. **Prices:** $500 to $5000. **Remarks:** Full-time makers; first knife sold in 1992. **Mark:** Last name over head of ram.

GRAVES, DAN,
4887 Dixie Garden Loop, Shreveport, LA 71105, Phone: 318-865-8166, Web: wwwtheknifemaker.com
Specialties: Traditional forged blades and Damascus. **Patterns:** Bowies (D guard also), fighters, hunters, large and small daggers. **Remarks:** Full-time maker. **Mark:** Initials with circle around them.

GRAY, BOB,
8206 N Lucia Court, Spokane, WA 99208, Phone: 509-468-3924
Specialties: Straight working knives of his own design or to customer specs. **Patterns:** Hunter, fillet and carving knives. **Technical:** Forges 5160, L6 and some 52100; grinds 440C. **Prices:** $100 to $600. **Remarks:** Part-time knifemaker; first knife sold in 1991. Doing business as Hi-Land Knives. **Mark:** HI-L.

GRAY, DANIEL,
GRAY KNIVES, 686 Main Rd., Brownville, ME 04414, Phone: 207-965-2191, mail@grayknives.com; Web: www.grayknives.com
Specialties: Straight knives, fantasy, folders, automatics and traditional of his own design. **Patterns:** Automatics, fighters, hunters. **Technical:** Grinds O1, 154CM and D2. **Prices:** From $155 to $750. **Remarks:** Full-time maker; first knife sold in 1974. **Mark:** Gray Knives.

GREBE, GORDON S,
PO Box 296, Anchor Point, AK 99556-0296, Phone: 907-235-8242
Specialties: Working straight knives and folders, some fancy. **Patterns:** Tantos, Bowies, boot fighter sets, locking folders. **Technical:** Grinds stainless steels; likes 1/4" inch stock and glass-bead finishes. **Prices:** $75 to $250; some to $2000. **Remarks:** Full-time maker; first knife sold in 1968. **Mark:** Initials in lightning logo.

GRECO, JOHN,
100 Mattie Jones Rd, Greensburg, KY 42743, Phone: 270-932-3335, johngreco@grecoknives.com; Web: www.grecoknives.com
Specialties: Limited edition knives and swords. **Patterns:** Tactical, fighters, camp knives, short swords. **Technical:** Stock removal carbon steel. **Prices:** Affordable. **Remarks:** Full-time maker since 1986. First knife sold in 1979. **Mark:** Greco and w/mo mark.

GREEN, BILL,
6621 Eastview Dr, Sachse, TX 75048, Phone: 972-463-3147
Specialties: High-art and working straight knives and folders of his design and to customer specs. **Patterns:** Bowies, hunters, kitchen knives and locking folders. **Technical:** Grinds ATS-34, D2 and 440V. Hand-tooled custom sheaths. **Prices:** $70 to $350; some to $750. **Remarks:** Part-time maker; first knife sold in 1990. **Mark:** Last name.

GREEN, WILLIAM (BILL),
46 Warren Rd, View Bank Vic., AUSTRALIA 3084, Fax: 03-9459-1529
Specialties: Traditional high-tech straight knives and folders. **Patterns:** Japanese-influenced designs, hunters, Bowies, folders and miniatures. **Technical:** Forges O1, D2 and his own Damascus. Offers lost wax castings for bolsters and pommels. Likes natural handle materials, gems, silver and gold. **Prices:** $400 to $750; some to $1200. **Remarks:** Full-time maker. **Mark:** Initials.

GREENAWAY, DON,
3325 Dinsmore Tr, Fayetteville, AR 72704, Phone: 501-521-0323

GREENE, CHRIS,
707 Cherry Lane, Shelby, NC 28150, Phone: 704-434-5620

GREENE, DAVID,
570 Malcom Rd, Covington, GA 30209, Phone: 770-784-0657
Specialties: Straight working using knives. **Patterns:** Hunters. **Technical:** Forges mosaic and twist Damascus. Prefers stag and desert ironwood for handle material.

GREENE, STEVE,
DUNN KNIVES INC, 2923 Holly Berry Ct., Kissimmee, FL 34743, Phone: 800-245-6483, steve.greene@dunnknives.com; Web: www.dunnknives.com
Specialties: Skinning & fillet knives. **Patterns:** Skinning, drop points, clip points and fillets. **Technical:** S60V, S90V and 20 CV powdered metal steel. **Prices:** $90 to $250. **Mark:** Dunn by Greene and year. **Remarks:** Full-time knifemaker. First knife sold in 1972.

GREENFIELD, G O,
2605 15th St #310, Everett, WA 98201, garyg1946@yahoo.com
Specialties: High-tech and working straight knives and folders of his design. **Patterns:** Boots, daggers, hunters and one-of-a-kinds. **Technical:** Grinds ATS-34, D2, 440C and T-440V. Makes sheaths for each knife. **Prices:** $100 to $800; some to $10,000. **Remarks:** Part-time maker; first knife sold in 1978. **Mark:** Springfield®, serial number.

GREGORY, MICHAEL,
211 Calhoun Rd, Belton, SC 29627, Phone: 864-338-8898
Specialties: Working straight knives and folders. **Patterns:** Hunters, tantos, locking folders and slip-joints, boots and fighters. **Technical:** Grinds 440C, 154CM and ATS-34; mirror finishes. **Prices:** $95 to $200; some to $1000. **Remarks:** Part-time maker; first knife sold in 1980. **Mark:** Name, city in logo.

GREINER, RICHARD,
1073 E County Rd 32, Green Springs, OH 44836

GREISS, JOCKL,
Herrenwald 15, D 77773 Schenkenzell, GERMANY, Phone: +49 7836 95 71 69 or +49 7836 95 55 76, www.jocklgreiss@yahoo.com
Specialties: Classic and working using straight knives of his design. **Patterns:** Bowies, daggers and hunters. **Technical:** Uses only Jerry Rados Damascus. All knives are one-of-a-kind made by hand; no machines are used. **Prices:** $700 to $2000; some to $3000. **Remarks:** Full-time maker; first knife sold in 1984. **Mark:** An "X" with a long vertical line through it.

GREY, PIET,
PO Box 363, Naboomspruit 0560, SOUTH AFRICA, Phone: 014-743-3613
Specialties: Fancy working and using straight knives of his design. **Patterns:** Fighters, hunters and utility/camp knives. **Technical:** Grinds ATS-34 and AEB-L; forges and grinds Damascus. Solder less fitting of guards. Engraves and scrimshaws. **Prices:** $125 to $750; some to $1500. **Remarks:** Part-time maker; first knife sold in 1970. **Mark:** Last name.

GRIFFIN, RENDON AND MARK,
9706 Cedardale, Houston, TX 77055, Phone: 713-468-0436
Specialties: Working folders and automatics of their designs. **Patterns:** Standard lockers and slip-joints. **Technical:** Most blade steels; stock removal. **Prices:** Start at $350. **Remarks:** Rendon's first knife sold in 1966; Mark's in 1974. **Mark:** Last name logo.

GRIFFIN JR., HOWARD A.,
14299 SW 31st Ct, Davie, FL 33330, Phone: 954-474-5406, mgriffin18@aol.com
Specialties: Working straight knives and folders. **Patterns:** Hunters, Bowies, locking folders with his own push-button lock design. **Technical:** Grinds 440C. **Prices:** $100 to $200; some to $500. **Remarks:** Part-time maker; first knife sold in 1983. **Mark:** Initials.

GROSPITCH, ERNIE,
18440 Amityville Dr, Orlando, FL 32820, Phone: 407-568-5438, shrpknife@aol.com; Web: www.erniesknives.com
Specialties: Bowies, hunting, fishing, kitchen, lockback folders, leather craft. **Patterns:** His design or customer. **Technical:** Stock removal using most available steels. **Prices:** $140 and up. **Remarks:** Full-time maker, sold first knife in 1990. **Mark:** Etched name/maker city and state.

GROSS, W W,
109 Dylan Scott Dr, Archdale, NC 27263-3858
Specialties: Working knives. **Patterns:** Hunters, boots, fighters. **Technical:** Grinds. **Prices:** Moderate. **Remarks:** Full-time maker. **Mark:** Name.

GROSSMAN, STEWART,
24 Water St #419, Clinton, MA 01510, Phone: 508-365-2291; 800-mysword
Specialties: Miniatures and full-size knives and swords. **Patterns:** One-of-a-kind miniatures—jewelry, replicas—and wire-wrapped figures. Full-size art, fantasy and combat knives, daggers and modular systems. **Technical:** Forges and grinds most metals and Damascus. Uses gems, crystals, electronics and motorized mechanisms. **Prices:** $20 to $300; some to $4500 and higher. **Remarks:** Full-time maker; first knife sold in 1985. **Mark:** G1.

GRUSSENMEYER, PAUL G,
310 Kresson Rd, Cherry Hill, NJ 08034, Phone: 856-428-1088, pgrussentne@comcast.net; Web: www.pgcarvings.com
Specialties: Assembling fancy and fantasy straight knives with his own carved handles. **Patterns:** Bowies, daggers, folders, swords, hunters and miniatures. **Technical:** Uses forged steel and Damascus, stock removal and knapped obsidian blades. **Prices:** $250 to $4000. **Remarks:** Spare-time maker; first knife sold in 1991. **Mark:** First and last initial hooked together on handle.

GUARNERA, ANTHONY R,
42034 Quail Creek Dr, Quartzhill, CA 93536, Phone: 661-722-4032
Patterns: Hunters, camp, Bowies, kitchen, fighter knives. **Technical:** Forged and stock removal. **Prices:** $100 and up.

GUIDRY, BRUCE,
24550 Adams Ave, Murrieta, CA 92562, Phone: 909-677-2384

GUINN, TERRY,
13026 Hwy 6 South, Eastland, TX 76448, Phone: 254-629-8603, Web: www.terryguinn.com
Specialties: Working fixed blades and balisongs. **Patterns:** Almost all types of folding and fixed blades, from patterns and "one of a kind". **Technical:** Stock removal all types of blade steel with preference for air hardening steel. Does own heat treating, all knives Rockwell tested in shop. **Prices:** $200 to $2,000. **Remarks:** Part time maker since 1982, sold first knife 1990. **Mark:** Full name with cross in the middle.

GUNTER, BRAD,
13 Imnaha Rd., Tijeras, NM 87059, Phone: 505-281-8080

GUNTHER, EDDIE,
11 Nedlands Pl Burswood, 2013 Auckland, NEW ZEALAND, Phone: 006492722373, eddit.gunther49@gmail.com
Specialties: Drop point hunters, boot, Bowies. All mirror finished. **Technical:** Grinds D2, 440C, 12c27. **Prices:** $250 to $800. **Remarks:** Part-time maker, first knife sold in 1986. **Mark:** Name, city, country.

GURGANUS, CAROL,
2553 NC 45 South, Colerain, NC 27924, Phone: 252-356-4831, Fax: 252-356-4650
Specialties: Working and using straight knives. **Patterns:** Fighters, hunters and kitchen knives. **Technical:** Grinds D2, ATS-34 and Damascus steel. Uses stag, and exotic wood handles. **Prices:** $100 to $300. **Remarks:** Part-time maker; first knife sold in 1992. **Mark:** Female symbol, last name, city, state.

GURGANUS, MELVIN H,
2553 NC 45 South, Colerain, NC 27924, Phone: 252-356-4831, Fax: 252-356-4650
Specialties: High-tech working folders. **Patterns:** Leaf-lock and back-lock designs, bolstered and interframe. **Technical:** D2 and 440C; Heat-treats, carves and offers lost wax casting. **Prices:** $300 to $3000. **Remarks:** Part-time maker; first knife sold in 1983. **Mark:** First initial, last name and maker.

GUTHRIE, GEORGE B,
1912 Puett Chapel Rd, Bassemer City, NC 28016, Phone: 704-629-3031
Specialties: Working knives of his design or to customer specs. **Patterns:** Hunters, boots, fighters, locking folders and slip-joints in traditional styles. **Technical:** Grinds D2, 440C and 154CM. **Prices:** $105 to $300; some to $450. **Remarks:** Part-time maker; first knife sold in 1978. **Mark:** Name in state.

H

HACKNEY, DANA A.,
33 Washington St., Monument, CO 80132, Phone: 719-481-3940, shacknee@peoplepc.com
Specialties: Hunters, bowies, and everyday carry knives, and some kitchen cutlery. **Technical:** Forges 1080 series, 5160, 0-1, W-2, and his own damascus. Uses 13C26 mostly for stainless knives. **Prices:** $100 and up. **Remarks:** Sole ownership knives and sheaths. Part-time maker. Sold first knife in 2005. ABS, MKA, and PKA member. **Mark:** Last name, HACKNEY on left-side ricasso.

HAGEN, DOC,
PO Box 58, 41780 Kansas Point Ln, Pelican Rapids, MN 56572, Phone: 218-863-8503, dhagen@prtel.com; Web: www.dochagencustomknives.com
Specialties: Folders. Autos:bolster release-dual action. Slipjoint folders **Patterns:** Defense-related straight knives; wide variety of folders. **Technical:** Dual action release, bolster release autos. **Prices:** $300 to $800; some to $3000. **Remarks:** Full-time maker; first knife sold in 1975. Makes his own Damascus. **Mark:** DOC HAGEN in shield, knife, banner logo; or DOC.

HAGGERTY, GEORGE S,
PO Box 88, Jacksonville, VT 05342, Phone: 802-368-7437, swewater@verizon.net
Specialties: Working straight knives and folders. **Patterns:** Hunters, claws, camp and fishing knives, locking folders and backpackers. **Technical:** Forges and grinds W2, 440C and 154CM. **Prices:** $85 to $300. **Remarks:** Part-time maker; first knife sold in 1981. **Mark:** Initials or last name.

HAGUE, GEOFF,
Unit 5, Project Workshops, Laines Farm, Quarley, SP11 8PX, UK, Phone: (+44) 01672-870212, Fax: (+44) 01672 870212, geoff@hagueknives.com; Web: www.hagueknives.com
Specialties: Quality folding knives. **Patterns:** Back lock, locking liner, slip joint, and friction folders. **Technical:** RWL34, D2, titanium, and some gold decoraqtion. Mainly natural handle materials. **Prices:** $900 to $2,000. **Remarks:** Full-time maker. **Mark:** Last name.

HAINES, JEFF HAINES CUSTOM KNIVES,
302 N Mill St, Wauzeka, WI 53826, Phone: 608-875-5325, jeffhaines@centurytel.net
Patterns: Hunters, skinners, camp knives, customer designs welcome. **Technical:** Forges 1095, 5160, and Damascus, grinds A2. **Prices:** $50 and up. **Remarks:** Part-time maker since 1995. **Mark:** Last name.

HALFRICH, JERRY,
340 Briarwood, San Marcos, TX 78666, Phone: 512-353-2582, Fax: 512-392-3659, jerryhalfrich@earthlink.net; Web: www.halfrichknives.com
Specialties: Working knives and specialty utility knives for the professional and serious hunter. Uses proven designs in both straight and folding knives. Plays close attention to fit and finish. Art knives on special request. **Patterns:** Hunters, skinners, lock back liner lock. **Technical:** Grinds both flat and hollow D2, damasteel, BG42 makes high precision folders. **Prices:** $300 to $600, sometimes $1000. **Remarks:** Full-time maker since 2000. DBA Halfrich Custom Knives. **Mark:** Halfrich, San Marcos, TX in a football shape.

HALL, JEFF,
PO Box 435, Los Alamitos, CA 90720, Phone: 562-594-4740, jhall10176@aol.com
Specialties: Collectible and working folders of his design. **Technical:** Grinds S30V, 154CM, and various makers' Damascus. **Patterns:** Fighters, gentleman's, hunters and utility knives. **Prices:** $400 to $600; some to $1000. **Remarks:** Full-time maker. First knife sold 1998. **Mark:** Last name.

HALLIGAN, ED,
14 Meadow Way, Sharpsburg, GA 30277, Phone: 770-251-7720, Fax: 770-251-7720
Specialties: Working straight knives and folders, some fancy. **Patterns:** Liner locks, hunters, skinners, boots, fighters and swords. **Technical:** Grinds ATS-34; forges 5160; makes cable and pattern Damascus. **Prices:** $160 to $2500. **Remarks:** Full-time maker; first knife sold in 1985. Doing business as Halligan Knives. **Mark:** Last name, city, state and USA.

HAMLET JR., JOHNNY,
300 Billington, Clute, TX 77531, Phone: 979-265-6929, nifeman@swbell.net; Web: www.hamlets-handmade-knives.com
Specialties: Working straight knives and folders. **Patterns:** Hunters, fighters, fillet and kitchen knives, locking folders. Likes upswept knives and trailing-points. **Technical:** Grinds 440C, D2, ATS-34. Makes sheaths. **Prices:** $125 and up. **Remarks:** Full-time maker; sold first knife in 1988. **Mark:** Hamlet's Handmade in script.

HAMMOND, HANK,
189 Springlake Dr, Leesburg, GA 31763, Phone: 229-434-1295, godogs57@bellsouth.net
Specialties: Traditional hunting and utility knives of his design. Will also design and produce knives to customer's specifications. **Patterns:** Straight or sheath knives, hunters skinners as well as Bowies and fighters. **Technical:** Grinds (hollow and flat grinds) CPM 154CM, ATS-34. Also uses Damascus and forges 52100. Offers filework on blades. Handle materials include all exotic woods, red stag, sambar stag, deer, elk, oosic, bone, fossil ivory, Micarta, etc. All knives come with sheath handmade for that individual knife. **Prices:** $100 up to $500. **Remarks:** Part-time maker. Sold first knife in 1981. Doing business as Double H Knives. **Mark:** "HH" inside 8 point deer rack.

HAMMOND, JIM,
PO Box 486, Arab, AL 35016, Phone: 256-586-4151, Fax: 256-586-0170, jim@jimhammondknives.com; Web: www.jimhammondknives.com
Specialties: High-tech fighters and folders. **Patterns:** Proven-design fighters. **Technical:** Grinds 440C, 440V, ATS-34 and other specialty steels. **Prices:** $385 to $1200; some to $9200. **Remarks:** Full-time maker; first knife sold in 1977. Designer for Columbia River Knife and Tool. **Mark:** Full name, city, state in shield logo.

HANCOCK, TIM,
10805 N. 83rd St, Scottsdale, AZ 85260, Phone: 480-998-8849
Specialties: High-art and working straight knives and folders of his design and to customer preferences. **Patterns:** Bowies, fighters, daggers, tantos, swords, folders. **Technical:** Forges Damascus and 52100; grinds ATS-34. Makes Damascus. Silver-wire inlays; offers carved fittings and file work. **Prices:** $500 to $10,000. **Remarks:** Full-time maker; first knife sold in 1988. Master Smith ABS. **Mark:** Last name or heart.

HAND, BILL,
PO Box 717, 1103 W. 7th St., Spearman, TX 79081, Phone: 806-659-2967, Fax: 806-659-5139, klinker@arn.net
Specialties: Traditional working and using straight knives and folders of his design or to customer specs. **Patterns:** Hunters, Bowies, folders and fighters. **Technical:** Forges 5160, 52100 and Damascus. **Prices:** Start at $150. **Remarks:** Part-time maker; Journeyman Smith. Current delivery time 12 to 16 months. **Mark:** Stylized initials.

HANSEN, LONNIE,
PO Box 4956, Spanaway, WA 98387, Phone: 253-847-4632, lonniehansen@msn.com; Web: lchansen.com
Specialties: Working straight knives of his design. **Patterns:** Tomahawks, tantos, hunters, fillet. **Technical:** Forges 1086, 52100, grinds 440V, BG-42. **Prices:** Starting at $300. **Remarks:** Part-time maker since 1989. **Mark:** First initial and last name. Also first and last initial.

HANSEN, ROBERT W,
35701 University Ave NE, Cambridge, MN 55008, Phone: 763-689-3242
Specialties: Working straight knives, folders and integrals. **Patterns:** From hunters to minis, camp knives to miniatures; folding lockers and slip-joints in original styles. **Technical:** Grinds O1, 440C and 154CM; likes filework. **Prices:** $100 to $450; some to $600. **Remarks:** Part-time maker; first knife sold in 1983. **Mark:** Fish with last initial inside.

HANSON III, DON L.,
PO Box 13, Success, MO 65570-0013, Phone: 573-674-3045, Web: www.sunfishforge.com; Web: www.donhansonknives.com
Specialties: One-of-a-kind Damascus folders and forged fixed blades. **Patterns:** Small, fancy pocket knives, large folding fighters and Bowies. **Technical:** Forges own pattern welded Damascus, file work and carving also carbon steel blades with hamons. **Prices:** $800 and up. **Remarks:** Full-time maker, first knife sold in 1984. ABS mastersmith. **Mark:** Sunfish.

HARA, KOUJI,
292-2 Osugi, Seki-City, Gifu-Pref. 501-3922, JAPAN, Phone: 0575-24-7569, Fax: 0575-24-7569, info@knifehousehara.com; Web: www.knifehousehara.com
Specialties: High-tech and working straight knives of his design; some folders. **Patterns:** Hunters, locking folders and utility/camp knives. **Technical:** Grinds Cowry X, Cowry Y and ATS-34. Prefers high mirror polish; pearl handle inlay. **Prices:** $400 to $2500. **Remarks:** Full-time maker; first knife sold in 1980. Doing business as Knife House "Hara." **Mark:** First initial, last name in fish.

HARDY, DOUGLAS E,
114 Cypress Rd, Franklin, GA 30217, Phone: 706-675-6305

HARDY, SCOTT,
639 Myrtle Ave, Placerville, CA 95667, Phone: 530-622-5780, Web: www.innercite.com/~shardy
Specialties: Traditional working and using straight knives of his design. **Patterns:** Most anything with an edge. **Technical:** Forges carbon steels. Japanese stone polish. Offers mirror finish; differentially tempers. **Prices:** $100 to $1000. **Remarks:** Part-time maker; first knife sold in 1982. **Mark:** First initial, last name and Handmade with bird logo.

HARKINS, J A,
PO Box 218, Conner, MT 59827, Phone: 406-821-1060, kutter@customknives.net; Web: customknives.net
Specialties: OTFs. **Patterns:** OTFs, Automatics, Folders. **Technical:** Grinds ATS-34. Engraves; offers gem work. **Prices:** $1500 and up. **Remarks:** Celebrating 20th year as full-time maker . **Mark:** First and middle initials, last name.

HARLEY, LARRY W,
348 Deerfield Dr, Bristol, TN 37620, Phone: 423-878-5368 (shop)/Cell 423-571-0638, Fax: 276-466-6771, Web: www.lonesomepineknives.com
Specialties: One-of-a-kind Persian in one-of-a-kind Damascus. Working knives, period pieces. **Technical:** Forges and grinds ATS-34, 440c, 15, 20, 1084, and 52100. **Patterns:** Full range of straight knives, tomahawks, razors, buck skinners and hog spears. **Prices:** $200 and up. **Mark:** Pine tree.

HARLEY, RICHARD,
348 Deerfield Dr, Bristol, TN 37620, Phone: 423-878-5368/423-571-0638
Specialties: Hunting knives, Bowies, friction folders, one-of-a-kind. **Technical:** Forges 1084, S160, 52100, Lg. **Prices:** $150 to $1000. **Mark:** Pine tree with name.

HARM, PAUL W,
818 Young Rd, Attica, MI 48412, Phone: 810-724-5582, harm@blclinks.net
Specialties: Early American working knives. **Patterns:** Hunters, skinners, patch knives, fighters, folders. **Technical:** Forges and grinds 1084, O1, 52100 and own Damascus. **Prices:** $75 to $1000. **Remarks:** First knife sold in 1990. **Mark:** Connected initials.

HARNER, LLOYD R. "BUTCH",
4865 Hanover Rd., Hanover, PA 17331, harnerknives@gmail.com; Web: www.harnerknives.com
Specialties: Kitchen knives and razors. **Technical:** CPM3V, CPM154, and crucible super-alloy blade steels. **Remarks:** Full-time maker since 2007. **Mark:** Maker's name, "L R Harner."

HARRINGTON, ROGER,
P.O. Box 157, Battle, East Sussex, ENGLAND TN 33 3 DD, Phone: 0854-838-7062, info@bisonbushcraft.co.uk; Web: www.bisonbushcraft.co.uk
Specialties: Working straight knives to his or customer's designs, flat saber Scandinavia-style grinds on full tang knives, also hollow and convex grinds. **Technical:** Grinds O1, D2, Damascus. **Prices:** $200 to $800. **Remarks:** First knife made by hand in 1997 whilst traveling around the world. **Mark:** Bison with bison written under.

HARRIS, CASS,
19855 Fraiser Hill Ln, Bluemont, VA 20135, Phone: 540-554-8774, Web: www.tdogforge.com
Prices: $160 to $500.

HARRIS, JAY,
991 Johnson St, Redwood City, CA 94061, Phone: 415-366-6077
Specialties: Traditional high-tech straight knives and folders of his design. **Patterns:** Daggers, fighters and locking folders. **Technical:** Uses 440C, ATS-34 and CPM. **Prices:** $250 to $850. **Remarks:** Spare-time maker; first knife sold in 1980.

HARRIS, JEFFERY A,
214 Glen Cove Dr, Chesterfield, MO 63017, Phone: 314-469-6317, Fax: 314-469-6374, jeffro135@aol.com
Remarks: Purveyor and collector of handmade knives.

HARRIS, JOHN,
14131 Calle Vista, Riverside, CA 92508, Phone: 951-653-2755, johnharrisknives@yahoo.com
Specialties: Hunters, daggers, Bowies, bird and trout, period pieces, Damascus and carbon steel knives, forged and stock removal. **Prices:** $200 to $1000.

HARRIS, RALPH DEWEY,
2607 Bell Shoals Rd, Brandon, FL 33511, Phone: 813-681-5293, Fax: 813-654-8175
Specialties: Collector quality interframe folders. **Patterns:** High tech locking folders of his own design with various mechanisms. **Technical:** Grinds 440C, ATS-34 and commercial Damascus. Offers various frame materials including 416ss, and titanium; file worked frames and his own engraving. **Prices:** $400 to $3000. **Remarks:** Full-time maker; first knife sold in 1978. **Mark:** Last name, or name and city.

HARRISON, BRIAN,
BFH KNIVES, 2359 E Swede Rd, Cedarville, MI 49719, Phone: 906-484-2011, bfhknives@easternup.net; Web: www.bfhknives.com
Specialties: Many sizes & variety of patterns from small pocket carries to large combat and camp knives. Mirror and bead blast finishes. All handles of high grade materials from ivory to highly figured stabilized woods to stag, deer & moose horn and Micarta. Hand sewn fancy sheaths for pocket or belt. **Technical:** Flat & hollow grinds usually ATS-34 but some O1, L6 and stellite 6K. **Prices:** $150 to $1200. **Remarks:** Full-time maker, sole authorship. Made first knife in 1980, sold first knife in 1999. Received much knowledge from the following makers: George Young, Eric Erickson, Webster Wood, Ed Kalfayan who are all generous men.**Mark:** Engraved blade outline w/BFH Knives over the top edge, signature across middle & Cedarville, MI underneath.

HARRISON, JIM (SEAMUS),
721 Fairington View Dr, St. Louis, MO 63129, Phone: 314-894-2525; Cell: 314-791-6350, jrh@seamusknives.com; Web: www.seamusknives.com
Specialties: Gents and fancy tactical locking-liner folders. Compact straight blades for hunting, backpacking and canoeing. **Patterns:** Liner-Lock® folders. Compact 3 fingered fixed blades often with modified wharncliffes. Survival knife with mortised handles. **Technical:** Grinds talonite, S30V, Mike Norris and Devin Thomas S.S. Damascus, 440-C. Heat treats. **Prices:** Folders $400 to $1,200. Fixed blades $400 to $600. **Remarks:** Full-time maker. **Mark:** Seamus

HARSEY, WILLIAM H,
82710 N. Howe Ln, Creswell, OR 97426, Phone: 519-895-4941, harseyjr@cs.com
Specialties: High-tech kitchen and outdoor knives. **Patterns:** Folding hunters, trout and bird folders; straight hunters, camp knives and axes. **Technical:** Grinds; etches. **Prices:** $125 to $300; some to $1500. Folders start at $350. **Remarks:** Full-time maker; first knife sold in 1979. **Mark:** Full name, state, U.S.A.

HART, BILL,
647 Cedar Dr, Pasadena, MD 21122, Phone: 410-255-4981
Specialties: Fur-trade era working straight knives and folders. **Patterns:** Springback folders, skinners, Bowies and patch knives. **Technical:** Forges and stock removes 1095 and 5160 wire Damascus. **Prices:** $100 to $600. **Remarks:** Part-time maker; first knife sold in 1986. **Mark:** Name.

HARTMAN, ARLAN (LANNY),
6102 S Hamlin Cir, Baldwin, MI 49304, Phone: 231-745-4029
Specialties: Working straight knives and folders. **Patterns:** Drop-point hunters, coil spring lockers, slip-joints. **Technical:** Flat-grinds D2, 440C and ATS-34. **Prices:** $300 to $2000. **Remarks:** Part-time maker; first knife sold in 1982. **Mark:** Last name.

HARTMAN, TIM,
3812 Pedroncelli Rd NW, Albuquerque, NM 87107, Phone: 505-385-6924, tbonz1@comcast.net
Specialties: Exotic wood scales, sambar stag, filework, hunters. **Patterns:** Fixed blade hunters, skinners, utility and hiking. **Technical:** 154CM, Ats-34 and D2. Mirror finish and contoured scales. **Prices:** Start at $200-$450. **Remarks:** Started making knives in 2004. **Mark:** 3 lines Ti Hartman, Maker, Albuquerque NM

HARVEY, HEATHER,
HEAVIN FORGE, PO Box 768, Belfast 1100, SOUTH AFRICA, Phone: 27-13-253-0914, heather@heavinforge.co.za; Web: www.heavinforge.co.za
Specialties: Integral hand forged knives, traditional African weapons, primitive folders and by-gone forged-styles. **Patterns:** All forged knives, war axes, spears, arrows, forks, spoons, and swords. **Technical:** Own carbon Damascus and mokume. Also forges stainless, brass, copper and titanium. Traditional forging and heat-treatment methods used. **Prices:** $300 to $5000, average $1000. **Remarks:** Full-time maker and knifemaking instructor. Master bladesmith with ABS. First Damascus sold in 1995, first knife sold in 1998. Often collaborate with husband, Kevin (ABS MS) using the logo "Heavin." **Mark:** First name and sur name, oval shape with "M S" in middle.

HARVEY, KEVIN,
HEAVIN FORGE, PO Box 768, Belfast 1100, SOUTH AFRICA, Phone: 27-13-253-0914, info@heavinforge.co.za Web: www.heavinforge.co.za
Specialties: Large knives of presentation quality and creative art knives. **Patterns:** Fixed blades of Bowie, dagger and fighter-styles, occasionally folders and swords. **Technical:** Stock removal of stainless and forging of carbon steel and own Damascus. Indigenous African handle materials preferred. Own engraving Often collaborate with wife, Heather (ABS MS) under the logo "Heavin." **Prices:** $500 to $5000 average $1500. **Remarks:** Full-time maker and knifemaking instructor. Master bladesmith with ABS. First knife sold in 1984. **Mark:** First name and surnname, oval with "M S" in the middle.

HARVEY, MAX,
14 Bass Rd, Bull Creek, Perth 6155, Western Australia, AUSTRALIA, Phone: 09-332-7585
Specialties: Daggers, Bowies, fighters and fantasy knives. **Patterns:** Hunters, Bowies, tantos and skinners. **Technical:** Hollow-and flat-grinds 440C, ATS-34, 154CM and Damascus. Offers gem work. **Prices:** $250 to $4000. **Remarks:** Part-time maker; first knife sold in 1981. **Mark:** First and middle initials, last name.

HARVEY, MEL,
P.O. Box 176, Nenana, AK 99760, Phone: 907-832-5560, tinker1@nenana.net
Specialties: Fixed blade knives for hunting and fishing. **Patterns:** Hunters, skinners. **Technical:** Stock removal on ATS-34, 440C, 01, 1095; Damascus blades using 1095 and 15N20. **Prices:** Starting at $350. **Remarks:** New maker. **Mark:** HARVEY-HOUSE.

HASLINGER, THOMAS,
164 Fairview Dr SE, Calgary, AB, CANADA T2H 1B3, Phone: 403-253-9628, Web: www.haslinger-knives.com
Specialties: One-of-a-kind using, working and art knives HCK signature sweeping grind lines. Maker of New Generation Chef series. Differential heat treated stainless steel. **Patterns:** No fixed patterns, likes to work with customers on design. **Technical:** Grinds various specialty alloys, including Damascus, High end satin finish. Prefers natural handle materials e.g. ancient ivory stag, pearl, abalone, stone and exotic woods. Does inlay work with stone, some sterling silver, niobium and gold wire work. Custom sheaths using matching woods or hand stitched with unique leather like sturgeon, Nile perch or carp. Offers engraving. **Prices:** $300 and up. **Remarks:** Full-time maker; first knife sold in 1994. **Mark:** Two marks used, high end work uses stylized initials, other uses elk antler with Thomas Haslinger, Canada, handcrafted above.

HAWES, CHUCK,
HAWES FORGE, PO Box 176, Weldon, IL 61882, Phone: 217-736-2479
Specialties: 95 percent of all work in own Damascus. **Patterns:** Slip-joints liner locks, hunters, Bowie's, swords, anything in between. **Technical:** Forges everything, uses all high-carbon steels, no stainless. **Prices:** $150 to $4000. **Remarks:** Like to do custom orders, his style or yours. Sells Damascus. Full-time maker since 1995. **Mark:** Small football shape. Chuck Hawes maker Weldon, IL.

HAWK, GRANT AND GAVIN,
Box 401, Idaho City, ID 83631, Phone: 208-392-4911, Web: www.9-hawkknives.com
Specialties: Large folders with unique locking systems D.O.G. lock, toad lock. **Technical:** Grinds ATS-34, titanium folder parts. **Prices:** $450 and up. **Remarks:** Full-time maker. **Mark:** First initials and last names.

HAWKINS, BUDDY,
PO Box 5969, Texarkana, TX 75505-5969, Phone: 903-838-7917, buddyhawkins@cableone.net

HAWKINS, RADE,
110 Buckeye Rd, Fayetteville, GA 30214, Phone: 770-964-1177, Fax: 770-306-2877, radeh@bellsouth.net; Web: wwwhawkinscustomknives.com
Specialties: All styles. **Patterns:** All styles. **Technical:** Grinds and forges. Makes own Damascus **Prices:** Start at $190. **Remarks:** Full-time maker; first knife sold in 1972. Member knifemakers guild, ABS Journeyman Smith. **Mark:** Rade Hawkins Custom Knives.

HAYES, SCOTTY,
Texarkana College, 2500 N Robinson Rd., Tesarkana, TX 75501, Phone: 903-838-4541, ext. 3236, Fax: 903-832-5030, shayes@texakanacollege.edu; Web: www.americanbladesmith.com/2005ABSo/o20schedule.htm
Specialties: ABS School of Bladesmithing.

HAYES, WALLY,
9960, 9th Concession, RR#1, Essex, Ont., CANADA N8M-2X5, Phone: 519-776-1284, Web: www.hayesknives.com
Specialties: Classic and fancy straight knives and folders. **Patterns:** Daggers, Bowies, fighters, tantos. **Technical:** Forges own Damascus and O1; engraves. **Prices:** $150 to $14,000. **Mark:** Last name, M.S. and serial number.

HAYNES, JERRY,
260 Forest Meadow Dr, Gunter, TX 75058, Phone: 210-599-2928, jhaynes@arrow-head.com; Web: http://www.arrow-head.com
Specialties: Working straight knives and folders of his design, also historical blades. **Patterns:** Hunters, skinners, carving knives, fighters, renais-

sance daggers, locking folders and kitchen knives. **Technical:** Grinds ATS-34, CPM, Stellite 6K, D2 and acquired Damascus. Prefers exotic handle materials. Has B.A. in design. Studied with R. Buckminster Fuller. **Prices:** $200 to $1200. **Remarks:** Part-time maker. First knife sold in 1953. **Mark:** Arrowhead and last name.

HAYS, MARK,
HAYS HANDMADE KNIVES, 1008 Kavanagh Dr., Austin, TX 78748, Phone: 512-292-4410, markhays@austin.rr.com
Specialties: Working straight knives and folders. Patterns inspired by Randall and Stone. **Patterns:** Bowies, hunters and slip-joint folders. **Technical:** 440C stock removal. Repairs and restores Stone knives. **Prices:** Start at $200. **Remarks:** Part-time maker, brochure available, with Stone knives 1974-1983, 1990-1991. **Mark:** First initial, last name, state and serial number.

HAZEN, MARK,
9600 Surrey Rd, Charlotte, NC 28227, Phone: 704-573-0052, Fax: 704-573-0052, mhazen@carolina.rr.com
Specialties: Working/using straight knives of his design. **Patterns:** Hunters/skinners, fillet, utility/camp, fighters, short swords. **Technical:** Grinds 154 CM, ATS-34, 440C. **Prices:** $75 to $450; some to $1500. **Remarks:** Part-time maker. First knife sold 1982. **Mark:** Name with cross in it, etched in blade.

HEADRICK, GARY,
122 Wilson Blvd, Juane Les Pins, FRANCE 06160, Phone: 033 0610282885, headrick-gary@wanadoo.fr
Specialties: Hi-tech folders with natural furnishings. Back lock & back spring. **Patterns:** Damascus and mokumes. **Technical:** Self made Damascus all steel (no nickel). **Prices:** $500 to $2000. **Remarks:** Full-time maker for last 7 years. German Guild-French Federation. 10 years active. **Mark:** HEADRICK on ricosso is new marking.

HEANEY, JOHN D,
9 Lefe Court, Haines City, FL 33844, Phone: 863-422-5823, jdh199@msn.com; Web: www.heaneyknives.com
Specialties: Forged 5160, O1 and Damascus. Prefers using natural handle material such as bone, stag and oosic. Plans on using some of the various ivories on future knives. **Prices:** $250 and up. **Remarks:** ABS member. Received journeyman smith stamp in June. **Mark:** Heaney JS.

HEASMAN, H G,
28 St Mary's Rd, Llandudno, N. Wales, UNITED KINGDOM LL302UB, Phone: (UK)0492-876351
Specialties: Miniatures only. **Patterns:** Bowies, daggers and swords. **Technical:** Files from stock high-carbon and stainless steel. **Prices:** $400 to $600. **Remarks:** Part-time maker; first knife sold in 1975. Doing business as Reduced Reality. **Mark:** NA.

HEATH, WILLIAM,
PO Box 131, Bondville, IL 61815, Phone: 217-863-2576
Specialties: Classic and working straight knives, folders. **Patterns:** Hunters and Bowies LinerLock® folders. **Technical:** Grinds ATS-34, 440C, 154CM, Damascus, handle materials Micarta, woods to exotic materials snake skins cobra, rattle snake, African flower snake. Does own heat treating. **Prices:** $75 to $300 some $1000. **Remarks:** Full-time maker. First knife sold in 1979. **Mark:** W. D. HEATH.

HEDLUND, ANDERS,
Samstad 400, 454 91, Brastad, SWEDEN, Phone: 46-523-13948, anderskniv@passagen.se; Web: http://hem.passagen.se/anderskniv
Specialties: Fancy high-end collectible folders, high-end collectible Nordic hunters with leather carvings on the sheath. Carvings combine traditional designs with own designs. **Patterns:** Own designs. **Technical:** Grinds most steels, but prefers mosaic Damascus and RWL-34. Prefers mother-of-pearl, mammoth, and mosaic steel for folders. Prefers desert ironwood, mammoth, stabilized arctic birch, willow burl, and Damascus steel or RWL-34 for stick tang knives. **Prices:** Starting at $750 for stick tang knives and staring at $1500 for folders. **Remarks:** Part-time maker, first knife sold in 1988. Nordic champion (five countries) several times and Swedish champion 20 times in different classes. **Mark:** Stylized initials or last name.

HEDRICK, DON,
131 Beechwood Hills, Newport News, VA 23608, Phone: 757-877-8100, donaldhedrick@cox.net
Specialties: Working straight knives; period pieces and fantasy knives. **Patterns:** Hunters, boots, Bowies and miniatures. **Technical:** Grinds 440C and commercial Damascus. Also makes micro-mini Randall replicas. **Prices:** $150 to $550; some to $1200. **Remarks:** Part-time maker; first knife sold in 1982. **Mark:** First initial, last name in oval logo.

HEFLIN, CHRISTOPHER M,
6013 Jocely Hollow Rd, Nashville, TN 37205, Phone: 615-352-3909, blix@bellsouth.net

HEGWALD, J L,
1106 Charles, Humboldt, KS 66748, Phone: 316-473-3523
Specialties: Working straight knives, some fancy. **Patterns:** Makes Bowies, miniatures. **Technical:** Forges or grinds O1, L6, 440C; mixes materials in handles. **Prices:** $35 to $200; some higher. **Remarks:** Part-time maker; first knife sold in 1983. **Mark:** First and middle initials.

HEHN, RICHARD KARL,
Lehnmuehler Str 1, 55444 Dorrebach, GERMANY, Phone: 06724 3152
   Specialties: High-tech, full integral working knives. **Patterns:** Hunters, fighters and daggers. **Technical:** Grinds CPM T-440V, CPM T-420V, forges his own stainless Damascus. **Prices:** $1000 to $10,000. **Remarks:** Full-time maker; first knife sold in 1963. **Mark:** Runic last initial in logo.

HEIMDALE, J E,
7749 E 28 CT, Tulsa, OK 74129, Phone: 918-640-0784, heimdale@sbcglobal.net
   Specialties: Art knives **Patterns:** Bowies, daggers **Technical:** Makes allcomponents and handles - exotic woods and sheaths. Uses Damascus blades by other Blademakers, notably R.W. Wilson. **Prices:** $300 and up. **Remarks:** Part-time maker. First knife sold in 1999. **Marks:** JEHCO

HEINZ, JOHN,
611 Cafferty Rd, Upper Black Eddy, PA 18972, Phone: 610-847-8535, Web: www.herugrim.com
   Specialties: Historical pieces / copies. **Technical:** Makes his own steel. **Prices:** $150 to $800. **Mark:** "H."

HEITLER, HENRY,
8106 N Albany, Tampa, FL 33604, Phone: 813-933-1645
   Specialties: Traditional working and using straight knives of his design and to customer specs. **Patterns:** Fighters, hunters, utility/camp knives and fillet knives. **Technical:** Flat-grinds ATS-34; offers tapered tangs. **Prices:** $135 to $450; some to $600. **Remarks:** Part-time maker; first knife sold in 1990. **Mark:** First initial, last name, city, state circling double H's.

HELSCHER, JOHN W,
2645 Highway 1, Washington, IA 52353, Phone: 319-653-7310

HELTON, ROY,
HELTON KNIVES, 2941 Comstock St., San Diego, CA 92111, Phone: 858-277-5024

HEMBROOK, RON,
HEMBROOK KNIVES, PO Box 201, Neosho, WI 53059, Phone: 920-625-3607, rhembrook3607@charter.net; Web: www.hembrookcustomknives.com
   Specialties: Hunters, working knives. **Technical:** Grinds ATS-34, 440C, O1 and Damascus. **Prices:** $125 to $750, some to $1000. **Remarks:** First knife sold in 1980. **Mark:** Hembrook plus a serial number. Part-time maker, makes hunters, daggers, Bowies, folders and miniatures.

HEMPERLEY, GLEN,
13322 Country Run Rd, Willis, TX 77318, Phone: 936-228-5048, hemperley.com
   Specialties: Specializes in hunting knives, does fixed and folding knives.

HENDRICKS, SAMUEL J,
2162 Van Buren Rd, Maurertown, VA 22644, Phone: 703-436-3305
   Specialties: Integral hunters and skinners of thin design. **Patterns:** Boots, hunters and locking folders. **Technical:** Grinds ATS-34, 440C and D2. Integral liners and bolsters of N-S and 7075 T6 aircraft aluminum. Does leatherwork. **Prices:** $50 to $250; some to $500. **Remarks:** Full-time maker; first knife sold in 1992. **Mark:** First and middle initials, last name, city and state in football-style logo.

HENDRICKSON, E JAY,
4204 Ballenger Creek Pike, Frederick, MD 21703, Phone: 301-663-6923, Fax: 301-663-6923, ejayhendrickson@comcast.net
   Specialties: Specializes in silver wire inlay. **Patterns:** Bowies, Kukri's, camp, hunters, and fighters. **Technical:** Forges 06, 1084, 5160, 52100, D2, L6 and W2; makes Damascus. Moran-styles on order. **Prices:** $400 to $5000. **Remarks:** Full-time maker; first knife sold in 1975. **Mark:** Last name, M.S.

HENDRICKSON, SHAWN,
2327 Kaetzel Rd, Knoxville, MD 21758, Phone: 301-432-4306
   Specialties: Hunting knives. **Patterns:** Clip points, drop points and trailing point hunters. **Technical:** Forges 5160, 1084 and L6. **Prices:** $175 to $400.

HENDRIX, JERRY,
HENDRIX CUSTOM KNIVES, 175 Skyland Dr. Ext., Clinton, SC 29325, Phone: 864-833-2659, jhendrix@backroads.net
   Specialties: Traditional working straight knives of all designs. **Patterns:** Hunters, utility, boot, bird and fishing. **Technical:** Grinds ATS-34 and 440C. **Prices:** $85 to $275. **Remarks:** Full-time maker. Hand stitched, waxed leather sheaths. **Mark:** Full name in shape of knife.

HENDRIX, WAYNE,
9636 Burton's Ferry Hwy, Allendale, SC 29810, Phone: 803-584-3825, Fax: 803-584-3825, knives@barnwellsc.com; Web: www.hendrixknives.com
   Specialties: Working/using knives of his design. **Patterns:** Hunters and fillet knives. **Technical:** Grinds ATS-34, D2 and 440C. **Prices:** $100 and up. **Remarks:** Full-time maker; first knife sold in 1985. **Mark:** Last name.

HENRIKSEN, HANS J,
Birkegaardsvej 24, DK 3200 Helsinge, DENMARK, Fax: 45 4879 4899
   Specialties: Zirconia ceramic blades. **Patterns:** Customer designs. **Technical:** Slip-cast zirconia-water mix in plaster mould; offers hidden or full tang. **Prices:** White blades start at $10cm; colored +50 percent. **Remarks:** Part-time maker; first ceramic blade sold in 1989. **Mark:** Initial logo.

HENSLEY, WAYNE,
PO Box 904, Conyers, GA 30012, Phone: 770-483-8938
   Specialties: Period pieces and fancy working knives. **Patterns:** Boots to Bowies, locking folders to miniatures. Large variety of straight knives. **Technical:** Grinds ATS-34, 440C, D2 and commercial Damascus. **Prices:** $85 and up. **Remarks:** Full-time maker; first knife sold in 1974. **Mark:** Last name.

HERB, MARTIN,
2500 Starwood Dr, Richmond, VA 23229

HERBST, PETER,
Komotauer Strasse 26, 91207 Lauf a.d. Pegn., GERMANY, Phone: 09123-13315, Fax: 09123-13379
   Specialties: Working/using knives and folders of his design. **Patterns:** Hunters, fighters and daggers; interframe and integral. **Technical:** Grinds CPM-T-440V, UHB-Elmax, ATS-34 and stainless Damascus. **Prices:** $300 to $3000; some to $8000. **Remarks:** Full-time maker; first knife sold in 1981. **Mark:** First initial, last name.

HERBST, THINUS,
PO Box 59158, Karenpark 0118, Akasia, South Africa, Phone: +27 82 254 8016, thinus@herbst.co.za; Web: www.herbst.co.za
   Specialties: Plain and fancy working straight knives of own design and liner lock folders. **Patterns:** Hunters, utility knives, art knives, and liner lock folders. **Technical:** Prefer exotic materials for handles. Most knives embellished with file work, carving and scrimshaw. **Prices:** $200 to $2000. **Remarks:** Full-time maker, member of the Knifemakers Guild of South Africa.

HERMAN, TIM,
517 E. 126 Terrace, Olathe, KS 66061-2731, Phone: 913-839-1924, HermanKnives@comcast.net
   Specialties: Investment-grade folders of his design; interframes and bolster frames. **Patterns:** Interframes and new designs in carved stainless. **Technical:** Grinds ATS-34 and damasteel Damascus. Engraves and gold inlays with pearl, jade, lapis and Australian opal. **Prices:** $1500 to $20,000 and up. **Remarks:** Full-time maker; first knife sold in 1978. **Mark:** Etched signature.

HERNDON, WM R "BILL",
32520 Michigan St, Acton, CA 93510, Phone: 661-269-5860, Fax: 661-269-4568, bherndons1@roadrunner.com
   Specialties: Straight knives, plain and fancy. **Technical:** Carbon steel (white and blued), Damascus, stainless steels. **Prices:** Start at $175. **Remarks:** Full-time maker; first knife sold in 1976. American Bladesmith Society journeyman smith. **Mark:** Signature and/or helm logo.

HERRING, MORRIS,
Box 85 721 W Line St, Dyer, AR 72935, Phone: 501-997-8861, morrish@ipa.com

HETHCOAT, DON,
Box 1764, Clovis, NM 88101, Phone: 575-762-5721, dhethcoat@plateautel.net; Web: www.donhethcoat.com
   Specialties: Liner lock-locking and multi-blade folders **Patterns:** Hunters, Bowies. **Technical:** Grinds stainless; forges Damascus. **Prices:** Moderate to upscale. **Remarks:** Full-time maker; first knife sold in 1969. **Mark:** Last name on all.

HIBBEN, DARYL,
PO Box 172, LaGrange, KY 40031-0172, Phone: 502-222-0983, dhibben1@bellsouth.net
   Specialties: Working straight knives, some fancy to customer specs. **Patterns:** Hunters, fighters, Bowies, short sword, art and fantasy. **Technical:** Grinds 440C, ATS-34, 154CM, Damascus; prefers hollow-grinds. **Prices:** $175 to $3000. **Remarks:** Full-time maker; first knife sold in 1979. **Mark:** Etched full name in script.

HIBBEN, GIL,
PO Box 13, LaGrange, KY 40031, Phone: 502-222-1397, Fax: 502-222-2676, hibbenknives.com; Web: www.gil_hibben@bellsouth.net
   Specialties: Working knives and fantasy pieces to customer specs. **Patterns:** Full range of straight knives, including swords, axes and miniatures; some locking folders. **Technical:** Grinds ATS-34, 440C and D2. **Prices:** $300 to $2000; some to $10,000. **Remarks:** Full-time maker; first knife sold in 1957. Maker and designer of *Rambo III* knife; made swords for movie *Marked for Death* and throwing knife for movie *Under Seige*; made belt buckle knife and knives for movie *Perfect Weapon*; made knives featured in movie *Star Trek the Next Generation* , *Star Trek Nemesis*. 1990 inductee Cutlery Hall of Fame; designer for United Cutlery. Official klingon armourer for Star Trek, over 37 movies and TV productions. Celebrating 50 years since first knife sold. **Mark:** Hibben Knives. City and state, or signature.

HIBBEN, JOLEEN,
PO Box 172, LaGrange, KY 40031, Phone: 502-222-0983, dhibben1@bellsouth.net
   Specialties: Miniature straight knives of her design; period pieces. **Patterns:** Hunters, axes and fantasy knives. **Technical:** Grinds Damascus, 1095 tool steel and stainless 440C or ATS-34. Uses wood, ivory, bone, feathers and claws on/for handles. **Prices:** $60 to $600. **Remarks:** Spare-time maker; first knife sold in 1991. Design knives, make & tool leather sheathes. Produced first inlaid handle in 2005, used by Daryl on a dagger. **Mark:** Initials or first name.

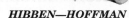

HIBBEN, WESTLEY G,
14101 Sunview Dr, Anchorage, AK 99515
Specialties: Working straight knives of his design or to customer specs. **Patterns:** Hunters, fighters, daggers, combat knives and some fantasy pieces. **Technical:** Grinds 440C mostly. Filework available. **Prices:** $200 to $400; some to $3000. **Remarks:** Part-time maker; first knife sold in 1988. **Mark:** Signature.

HICKS, GARY,
341 CR 275, Tuscola, TX 79562, Phone: 325-554-9762

HIGH, TOM,
5474 S 1128 Rd, Alamosa, CO 81101, Phone: 719-589-2108, www.rockymountainscrimshaw.com
Specialties: Hunters, some fancy. **Patterns:** Drop-points in several shapes; some semi-skinners. Knives designed by and for top outfitters and guides. **Technical:** Grinds ATS-34; likes hollow-grinds, mirror finishes; prefers scrimable handles. **Prices:** $300 to $8000.. **Remarks:** Full-time maker; first knife sold in 1965. Limited edition wildlife series knives. **Mark:** Initials connected; arrow through last name.

HILKER, THOMAS N,
PO Box 409, Williams, OR 97544, Phone: 541-846-6461
Specialties: Traditional working straight knives and folders. **Patterns:** Folding skinner in two sizes, Bowies, fork and knife sets, camp knives and interchangeable. **Technical:** Grinds D2, 440C and ATS-34. Heat-treats. **Prices:** $50 to $350; some to $400. Doing business as Thunderbolt Artisans. Only limited production models available; not currently taking orders. **Remarks:** Full-time maker; first knife sold in 1983. **Mark:** Last name.

HILL, HOWARD E,
41785 Mission Lane, Polson, MT 59860, Phone: 406-883-3405, Fax: 406-883-3486, knifeman@bigsky.net
Specialties: Autos, complete new design, legal in Montana (with permit). **Patterns:** Bowies, daggers, skinners and lockback folders. **Technical:** Grinds 440C; uses micro and satin finish. **Prices:** $150 to $1000. **Remarks:** Full-time maker; first knife sold in 1981. **Mark:** Persuader.

HILL, RICK,
20 Nassau, Maryville, IL 62062-5618, Phone: 618-288-4370
Specialties: Working knives and period pieces to customer specs. **Patterns:** Hunters, skinners, fighters and daggers. **Technical:** Grinds D2, 440C and 154CM; forges his own Damascus. **Prices:** $75 to $500; some to $3000. **Remarks:** Part-time maker; first knife sold in 1983. **Mark:** Full name in hill shape logo.

HILL, STEVE E,
40 Rand Pond Rd, Goshen, NH 03752, Phone: 603-863-4762, Fax: 603-863-4762, kingpirateboy2@juno.com; Web: www.stevehillknives.com
Specialties: Fancy manual and automatic LinerLock® folders, small fixed blades and classic Bowie knives. **Patterns:** Classic to cool folding and fixed blade designs. **Technical:** Grinds Damascus and occasional 440C, D2. Prefers natural handle materials; offers elaborate filework, carving, and inlays. **Prices:** $400 to $6000, some higher. **Remarks:** Full-time maker; first knife sold in 1978. Google search: Steve Hill custom knives. **Mark:** First initial, last name and handmade. (4400, D2). Damascus folders: mark inside handle.

HILLMAN, CHARLES,
225 Waldoboro Rd, Friendship, ME 04547, Phone: 207-832-4634
Specialties: Working knives of his own or custom design. Heavy Scagel influence. **Patterns:** Hunters, fishing, camp and general utility. Occasional folders. **Technical:** Grinds D2 and 440C. File work, blade and handle carving, engraving. Natural handle materials–antler, bone, leather, wood, horn. Sheaths made to order. **Prices:** $60 to $500. **Remarks:** Part-time maker; first knife sold 1986. **Mark:** Last name in oak leaf.

HINDERER, RICK,
5373 Columbus Rd., Shreve, OH 44676, Phone: 330-263-0962, Fax: 330-263-0962, rhind64@earthlink.net; Web: www.rickhindererknives.com
Specialties: Working tactical knives, and some one-of-a kind. **Patterns:** Makes his own. **Technical:** Grinds Duratech 20 CV and CPM S30V. **Prices:** $150 to $4000. **Remarks:** Full-time maker doing business as Rick Hinderer Knives; first knife sold in 1988. **Mark:** R. Hinderer.

HINDMARCH, G,
PO Box 135, Carlyle SK S0C 0R0, CANADA, Phone: 306-453-2568
Specialties: Working and fancy straight knives, Bowies. **Patterns:** Hunters, skinners, Bowies. **Technical:** Grind 440C, ATS-34, some Damascus. **Prices:** $175 - $700. **Remarks:** Part-time maker; first knife sold 1994. All knives satin finish. Does file work, offers engraving, stabilized wood, Giraffe bone, some Micarta. **Mark:** First initial last name, city, province.

HINK III, LES,
1599 Aptos Lane, Stockton, CA 95206, Phone: 209-547-1292
Specialties: Working straight knives and traditional folders in standard patterns or to customer specs. **Patterns:** Hunting and utility/camp knives; others on request. **Technical:** Grinds carbon and stainless steels. **Prices:** $80 to $200; some higher. **Remarks:** Part-time maker; first knife sold in 1980. **Mark:** Last name, or last name 3.

HINMAN, THEODORE,
186 Petty Plain Road, Greenfield, MA 01301, Phone: 413-773-0448, armenemargosian@verizon.net
Specialties: Tomahawks and axes. Offers classes in bladesmithing and toolmaking.

HINSON AND SON, R,
2419 Edgewood Rd, Columbus, GA 31906, Phone: 706-327-6801
Specialties: Working straight knives and folders. **Patterns:** Locking folders, liner locks, combat and commercial Damascus. **Technical:** Grinds 440C and commercial Damascus. **Prices:** $200 to $450; some to $1500. **Remarks:** Part-time maker; first knife sold in 1983. Son Bob is co-worker. **Mark:** HINSON, city and state.

HINTZ, GERALD M,
5402 Sahara Ct, Helena, MT 59602, Phone: 406-458-5412
Specialties: Fancy, high-art, working/using knives of his design. **Patterns:** Bowies, hunters, daggers, fish fillet and utility/camp knives. **Technical:** Forges ATS-34, 440C and D2. Animal art in horn handles or in the blade. **Prices:** $75 to $400; some to $1000. **Remarks:** Part-time maker; first knife sold in 1980. Doing business as Big Joe's Custom Knives. Will take custom orders. **Mark:** F.S. or W.S. with first and middle initials and last name.

HIRAYAMA, HARUMI,
4-5-13 Kitamachi, Warabi City, Saitama Pref. 335-0001, JAPAN, Phone: 048-443-2248, Fax: 048-443-2248, Web: www.ne.jp/asahi/harumi/knives
Specialties: High-tech working knives of her design. **Patterns:** Locking folders, interframes, straight gents and slip-joints. **Technical:** Grinds 440C or equivalent; uses natural handle materials and gold. **Prices:** Start at $1500. **Remarks:** Part-time maker; first knife sold in 1985. **Mark:** First initial, last name.

HIROTO, FUJIHARA,
2-34-7 Koioosako Nishi-ku Hiroshima-city, Hiroshima, JAPAN, Phone: 082-271-8389, fjhr8363@crest.ocn.ne.jp

HITCHMOUGH, HOWARD,
95 Old Street Rd, Peterborough, NH 03458-1637, Phone: 603-924-9646, Fax: 603-924-9595, howard@hitchmoughknives.com; Web: www.hitchmoughknives.com
Specialties: High class folding knives. **Patterns:** Lockback folders, liner locks, pocket knives. **Technical:** Uses ATS-34, stainless Damascus, titanium, gold and gemstones. Prefers hand-rubbed finishes and natural handle materials. **Prices:** $2500 - $7500. **Remarks:** Full-time maker; first knife sold in 1967. **Mark:** Last name.

HOBART, GENE,
100 Shedd Rd, Windsor, NY 13865, Phone: 607-655-1345

HOCKENSMITH, DAN,
12620 WCR 108, Carr, CO 80612, Phone: 970-231-6506, blademan@skybeam.com
Specialties: Traditional working and using straight knives of his design. **Patterns:** Hunters, Bowies, folders and utility/camp knives. **Technical:** Uses his Damascus, 5160, carbon steel, 52100 steel and 1084 steel. Hand forged. **Prices:** $250 to $1500. **Remarks:** Part-time maker; first knife sold in 1987. **Mark:** Last name or stylized "D" with H inside.

HODGE III, JOHN,
422 S 15th St, Palatka, FL 32177, Phone: 904-328-3897
Specialties: Fancy straight knives and folders. **Patterns:** Various. **Technical:** Pattern-welded Damascus—"Southern-style." **Prices:** To $1000. **Remarks:** Part-time maker; first knife sold in 1981. **Mark:** JH3 logo.

HOEL, STEVE,
PO Box 283, Pine, AZ 85544, Phone: 602-476-4278
Specialties: Investor-class folders, straight knives and period pieces of his design. **Patterns:** Folding interframes lockers and slip-joints; straight Bowies, boots and daggers. **Technical:** Grinds 154CM, ATS-34 and commercial Damascus. **Prices:** $600 to $1200; some to $7500. **Remarks:** Full-time maker. **Mark:** Initial logo with name and address.

HOFER, LOUIS,
BOX 125, Rose Prairie, B.C., CANADA V0C 2H0, Phone: 250-827-3999, ldhofer@xplornet.com
Specialties: Damascus knives, working knives, fixed blade bowies, daggers. **Patterns:** Hunting, skinning, custom. **Technical:** Wild damascus, random damascus. **Prices:** $450 and up. **Remarks:** Part-time maker since 1995. **Mark:** Logo of initials.

HOFFMAN, KEVIN L,
28 Hopeland Dr, Savannah, GA 31419, Phone: 912-920-3579, Fax: 912-920-3579, kevh052475@aol.com; Web: www.KLHoffman.com
Specialties: Distinctive folders and fixed blades. **Patterns:** Titanium frame lock folders. **Technical:** Sculpted guards and fittings cast in sterling silver and 14k gold. Grinds ATS-34, CPM S30V Damascus. Makes kydex sheaths for his fixed blade working knives. **Prices:** $400 and up. **Remarks:** Full-time maker since 1981. **Mark:** KLH.

HOGAN, THOMAS R,
2802 S. Heritage Ave, Boise, ID 83709, Phone: 208-362-7848

HOGSTROM, ANDERS T,
Halmstadsvagen 36, 121 53, Johanneshov, SWEDEN, Phone: 46 702 674 574, andershogstrom@hotmail.com or info@andershogstrom.com; Web: www.andershogstrom.com

Specialties: Short and long daggers, fighters and swords For select pieces makes wooden display stands. **Patterns:** Daggers, fighters, short knives and swords and an occasional sword. **Technical:** Grinds 1050 High Carbon, Damascus and stainless, forges own Damasus on occasion, fossil ivories. Does clay tempering and uses exotic hardwoods. **Prices:** Start at $850. **Marks:** Last name in maker's own signature.

HOKE, THOMAS M,
3103 Smith Ln, LaGrange, KY 40031, Phone: 502-222-0350

Specialties: Working/using knives, straight knives. Own designs and customer specs. **Patterns:** Daggers, Bowies, hunters, fighters, short swords. **Technical:** Grind 440C, Damascus and ATS-34. Filework on all knives. Tooling on sheaths (custom fit on all knives). Any handle material, mostly exotic. **Prices:** $100 to $700; some to $1500. **Remarks:** Full-time maker, first knife sold in 1986. **Mark:** Dragon on banner which says T.M. Hoke.

HOLBROOK, H L,
PO Box 483, Sandy Hook, KY 41171, Phone: 606-738-9922 home, hhknives@mrtc.com

Specialties: Traditional working using straight knives of his design, to customer specs and in standard patterns. Stabilized wood. **Patterns:** Hunters, mild tacticals and neck knives with kydex sheaths. **Technical:** Grinds CPM154CM, 154CM. Blades have hand-rubbed satin finish. Uses exotic woods, stag and Micarta. Hand-sewn sheath with each straight knife. **Prices:** $100 - $300. **Remarks:** Part-time maker; first knife sold in 1983. Doing business as Holbrook Knives. **Mark:** Name, city, state.

HOLDER, D'ALTON,
18910 McNeil Rd., Wickenburg, AZ 85390, Phone: 928-684-2025, Fax: 623-878-3964, dholderknives@cox.net; Web: d'holder.com

Specialties: Deluxe working knives and high-art hunters. **Patterns:** Drop-point hunters, fighters, Bowies. **Technical:** Grinds ATS-34; uses amber and other materials in combination on stick tangs. **Prices:** $400 to $1000; some to $2000. **Remarks:** Full-time maker; first knife sold in 1966. **Mark:** D'HOLDER, city and state.

HOLLOWAY, PAUL,
714 Burksdale Rd, Norfolk, VA 23518, Phone: 757-547-6025

Specialties: Working straight knives and folders to customer specs. **Patterns:** Lockers and slip-joints; fighters and boots; fishing and push knives, from swords to miniatures. **Technical:** Grinds A2, D2, 154CM, 440C and ATS-34. **Prices:** $195 to $900; some to $1200. **Remarks:** Part-time maker; first knife sold in 1981. **Mark:** Last name, or last name and city in logo.

HOOK, BOB,
3247 Wyatt Rd, North Pole, AK 99705, Phone: 907-488-8886, grayling@alaska.net; Web: www.alaskaknifeandforge.com

Specialties: Forged carbon steel. Damascus blades. **Patterns:** Pronghorns, bowies, drop point hunters and knives for the kitchen. **Technical:** 5160, 52100, carbon steel and 1084 and 15N20 pattern welded steel blades are forged. Heat treated and ground by maker. Handles are natural materials from Alaska. I favor sole authorship of each piece. **Prices:** $300-$1000. **Remarks:** Journeyman smith with ABS. I have attended the Bill Moran School of Bladesmithing. Knife maker since 2000. **Mark:** Hook.

HORN, DES,
PO Box 322, Onrusrivier 7201, SOUTH AFRICA, Phone: 27283161795, Fax: 27283161795, deshorn@usa.net

Specialties: Folding knives. **Patterns:** Ball release side lock mechanism and interframe automatics. **Technical:** Prefers working in totally stainless materials. **Prices:** $800 to $7500. **Remarks:** Full-time maker. Enjoys working in gold, titanium, meteorite, pearl and mammoth. **Mark:** Des Horn.

HORN, JESS,
2526 Lansdown Rd, Eugene, OR 97404, Phone: 541-463-1510, jandahorn@earthlink.net

Specialties: Investor-class working folders; period pieces; collectibles. **Patterns:** High-tech design and finish in folders; liner locks, traditional slip-joints, and featherweight models. **Technical:** Grinds ATS-34, 154CM. **Prices:** Start at $1000. **Remarks:** Full-time maker; first knife sold in 1968. **Mark:** Full name or last name.

HORNE, GRACE,
182 Crimicar Ln, Sheffield Britain, UNITED KINGDOM S10 4EJ, gracehorne@hotmail.co.uk

Specialties: Knives of own design including kitchen and utility knives for people with reduced hand use. **Technical:** Working at Sheffield Hallam University researching innovative, contemporary Damascus steels using non-traditional methods of manufacture. **Remarks:** Spare-time maker/full-time researcher. **Mark:** 'gH' and 'Sheffield'.

HORTON, SCOT,
PO Box 451, Buhl, ID 83316, Phone: 208-543-4222

Specialties: Traditional working stiff knives and folders. **Patterns:** Hunters, skinners, utility and show knives. **Technical:** Grinds ATS-34. Uses exotic woods and Micarta. **Prices:** $350 to $2500. **Remarks:** First knife sold in 1990. **Mark:** Full name in arch underlined with arrow, city, state.

HOSSOM, JERRY,
3585 Schilling Ridge, Duluth, GA 30096, Phone: 770-449-7809, jerry@hossom.com; Web: www.hossom.com

Specialties: Working straight knives of his own design. **Patterns:** Fighters, combat knives, modern Bowies and daggers, modern swords, concealment knives for military and LE uses. **Technical:** Grinds 154CM, S30V, CPM-3V, CPM-154 and stainless Damascus. Uses natural and synthetic handle materials. **Prices:** $350-1500, some higher. **Remarks:** Full-time maker since 1997. First knife sold in 1983. **Mark:** First initial and last name, includes city and state since 2002.

HOUSE, GARY,
2851 Pierce Rd, Ephrata, WA 98823, Phone: 509-754-3272, spindry101@aol.com

Specialties: Mosaic Damascus bar stock. Forged blades. **Patterns:** Unlimited, SW Indian designs, geometric patterns, using 1084, 15N20 and some nickel. Bowies, hunters and daggers. **Technical:** Forged company logos and customer designs in mosaic damascus. **Prices:** $500 & up. **Remarks:** Some of the finest and most unique patterns available. ABS Journeyman Smith. **Marks:** Initials GTH, G hanging T, H.

HOWARD, DURVYN M,
4220 McLain St S, Hokes Bluff, AL 35903, Phone: 256-492-5720

Specialties: Collectible upscale folders; one-of-a-kind, gentlemen's folders. Multiple patents. **Patterns:** Conceptual designs; each unique and different. **Technical:** Uses natural and exotic materials and precious metals. **Prices:** $5000 to $25,000. **Remarks:** Full-time maker; by commission or available work. Work displayed at select shows, K.G. Show etc. **Mark:** Howard: new for 2000; Howard in Garamond Narrow "etched."

HOWE, TORI,
30020 N Stampede Rd, Athol, ID 83801, Phone: 208-449-1509, wapiti@knifescales.com; Web:www.knifescales.com

Specialties: Custom knives, knife scales & Damascus blades. **Remarks:** Carry James Luman polymer clay knife scales.

HOWELL, JASON G,
1112 Sycamore, Lake Jackson, TX 77566, Phone: 979-297-9454, tinyknives@yahoo.com; Web:www.howellbladesmith.com

Specialties: Fixed blades and LinerLock® folders. Makes own Damascus. **Patterns:** Clip and drop point. **Prices:** $150 to $750. **Remarks:** Likes making Mosaic Damascus out of the ordinary stuff. Member of TX Knifemakers and Collectors Association; apprentice in ABS; working towards Journeyman Stamp. **Mark:** Name, city, state.

HOWELL, LEN,
550 Lee Rd 169, Opelika, AL 36804, Phone: 334-749-1942

Specialties: Traditional and working knives of his design and to customer specs. **Patterns:** Buckskinner, hunters and utility/camp knives. **Technical:** Forges cable Damascus, 1085 and 5160; makes own Damascus. **Mark:** Engraved last name.

HOWELL, TED,
1294 Wilson Rd, Wetumpka, AL 36092, Phone: 205-569-2281, Fax: 205-569-1764

Specialties: Working/using straight knives and folders of his design; period pieces. **Patterns:** Bowies, fighters, hunters. **Technical:** Forges 5160, 1085 and cable. Offers light engraving and scrimshaw; filework. **Prices:** $75 to $250; some to $450. **Remarks:** Part-time maker; first knife sold in 1991. Doing business as Howell Co. **Mark:** Last name, Slapout AL.

HOWSER, JOHN C,
54 Bell Ln, Frankfort, KY 40601, Phone: 502-875-3678

Specialties: Slip joint folders (old patterns-multi blades). **Patterns:** Traditional slip joint folders, lockbacks, hunters and fillet knives. **Technical:** Steel S30V, CPM154, ATS-34 and D2. **Prices:** $200 to $600 some to $800. **Remarks:** Full-time maker; first knife sold in 1974. **Mark:** Signature or stamp.

HOY, KEN,
54744 Pinchot Dr, North Fork, CA 93643, Phone: 209-877-7805

HRISOULAS, JIM,
SALAMANDER ARMOURY, 284-C Lake Mead Pkwy #157, Henderson, NV 89105, Phone: 702-566-8551

Specialties: Working straight knives; period pieces. **Patterns:** Swords, daggers and sgian dubhs. **Technical:** Double-edged differential heat treating. **Prices:** $85 to $175; some to $600 and higher. **Remarks:** Full-time maker; first knife sold in 1973. Author of *The Complete Bladesmith*, *The Pattern Welded Blade* and *The Master Bladesmith*. Doing business as Salamander Armory. **Mark:** 8R logo and sword and salamander.

HUCKABEE, DALE,
254 Hwy 260, Maylene, AL 35114, Phone: 205-664-2544, dalehuckabee@hotmail.com

Specialties: Fixed blade hunter and Bowies of his design. **Technical:** Steel used: 5160, 1084, and Damascus. **Prices:** $225 and up, depending on materials used. **Remarks:** Hand forged. Journeyman Smith. Part-time maker. **Mark:** Stamped Huckabee J.S.

HUCKS, JERRY,
KNIVES BY HUCKS, 1807 Perch Road, Moncks Corner, SC 29461, Phone: 843-761-6481, knivesbyhucks@netrockets.com
Specialties: Oyster knives, hunters, Bowies, fillets. Bowies are the maker's favorite with stag & ivory. **Patterns:** Yours and his. **Technical:** ATS-34, BG-42, CPM-154, maker's cable Damascus, also 1084 & 15N20. **Prices:** $125 and up. **Remarks:** Full-time maker, retired as a machinist in 1990. **Mark:** Robin Hood hat with moncke corner, S.C. in oval.

HUDSON, ANTHONY B,
PO Box 368, Amanda, OH 43102, Phone: 740-969-4200, jjahudson@wmconnect.com
Specialties: Hunting knives, fighters, survival. **Remarks:** ABS Journeyman Smith. **Mark:** A.B. HUDSON.

HUDSON, C ROBBIN,
497 Groton Hollow Rd, Rummney, NH 03266, Phone: 603-786-9944
Specialties: High-art working knives. **Patterns:** Hunters, Bowies, fighters and kitchen knives. **Technical:** Forges W2, nickel steel, pure nickel steel, composite and mosaic Damascus; makes knives one-at-a-time. **Prices:** 500 to $1200; some to $5000. **Remarks:** Full-time maker; first knife sold in 1970. **Mark:** Last name and MS.

HUDSON, ROB,
340 Roush Rd, Northumberland, PA 17857, Phone: 570-473-9588, robscustknives@aol.com Web:www.robscustomknives.com
Specialties: Presentation hunters and Bowies. **Technical:** Hollow grinds CPM-154 stainless and stainless Damascus. **Prices:** $400 to $2000. **Remarks:** Full-time maker. Does business as Rob's Custom Knives. **Mark:** Capital R, Capital H in script.

HUDSON, ROBERT,
3802 Black Cricket Ct, Humble, TX 77396, Phone: 713-454-7207
Specialties: Working straight knives of his design. **Patterns:** Bowies, hunters, skinners, fighters and utility knives. **Technical:** Grinds D2, 440C, 154CM and commercial Damascus. **Prices:** $85 to $350; some to $1500. **Remarks:** Part-time maker; first knife sold in 1980. **Mark:** Full name, hand-made, city and state.

HUGHES, DAN,
301 Grandview Bluff Rd, Spencer, TN 38585, Phone: 931-946-3044
Specialties: Working straight knives to customer specs. **Patterns:** Hunters, fighters, fillet knives. **Technical:** Grinds 440C and ATS-34. **Prices:** $55 to $175; some to $300. **Remarks:** Part-time maker; first knife sold in 1984. **Mark:** Initials.

HUGHES, DARYLE,
10979 Leonard, Nunica, MI 49448, Phone: 616-837-6623, hughes.builders@verizon.net
Specialties: Working knives. **Patterns:** Buckskinners, hunters, camp knives, kitchen and fishing knives. **Technical:** Forges and grinds 52100 and Damascus. **Prices:** $125 to $1000. **Remarks:** Part-time maker; first knife sold in 1979. **Mark:** Name and city in logo.

HUGHES, ED,
280 1/2 Holly Lane, Grand Junction, CO 81503, Phone: 970-243-8547, edhughes26@msn.com
Specialties: Working and art folders. **Patterns:** Buys Damascus. **Technical:** Grinds stainless steels. Engraves. **Prices:** $300 and up. **Remarks:** Full-time maker; first knife sold in 1978. **Mark:** Name or initials.

HUGHES, LAWRENCE,
207 W Crestway, Plainview, TX 79072, Phone: 806-293-5406
Specialties: Working and display knives. **Patterns:** Bowies, daggers, hunters, buckskinners. **Technical:** Grinds D2, 440C and 154CM. **Prices:** $125 to $300; some to $2000. **Remarks:** Full-time maker; first knife sold in 1979. **Mark:** Name with buffalo skull in center.

HULETT, STEVE,
115 Yellowstone Ave, West Yellowstone, MT 59758-0131, Phone: 406-646-4116, Web: www.seldomseenknives.com
Specialties: Classic, working/using knives, straight knives, folders. Your design, custom specs. **Patterns:** Utility/camp knives, hunters, and Liner-Lock folders, lock back pocket knives. **Technical:** Grinds 440C stainless steel, O1 Carbon, 1095. Shop is retail and knife shop; people watch their knives being made. We do everything in house: "all but smelt the ore, or tan the hide." **Prices:** Strarting $250 to $7000. **Remarks:** Full-time maker; first knife sold in 1994. **Mark:** Seldom seen knives/West Yellowstone Montana.

HULL, MICHAEL J,
1330 S Hermits Circle, Cottonwood, AZ 86326, Phone: 928-634-2871, mjwhull@earthlink.net
Specialties: Period pieces and working knives. **Patterns:** Hunters, fighters, Bowies, camp and Mediterranean knives, etc. **Technical:** Grinds 440C, ATS-34 and BG42 and S30V. **Prices:** $125 to $750; some to $1000. **Remarks:** Due to health reasons, I have had to go part time; make knives of my design only and when able. First knife sold in 1983. **Mark:** Name, city, state.

HULSEY, HOYT,
379 Shiloh, Attalla, AL 35954, Phone: 256-538-6765
Specialties: Traditional working straight knives and folders of his design. **Patterns:** Hunters and utility/camp knives. **Technical:** Grinds 440C, ATS-34, O1 and A2. **Prices:** $75 to $250. **Remarks:** Part-time maker; first knife sold in 1989. **Mark:** Hoyt Hulsey Attalla AL.

HUME, DON,
2731 Tramway Circle NE, Albuquerque, NM 87122, Phone: 505-796-9451

HUMENICK, ROY,
PO Box 55, Rescue, CA 95672
Specialties: Multiblade folders. **Patterns:** Original folder and fixed blade designs, also traditional patterns. **Technical:** Grinds premium steels and Damascus. **Prices:** $350 and up; some to $1500. **Remarks:** First knife sold in 1984. **Mark:** Last name in ARC.

HUMPHREY, LON,
83 Wilwood Ave., Newark, OH 43055, Phone: 740-644-1137, ironcrossforge@hotmail.com
Specialties: Hunters, tacticals, and bowie knives. **Prices:** I make knives that start in the $150 range and go up to $1000 for a large bowie. **Remarks:** Has been blacksmithing since age 13 and progressed to the forged blade.

HUMPHREYS, JOEL,
90 Boots Rd, Lake Placid, FL 33852, Phone: 863-773-0439
Specialties: Traditional working/using straight knives and folders of his design and in standard patterns. **Patterns:** Hunters, folders and utility/camp knives. **Technical:** Grinds ATS-34, D2, 440C. All knives have tapered tangs, mitered bolster/handle joints, handles of horn or bone fitted sheaths. **Prices:** $135 to $225; some to $350. **Remarks:** Part-time maker; first knife sold in 1990. Doing business as Sovereign Knives. **Mark:** First name or "H" pierced by arrow.

HUNT, MAURICE,
10510 N CR 650 E, Winter: 2925 Argyle Rd. Venice FL 34293, Brownsburg, IN 46112, Phone: 317-892-2982/Winter: 941-493-4027, mdhuntknives@juno.com
Patterns: Bowies, hunters, fighters. **Prices:** $200 to $800. **Remarks:** Part-time maker. Journeyman Smith.

HUNTER, HYRUM,
285 N 300 W, PO Box 179, Aurora, UT 84620, Phone: 435-529-7244
Specialties: Working straight knives of his design or to customer specs. **Patterns:** Drop and clip, fighters dagger, some folders. **Technical:** Forged from two-piece Damascus. **Prices:** Prices are adjusted according to size, complexity and material used. **Remarks:** Will consider any design you have. Part-time maker; first knife sold in 1990. **Mark:** Initials encircled with first initial and last name and city, then state. Some patterns are numbered.

HUNTER, RICHARD D,
7230 NW 200th Ter, Alachua, FL 32615, Phone: 386-462-3150
Specialties: Traditional working/using knives of his design or customer suggestions; filework. **Patterns:** Folders of various types, Bowies, hunters, daggers. **Technical:** Traditional blacksmith; hand forges high-carbon steel (5160, 1084, 52100) and makes own Damascus; grinds 440C and ATS-34. **Prices:** $200 and up. **Remarks:** Part-time maker; first knife sold in 1992. **Mark:** Last name in capital letters.

HURST, COLE,
1583 Tedford, E. Wenatchee, WA 98802, Phone: 509-884-9206
Specialties: Fantasy, high-art and traditional straight knives. **Patterns:** Bowies, daggers and hunters. **Technical:** Blades are made of stone; handles are made of stone, wood or ivory and embellished with fancy woods, ivory or antlers. **Prices:** $100 to $300; some to $2000. **Remarks:** Spare-time maker; first knife sold in 1985. **Mark:** Name and year.

HURST, JEFF,
PO Box 247, Rutledge, TN 37861, Phone: 865-828-5729, jhurst@esper.com
Specialties: Working straight knives and folders of his design. **Patterns:** Tomahawks, hunters, boots, folders and fighters. **Technical:** Forges W2, O1 and his own Damascus. Makes mokume. **Prices:** $250 to $600. **Remarks:** Full-time maker; first knife sold in 1984. Doing business as Buzzard's Knob Forge. **Mark:** Last name; partnered knives are marked with Newman L. Smith, handle artisan, and SH in script.

HURT, WILLIAM R,
9222 Oak Tree Cir, Frederick, MD 21701, Phone: 301-898-7143
Specialties: Traditional and working/using straight knives. **Patterns:** Bowies, hunters, fighters and utility knives. **Technical:** Forges 5160, O1 and O6; makes own Damascus. Offers silver wire inlay. **Prices:** $200 to $600; some higher. **Remarks:** Full-time maker; first knife sold in 1989. **Mark:** First and middle initials, last name.

HUSIAK, MYRON,
PO Box 238, Altona 3018, Victoria, AUSTRALIA, Phone: 03-315-6752
Specialties: Straight knives and folders of his design or to customer specs. **Patterns:** Hunters, fighters, lock-back folders, skinners and boots. **Technical:** Forges and grinds his own Damascus, 440C and ATS-34. **Prices:** $200 to $900. **Remarks:** Part-time maker; first knife sold in 1974. **Mark:** First initial, last name in logo and serial number.

HUTCHESON, JOHN,
SURSUM KNIFE WORKS, 1237 Brown's Ferry Rd., Chattanooga, TN 37419, Phone: 423-667-6193, sursum5071@aol.com; Web: www.sursumknife.com
Specialties: Straight working knives, hunters. **Patterns:** Customer designs, hunting, speciality working knives. **Technical:** Grinds D2, S7, O1 and 5160, ATS-34 on request. **Prices:** $100 to $300, some to $600. **Remarks:** First knife sold 1985, also produces a mid-tech line. Doing business as Sursum Knife Works. **Mark:** Family crest boar's head over 3 arrows.

HYTOVICK, JOE "HY",
14872 SW 111th St, Dunnellon, FL 34432, Phone: 800-749-5339, Fax: 352-489-3732, hyclassknives@aol.com
  Specialties: Straight, folder and miniature. **Technical:** Blades from Wootz, Damascus and Alloy steel. **Prices:** To $5000. **Mark:** HY.

I

IAMES, GARY,
PO Box 8493, South Lake, Tahoe, CA 96158, Phone: 530-541-2250, iames@charter.net
  Specialties: Working and fancy straight knives and folders. **Patterns:** Bowies, hunters, wedding sets and liner locking folders. **Technical:** Grinds 440C, ATS-34, forges 5160 and 1080, makes Damascus. **Prices:** $300 and up. **Mark:** Initials and last name, city or last name.

IMBODEN II, HOWARD L.,
620 Deauville Dr, Dayton, OH 45429, Phone: 513-439-1536
  Specialties: One-of-a-kind hunting, flint, steel and art knives. **Technical:** Forges and grinds stainless, high-carbon and Damascus. Uses obsidian, cast sterling silver, 14K and 18K gold guards. Carves ivory animals and more. **Prices:** $65 to $25,000. **Remarks:** Full-time maker; first knife sold in 1986. Doing business as Hill Originals. **Mark:** First and last initials, II.

IMEL, BILLY MACE,
1616 Bundy Ave, New Castle, IN 47362, Phone: 765-529-1651
  Specialties: High-art working knives, period pieces and personal cutlery. **Patterns:** Daggers, fighters, hunters; locking folders and slip-joints with interframes. **Technical:** Grinds D2, 440C and 154CM. **Prices:** $300 to $2000; some to $6000. **Remarks:** Part-time maker; first knife sold in 1973. **Mark:** Name in monogram.

IRIE, MICHAEL L,
MIKE IRIE HANDCRAFT, 1606 Auburn Dr., Colorado Springs, CO 80909, Phone: 719-572-5330, mikeirie@aol.com
  Specialties: Working fixed blade knives and handcrafted blades for the do-it-yourselfer. **Patterns:** Twenty standard designs along with custom. **Technical:** Blades are ATS-34, BG-43, 440C with some outside Damascus. **Prices:** Fixed blades $95 and up, blade work $45 and up. **Remarks:** Formerly dba Wood, Irie and Co. with Barry Wood. Full-time maker since 1991. **Mark:** Name.

IRON WOLF FORGE, SEE NELSON KEN,

ISAO, OHBUCHI,
702-1 Nouso Yame-City, Fukuoka, JAPAN, Phone: 0943-23-4439, www.5d.biglobe.ne.jp/~ohisao/

ISGRO, JEFFERY,
1516 First St, West Babylon, NY 11704, Phone: 631-235-1896
  Specialties: File work, glass beading, kydex, leather. **Patterns:** Tactical use knives, skinners, capers, Bowies, camp, hunters. **Technical:** ATS-34, 440C and D2. **Price:** $120 to $600. **Remarks:** Part-time maker. **Mark:** First name, last name, Long Island, NY.

ISHIHARA, HANK,
86-18 Motomachi, Sakura City, Chiba Pref., JAPAN, Phone: 043-485-3208, Fax: 043-485-3208
  Specialties: Fantasy working straight knives and folders of his design. **Patterns:** Boots, Bowies, daggers, fighters, hunters, fishing, locking folders and utility camp knives. **Technical:** Grinds ATS-34, 440C, D2, 440V, CV-134, COS25 and Damascus. Engraves. **Prices:** $250 to $1000; some to $10,000. **Remarks:** Full-time maker; first knife sold in 1987. **Mark:** HANK.

J

JACKS, JIM,
344 S. Hollenbeck Ave, Covina, CA 91723-2513, Phone: 626-331-5665
  Specialties: Working straight knives in standard patterns. **Patterns:** Bowies, hunters, fighters, fishing and camp knives, miniatures. **Technical:** Grinds Stellite 6K, 440C and ATS-34. **Prices:** Start at $100. **Remarks:** Spare-time maker; first knife sold in 1980. **Mark:** Initials in diamond logo.

JACKSON, CHARLTON R,
6811 Leyland Dr, San Antonio, TX 78239, Phone: 210-601-5112

JACKSON, DAVID,
214 Oleander Ave, Lemoore, CA 93245, Phone: 559-925-8547, jnbcrea@lemoorenet.com
  Specialties: Forged steel. **Patterns:** Hunters, camp knives, Bowies. **Prices:** $150 and up. **Mark:** G.D. Jackson - Maker - Lemoore CA.

JACKSON, JIM,
7 Donnington Close, Chapel Row Bucklebury RG7 6PU, ENGLAND, Phone: 011-89-712743, Fax: 011-89-710495, jlandsejackson@aol.com
  Specialties: Large Bowies, concentrating on form and balance; collector quality Damascus daggers. **Patterns:** With fancy filework and engraving available. **Technical:** Forges O1, 5160 and CS70 and 15N20 Damascus. **Prices:** From $1000. **Remarks:** Part-time maker. All knives come with a custom tooled leather swivel sheath of exotic material. **Mark:** Jackson England with in a circle M.S.

JACQUES, ALEX,
16 Tupelo Rd., Wakefield, RI 02879, Phone: 617-771-4441, customrazors@gmail.com Web: www.customrazors.com
  Specialties: Functional, fully custom STRAIGHT RAZORS. **Technical:** Damascus, 01, CPM154, and various other high carbon and stainless steels using the stock removal method. **Prices:** $350 - $1000. **Remarks:** Slowly transitioning to full-time maker; first knife made in 2008. **Mark:** Jack-O-Lantern logo with "A. Jacques" underneath.

JAKSIK JR., MICHAEL,
427 Marschall Creek Rd, Fredericksburg, TX 78624, Phone: 830-997-1119
  Mark: MJ or M. Jaksik.

JARVIS, PAUL M,
30 Chalk St, Cambridge, MA 02139, Phone: 617-547-4355 or 617-666-9090
  Specialties: High-art knives and period pieces of his design. **Patterns:** Japanese and Mid-Eastern knives. **Technical:** Grinds Myer Damascus, ATS-34, D2 and O1. Specializes in height-relief Japanese-style carving. Works with silver, gold and gems. **Prices:** $200 to $17,000. **Remarks:** Part-time maker; first knife sold in 1978.

JEAN, GERRY,
25B Cliffside Dr, Manchester, CT 06040, Phone: 860-649-6449
  Specialties: Historic replicas. **Patterns:** Survival and camp knives. **Technical:** Grinds A2, 440C and 154CM. Handle slabs applied in unique tongue-and-groove method. **Prices:** $125 to $250; some to $1000. **Remarks:** Spare-time maker; first knife sold in 1973. **Mark:** Initials and serial number.

JEFFRIES, ROBERT W,
Route 2 Box 227, Red House, WV 25168, Phone: 304-586-9780, wvknifeman@hotmail.com; Web: www.jeffrieskniveswv.tripod.com
  Specialties: Hunters, Bowies, daggers, lockback folders and LinerLock push buttons. **Patterns:** Skinning types, drop points, typical working hunters, folders one-of-a-kind. **Technical:** Grinds all types of steel. Makes his own Damascus. **Prices:** $125 to $600. Private collector pieces to $3000. **Remarks:** Starting engraving. Custom folders of his design. Part-time maker since 1988. **Mark:** Name etched or on plate pinned to blade.

JENKINS, MITCH,
194 East 500 South, Manti, Utah 84642, mitch.jenkins@gmail.com
  Specialties: Hunters, working knives. **Patterns:** Johnson and Loveless Style. Drop points, skinners and semi-skinners, Capers and utilities. **Technical:** 154CM and ATS-34. Experimenting with S30V and love working with Damascus on occasion. **Prices:** $150 and up. **Remarks:** Slowly transitioning to full-time maker; first knife made in 2008. **Mark:** Jenkins Manti, Utah and M. Jenkins, Utah.

JENSEN, JOHN LEWIS,
JENSEN KNIVES, PO Box 50041, Pasadena, CA 91116, Phone: 323-559-7454, Fax: 626-449-1148, john@jensenknives.com; Web: www.jensenknives.com
  Specialties: Designer and fabricator of modern, original one-of-a-kind, hand crafted, custom ornamental edged weaponry. Combines skill, precision, distinction and the finest materials, geared toward the discriminating art collector. **Patterns:** Folding knives and fixed blades, daggers, fighters and swords. **Technical:** High embellishment, BFA 96 Rhode Island School of Design: jewelry and metalsmithing. Grinds 440C, ATS-34, Damascus. Works with custom made Damascus to his specs. Uses gold, silver, gemstones, pearl, titanium, fossil mastodon and walrus ivories. Carving, file work, soldering, deep etches Damascus, engraving, layers, bevels, blood grooves. Also forges his own Damascus. **Prices:** Start at $10,000. **Remarks:** Available on a first come basis and via commission based on his designs. Knifemakers Guild voting member and ABS apprenticesmith and member of the Society of North American Goldsmiths. **Mark:** Maltese cross/butterfly shield.

JERNIGAN, STEVE,
3082 Tunnel Rd., Milton, FL 32571, Phone: 850-994-0802, Fax: 850-994-0802, jerniganknives@mchsi.com
  Specialties: Investor-class folders and various theme pieces. **Patterns:** Array of models and sizes in side plate locking interframes and conventional liner construction. **Technical:** Grinds ATS-34, CPM-T-440V and Damascus. Inlays mokume (and minerals) in blades and sculpts marble cases. **Prices:** $650 to $1800; some to $6000. **Remarks:** Full-time maker, first knife sold in 1982. **Mark:** Last name.

JOBIN, JACQUES,
46 St Dominique, Levis Quebec, CANADA G6V 2M7, Phone: 418-833-0283, Fax: 418-833-8378
  Specialties: Fancy and working straight knives and folders; miniatures. **Patterns:** Minis, fantasy knives, fighters and some hunters. **Technical:** ATS-34, some Damascus and titanium. Likes native snake wood. Heat-treats. **Prices:** Start at $250. **Remarks:** Full-time maker; first knife sold in 1986. **Mark:** Signature on blade.

JOEHNK, BERND,
Posadowskystrasse 22, 24148 Kiel, GERMANY, Phone: 0431-7297705, Fax: 0431-7297705
  Specialties: One-of-a-kind fancy/embellished and traditional straight knives of his design and from customer drawing. **Patterns:** Daggers, fighters, hunters and letter openers. **Technical:** Grinds and file 440C, ATS-34, powder metal orgical, commercial Damascus and various stainless and corrosion-resistant steels. **Prices:** Upscale. **Remarks:** Likes filework. Leather sheaths. Offers engraving. Part-time maker; first knife sold in1990. Doing business as metal design kiel. All knives made by hand. **Mark:** From 2005 full name and city, with certificate.

JOHANNING CUSTOM KNIVES, TOM,
1735 Apex Rd, Sarasota, FL 34240 9386, Phone: 941-371-2104, Fax: 941-378-9427, Web: www.survivalknives.com
    Specialties: Survival knives. **Prices:** $375 to $775.

JOHANSSON, ANDERS,
Konstvartarevagen 9, S-772 40 Grangesberg, SWEDEN, Phone: 46 240 23204, Fax: +46 21 358778, www.scrimart.u.se
    Specialties: Scandinavian traditional and modern straight knives. **Patterns:** Hunters, fighters and fantasy knives. **Technical:** Grinds stainless steel and makes own Damascus. Prefers water buffalo and mammoth for handle material. **Prices:** Start at $100. **Remarks:** Spare-time maker; first knife sold in 1994. Works together with scrimshander Viveca Sahlin. **Mark:** Stylized initials.

JOHNS, ROB,
1423 S. Second, Enid, OK 73701, Phone: 405-242-2707
    Specialties: Classic and fantasy straight knives of his design or to customer specs; fighters for use at Medieval fairs. **Patterns:** Bowies, daggers and swords. **Technical:** Forges and grinds 440C, D2 and 5160. Handles of nylon, walnut or wire-wrap. **Prices:** $150 to $350; some to $2500. **Remarks:** Full-time maker; first knife sold in 1980. **Mark:** Medieval Customs, initials.

JOHNSON, C E GENE,
1240 Coan Street, Chesterton, IN 46304, Phone: 219-787-8324, ddjlady55@aol.com
    Specialties: Lock-back folders and springers of his design or to customer specs. **Patterns:** Hunters, Bowies, survival lock-back folders. **Technical:** Grinds D2, 440C, A18, O1, Damascus; likes filework. **Prices:** $100 to $2000. **Remarks:** Full-time maker; first knife sold in 1975. **Mark:** Gene.

JOHNSON, DAVID A,
1791 Defeated Creek Rd, Pleasant Shade, TN 37145, Phone: 615-774-3596, artsmith@mwsi.net

JOHNSON, GORDEN W,
5426 Sweetbriar, Houston, TX 77017, Phone: 713-645-8990
    Specialties: Working knives and period pieces. **Patterns:** Hunters, boots and Bowies. **Technical:** Flat-grinds 440C; most knives have narrow tang. **Prices:** $90 to $450. **Remarks:** Full-time maker; first knife sold in 1974. **Mark:** Name, city, state.

JOHNSON, GORDON A.,
981 New Hope Rd, Choudrant, LA 71227, Phone: 318-768-2613
    Specialties: Using straight knives and folders of my design, or customers. Offering filework and hand stitched sheaths. **Patterns:** Hunters, bowies, folders and miniatures. **Technical:** Forges 5160, 1084, 52100 and my own Damascus. Some stock removal on working knives and miniatures. **Prices:** Mid range. **Remarks:** First knife sold in 1990. ABS apprentice smith. **Mark:** Interlocking initials G.J. or G. A. J.

JOHNSON, JERRY,
PO Box 491, Spring City, Utah 84662, Phone: 435-851-3604, Web: sanpetesilver.com
    Specialties: Hunter, fighters, camp. **Patterns:** Multiple. **Prices:** $175 - $200. **Mark:** Jerry E. Johnson Spring City, UT in several fonts.

JOHNSON, JOHN R,
PO Box 246, New Buffalo, PA 17069, Phone: 717-834-6265, jrj@jrjknives.com; Web: www.jrjknives.com
    Specialties: Working hunting and tactical fixed blade sheath knives. **Patterns:** Hunters, tacticals, Bowies, daggers, neck knives and primitives. **Technical:** Flat, convex and hollow grinds. ATS-34, CPM154CM, L6, O1, D2, 5160, 1095 and Damascus. **Prices:** $60 to $700. **Remarks:** Full-time maker, first knife sold in 1996. Doing business as JRJ Knives. Custom sheath made by maker for every knife, **Mark:** Initials connected.

JOHNSON, JOHN R,
5535 Bob Smith Ave, Plant City, FL 33565, Phone: 813-986-4478, rottyjohn@msn.com
    Specialties: Hand forged and stock removal. **Technical:** High tech. Folders. **Mark:** J.R. Johnson Plant City, FL.

JOHNSON, MIKE,
38200 Main Rd, Orient, NY 11957, Phone: 631-323-3509, mjohnsoncustomknives@hotmail.com
    Specialties: Large Bowie knives and cutters, fighters and working knives to customer specs. **Technical:** Forges 5160, O1. **Prices:** $325 to $1200. **Remarks:** Full-time bladesmith. **Mark:** Johnson.

JOHNSON, R B,
Box 11, Clearwater, MN 55320, Phone: 320-558-6128, Fax: 320-558-6128, rbjohnson@mywdo.comorrb@rbjohnsonknives.com; Web: rbjohnsonknives.com
    Specialties: Liner locks with titanium, mosaic Damascus. **Patterns:** LinerLock® folders, skeleton hunters, frontier Bowies. **Technical:** Damascus, mosaic Damascus, A-2, O1, 1095. **Prices:** $200 and up. **Remarks:** Full-time maker since 1973. Not accepting orders. **Mark:** R B Johnson (signature).

JOHNSON, RANDY,
2575 E Canal Dr, Turlock, CA 95380, Phone: 209-632-5401
    Specialties: Folders. **Patterns:** Locking folders. **Technical:** Grinds Damascus. **Prices:** $200 to $400. **Remarks:** Spare-time maker; first knife sold in 1989. Doing business as Puedo Knifeworks. **Mark:** PUEDO.

JOHNSON, RICHARD,
W165 N10196 Wagon Trail, Germantown, WI 53022, Phone: 262-251-5772, rlj@execpc.com; Web: http://www.execpc.com/~rlj/index.html
    Specialties: Custom knives and knife repair.

JOHNSON, RUFFIN,
215 LaFonda Dr, Houston, TX 77060, Phone: 281-448-4407
    Specialties: Working straight knives and folders. **Patterns:** Hunters, fighters and locking folders. **Technical:** Grinds 440C and 154CM; hidden tangs and fancy handles. **Prices:** $450 to $650; some to $1350. **Remarks:** Full-time maker; first knife sold in 1972. **Mark:** Wolf head logo and signature.

JOHNSON, RYAN M,
7320 Foster Hixson Cemetery Rd, Hixson, TN 37343, Phone: 615-842-9323
    Specialties: Working and using straight knives of his design and to customer specs. **Patterns:** Bowies, hunters and utility/camp knives. **Technical:** Forges 5160, Damascus and files. **Prices:** $70 to $400; some to $800. **Remarks:** Full-time maker; first knife sold in 1986. **Mark:** Sledge-hammer with halo.

JOHNSON, STEVEN R,
202 E 200 N, PO Box 5, Manti, UT 84642, Phone: 435-835-7941, Fax: 435-835-7941, srj@mail.manti.com; Web: www.srjknives.com
    Specialties: Investor-class working knives. **Patterns:** Hunters, fighters, boots. **Technical:** Grinds 154-CM, ATS-34, CPM 154-CM. **Prices:** $1,500 to $20,000. **Remarks:** Full-time maker; first knife sold in 1972. Also see SR Johnson forum on www.knifenetwork.com. **Mark:** Registered trademark, including name, city, state, and optional signature mark.

JOHNSTON, DR. ROBT,
PO Box 9887 1 Lomb Mem Dr, Rochester, NY 14623

JOKERST, CHARLES,
9312 Spaulding, Omaha, NE 68134, Phone: 402-571-2536
    Specialties: Working knives in standard patterns. **Patterns:** Hunters, fighters and pocketknives. **Technical:** Grinds 440C, ATS-34. **Prices:** $90 to $170. **Remarks:** Spare-time maker; first knife sold in 1984. **Mark:** Early work marked RCJ; current work marked with last name and city.

JONES, BARRY M AND PHILLIP G,
221 North Ave, Danville, VA 24540, Phone: 804-793-5282
    Specialties: Working and using straight knives and folders of their design and to customer specs; combat and self-defense knives. **Patterns:** Bowies, fighters, daggers, swords, hunters and LinerLock® folders. **Technical:** Grinds 440C, ATS-34 and D2; flat-grinds only. All blades hand polished. **Prices:** $100 to $1000, some higher. **Remarks:** Part-time makers; first knife sold in 1989. **Mark:** Jones Knives, city, state.

JONES, CURTIS J,
210 Springfield Ave, Washington, PA 15301-5244, Phone: 724-225-8829
    Specialties: Big Bowies, daggers, his own style of hunters. **Patterns:** Bowies, daggers, hunters, swords, boots and miniatures. **Technical:** Grinds 440C, ATS-34 and D2. Fitted guards only; does not solder. Heat-treats. Custom sheaths: hand-tooled and stitched. **Prices:** $125 to $1500; some to $3000. **Remarks:** Full-time maker; first knife sold in 1975. Mail orders accepted. **Mark:** Stylized initials on either side of three triangles interconnected.

JONES, ENOCH,
7278 Moss Ln, Warrenton, VA 20187, Phone: 540-341-0292
    Specialties: Fancy working straight knives. **Patterns:** Hunters, fighters, boots and Bowies. **Technical:** Forges and grinds O1, W2, 440C and Damascus. **Prices:** $100 to $350; some to $1000. **Remarks:** Part-time maker; first knife sold in 1982. **Mark:** First name.

JONES, FRANKLIN (FRANK) W,
6030 Old Dominion Rd, Columbus, GA 31909, Phone: 706-563-6051, frankscuba@bellsouth.net
    Specialties: Traditional/working/tactical/period straight knives of his or your design. **Patterns:** Hunters, skinners, utility/camp, Bowies, fighters, kitchen, neck knives, Harley chains. **Technical:** Forges using 5160, O1, 52100, 1084 1095 and Damascus. Also stock removal of stainless steel. **Prices:** $150 to $1000. **Remarks:** Full-time, American Bladesmith Society Journeyman Smith. **Mark:** F.W. Jones, Columbus, GA.

JONES, JACK P.,
17670 Hwy. 2 East, Ripley, MS 38663, Phone: 662-837-3882, jacjones@ripleyealy.net
    Specialties: Working knives in classic design. **Patterns:** Hunters, fighters, and Bowies. **Technical:** Grinds ATS-34, D2, A2, CPM-154 CM. **Prices:** $200 and up. **Remarks:** Full-time maker since retirement in 2005, first knife sold in 1976. **Mark:** J.P. Jones, Ripley, MS.

JONES, JOHN,
62 Sandy Creek Rd, Gympie, Queensland 4570, AUSTRALIA, Phone: 07-54838731, jaj36@bigpond.com
    Specialties: Straight knives, gents folders and folders. **Patterns:** Hunters, Bowies, and art knives. **Technical:** Grinds 440C, AT34, Damasteel. **Prices:** $250 to $2000. **Remarks:** Using knives and collectibles. Prefer natural materials. Full-time maker. **Mark:** Jones in script and year of manufacture.

JONES, JOHN A,
779 SW 131 Hwy, Holden, MO 64040, Phone: 816-850-4318
Specialties: Working, using knives. Hunters, skinners and fighters. **Technical:** Grinds D2, O1, 440C, 1095. Prefers forging; creates own Damascus. File working on most blades. **Prices:** $50 to $500. **Remarks:** Part-time maker; first knife sold in 1996. Doing business as Old John Knives. **Mark:** OLD JOHN and serial number.

JONES, ROGER MUDBONE,
GREENMAN WORKSHOP, 320 Prussia Rd, Waverly, OH 45690, Phone: 740-739-4562, greenmanworkshop@yahoo.com
Specialties: Working in cutlery to suit working woodsman and fine collector. **Patterns:** Bowies, hunters, folders, hatchets in both period and modern style, scale miniatures a specialty. **Technical:** All cutlery hand forged to shape with traditional methods; multiple quench and draws, limited Damascus production hand carves wildlife and historic themes in stag/antler/ivory, full line of functional and high art leather. All work sole authorship. **Prices:** $50 to $5000 **Remarks:** Full-time maker/first knife sold in 1979. **Mark:** Stamped R. Jones hand made or hand engraved sig. W/Bowie knife mark.

JUSTICE, SHANE,
425 South Brooks St, Sheridan, WY 82801, Phone: 307-673-4432, justicecustomknives@yahoo.com
Specialties: Fixed blade working knives. **Patterns:** Hunters, skinners and camp knives. Other designs produced on a limited basis. **Technical:** Hand forged 5160 and 52100. **Remarks:** Part-time maker. Sole author. **Mark:** Last name.

K

K B S, KNIVES,
RSD 181, North Castlemaine, Vic 3450, AUSTRALIA, Phone: 0011 61 3 54 705864, Fax: 0011 61 3 54 706233
Specialties: Bowies, daggers and miniatures. **Patterns:** Art daggers, traditional Bowies, fancy folders and miniatures. **Technical:** Hollow or flat grind, most steels. **Prices:** $200 to $600+. **Remarks:** Full-time maker; first knife sold in 1983. **Mark:** Initials and address in Southern Cross motif.

KACZOR, TOM,
375 Wharncliffe Rd N, Upper London, Ont., CANADA N6G 1E4, Phone: 519-645-7640

KAGAWA, KOICHI,
1556 Horiyamashita, Hatano-Shi, Kanagawa, JAPAN
Specialties: Fancy high-tech straight knives and folders to customer specs. **Patterns:** Hunters, locking folders and slip-joints. **Technical:** Uses 440C and ATS-34. **Prices:** $500 to $2000; some to $20,000. **Remarks:** Part-time maker; first knife sold in 1986. **Mark:** First initial, last name-YOKOHAMA.

KAIN, CHARLES,
KAIN DESIGNS, 38 South Main St, Indianapolis, IN 46227, Phone: 317-781-8556, Fax: 317-781-8521, charles@kaincustomknives.com; Web: www.kaincustomknives.com
Specialties: Unique Damascus art folders. **Patterns:** Any. **Technical:** Specialized & patented mechanisms. **Remarks:** Unique knife & knife mechanism design. **Mark:** Kain and Signet stamp for unique pieces.

KAJIN, AL,
PO Box 1047, 342 South 6th Ave, Forsyth, MT 59327, Phone: 406-346-2442, kajinknives@cablemt.net
Specialties: Utility/working knives, hunters, kitchen cutlery. Produces own Damascus steel from 15N20 and 1084 and cable. Forges 52100, 5160, 1084, 15N20 and O1. Stock removal ATS-34, D2, O1, and L6. Patterns: All types, especially like to work with customer on their designs. Technical: Maker since 1989. ABS member since 1995. Does own differential heat treating, cryogenic soaking when appropriate. Does all leather work. Prices: Stock removal starts at $250. Forged blades and Damascus starts at $300. Kitchen cutlery starts at $100. Remarks: Likes to use exotic woods. Mark: Interlocked AK on forged blades, etched stylized Kajin in outline of Montana on stock removal knives.

KANDA, MICHIO,
7-32-5 Shinzutumi-cho, Shunan-shi, Yamaguchi 7460033, JAPAN, Phone: 0834-62-1910, Fax: 011-81-83462-1910
Specialties: Fantasy knives of his design. **Patterns:** Animal knives. **Technical:** Grinds ATS-34. **Prices:** $300 to $3000. **Remarks:** Full-time maker; first knife sold in 1985. Doing business as Shusui Kanda. **Mark:** Last name inside "M."

KANKI, IWAO,
691-2 Tenjincho, Ono-City, Hyogo, JAPAN 675-1316, Phone: 07948-3-2555, Web: www.chiyozurusadahide.jp
Specialties: Plane, knife. **Prices:** Not determined yet. **Remarks:** Masters of traditional crafts designated by the Minister of International Trade and Industry (Japan). **Mark:** Chiyozuru Sadahide.

KANSEI, MATSUNO,
109-8 Uenomachi Nishikaiden, Gitu-city, JAPAN 501-1168, Phone: 81-58-234-8643
Specialties: Folders of original design. **Patterns:** LinerLock® folder. **Technical:** Grinds VG-10, Damascus. **Prices:** $350 to $2000. **Remarks:** Full-time maker. First knife sold in 1993. **Mark:** Name.

KANTER, MICHAEL,
ADAM MICHAEL KNIVES, 14550 West Honey Ln., New Berlin, WI 53151, Phone: 262-860-1136, mike@adammichaelknives.com; Web: www.adammichaelknives.com
Specialties: Fixed blades and folders. **Patterns:** Drop point hunters, Bowies and fighters. **Technical:** Jerry Rados Damascus, BG42, CPM, S60V and S30V. **Prices:** $375 and up. **Remarks:** Ivory, mammoth ivory, stabilized woods, and pearl handles. **Mark:** Engraved Adam Michael.

KARP, BOB,
PO Box 47304, Phoenix, AZ 85068, Phone: 602 870-1234
602 870-1234, Fax: 602-331-0283
Remarks: Bob Karp "Master of the Blade."

KATO, SHINICHI,
Rainbow Amalke 402, Ohoragnchi, Nakashidami, Moriyama-ku Nagoya, JAPAN 463-0002, Phone: 81-52-736-6032, skato-402@u0l.gate01.com
Specialties: Flat grind and hand finish. **Patterns:** Bowie, fighter. Hunting and folding knives. **Technical:** Hand forged,flat grind. **Prices:** $100 to $2000. **Remarks:** Part-time maker. **Mark:** Name.

KATSUMARO, SHISHIDO,
2-6-11 Kamiseno Aki-ku, Hiroshima, JAPAN, Phone: 090-3634-9054, Fax: 082-227-4438, shishido@d8.dion.ne.jp

KAUFFMAN, DAVE,
4 Clark Creek Loop, Montana City, MT 59634, Phone: 406-442-9328
Specialties: Field grade and exhibition grade hunting knives and ultra light folders. **Patterns:** Fighters, Bowies and drop-point hunters. **Technical:** S30V and SS Damascus. **Prices:** $155 to $1200. **Remarks:** Full-time maker; first knife sold in 1989. On the cover of *Knives '94*. **Mark:** First and last name, city and state.

KAWASAKI, AKIHISA,
11-8-9 Chome Minamiamachi, Suzurandai Kita-Ku, Kobe, JAPAN, Phone: 078-593-0418, Fax: 078-593-0418
Specialties: Working/using knives of his design. **Patterns:** Hunters, kit knives. **Technical:** Forges and grinds Molybdenum Panadium. Grinds ATS-34 and stainless steel. Uses Chinese Quince wood, desert ironwood and cow leather. **Prices:** $300 to $800; some to $1000. **Remarks:** Full-time maker. **Mark:** A.K.

KAY, J WALLACE,
332 Slab Bridge Rd, Liberty, SC 29657

KAZSUK, DAVID,
PO Box 39, Perris, CA 92572-0039, Phone: 909-780-2288, ddkaz@hotmail.com
Specialties: Hand forged. **Prices:** $150+. **Mark:** Last name.

KEARNEY, JAROD,
10 Park St Hamlet, Bordentown, NJ 08505, Phone: 336-656-4617, jarodk@mindspring.com; Web: www.jarodsworkshop.com

KEESLAR, JOSEPH F,
391 Radio Rd, Almo, KY 42020, Phone: 270-753-7919, Fax: 270-753-7919, sjkees@apex.net
Specialties: Classic and contemporary Bowies, combat, hunters, daggers and folders. **Patterns:** Decorative filework, engraving and custom leather sheaths available. **Technical:** Forges 5160, 52100 and his own Damascus steel. **Prices:** $300 to $3000. **Remarks:** Full-time maker; first knife sold in 1976. ABS Master Smith. **Mark:** First and middle initials, last name in hammer, knife and anvil logo, M.S.

KEESLAR, STEVEN C,
115 Lane 216 Hamilton Lake, Hamilton, IN 46742, Phone: 260-488-3161, sskeeslar@hotmail.com
Specialties: Traditional working/using straight knives of his design and to customer specs. **Patterns:** Bowies, hunters, utility/camp knives. **Technical:** Forges 5160, files 52100 Damascus. **Prices:** $100 to $600; some to $1500. **Remarks:** Part-time maker; first knife sold in 1976. ABS member. **Mark:** Fox head in flames over Steven C. Keeslar.

KEETON, WILLIAM L,
6095 Rehobeth Rd SE, Laconia, IN 47135-9550, Phone: 812-969-2836, wlkeeton@hughes.net; Web: www.keetoncustomknives.com
Specialties: Plain and fancy working knives. **Patterns:** Hunters and fighters; locking folders and slip-joints. Names patterns after Kentucky Derby winners. **Technical:** Grinds any of the popular alloy steels. **Prices:** $175 to $4000. **Remarks:** Full-time maker; first knife sold in 1971. **Mark:** Logo of key.

KEHIAYAN, ALFREDO,
Cuzco 1455 Ing. Maschwitz, CP B1623GXU Buenos Aires, ARGENTINA, Phone: 54-03488-442212, Fax: 54-077-75-4493-5359, alfredo@kehiayan.com.ar; Web: www.kehiayan.com.ar
Specialties: Functional straight knives. **Patterns:** Utility knives, skinners, hunters and boots. **Technical:** Forges and grinds SAE 52.100, SAE 6180, SAE 9260, SAE 5160, 440C and ATS-34, titanium with nitride. All blades mirror-polished; makes leather sheath and wood cases. **Prices:** $70 to $800; some to $6000. **Remarks:** Full-time maker; first knife sold in 1983. Some knives are satin finish (utility knives). **Mark:** Name.

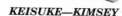

KEISUKE, GOTOH,
105 Cosumo-City, Otozu 202 Ohita-city, Ohita, JAPAN, Phone: 097-523-0750, k-u-an@ki.rim.or.jp

KELLER, BILL,
12211 Las Nubes, San Antonio, TX 78233, Phone: 210-653-6609
Specialties: Primarily folders, some fixed blades. **Patterns:** Autos, liner locks and hunters. **Technical:** Grinds stainless and Damascus. **Prices:** $400 to $1000, some to $4000. **Remarks:** Part-time maker, first knife sold 1995. **Mark:** Last name inside outline of Alamo.

KELLEY, GARY,
17485 SW Pheasant Lane, Aloha, OR 97006, Phone: 503-649-7867, garykelley@theblademaker.com; Web: wwwtheblademaker.com
Specialties: Primitive knives and blades. **Patterns:** Fur trade era rifleman's knives, fur trade, cowboy action, hunting knives. **Technical:** Hand-forges and precision investment casts. **Prices:** $35 to $125. **Remarks:** Family business. Doing business as The Blademaker. **Mark:** Fir tree logo.

KELLY, DAVE,
865 S. Shenandoah St., Los Angeles, CA 90035, Phone: 310-657-7121, dakcon@sbcglobal.net
Specialties: Collector and user one-of-a-kind (his design) fixed blades, liner lock folders, and leather sheaths. **Patterns:** Utility and hunting fixed blade knives with hand-sewn leather sheaths, Gentleman liner lock folders. **Technical:** Grinds carbon steels, hollow, convex, and flat. Offers clay differentially hardened blades, etched and polished. Uses Sambar stag, mammoth ivory, and high-grade burl woods. Hand-sewn leather sheaths for fixed blades and leather pouch sheaths for folders. **Prices:** $250 to $750, some higher. **Remarks:** Full-time maker, first knife made in 2003. **Mark:** First initial, last name with large K.

KELLY, STEVEN,
11407 Spotted Fawn Ln., Bigfork, MT 59911, Phone: 406-837-1489, www.skknives.com
Technical: Damascus from 1084 or 1080 and 15n20. 52100.

KELSEY, NATE,
3401 Cherry St, Anchorage, AK 99504, Phone: 907-360-4469, edgealaska@mac.com; Web: www.edgealaska.com
Specialties: Hand forges or stock removal traditional working knives of own or customer design. Forges own Damascus, makes custom leather sheaths, does fine engraving and scrimshaw. **Technical:** Forges 52100, 1084/15N20, 5160. Grinds ATS-34, 154CM. Prefers natural handle materials. **Prices:** $300 to $1500. **Remarks:** Part-time maker since 1990. Member ABS, Arkansas Knifemakers Assoc. **Mark:** Name and city.

KELSO, JIM,
577 Collar Hill Rd, Worcester, VT 05682, Phone: 802-229-4254, Fax: 802-229-0595, kelsonmaker@gmail.com; Web:www.jimkelso.com
Specialties: Fancy high-art straight knives and folders that mix Eastern and Western influences. Only uses own designs. **Patterns:** Daggers, swords and locking folders. **Technical:** Grinds only custom Damascus. Works with top Damascus bladesmiths. **Prices:** $6000 to $20,000. **Remarks:** Full-time maker; first knife sold in 1980. **Mark:** Stylized initials.

KEMP, LAWRENCE,
8503 Water Tower Rd, Ooletwah, TN 37363, Phone: 423-344-2357, larry@kempknives.com Web: www.kempknives.com
Specialties: Bowies, hunters and working knives. **Patterns:** Bowies, camp knives, hunters and skinners. **Technical:** Forges carbon steel, and his own Damascus. **Prices:** $250 to $1500. **Remarks:** Part-time maker, first knife sold in 1991. ABS Journeyman Smith. **Mark:** L.A. Kemp.

KENNEDY JR., BILL,
PO Box 850431, Yukon, OK 73085, Phone: 405-354-9150
Specialties: Working straight knives. **Patterns:** Hunters, fighters, minis and fishing knives. **Technical:** Grinds D2, 440C, ATS-34, BG42. **Prices:** $110 and up. **Remarks:** Part-time maker; first knife sold in 1980. **Mark:** Last name and year made.

KERANEN, PAUL,
16 Duncan St., P.O. Box 261, Ahmeek, MI 49901, Phone: 906-337-0774, pkknives@gmail.com
Specialties: Specializes in Japanese style knives and swords. Most clay tempered with hamon. **Patterns:** Does bowies, fighters and hunters. **Technical:** Forges and grinds carbons steel only. Make my own Damascus. **Prices:** $75 to $800. **Mark:** PK etched.

KERN, R W,
20824 Texas Trail W, San Antonio, TX 78257-1602, Phone: 210-698-2549, rkern@ev1.net
Specialties: Damascus, straight and folders. **Patterns:** Hunters, Bowies and folders. **Technical:** Grinds ATS-34, 440C and BG42. Forges own Damascus. **Prices:** $200 and up. **Remarks:** First knives 1980; retired; work as time permits. Member ABS, Texas Knifemaker and Collectors Association. **Mark:** Outline of Alamo with kern over outline.

KEYES, DAN,
6688 King St, Chino, CA 91710, Phone: 909-628-8329

KEYES, GEOFF P.,
13027 Odell Rd NE, Duvall, WA 98019, Phone: 425-844-0758, 5ef@polarisfarm.com; Web: www5elementsforge.com
Specialties: Working grade fixed blades, 19th century style gents knives. **Patterns:** Fixed blades, your design or mine. **Technical:** Hnad-forged 5160, 1084, and own designs. **Prices:** $200 and up. **Remarks:** Geoff Keyes DBA 5 Elements Forge, ABS Journeyman Smith. **Mark:** Early mark KEYES etched in script. New mark as of 2009: pressed GPKeyes.

KHALSA, JOT SINGH,
368 Village St, Millis, MA 02054, Phone: 508-376-8162, Fax: 508-532-0517, jotkhalsa@comcast.net; Web: www.khalsakirpans.com, www.lifeknives.com, and www.thekhalsaraj.com
Specialties: Liner locks, one-of-a-kind daggers, swords, and kirpans (Sikh daggers) all original designs. **Technical:** Forges own Damascus, uses others high quality Damascus including stainless, and grinds stainless steels. Uses natural handle materials frequently unusual minerals. Pieces are frequently engraved and more recently carved. **Prices:** Start at $700.

KHARLAMOV, YURI,
Oboronnay 46, 2, Tula, 300007, RUSSIA
Specialties: Classic, fancy and traditional knives of his design. **Patterns:** Daggers and hunters. **Technical:** Forges only Damascus with nickel. Uses natural handle materials; engraves on metal, carves on nut-tree; silver and pearl inlays. **Prices:** $600 to $2380; some to $4000. **Remarks:** Full-time maker; first knife sold in 1988. **Mark:** Initials.

KI, SHIVA,
5222 Ritterman Ave, Baton Rouge, LA 70805, Phone: 225-356-7274, shivakicustomknives@netzero.net; Web: www.shivakicustomknives.com
Specialties: Working straight knives and folders. **Patterns:** Emphasis on personal defense knives, martial arts weapons. **Technical:** Forges and grinds; makes own Damascus; prefers natural handle materials. **Prices:** $135 to $850; some to $1800. **Remarks:** Full-time maker; first knife sold in 1981. **Mark:** Name with logo.

KIEFER, TONY,
112 Chateaugay Dr, Pataskala, OH 43062, Phone: 740-927-6910
Specialties: Traditional working and using straight knives in standard patterns. **Patterns:** Bowies, fighters and hunters. **Technical:** Grinds 440C and D2; forges D2. Flat-grinds Bowies; hollow-grinds drop-point and trailing-point hunters. **Prices:** $110 to $300; some to $200. **Remarks:** Spare-time maker; first knife sold in 1988. **Mark:** Last name.

KILBY, KEITH,
1902 29th St, Cody, WY 82414, Phone: 307-587-2732
Specialties: Works with all designs. **Patterns:** Mostly Bowies, camp knives and hunters of his design. **Technical:** Forges 52100, 5160, 1095, Damascus and mosaic Damascus. **Prices:** $250 to $3500. **Remarks:** Part-time maker; first knife sold in 1974. Doing business as Foxwood Forge. **Mark:** Name.

KILEY, MIKE AND JANDY,
ROCKING K KNIVES, 1325 Florida, Chino Valley, AZ 86323, Phone: 928-910-2647
Specialties: Period knives for cowboy action shooters and mountain men. **Patterns:** Bowies, drop-point hunters, skinners, sheepsfoot blades and spear points. **Technical:** Steels are 1095, 0-1, Damascus and others upon request. Handles include all types of wood, with cocobolo, ironwood, rosewood, maple and bacote being favorites as well as buffalo horn, stag, elk antler, mammoth ivory, giraffe bone, sheep horn and camel bone. **Prices:** $100 to $500 depending on style and materials. Hand-tooled leather sheaths by Jan and Mike. **Mark:** Stylized K on one side; Kiley on the other.

KILPATRICK, CHRISTIAN A,
6925 Mitchell Ct, Citrus Hieghts, CA 95610, Phone: 916-729-0733, crimsonkil@gmail.com; Web:www.crimsonknives.com
Specialties: All forged weapons (no firearms) from ancient to modern. All blades produced are first and foremost useable tools, and secondly but no less importantly, artistic expressions. **Patterns:** Hunters, bowies, daggers, swords, axes, spears, boot knives, bird knives, ethnic blades and historical reproductions. Customer designs welcome. **Technical:** Forges and grinds, makes own Damascus. Does file work. **Prices:** $125 to $3200. **Remarks:** 26 year part time maker. First knife sold in 2002.

KIMBERLEY, RICHARD L.,
86-B Arroyo Hondo Rd, Santa Fe, NM 87508, Phone: 505-820-2727
Specialties: Fixed-blade and period knives. **Technical:** O1, 52100, 9260 steels. **Remarks:** Member ABS. Marketed under "Kimberleys of Santa Fe." **Mark:** "By D. KIMBERLEY SANTA FE NM."

KIMSEY, KEVIN,
198 Cass White Rd. NW, Cartersville, GA 30121, Phone: 770-387-0779 and 770-655-8879
Specialties: Tactical fixed blades and folders. **Patterns:** Fighters, folders, hunters and utility knives. **Technical:** Grinds 440C, ATS-34 and D2 carbon. **Prices:** $100 to $400; some to $600. **Remarks:** Three-time *Blade* magazine award winner, knifemaker since 1983. **Mark:** Rafter and stylized KK.

KING, BILL,
14830 Shaw Rd, Tampa, FL 33625, Phone: 813-961-3455
Specialties: Folders, lockbacks, liner locks, automatics and stud openers. **Patterns:** Wide varieties; folders. **Technical:** ATS-34 and some Damascus; single and double grinds. Offers filework and jewel embellishment; nickel-silver Damascus and mokume bolsters. **Prices:** $150 to $475; some to $850. **Remarks:** Full-time maker; first knife sold in 1976. All titanium fitting on liner-locks; screw or rivet construction on lock-backs. **Mark:** Last name in crown.

KING, FRED,
430 Grassdale Rd, Cartersville, GA 30120, Phone: 770-382-8478, Web: http://www.fking83264@aol.com
Specialties: Fancy and embellished working straight knives and folders. **Patterns:** Hunters, Bowies and fighters. **Technical:** Grinds ATS-34 and D2; forges 5160 and Damascus. Offers filework. **Prices:** $100 to $3500. **Remarks:** Spare-time maker; first knife sold in 1984. **Mark:** Kings Edge.

KING, JASON M,
5170 Rockenham Rd, St. George, KS 66423, Phone: 785-494-8377, Web: www.jasonmkingknives.com
Specialties: Working and using straight knives of his design and some-times to customer specs. Some slip joint and lockback folders. **Patterns:** Hunters, Bowies, tacticals, fighters; some miniatures. **Technical:** Grinds D2, 440C and other Damascus. **Prices:** $75 to $200; some up to $500. **Remarks:** First knife sold in 1998. Likes to use height quality stabilized wood. **Mark:** JMK.

KING JR., HARVEY G,
32170 Hwy K4, Alta Vista, KS 66834, Phone: 785-499-5207, Web: www.harveykingknives.com
Specialties: Traditional working and using straight knives of his design and to customer specs. **Patterns:** Hunters, Bowies and fillet knives. **Technical:** Grinds O1, A2 and D2. Prefers natural handle materials; offers leatherwork. **Prices:** Start at $100. **Remarks:** Part-time maker; first knife sold in 1988. **Mark:** Name, city, state, and serial number.

KINKER, MIKE,
8755 E County Rd 50 N, Greensburg, IN 47240, Phone: 812-663-5277, Fax: 812-662-8131, mokinker@hsonline.net
Specialties: Working/using knives, straight knives. Starting to make fold-ers. Your design. **Patterns:** Boots, daggers, hunters, skinners, hatchets. **Technical:** Grind 440C and ATS-34, others if required. Damascus, dovetail bolsters, jeweled blade. **Prices:** $125 to 375; some to $1000. **Remarks:** Part-time maker; first knife sold in 1991. Doing business as Kinker Knives. **Mark:** Kinker and Kinker plus year.

KINNIKIN, TODD,
EUREKA FORGE, 7 Capper Dr., Pacific, MO 63069-3603, Phone: 314-938-6248
Specialties: Mosaic Damascus. **Patterns:** Hunters, fighters, folders and automatics. **Technical:** Forges own mosaic Damascus with tool steel Da-mascus edge. Prefers natural, fossil and artifact handle materials. **Prices:** $400 to $2400. **Remarks:** Full-time maker; first knife sold in 1994. **Mark:** Initials connected.

KIOUS, JOE,
1015 Ridge Pointe Rd, Kerrville, TX 78028, Phone: 830-367-2277, kious@hctc.net
Specialties: Investment-quality interframe and bolstered folders. **Patterns:** Folder specialist, all types. **Technical:** Both stainless and non-stainless Damascus. **Prices:** $1300 to $5000; some to $10,000. **Remarks:** Full-time maker; first knife sold in 1969. **Mark:** Last name, city and state or last name only.

KIRK, RAY,
PO Box 1445, Tahlequah, OK 74465, Phone: 918-456-1519, ray@rakerknives.com; Web: www.rakerknives.com
Specialties: Folders, skinners fighters, and Bowies. **Patterns:** Neck knives and small hunters and skinners. **Technical:** Forges all knives from 52100 and own Damascus. **Prices:** $65 to $3000. **Remarks:** Started forging in 1989; makes own Damascus. Does custom steel rolling. Has some 52100 and Damascus in custom flat bar 52100 for sale **Mark:** Stamped "Raker" on blade.

KITSMILLER, JERRY,
67277 Las Vegas Dr, Montrose, CO 81401, Phone: 970-249-4290
Specialties: Working straight knives in standard patterns. **Patterns:** Hunt-ers, boots. **Technical:** Grinds ATS-34 and 440C only. **Prices:** $75 to $200; some to $300. **Remarks:** Spare-time maker; first knife sold in 1984. **Mark:** JandS Knives.

KLAASEE, TINUS,
PO Box 10221, George 6530, SOUTH AFRICA
Specialties: Hunters, skinners and utility knives. **Patterns:** Uses own de-signs and client specs. **Technical:** N690 stainless steel 440C Damascus. **Prices:** $700 and up. **Remarks:** Use only indigenous materials. Hardwood, horns and ivory. Makes his own sheaths and boxes. **Mark:** Initials and sur name over warthog.

KNAPP, MARK,
Mark Knapp Custom Knives, 1971 Fox Ave, Fairbanks, AK 99701, Phone: 907-452-7477, info@markknappcustomknives.com; Web: www.markknappcustomknives.com
Specialties: Mosaic handles of exotic natural materials from Alaska and around the world. Folders, fixed blades, full and hidden tangs. **Patterns:** Folders, hunters, skinners, and camp knives. **Technical:** Forges own Damascus, uses both forging and stock removal with ATS-34, 154CM, stainless Damascus, carbon steel and carbon Damascus. **Prices:** $800-$3000. **Remarks:** Full time maker, sold first knife in 2000. **Mark:** Mark Knapp Custom Knives Fairbanks, AK.

KNICKMEYER, HANK,
6300 Crosscreek, Cedar Hill, MO 63016, Phone: 314-285-3210
Specialties: Complex mosaic Damascus constructions. **Patterns:** Fixed blades, swords, folders and automatics. **Technical:** Mosaic Damascus with all tool steel Damascus edges. **Prices:** $500 to $2000; some $3000 and higher. **Remarks:** Part-time maker; first knife sold in 1989. Doing business as Dutch Creek Forge and Foundry. **Mark:** Initials connected.

KNICKMEYER, KURT,
6344 Crosscreek, Cedar Hill, MO 63016, Phone: 314-274-0481

KNIGHT, JASON,
110 Paradise Pond Ln, Harleyville, SC 29448, Phone: 843-452-1163, jasonknightknives.com
Specialties: Bowies. **Patterns:** Bowies and anything from history or his own design. **Technical:** 1084, 5160, O1, 52102, Damascus/forged blades. **Prices:** $200 and up. **Remarks:** Bladesmith. **Mark:** KNIGHT.

KNIPSCHIELD, TERRY,
808 12th Ave NE, Rochester, MN 55906, Phone: 507-288-7829, terry@knipknives.com; Web: www.knipknives.com
Specialties: Folders and fixed blades and woodcarving knives. **Patterns:** Variations of traditional patterns and his own new designs. **Technical:** Stock removal. Grinds CPM-154CM, ATS-34, stainless Damascus, 01.**Prices:** $60 to $1200 and higher for upscale folders. **Mark:** Etchd logo on blade, KNIP with shield image.

KNIPSTEIN, R C (JOE),
731 N Fielder, Arlington, TX 76012, Phone: 817-265-0573;817-265-2021, Fax: 817-265-3410
Specialties: Traditional pattern folders along with custom designs. **Patterns:** Hunters, Bowies, folders, fighters, utility knives. **Technical:** Grinds 440C, D2, 154CM and ATS-34. Natural handle materials and full tangs are standard. **Prices:** Start at $300. **Remarks:** Part-time maker; first knife sold in 1989. **Mark:** Last name.

KNOTT, STEVE,
KNOTT KNIVES, 203 Wild Rose, Guyton, GA 31312, Phone: 912-772-7655
Technical: Uses ATS-34/440C and some commercial Damascus, single and double grinds with mirror or satin finishes. **Patters:** Hunters, boot knives, Bowies, and tantos, slip joint and lock-back folders. Uses a wide variety of handle materials to include ironwood, coca-bola and colored sta-bilized wood, also horn, bone and ivory upon customer request. **Remarks:** First knife sold in 1991. Part-time maker.

KNUTH, JOSEPH E,
3307 Lookout Dr, Rockford, IL 61109, Phone: 815-874-9597
Specialties: High-art working straight knives of his design or to customer specs. **Patterns:** Daggers, fighters and swords. **Technical:** Grinds 440C, ATS-34 and D2. **Prices:** $150 to $1500; some to $15,000. **Remarks:** Full-time maker; first knife sold in 1989. **Mark:** Initials on bolster face.

KOHLS, JERRY,
N4725 Oak Rd, Princeton, WI 54968, Phone: 920-295-3648
Specialties: Working knives and period pieces. **Patterns:** Hunters-boots and Bowies, your designs or his. **Technical:** Grinds, ATS-34 440c 154CM and 1095 and commercial Damascus. **Remarks:** Part-time maker. **Mark:** Last name.

KOJETIN, W,
20 Bapaume Rd Delville, Germiston 1401, SOUTH AFRICA, Phone: 27118733305/mobile 27836256208
Specialties: High-art and working straight knives of all designs. **Patterns:** Daggers, hunters and his own Man hunter Bowie. **Technical:** Grinds D2 and ATS-34; forges and grinds 440B/C. Offers "wrap-around" pava and abalone handles, scrolled wood or ivory, stacked filework and setting of faceted semi-precious stones. **Prices:** $185 to $600; some to $11,000. **Remarks:** Spare-time maker; first knife sold in 1962. **Mark:** Billy K.

KOLITZ, ROBERT,
W9342 Canary Rd, Beaver Dam, WI 53916, Phone: 920-887-1287
Specialties: Working straight knives to customer specs. **Patterns:** Bowies, hunters, bird and trout knives, boots. **Technical:** Grinds O1, 440C; com-mercial Damascus. **Prices:** $50 to $100; some to $500. **Remarks:** Spare-time maker; first knife sold in 1979. **Mark:** Last initial.

KOMMER, RUSS,
4609 35th Ave N, Fargo, NC 58102, Phone: 907-346-3339
Specialties: Working straight knives with the outdoorsman in mind. **Patterns:** Hunters, semi-skinners, fighters, folders and utility knives, art knives. **Technical:** Hollow-grinds ATS-34, 440C and 440V. **Prices:** $125 to $850; some to $3000. **Remarks:** Full-time maker; first knife sold in 1995. **Mark:** Bear paw—full name, city and state or full name and state.

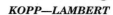

KOPP, TODD M,
PO Box 3474, Apache Jct., AZ 85217, Phone: 480-983-6143, tmkopp@msn.com
Specialties: Classic and traditional straight knives. Fluted handled daggers. **Patterns:** Bowies, boots, daggers, fighters, hunters, swords and folders. **Technical:** Grinds 5160, 440C, ATS-34. All Damascus steels, or customers choice. Some engraving and filework. **Prices:** $200 to $1200; some to $4000. **Remarks:** Part-time maker; first knife sold in 1989. **Mark:** Last name in Old English, some others name, city and state.

KOSTER, STEVEN C,
16261 Gentry Ln, Huntington Beach, CA 92647, Phone: 714-840-8621, hbkosters@verizon.net
Specialties: Bowies, daggers, skinners, camp knives. **Technical:** Use 5160, 52100, 1084, 1095 steels. **Prices:** $200 to $1000. **Remarks:** Wood and leather sheaths with silver furniture. ABS Journeyman 2003. **Mark:** Koster squeezed between lines.

KOVACIK, ROBERT,
Erenburgova 23, 98401 Lucenec, SLOVAKIA, Phone: 00421474332566 Mobil:00421470907644800, Fax: 00421470907644800, robert.kovacik@post.sk Web: www.robertkovacik.com
Specialties: Engraved hunting knives, guns engraved; Knifemakers. **Technical:** Fixed blades, folder knives, miniatures. **Prices:** $350 to $20,000 U.S. **Mark:** R.

KOVAR, EUGENE,
2626 W 98th St., Evergreen Park, IL 60642, Phone: 708-636-3724/708-790-4115, baldemaster333@aol.com
Specialties: One-of-a-kind miniature knives only. **Patterns:** Fancy to fantasy miniature knives; knife pendants and tie tacks. **Technical:** Files and grinds nails, nickel-silver and sterling silver. **Prices:** $5 to $35; some to $100. **Mark:** GK.

KOYAMA, CAPTAIN BUNSHICHI,
3-23 Shirako-cho, Nakamura-ku, Nagoya City 453-0817, JAPAN, Phone: 052-461-7070, Fax: 052-461-7070
Specialties: Innovative folding knife. **Patterns:** General purpose one hand. **Technical:** Grinds ATS-34 and Damascus. **Prices:** $400 to $900; some to $1500. **Remarks:** Part-time maker; first knife sold in 1994. **Mark:** Captain B. Koyama and the shoulder straps of CAPTAIN.

KRAFT, STEVE,
408 NE 11th St, Abilene, KS 67410, Phone: 785-263-1411
Specialties: Folders, lockbacks, scale release auto, push button auto. **Patterns:** Hunters, boot knives and fighters. **Technical:** Grinds ATS-34, Damascus; uses titanium, pearl, ivory etc. **Prices:** $500 to $2500. **Remarks:** Part-time maker; first knife sold in 1984. **Mark:** Kraft.

KRAPP, DENNY,
1826 Windsor Oak Dr, Apopka, FL 32703, Phone: 407-880-7115
Specialties: Fantasy and working straight knives of his design. **Patterns:** Hunters, fighters and utility/camp knives. **Technical:** Grinds ATS-34 and 440C. **Prices:** $85 to $300; some to $800. **Remarks:** Spare-time maker; first knife sold in 1988. **Mark:** Last name.

KRAUSE, ROY W,
22412 Corteville, St. Clair Shores, MI 48081, Phone: 810-296-3995, Fax: 810-296-2663
Specialties: Military and law enforcement/Japanese-style knives and swords. **Patterns:** Combat and back-up, Bowies, fighters, boot knives, daggers, tantos, wakazashis and katanas. **Technical:** Grinds ATS-34, A2, D2, 1045, O1 and commercial Damascus; differentially hardened Japanese-style blades. **Prices:** Moderate to upscale. **Remarks:** Full-time maker. **Mark:** Last name on traditional knives; initials in Japanese characters on Japanese-style knives.

KREGER, THOMAS,
1996 Dry Branch Rd., Lugoff, SC 29078, Phone: 803-438-4221, tdkreger@bellsouth.net
Specialties: South Carolina/George Herron style working/using knives. Customer designs considered. **Patterns:** Hunters, skinners, fillet, liner lock folders, kitchen, and camp knives. **Technical:** Hollow and flat grinds of ATS-34, CPM154CM, and 5160. **Prices:** $100 and up. **Remarks:** Full-time maker. President of the South Carolina Association of Knifemakers 2002-06. **Mark:** TDKreger.

KREH, LEFTY,
210 Wichersham Way, "Cockeysville", MD 21030

KREIBICH, DONALD L.,
1638 Commonwealth Circle, Reno, NV 89503, Phone: 775-746-0533, dmkreno@sbcglobal.net
Specialties: Working straight knives in standard patterns. **Patterns:** Bowies, boots and daggers; camp and fishing knives. **Technical:** Grinds 440C, 154CM and ATS-34; likes integrals. **Prices:** $100 to $200; some to $500. **Remarks:** Part-time maker; first knife sold in 1980. **Mark:** First and middle initials, last name.

KRESSLER, D F,
Mittelweg 31 i, D-28832 Achim, GERMANY, Phone: 49-4202765742, Fax: 49-042 02/7657 41, info@kresslerknives.com; Web: www.kresslerknives.com
Specialties: High-tech integral and interframe knives. **Patterns:** Hunters, fighters, daggers. **Technical:** Grinds new state-of-the-art steels; prefers natural handle materials. **Prices:** Upscale. **Mark:** Name in logo.

KRETSINGER JR., PHILIP W,
17536 Bakersville Rd, Boonsboro, MD 21713, Phone: 301-432-6771
Specialties: Fancy and traditional period pieces. **Patterns:** Hunters, Bowies, camp knives, daggers, carvers, fighters. **Technical:** Forges W2, 5160 and his own Damascus. **Prices:** Start at $200. **Remarks:** Full-time knifemaker. **Mark:** Name.

KUBASEK, JOHN A,
74 Northhampton St, Easthampton, MA 01027, Phone: 413-527-7917, jaknife01@verizon.net
Specialties: Left- and right-handed LinerLock® folders of his design or to customer specs. Also new knives made with Ripcord patent. **Patterns:** Fighters, tantos, drop points, survival knives, neck knives and belt buckle knives. **Technical:** Grinds 154CM, S30 and Damascus. **Prices:** $395 to $1500. **Remarks:** Part-time maker; first knife sold in 1985. **Mark:** Name and address etched.

KUKULKA, WOLFGANG,
Dubai, United Arab Emirates, wolfgang.kukulka@hotmail.com
Specialties: Fully handmade from various steels: Damascus Steel, Japanese Steel, 1.2842, 1.2379, K110, K360, M390 microclean **Patterns:** Handles made from stabilized wood, different hard woods, horn and various materials **Technical:** <BNHardness of blades: 58-67 HRC.

L

LADD, JIM S,
1120 Helen, Deer Park, TX 77536, Phone: 713-479-7286
Specialties: Working knives and period pieces. **Patterns:** Hunters, boots and Bowies plus other straight knives. **Technical:** Grinds D2, 440C and 154CM. **Prices:** $125 to $225; some to $550. **Remarks:** Part-time maker; first knife sold in 1965. Doing business as The Tinker. **Mark:** First and middle initials, last name.

LADD, JIMMIE LEE,
1120 Helen, Deer Park, TX 77536, Phone: 713-479-7186
Specialties: Working knives. **Patterns:** Hunters, skinners and utility knives. **Technical:** Grinds 440C and D2. **Prices:** $75 to $225. **Remarks:** First knife sold in 1979. **Mark:** First and middle initials, last name.

LAGRANGE, FANIE,
12 Canary Crescent, Table View 7441, SOUTH AFRICA, Phone: 27 21 55 76 805
Specialties: African-influenced styles in folders and fixed blades. **Patterns:** All original patterns with many one-of-a-kind. **Technical:** Mostly stock removal in 12C27, ATS-34, stainless Damascus. **Prices:** $350 to $3000. **Remarks:** Professional maker. SA Guild member. **Mark:** Name over spear.

LAINSON, TONY,
114 Park Ave, Council Bluffs, IA 51503, Phone: 712-322-5222
Specialties: Working straight knives, liner locking folders. **Technical:** Grinds 154CM, ATS-34, 440C buys Damascus. Handle materials include Micarta, carbon fiber G-10 ivory pearl and bone. **Prices:** $95 to $600. **Remarks:** Part-time maker; first knife sold in 1987. **Mark:** Name and state.

LAIRSON SR., JERRY,
H C 68 Box 970, Ringold, OK 74754, Phone: 580-876-3426, bladesmt@brightok.net; Web: www.lairson-custom-knives.net
Specialties: Damascus collector grade knives & high performance field grade hunters & cutting competition knives. **Patterns:** Damascus, random, raindrop, ladder, twist and others. **Technical:** All knives hammer forged. Mar Tempering**Prices:** Field grade knives $300. Collector grade $400 & up. **Mark:** Lairson. **Remarks:** Makes any style knife but prefer fighters and hunters. ABS Mastersmith, AKA member, KGA member. Cutting competition competitor.

LAKE, RON,
3360 Bendix Ave, Eugene, OR 97401, Phone: 541-484-2683
Specialties: High-tech working knives; inventor of the modern interframe folder. **Patterns:** Hunters, boots, etc.; locking folders. **Technical:** Grinds 154CM and ATS-34. Patented interframe with special lock release tab. **Prices:** $2200 to $3000; some higher. **Remarks:** Full-time maker; first knife sold in 1966. **Mark:** Last name.

LALA, PAULO RICARDO P AND LALA, ROBERTO P.,
R Daniel Martins 636, Centro, Presidente Prudente, SP-19031-260, BRAZIL, Phone: 0182-210125, Web: http://www.orbita.starmedia/~korth
Specialties: Straight knives and folders of all designs to customer specs. **Patterns:** Bowies, daggers fighters, hunters and utility knives. **Technical:** Grinds and forges D6, 440C, high-carbon steels and Damascus. **Prices:** $60 to $400; some higher. **Remarks:** Full-time makers; first knife sold in 1991. All stainless steel blades are ultra sub-zero quenched. **Mark:** Sword carved on top of anvil under KORTH.

LAMB, CURTIS J,
3336 Louisiana Ter, Ottawa, KS 66067-8996, Phone: 785-242-6657

LAMBERT, JARRELL D,
2321 FM 2982, Granado, TX 77962, Phone: 512-771-3744
Specialties: Traditional working and using straight knives of his design and to customer specs. **Patterns:** Bowies, hunters, tantos and utility/camp knives. **Technical:** Grinds ATS-34; forges W2 and his own Damascus. Makes own sheaths. **Prices:** $80 to $600; some to $1000. **Remarks:** Part-time maker; first knife sold in 1982. **Mark:** Etched first and middle initials, last name; or stamped last name.

LAMBERT, KIRBY,
536 College Ave, Regina Saskatchewan S4N X3, CANADA, kirby@lambertknives.com; Web: www.lambertknives.com
Specialties: Tactical/utility folders. Tactical/utility Japanese style fixed blades. Prices: $200 to $1500 U.S. Remarks: Full-time maker since 2002. Mark: Black widow spider and last name Lambert.

LAMEY, ROBERT M,
15800 Lamey Dr, Biloxi, MS 39532, Phone: 228-396-9066, Fax: 228-396-9022, rmlamey@ametro.net; Web: www.lameyknives.com
Specialties: Bowies, fighters, hard use knives. Patterns: Bowies, fighters, hunters and camp knives. Technical: Forged and stock removal. Prices: $125 to $350. Remarks: Lifetime reconditioning; will build to customer designs, specializing in hard use, affordable knives. Mark: LAMEY.

LAMPSON, FRANK G,
3215 Saddle Bag Circle, Rimrock, AZ 86335, Phone: 928-567-7395, fglampson@yahoo.com
Specialties: Working folders; one-of-a-kinds. Patterns: Folders, hunters, utility knives, fillet knives and Bowies. Technical: Grinds ATS-34, 440C and 154CM. Prices: $100 to $750; some to $3500. Remarks: Full-time maker; first knife sold in 1971. Mark: Name in fish logo.

LANCASTER, C G,
No 2 Schoonwinkel St, Parys, Free State, SOUTH AFRICA, Phone: 0568112090
Specialties: High-tech working and using knives of his design and to customer specs. Patterns: Hunters, locking folders and utility/camp knives. Technical: Grinds Sandvik 12C27, 440C and D2. Offers anodized titanium bolsters. Prices: $450 to $750; some to $1500. Remarks: Part-time maker; first knife sold in 1990. Mark: Etched logo.

LANCE, BILL,
PO Box 4427, Eagle River, AK 99577, Phone: 907-694-1487
Specialties: Ooloos and working straight knives; limited issue sets. Patterns: Several ulu patterns, drop-point skinners. Technical: Uses ATS-34, Vascomax 350; ivory, horn and high-class wood handles. Prices: $85 to $300; art sets to $3000. Remarks: First knife sold in 1981. Mark: Last name over a lance.

LANDERS, JOHN,
758 Welcome Rd, Newnan, GA 30263, Phone: 404-253-5719
Specialties: High-art working straight knives and folders of his design. Patterns: Hunters, fighters and slip-joint folders. Technical: Grinds 440C, ATS-34, 154CM and commercial Damascus. Prices: $85 to $250; some to $500. Remarks: Part-time maker; first knife sold in 1989. Mark: Last name.

LANER, DEAN,
1480 Fourth St, Susanville, CA 96130, Phone: 530-310-1917, laner54knives@yahoo.com
Specialties: Fancy working fixed blades, of his design, will do custom orders. Patterns: Hunters, fighters, combat, fishing, Bowies, utility, and kitchen knives. Technical: Grinds 154CM, ATS-34, D2, buys Damascus. Does mostly hallow grinding, some flat grinds. Uses Micarta, mastodon ivory, hippo ivory, exotic woods. Loves doing spacer work on stick tang knives. A leather or kydes sheath comes with every knife. Life-time warrantee and free sharpening also. Remarks: Part-time maker, first knife sold in 1993. Prices: $150 to $1000. Mark: LANER CUSTOM KNIVES over D next to a tree.

LANG, DAVID,
6153 Cumulus Circle, Kearns, UT 84118, Phone: 801-809-1241, dknifeguy@msn.com
Specialties: Hunters, Fighters, Push Daggers, Upscale Art Knives, Folders. Technical: Flat grind, hollow grind, hand carving, casting. Remarks: Will work from my designs or to your specifications. I have been making knives 10 years and have gleaned help from Jerry Johnson, Steven Rapp, Earl Black, Steven Johnson, and many others. Prices: $225 - $3000. Mark: Dland over UTAH.

LANGLEY, GENE H,
1022 N. Price Rd, Florence, SC 29506, Phone: 843-669-3150
Specialties: Working knives in standard patterns. Patterns: Hunters, boots, fighters, locking folders and slip-joints. Technical: Grinds 440C, 154CM and ATS-34. Prices: $125 to $450; some to $1000. Remarks: Part-time maker; first knife sold in 1979. Mark: Name.

LANGLEY, MICK,
1015 Centre Crescent, Qualicum Beach, B.C., CANADA V9K 2G6, Phone: 250-752-4261
Specialties: Period pieces and working knives. Patterns: Bowies, push daggers, fighters, boots. Technical: Forges 5160, 1084, W2 and his own Damascus. Prices: $250 to $2500; some to $4500. Remarks: Full-time maker, first knife sold in 1977. Mark: Langley with M.S. (for ABS Master Smith)

LANKTON, SCOTT,
8065 Jackson Rd. R-11, Ann Arbor, MI 48103, Phone: 313-426-3735
Specialties: Pattern welded swords, krisses and Viking period pieces. Patterns: One-of-a-kind. Technical: Forges W2, L6 nickel and other steels. Prices: $600 to $12,000. Remarks: Part-time bladesmith, full-time smith; first knife sold in 1976. Mark: Last name logo.

LAOISLAV, SANTA-LASKY,
Hrochot 264, 976 37 Hrochot, Okres Banska Bystrica, Slovensko (Slovakia), Phone: +421-905-544-280, santa.ladislav@pobox.sk; Web: www.lasky.sk
Specialties: Damascus hunters, daggers and swords. Patterns: Carious Damascus patterns. Prices: $300 to $6000 U.S. Mark: L or Lasky.

LAPEN, CHARLES,
Box 529, W. Brookfield, MA 01585
Specialties: Chef's knives for the culinary artist. Patterns: Camp knives, Japanese-style swords and wood working tools, hunters. Technical: Forges 1075, car spring and his own Damascus. Favors narrow and Japanese tangs. Prices: $200 to $400; some to $2000. Remarks: Part-time maker; first knife sold in 1972. Mark: Last name.

LAPLANTE, BRETT,
4545 CR412, McKinney, TX 75071, Phone: 972-838-9191, blap007@aol.com
Specialties: Working straight knives and folders to customer specs. Patterns: Survival knives, Bowies, skinners, hunters. Technical: Grinds D2 and 440C. Heat-treats. Prices: $200 to $800. Remarks: Part-time maker; first knife sold in 1987. Mark: Last name in Canadian maple leaf logo.

LARAMIE, MARK,
301 McCain St., Raeford, NC 28376, Phone: 978-502-2726, mark@malknives.com; Web: www.malknives.com
Specialties: Traditional fancy & art knives. Patterns: Slips, back-lock L/L, automatics, single and multi blades. Technical: Free hand ground blades of D2, 440, and Damascus. Mark: M.A.L. Knives w/fish logo.

LARGIN,
KELGIN KNIVES, 104 Knife Works Ln, Sevierville, TN 37876, Phone: 765-969-5012, kelginfinecutlery@hotmail.com; Web: wwwkelgin.com
Specialties: Retired from general knife making. Only take limited orders in meteorite Damascus or solid meteorite blades. Patterns: Any. Technical: Stock removal or forged. Prices: $500 & up. Remarks: Run the Kelgin Knife Makers Co-op at Smoky Mtn. Knife Works. Mark: K.C. Largin - Kelgin mark retired in 2004.

LARSON, RICHARD,
549 E Hawkeye Ave, Turlock, CA 95380, Phone: 209-668-1615, lebatardknives@aol.com
Specialties: Sound working knives, lightweight folders, practical tactical knives. Patterns: Hunters, trout and bird knives, fish fillet knives, Bowies, tactical sheath knives, one- and two-blade folders. Technical: Grinds ATS-34, A2, D2, CPM 3V and commercial. Damascus; forges and grinds 52100, O1 and 1095. Machines folder frames from aircraft aluminum. Prices: $40 to $650. Remarks: Full-time maker. First knife made in 1974. Offers knife repair, restoration and sharpening. All knives are serial numbered and registered in the name of original purchaser. Mark: Stamped last name or etched logo of last name, city, and state.

LARY, ED,
951 Rangeline Rd, Mosinee, WI 54476, Phone: 715-693-3940, laryblades@hotmail.com
Specialties: Upscale hunters and art knives with display presentations. Patterns: Hunters, period pieces. Technical: Grinds all steels, heat treats, fancy file work and engraving. Prices: Upscale. Remarks: Full-time maker since 1974. Mark: Hand engraved "Ed Lary" in script.

LAURENT, KERMIT,
1812 Acadia Dr, LaPlace, LA 70068, Phone: 504-652-5629
Specialties: Traditional and working straight knives and folders of his design. Patterns: Bowies, hunters, utilities and folders. Technical: Forges own Damascus, plus uses most tool steels and stainless. Specializes in altering cable patterns. Uses stabilized handle materials, especially select exotic woods. Prices: $100 to $2500; some to $50,000. Remarks: Full-time maker; first knife sold in 1982. Doing business as Kermit's Knife Works. Favorite material is meteorite Damascus. Mark: First name.

LAWRENCE, ALTON,
201 W Stillwell, De Queen, AR 71832, Phone: 870-642-7643, Fax: 870-642-4023, uncle21@riversidemachine.net; Web: riversidemachine.net
Specialties: Classic straight knives and folders to customer specs. Patterns: Bowies, hunters, folders and utility/camp knives. Technical: Forges 5160, 1095, 1084, Damascus and railroad spikes. Prices: Start at $100. Remarks: Part-time maker; first knife sold in 1988. Mark: Last name inside fish symbol.

LAY, L J,
602 Mimosa Dr, Burkburnett, TX 76354, Phone: 940-569-1329
Specialties: Working straight knives in standard patterns; some period pieces. Patterns: Drop-point hunters, Bowies and fighters. Technical: Grinds ATS-34 to mirror finish; likes Micarta handles. Prices: Moderate. Remarks: Full-time maker; first knife sold in 1985. Mark: Name or name with ram head and city or stamp L J Lay.

LAY, R J (BOB),
Box 1225, Logan Lake, B.C., CANADA V0K 1W0, Phone: 250-523-9923, Fax: SAME, rjlay@telus.net
Specialties: Traditional-styled, fancy straight knifes of his design. Specializing in hunters. Patterns: Bowies, fighters and hunters. Technical: Grinds 440C, ATS-34, S30V, CPM-154CM. Uses exotic handle and spacer material. File cut, prefers narrow tang. Sheaths available. Price: $200 to $500, some to $5000. Remarks: Full-time maker, first knife sold in 1976. Doing business as Lay's Custom Knives. Mark: Signature acid etched.

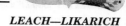

LEACH, MIKE J,
5377 W Grand Blanc Rd., Swartz Creek, MI 48473, Phone: 810-655-4850
Specialties: Fancy working knives. **Patterns:** Hunters, fighters, Bowies and heavy-duty knives; slip-joint folders and integral straight patterns. **Technical:** Grinds D2, 440C and 154CM; buys Damascus. **Prices:** Start at $300. **Remarks:** Full-time maker; first knife sold in 1952. **Mark:** First initial, last name.

LEAVITT JR., EARL F,
Pleasant Cove Rd Box 306, E. Boothbay, ME 04544, Phone: 207-633-3210
Specialties: 1500-1870 working straight knives and fighters; pole arms. **Patterns:** Historically significant knives, classic/modern custom designs. **Technical:** Flat-grinds O1; heat-treats. Filework available. **Prices:** $90 to $350; some to $1000. **Remarks:** Full-time maker; first knife sold in 1981. Doing business as Old Colony Manufactory. **Mark:** Initials in oval.

LEBATARD, PAUL M,
14700 Old River Rd, Vancleave, MS 39565, Phone: 228-826-4137, Fax: Cell phone 228-238-7461, lebatardknives@aol.com
Specialties: Sound working hunting and fillet knives, folding knives, practical tactical knives. **Patterns:** Hunters, trout and bird knives, fish fillet knives, kitchen knives, Bowies, tactical sheath knives, one- and two-blade folders. **Technical:** Grinds ATS-34, D-2, CPM 3-V, CPM-154CM, and commercial Damascus; forges and grinds 1095, 01, and 52100. **Prices:** $75 to $650; some to $1200. **Remarks:** Full-time maker, first knife made in 1974. Charter member Gulf Coast Custom Knifemakers; Voting member Knifemaker's Guild. **Mark:** Stamped last name, or etched logo of last name, city, and state. **Other:** All knives are serial numbered and registered in the name of the original purchaser.

LEBER, HEINZ,
Box 446, Hudson's Hope, B.C., CANADA V0C 1V0, Phone: 250-783-5304
Specialties: Working straight knives of his design. **Patterns:** 20 models, from capers to Bowies. **Technical:** Hollow-grinds D2 and M2 steel; mirror-finishes and full tang only. Likes moose, elk, stone sheep for handles. **Prices:** $175 to $1000. **Remarks:** Full-time maker; first knife sold in 1975. **Mark:** Initials connected.

LECK, DAL,
Box 1054, Hayden, CO 81639, Phone: 970-276-3663
Specialties: Classic, traditional and working knives of his design and in standard patterns; period pieces. **Patterns:** Boots, daggers, fighters, hunters and push daggers. **Technical:** Forges O1 and 5160; makes his own Damascus. **Prices:** $175 to $700; some to $1500. **Remarks:** Part-time maker; first knife sold in 1990. Doing business as The Moonlight Smithy. **Mark:** Stamped: hammer and anvil with initials.

LEE, RANDY,
PO Box 1873, St. Johns, AZ 85936, Phone: 928-337-2594, Fax: 928-337-5002, randyleeknives@yahoo.com; Web.www.randyleeknives.com
Specialties: Traditional working and using straight knives of his design. **Patterns:** Bowies, fighters, hunters, daggers. **Technical:** Grinds ATS-34, 440C Damascus, and 154CPM. Offers sheaths. **Prices:** $325 to $2500. **Remarks:** Part-time maker; first knife sold in 1979. **Mark:** Full name, city, state.

LELAND, STEVE,
2300 Sir Francis Drake Blvd, Fairfax, CA 94930-1118, Phone: 415-457-0318, Fax: 415-457-0995, Web: www.stephenleland@comcast.net
Specialties: Traditional and working straight knives and folders of his design. **Patterns:** Hunters, fighters, Bowies, chefs. **Technical:** Grinds O1, ATS-34 and 440C. Does own heat treat. Makes nickel silver sheaths. **Prices:** $150 to $750; some to $1500. **Remarks:** Part-time maker; first knife sold in 1987. Doing business as Leland Handmade Knives. **Mark:** Last name.

LEMCKE, JIM L,
10649 Haddington Ste 180, Houston, TX 77043, Phone: 888-461-8632, Fax: 713-461-8221, jimll@hal-pc.org; Web: www.texasknife.com
Specialties: Large supply of custom ground and factory finished blades; knife kits; leather sheaths; in-house heat treating and cryogenic tempering; exotic handle material (wood, ivory, oosik, horn, stabilized woods); machines and supplies for knifemaking; polishing and finishing supplies; heat treat ovens; etching equipment; bar, sheet and rod material (brass, stainless steel, nickel silver); titanium sheet material. Catalog. $4.

LENNON, DALE,
459 County Rd 1554, Alba, TX 75410, Phone: 903-765-2392, devildaddy1@netzero.net
Specialties: Working / using knives. **Patterns:** Hunters, fighters and Bowies. **Technical:** Grinds high carbon steels, ATS-34, forges some. **Prices:** Starts at $120. **Remarks:** Part-time maker, first knife sold in 2000. **Mark:** Last name.

LEONARD, RANDY JOE,
188 Newton Rd, Sarepta, LA 71071, Phone: 318-994-2712

LEONE, NICK,
9 Georgetown, Pontoon Beach, IL 62040, Phone: 618-797-1179, nickleone@sbcglobal.net
Specialties: 18th century period straight knives. **Patterns:** Skinners, hunters, neck, leg and friction folders. **Technical:** Forges 5160, W2, O1, 1098, 52100 and his own Damascus. **Prices:** $100 to $1000; some to $3500. **Remarks:** Full-time maker; first knife sold in 1987. Doing business as Anvil Head Forge. **Mark:** Last name, NL, AHF.

LERCH, MATTHEW,
N88 W23462 North Lisbon Rd, Sussex, WI 53089, Phone: 262-246-6362, Web: www.lerchcustomknives.com
Specialties: Folders and folders with special mechanisms. **Patterns:** Interframe and integral folders; lock backs, assisted openers, side locks, button locks and liner locks. **Technical:** Grinds ATS-34, 1095, 440 and Damascus. Offers filework and embellished bolsters. **Prices:** $900 and up. **Remarks:** Part-time maker; first knife sold in 1995. **Mark:** Last name.

LEVENGOOD, BILL,
15011 Otto Rd, Tampa, FL 33624, Phone: 813-961-5688, bill.levengood@verison.net; Web: www.levengoodknives.com
Specialties: Working straight knives and folders. **Patterns:** Hunters, Bowies, folders and collector pieces. **Technical:** Grinds ATS-34, S-30V, CPM-154 and Damascus. **Prices:** $175 to $1500. **Remarks:** Full time maker; first knife sold in 1983. **Mark:** Last name, city, state.

LEVIN, JACK,
7216 Bay Pkwy, Brooklyn, NY 11204, Phone: 718-232-8574, jacklevin1@yahoo.com
Specialties: Folders with mechanisms.

LEVINE, BOB,
101 Westwood Dr, Tullahoma, TN 37388, Phone: 931-454-9943, levineknives@msn.com
Specialties: Working left- and right-handed LinerLock® folders. **Patterns:** Hunters and folders. **Technical:** Grinds ATS-34, 440C, D2, O1 and some Damascus; hollow and some flat grinds. Uses sheep horn, fossil ivory, Micarta and exotic woods. Provides custom leather sheath with each fixed knife. **Prices:** Starting at $275. **Remarks:** Full-time maker; first knife sold in 1984. Voting member Knifemakers Guild, German Messermaker Guild. **Mark:** Name and logo.

LEWIS, BILL,
PO Box 63, Riverside, IA 52327, Phone: 319-629-5574, wildbill37@geticonnect.com
Specialties: Folders of all kinds including those made from one-piece of white tail antler with or without the crown. **Patterns:** Hunters, folding hunters, fillet, Bowies, push daggers, etc. **Prices:** $20 to $200. **Remarks:** Full-time maker; first knife sold in 1978. **Mark:** W.E.L.

LEWIS, MIKE,
21 Pleasant Hill Dr, DeBary, FL 32713, Phone: 386-753-0936, dragonsteel@prodigy.net
Specialties: Traditional straight knives. **Patterns:** Swords and daggers. **Technical:** Grinds 440C, ATS-34 and 5160. Frequently uses cast bronze and cast nickel guards and pommels. **Prices:** $100 to $750. **Remarks:** Part-time maker; first knife sold in 1988. **Mark:** Dragon Steel and serial number.

LEWIS, TOM R,
1613 Standpipe Rd, Carlsbad, NM 88220, Phone: 575-885-3616, lewisknives@carlsbadnm.com; Web: www.cavemen.net/lewisknives/
Specialties: Traditional working straight knives. **Patterns:** Outdoor knives, hunting knives and Bowies. **Technical:** Grinds ATS-34 forges 5168 and O1. Makes wire, pattern welded and chainsaw Damascus. **Prices:** $140 to $1500. **Remarks:** Part-time maker; first knife sold in 1980. Doing business as TR Lewis Handmade Knives. **Mark:** Lewis family crest.

LICATA, STEVEN,
LICATA CUSTOM KNIVES, 146 Wilson St. 1st Floor, Boonton, NJ 07005, Phone: 973-588-4909, steven.licata@att.net; Web: www.licataknives.com
Specialties: Fantasy swords and knives. One-of-a-kind sculptures in steel. **Prices:** $200 to $25,000.

LIEBENBERG, ANDRE,
8 Hilma Rd, Bordeauxrandburg 2196, SOUTH AFRICA, Phone: 011-787-2303
Specialties: High-art straight knives of his design. **Patterns:** Daggers, fighters and swords. **Technical:** Grinds 440C and 12C27. **Prices:** $250 to $500; some $4000 and higher. Giraffe bone handles with semi-precious stones. **Remarks:** Spare-time maker; first knife sold in 1990. **Mark:** Initials.

LIEGEY, KENNETH R,
132 Carney Dr, Millwood, WV 25262, Phone: 304-273-9545
Specialties: Traditional working/using straight knives of his design and to customer specs. **Patterns:** Hunters, utility/camp knives, miniatures. **Technical:** Grinds 440C. **Prices:** $75 to $150; some to $300. **Remarks:** Spare-time maker; first knife sold in 1977. **Mark:** First and middle initials, last name.

LIGHTFOOT, GREG,
RR #2, Kitscoty, AB, CANADA T0B 2P0, Phone: 780-846-2812, Pitbull@lightfootknives.com; Web: www.lightfootknives.com
Specialties: Stainless steel and Damascus. **Patterns:** Boots, fighters and locking folders. **Technical:** Grinds BG-42, 440C, D2, CPM steels, Stellite 6K. Offers engraving. **Prices:** $500 to $2000. **Remarks:** Full-time maker; first knife sold in 1988. Doing business as Lightfoot Knives. **Mark:** Shark with Lightfoot Knives below.

LIKARICH, STEVE,
PO Box 961, Colfax, CA 95713, Phone: 530-346-8480
Specialties: Fancy working knives; art knives of his design. **Patterns:** Hunters, fighters and art knives of his design. **Technical:** Grinds ATS-34, 154CM and 440C; likes high polishes and filework. **Prices:** $200 to $2000; some higher. **Remarks:** Full-time maker; first knife sold in 1987. **Mark:** Name.

LINKLATER, STEVE,
8 Cossar Dr, Aurora, Ont., CANADA L4G 3N8, Phone: 905-727-8929, knifman@sympatico.ca

> **Specialties:** Traditional working/using straight knives and folders of his design. **Patterns:** Fighters, hunters and locking folders. **Technical:** Grinds ATS-34, 440V and D2. **Prices:** $125 to $350; some to $600. **Remarks:** Part-time maker; first knife sold in 1987. Doing business as Links Knives. **Mark:** LINKS.

LISCH, DAVID K,
9239 8th Ave. SW, Seattle, WA 98106, Phone: 206-919-5431, Web: www.davidlisch.com

> **Specialties:** One-of-a-kind collectibles, straight knives of own design and to customer specs. **Patterns:** Hunters, skinners, Bowies, and daggers. **Technical:** Forges all his own Damascus under 360-pound air hammer. Forges and chisels wrought iron, pure iron, and bronze butt caps. **Prices:** Starting at $350. **Remarks:** Full-time blacksmith, part-time bladesmith. **Mark:** D. Lisch J.S.

LISTER JR., WELDON E,
9140 Sailfish Dr, Boerne, TX 78006, Phone: 210-981-2210

> **Specialties:** One-of-a-kind fancy and embellished folders. **Patterns:** Locking and slip-joint folders. **Technical:** Commercial Damascus and O1. All knives embellished. Engraves, inlays, carves and scrimshaws. **Prices:** Upscale. **Remarks:** Spare-time maker; first knife sold in 1991. **Mark:** Last name.

LITTLE, GARY M,
HC84 Box 10301, PO Box 156, Broadbent, OR 97414, Phone: 503-572-2656

> **Specialties:** Fancy working knives. **Patterns:** Hunters, tantos, Bowies, axes and buckskinners; locking folders and interframes. **Technical:** Forges and grinds O1, L6, 1095; makes his own Damascus; bronze fittings. **Prices:** $85 to $300; some to $2500. **Remarks:** Full-time maker; first knife sold in 1979. Doing business as Conklin Meadows Forge. **Mark:** Name, city and state.

LITTLE, LARRY,
1A Cranberry Ln, Spencer, MA 01562, Phone: 508-885-2301, littcran@aol.com

> **Specialties:** Working straight knives of his design or to customer specs. Likes Scagel-style. **Patterns:** Hunters, fighters, Bowies, folders. **Technical:** Grinds and forges L6, O1, 5160, 1095, 1080. Prefers natural handle material especially antler. Uses nickel silver. Makes own heavy duty leather sheath. **Prices:** Start at $125. **Remarks:** Part-time maker. First knife sold in 1985. Offers knife repairs. **Mark:** Little on one side, LL brand on the other.

LIVELY, TIM AND MARIAN,
PO Box 1172, Marble Falls, TX 78654, Web: www.livelyknives.com

> **Specialties:** Multi-cultural primitive knives of their design on speculation. **Patterns:** Old world designs. **Technical:** Hand forges using ancient techniques without electricity; hammer finish. **Prices:** High. **Remarks:** Retired 2009. Offers knifemaking DVD online. **Mark:** Last name.

LIVESAY, NEWT,
3306 S. Dogwood St, Siloam Springs, AR 72761, Phone: 479-549-3356, Fax: 479-549-3357, newt@newtlivesay.com; Web:www.newtlivesay.com

> **Specialties:** Combat utility knives, hunting knives, titanium knives, swords, axes, KYDWX sheaths for knives and pistols, custom orders.

LIVINGSTON, ROBERT C,
PO Box 6, Murphy, NC 28906, Phone: 704-837-4155

> **Specialties:** Art letter openers to working straight knives. **Patterns:** Minis to machetes. **Technical:** Forges and grinds most steels. **Prices:** Start at $20. **Remarks:** Full-time maker; first knife sold in 1988. Doing business as Mystik Knifeworks. **Mark:** MYSTIK.

LOCKETT, STERLING,
527 E Amherst Dr, Burbank, CA 91504, Phone: 818-846-5799

> **Specialties:** Working straight knives and folders to customer specs. **Patterns:** Hunters and fighters. **Technical:** Grinds. **Prices:** Moderate. **Remarks:** Spare-time maker. **Mark:** Name, city with hearts.

LOERCHNER, WOLFGANG,
WOLFE FINE KNIVES, PO Box 255, Bayfield, Ont., CANADA N0M 1G0, Phone: 519-565-2196

> **Specialties:** Traditional straight knives, mostly ornate. **Patterns:** Small swords, daggers and stilettos; locking folders and miniatures. **Technical:** Grinds D2, 440C and 154CM; all knives hand-filed and flat-ground. **Prices:** $300 to $5000; some to $10,000. **Remarks:** Part-time maker; first knife sold in 1983. Doing business as Wolfe Fine Knives. **Mark:** WOLFE.

LONEWOLF, J AGUIRRE,
481 Hwy 105, Demorest, GA 30535, Phone: 706-754-4660, Fax: 706-754-8470, lonewolfandsons@windstream.net, Web: www.knivesbylonewolf.com www.scrimshawbywei.com

> **Specialties:** High-art working and using straight knives of his design. **Patterns:** Bowies, hunters, utility/camp knives and fine steel blades. **Technical:** Forges Damascus and high-carbon steel. Most knives have hand-carved moose antler handles. **Prices:** $55 to $500; some to $2000. **Remarks:** Full-time maker; first knife sold in 1980. Doing business as Lonewolf and Sons LLC. **Mark:** Stamp.

LONG, GLENN A,
10090 SW 186th Ave, Dunnellon, FL 34432, Phone: 352-489-4272, galong99@att.net

> **Specialties:** Classic working and using straight knives of his design and to customer specs. **Patterns:** Hunters, Bowies, utility. **Technical:** Grinds 440C D2 and 440V. **Prices:** $85 to $300; some to $800. **Remarks:** Part-time maker; first knife sold in 1990. **Mark:** Last name inside diamond.

LONGWORTH, DAVE,
PO Box 222, Neville, OH 45156, Phone: 513-876-2372

> **Specialties:** High-tech working knives. **Patterns:** Locking folders, hunters, fighters and elaborate daggers. **Technical:** Grinds O1, ATS-34, 440C; buys Damascus. **Prices:** $125 to $600; some higher. **Remarks:** Part-time maker; first knife sold in 1980. **Mark:** Last name.

LOOS, HENRY C,
210 Ingraham, New Hyde Park, NY 11040, Phone: 516-354-1943, hcloos@optonline.net

> **Specialties:** Miniature fancy knives and period pieces of his design. **Patterns:** Bowies, daggers and swords. **Technical:** Grinds O1 and 440C. Uses sterling, 18K, rubies and emeralds. All knives come with handmade hardwood cases. **Prices:** $90 to $195; some to $250. **Remarks:** Spare-time maker; first knife sold in 1990. **Mark:** Script last initial.

LORO, GENE,
2457 State Route 93 NE, Crooksville, OH 43731, Phone: 740-982-4521, Fax: 740-982-1249, geney@aol.com

> **Specialties:** Hand forged knives. **Patterns:** Damascus, Random, Ladder, Twist, etc. **Technical:** ABS Journeyman Smith. **Prices:** $200 and up. **Remarks:** Loro and hand forged by Gene Loro. **Mark:** Loro. Retired engineer.

LOTT, SHERRY,
1100 Legion Park Rd, Greensburg, KY 42743, Phone: 270-932-2212, sherrylott@alltel.net

> **Specialties:** One-of-a-kind, usually carved handles. **Patterns:** Art. **Technical:** Carbon steel, stock removal. **Prices:** Moderate. **Mark:** Sherry Lott. **Remarks:** First knife sold in 1994.

LOVE, ED,
19443 Mill Oak, San Antonio, TX 78258, Phone: 210-497-1021, Fax: 210-497-1021, annaedlove@sbcglobal.net

> **Specialties:** Hunting, working knives and some art pieces. **Technical:** Grinds ATS-34, and 440C. **Prices:** $150 and up. **Remarks:** Part-time maker. First knife sold in 1980. **Mark:** Name in a weeping heart.

LOVELESS, R W,
PO Box 7836, Riverside, CA 92503, Phone: 951-689-7800

> **Specialties:** Working knives, fighters and hunters of his design. **Patterns:** Contemporary hunters, fighters and boots. **Technical:** Grinds 154CM and ATS-34. **Prices:** $850 to $4950. **Remarks:** Full-time maker since 1969. **Mark:** Name in logo.

LOVESTRAND, SCHUYLER,
1136 19th St SW, Vero Beach, FL 32962, Phone: 772-778-0282, Fax: 772-466-1126, lovestranded@aol.com

> **Specialties:** Fancy working straight knives of his design and to customer specs; unusual fossil ivories. **Patterns:** Hunters, fighters, Bowies and fishing knives. **Technical:** Grinds stainless steel. **Prices:** $450 and up. **Remarks:** Part-time maker; first knife sold in 1982. **Mark:** Name in logo.

LOVETT, MICHAEL,
PO Box 121, Mound, TX 76558, Phone: 254-865-9956, michaellovett@embarqmail.com

> **Specialties:** The Loveless Connection Knives as per R.W. Loveless-Jim Merritt. **Patterns:** All Loveless Patterns and Original Lovett Patterns. **Technical:** Complicated double grinds and premium fit and finish. **Prices:** $1000 and up. **Remarks:** High degree of fit and finish - Authorized collection by R. W. Loveless **Mark:** Loveless Authorized football or double nude.

LOZIER, DON,
5394 SE 168th Ave, Ocklawaha, FL 32179, Phone: 352-625-3576

> **Specialties:** Fancy and working straight knives of his design and in standard patterns. **Patterns:** Daggers, fighters, boot knives, and hunters. **Technical:** Grinds ATS-34, 440C and Damascus. Most pieces are highly embellished by notable artisans. Taking limited number of orders per annum. **Prices:** Start at $250; most are $1250 to $3000; some to $12,000. **Remarks:** Full-time maker. **Mark:** Name.

LUCHAK, BOB,
15705 Woodforest Blvd, Channelview, TX 77530, Phone: 281-452-1779

> **Specialties:** Presentation knives; start of The Survivor series. **Patterns:** Skinners, Bowies, camp axes, steak knife sets and fillet knives. **Technical:** Grinds 440C. Offers electronic etching; filework. **Prices:** $50 to $1500. **Remarks:** Full-time maker; first knife sold in 1983. Doing business as Teddybear Knives. **Mark:** Full name, city and state with Teddybear logo.

LUCHINI, BOB,
1220 Dana Ave, Palo Alto, CA 94301, Phone: 650-321-8095, rwluchin@bechtel.com

LUCIE, JAMES R,
4191 E. Fruitport R, Fruitport, MI 49415, Phone: 231-865-6390, scagel@netonecom.net

> **Specialties:** Hand-forges William Scagel-style knives. **Patterns:** Authen-

tic scagel-style knives and miniatures. **Technical:** Forges 5160, 52100 and 1084 and forges his own pattern welded Damascus steel. **Prices:** Start at $750. **Remarks:** Full-time maker; first knife sold in 1975. Believes in sole authorship of his work. ABS Journeyman Smith. **Mark:** Scagel Kris with maker's name and address.

LUCKETT, BILL,
108 Amantes Ln, Weatherford, TX 76088, Phone: 817-594-9288, bill_luckett@hotmail.com Web: www.billluckettcustomknives.com
Specialties: Uniquely patterned robust straight knives. **Patterns:** Fighters, Bowies, hunters. **Technical:** 154CM stainless.**Prices:** $550 to $1500. **Remarks:** Part-time maker; first knife sold in 1975. Knifemakers Guild Member. **Mark:** Last name over Bowie logo.

LUDWIG, RICHARD O,
57-63 65 St, Maspeth, NY 11378, Phone: 718-497-5969
Specialties: Traditional working/using knives. **Patterns:** Boots, hunters and utility/camp knives folders. **Technical:** Grinds 440C, ATS-34 and BG42. File work on guards and handles; silver spacers. Offers scrimshaw. **Prices:** $325 to $400; some to $2000. **Remarks:** Full-time maker. **Mark:** Stamped first initial, last name, state.

LUI, RONALD M,
4042 Harding Ave, Honolulu, HI 96816, Phone: 808-734-7746
Specialties: Working straight knives and folders in standard patterns. **Patterns:** Hunters, boots and liner locks. **Technical:** Grinds 440C and ATS-34. **Prices:** $100 to $700. **Remarks:** Spare-time maker; first knife sold in 1988. **Mark:** Initials connected.

LUMAN, JAMES R,
Clear Creek Trail, Anaconda, MT 59711, Phone: 406-560-1461
Specialties: San Mai and composite end patterns. **Patterns:** Pool and eye Spirograph southwest composite patterns. **Technical:** All patterns with blued steel; all made by him. **Prices:** $200 to $800. **Mark:** Stock blade removal. Pattern welded steel. Bottom ricasso JRL.

LUNDSTROM, JAN-AKE,
Mastmostigen 8, 66010 Dals-Langed, SWEDEN, Phone: 0531-40270
Specialties: Viking swords, axes and knives in cooperation with handle makers. **Patterns:** All traditional-styles, especially swords and inlaid blades. **Technical:** Forges his own Damascus and laminated steel. **Prices:** $200 to $1000. **Remarks:** Full-time maker; first knife sold in 1985; collaborates with museums. **Mark:** Runic.

LUNN, GAIL,
434 CR 1422, Mountain Home, AR 72653, Phone: 870-424-2662, gail@lunnknives.com; Web: www.lunnknives.com
Specialties: Fancy folders and double action autos, some straight blades. **Patterns:** One-of-a-kind, all types. **Technical:** Stock removal, hand made. **Prices:** $300 and up. **Remarks:** Fancy file work, exotic materials, inlays, stone etc. **Mark:** Name in script.

LUNN, LARRY A,
434 CR 1422, Mountain Home, AR 72653, Phone: 870-424-2662, larry@lunnknives.com; Web: www.lunnknives.com
Specialties: Fancy folders and double action autos; some straight blades. **Patterns:** All types; his own designs. **Technical:** Stock removal; commercial Damascus. **Prices:** $125 and up. **Remarks:** File work inlays and exotic materials. **Mark:** Name in script.

LUPOLE, JAMIE G,
KUMA KNIVES, 285 Main St., Kirkwood, NY 13795, Phone: 607-775-9368, jlupole@stny.rr.com
Specialties: Working and collector grade fixed blades, ethnic-styled blades. **Patterns:** Fighters, Bowies, tacticals, hunters, camp, utility, personal carry knives, some swords. **Technical:** Forges and grinds 10XX series and other high-carbon steels, grinds ATS-34 and 440C, will use just about every handle material available. **Prices:** $80 to $500 and up. **Remarks:** Part-time maker since 1999. **Marks:** "KUMA" hot stamped, name, city and state-etched, or "Daiguma saku" in kanji.

LUTZ, GREG,
127 Crescent Rd, Greenwood, SC 29646, Phone: 864-229-7340
Specialties: Working and using knives and period pieces of his design and to customer specs. **Patterns:** Fighters, hunters and swords. **Technical:** Forges 1095 and O1; grinds ATS-34. Differentially heat-treats forged blades; uses cryogenic treatment on ATS-34. **Prices:** $50 to $350; some to $1200. **Remarks:** Part-time maker; first knife sold in 1986. Doing business as Scorpion Forge. **Mark:** First initial, last name.

LYLE III, ERNEST L,
LYLE KNIVES, PO Box 1755, Chiefland, FL 32644, Phone: 352-490-6693, ernestlyle@msn.com
Specialties: Fancy period pieces; one-of-a-kind and limited editions. **Patterns:** Arabian/Persian influenced fighters, military knives, Bowies and Roman short swords; several styles of hunters. **Technical:** Grinds 440C, D2 and 154 CM. Engraves. **Prices:** Upscale. **Remarks:** Full-time maker; first knife sold in 1972. **Mark:** Last name in capital letters - LYLE over a much smaller Chief land.

LYNCH, TAD,
140 Timberline Dr., Beene, AR 72012, Phone: 501-626-1647, lynchknives@yahoo.com
Specialties: Forged fixed blades of original design and Bowies based on

19th century examples. **Patterns:** Hunters, skinners, Bowies, tomahawks, neck knives. **Technical:** Hand-forged 1084, 1095, clay/edge quenched; 52100; Damascus, san mai. **Prices:** Starting at $250. **Remarks:** Part-time maker, also offers custom leather work via wife Amy Lynch. **Mark:** T.D. Lynch over anvil.

LYNN, ARTHUR,
29 Camino San Cristobal, Galisteo, NM 87540, Phone: 505-466-3541, lynnknives@aol.com
Specialties: Handforged Damascus knives. **Patterns:** Folders, hunters, Bowies, fighters, kitchen. **Technical:** Forges own Damascus. **Prices:** Moderate.

LYTTLE, BRIAN,
Box 5697, High River, AB, CANADA T1V 1M7, Phone: 403-558-3638, brian@lyttleknives.com; Web: www.lyttleknives.com
Specialties: Fancy working straight knives and folders; art knives. **Patterns:** Bowies, daggers, dirks, sgian dubhs, folders, dress knives, tantos, short swords. **Technical:** Forges Damascus steel; engraving; scrimshaw; heat-treating; classes. **Prices:** $450 to $15,000. **Remarks:** Full-time maker; first knife sold in 1983. **Mark:** Last name, country.

M

MACDONALD, DAVID,
2824 Hwy 47, Los Lunas, NM 87031, Phone: 505-866-5866

MACDONALD, JOHN,
9 David Dr, Raymond, NH 03077, Phone: 603-895-0918
Specialties: Working/using straight knives of his design and to customer specs. **Patterns:** Japanese cutlery, Bowies, hunters and working knives. **Technical:** Grinds O1, L6 and ATS-34. Swords have matching handles and scabbards with Japanese flair. **Prices:** $70 to $250; some to $500. **Remarks:** Part-time maker; first knife sold in 1988. Wood/glass-topped custom cases. Doing business as Mac the Knife. **Mark:** Initials.

MACKIE, JOHN,
13653 Lanning, Whittier, CA 90605, Phone: 562-945-6104
Specialties: Forged. **Patterns:** Bowie and camp knives. **Technical:** Attended ABS Bladesmith School. **Prices:** $75 to $500. **Mark:** JSM in a triangle.

MACKRILL, STEPHEN,
PO Box 1580, Pinegowrie, JHB 2123, SOUTH AFRICA, Phone: 27-11-474-7139, Fax: 27-11-474-7139, info@mackrill.co.za; Web: www.mackrill.net
Specialties: Art fancy, historical, collectors and corporate gifts cutlery. **Patterns:** Fighters, hunters, camp, custom lock back and LinerLock® folders. **Technical:** N690, 12C27, ATS-34, silver and gold inlay on handles; wooden and silver sheaths. **Prices:** $330 and upwards. **Remarks:** First knife sold in 1978. **Mark:** Mackrill fish with country of origin.

MADRULLI, MME JOELLE,
Residence Ste Catherine B1, Salon De Provence, FRANCE 13330

MAE, TAKAO,
1-119 1-4 Uenohigashi, Toyonaka, Osaka, JAPAN 560-0013, Phone: 81-6-6852-2758, Fax: 81-6-6481-1649, takamae@nifty.com
Remarks: Distinction stylish in art-forged blades, with lacquered ergonomic handles.

MAESTRI, PETER A,
S11251 Fairview Rd, Spring Green, WI 53588, Phone: 608-546-4481
Specialties: Working straight knives in standard patterns. **Patterns:** Camp and fishing knives, utility green-river-styled. **Technical:** Grinds 440C, 154CM and 440A. **Prices:** $15 to $45; some to $150. **Remarks:** Full-time maker; first knife sold in 1981. Provides professional cutler service to professional cutters. **Mark:** CARISOLO, MAESTRI BROS., or signature.

MAGEE, JIM,
741 S. Ohio St., Salina, KS 67401, Phone: 785-820-6928, jimmagee@cox.net
Specialties: Working and fancy folding knives. **Patterns:** Liner locking folders, favorite is his Persian. **Technical:** Grinds ATS-34, Devin Thomas & Eggerling Damascus, titanium. Liners Prefer mother-of-pearl handles. **Prices:** Start at $225 to $1200. **Remarks:** Part-time maker, first knife sold in 2001. Purveyor since 1982. Past president of the Professional Knifemakers Association **Mark:** Last name.

MAGRUDER, JASON,
10W Saint Elmo Ave, Colorado Springs, CO 80906, Phone: 719-210-1579, belstain@hotmail.com
Specialties: Fancy/embellished and working/using knives of his own design or to customer specs. Fancy filework and carving. **Patterns:** Tactical straight knives, hunters, Bowies and lockback folders. **Technical:** Flats grinds S30V, CPM3V, and 1080. Forges own Damascus. **Prices:** $150 and up. **Remarks:** Part-time maker; first knife sold in 2000. **Mark:** Magruder, or initials J M.

MAHOMEDY, A R,
PO Box 76280, Marble Ray KZN, 4035, SOUTH AFRICA, Phone: +27 31 577 1451, arm-koknives@mweb.co.za; Web: www.arm-koknives.co.za
Specialties: Daggers, elegant folders, hunters & utilities. Prefers to work to commissions, collections & presentations. With handles of mother-of-pearl, fossil & local ivories. Exotic dyed/stablized burls, giraffe bone and horns. **Technical:** Via stock removal grinds Damasteel, carbon and mosaic Damascus, ATS-34, N690, 440A, 440B, 12 C 27 and RWL 34. **Prices:** $500 and up. **Remarks:** Part-time maker. First knife sold in 1995. Member knifemakers guild of SA. **Mark:** Logo of initials A R M crowned with a "Minaret."

MAIENKNECHT, STANLEY,
38648 S R 800, Sardis, OH 43946

MAINES, JAY,
SUNRISE RIVER CUSTOM KNIVES, 5584 266th St., Wyoming, MN 55092, Phone: 651-462-5301, jaymaines@fronternet.net; Web: http://www.sunrisecustomknives.com
Specialties: Heavy duty working, classic and traditional fixed blades. Some high-tech and fancy embellished knives available. **Patterns:** Hunters, skinners, fillet, bowies tantos, boot daggers etc. etc. **Technical:** Hollow ground, stock removal blades of 440C, ATS-34 and CPM S-90V. Prefers natural handle materials, exotic hard woods, and stag, rams and buffalo horns. Offers dovetailed bolsters in brass, stainless steel and nickel silver. Custom sheaths from matching wood or hand-stitched from heavy duty water buffalo hide. **Prices:** Moderate to up-scale. **Remarks:** Part-time maker; first knife sold in 1992. Doing business as Sunrise River Custom Knives. Offers fixed blade knives repair and handle conversions. **Mark:** Full name under a Rising Sun logo.

MAISEY, ALAN,
PO Box 197, Vincentia 2540, NSW, AUSTRALIA, Phone: 2-4443 7829, tosanaji@excite.com
Specialties: Daggers, especially krisses; period pieces. **Technical:** Offers knives and finished blades in Damascus and nickel Damascus. **Prices:** $75 to $2000; some higher. **Remarks:** Part-time maker; provides complete restoration service for krisses. Trained by a Japanese Kris smith. **Mark:** None, triangle in a box, or three peaks.

MAKOTO, KUNITOMO,
3-3-18 Imazu-cho, Fukuyama-city, Hiroshima, JAPAN, Phone: 084-933-5874, kunitomo@po.iijnet.or.jp

MALABY, RAYMOND J,
835 Calhoun Ave, Juneau, AK 99801, Phone: 907-586-6981, Fax: 907-523-8031, malaby@gci.net
Specialties: Straight working knives. **Patterns:** Hunters, skiners, Bowies, and camp knives. **Technical:** Hand forged 1084, 5160, O1 and grinds ATS-34 stainless. **Prices:** $195 to $400. **Remarks:** First knife sold in 1994. **Mark:** First initial, last name, city and state.

MALLOY, JOE,
1039 Schwabe St, Freeland, PA 18224, Phone: 570-636-2781, jdmalloy@msn.com
Specialties: Working straight knives and lock back folders—plain and fancy—of his design. **Patterns:** Hunters, utility, Bowie, survival knives, folders. **Technical:** Grinds ATS-34, 440C, D2 and A2 and Damascus. Makes own leather and kydex sheaths. **Prices:** $100 to $1800. **Remarks:** Part-time maker; first knife sold in 1982. **Mark:** First and middle initials, last name, city and state.

MANDT, JOE,
3735 Overlook Dr. NE, St. Petersburg, FL 33703, Phone: 813-244-3816, jmforge@mac.com
Specialties: Forged Bowies, camp knives, hunters, skinners, fighters, boot knives, military style field knives. **Technical:** Forges plain carbon steel and high carbon tool steels, including W2, 1084, 5160, O1, 9260, 15N20, cable Damascus, pattern welded Damascus, flat and convex grinds. Prefers natural handle materials, hand-rubbed finishes, and stainless low carbon steel, Damascus and wright iron fittings. Does own heat treat. **Prices:** $150 to $750. **Remarks:** Part-time maker, first knife sold in 206. **Mark:** "MANDT".

MANEKER, KENNETH,
RR 2, Galiano Island, B.C., CANADA V0N 1P0, Phone: 604-539-2084
Specialties: Working straight knives; period pieces. **Patterns:** Camp knives and hunters; French chef knives. **Technical:** Grinds 440C, 154CM and Vascowear. **Prices:** $50 to $200; some to $300. **Remarks:** Part-time maker; first knife sold in 1981. Doing business as Water Mountain Knives. **Mark:** Japanese Kanji of initials, plus glyph.

MANKEL, KENNETH,
7836 Cannonsburg Rd, PO Box 35, Cannonsburg, MI 49317, Phone: 616-874-6955, Fax: 616-8744-4053

MANLEY, DAVID W,
3270 Six Mile Hwy, Central, SC 29630, Phone: 864-654-1125, dmanleyknives@wmconnect.com
Specialties: Working straight knives of his design or to custom specs. **Patterns:** Hunters, boot and fighters. **Technical:** Grinds 440C and ATS-34. **Prices:** $60 to $250. **Remarks:** Part-time maker; first knife sold in 1994. **Mark:** First initial, last name, year and serial number.

MANN, MICHAEL L,
IDAHO KNIFE WORKS, PO Box 144, Spirit Lake, ID 83869, Phone: 509 994-9394, Web: www.idahoknifeworks.com
Specialties: Good working blades-historical reproduction, modern or custom design. **Patterns:** Cowboy Bowies, Mountain Man period blades, old-style folders, designer and maker of "The Cliff Knife", hunter knives, hand ax and fish fillet. **Technical:** High-carbon steel blades-hand forged 5160. Stock removed 15N20 steel. Also Damascus. **Prices:** $130 to $670+. **Remarks:** Made first knife in 1965. Full-time making knives as Idaho Knife Works since 1986. Functional as well as collectible. Each knife truly unique! **Mark:** Four mountain peaks are his initials MM.

MANN, TIM,
BLADEWORKS, PO Box 1196, Honokaa, HI 96727, Phone: 808-775-0949, Fax: 808-775-0949, birdman@shaka.com
Specialties: Hand-forged knives and swords. **Patterns:** Bowies, tantos, pesh kabz, daggers. **Technical:** Use 5160, 1050, 1075, 1095 and ATS-34 steels, cable Damascus. **Prices:** $200 to $800. **Remarks:** Just learning to forge Damascus. **Mark:** None yet.

MARAGNI, DAN,
RD 1 Box 106, Georgetown, NY 13072, Phone: 315-662-7490
Specialties: Heavy-duty working knives, some investor class. **Patterns:** Hunters, fighters and camp knives, some Scottish types. **Technical:** Forges W2 and his own Damascus; toughness and edge-holding a high priority. **Prices:** $125 to $500; some to $1000. **Remarks:** Full-time maker; first knife sold in 1975. **Mark:** Celtic initials in circle.

MARINGER, TOM,
2692 Powell St., Springdale, AR 72764, maringer@arkansas.net; Web: shirepost.com/cutlery.
Specialties: Working straight and curved blades with stainless steel furniture and wire-wrapped handles. **Patterns:** Subhilts, daggers, boots, swords. **Technical:** Grinds D-2, A-2, ATS-34. May be safely disassembled by the owner via pommel screw or pegged construction. **Prices:** $2000 to $3000, some to $20,000. **Remarks:** Former full-time maker, now part-time. First knife sold in 1975. **Mark:** Full name, year, and serial number etched on tang under handle.

MARKLEY, KEN,
7651 Cabin Creek Lane, Sparta, IL 62286, Phone: 618-443-5284
Specialties: Traditional working and using knives of his design and to customer specs. **Patterns:** Fighters, hunters and utility/camp knives. **Technical:** Forges 5160, 1095 and L6; makes his own Damascus; does file work. **Prices:** $150 to $800; some to $2000. **Remarks:** Part-time maker; first knife sold in 1991. Doing business as Cabin Creek Forge. **Mark:** Last name, JS.

MARLOWE, CHARLES,
10822 Poppleton Ave, Omaha, NE 68144, Phone: 402-933-5065, cmarlowe1@cox.net; Web: www.marloweknives.com
Specialties: Folding knives and balisong. **Patterns:** Tactical pattern folders. **Technical:** Grind ATS-34, S30V, CPM154, 154CM, Damasteel, others on request. Forges/grinds 1095 on occasion. **Prices:** Start at $450. **Remarks:** First knife sold in 1993. Full-time since 1999. **Mark:** Turtle logo with Marlowe above, year below.

MARLOWE, DONALD,
2554 Oakland Rd, Dover, PA 17315, Phone: 717-764-6055
Specialties: Working straight knives in standard patterns. **Patterns:** Bowies, fighters, boots and utility knives. **Technical:** Grinds D2 and 440C. Integral design hunter models. **Prices:** $130 to $850. **Remarks:** Spare-time maker; first knife sold in 1977. **Mark:** Last name.

MARSH, JEREMY,
6169 3 Mile NE, Ada, MI 49301, Phone: 616-889-1945, steelbean@hotmail.com; Web: www.marshcustomknives.com
Specialties: Locking liner folders, dressed-up gents knives, tactical knives, and dress tacticals. **Technical:** CPM S30V stainless and Damascus blade steels using the stock-removal method of bladesmithing. **Prices:** $450 to $1500. **Remarks:** Self-taught, part-time knifemaker; first knife sold in 2004. **Mark:** Maker's last name and large, stylized M.

MARSHALL, GLENN,
PO Box 1099, 305 Hoffmann St., Mason, TX 76856, Phone: 325-347-6207
Specialties: Working knives, hunting knives, special folders, period pieces, and commemmorative knives. **Patterns:** Straight and folding knives, fighters and camp knives. **Technical:** Steel used 440C, D2, CPM and 440V. **Prices:** $200 and up according to options. **Remarks:** Full-time maker; first knife sold in 1930. Sold #1 in 1932. **Mark:** First initial, last name, city and state with anvil logo.

MARSHALL, STEPHEN R,
975 Harkreader Rd, Mt. Juliet, TN 37122

MARTIN, BRUCE E,
Rt. 6, Box 164-B, Prescott, AR 71857, Phone: 501-887-2023
Specialties: Fancy working straight knives of his design. **Patterns:** Bowies, camp knives, skinners and fighters. **Technical:** Forges 5160, 1095 and his own Damascus. Uses natural handle materials; filework available. **Prices:** $75 to $350; some to $500. **Remarks:** Full-time maker; first knife sold in 1979. **Mark:** Name in arch.

MARTIN, GENE,
PO Box 396, Williams, OR 97544, Phone: 541-846-6755, bladesmith@customknife.com
Specialties: Straight knives and folders. **Patterns:** Fighters, hunters, skinners, boot knives, spring back and lock back folders. **Technical:** Grinds ATS-34, 440C, Damascus and 154CM. Forges; makes own Damascus; scrimshaws. **Prices:** $150 to $2500. **Remarks:** Full-time maker; first knife sold in 1993. Doing business as Provision Forge. **Mark:** Name and/or crossed staff and sword.

MARTIN, HAL W,
781 Hwy 95, Morrilton, AR 72110, Phone: 501-354-1682, hal.martin@sbcglobal.net
Specialties: Hunters, Bowies and fighters. **Prices:** $250 and up. **Mark:** MARTIN.

MARTIN, HERB,
2500 Starwood Dr, Richmond, VA 23229, Phone: 804-747-1675, hamjlm@hotmail.com
Specialties: Working straight knives. **Patterns:** Skinners, hunters and utility. **Technical:** Hollow grinds ATS-34, and Micarta handles. **Prices:** $85 to $125. **Remarks:** Part-time Maker. First knife sold in 2001. **Mark:** HA MARTIN.

MARTIN, MICHAEL W,
Box 572, Jefferson St, Beckville, TX 75631, Phone: 903-678-2161
Specialties: Classic working/using straight knives of his design and in standard patterns. **Patterns:** Hunters. **Technical:** Grinds ATS-34, 440C, O1 and A2. Bead blasted, Parkerized, high polish and satin finishes. Sheaths are handmade. Also hand forges cable Damascus. **Prices:** $185 to $280 some higher. **Remarks:** Part-time maker; first knife sold in 1995. Doing business as Michael W. Martin Knives. **Mark:** Name and city, state in arch.

MARTIN, PETER,
28220 N. Lake Dr, Waterford, WI 53185, Phone: 262-706-3076, Web: www.petermartinknives.com
Specialties: Fancy, fantasy and working straight knives and folders of his design and in standard patterns. **Patterns:** Bowies, fighters, hunters, locking folders and liner locks. **Technical:** Forges own Mosaic Damascus, powdered steel and his own Damascus. Prefers natural handle material; offers file work and carved handles. **Prices:** Moderate. **Remarks:** Full-time maker; first knife sold in 1988. Doing business as Martin Custom Products. **Mark:** Martin Knives.

MARTIN, RANDALL J,
51 Bramblewood St, Bridgewater, MA 02324, Phone: 508-279-0682
Specialties: High tech folding and fixed blade tactical knives employing the latest blade steels and exotic materials. Employs a unique combination of 3d-CNC machining and hand work on both blades and handles. All knives are designed for hard use. Clean, radical grinds and ergonomic handles are hallmarks of RJ's work, as is his reputation for producing "Scary Sharp" knives. **Technical:** Grinds CPM30V, CPM 3V, CPM154CM, A2 and stainless Damascus. Other CPM alloys used on request. Performs all heat treating and cryogenic processing in-house. **Remarks:** Full-time maker since 2001 and materials engineer. Former helicopter designer. First knife sold in 1976.

MARTIN, TONY,
PO Box 10, Arcadia, MO 63621, Phone: 573-546-2254, arcadian@charter.net; Web: www.arcadianforge.com
Specialties: Specializes in historical designs, esp. puukko, skean dhu. **Remarks:** Premium quality blades, exotic wood handles, unmatched fit and finish. **Mark:** AF.

MARTIN, WALTER E,
570 Cedar Flat Rd, Williams, OR 97544, Phone: 541-846-6755

MARTIN

MARTIN, JOHN ALEXANDER,
821 N Grand Ave, Okmulgee, OK 74447, Phone: 918-758-1099, jam@jamblades.com; Web: www.jamblades.com
Specialties: Inlaid and engraved handles. **Patterns:** Bowies, fighters, hunters and traditional patterns. Swords, fixed blade knives, folders and axes. **Technical:** Forges 5160, 1084, 10XX, O1, L6 and his own Damascus. **Prices:** Start at $300. **Remarks:** Part-time maker. **Mark:** Two initials with last name and MS or 5 pointed star.

MARZITELLI, PETER,
19929 35A Ave, Langley, B.C., CANADA V3A 2R1, Phone: 604-532-8899, marzitelli@shaw.ca
Specialties: Specializes in unique functional knife shapes and designs using natural and synthetic handle materials. **Patterns:** Mostly folders, some daggers and art knives. **Technical:** Grinds ATS-34, S/S Damascus and others. **Prices:** $220 to $1000 (average $375). **Remarks:** Full-time maker; first knife sold in 1984. **Mark:** Stylized logo reads "Marz."

MASON, BILL,
1114 St Louis #33, Excelsior Springs, MO 64024, Phone: 816-637-7335
Specialties: Combat knives; some folders. **Patterns:** Fighters to match knife types in book *Cold Steel*. **Technical:** Grinds O1, 440C and ATS-34. **Prices:** $115 to $250; some to $350. **Remarks:** Spare-time maker; first knife sold in 1979. **Mark:** Initials connected.

MASSEY, AL,
Box 14 Site 15 RR#2, Mount Uniacke, Nova Scotia, CANADA B0N 1Z0, Phone: 902-866-4754, armjan@eastlink.ca
Specialties: Working knives and period pieces. **Patterns:** Swords and daggers of Celtic to medieval design, Bowies. **Technical:** Forges 5160, 1084 and 1095. Makes own Damascus. **Prices:** $200 to $500, damascus $300-$1000. **Remarks:** Part-time maker, first blade sold in 1988. **Mark:** Initials and JS on Ricasso.

MASSEY, ROGER,
4928 Union Rd, Texarkana, AR 71854, Phone: 870-779-1018
Specialties: Traditional and working straight knives and folders of his design and to customer specs. **Patterns:** Bowies, hunters, daggers and utility knives. **Technical:** Forges 1084 and 52100, makes his own Damascus. Offers filework and silver wire inlay in handles. **Prices:** $200 to $1500; some to $2500. **Remarks:** Part-time maker; first knife sold in 1991. **Mark:** Last name, M.S.

MASSEY, RON,
61638 El Reposo St., Joshua Tree, CA 92252, Phone: 760-366-9239 after 5 p.m., Fax: 763-366-4620
Specialties: Classic, traditional, fancy/embellished, high art, period pieces, working/using knives, straight knives, folders, and automatics. Your design, customer specs, about 175 standard patterns. **Patterns:** Automatics, hunters and fighters. All folders are side-locking folders. Unless requested as lock books slip joint he specializes or custom designs. **Technical:** ATS-34, 440C, D-2 upon request. Engraving, filework, scrimshaw, most of the exotic handle materials. All aspects are performed by him: inlay work in pearls or stone, handmade Pem' work. **Prices:** $110 to $2500; some to $6000. **Remarks:** Part-time maker; first knife sold in 1976.

MATA, LEONARD,
3583 Arruza St, San Diego, CA 92154, Phone: 619-690-6935

MATHEWS, CHARLIE AND HARRY,
TWIN BLADES, 121 Mt Pisgah Church Rd., Statesboro, GA 30458, Phone: 912-865-9098, twinxblades@bulloch.net; Web: www.twinxblades.com
Specialties: Working straight knives, carved stag handles. **Patterns:** Hunters, fighters, Bowies and period pieces. **Technical:** Grinds D2, CPMS30V, CPM3V, ATS-34 and commercial Damascus; handmade sheaths some with exotic leather, file work. Forges 1095, 1084, and 5160. **Prices:** Starting at $125. **Remarks:** Twin brothers making knives full-time under the label of Twin Blades. Charter members Georgia Custom Knifemakers Guild. Members of The Knifemakers Guild. **Mark:** Twin Blades over crossed knives, reverse side steel type.

MATSUNO, KANSEI,
109-8 Uenomachi Nishikaiden, Gifu-City 501-1168, JAPAN, Phone: 81 58 234 8643

MATSUOKA, SCOT,
94-415 Ukalialii Place, Mililani, HI 96789, Phone: 808-625-6658, Fax: 808-625-6658, scottym@hawaii.rr.com; Web: www.matsuokaknives.com
Specialties: Folders, fixed blades with custom hand-stitched sheaths. **Patterns:** Gentleman's knives, hunters, tactical folders. **Technical:** CPM 154CM, 440C, 154, BG42, bolsters, file work, and engraving. **Prices:** Starting price $350. **Remarks:** Part-time maker, first knife sold in 2002. **Mark:** Logo, name and state.

MATSUSAKI, TAKESHI,
MATSUSAKI KNIVES, 151 Ono-Cho Sasebo-shi, Nagasaki, JAPAN, Phone: 0956-47-2938, Fax: 0956-47-2938
Specialties: Working and collector grade front look and slip joint. **Patterns:** Sheffierd type folders. **Technical:** Grinds ATS-34 k-120. **Price:** $250 to $1000, some to $8000. **Remarks:** Part-time maker, first knife sold in 1990. **Mark:** Name and initials.

MAXEN, MICK,
2 Huggins Welham Green, "Hatfield, Herts", UNITED KINGDOM AL97LR, Phone: 01707 261213, mmaxen@aol.com
Specialties: Damascus and Mosaic. **Patterns:** Medieval-style daggers and Bowies. **Technical:** Forges CS75 and 15N20 / nickel Damascus. **Mark:** Last name with axe above.

MAXFIELD, LYNN,
382 Colonial Ave, Layton, UT 84041, Phone: 801-544-4176, maxfieldknives@q.com
Specialties: Sporting knives, some fancy. **Patterns:** Hunters, fishing, fillet, special purpose: some locking folders. **Technical:** Grinds 440-C, 154-CM, CPM154, D2, CPM S30V, and Damascus. **Prices:** $125 to $400; some to $900. **Remarks:** Part-time maker; first knife sold in 1979. **Mark:** Name, city and state.

MAXWELL, DON,
1484 Celeste Ave, Clovis, CA 93611, Phone: 559-299-2197, maxwellknives@aol.com; Web: maxwellknives.com
Specialties: Fancy folding knives and fixed blades of his design. **Patterns:** Hunters, fighters, utility/camp knives, LinerLock® folders, flippers and fantasy knives. **Technical:** Grinds 440C, ATS-34, D2, CPM 154, and commercial Damascus. **Prices:** $250 to $1000; some to $2500. **Remarks:** Full-time maker; first knife sold in 1987. **Mark:** Last name only or Maxwell MAX-TAC.

MAY, CHARLES,
10024 McDonald Rd., Aberdeen, MS 39730, Phone: 662-369-0404, charlesmayknives@yahoo.com; Web: www.charlesmayknives.blademakers.com
Specialties: Fixed-blade sheath knives. **Patterns:** Hunters and fillet knives. **Technical:** Scandinavian-ground D2 and S30V blades, black micarta and wood handles, nickel steel pins with maker's own pocket carry or belt-loop pouches. **Prices:** $215 to $495. **Mark:** "Charles May Knives" and a knife in a circle.

MAYNARD, LARRY JOE,
PO Box 493, Crab Orchard, WV 25827
Specialties: Fancy and fantasy straight knives. **Patterns:** Big knives; a Bowie with a full false edge; fighting knives. **Technical:** Grinds standard steels. **Prices:** $350 to $500; some to $1000. **Remarks:** Full-time maker; first knife sold in 1986. **Mark:** Middle and last initials.

MAYNARD, WILLIAM N.,
2677 John Smith Rd, Fayetteville, NC 28306, Phone: 910-425-1615
Specialties: Traditional and working straight knives of all designs. **Patterns:** Combat, Bowies, fighters, hunters and utility knives. **Technical:** Grinds 440C, ATS-34 and commercial Damascus. Offers fancy filework; handmade sheaths. **Prices:** $100 to $300; some to $750. **Remarks:** Full-time maker; first knife sold in 1988. **Mark:** Last name.

MAYO JR., HOMER,
18036 Three Rivers Rd., Biloxi, MS 39532, Phone: 228-326-8298
Specialties: Traditional working straight knives, folders and tactical. **Patterns:** Hunters, fighters, tactical, bird, Bowies, fish fillet knives and lightweight folders. **Technical:** Grinds 440C, ATS-34, D-2, Damascus, forges and grinds 52100 and custom makes sheaths. **Prices:** $100 to $1000. **Remarks:** Part-time maker **Mark:** All knives are serial number and registered in the name of the original purchaser, stamped last name or etched.

MAYO JR., TOM,
67 412 Alahaka St, Waialua, HI 96791, Phone: 808-637-6560, mayot001@hawaii.rr.com; Web: www.mayoknives.com
Specialties: Framelocks/tactical knives. **Patterns:** Combat knives, hunters, Bowies and folders. **Technical:** Titanium/stellite/S30V. **Prices:** $500 to $1000. **Remarks:** Full-time maker; first knife sold in 1982. **Mark:** Volcano logo with name and state.

MAYVILLE, OSCAR L,
2130 E. County Rd 910S, Marengo, IN 47140, Phone: 812-338-4159
Specialties: Working straight knives; period pieces. **Patterns:** Kitchen cutlery, Bowies, camp knives and hunters. **Technical:** Grinds A2, O1 and 440C. **Prices:** $50 to $350; some to $500. **Remarks:** Full-time maker; first knife sold in 1984. **Mark:** Initials over knife logo.

MCABEE, WILLIAM,
27275 Norton Grade, Colfax, CA 95713, Phone: 530-389-8163
Specialties: Working/using knives. **Patterns:** Fighters, Bowies, Hunters. **Technical:** Grinds ATS-34. **Prices:** $75 to $200; some to $350. **Remarks:** Part-time maker; first knife sold in 1990. **Mark:** Stylized WM stamped.

MCCALLEN JR., HOWARD H,
110 Anchor Dr, So Seaside Park, NJ 08752

MCCARLEY, JOHN,
4165 Harney Rd, Taneytown, MD 21787
Specialties: Working straight knives; period pieces. **Patterns:** Hunters, Bowies, camp knives, miniatures, throwing knives. **Technical:** Forges W2, O1 and his own Damascus. **Prices:** $150 to $300; some to $1000. **Remarks:** Part-time maker; first knife sold in 1977. **Mark:** Initials in script.

MCCARTY, HARRY,
1479 Indian Ridge Rd, Blaine, TN 37709
Specialties: Period pieces. **Patterns:** Trade knives, Bowies, 18th and 19th century folders and hunting swords. **Technical:** Forges and grinds high-carbon steel. **Prices:** $75 to $1300. **Remarks:** Full-time maker; first knife sold in 1977. Doing business as Indian Ridge Forge. **Mark:** Stylized initials inside a shamrock.

MCCLURE, JERRY,
3052 Isim Rd, Norman, OK 73026, Phone: 405-321-3614, jerry@jmcclureknives.net; Web: www.jmcclureknives.net
Specialties: Gentleman's folder, linerlock with my jeweled pivot system of eight rubies, forged one-of-a-kind Damascus Bowies, and a line of hunting/camp knives. **Patterns:** Folders, Bowie, and hunting/camp **Technical** Forges own Damascus, also uses Damasteel and does own heat treating. **Prices** $500 to $3,000 and up **Remarks** Full-time maker, made first knife in 1965. **Mark** J.MCCLURE

MCCLURE, MICHAEL,
803 17th Ave, Menlo Park, CA 94025, Phone: 650-323-2596, mikesknives@comcast.net
Specialties: Working/using straight knives of his design and to customer specs. **Patterns:** Bowies, hunters, skinners, utility/camp, tantos, fillets and boot knives. **Technical:** Forges high-carbon and Damascus; also grinds stainless, all grades. **Prices:** Start at $200. **Remarks:** Part-time maker; first knife sold in 1991. ABS Journeyman Smith. **Mark:** Mike McClure.

MCCONNELL JR., LOYD A,
309 County Road 144-B, Marble Falls, TX 78654, Phone: 830-798-8087, ccknives@ccknives.com; Web: www.ccknives.com
Specialties: Working straight knives and folders, some fancy. **Patterns:** Hunters, boots, Bowies, locking folders and slip-joints. **Technical:** Grinds CPM Steels, ATS-34 and BG-42 and commercial Damascus. **Prices:** $450 to $10,000. **Remarks:** Full-time maker; first knife sold in 1975. Doing business as Cactus Custom Knives. Markets product knives under name: Lone Star Knives. **Mark:** Name, city and state in cactus logo.

MCCORNOCK, CRAIG,
MCC MTN OUTFITTERS, 4775 Rt. 212/PO 162, Willow, NY 12495, Phone: 845-679-9758, Mccmtn@aol.com; Web: www.mccmtn.com
Specialties: Carry, utility, hunters, defense type knives and functional swords. **Patterns:** Drop points, hawkbills, tantos, wakizashis, katanas **Technical:** Stock removal, forged and Damascus, (yes, he still flints knap). **Prices:** $200 to $2000. **Mark:** McM.

MCCOUN, MARK,
14212 Pine Dr, DeWitt, VA 23840, Phone: 804-469-7631, mccounandsons@live.com
Specialties: Working/using straight knives of his design and in standard patterns; custom miniatures. **Patterns:** Locking liners, integrals. **Technical:** Grinds Damascus, ATS-34 and 440C. **Prices:** $150 to $500. **Remarks:** Part-time maker; first knife sold in 1989. **Mark:** Name, city and state.

MCCRACKIN, KEVIN,
3720 Hess Rd, House Spings, MO 63051, Phone: 636-677-6066

MCCRACKIN AND SON, V J,
3720 Hess Rd, House Springs, MO 63051, Phone: 636-677-6066
Specialties: Working straight knives in standard patterns. **Patterns:** Hunters, Bowies and camp knives. **Technical:** Forges L6, 5160, his own Damascus, cable Damascus. **Prices:** $125 to $700; some to $1500. **Remarks:** Part-time maker; first knife sold in 1983. Son Kevin helps make the knives. **Mark:** Last name, M.S.

MCCULLOUGH, JERRY,
274 West Pettibone Rd, Georgiana, AL 36033, Phone: 334-382-7644, ke4er@alaweb.com
Specialties: Standard patterns or custom designs. **Technical:** Forge and grind scrap-tool and Damascus steels. Use natural handle materials and turquoise trim on some. Filework on others. **Prices:** $65 to $250 and up. **Remarks:** Part-time maker. **Mark:** Initials (JM) combined.

MCDONALD, RICH,
4590 Kirk Rd, Columbiana, OH 44408, Phone: 330-482-0007, Fax: 330-482-0007
Specialties: Traditional working/using and art knives of his design. **Patterns:** Bowies, hunters, folders, primitives and tomahawks. **Technical:** Forges 5160, 1084, 1095, 52100 and his own Damascus. Fancy filework. **Prices:** $200 to $1500. **Remarks:** Full-time maker; first knife sold in 1994. **Mark:** First and last initials connected.

MCDONALD, ROBERT J,
14730 61 Court N, Loxahatchee, FL 33470, Phone: 561-790-1470
Specialties: Traditional working straight knives to customer specs. **Patterns:** Fighters, swords and folders. **Technical:** Grinds 440C, ATS-34 and forges own Damascus. **Prices:** $150 to $1000. **Remarks:** Part-time maker; first knife sold in 1988. **Mark:** Electro-etched name.

MCDONALD, ROBIN J,
7300 Tolleson Ave NW, Albuquerque, NM 87114-3546
Specialties: Working knives of maker's design. **Patterns:** Bowies, hunters, camp knives and fighters. **Technical:** Forges primarily 5160. **Prices:** $100 to $500. **Remarks:** Part-time maker; first knife sold in 1999. **Mark:** Initials RJM.

MCDONALD, W J "JERRY",
7173 Wickshire Cove E, Germantown, TN 38138, Phone: 901-756-9924, wjmcdonaldknives@email.msn.com; Web: www.mcdonaldknives.com
Specialties: Classic and working/using straight knives of his design and in standard patterns. **Patterns:** Bowies, hunters kitchen and traditional spring back pocket knives. **Technical:** Grinds ATS-34, 154CM, D2, 440V, BG42 and 440C. **Prices:** $125 to $1000. **Remarks:** Full-time maker; first knife sold in 1989. **Mark:** First and middle initials, last name, maker, city and state. Some of his knives are stamped McDonald in script.

MCFALL, KEN,
PO Box 458, Lakeside, AZ 85929, Phone: 928-537-2026, Fax: 928-537-8066, knives@citlink.net
Specialties: Fancy working straight knives and some folders. **Patterns:** Daggers, boots, tantos, Bowies; some miniatures. **Technical:** Grinds D2, ATS-34 and 440C. Forges his own Damascus. **Prices:** $200 to $1200. **Remarks:** Part-time maker; first knife sold in 1984. **Mark:** Name, city and state.

MCFARLIN, ERIC E,
PO Box 2188, Kodiak, AK 99615, Phone: 907-486-4799
Specialties: Working knives of his design. **Patterns:** Bowies, skinners, camp knives and hunters. **Technical:** Flat and convex grinds 440C, A2 and AEB-L. **Prices:** Start at $200. **Remarks:** Part-time maker; first knife sold in 1989. **Mark:** Name and city in rectangular logo.

MCFARLIN, J W,
3331 Pocohantas Dr, Lake Havasu City, AZ 86404, Phone: 928-453-7612, Fax: 928-453-7612, aztheedge@NPGcable.com
Technical: Flat grinds, D2, ATS-34, 440C, Thomas and Peterson Damascus. **Remarks:** From working knives to investment. Customer designs always welcome. 100 percent handmade. Made first knife in 1972. **Prices:** $150 to $3000. **Mark:** Hand written in the blade.

MCGILL, JOHN,
PO Box 302, Blairsville, GA 30512, Phone: 404-745-4686
Specialties: Working knives. **Patterns:** Traditional patterns; camp knives. **Technical:** Forges L6 and 9260; makes Damascus. **Prices:** $50 to $250; some to $500. **Remarks:** Full-time maker; first knife sold in 1982. **Mark:** XYLO.

MCGOWAN, FRANK E,
12629 Howard Lodge Dr, Summer address, Sykesville, MD 21784, Phone: 443-285-3815, fmcgowan1@comcast.net
Specialties: Fancy working knives and folders to customer specs. **Patterns:** Survivor knives, fighters, fishing knives, folders and hunters. **Technical:** Grinds and forges O1, 440C, 5160, ATS-34, 52100, or customer choice. **Prices:** $100 to $1000; some more. **Remarks:** Full-time maker; first knife sold in 1986. **Mark:** Last name.

MCGOWAN, FRANK E,
2023 Robin Ct, Winter address, Sebring, FL 33870, Phone: 443-285-3815, fmcgowan1@comcast.net
Specialties: Fancy working knives and folders to customer specs. **Patterns:** Survivor knives, fighters, fishing knives, folders and hunters. **Technical:** Grinds and forges O1, 440C, 5160, ATS-34, 52100 or customer choice. **Prices:** $100 to $1000, some more. **Remarks:** Full-time maker. First knife sold in 1986. **Mark:** Last name.

MCGRATH, PATRICK T,
8343 Kenyon Ave, Westchester, CA 90045, Phone: 310-338-8764, hidinginLA@excite.com

MCGRODER, PATRICK J,
5725 Chapin Rd, Madison, OH 44057, Phone: 216-298-3405, Fax: 216-298-3405
Specialties: Traditional working/using knives of his design. **Patterns:** Bowies, hunters and utility/camp knives. **Technical:** Grinds ATS-34, D2 and customer requests. Does reverse etching; heat-treats; prefers natural materials; custom made sheath with each knife. **Prices:** $125 to $250. **Remarks:** Part-time maker. **Mark:** First and middle initials, last name, maker, city and state.

MCGUANE IV, THOMAS F,
410 South 3rd Ave, Bozeman, MT 59715, Phone: 406-586-0248, Web: http://www.thomasmcguane.com
Specialties: Multi metal inlaid knives of handmade steel. **Patterns:** Lock back and LinerLock® folders, fancy straight knives. **Technical:** 1084/1SN20 Damascus and Mosaic steel by maker. **Prices:** $1000 and up. **Mark:** Surname or name and city, state.

MCHENRY, WILLIAM JAMES,
Box 67, Wyoming, RI 02898, Phone: 401-539-8353
Specialties: Fancy high-tech folders of his design. **Patterns:** Locking folders with various mechanisms. **Technical:** One-of-a-kind only, no duplicates. Inventor of the Axis Lock. Most pieces disassemble and feature top-shelf materials including gold, silver and gems. **Prices:** Upscale. **Remarks:** Full-time maker; first knife sold in 1988. Former goldsmith. **Mark:** Last name or first and last initials.

MCINTYRE, SHAWN,
71 Leura Grove, Hawthorn East Victoria, AUSTRALIA 3123, Phone: 61 3 9813 2049/Cell 61 412 041 062, macpower@netspace.net.au; Web: www.mcintyreknives.com
Specialties: Damascus & CS fixed blades and art knives. **Patterns:** Bowies, hunters, fighters, kukris, integrals. **Technical:** Forges, makes own Damascus including pattern weld, mosaic, and composite multi-bars form O1 & 15N20 Also uses 1084, W2, and 52100. **Prices:** $275 to $2000. **Remarks:** Full-time maker since 1999. **Mark:** Mcintyre in script.

MCKEE, NEIL,
674 Porter Hill Rd., Stevensville, MT 59870, Phone: 406-777-3507, mckeenh@peoplepc.com
Specialties: Early American. **Patterns:** Nessmuk, DeWeese, French folders, art pieces. **Technical:** Engraver. **Prices:** $150 to $1000. **Mark:** Oval with initials.

MCKENZIE, DAVID BRIAN,
2311 B Ida Rd, Campbell River B, CANADA V9W-4V7

MCKIERNAN, STAN,
11751 300th St, Lamoni, IA 50140, Phone: 641-784-6873/641-781-0368, slmck@hotmailc.om
Specialties: Self-sheathed knives and miniatures. **Patterns:** Daggers, ethnic designs and individual styles. **Technical:** Grinds Damascus and 440C. **Prices:** $200 to $500, some to $1500. **Mark:** "River's Bend" inside two concentric circles.

MCLENDON, HUBERT W,
125 Thomas Rd, Waco, GA 30182, Phone: 770-574-9796
Specialties: Using knives; his design or customer's. **Patterns:** Bowies and hunters. **Technical:** Hand ground or forged ATS-34, 440C and D2. **Prices:** $100 to $300. **Remarks:** First knife sold in 1978. **Mark:** McLendon or Mc.

MCLUIN, TOM,
36 Fourth St, Dracut, MA 01826, Phone: 978-957-4899, tmcluin@comcast.net; Web: www.mcluinknives.com
Specialties: Working straight knives and folders of his design. **Patterns:** Boots, hunters and folders. **Technical:** Grinds ATS-34, 440C, O1 and Damascus; makes his own mokume. **Prices:** $100 to $400; some to $700. **Remarks:** Part-time maker; first knife sold in 1991. **Mark:** Last name.

MCLURKIN, ANDREW,
2112 Windy Woods Dr, Raleigh, NC 27607, Phone: 919-834-4693, mclurkincustomknives.com
Specialties: Collector grade folders, working folders, fixed blades, and miniatures. Knives made to order and to his design. **Patterns:** Locking liner and lock back folders, hunter, working and tactical designs. **Technical:** Using patterned Damascus, Mosaic Damascus, ATS-34, BG-42, and CPM steels. Prefers natural handle materials such as pearl, ancient ivory and stabilized wood. Also using synthetic materials such as carbon fiber, titanium, and G10. **Prices:** $250 and up. **Mark:** Last name. Mark is often on inside of folders.

MCMANUS, DANNY,
413 Fairhaven Drive, Taylors, SC 29687, Phone: 864-268-9849, Fax: 864-268-9699, DannyMcManus@bigfoot.com
Specialties: High-tech and traditional working/using straight knives of his design, to customer specs and in standard patterns. **Patterns:** Boots, Bowies, fighters, hunters and utility/camp knives. **Technical:** Forges stainless steel Damascus; grinds ATS-34. Offers engraving and scrimshaw. **Prices:** $300 to $2000; some to $3000. **Remarks:** Full-time maker; first knife sold in 1997. Doing business as Stamascus KnifeWorks Corp. **Mark:** Stamascus.

MCNABB, TOMMY,
CAROLINA CUSTOM KNIVES, PO Box 327, Bethania, NC 27010, Phone: 336-924-6053, Fax: 336-924-4854, tommy@tmcnabb.com; Web: carolinaknives.com
Specialties: Classic and working knives of his own design or to customer's specs. **Patterns:** Traditional bowies. Tomahawks, hunters and customer designs. **Technical:** Forges his own Damascus steel, hand forges or grinds ATS-34 and other hi-tech steels. Prefers mirror finish or satin finish on working knives. Uses exotic or natural handle material and stabilized woods. **Price:** $300-$3500. **Remarks:** Full time maker. Made first knife in 1982. **Mark:** "Carolina Custom Knives" on stock removal blades "T. McNabb" on custom orders and Damascus knives.

MCRAE, J MICHAEL,
6100 Lake Rd, Mint Hill, NC 28227, Phone: 704-545-2929, scotia@carolina.rr.com; Web: www.scotiametalwork.com
Specialties: Scottish dirks, sgian dubhs, broadswords. **Patterns:** Traditional blade styles with traditional and slightly non-traditional handle treatments. **Technical:** Forges 5160 and his own Damascus. Prefers stag and exotic hardwoods for handles, many intricately carved. **Prices:** Starting at $125, some to $3500. **Remarks:** Journeyman Smith in ABS, member of North Carolina Custom Knifemakers Guild and ABANA. Full-time maker, first knife sold in 1982. Doing business as Scotia Metalwork. **Mark:** Last name underlined with a claymore.

MEERDINK, KURT,
248 Yulan Barryville Rd., Barryville, NY 12719-5305, Phone: 845-557-0783
Specialties: Working straight knives. **Patterns:** Hunters, Bowies, tactical and neck knives. **Technical:** Grinds ATS-34, 440C, D2, Damascus. **Prices:** $95 to $1100. **Remarks:** Full-time maker, first knife sold in 1994. **Mark:** Meerdink Maker, Rio NY.

MEIER, DARYL,
75 Forge Rd, Carbondale, IL 62901, Phone: 618-549-3234, Web: www.meiersteel.com
Specialties: One-of-a-kind knives and swords. **Patterns:** Collaborates on blades. **Technical:** Forges his own Damascus, W1 and A203E, 440C, 431, nickel 200 and clad steel. **Prices:** $250 to $450; some to $6000. **Remarks:** Full-time smith and researcher since 1974; first knife sold in 1974. **Mark:** Name or circle/arrow symbol or SHAWNEE.

MELIN, GORDON C,
14207 Coolbank Dr, La Mirada, CA 90638, Phone: 562-946-5753

MELLARD, J R,
17006 Highland Canyon Dr., Houston, TX 77095, Phone: 281-550-9464

MELOY, SEAN,
7148 Rosemary Lane, Lemon Grove, CA 91945-2105, Phone: 619-465-7173
Specialties: Traditional working straight knives of his design. **Patterns:** Bowies, fighters and utility/camp knives. **Technical:** Grinds 440C, ATS-34 and D2. **Prices:** $125 to $300. **Remarks:** Part-time maker; first knife sold in 1985. **Mark:** Broz Knives.

MENEFEE, RICKY BOB,
2440 County Road 1322, Blawchard, OK 73010, rmenefee@pldi.net
Specialties: Working straight knives and pocket knives. **Patterns:** Hunters, fighters, minis & Bowies. **Technical:** Grinds ATS-34, 440C, D2, BG42 and S30V. **Price:** $130 to $1000. **Remarks:** Part-time maker, first knife sold in 2001. Member of KGA of Oklahoma, also Knifemakers Guild. **Mark:** Menefee made or Menefee stamped in blade.

MENSCH, LARRY C,
Larry's Knife Shop, 578 Madison Ave, Milton, PA 17847, Phone: 570-742-9554
Specialties: Custom orders. **Patterns:** Bowies, daggers, hunters, tantos, short swords and miniatures. **Technical:** Grinds ATS-34, stainless steel Damascus; blade grinds hollow, flat and slack. Filework; bending guards and fluting handles with finger grooves. Offers engraving and scrimshaw. **Prices:** $200 and up. **Remarks:** Full-time maker; first knife sold in 1993. Doing business as Larry's Knife Shop. **Mark:** Connected capital "L" and small "m" in script.

MERCER, MIKE,
149 N. Waynesville Rd, Lebanon, OH 45036, Phone: 513-932-2837, mmercer08445@roadrunner.com
Specialties: Miniatures and autos. **Patterns:** All folder patterns. **Technical:** Diamonds and gold, one-of-a-kind, Damascus, O1, stainless steel blades. **Prices:** $500 to $5000. **Remarks:** Carved wax - lost wax casting. **Mark:** Stamp - Mercer.

MERCHANT, TED,
7 Old Garrett Ct, White Hall, MD 21161, Phone: 410-343-0380
Specialties: Traditional and classic working knives. **Patterns:** Bowies, hunters, camp knives, fighters, daggers and skinners. **Technical:** Forges W2 and 5160; makes own Damascus. Makes handles with wood, stag, horn, silver and gem stone inlay; fancy filework. **Prices:** $125 to $600; some to $1500. **Remarks:** Full-time maker; first knife sold in 1985. **Mark:** Last name.

MERZ III, ROBERT L,
1447 Winding Canyon, Katy, TX 77493, Phone: 281-391-2897, bobmerz@consolidated.net; Web: www.merzknives.com
Specialties: Folders. **Prices:** $350 to $1,400. **Remarks:** Full time maker; first knife sold in 1974. **Mark:** MERZ.

MESHEJIAN, MARDI,
5 Bisbee Court 109 PMB 230, Santa Fe, NM 87508, Phone: 505-310-7441, toothandnail13@yahoo.com
Specialties: One-of-a-kind fantasy and high art straight knives & folders. **Patterns:** Swords, daggers, folders and other weapons. **Technical:** Forged steel Damascus and titanium Damascus. **Prices:** $300 to $5000 some to $7000. **Mark:** Stamped stylized "M."

MESSER, DAVID T,
134 S Torrence St, Dayton, OH 45403-2044, Phone: 513-228-6561
Specialties: Fantasy period pieces, straight and folding, of his design. **Patterns:** Bowies, daggers and swords. **Technical:** Grinds 440C, O1, 06 and commercial Damascus. Likes fancy guards and exotic handle materials. **Prices:** $100 to $225; some to $375. **Remarks:** Spare-time maker; first knife sold in 1991. **Mark:** Name stamp.

METHENY, H A "WHITEY",
7750 Waterford Dr, Spotsylvania, VA 22553, Phone: 540-582-3095, Fax: 540-582-3095, hametheny@aol.com; Web: www.methenyknives.com
Specialties: Working and using straight knives of his design and to customer specs. **Patterns:** Hunters and kitchen knives. **Technical:** Grinds 440C and ATS-34. Offers filework; tooled custom sheaths. **Prices:** $200 to $350. **Remarks:** Spare-time maker; first knife sold in 1990. **Mark:** Initials/full name football logo.

METSALA, ANTHONY,
30557 103rd St. NW, Princeton, MN 55371, Phone: 763-389-2628, acmetsala@izoom.net; Web: www.metsalacustomknives.com
Specialties: Sole authorship one-off mosaic Damascus liner locking folders, sales of makers finished one-off mosaic Damascus blades. **Patterns:** Except for a couple EDC folding knives, maker does not use patterns. **Technical:** Forges own mosaic Damascus carbon blade and bolster material. All stainless steel blades are heat treated by Paul Bos. **Prices:** $250 to $1500. **Remarks:** Full-time knifemaker and Damascus steel maker, first knife sold in 2005. **Mark:** A.C. Metsala or Metsala.

METZ, GREG T,
c/o James Ranch HC 83, Cascade, ID 83611, Phone: 208-382-4336, metzenterprise@yahoo.com
Specialties: Hunting and utility knives. **Prices:** $350 and up. **Remarks:** Natural handle materials; hand forged blades; 1084 and 1095. **Mark:** METZ (last name).

MEYER, CHRISTOPHER J,
737 Shenipsit Lake Rd, Tolland, CT 06084, Phone: 860-875-1826, shenipsitforge.cjm@gmail.com
Specialties: Hand forged tool steels. **Patterns:** Bowies, fighters, hunters, and camp knives. **Technical:** Forges O1, 1084, W2, Grinds ATS-34, O1, D2, CPM154CM. **Remarks:** Spare-time maker, sold first knife in 2003. **Mark:** Name or "Shenipsit forge, Meyer".

MICHINAKA, TOSHIAKI,
I-679 Koyamacho-nishi Tottori-shi, Tottori 680-0947, JAPAN, Phone: 0857-28-5911
Specialties: Art miniature knives. **Patterns:** Bowies, hunters, fishing, camp knives & miniatures. **Technical:** Grinds ATS-34 and 440C. **Prices:** $300 to $900 some higher. **Remarks:** Part-time maker. First knife sold in 1982. **Mark:** First initial, last name.

MICHO, KANDA,
7-32-5 Shinzutsumi-cho, Shinnanyo-city, Yamaguchi, JAPAN, Phone: 0834-62-1910

MICKLEY, TRACY,
42112 Kerns Dr, North Mankato, MN 56003, Phone: 507-947-3760, tracy@mickleyknives.com; Web: www.mickleyknives.com
Specialties: Working and collectable straight knives using mammoth ivory or burl woods, LinerLock® folders. **Patterns:** Custom and classic hunters, utility, fighters and Bowies. **Technical:** Grinding 154-CM, BG-42 forging O1 and 52100. **Prices:** Starting at $325 **Remarks:** Part-time since 1999. **Mark:** Last name.

MILES JR., C R "IRON DOCTOR",
1541 Porter Crossroad, Lugoff, SC 29078, Phone: 803-438-5816
Specialties: Traditional working straight knives of his design or made to custom specs. **Patterns:** Hunters, fighters, utility camp knives and hatches. **Technical:** Grinds O1, D2, ATS-34, 440C, and 1095. Forges 18th century style cutlery of high carbon steels. Also forges and grinds old files to make knives. Custom leather sheaths. **Prices:** $100 and up. **Remarks:** Part-time maker, first knife sold in 1997. Member of South Carolina Association of Knifemakers since 1997. **Mark:** Iron doctor plus name and serial number.

MILITANO, TOM,
CUSTOM KNIVES, 77 Jason Rd., Jacksonville, AL 36265-6655, Phone: 256-435-7132, jeffkin57@aol.com
Specialties: Fixed blade, one-of-a-kind knives. **Patterns:** Bowies, fighters, hunters and tactical knives. **Technical:** Grinds 440C, ATS-34, A2, and Damascus. Hollow grinds, flat grinds, and decorative filework. **Prices:** $150 plus. **Remarks:** Part-time maker. Sold first knives in the mid to late 1980s. Memberships: Founding member of New England Custom Knife Association. **Mark:** Name engraved in ricasso area - type of steel on reverse side.

MILLARD, FRED G,
27627 Kopezyk Ln, Richland Center, WI 53581, Phone: 608-647-5376
Specialties: Working/using straight knives of his design or to customer specs. **Patterns:** Bowies, hunters, utility/camp knives, kitchen/steak knives. **Technical:** Grinds ATS-34, O1, D2 and 440C. Makes sheaths. **Prices:** $110 to $300. **Remarks:** Full-time maker; first knife sold in 1993. Doing business as Millard Knives. **Mark:** Mallard duck in flight with serial number.

MILLER, BOB,
7659 Fine Oaks Pl, Oakville, MO 63129, Phone: 314-846-8934
Specialties: Mosaic Damascus; collector straight knives and folders. **Patterns:** Hunters, Bowies, utility/camp knives, daggers. **Technical:** Forges own Damascus, mosaic-Damascus and 52100. **Prices:** $125 to $500. **Remarks:** Part-time maker; first knife sold in 1983. **Mark:** First and middle initials and last name, or initials.

MILLER, DON,
1604 Harrodsburg Rd, Lexington, KY 40503, Phone: 606-276-3299

MILLER, HANFORD J,
Box 97, Cowdrey, CO 80434, Phone: 970-723-4708
Specialties: Working knives in Moran styles, Bowie, period pieces, Cinquedea. **Patterns:** Daggers, Bowies, working knives. **Technical:** All work forged: W2, 1095, 5160 and Damascus. ABS methods; offers fine silver repousse, scabboard mountings and wire inlay, oak presentation cases. **Prices:** $400 to $1000; some to $3000 and up. **Remarks:** Full-time maker; first knife sold in 1968. **Mark:** Initials or name within Bowie logo.

MILLER, JAMES P,
9024 Goeller Rd, RR 2, Box 28, Fairbank, IA 50629, Phone: 319-635-2294, Web: www.damascusknives.biz
Specialties: All tool steel Damascus; working knives and period pieces. **Patterns:** Hunters, Bowies, camp knives and daggers. **Technical:** Forges and grinds 1095, 52100, 440C and his own Damascus. **Prices:** $175 to $500; some to $1500. **Remarks:** Full-time maker; first knife sold in 1970. **Mark:** First and middle initials, last name with knife logo.

MILLER, M A,
11625 Community Center Dr, Unit #1531, Northglenn, CO 80233, Phone: 303-280-3816
Specialties: Using knives for hunting. 3-1/2"-4" Loveless drop-point. Made to customer specs. **Patterns:** Skinners and camp knives. **Technical:** Grinds 440C, D2, O1 and ATS-34 Damascus miniatures. **Prices:** $225 to $350; miniatures $75 to $150. **Remarks:** Part-time maker; first knife sold in 1988. **Mark:** Last name stamped in block letters or first and middle initials, last name, maker, city and state with triangles on either side etched.

MILLER, MICHAEL,
3030 E Calle Cedral, Kingman, AZ 86401, Phone: 928-757-1359, mike@mmilleroriginals.com
Specialties: Hunters, Bowies, and skinners with exotic burl wood, stag, ivory and gemstone handles. **Patterns:** High carbon steel knives. **Technical:** High carbon and nickel alloy Damascus and high carbon and meteorite Damascus. Also mosaic Damascus. **Prices:** $235 to $4500. **Remarks:** Full-time maker since 2002, first knife sold 2000; doing business as M Miller Originals. **Mark:** First initial and last name with 'handmade' underneath.

MILLER, MICHAEL E,
910146 S. 3500 Rd., Chandler, OK 74834, Phone: 918-377-2411, mimiller1@brightok.net
Specialties: Traditional working/using knives of his design. **Patterns:** Bowies, hunters and kitchen knives. **Technical:** Grinds ATS-34, CPM440V; forges Damascus and cable Damascus and 52100. Prefers scrimshaw, fancy pins, basket weave and embellished sheaths. **Prices:** $80 to $300; some to $500. **Remarks:** Part-time maker; first knife sold in 1984. Doing business as Miller Custom Knives. Member of KGA of Oklahoma and Salt Fork Blacksmith Association. **Mark:** First and middle initials, last name, maker.

MILLER, NATE,
Sportsman's Edge, 1075 Old Steese Hwy N, Fairbanks, AK 99712, Phone: 907-479-4774, sportsmansedge@gci.net
Specialties: Fixed blade knives for hunting, fishing, kitchen and collector pieces. **Patterns:** Hunters, skinners, utility, tactical, fishing, camp knives-

your pattern or mine. **Technical:** Stock removal maker, ATS-34, 154CM, D2, 1095, other steels on request. Handle material includes micarta, horn, antler, fossilized ivory and bone, wide selection of woods. **Prices:** $225-$800. **Remarks:** Full time maker since 2002. **Mark:** Nate Miller, Fairbanks, AK.

MILLER, R D,
10526 Estate Lane, Dallas, TX 75238, Phone: 214-348-3496
Specialties: One-of-a-kind collector-grade knives. **Patterns:** Boots, hunters, Bowies, camp and utility knives, fishing and bird knives, miniatures. **Technical:** Grinds a variety of steels to include O1, D2, 440C, 154CM and 1095. **Prices:** $65 to $300; some to $900. **Remarks:** Full-time maker; first knife sold in 1984. **Mark:** R.D. Custom Knives with date or bow and arrow logo.

MILLER, RICK,
516 Kanaul Rd, Rockwood, PA 15557, Phone: 814-926-2059
Specialties: Working/using straight knives of his design and in standard patterns. **Patterns:** Bowies, daggers, hunters and friction folders. **Technical:** Grinds L6. Forges 5160, L6 and Damascus. Patterns for Damascus are random, twist, rose or ladder. **Prices:** $75 to $250; some to $400. **Remarks:** Part-time maker; first knife sold in 1982. **Mark:** Script stamp "R.D.M."

MILLER, RON,
NORTH POLE KNIVES, PO BOX 55301, NORTH POLE, AK 99705, Phone: 907-488-5902, JTMRON@NESCAPE.NET
Specialties: Custom handmade hunting knives built for the extreme conditions of Alaska. Custom fillet blades, tactical fighting knives, custom kitchen knives. Handles are made from mammoth ivory, musk ox, fossilized walrus tusk. Hunters have micarta handles. **Patterns:** Hunters, skinners, fillets, fighters. **Technical:** Stock removal for D2, ATS-34, 109HR, 154CM, and Damascus. **Prices:** $180 and up. **Remarks:** Makes custom sheaths for the above knives. **Mark:** Ron Miller, circle with North Pole Knives with bowie style blade through circle.

MILLER, RONALD T,
12922 127th Ave N, Largo, FL 34644, Phone: 813-595-0378 (after 5 p.m.)
Specialties: Working straight knives in standard patterns. **Patterns:** Combat knives, camp knives, kitchen cutlery, fillet knives, locking folders and butterflies. **Technical:** Grinds D2, 440C and ATS-34; offers brass inlays and scrimshaw. **Prices:** $45 to $325; some to $750. **Remarks:** Part-time maker; first knife sold in 1984. **Mark:** Name, city and state in palm tree logo.

MILLER, TERRY,
P.O. Box 262, Healy, AK 99743, Phone: 907-683-1239, terry@denalidomehome.com
Specialties: Alaskan ulas with wood or horn. **Remarks:** New to knifemaking (4 years).

MILLS, LOUIS G,
9450 Waters Rd, Ann Arbor, MI 48103, Phone: 734-668-1839
Specialties: High-art Japanese-style period pieces. **Patterns:** Traditional tantos, daggers and swords. **Technical:** Makes steel from iron; makes his own Damascus by traditional Japanese techniques. **Prices:** $900 to $2000; some to $8000. **Remarks:** Spare-time maker. **Mark:** Yasutomo in Japanese Kanji.

MILLS, MICHAEL,
151 Blackwell Rd, Colonial Beach, VA 22443-5054, Phone: 804-224-0265
Specialties: Working knives, hunters, skinners, utility and Bowies. **Technical:** Forge 5160 differential heat-treats. **Prices:** $300 and up. **Remarks:** Part-time maker, ABS Journeyman. **Mark:** Last name in script.

MINK, DAN,
PO Box 861, 196 Sage Circle, Crystal Beach, FL 34681, Phone: 727-786-5408, blademkr@gmail.com
Specialties: Traditional and working knives of his design. **Patterns:** Bowies, fighters, folders and hunters. **Technical:** Grinds ATS-34, 440C and D2. Blades and tanges embellished with fancy filework. Uses natural and rare handle materials. **Prices:** $125 to $450. **Remarks:** Part-time maker; first knife sold in 1985. **Mark:** Name and star encircled by custom made, city, state.

MINNICK, JIM,
144 North 7th St, Middletown, IN 47356, Phone: 765-354-4108
Specialties: Lever-lock folding art knives, liner-locks. **Patterns:** Stilettos, Persian and one-of-a-kind folders. **Technical:** Grinds and carves Damascus, stainless, and high-carbon. **Prices:** $950 to $7000. **Remarks:** Part-time maker; first knife sold in 1976. Husband and wife team. **Mark:** Minnick and JMJ.

MIRABILE, DAVID,
1715 Glacier Ave, Juneau, AK 99801, Phone: 907-463-3404
Specialties: Elegant edged weapons. **Patterns:** Fighters, Bowies, claws, tklinget daggers, executive desk knives. **Technical:** Forged high-carbon steels, his own Damascus; uses ancient walrus ivory and prehistoric bone extensively, very rarely uses wood. **Prices:** $350 to $7000. **Remarks:** Full-time maker. Knives sold through art gallery in Juneau, AK. **Mark:** Last name etched or engraved.

MITCHELL, JAMES A,
PO Box 4646, Columbus, GA 31904, Phone: 404-322-8582
Specialties: Fancy working knives. **Patterns:** Hunters, fighters, Bowies and locking folders. **Technical:** Grinds D2, 440C and commercial Damascus. **Prices:** $100 to $400; some to $900. **Remarks:** Part-time maker; first knife sold in 1976. Sells knives in sets. **Mark:** Signature and city.

MITCHELL, MAX DEAN AND BEN,
3803 VFW Rd, Leesville, LA 71440, Phone: 318-239-6416
Specialties: Hatchet and knife sets with folder and belt and holster all match. **Patterns:** Hunters, 200 L6 steel. **Technical:** L6 steel; soft back, hand edge. **Prices:** $300 to $500. **Remarks:** Part-time makers; first knife sold in 1965. Custom orders only; no stock. **Mark:** First names.

MITCHELL, WM DEAN,
PO Box 2, Warren, TX 77664, Phone: 409-547-2213
Specialties: Functional and collectable cutlery. **Patterns:** Personal and collector's designs. **Technical:** Forges own Damascus and carbon steels. **Prices:** Determined by the buyer. **Remarks:** Gentleman knifemaker. ABS Master Smith 1994. **Mark:** Full name with anvil and MS or WDM and MS.

MITSUYUKI, ROSS,
PO Box 29577, Honolulu, HI 96820, Phone: 808-671-3335, Fax: 808-671-3335, rossman@hawaiiantel.net; Web: www.picturetrail.com/homepage/mrbing
Specialties: Working straight knives and folders/engraving titanium & 416 S.S. **Patterns:** Hunting, fighters, utility knives and boot knives. **Technical:** 440C, BG42, ATS-34, 530V, and Damascus. **Prices:** $100 and up. **Remarks:** Spare-time maker, first knife sold in 1998. **Mark:** (Honu) Hawaiian sea turtle.

MIVILLE-DESCHENES, ALAIN,
1952 Charles A Parent, Quebec, CANADA G2B 4B2, Phone: 418-845-0950, Fax: 418-845-0950, amd@miville-deschenes.com; Web: www.miville-deschenes.com
Specialties: Working knives of his design or to customer specs and art knives. **Patterns:** Bowies, skinner, hunter, utility, camp knives, fighters, art knives. **Technical:** Grinds ATS-34, CPMS30V, 0-1, D2, and sometime forge carbon steel. **Prices:** $250 to $700; some higher. **Remarks:** Part-time maker; first knife sold in 2001. **Mark:** Logo (small hand) and initials (AMD).

MOJZIS, JULIUS,
B S Timravy 6, 98511 Halic, SLOVAKIA, mojzisj@stoneline.sk; Web: www.juliusmojzis.com
Specialties: Art Knives. **Prices:** USD $2000. **Mark:** MOJZIS.

MONCUS, MICHAEL STEVEN,
1803 US 19 N, Smithville, GA 31787, Phone: 912-846-2408

MONTANO, GUS A,
11217 Westonhill Dr, San Diego, CA 92126-1447, Phone: 619-273-5357
Specialties: Traditional working/using straight knives of his design. **Patterns:** Boots, Bowies and fighters. **Technical:** Grinds 1095 and 516O; grinds and forges cable. Double or triple hardened and triple drawn; hand-rubbed finish. Prefers natural handle materials. **Prices:** $200 to $400; some to $600. **Remarks:** Spare-time maker; first knife sold in 1997. **Mark:** First initial and last name.

MONTEIRO, VICTOR,
31 Rue D'Opprebais, 1360 Maleves Ste Marie, BELGIUM, Phone: 010 88 0441, victor.monteiro@skynet.be
Specialties: Working and fancy straight knives, folders and integrals of his design. **Patterns:** Fighters, hunters and kitchen knives. **Technical:** Grinds ATS-34, 440C, D2, Damasteel and other commercial Damascus, embellishment, filework and domed pins. **Prices:** $300 to $1000, some higher. **Remarks:** Part-time maker; first knife sold in 1989. **Mark:** Logo with initials connected.

MONTJOY, CLAUDE,
706 Indian Creek Rd, Clinton, SC 29325, Phone: 864-697-6160
Specialties: Folders, slip joint, lock, lock liner and interframe. **Patterns:** Hunters, boots, fighters, some art knives and folders. **Technical:** Grinds ATS-34 and Damascus. Offers inlaid handle scales. **Prices:** $100 to $500. **Remarks:** Full-time maker; first knife sold in 1982. Custom orders, no catalog. **Mark:** Montjoy.

MOONEY, MIKE,
19432 E Cloud Rd, Queen Creek, AZ 85142, Phone: 480-987-3576, mike@moonblades.com; Web: www.moonblades.com
Specialties: Fancy working straight knives of his design or customers. **Patterns:** Fighters, Bowies, daggers, hunters, kitchen, camp. **Technical:** Flat-grind, hand-rubbed finish, S30V, commercial Damascus, CPM154. **Prices:** $250 to $2000. **Remarks:** Doing business as moonblades.com. **Mark:** M. Mooney followed by crescent moon.

MOORE, JAMES B,
1707 N Gillis, Ft. Stockton, TX 79735, Phone: 915-336-2113
Specialties: Classic working straight knives and folders of his design. **Patterns:** Hunters, Bowies, daggers, fighters, boots, utility/camp knives, locking folders and slip-joint folders. **Technical:** Grinds 440C, ATS-34, D2, L6, CPM and commercial Damascus. **Prices:** $85 to $700; exceptional knives to $1500. **Remarks:** Full-time maker; first knife sold in 1972. **Mark:** Name, city and state.

MOORE, JON P,
304 South N Rd, Aurora, NE 68818, Phone: 402-849-2616, Web: www.sharpdecisionknives.com
Specialties: Working and fancy straight knives using antler, exotic bone, wood and Micarta. Will use customers antlers on request. **Patterns:** Hunters, skinners, camp Bowies. **Technical:** Hand forged high carbon steel. Makes his own Damascus. **Remarks:** Part-time maker, sold first knife in 2003, member of ABS - apprentice. Does on location knife forging demonstrations. **Mark:** Signature.

MOORE, MARVE,
HC 89 Box 393, Willow, AK 99688, Phone: 907-232-0478, marvemoore@aol.com
    Specialties: Fixed blades forged and stock removal. **Patterns:** Hunter, skinners, fighter, short swords. **Technical:** 100 percent of his work is done by hand. **Prices:** $100 to $500. **Remarks:** Also makes his own sheaths. **Mark:** -MM-.

MOORE, MICHAEL ROBERT,
70 Beauliew St, Lowell, MA 01850, Phone: 978-479-0589, Fax: 978-441-1819

MOORE, TED,
340 E Willow St, Elizabethtown, PA 17022, Phone: 717-367-3939, tedmoore@supernet.com; Web: www.tedmooreknives.com
    Specialties: Damascus folders, cigar cutters. **Patterns:** Locking folders and slip joint. **Technical:** Grinds Damascus, high-carbon and stainless; also ATS-34 and D2. **Prices:** $250 to $1500. **Remarks:** Part-time maker; first knife sold 1993. Knife and gun leather also. **Mark:** Moore U.S.A.

MORETT, DONALD,
116 Woodcrest Dr, Lancaster, PA 17602-1300, Phone: 717-746-4888

MORGAN, JEFF,
9200 Arnaz Way, Santee, CA 92071, Phone: 619-448-8430
    Specialties: Early American style knives. **Patterns:** Hunters, bowies, etc. **Technical:** Carbon steel and carbon steel damascus. **Prices:** $60 to $400

MORGAN, TOM,
14689 Ellett Rd, Beloit, OH 44609, Phone: 330-537-2023
    Specialties: Working straight knives and period pieces. **Patterns:** Hunters, boots and presentation tomahawks. **Technical:** Grinds O1, 440C and 154CM. **Prices:** Knives, $65 to $200; tomahawks, $100 to $325. **Remarks:** Full-time maker; first knife sold in 1977. **Mark:** Last name and type of steel used.

MORRIS, C H,
1590 Old Salem Rd, Frisco City, AL 36445, Phone: 334-575-7425
    Specialties: LinerLock® folders. **Patterns:** Interframe liner locks. **Technical:** Grinds 440C and ATS-34. **Prices:** Start at $350. **Remarks:** Full-time maker; first knife sold in 1973. Doing business as Custom Knives. **Mark:** First and middle initials, last name.

MORRIS, DARRELL PRICE,
92 Union, St. Plymouth, Devon, ENGLAND PL1 3EZ, Phone: 0752 223546
    Specialties: Traditional Japanese knives, Bowies and high-art knives. **Technical:** Nickel Damascus and mokume. **Prices:** $1000 to $4000. **Remarks:** Part-time maker; first knife sold in 1990. **Mark:** Initials and Japanese name—Kuni Shigae.

MORRIS, ERIC,
306 Ewart Ave, Beckley, WV 25801, Phone: 304-255-3951

MORRIS, MICHAEL S.,
609 S. Main St., Yale, MI 48097, Phone: 810-887-7817, mykulmorris@yahoo.com
    Specialties: Hunting and Tactical fixed blade knives of his design made from files. **Technical:** All knives hollow ground on 12" wheel. Hand stitches his own sheaths also. **Prices:** From $60 to $350 with most in the $90 to $125 range. **Remarks:** Machinist since 1980, made his first knife in 1984, sold his first knife in 2004. Now full-time maker. **Mark:** Last name with date of manufacture.

MOSES, STEVEN,
1610 W Hemlock Way, Santa Ana, CA 92704

MOSIER, DAVID,
1725 Millburn Ave., Independence, MO 64056, Phone: 816-796-3479, dmknives@aol.com
    Specialties: Tactical folders and fixed blades. **Patterns:** Fighters and concealment blades. **Technical:** Uses S30V, 154CM, ATS-34, 440C, A2, D2, Stainless damascus, and Damasteel. Fixed blades come with Kydex sheaths made by maker. **Prices:** $150 to $1000. **Remarks:** Full-time maker, business name is DM Knives. **Mark:** David Mosier Knives encircling sun.

MOSIER, JOSHUA J,
SPRING CREEK KNIFE WORKS, PO Box 476/608 7th St, Deshler, NE 68340, Phone: 402-365-4386, joshm@sl-kw.com; Web:www.sc-kw.com
    Specialties: Working straight and folding knives of his designs with customer specs. **Patterns:** Hunter/utility LinerLock® folders. **Technical:** Forges random pattern Damascus, 01, and 5160. **Prices:** $85 and up. **Remarks:** Part-time maker, sold first knife in 1986. **Mark:** SCKW.

MOULTON, DUSTY,
135 Hillview Lane, Loudon, TN 37774, Phone: 865-408-9779, Web: www.moultonknives.com
    Specialties: Fancy and working straight knives. **Patterns:** Hunters, fighters, fantasy and miniatures. **Technical:** Grinds ATS-34 and Damascus. **Prices:** $300 to $2000. **Remarks:** Full-time maker; first knife sold in 1991. Now doing engraving on own knives as well as other makers. **Mark:** Last name.

MOUNT, DON,
4574 Little Finch Ln, Las Vegas, NV 89115, Phone: 702-531-2925
    Specialties: High-tech working and using straight knives of his design. **Patterns:** Bowies, fighters and utility/camp knives. **Technical:** Uses 440C and ATS-34. **Prices:** $150 to $300; some to $1000. **Remarks:** Part-time maker; first knife sold in 1985. **Mark:** Name below a woodpecker.

MOYER, RUSS,
1266 RD 425 So, Havre, MT 59501, Phone: 406-395-4423
    Specialties: Working knives to customer specs. **Patterns:** Hunters, Bowies and survival knives. **Technical:** Forges W2 & 5160. **Prices:** $150 to $350. **Remarks:** Part-time maker; first knife sold in 1976. **Mark:** Initials in logo.

MULKEY, GARY,
533 Breckenridge Rd., Branson, MO 65616, Phone: 417-335-0123, gary@mulkeyknives.com; Web: www.mulkeyknives.com
    Specialties: Working and fancy fixed blades and folders of his design and to customer's specs. **Patterns:** Hunters, Bowies, fighters, folders, and lock backs. **Technical:** Prefers 1095 or D2 with Damascus, filework, inlets or clay coated blades available on order. **Prices:** $200 to $1000 plus. **Remarks:** Sponsors Branson Knife Show/Hammer-In in June. Full-time maker since 1997. Shop/showroom open to public. Member ABS, KGA. **Mark:** MUL above skeleton key.

MULLER, JODY,
3359 S. 225th Rd., Goodson, MO 65663, Phone: 417-852-4306/417-752-3260, mullerforge2@hotmail.com; Web: www.mullerforge.com
    Specialties: Hand engraving, carving and inlays, fancy folders and oriental styles. **Patterns:** One-of-a-kind fixed blades and folders in all styles. **Technical:** Forges own Damascus and high carbon steel. **Prices:** $300 and up. **Remarks:** Full-time Journeyman Smith, knifemaker, does hand engraving, carving and inlay. All work done by maker. **Mark:** Muller J.S.

MURSKI, RAY,
12129 Captiva Ct, Reston, VA 22091-1204, Phone: 703-264-1102, murski@vtisp.com
    Specialties: Fancy working/using folders of his design. **Patterns:** Hunters, slip-joint folders and utility/camp knives. **Technical:** Grinds CPM-3V **Prices:** $125 to $500. **Remarks:** Spare-time maker; first knife sold in 1996. **Mark:** Engraved name with serial number under name.

MUTZ, JEFF,
8210 Rancheria Dr. Unit 7, Rancho Cucamonga, CA 91730, Phone: 909-931-9829, jmutzknives@hotmail.com; Web: www.jmutzknives.com
    Specialties: Traditional working/using fixed blade and slip-jointed knives of own design and customer specs. **Patterns:** Hunters, skinners, and folders. **Technical:** Grinds 440C. Offers scrimshaw. **Prices:** $145 to $500. **Remarks:** Full-time maker, first knife sold in 1998. **Mark:** First initial, last name over "maker."

MYERS, PAUL,
644 Maurice St, Wood River, IL 62095, Phone: 618-258-1707
    Specialties: Fancy working straight knives and folders. **Patterns:** Full range of folders, straight hunters and Bowies; tie tacks; knife and fork sets. **Technical:** Grinds D2, 440C, ATS-34 and 154CM. **Prices:** $100 to $350; some to $3000. **Remarks:** Full-time maker; first knife sold in 1974. **Mark:** Initials with setting sun on front; name and number on back.

MYERS, STEVE,
903 Hickory Rd., Virginia, IL 62691-8716, Phone: 217-452-3157, Web: www.myersknives.net
    Specialties: Working straight knives and integrals. **Patterns:** Camp knives, hunters, skinners, Bowies, and boot knives. **Technical:** Forges own Damascus and high carbon steels. **Prices:** $250 to $1,000. **Remarks:** Full-time maker, first knife sold in 1985. **Mark:** Last name in logo.

N

NATEN, GREG,
1804 Shamrock Way, Bakersfield, CA 93304-3921
    Specialties: Fancy and working/using folders of his design. **Patterns:** Fighters, hunters and locking folders. **Technical:** Grinds 440C, ATS-34 and CPM440V. Heat-treats; prefers desert ironwood, stag and mother-of-pearl. Designs and sews leather sheaths for straight knives. **Prices:** $175 to $600; some to $950. **Remarks:** Spare-time maker; first knife sold in 1992. **Mark:** Last name above battle-ax, handmade.

NAUDE, LOUIS,
3 Flamingo, Protea Heights, Cape Town, Western Cape 7560, www.louisnaude.co.za

NEALY, BUD,
RR1, Box 1439, Stroudsburg, PA 18360, Phone: 570-402-1018, Fax: 570-402-1018, budnealy@ptd.net; Web: www.budnealyknifemaker.com
    Specialties: Original design concealment knives with designer multi-concealment sheath system. **Patterns:** Concealment knives, boots, combat and collector pieces. **Technical:** Grinds CPM 154, S30V & Damascus. **Prices:** $200 to $2500. **Remarks:** Full-time maker; first knife sold in 1980. **Mark:** Name, city, state or signature.

NEDVED, DAN,
206 Park Dr, Kalispell, MT 59901, bushido2222@yahoo.com
    Specialties: Slip joint folders, liner locks, straight knives. **Patterns:** Mostly traditional or modern blend with traditional lines. **Technical:** Grinds ATS-34, 440C, 1095 and uses other makers Damascus. **Prices:** $95 and up. Mostly in the $150 to $200 range. **Remarks:** Part-time maker, averages 2 a month. **Mark:** Dan Nedved or Nedved with serial # on opposite side.

NEELY, GREG,
5419 Pine St, Bellaire, TX 77401, Phone: 713-991-2677, ediiorio@houston.rr.com
Specialties: Traditional patterns and his own patterns for work and/or collecting. **Patterns:** Hunters, Bowies and utility/camp knives. **Technical:** Forges own Damascus, 1084, 5160 and some tool steels. Differentially tempers. **Prices:** $225 to $5000. **Remarks:** Part-time maker; first knife sold in 1987. **Mark:** Last name or interlocked initials, MS.

NEILSON, J,
RR 2 Box 16, Wyalusing, PA 18853, Phone: 570-746-4944, mountainhollow@epix.net; Web: www.mountainhollow.net
Specialties: Working and collectable fixed blade knives. **Patterns:** Hunter/fighters, Bowies, neck knives and daggers. **Technical:** 1084, 1095, 5160, W-2, 52100, maker's own Damascus. **Prices:** $175 to $2500. **Remarks:** ABS Master Smith, full-time maker, first knife sold in 2000, doing business as Neilson's Mountain Hollow. Each knife comes with a sheath. **Mark:** J. Neilson MS.

NELSON, DR CARL,
2500 N Robison Rd, Texarkana, TX 75501

NELSON, KEN,
PO BOX 272, Pittsville, WI 54466, Phone: 715-323-0538 or 715-884-6448, ken@ironwolfonline.com Web: www.ironwolfonline.com
Specialties: Working straight knives, period pieces. **Patterns:** Utility, hunters, dirks, daggers, throwers, hawks, axes, swords, pole arms and blade blanks as well. **Technical:** Forges 5160, 52100, W2, 10xx, L6, carbon steels and own Damascus. Does his own heat treating. **Prices:** $50 to $350, some to $3000. **Remarks:** Part-time maker. First knife sold in 1995. Doing business as Iron Wolf Forge. **Mark:** Stylized wolf paw print.

NELSON, TOM,
PO Box 2298, Wilropark 1731, Gauteng, SOUTH AFRICA, Phone: 27 11 7663991, Fax: 27 11 7687161, tom.nelson@telkomsa.net
Specialties: Own Damascus (Hosaic etc.) **Patterns:** One-of-a-kind art knives, swords and axes. **Prices:** $500 to $1000.

NETO JR., NELSON AND DE CARVALHO, HENRIQUE M.,
R. Joao Margarido No 20-V, Guerra, Braganca Paulista, SP-12900-000, BRAZIL, Phone: 011-7843-6889, Fax: 011-7843-6889
Specialties: Straight knives and folders. **Patterns:** Bowies, katanas, jambyias and others. **Technical:** Forges high-carbon steels. **Prices:** $70 to $3000. **Remarks:** Full-time makers; first knife sold in 1990. **Mark:** HandN.

NEUHAEUSLER, ERWIN,
Heiligenangerstrasse 15, 86179 Augsburg, GERMANY, Phone: 0821/81 49 97, ERWIN@AUASBURGKNIVES.DE
Specialties: Using straight knives of his design. **Patterns:** Hunters, boots, Bowies and folders. **Technical:** Grinds ATS-34, RWL-34 and Damascus. **Prices:** $200 to $750. **Remarks:** Spare-time maker; first knife sold in 1991. **Mark:** Etched logo, last name and city.

NEVLING, MARK,
BURR OAK KNIVES, PO Box 9, Hume, IL 61932, Phone: 217-887-2522, burroakknives@aol.com; Web: www.burroakknives.com
Specialties: Straight knives and folders of his own design. **Patterns:** Hunters, fighters, Bowies, folders, and small executive knives. **Technical:** Convex grinds, Forges, uses only high-carbon and Damascus. **Prices:** $200 to $2000. **Remarks:** Full-time maker, first knife sold 1988. Apprentice Damascus smith to George Werth.

NEWCOMB, CORBIN,
628 Woodland Ave, Moberly, MO 65270, Phone: 660-263-4639
Specialties: Working straight knives and folders; period pieces. **Patterns:** Hunters, axes, Bowies, folders, buckskinned blades and boots. **Technical:** Hollow-grinds D2, 440C and 154CM; prefers natural handle materials. Makes own Damascus; offers cable Damascus. **Prices:** $100 to $500. **Remarks:** Full-time maker; first knife sold in 1982. Doing business as Corbin Knives. **Mark:** First name and serial number.

NEWHALL, TOM,
3602 E 42nd Stravenue, Tucson, AZ 85713, Phone: 520-721-0562, gggaz@aol.com

NEWTON, LARRY,
1758 Pronghorn Ct, Jacksonville, FL 32225, Phone: 904-221-2340, CNewton1234@aol.com
Specialties: Traditional and slender high-grade gentlemen's automatic folders, locking liner type tactical, and working straight knives. **Patterns:** Front release locking folders, interframes, hunters, and skinners. **Technical:** Grinds Damascus, ATS-34, 440C and D2. **Prices:** Folders start at $350, straights start at $150. **Remarks:** Retired teacher. Full-time maker. First knife sold in 1989. Won Best Folder for 2008 - Blade Magazine. **Mark:** Last name.

NEWTON, RON,
223 Ridge Ln, London, AR 72847, Phone: 479-293-3001, rnewton@cei.net
Specialties: Mosaic Damascus folders with accelerated actions. **Patterns:** One-of-a-kind. **Technical:** 1084-15N20 steels used in his mosaic Damascus steels. **Prices:** $1000 to $5000. **Remarks:** Also making antique Bowie repros and various fixed blades. **Mark:** All capital letters in NEWTON "Western Invitation" font.

NICHOLS, CHAD,
1125 Cr 185, Blue Springs, MS 38828, Phone: 662-538-5966, chadn28@hotmail.com Web: chadnicholsdamascus.com
Specialties: Gents folders and everyday tactical/utility style knives and fixed hunters. **Technical:** Makes own stainless damascus, mosaic damascus, and high carbon damascus. **Prices:** $450 - $1000. **Mark:** Name and Blue Springs.

NICHOLSON, R. KENT,
PO Box 204, Phoenix, MD 21131, Phone: 410-323-6925
Specialties: Large using knives. **Patterns:** Bowies and camp knives in the Moran-style. **Technical:** Forges W2, 9260, 5160; makes Damascus. **Prices:** $150 to $995. **Remarks:** Part-time maker; first knife sold in 1984. **Mark:** Name.

NIELSON, JEFF V,
1060 S Jones Rd, Monroe, UT 84754, Phone: 435-527-4242, jvn1u205@hotmail.com
Specialties: Classic knives of his design and to customer specs. **Patterns:** Fighters, hunters; miniatures. **Technical:** Grinds 440C stainless and Damascus. **Prices:** $100 to $1200. **Remarks:** Part-time maker; first knife sold in 1991. **Mark:** Name, location.

NIEMUTH, TROY,
3143 North Ave, Sheboygan, WI 53083, Phone: 414-452-2927
Specialties: Period pieces and working/using straight knives of his design and to customer specs. **Patterns:** Hunters and utility/camp knives. **Technical:** Grinds 440C, 1095 and A2. **Prices:** $85 to $350; some to $500. **Remarks:** Full-time maker; first knife sold in 1995. **Mark:** Etched last name.

NILSSON, JONNY WALKER,
Tingsstigen 11, SE-933 33 Arvidsjaur, SWEDEN, Phone: (46) 960-13048, 0960.1304@telia.com; Web: www.jwnknives.com
Specialties: High-end collectible Nordic hunters, engraved reindeer antler. World class freehand engravings. Matching engraved sheaths in leather, bone and Arctic wood with inlays. Combines traditional techniques and design with his own innovations. Master Bladesmith who specializes in forging mosaic Damascus. Sells unique mosaic Damascus bar stock to folder makers. **Patterns:** Own designs and traditional Sami designs. **Technical:** Mosaic Damascus of UHB 20 C 15N20 with pure nickel, hardness HRC 58-60. **Prices:** $1500 to $6000. **Remarks:** Full-time maker since 1988. Nordic Champion (5 countries) numerous times, 50 first prizes in Scandinavian shows. Yearly award in his name in Nordic Championship. Knives inspired by 10,000 year old indigenous Sami culture. **Mark:** JN on sheath, handle, custom wood box. JWN on blade.

NIRO, FRANK,
2469 Waverly Dr., Blind Bay, B.C. Canada V0E1H1, Phone: 250-675-4234, niro@telus.net
Specialties: Liner locking folding knives in his designs in what might be called standard patterns. **Technical:** Enjoys grinding mosaic Damascus with pure nickel of the make up for blades that are often double ground; as well as meteorite for bolsters which are then etched and heat colored. Uses 416 stainless for spacers with inlays of natural materials, gem stones with also file work. Liners are made from titanium are most often fully file worked and anodized. Only uses natural materials particularly mammoth ivory for scales. **Prices:** $500 to $1500 **Remarks:** Full time maker. Has been selling knives for over thirty years. **Mark:** Last name on the inside of the spacer.

NISHIUCHI, MELVIN S,
6121 Forest Park Dr, Las Vegas, NV 89156, Phone: 702-501-3724, msnknives@yahoo.com
Specialties: Collectable quality using/working knives. **Patterns:** Locking liner folders, fighters, hunters and fancy personal knives. **Technical:** Grinds ATS-34 and Devin Thomas Damascus; prefers semi-precious stone and exotic natural handle materials. **Prices:** $375 to $2000. **Remarks:** Part-time maker; first knife sold in 1985. **Mark:** Circle with a line above it.

NOLEN, STEVE,
105 Flowingwells Rd, Pottsboro, TX 75076, Phone: 903-786-2454, blademaster@nolenknives.com; Web: www.nolenknives.com
Specialties: Working knives; display pieces. **Patterns:** Wide variety of straight knives, butterflies and buckles. **Technical:** Grind D2, 440C and 154CM. Offer filework; make exotic handles. **Prices:** $150 to $800; some higher. **Remarks:** Full-time maker; Steve is third generation maker. **Mark:** NK in oval logo.

NORDELL, INGEMAR,
Skarpå 2103, 82041 Färila, SWEDEN, Phone: 0651-23347
Specialties: Classic working and using straight knives. **Patterns:** Hunters, Bowies and fighters. **Technical:** Forges and grinds ATS-34, D2 and Sandvik. **Prices:** $120 to $1500. **Remarks:** Part-time maker; first knife sold in 1985. **Mark:** Initials or name.

NOREN, DOUGLAS E,
14676 Boom Rd, Springlake, MI 49456, Phone: 616-842-4247, gnoren@icsdata.com
Specialties: Hand forged blades, custom built and made to order. Hand file work, carving and casting. Stag and stacked handles. Replicas of Scagel and Joseph Rogers. Hand tooled custom made sheaths. **Technical:** Master smith, 5160, 52100 and 1084 steel. **Prices:** Start at $250. **Remarks:** Sole authorship, works in all mediums, ABS Mastersmith, all knives come with a custom hand-tooled sheath. Also makes anvils. Enjoys the challenge and meeting people.

NORFLEET, ROSS W,
4110 N Courthouse Rd, Providence Forge, VA 23140-3420, Phone: 804-966-2596, rossknife@aol.com
Specialties: Classic, traditional and working/using knives of his design or in standard patterns. **Patterns:** Hunters and folders. **Technical:** Hollow-grinds 440C and ATS-34. **Prices:** $150 to $550. **Remarks:** Part-time maker; first knife sold in 1992. **Mark:** Last name.

NORTON, DON,
95N Wilkison Ave, Port Townsend, WA 98368-2534, Phone: 306-385-1978
Specialties: Fancy and plain straight knives. **Patterns:** Hunters, small Bowies, tantos, boot knives, fillets. **Technical:** Prefers 440C, Micarta, exotic woods and other natural handle materials. Hollow-grinds all knives except fillet knives. **Prices:** $185 to $2800; average is $200. **Remarks:** Full-time maker; first knife sold in 1980. **Mark:** Full name, Hsi Shuai, city, state.

NOTT, RON P,
PO Box 281, Summerdale, PA 17093, Phone: 717-732-2763, neitznott@aol.com
Specialties: High-art folders and some straight knives. **Patterns:** Scale release folders. **Technical:** Grinds ATS-34, 416 and nickel-silver. Engraves, inlays gold. **Prices:** $250 to $3000. **Remarks:** Full-time maker; first knife sold in 1993. Doing business as Knives By Nott, customer engraving. **Mark:** First initial, last name and serial number.

NOWLAND, RICK,
3677 E Bonnie Rd, Waltonville, IL 62894, Phone: 618-279-3170, ricknowland@frontiernet.net
Specialties: Slip joint folders in traditional patterns. **Patterns:** Trapper, whittler, sowbelly, toothpick and copperhead. **Technical:** Uses ATS-34, bolsters and liners have integral construction. **Prices:** $225 to $1000. **Remarks:** Part-time maker. **Mark:** Last name.

NUNN, GREGORY,
HC64 Box 2107, Castle Valley, UT 84532, Phone: 435-259-8607
Specialties: High-art working and using knives of his design; new edition knife with handle made from anatomized dinosaur bone, first ever made. **Patterns:** Flaked stone knives. **Technical:** Uses gem-quality agates, jaspers and obsidians for blades. **Prices:** $250 to $2300. **Remarks:** Full-time maker; first knife sold in 1989. **Mark:** Name, knife and edition numbers, year made.

O

OCHS, CHARLES F,
124 Emerald Lane, Largo, FL 33771, Phone: 727-536-3827, Fax: 727-536-3827, chuckandbelle@juno.com
Specialties: Working knives; period pieces. **Patterns:** Hunters, fighters, Bowies, buck skinners and folders. **Technical:** Forges 52100, 5160 and his own Damascus. **Prices:** $150 to $1800; some to $2500. **Remarks:** Full-time maker; first knife sold in 1978. **Mark:** OX Forge.

O'DELL, CLYDE,
176 Ouachita 404, Camden, AR 71701, Phone: 870-574-2754, abcodell@arkansas.net
Specialties: Working knives. **Patterns:** Hunters, camp knives, Bowies, daggers, tomahawks. **Technical:** Forges 5160 and 1084. **Prices:** Starting at $125. **Remarks:** Spare-time maker. **Mark:** Last name.

ODGEN, RANDY W,
10822 Sage Orchard, Houston, TX 77089, Phone: 713-481-3601

ODOM JR., VICTOR L.,
PO Box 572, North, SC 29112, Phone: 803-247-2749, cell 803-608-0829, vlodom3@tds.net
Specialties: Forged knives and tomahawks; stock removal knives. **Patterns:** Hunters, Bowies and folders. **Technical:** Use 1095, 5160, 52100 high carbon and alloy steels, ATS-34, and 55. **Prices:** Straight knives $60 and up. Folders @$250 and up. **Remarks:** Student of Mr. George Henron. SCAK.ORG. Secretary of the Couth Carolina Association of Knifemakers. **Mark:** Steel stamp "ODOM" and etched "Odom Forge North, SC" plus a serial number.

OGDEN, BILL,
OGDEN KNIVES, PO Box 52, Avis
AVIS, PA 17721, Phone: 570-974-9114
Specialties: One-of-a-kind, liner-lock folders, hunters, skinners, minis. **Technical:** Grinds ATS-34, 440-C, D2, 52100, Damascus, natural and unnatural handle materials, hand-stitched custom sheaths. **Prices:** $50 and up. **Remarks:** Part-time maker since 1992. **Marks:** Last name or "OK" stamp (Ogden Knives).

OGLETREE JR., BEN R,
2815 Israel Rd, Livingston, TX 77351, Phone: 409-327-8315
Specialties: Working/using straight knives of his design. **Patterns:** Hunters, kitchen and utility/camp knives. **Technical:** Grinds ATS-34, W1 and 1075; heat-treats. **Prices:** $200 to $400. **Remarks:** Part-time maker; first knife sold in 1955. **Mark:** Last name, city and state in oval with a tree on either side.

O'HARE, SEAN,
1831 Rte. 776, Grand Manan, NB, CANADA E5G 2H9, Phone: 506-662-8524, sean@ohareknives.com; Web: www.ohareknives.com
Specialties: Fixed blade hunters and folders. **Patterns:** Small to large

hunters and daily carry folders. **Technical:** Stock removal, flat ground. **Prices:** $220 USD to $800 USD. **Remarks:** Strives to balance aesthetics, functionality and durability. **Mark:** 1st line - "OHARE KNIVES", 2nd line - "CANADA."

OLIVE, MICHAEL E,
6388 Angora Mt Rd, Leslie, AR 72645, Phone: 870-363-4668
Specialties: Fixed blades. **Patterns:** Bowies, camp knives, fighters and hunters. **Technical:** Forged blades of 1084, W2, 5160, Damascus of 1084, and1572. **Prices:** $250 and up. **Remarks:** Received J.S. stamp in 2005. **Mark:** Olive.

OLIVER, TODD D,
894 Beaver Hollow, Spencer, IN 47460, Phone: 812-829-1762
Specialties: Damascus hunters and daggers. High-carbon as well. **Patterns:** Ladder, twist random. **Technical:** Sole author of all his blades. **Prices:** $350 and up. **Remarks:** Learned bladesmithing from Jim Batson at the ABS school and Damascus from Billy Merritt in Indiana. **Mark:** T.D. Oliver Spencer IN. Two crossed swords and a battle ax.

OLSON, DARROLD E,
PO Box 1539, Springfield, OR 97477, Phone: 541-285-1412
Specialties: Straight knives and folders of his design and to customer specs. **Patterns:** Hunters, liner locks and locking folders. **Technical:** Grinds 440C, ATS-34 and 154CM. Uses anodized titanium; sheaths wet-molded. **Prices:** $250 to $550. **Remarks:** Part-time maker; first knife sold in 1989. **Mark:** Etched logo, year, type of steel and name.

OLSON, ROD,
Box 5973, High River, AB, CANADA T1V 1P6, Phone: 403-652-2744, Fax: 403-646-5838
Specialties: Lockback folders with gold toothpicks. **Patterns:** Locking folders. **Technical:** Grinds ATS-34 blades and spring, filework-14kt bolsters and liners. **Prices:** Mid range. **Remarks:** Part-time maker; first knife sold in 1979. **Mark:** Last name on blade.

OLSON, WAYNE C,
890 Royal Ridge Dr, Bailey, CO 80421, Phone: 303-816-9486
Specialties: High-tech working knives. **Patterns:** Hunters to folding lockers; some integral designs. **Technical:** Grinds 440C, 154CM and ATS-34; likes hand-finishes; precision-fits stainless steel fittings—no solder, no nickel silver. **Prices:** $275 to $600; some to $3000. **Remarks:** Part-time maker; first knife sold in 1979. **Mark:** Name, maker.

OLSZEWSKI, STEPHEN,
1820 Harkney Hill Rd, Coventry, RI 02816, Phone: 401-397-4774, blade5377@yahoo.com; Web: www.olszewskiknives.com
Specialties: Lock back, liner locks, automatics (art knives). **Patterns:** One-of-a-kind art knives specializing in figurals. **Technical:** Damascus steel, titanium file worked liners, fossil ivory and pearl. Double actions. **Prices:** $1750 to $20,000. **Remarks:** Will custom build to your specifications. Quality work with guarantee. **Mark:** SCO inside fish symbol. Also "Olszewski."

O'MACHEARLEY, MICHAEL,
129 Lawnview Dr., Wilmington, OH 45177, Phone: 937-728-2818, omachearleycustomknives@yahoo.com
Specialties: Forged and Stock removal; hunters, skinners, bowies, plain to fancy. **Technical:** ATS-34 and 5160, forges own Damascus. **Prices:** $180-$1000 and up. **Remarks:** Full-time maker, first knife made in 1999. **Mark:** Last name and shamrock.

O'MALLEY, DANIEL,
4338 Evanston Ave N, Seattle, WA 98103, Phone: 206-527-0315
Specialties: Custom chef's knives. **Remarks:** Making knives since 1997.

ONION, KENNETH J,
47-501 Hui Kelu St, Kaneohe, HI 96744, Phone: 808-239-1300, Fax: 808-289-1301, shopjunky@aol.com; Web: www.kenonionknives.com
Specialties: Folders featuring speed safe as well as other invention gadgets. **Patterns:** Hybrid, art, fighter, utility. **Technical:** S30V, CPM 154V, Cowry Y, SQ-2 and Damascus. **Prices:** $500 to $20,000. **Remarks:** Full-time maker; designer and inventor. First knife sold in 1991. **Mark:** Name and state.

ORFORD, BEN,
Nethergreen Farm, Ridgeway Cross, Malvern, Worcestershire, England WR13 5JS, Phone: 44 01886 880410, web: www.benorford.com
Specialties: Working knives for woodcraft and the outdoorsman, made to his own designs. **Patterns:** Mostly flat Scandinavian grinds, full and partial tang. Also makes specialist woodcraft tools and hook knives. Custom leather sheaths by Lois, his wife. **Technical:** Grinds and forges 01, EN9, EN43, EN45 plus recycled steels. Heat treats. **Prices:** $25 - $650. **Remarks:** Full-time maker; first knife made in 1997. **Mark:** Celtic knot with name underneath.

ORTEGA, BEN M,
165 Dug Rd, Wyoming, PA 18644, Phone: 717-696-3234

ORTON, RICH,
3625 Fleming St, Riverside, CA 92509, Phone: 951-685-3019, ortonknifeworks@att.net
Specialties: Straight knives only. **Patterns:** Fighters, hunters, skinners. **Technical:** Grinds ATS-34. Heat treats by Paul Bos. **Prices:** $100 to $1000. **Remarks:** Full-time maker; first knife sold in 1992. Doing business as Orton Knife Works. **Mark:** Last name, city state (maker)

OSBORNE, DONALD H,
5840 N McCall, Clovis, CA 93611, Phone: 559-299-9483, Fax: 559-298-1751, oforge@sbcglobal.net
Specialties: Traditional working using straight knives and folder of his design. **Patterns:** Working straight knives, Bowies, hunters, camp knives and folders. **Technical:** Forges carbon steels and makes Damascus. Grinds ATS-34, 154CM, and 440C. **Prices:** $150 and up. **Remarks:** Part-time maker. **Mark:** Last name logo and J.S.

OSBORNE, WARREN,
#2-412 Alysa Ln, Waxahachie, TX 75167, Phone: 972-935-0899, Fax: 972-937-9004, ossie1@worldnet.att.net; Web: www.osborneknives.com
Specialties: Investment grade collectible, interframes, one-of-a-kinds; unique locking mechanisms and cutting competition knives. **Patterns:** Folders; bolstered and interframes; conventional lockers, front lockers and back lockers; some slip-joints; some high-art pieces. **Technical:** Grinds CPM M4, BG42, CPM S30V, Damascus - some forged and stock removed cutting competition knives. **Prices:** $1200 to $3500; some to $5000. Interframes $1250 to $3000. **Remarks:** Full-time maker; first knife sold in 1980. **Mark:** Last name in boomerang logo.

OTT, FRED,
1257 Rancho Durango Rd, Durango, CO 81303, Phone: 970-375-9669, fredsknives@durango.net
Patterns: Bowies, hunters tantos and daggers. **Technical:** Forges 1086M, W2 and Damascus. **Prices:** $250 to $1000. **Remarks:** Full-time maker. **Mark:** Last name.

OUYE, KEITH,
PO Box 25307, Honolulu, HI 96825, Phone: 808-395-7000, keithouyeknives@yahoo.com; Web: www.keithouyeknives.com
Specialties: Folders with 1/8 blades and titanium handles. **Patterns:** Tactical design with liner lock and flipper. **Technical:** Blades are stainless steel ATS 34, CPM154 and S30V. Titanium liners (.071) and scales 3/16 pivots and stop pin, titanium pocket clip. Heat treat by Paul Bos.**Prices:** $450-$600 with engraved knives starting at $995 and up. **Remarks:** Engraving done by C.J. Cal (www.caiengraving.com) and Bruce Shaw Retired, so basically a full time knifemaker. Sold first fixed blade in 2004 and first folder in 2005. **Mark:** Ouye/Hawaii with steel type on back side **Other:** Selected by Blade Magazine (March 2006 issue) as one of five makers to watch in 2006.

OVEREYNDER, T R,
1800 S. Davis Dr, Arlington, TX 76013, Phone: 817-277-4812, Fax: 817-277-4812, trovereynderknives@sbcglobal.net; Web: www.overeynderknives.com
Specialties: Highly finished collector-grade knives. Multi-blades. **Patterns:** Fighters, Bowies, daggers, locking folders, 70 percent collector-grade multi blade slip joints, 25 percent interframe, 5 percent fixed blade **Technical:** Grinds CPM-D2, BG-42, S60V, S30V, CPM154, CPM M4, RWL-34 vendor supplied Damascus. Has been making titanium-frame folders since 1977. **Prices:** $750 to $2000, some to $7000. **Remarks:** Full-time maker; first knife sold in 1977. Doing business as TRO Knives. **Mark:** T.R. OVEREYNDER KNIVES, city and state.

OWENS, DONALD,
2274 Lucille Ln, Melbourne, FL 32935, Phone: 321-254-9765

OWENS, JOHN,
14500 CR 270, Nathrop, CO 81236, Phone: 719-395-0870
Specialties: Hunters. **Prices:** $200 to $375 some to $650. **Remarks:** Spare-time maker. **Mark:** Last name.

OWNBY, JOHN C,
708 Morningside Tr., Murphy, TX 75094-4365, Phone: 972-442-7352, john@johnownby.com; Web: www.johnownby.com
Specialties: Hunters, utility/camp knives. **Patterns:** Hunters, locking folders and utility/camp knives. **Technical:** 440C, D2 and ATS-34. All blades are flat ground. Prefers natural materials for handles—exotic woods, horn and antler. **Prices:** $150 to $350; some to $500. **Remarks:** Part-time maker; first knife sold in 1993. Doing business as John C. Ownby Handmade Knives. **Mark:** Name, city, state.

OYSTER, LOWELL R,
543 Grant Rd, Corinth, ME 04427, Phone: 207-884-8663
Specialties: Traditional and original designed multi-blade slip-joint folders. **Patterns:** Hunters, minis, camp and fishing knives. **Technical:** Grinds O1; heat-treats. **Prices:** $55 to $450; some to $750. **Remarks:** Full-time maker; first knife sold in 1981. **Mark:** A scallop shell.

P

PACHI, FRANCESCO,
Via Pometta 1, 17046 Sassello (SV), ITALY, Phone: 019 720086, Fax: 019 720086, Web: www.pachi-knives.com
Specialties: Folders and straight knives of his design. **Patterns:** Utility, hunters and skinners. **Technical:** Grinds RWL-34, CPM S30V and Damascus. **Prices:** $800 to $3500. **Remarks:** Full-time maker; first knife sold in 1991. **Mark:** Logo with last name.

PACKARD, BOB,
PO Box 311, Elverta, CA 95626, Phone: 916-991-5218
Specialties: Traditional working/using straight knives of his design and to customer specs. **Patterns:** Hunters, fishing knives, utility/camp knives.

Technical: Grinds ATS-34, 440C; Forges 52100, 5168 and cable Damascus. **Prices:** $75 to $225. **Mark:** Engraved name and year.

PADILLA, GARY,
PO Box 5706, Bellingham, WA 98227, Phone: 360-756-7573, gkpadilla@yahoo.com
Specialties: Unique knives of all designs and uses. **Patterns:** Hunters, kitchen knives, utility/camp knives and obsidian ceremonial knives. **Technical:** Grinds 440C, ATS-34, O1 and Damascus. **Prices:** Generally $100 to $200. **Remarks:** Part-time maker; first knife sold in 1977. **Mark:** Stylized name.

PAGE, LARRY,
1200 Mackey Scott Rd, Aiken, SC 29801-7620, Phone: 803-648-0001
Specialties: Working knives of his design. **Patterns:** Hunters, boots and fighters. **Technical:** Grinds ATS-34. **Prices:** Start at $85. **Remarks:** Part-time maker; first knife sold in 1983. **Mark:** Name, city and state in oval.

PAGE, REGINALD,
6587 Groveland Hill Rd, Groveland, NY 14462, Phone: 716-243-1643
Specialties: High-art straight knives and one-of-a-kind folders of his design. **Patterns:** Hunters, locking folders and slip-joint folders. **Technical:** Forges O1, 5160 and his own Damascus. Prefers natural handle materials but will work with Micarta. **Remarks:** Spare-time maker; first knife sold in 1985. **Mark:** First initial, last name.

PAINTER, TONY,
87 Fireweed Dr, Whitehorse Yukon, CANADA Y1A 5T8, Phone: 867-633-3323, jimmies@klondiker.com; Web: www.tonypainterdesigns.com
Specialties: One-of-a-kind using knives, some fancy, fixed and folders. **Patterns:** No fixed patterns. **Technical:** Grinds ATS-34, D2, O1, S30V, Damascus satin finish. Prefers to use exotic woods and other natural materials. Micarta and G10 on working knives. **Prices:** Starting at $200. **Remarks:** Full-time knifemaker and carver. First knife sold in 1996. **Mark:** Two stamps used: initials TP in a circle and painter.

PALM, RIK,
10901 Scripps Ranch Blvd, San Diego, CA 92131, Phone: 858-530-0407, rikpalm@knifesmith.com; Web: www.knifesmith.com
Specialties: Sole authorship of one-of-a-kind unique art pieces, working/using knives and sheaths. **Patterns:** Carved nature themed knives, camp, hunters, friction folders, tomahawks, and small special pocket knives. **Technical:** Makes own Damascus, forges 5160H, 1084, 1095, W2, O1. Does his own heat treating including clay hardening. **Prices:** $80 and up. **Remarks:** American Bladesmith Society Journeyman Smith. First blade sold in 2000. **Mark:** Stamped, hand signed, etched last name signature.

PALMER, TAYLOR,
TAYLOR-MADE SCENIC KNIVES INC., Box 97, Blanding, UT 84511, Phone: 435-678-2523, taylormadewoodeu@citlink.net
Specialties: Bronze carvings inside of blade area. **Prices:** $250 and up. **Mark:** Taylor Palmer Utah.

PANAK, PAUL S,
9128 Stanhope-Kellogsville Rd, Kinsman, OH 44428, Phone: 330-876-2210, burn@burnknives.com; Web: www.burnknives.com
Specialties: Italian-styled knives. DA OTF's, Italian style stilettos. **Patterns:** Vintage-styled Italians, fighting folders and high art gothic-styles all with various mechanisms. **Technical:** Grinds ATS-34, 154 CM, 440C and Damascus. **Prices:** $800 to $3000. **Remarks:** Full-time maker, first knife sold in 1998. **Mark:** "Burn."

PARDUE, JOE,
PO Box 693, Spurger, TX 77660, Phone: 409-429-7074, Fax: 409-429-5657

PARDUE, MELVIN M,
4461 Jerkins Rd., Repton, AL 36475, Phone: 251-248-2686, mpardue@frontiernet.net; Web: www.pardueknives.com
Specialties: Folders, collectable, combat, utility and tactical. **Patterns:** Lockback, liner lock, push button; all blade and handle patterns. **Technical:** Grinds 154CM, 440C, 12C27. Forges mokume and Damascus. Uses titanium. **Prices:** $400 to $1600. **Remarks:** Full-time maker, Guild member, ABS member, AFC member. First knife made in 1957; first knife sold professionally in 1974. **Mark:** Mel Pardue.

PARKER, CLIFF,
6350 Tulip Dr, Zephyrhills, FL 33544, Phone: 813-973-1682, cooldamascus@aol.com Web: cliffparkerknives.com
Specialties: Damascus gent knives. **Patterns:** Locking liners, some straight knives. **Technical:** Mostly use 1095, 1084, 15N20, 203E and powdered steel. **Prices:** $700 to $2100. **Remarks:** Making own Damascus and specializing in mosaics; first knife sold in 1996. Full-time beginning in 2000. **Mark:** CP.

PARKER, J E,
11 Domenica Cir, Clarion, PA 16214, Phone: 814-226-4837, jimparkerknives@hotmail.com Web:www.jimparkerknives.com
Specialties: Fancy/embellished, traditional and working straight knives of his design and to customer specs. Engraving and scrimshaw by the best in the business. **Patterns:** Bowies, hunters and LinerLock® folders. **Technical:** Grinds 440C, 440V, ATS-34 and nickel Damascus. Prefers mastodon, oosik, amber and malachite handle material. **Prices:** $75 to $5200. **Remarks:** Full-time maker; first knife sold in 1991. Doing business as Custom Knife. **Mark:** J E Parker and Clarion PA stamped or etched in blade.

PARKER, ROBERT NELSON,
1527 E Fourth St, Royal Oak, MI 48067, Phone: 248-545-8211, rnparkerknives@wowway.com; Web: classicknifedesign@wowway.com
Specialties: Traditional working and using straight knives of his design. **Patterns:** Chutes, subhilts, hunters, and fighters. **Technical:** Grinds ATS-34; GB-42, S-30V, BG-42, ATS, 34-D-Z, no forging, hollow and flat grinds, full and hidden tangs. Hand-stitched leather sheaths. **Prices:** $400 to $1400; some to $2000. **Remarks:** Full-time maker; first knife sold in 1986. I do forge sometimes. **Mark:** Full name.

PARKS, BLANE C,
15908 Crest Dr, Woodbridge, VA 22191, Phone: 703-221-4680
Specialties: Knives of his design. **Patterns:** Boots, Bowies, daggers, fighters, hunters, kitchen knives, locking and slip-joint folders, utility/camp knives, letter openers and friction folders. **Technical:** Grinds ATS-34, 440C, D2 and other carbon steels. Offers filework, silver wire inlay and wooden sheaths. **Prices:** Start at $250 to $650; some to $1000. **Remarks:** Part-time maker; first knife sold in 1993. Doing business as B.C. Parks Knives. **Mark:** First and middle initials, last name.

PARKS, JOHN,
3539 Galilee Church Rd, Jefferson, GA 30549, Phone: 706-367-4916
Specialties: Traditional working and using straight knives of his design. **Patterns:** Hunters, integral bolsters, and personal knives. **Technical:** Forges 1095 and 5168. **Prices:** $275 to $600; some to $800. **Remarks:** Part-time maker; first knife sold in 1989. **Mark:** Initials.

PARLER, THOMAS O,
11 Franklin St, Charleston, SC 29401, Phone: 803-723-9433

PARRISH, ROBERT,
271 Allman Hill Rd, Weaverville, NC 28787, Phone: 828-645-2864
Specialties: Heavy-duty working knives of his design or to customer specs. **Patterns:** Survival and duty knives; hunters and fighters. **Technical:** Grinds 440C, D2, O1 and commercial Damascus. **Prices:** $200 to $300; some to $6000. **Remarks:** Part-time maker; first knife sold in 1970. **Mark:** Initials connected, sometimes with city and state.

PARRISH III, GORDON A,
940 Lakloey Dr, North Pole, AK 99705, Phone: 907-488-0357, ga-parrish@gci.net
Specialties: Classic and high-art straight knives of his design and to customer specs; working and using knives. **Patterns:** Bowies and hunters. **Technical:** Grinds tool steel and ATS-34. Uses mostly Alaskan handle materials. **Prices:** Starting at $225. **Remarks:** Spare-time maker; first knife sold in 1980. **Mark:** Last name, FBKS. ALASKA

PARSONS, LARRY,
1038 W Kyle Way, Mustang, OK 73064, Phone: 405-376-9408, Fax: 405-376-9408, l.j.parsons@sbcglobal.net
Specialties: Variety of sheaths from plain leather, geometric stamped, also inlays of various types. **Prices:** Starting at $35 and up

PARSONS, MICHAEL R,
MCKEE KNIVES, 7042 McFarland Rd., Indianapolis, IN 46227, Phone: 317-784-7943, mparsons@comcast.net
Specialties: Hand-forged fixed-blade and folding knives, all fancy but all are useable knives. **Patterns:** Engraves, carves, wire inlay, and leather work. All knives one-of-a-kind. **Technical:** Blades forged from files, all work hand done. Doing business as McKee Knives. **Prices:** $350 to $2000. **Mark:** McKee.

PARSONS, PETE,
5905 High Country Dr., Helena, MT 59602, Phone: 406-202-0181, Parsons14@MT.net; Web: www.ParsonsMontanaKnives.com
Specialties: Forged utility blades in straight steel or Damascus (will grind stainless on customer request). Folding knives of my own design. **Patterns:** Hunters, fighters, Bowies, hikers, camp knives, everyday carry folders, tactical folders, gentleman's folders. Some customer designed pieces. **Technical:** Forges carbon steel, grinds carbon steel and some stainless. Forges own Damascus. **Mark:** Left side of blade PARSONS stamp or Parsons Helena, MT etch.

PARTRIDGE, JERRY D.,
P.O. Box 977, DeFuniak Springs, FL 32435, Phone: 850-585-0458, jerry@partridgeknives.com; Web: www.partridgeknives.com
Specialties: Various-sized skinners and fighting knives of carbon Damascus and 440C stainless (both plain and fileworked). I primarily use mammoth tooth, exotic woods (such as ebonywood, cocobolo, kingwood, blackwood, rosewood, and bloodwood) and giraffe bone. **Prices:** $250 and up, depending on materials used. **Remarks:** First knife sold in 2007. **Mark:** Partridge Knives logo on the blade.

PASSMORE, JIMMY D,
316 SE Elm, Hoxie, AR 72433, Phone: 870-886-1922

PATRICK, BOB,
12642 24A Ave, S. Surrey, B.C., CANADA V4A 8H9, Phone: 604-538-6214, Fax: 604-888-2683, bob@knivesonnet.com; Web: www.knivesonnet.com
Specialties: Maker's designs only, No orders. **Patterns:** Bowies, hunters, daggers, throwing knives. **Technical:** D2, 5160, Damascus. **Prices:** Good value. **Remarks:** Full-time maker; first knife sold in 1987. Doing business as Crescent Knife Works. **Mark:** Logo with name and province or Crescent Knife Works.

PATRICK, CHUCK,
PO Box 127, Brasstown, NC 28902, Phone: 828-837-7627
Specialties: Period pieces. **Patterns:** Hunters, daggers, tomahawks, pre-Civil War folders. **Technical:** Forges hardware, his own cable and Damascus, available in fancy pattern and mosaic. **Prices:** $150 to $1000; some higher. **Remarks:** Full-time maker. **Mark:** Hand-engraved name or flying owl

PATRICK, PEGGY,
PO Box 127, Brasstown, NC 28902, Phone: 828-837-7627
Specialties: Authentic period and Indian sheaths, braintan, rawhide, beads and quill work. **Technical:** Does own braintan, rawhide; uses only natural dyes for quills, old color beads.

PATRICK, WILLARD C,
PO Box 5716, Helena, MT 59604, Phone: 406-458-6552, Fax: 406-458-7068, wkamar2@onewest.net
Specialties: Working straight knives and one-of-a-kind art knives of his design or to customer specs. **Patterns:** Hunters, Bowies, fish, patch and kitchen knives. **Technical:** Grinds ATS-34, 1095, O1, A2 and Damascus. **Prices:** $100 to $2000. **Remarks:** Full-time maker; first knife sold in 1989. Doing business as Wil-A-Mar Cutlery. **Mark:** Shield with last name and a dagger.

PATTAY, RUDY,
510 E. Harrison St, Long Beach, NY 11561, Phone: 516-431-0847, dolphinp@optonline.net; Web: www.pattayknives.com
Specialties: Fancy and working straight knives of his design. **Patterns:** Bowies, hunters, utility/camp knives, drop point, skinners. **Technical:** Hollow-grinds ATS-34, 440C, O1. Offers commercial Damascus, stainless steel soldered guards; fabricates guard and butt cap on lathe and milling machine. Heat-treats. Prefers synthetic handle materials. Offers hand-sewn sheaths. **Prices:** $100 to $350; some to $500. **Remarks:** Full-time maker; first knife sold in 1990. **Mark:** First initial, last name in sorcerer logo.

PATTERSON, PAT,
Box 246, Barksdale, TX 78828, Phone: 830-234-3586, pat@pattersonknives.com
Specialties: Traditional fixed blades and LinerLock folders. **Patterns:** Hunters and folders. **Technical:** Grinds 440C, ATS-34, D2, O1 and Damascus. **Prices:** $250 to $1000. **Remarks:** Full-time maker. First knife sold in 1991. **Mark:** Name and city.

PATTON, DICK AND ROB,
6803 View Ln, Nampa, ID 83687, Phone: 208-468-4123, grpatton@pattonknives.com; Web: www.pattonknives.com
Specialties: Custom Damascus, hand forged, fighting knives, Bowie and tactical. **Patterns:** Mini Bowie, Merlin Fighter, Mandrita Fighting Bowie. **Prices:** $100 to $2000.

PATTON, PHILLIP,
PO BOX 113, Yoder, IN 46798, phillip@pattonblades.com Web: www.pattonblades.com
Specialties: Tactical fixed blades, including fighting, camp, and general utility blades. Also makes Bowies and daggers. Known for leaf and recurve blade shapes. **Technical:** Forges carbon, stainless, and high alloy tool steels. Makes own damascus using 1084/15n20 or O1/L6. Makes own carbon/stainless laminated blades. For handle materials, prefers high end woods and sythetics. Uses 416 ss and bronze for fittings. **Prices:** $175 - $1000 for knives; $750 and up for swords. **Remarks:** Full-time maker since 2005. Two-year backlog. ABS member. **Mark:** "Phillip Patton" with Phillip above Patton.

PAULO, FERNANDES R,
Raposo Tavares No 213, Lencois Paulista, 18680, Sao Paulo, BRAZIL, Phone: 014-263-4281
Specialties: An apprentice of Jose Alberto Paschoarelli, his designs are heavily based on the later designs. **Technical:** Grinds tool steels and stainless steels. Part-time knifemaker. **Prices:** Start from $100. **Mark:** P.R.F.

PAWLOWSKI, JOHN R,
111 Herman Melville Ave, Newport News, VA 23606, Phone: 757-870-4284, Fax: 757-223-5935, www.virginiacustomcutlery.com
Specialties: Traditional working and using straight knives and folders. **Patterns:** Hunters, Bowies, fighters and camp knives. **Technical:** Stock removal, grinds 440C, ATS-34, 154CM and buys Damascus. **Prices:** $150 to $500; some higher. **Remarks:** Part-time maker, first knife sold in 1983, Knifemaker Guild Member. **Mark:** Name with attacking eagle.

PEAGLER, RUSS,
PO Box 1314, Moncks Corner, SC 29461, Phone: 803-761-1008
Specialties: Traditional working straight knives of his design and to customer specs. **Patterns:** Hunters, fighters, boots. **Technical:** Hollow-grinds 440C, ATS-34 and O1; uses Damascus steel. Prefers bone handles. **Prices:** $85 to $300; some to $500. **Remarks:** Spare-time maker; first knife sold in 1983. **Mark:** Initials.

PEASE, W D,
657 Cassidy Pike, Ewing, KY 41039, Phone: 606-845-0387, Web: www.wdpeaseknives.com
Specialties: Display-quality working folders. **Patterns:** Fighters, tantos and boots; locking folders and interframes. **Technical:** Grinds ATS-34 and commercial Damascus; has own side-release lock system. **Prices:** $500 to

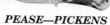

$1000; some to $3000. **Remarks:** Full-time maker; first knife sold in 1970. First and middle initials, last name and state. W. D. Pease Kentucky.

PEELE, BRYAN,
219 Ferry St, PO Box 1363, Thompson Falls, MT 59873, Phone: 406-827-4633, banana_peele@yahoo.com
Specialties: Fancy working and using knives of his design. **Patterns:** Hunters, Bowies and fighters. **Technical:** Grinds 440C, ATS-34, D2, O1 and commercial Damascus. **Prices:** $110 to $300; some to $900. **Remarks:** Part-time maker; first knife sold in 1985. **Mark:** The Elk Rack, full name, city, state.

PELLEGRIN, MIKE,
MP3 Knives, 107 White St., Troy, IL 62294-1126, Phone: 618-667-6777, Web: MP3knives.com
Specialties: Lockback folders with stone inlays, and one-of-a-kind art knives with stainless steel or damascus handles. **Technical:** Stock-removal method of blade making using 440C, Damasteel or high-carbon damascus blades. **Prices:** $800-$2000. **Remarks:** Making knives since 2000. **Mark:** MP (combined) 3.

PENDLETON, LLOYD,
24581 Shake Ridge Rd, Volcano, CA 95689, Phone: 209-296-3353, Fax: 209-296-3353
Specialties: Contemporary working knives in standard patterns. **Patterns:** Hunters, fighters and boots. **Technical:** Grinds and ATS-34; mirror finishes. **Prices:** $400 to $900 **Remarks:** Full-time maker; first knife sold in 1973. **Mark:** First initial, last name logo, city and state.

PENDRAY, ALFRED H,
13950 NE 20th St, Williston, FL 32696, Phone: 352-528-6124
Specialties: Working straight knives and folders; period pieces. **Patterns:** Fighters and hunters, axes, camp knives and tomahawks. **Technical:** Forges Wootz steel; makes his own Damascus; makes traditional knives from old files and rasps. **Prices:** $125 to $1000; some to $3500. **Remarks:** Part-time maker; first knife sold in 1954. **Mark:** Last initial in horseshoe logo.

PENFOLD, MICK,
PENFOLD KNIVES, 5 Highview Close, Tremar, Cornwall PL14 5SJ, ENGLAND/UK, Phone: 01579-345783, Fax: 01579-345783, mickpenfold@btinternet.com; Web: www.penfoldknives.com
Specialties: Hunters, fighters, Bowies. **Technical:** Grinds 440C, ATS-34, Damasteel, and Damascus. **Prices:** $200 to $1800. **Remarks:** Part-time maker. First knives sold in 1999. **Mark:** Last name.

PENNINGTON, C A,
163 Kainga Rd, Kainga Christchurch 8009, NEW ZEALAND, Phone: 03-3237292, capennington@xtra.co.nz
Specialties: Classic working and collectors knives. Folders a specialty. **Patterns:** Classical styling for hunters and collectors. **Technical:** Forges his own all tool steel Damascus. Grinds D2 when requested. **Prices:** $240 to $2000. **Remarks:** Full-time maker; first knife sold in 1988. Color brochure $3. **Mark:** Name, country.

PEPIOT, STEPHAN,
73 Cornwall Blvd, Winnipeg, Man., CANADA R3J-1E9, Phone: 204-888-1499
Specialties: Working straight knives in standard patterns. **Patterns:** Hunters and camp knives. **Technical:** Grinds 440C and industrial hack-saw blades. **Prices:** $75 to $125. **Remarks:** Spare-time maker; first knife sold in 1982. Not currently taking orders. **Mark:** PEP.

PERRY, CHRIS,
1654 W. Birch, Fresno, CA 93711, Phone: 559-246-7446, chris.perry4@comcast.net
Specialties: Traditional working/using straight knives of his design. **Patterns:** Boots, hunters and utility/camp knives. **Technical:** Grinds ATS-34, Damascus, 416ss fittings, silver and gold fittings, hand-rubbed finishes. **Prices:** Starting at $250. **Remarks:** Part-time maker, first knife sold in 1995. **Mark:** Name above city and state.

PERRY, JIM,
Hope Star PO Box 648, Hope, AR 71801, jenn@comfabinc.com

PERRY, JOHN,
9 South Harrell Rd, Mayflower, AR 72106, Phone: 501-470-3043, jpknives@cyberback.com
Specialties: Investment grade and working folders; Antique Bowies and slip joints. **Patterns:** Front and rear lock folders, liner locks, hunters and Bowies. **Technical:** Grinds CPM440V, D2 and making own Damascus. Offers filework. **Prices:** $375 to $1200; some to $3500. **Remarks:** Part-time maker; first knife sold in 1991. Doing business as Perry Custom Knives. **Mark:** Initials or last name in high relief set in a diamond shape.

PERRY, JOHNNY,
PO Box 35, Inman, SC 29349, Phone: 864-431-6390, perr3838@bellsouth.net
Mark: High Ridge Forge.

PERSSON, CONNY,
PL 588, 820 50 Loos, SWEDEN, Phone: +46 657 10305, Fax: +46 657 413 435, connyknives@swipnet.se; Web: www.connyknives.com
Specialties: Mosaic Damascus. **Patterns:** Mosaic Damascus. **Technical:** Straight knives and folders. **Prices:** $1000 and up. **Mark:** C. Persson.

PETEAN, FRANCISCO AND MAURICIO,
R. Dr. Carlos de Carvalho Rosa 52, Centro, Birigui, SP-16200-000, BRAZIL, Phone: 0186-424786
Specialties: Classic knives to customer specs. **Patterns:** Bowies, boots, fighters, hunters and utility knives. **Technical:** Grinds D6, 440C and high-carbon steels. Prefers natural handle material. **Prices:** $70 to $500. **Remarks:** Full-time maker; first knife sold in 1985. **Mark:** Last name, hand made.

PETERSEN, DAN L,
10610 SW 81st, Auburn, KS 66402, Phone: 785-256-2640, dan@petersenknives.com; Web: www.petersenknives.com
Specialties: Period pieces and forged integral hilts on hunters and fighters. **Patterns:** Texas-style Bowies, boots and hunters in high-carbon and Damascus steel. **Technical:** Austempers forged high-carbon sword blades. Precision heat treating using salt tanks. **Prices:** $400 to $5000. **Remarks:** First knife sold in 1978. ABS Master Smith. **Mark:** Stylized initials, MS.

PETERSON, CHRIS,
Box 143, 2175 W Rockyford, Salina, UT 84654, Phone: 435-529-7194
Specialties: Working straight knives of his design. **Patterns:** Large fighters, boots, hunters and some display pieces. **Technical:** Forges O1 and meteor. Makes and sells his own Damascus. Engraves, scrimshaws and inlays. **Prices:** $150 to $600; some to $1500. **Remarks:** Full-time maker; first knife sold in 1986. **Mark:** A drop in a circle with a line through it.

PETERSON, ELDON G,
368 Antelope Trl, Whitefish, MT 59937, Phone: 406-862-2204, draino@digisys.net; Web: http://www.kmg.org/egpeterson
Specialties: Fancy and working folders, any size. **Patterns:** Lockback interframes, integral bolster folders, liner locks, and two-blades. **Technical:** Grinds 440C and ATS-34. Offers gold inlay work, gem stone inlays and engraving. **Prices:** $285 to $5000. **Remarks:** Full-time maker; first knife sold in 1974. **Mark:** Name, city and state.

PETERSON, KAREN,
THE PEN AND THE SWORD LTD., PO Box 290741, Brooklyn, NY 11229-0741, Phone: 718-382-4847, Fax: 718-376-5745, info@pensword.com; Web: www.pensword.com

PETERSON, LLOYD (PETE) C,
64 Halbrook Rd, Clinton, AR 72031, Phone: 501-893-0000, wmblade@cyberback.com
Specialties: Miniatures and mosaic folders. **Prices:** $250 and up. **Remarks:** Lead time is 6-8 months. **Mark:** Pete.

PFANENSTIEL, DAN,
1824 Lafayette Ave, Modesto, CA 95355, Phone: 209-575-5937, dpfan@sbcglobal.net
Specialties: Japanese tanto, swords. One-of-a-kind knives. **Technical:** Forges simple carbon steels, some Damascus. **Prices:** $200 to $1000. **Mark:** Circle with wave inside.

PHILIPPE, D A,
PO Box 306, Cornish, NH 03746, Phone: 603-543-0662
Specialties: Traditional working straight knives. **Patterns:** Hunters, trout and bird, camp knives etc. **Technical:** Grinds ATS-34, 440C, A-2, Damascus, flat and hollow ground. Exotic woods and antler handles. Brass, nickel silver and stainless components. **Prices:** $125 to $800. **Remarks:** Full-time maker, first knife sold in 1984. **Mark:** First initial, last name.

PHILLIPS, ALISTAIR,
Amaroo, ACT, 2914, AUSTRALIA, alistair.phillips@knives.mutantdiscovery.com; Web: http://knives.mutantdiscovery.com
Specialties: Slipjoint folders, forged or stock removal fixed blades. **Patterns:** Single blade slipjoints, smaller neck knives, and hunters. **Technical:** Flat grnds O1, ATS-34, and forged 1055. **Prices:** $80 to $400. **Remarks:** Part-time maker, first knife made in 2005. **Mark:** Stamped signature.

PHILLIPS, DENNIS,
16411 West Bennet Rd, Independence, LA 70443, Phone: 985-878-8275
Specialties: Specializes in fixed blade military combat tacticals.

PHILLIPS, RANDY,
759 E. Francis St, Ontario, CA 91761, Phone: 909-923-4381
Specialties: Hunters, collector-grade liner locks and high-art daggers. **Technical:** Grinds D2, 440C and 154CM; embellishes. **Prices:** Start at $200. **Remarks:** Part-time maker; first knife sold in 1981. Not currently taking orders. **Mark:** Name, city and state in eagle head.

PHILLIPS, SCOTT C,
671 California Rd, Gouverneur, NY 13642, Phone: 315-287-1280, Web: www.mangusknives.com
Specialties: Sheaths in leather. Fixed blade hunters, boot knives, Bowies, buck skinners (hand forged and stock removal). **Technical:** 440C, 5160, 1095 and 52100. **Prices:** Start at $125. **Remarks:** Part-time maker; first knife sold in 1993. **Mark:** Before "2000" as above after S Mangus.

PICKENS, SELBERT,
2295 Roxalana Rd, Dunbar, WV 25064, Phone: 304-744-4048
Specialties: Using knives. **Patterns:** Standard sporting knives. **Technical:** Stainless steels; stock removal method. **Prices:** Moderate. **Remarks:** Part-time maker. **Mark:** Name.

PICKETT, TERRELL,
66 Pickett Ln, Lumberton, MS 39455, Phone: 601-794-6125, pickettfence66@bellsouth.net
Specialties: Fix blades, camp knives, Bowies, hunters, & skinners. Forge and stock removal and some firework. **Technical:** 5160, 1095, 52100, 440C and ATS-34. **Prices:** Range from $150 to $550. **Mark:** Logo on stock removal T.W. Pickett and on forged knives Terrell Pickett's Forge.

PIENAAR, CONRAD,
19A Milner Rd, Bloemfontein 9300, SOUTH AFRICA, Phone: 027 514364180, Fax: 027 514364180
Specialties: Fancy working and using straight knives and folders of his design, to customer specs and in standard patterns. **Patterns:** Hunters, locking folders, cleavers, kitchen and utility/camp knives. **Technical:** Grinds 12C27, D2 and ATS-34. Uses some Damascus. Scrimshaws; inlays gold. Knives come with wooden box and custom-made leather sheath. **Prices:** $300 to $1000. **Remarks:** Part-time maker; first knife sold in 1981. Doing business as C.P. Knifemaker. Makes slip joint folders and liner locking folders. **Mark:** Initials and serial number.

PIERCE, HAROLD L,
106 Lyndon Lane, Louisville, KY 40222, Phone: 502-429-5136
Specialties: Working straight knives, some fancy. **Patterns:** Big fighters and Bowies. **Technical:** Grinds D2, 440C, 154CM; likes sub-hilts. **Prices:** $150 to $450; some to $1200. **Remarks:** Full-time maker; first knife sold in 1982. **Mark:** Last name with knife through the last initial.

PIERCE, RANDALL,
903 Wyndam, Arlington, TX 76017, Phone: 817-468-0138

PIERGALLINI, DANIEL E,
4011 N. Forbes Rd, Plant City, FL 33565, Phone: 813-754-3908, Fax: 813-754-3908, coolnifedad@earthlink.net
Specialties: Traditional and fancy straight knives and folders of his design or to customer's specs. **Patterns:** Hunters, fighters, skinners, working and camp knives. **Technical:** Grinds 440C, O1, D2, ATS-34, some Damascus; forges his own mokume. Uses natural handle material. **Prices:** $450 to $800; some to $1800. **Remarks:** Part-time maker; sold first knife in 1994. **Mark:** Last name, city, state or last name in script.

PIESNER, DEAN,
1786 Sawmill Rd, Conestogo, Ont., CANADA N0B 1N0, Phone: 519-664-3648, dean47@rogers.com
Specialties: Classic and period pieces of his design and to customer specs. **Patterns:** Bowies, skinners, fighters and swords. **Technical:** Forges 5160, 52100, steel Damascus and nickel-steel Damascus. Makes own mokume gane with copper, brass and nickel silver. Silver wire inlays in wood. **Prices:** Start at $150. **Remarks:** Full-time maker; first knife sold in 1990. **Mark:** First initial, last name, JS.

PITMAN, DAVID,
PO Drawer 2566, Williston, ND 58802, Phone: 701-572-3325

PITT, DAVID F,
6812 Digger Pine Ln, Anderson, CA 96007, Phone: 530-357-2393
Specialties: Fixed blade, hunters and hatchets. Flat ground mirror finish. **Patterns:** Hatchets with gut hook, small gut hooks, guards, bolsters or guard less. **Technical:** Grinds A2, 440C, 154CM, ATS-34, D2. **Prices:** $150 to $750. **Remarks:** Guild member since 1982. **Mark:** Bear paw with name David F. Pitt.

PLUNKETT, RICHARD,
29 Kirk Rd, West Cornwall, CT 06796, Phone: 860-672-3419; Toll free: 888-KNIVES-8
Specialties: Traditional, fancy folders and straight knives of his design. **Patterns:** Slip-joint folders and small straight knives. **Technical:** Grinds O1 and stainless steel. Offers many different file patterns. **Prices:** $150 to $450. **Remarks:** Full-time maker; first knife sold in 1994. **Mark:** Signature and date under handle scales.

POLK, CLIFTON,
4625 Webber Creek Rd, Van Buren, AR 72956, Phone: 479-474-3828, cliffpolkknives1@aol.com; Web: www.polkknives.com
Specialties: Fancy working folders. **Patterns:** One blades spring backs in five sizes, LinerLock®, automatics, double blades spring back folder with standard drop & clip blade or bird knife with drop and vent hook or cowboy's knives with drop and hoof pick and straight knives. **Technical:** Uses D2 & ATS-34. Makes all own Damascus using 1084, 1095, O1, 15N20, 5160. Using all kinds of exotic woods. Stag, pearls, ivory, mastodon ivory and other bone and horns. **Prices:** $200 to $3000. **Remarks:** Retired fire fighter, made knives since 1974. **Mark:** Polk.

POLK, RUSTY,
5900 Wildwood Dr, Van Buren, AR 72956, Phone: 479-410-3661, polkknives@aol.com; Web: www.polkknives.com
Specialties: Skinners, hunters, Bowies, fighters and forging working knives fancy Damascus, daggers, boot knives and survival knives. **Patterns:** Drop point, and forge to shape. **Technical:** ATS-34, 440C, Damascus, D2, 51/60, 1084, 15N20, does all his forging. **Prices:** $200 to $1500. **Mark:** R. Polk all hand made. RP on miniatures.

POLKOWSKI, AL,
8 Cathy Lane, Chester, NJ 07930, Phone: 908-879-6030, Web: polkowskiknives.com
Specialties: High-tech straight knives and folders for adventurers and professionals. **Patterns:** Fighters, side-lock folders, boots and concealment knives. **Technical:** Grinds 154CM and S30V, satin and beadblast finishes; Kydex sheaths. **Prices:** Start at $100. **Remarks:** Full-time maker; first knife sold in 1985. **Mark:** Last name with lightning bolts.

POLLOCK, WALLACE J,
PO BOX 449, Reserve, NM 87830, Phone: 575-654-4039, wally@pollockknives.com Web: www.pollackknives.com
Specialties: Using knives, skinner, hunter, fighting, camp knives. **Patterns:** Use his own patterns or yours. Traditional hunters, daggers, fighters, camp knives. **Technical:** Grinds ATS-34, D-2, BG-42, makes own Damascus, D-2, 0-1, ATS-34, prefer D-2, handles exotic wood, horn, bone, ivory. **Remarks:** Full-time maker, sold first knife 1973. **Prices:** $250 to $2500. **Mark:** Last name, maker, city/state.

POLZIEN, DON,
1912 Inler Suite-L, Lubbock, TX 79407, Phone: 806-791-0766, blindinglightknives.net
Specialties: Traditional Japanese-style blades; restores antique Japanese swords, scabbards and fittings. **Patterns:** Hunters, fighters, one-of-a-kind art knives. **Technical:** 1045-1050 carbon steels, 440C, D2, ATS-34, standard and cable Damascus. **Prices:** $150 to $2500. **Remarks:** Full-time maker. First knife sold in 1990. **Mark:** Oriental characters inside square border.

PONZIO, DOUG,
10219 W State Rd 81, Beloit, WI 53511, Phone: 608-313-3223, prfgdoug@hughes.net; Web: www.ponziodamascus.com
Specialties: Mosaic Damascus, stainless Damascus. **Mark:** P.F.

POOLE, MARVIN O,
PO Box 552, Commerce, GA 30529, Phone: 803-225-5970
Specialties: Traditional working/using straight knives and folders of his design and in standard patterns. **Patterns:** Bowies, fighters, hunters, locking folders, bird and trout knives. **Technical:** Grinds 440C, D2, ATS-34. **Prices:** $50 to $150; some to $750. **Remarks:** Part-time maker; first knife sold in 1980. **Mark:** First initial, last name, year, serial number.

POSNER, BARRY E,
12501 Chandler Blvd Suite 104, N. Hollywood, CA 91607, Phone: 818-752-8005, Fax: 818-752-8006
Specialties: Working/using straight knives. **Patterns:** Hunters, kitchen and utility/camp knives. **Technical:** Grinds ATS-34; forges 1095 and nickel. **Prices:** $95 to $400. **Remarks:** Part-time maker; first knife sold in 1987. Doing business as Posner Knives. Supplier of finished mosaic handle pin stock. **Mark:** First and middle initials, last name.

POTIER, TIMOTHY F,
PO Box 711, Oberlin, LA 70655, Phone: 337-639-2229, tpotier@hotmail.com
Specialties: Classic working and using straight knives to customer specs; some collectible. **Patterns:** Hunters, Bowies, utility/camp knives and belt axes. **Technical:** Forges carbon steel and his own Damascus; offers filework. **Prices:** $300 to $1800; some to $4000. **Remarks:** Part-time maker; first knife sold in 1981. **Mark:** Last name, MS.

POTTER, BILLY,
6323 Hyland Dr., Dublin, OH 43017, Phone: 614-589-8324, potterknives@yahoo.com; Web: www.potterknives.com
Specialties: Working straight knives; his design or to customers patterns. **Patterns:** Bowie, fighters, utilities, skinners, hunters, folding lock blade, miniatures and tomahawks. **Technical:** Grinds and forges, carbon steel, L6, 0-1, 1095, 5160, 1084 and 52000. Grinds 440C stainless. Forges own Damascus. Handles: prefers exotic hardwood, curly and birdseye maples. Bone, ivory, antler, pearl and horn. Some scrimshaw. **Prices:** Start at $100 up to $800. **Remarks:** Part-time maker; first knife sold 1996. **Mark:** First and last name (maker).

POWELL, JAMES,
2500 North Robinson Rd, Texarkana, TX 75501

POWELL, ROBERT CLARK,
PO Box 321, 93 Gose Rd., Smarr, GA 31086, Phone: 478-994-5418
Specialties: Composite bar Damascus blades. **Patterns:** Art knives, hunters, combat, tomahawks. **Patterns:** Hand forges all blades. **Prices:** $300 and up. **Remarks:** ABS Journeyman Smith. **Mark:** Powell.

PRATER, MIKE,
PRATER AND COMPANY, 81 Sanford Ln., Flintstone, GA 30725, cmprater@aol.com; Web: www.casecustomknives.com
Specialties: Customizing factory knives. **Patterns:** Buck knives, case knives, hen and rooster knives. **Technical:** Manufacture of mica pearl. **Prices:** Varied. **Remarks:** First knife sold in 1980. **Mark:** Mica pearl.

PRESSBURGER, RAMON,
59 Driftway Rd, Howell, NJ 07731, Phone: 732-363-0816
Specialties: BG-42. Only knifemaker in U.S.A. that has complete line of affordable hunting knives made from BG-42. **Patterns:** All types hunting styles. **Technical:** Uses all steels; main steels are D-2 and BG-42. **Prices:** $75 to $500. **Remarks:** Full-time maker; has been making hunting knives for 30 years. Makes knives to your patterning. **Mark:** NA.

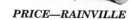

PRICE, TIMMY,
PO Box 906, Blairsville, GA 30514, Phone: 706-745-5111

PRIDGEN JR., LARRY,
PO BOX 707, Fitzgerald, GA 31750, Phone: 229-591-0013, pridgencustomknives@gmail.com Web: www.pridgencustomknives.com **Specialties:** Bowie and Liner Lock Folders. **Patterns:** Bowie, fighter, skinner, trout, liner lock, and custom orders. **Technical:** I do stock removal and use carbon and stainless Damascus and stainless steel. **Prices:** $250 and up. **Remarks:** Each knife comes with a hand-crafted custom sheath and life-time guarantee. **Mark:** Distinctive logo that looks like a brand with LP and a circle around it.

PRIMOS, TERRY,
932 Francis Dr, Shreveport, LA 71118, Phone: 318-686-6625, tprimos@sport.rr.com or terry@primosknives.com; Web: www.primosknives.com **Specialties:** Traditional forged straight knives. **Patterns:** Hunters, Bowies, camp knives, and fighters. **Technical:** Forges primarily 1084 and 5160; also forges Damascus. **Prices:** $250 to $600. **Remarks:** Full-time maker; first knife sold in 1993. **Mark:** Last name.

PRINSLOO, THEUNS,
PO Box 2263, Bethlehem, 9700, SOUTH AFRICA, Phone: 27824663885, theunmesa@telkomsa.net; Web: www.theunsprinsloo.com **Specialties:** Fancy folders. **Technical:** Own Damascus and mokume. **Prices:** $450 to $1500.

PRITCHARD, RON,
613 Crawford Ave, Dixon, IL 61021, Phone: 815-284-6005 **Specialties:** Plain and fancy working knives. **Patterns:** Variety of straight knives, locking folders, interframes and miniatures. **Technical:** Grinds 440C, 154CM and commercial Damascus. **Prices:** $100 to $200; some to $1500. **Remarks:** Part-time maker; first knife sold in 1979. **Mark:** Name and city.

PROVENZANO, JOSEPH D,
39043 Dutch Lane, Ponchatoula, LA 70454, Phone: 225-615-4846 **Specialties:** Working straight knives and folders in standard patterns. **Patterns:** Hunters, Bowies, folders, camp and fishing knives. **Technical:** Grinds ATS-34, 440C, 154CM, CPM 4400V, CPM420V and Damascus. Hollow-grinds hunters. **Prices:** $110 to $300; some to $1000. **Remarks:** Part-time maker; first knife sold in 1980. **Mark:** Joe-Pro.

PRYOR, STEPHEN L,
HC Rt 1, Box 1445, Boss, MO 65440, Phone: 573-626-4838, Fax: same, Knives4U3@juno.com; Web: www.stevescutler.com **Specialties:** Working and fancy straight knives, some to customer specs. **Patterns:** Bowies, hunting/fishing, utility/camp, fantasy/art. **Technical:** Grinds 440C, ATS-34, 1085, some Damascus, and does filework. Stag and exotic hardwood handles. **Prices:** $250 and up. **Remarks:** Full-time maker; first knife sold in 1991. **Mark:** Stylized first initial and last name over city and state.

PUGH, JIM,
PO Box 711, Azle, TX 76020, Phone: 817-444-2679, Fax: 817-444-5455 **Specialties:** Fancy/embellished limited editions by request. **Patterns:** 5- to 7-inch Bowies, wildlife art pieces, hunters, daggers and fighters; some commemoratives. **Technical:** Multi color transplanting in solid 18K gold, fine gems; grinds 440C and ATS-34. Offers engraving, fancy file etching and leather sheaths for wildlife art pieces. Ivory and coco bolo handle material on limited editions. Designs animal head butt caps and paws or bear claw guards; sterling silver heads and guards. **Prices:** $60,000 to $80,000 each in the Big Five 2000 edition. **Remarks:** Full-time maker; first knife sold in 1970. **Mark:** Pugh (Old English).

PULIS, VLADIMIR,
CSA 230-95, SL Republic, 96701 Kremnica, SLOVAKIA, Phone: 00421 903 340076, Fax: 00427 903 390076, vpulis@host.sk; Web: www.vpulis.host.sk **Specialties:** Fancy and high-art straight knives of his design. **Patterns:** Daggers and hunters. **Technical:** Forges Damascus steel. All work done by hand. **Prices:** $250 to $3000; some to $10,000. **Remarks:** Full-time maker; first knife sold in 1990. **Mark:** Initials in sixtagon.

PULLIAM, MORRIS C,
560 Jeptha Knob Rd, Shelbyville, KY 40065, Phone: 502-633-2261, mcpulliam@fastballinternet.com **Specialties:** Working knives, Cherokee River pattern Damascus. **Patterns:** Hunters and tomahawks. **Technical:** Forges L6, W2, 1095, Damascus and bar 320 layer Damascus. **Prices:** $165 to $1200. **Remarks:** Full-time maker; first knife sold in 1974. Makes knives for Native American festivals. Doing business as Knob Hill Forge. Member of Piqua Sept Shawnee of Ohio. Indian name Cherokee name Chewla (Fox). As a member of a state tribe, is an American Indian artist and craftsman by federal law. **Mark:** Small and large - Pulliam.

PURSLEY, AARON,
8885 Coal Mine Rd, Big Sandy, MT 59520, Phone: 406-378-3200 **Specialties:** Fancy working knives. **Patterns:** Locking folders, straight hunters and daggers, personal wedding knives and letter openers. **Technical:** Grinds O1 and 440C; engraves. **Prices:** $900 to $2500. **Remarks:** Full-time maker; first knife sold in 1975. **Mark:** Initials connected with year.

PURVIS, BOB AND ELLEN,
2416 N Loretta Dr, Tucson, AZ 85716, Phone: 520-795-8290, repknives2@cox.net **Specialties:** Hunter, skinners, Bowies, using knives, gentlemen folders and collectible knives. **Technical:** Grinds ATS-34, 440C, Damascus, Dama steel, heat-treats and cryogenically quenches. We do gold-plating, salt bluing, scrimshawing, filework and fashion handmade leather sheaths. Materials used for handles include exotic woods, mammoth ivory, mother-of-pearl, G-10 and Micarta. **Prices:** $165 to $800. **Remarks:** Knifemaker since retirement in 1984. Selling them since 1993. **Mark:** Script or print R.E. Purvis ~ Tucson, AZ or last name only.

PUTNAM, DONALD S,
590 Wolcott Hill Rd, Wethersfield, CT 06109, Phone: 860-563-9718, Fax: 860-563-9718, dpknives@cox.net **Specialties:** Working knives for the hunter and fisherman. **Patterns:** His design or to customer specs. **Technical:** Uses stock removal method, O1, W2, D2, ATS-34, 154CM, 440C and CPM REX 20; stainless steel Damascus on request. **Prices:** $250 and up. **Remarks:** Full-time maker; first knife sold in 1985. **Mark:** Last name with a knife outline.

Q

QUAKENBUSH, THOMAS C,
2426 Butler Rd, Ft Wayne, IN 46808, Phone: 219-483-0749

QUARTON, BARR,
PO Box 4335, McCall, ID 83638, Phone: 208-634-3641 **Specialties:** Plain and fancy working knives; period pieces. **Patterns:** Hunters, tantos and swords. **Technical:** Forges and grinds 154CM, ATS-34 and his own Damascus. **Prices:** $180 to $450; some to $4500. **Remarks:** Part-time maker; first knife sold in 1978. Doing business as Barr Custom Knives. **Mark:** First name with bear logo.

QUATTLEBAUM, CRAIG,
5065 Bennetts Pasture Rd., Suffolk, VA 23435-1443, Phone: 757-686-4635, mustang376@gci.net **Specialties:** Traditional straight knives and one-of-a-kind knives of his design; period pieces. **Patterns:** Bowies and fighters. **Technical:** Forges 5168, 1095 and own Damascus. **Prices:** $300 to $2000. **Remarks:** Part-time maker; first knife sold in 1988. **Mark:** Stylized initials.

QUESENBERRY, MIKE,
110 Evergreen Cricle, Blairsden, CA 96103, Phone: 775-233-1527, quesenberry@psln.com; Web: www.quesenberryknives.com **Specialties:** Hunters, daggers, Bowies, and integrals. **Technical:** Forges 52100, 1095, 1084, 5160. Makes own Damascus. Will use stainless on customer requests. Does own heat-treating and own leather work. **Prices:** Starting at $300. **Remarks:** Parttime maker. ABS member since 2006. Journeyman Bladesmith **Mark:** Last name.

R

RACHLIN, LESLIE S,
1200 W Church St, Elmira, NY 14905, Phone: 607-733-6889, lrachlin@stny.rr.com **Specialties:** Classic and working/using straight knives and folders of his design. **Patterns:** Hunters and utility/camp knives. **Technical:** Grinds 440C. **Prices:** $50 to $700. **Remarks:** Spare-time maker; first knife sold in 1989. Doing business as Tinkermade Knives. **Mark:** LSR

RADER, MICHAEL,
P.O. Box 393, Wilkeson, WA 98396, Phone: 253-255-7064, michael@raderblade.com; Web: www.raderblade.com **Specialties:** Swords, kitchen knives, integrals. **Patterns:** Non traditional designs. Inspired by various cultures. **Technical:** Damascus is made with 1084 and 15N-20, forged blades in 52100. **Prices:** $350 - $5,000 **Remarks:** ABS Journeyman Smith **Mark:** "Rader" on one side, "J.S." on other

RADOS, JERRY F,
7523 E 5000 N Rd, Grant Park, IL 60940, Phone: 815-472-3350, Fax: 815-472-3944 **Specialties:** Deluxe period pieces. **Patterns:** Hunters, fighters, locking folders, daggers and camp knives. **Technical:** Forges and grinds his own Damascus which he sells commercially; makes pattern-welded Turkish Damascus. **Prices:** Start at $900. **Remarks:** Full-time maker; first knife sold in 1981. **Mark:** Last name.

RAGSDALE, JAMES D,
3002 Arabian Woods Dr, Lithonia, GA 30038, Phone: 770-482-6739 **Specialties:** Fancy and embellished working knives of his design or to customer specs. **Patterns:** Hunters, folders and fighters. **Technical:** Grinds 440C, ATS-34 and A2. **Prices:** $150 and up. **Remarks:** Full-time maker; first knife sold in 1984. **Mark:** Fish symbol with name above, town below.

RAINVILLE, RICHARD,
126 Cockle Hill Rd, Salem, CT 06420, Phone: 860-859-2776, w1jo@snet.net **Specialties:** Traditional working straight knives. **Patterns:** Outdoor knives, including fishing knives. **Technical:** L6, 400C, ATS-34. **Prices:** $100 to $800. **Remarks:** Full-time maker; first knife sold in 1982. **Mark:** Name, city, state in oval logo.

RALEY, R. WAYNE,
825 Poplar Acres Rd, Collierville, TN 38017, Phone: 901-853-2026

RALPH, DARREL,
BRIAR KNIVES, 4185 S St Rt 605, Galena, OH 43021, Phone: 740-965-9970, dr@darrelralph.com; Web: www.darrelralph.com
Specialties: Fancy, high-art, high-tech, collectible straight knives and folders of his design and to customer specs; unique mechanisms, some disassemble. **Patterns:** Daggers, fighters and swords. **Technical:** Forges his own Damascus, nickel and high-carbon. Uses mokume and Damascus; mosaics and special patterns. Engraves and heat-treats. Prefers pearl, ivory and abalone handle material; uses stones and jewels. **Prices:** $250 to six figures. **Remarks:** Full-time maker; first knife sold in 1987. Doing business as Briar Knives. **Mark:** DDR.

RAMONDETTI, SERGIO,
VIA MARCONI N 24, 12013 CHIUSA DI PESIO (CN), ITALY, Phone: 0171 734490, Fax: 0171 734490, s.ramon@tin.it
Specialties: Folders and straight knives of his design. **Patterns:** Utility, hunters and skinners. **Technical:** Grinds RWL-34 and Damascus. **Prices:** $500 to $2000. **Remarks:** Part-time maker; first knife sold in 1999. **Mark:** Logo (S.Ramon) with last name.

RAMSEY, RICHARD A,
8525 Trout Farm Rd, Neosho, MO 64850, Phone: 417-451-1493, rams@direcway.com; Web: www.ramseyknives.com
Specialties: Drop point hunters. **Patterns:** Various Damascus. **Prices:** $125 to $1500. **Mark:** RR double R also last name-RAMSEY.

RANDALL, PATRICK,
160 Mesa Ave., Newbury Park, CA 91320, Phone: 805-754-8093, pat@patrickknives.com; Web: www.patrickknives.com
Specialties: EDC slipjoint folders, drop point hunters, and dive knives of own design. **Technical:** Materials are mostly O1, A2, and ATS-34. Wood, stag, jigged bone, and micarta handles. **Prices:** $125 to $225. **Remarks:** Part-time maker, 4 years of experience, makes about 50 knives per year.

RANDALL JR., JAMES W,
11606 Keith Hall Rd, Keithville, LA 71047, Phone: 318-925-6480, Fax: 318-925-1709, jw@jwrandall.com; Web: www.jwrandall.com
Specialties: Collectible and functional knives. **Patterns:** Bowies, hunters, daggers, swords, folders and combat knives. **Technical:** Forges 5160, 1084, O1 and his Damascus. **Prices:** $400 to $8000. **Remarks:** Part-time. First knife sold in 1998. **Mark:** JW Randall, MS.

RANDALL MADE KNIVES,
4857 South Orange Blossom Trail, Orlando, FL 32839, Phone: 407-855-8075, Fax: 407-855-9054, Web: http://www.randallknives.com
Specialties: Working straight knives. **Patterns:** Hunters, fighters and Bowies. **Technical:** Forges and grinds O1 and 440B. **Prices:** $170 to $550; some to $450. **Remarks:** Full-time maker; first knife sold in 1937. **Mark:** Randall made, city and state in scimitar logo.

RANDOW, RALPH,
4214 Blalock Rd, Pineville, LA 71360, Phone: 318-640-3369

RANKL, CHRISTIAN,
Possenhofenerstr 33, 81476 Munchen, GERMANY, Phone: 0049 01 71 3 66 26 79, Fax: 0049 8975967265, christian@crankl.de.
Specialties: Tail-lock knives. **Patterns:** Fighters, hunters and locking folders. **Technical:** Grinds ATS-34, D2, CPM1440V, RWL 34 also stainless Damascus. **Prices:** $450 to $950; some to $2000. **Remarks:** Full-time maker; first knife sold in 1989. **Mark:** Electrochemical etching on blade.

RAPP, STEVEN J,
8033 US Hwy 25-70, Marshall, NC 28753, Phone: 828-649-1092
Specialties: Gold quartz; mosaic handles. **Patterns:** Daggers, Bowies, fighters and San Francisco knives. **Technical:** Hollow- and flat-grinds 440C and Damascus. **Prices:** Start at $500. **Remarks:** Full-time maker; first knife sold in 1981. **Mark:** Name and state.

RAPPAZZO, RICHARD,
142 Dunsbach Ferry Rd, Cohoes, NY 12047, Phone: 518-783-6843
Specialties: Damascus locking folders and straight knives. **Patterns:** Folders, dirks, fighters and tantos in original and traditional designs. **Technical:** Hand-forges all blades; specializes in Damascus; uses only natural handle materials. **Prices:** $400 to $1500. **Remarks:** Part-time maker; first knife sold in 1985. **Mark:** Name, date, serial number.

RARDON, A D,
1589 SE Price Dr, Polo, MO 64671, Phone: 660-354-2330
Specialties: Folders, miniatures. **Patterns:** Hunters, buck skinners, Bowies, miniatures and daggers. **Technical:** Grinds O1, D2, 440C and ATS-34. **Prices:** $150 to $2000; some higher. **Remarks:** Full-time maker; first knife sold in 1954. **Mark:** Fox logo.

RARDON, ARCHIE F,
1589 SE Price Dr, Polo, MO 64671, Phone: 660-354-2330
Specialties: Working knives. **Patterns:** Hunters, Bowies and miniatures. **Technical:** Grinds O1, D2, 440C, ATS-34, cable and Damascus. **Prices:** $50 to $500. **Remarks:** Part-time maker. **Mark:** Boar hog.

RAY, ALAN W,
1287 FM 1280 E, Lovelady, TX 75851, awray@rayzblades.com; Web: www.rayzblades.com
Specialties: Working straight knives of his design. **Patterns:** Hunters. **Technical:** Forges O1, L6 and 5160 for straight knives. **Prices:** $200 to $1000. **Remarks:** Full-time maker; first knife sold in 1979. **Mark:** Stylized initials.

REBELLO, INDIAN GEORGE,
358 Elm St, New Bedford, MA 02740-3837, Phone: 508-951-2719, indgeo@juno.com; Web: www.indiangeorgesknives.com
Specialties: One-of-a-kind fighters and Bowies. **Patterns:** To customer's specs, hunters and utilities. **Technical:** Forges his own Damascus, 5160, 52100, 1084, 1095, cable and O1. Grinds S30V, ATS-34, 154CM, 440C, D2 and A2. **Prices:** Starting at $250. **Remarks:** Full-time maker, first knife sold in 1991. Doing business as Indian George's Knives. Founding father and President of the Southern New England Knife-Makers Guild. Member of the N.C.C.A. and A.B.S. **Mark:** Indian George's Knives.

RED, VERNON,
2020 Benton Cove, Conway, AR 72034, Phone: 501-450-7284, knivesvr@conwaycorp.net
Specialties: Custom design straight knives or folders of own design or customer's. **Patterns:** Hunters, fighters, Bowies, folders. **Technical:** Hollow grind, flat grind, stock removal and forged blades. Uses 440C, D-2, ATS-34, 1084, 1095, and Damascus. **Prices:** $150 and up. **Remarks:** Made first knife in 1982, first folder in 1992. Member of (AKA) Arkansas Knives Association. Doing business as Custom Made Knives by Vernon Red. **Mark:** Last name.

REDDIEX, BILL,
27 Galway Ave, Palmerston North, NEW ZEALAND, Phone: 06-357-0383, Fax: 06-358-2910
Specialties: Collector-grade working straight knives. **Patterns:** Traditional-style Bowies and drop-point hunters. **Technical:** Grinds 440C, D2 and O1; offers variety of grinds and finishes. **Prices:** $130 to $750. **Remarks:** Full-time maker; first knife sold in 1980. **Mark:** Last name around kiwi bird logo.

REED, DAVE,
Box 132, Brimfield, MA 01010, Phone: 413-245-3661
Specialties: Traditional styles. Makes knives from chains, rasps, gears, etc. **Patterns:** Bush swords, hunters, working minis, camp and utility knives. **Technical:** Forges 1075 and his own Damascus. **Prices:** Start at $50. **Remarks:** Part-time maker; first knife sold in 1970. **Mark:** Initials.

REED, JOHN M,
257 Navajo Dr, Oak Hill, FL 32759, Phone: 386-345-4763
Specialties: Hunter, utility, some survival knives. **Patterns:** Trailing Point, and drop point sheath knives. **Technical:** ATS-34, Rockwell 60 exotic wood or natural material handles. **Prices:** $135 to $300. Depending on handle material. **Remarks:** Likes the stock removal method. "Old Fashioned trailing point blades." Handmade and sewn leather sheaths. **Mark:** "Reed" acid etched on left side of blade.

REEVE, CHRIS,
2949 Victory View Way, Boise, ID 83709-2946, Phone: 208-375-0367, Fax: 208-375-0368, crkinfo@chrisreeve.com; Web: www.chrisreeve.com
Specialties: Originator and designer of the One Piece range of fixed blade utility knives and of the Sebenza Integral Lock folding knives made by Chris Reeve Knives. Currently makes only one or two pieces per year himself. **Patterns:** Art folders and fixed blades; one-of-a-kind. **Technical:** Grinds specialty stainless steels, Damascus and other materials to his own design. **Prices:** $1000 and upwards. **Remarks:** Full-time in knife business; first knife sold in 1982. **Mark:** Signature and date.

REEVES, J.R.,
5181 South State Line, Texarkana, Arkansas 71854, Phone: 870-773-5777, jos123@netscape.com
Specialties: Working straight knives of my design or customer design if a good flow. **Patterns:** Hunters, fighters, bowies, camp, bird, and trout knives. **Technical:** Forges and grinds 5160, 1084, 15n20, L6, 52100 and some damascus. Also some stock removal 440C, 01, D2, and 154 CM steels. I offer flat or hollow grinds. Natural handle material to include Sambar stag, desert Ironwood, sheep horn, other stabilized exotic woods and ivory. Custom filework offered. **Prices:** $200 - $1500. **Remarks:** Full-time maker, first knife sold in 1985. **Mark:** JR Reeves.

REGGIO JR., SIDNEY J,
PO Box 851, Sun, LA 70463, Phone: 504-886-5886
Specialties: Miniature classic and fancy straight knives of his design or in standard patterns. **Patterns:** Fighters, hunters and utility/camp knives. **Technical:** Grinds 440C, ATS-34 and commercial Damascus. Engraves; scrimshaws; offers filework. Hollow grinds most blades. Prefers natural handle material. Offers handmade sheaths. **Prices:** $85 to $250; some to $500. **Remarks:** Part-time maker; first knife sold in 1988. Doing business as Sterling Workshop. **Mark:** Initials.

REPKE, MIKE,
4191 N. Euclid Ave., Bay City, MI 48706, Phone: 517-684-3111
Specialties: Traditional working and using straight knives of his design or to customer specs; classic knives; display knives. **Patterns:** Hunters, Bowies, skinners, fighters boots, axes and swords. **Technical:** Grind 440C.

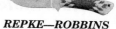

Offer variety of handle materials. **Prices:** $99 to $1500. **Remarks:** Full-time makers. Doing business as Black Forest Blades. **Mark:** Knife logo.

REVERDY, NICOLE AND PIERRE,
5 Rue de L'egalite', 26100 Romans, FRANCE, Phone: 334 75 05 10 15, Web: http://www.reverdy.com
　　Specialties: Art knives; legend pieces. Pierre and Nicole, his wife, are creating knives of art with combination of enamel on pure silver (Nicole) and poetic Damascus (Pierre) such as the "La dague a la unicorne." **Patterns:** Daggers, folding knives Damascus and enamel, Bowies, hunters and other large patterns. **Technical:** Forges his Damascus and "poetic Damascus"; where animals such as unicorns, stags, dragons or star crystals appear, works with his own EDM machine to create any kind of pattern inside the steel with his own touch. **Prices:** $2000 and up. **Remarks:** Full-time maker since 1989; first knife sold in 1986. Nicole (wife) collaborates with enamels. **Mark:** Reverdy.

REVISHVILI, ZAZA,
2102 Linden Ave, Madison, WI 53704, Phone: 608-243-7927
　　Specialties: Fancy/embellished and high-art straight knives and folders of his design. **Patterns:** Daggers, swords and locking knives. **Technical:** Uses Damascus; silver filigree, silver inlay in wood; enameling. **Prices:** $1000 to $9000; some to $15,000. **Remarks:** Full-time maker; first knife sold in 1987. **Mark:** Initials, city.

REXFORD, TODD,
518 Park Dr., Woodland Park, CO 80863, Phone: 719-650-6799, todd@rexfordknives.com; Web: www.rexfordknives.com
　　Specialties: Dress tactical and tactical folders and fixed blades. **Technical:** I work in stainless steels, stainless damascus, titanium, Stellite and other high performance alloys. All machining and part engineering is done in house.

REXROAT, KIRK,
527 Sweetwater Circle Box 224, Wright, WY 82732, Phone: 307-464-0166, rexknives@vcn.com; Web: www.rexroatknives.com
　　Specialties: Using and collectible straight knives and folders of his design or to customer specs. **Patterns:** Bowies, hunters, folders. **Technical:** Forges Damascus patterns, mosaic and 52100. **Prices:** $400 and up. **Remarks:** Part-time maker, Master Smith in the ABS; first knife sold in 1984. Doing business as Rexroat Knives. **Mark:** Last name.

REYNOLDS, DAVE,
Rt 2 Box 36, Harrisville, WV 26362, Phone: 304-643-2889, wvreynolds@zoominternet.net
　　Specialties: Working straight knives of his design. **Patterns:** Bowies, kitchen and utility knives. **Technical:** Grinds and forges L6, 1095 and 440C. Heat-treats. **Prices:** $50 to $85; some to $175. **Remarks:** Full-time maker; first knife sold in 1980. Doing business as Terra-Gladius Knives. **Mark:** Mark on special orders only; serial number on all knives.

REYNOLDS, JOHN C,
#2 Andover HC77, Gillette, WY 82716, Phone: 307-682-6076
　　Specialties: Working knives, some fancy. **Patterns:** Hunters, Bowies, tomahawks and buck skinners; some folders. **Technical:** Grinds D2, ATS-34, 440C and forges own Damascus and knives. Scrimshaws. **Prices:** $200 to $3000. **Remarks:** Spare-time maker; first knife sold in 1969. **Mark:** On ground blades JC Reynolds Gillette, WY, on forged blades, initials make the mark-JCR.

RHEA, LIN,
413 Grant 291020, Prattsville, AR 72129, Phone: 870-699-5095, lwrhea1@windstream.net; Web: www.rheaknives.com
　　Specialties: Traditional and early American styled Bowies in high carbon steel or Damascus. **Patterns:** Bowies, hunters and fighters. **Technical:** Filework wire inlay. Sole authorship of construction, Damascus and embellishment. **Prices:** $280 to $1500. **Remarks:** Serious part-time maker and rated as a Journeyman Bladesmith in the ABS.

RHO, NESTOR LORENZO,
Primera Junta 589, (6000) Junin, Buenos Aires, ARGENTINA, Phone: (02362) 15670686
　　Specialties: Classic and fancy straight knives of his design. **Patterns:** Bowies, fighters and hunters. **Technical:** Grinds 420C, 440C, 1084, 51-60, 52100, L6, and W1. Offers semi-precious stones on handles, acid etching on blades and blade engraving. **Prices:** $90 to $500, some to $1500. **Remarks:** Full-time maker; first knife sold in 1975. **Mark:** Name.

RIBONI, CLAUDIO,
Via L Da Vinci, Truccazzano (MI), ITALY, Phone: 02 95309010, Web: www.riboni-knives.com

RICARDO ROMANO, BERNARDES,
Ruai Coronel Rennò 1261, Itajuba MG, BRAZIL 37500, Phone: 0055-2135-622-5896
　　Specialties: Hunters, fighters, Bowies. **Technical:** Grinds blades of stainless and tools steels. **Patterns:** Hunters. **Prices:** $100 to $700. **Mark:** Romano.

RICHARD, RAYMOND,
31047 SE Jackson Rd., Gresham, OR 97080, Phone: 503-663-1219, rayskee13@hotmail.com; Web: www.hawknknives.com
　　Specialties: Hand-forged knives, tomahawks, axes, and spearheads, all one-of-a-kind. **Prices:** $200 and up, some to $3000. **Remarks:** Full-time maker since 1994. **Mark:** Name on spine of blades.

RICHARDS, CHUCK,
7243 Maple Tree Lane SE, Salem, OR 97317, Phone: 503-569-5549, chuck@woodforge.com; Web: www.woodchuckforge.com
　　Specialties: Fixed blade Damascus. One-of-a-kind. **Patterns:** Hunters, fighters. **Prices:** $200 to $1200. **Remarks:** Likes to work with customers on a truly custom knife. **Mark:** A C Richards or ACR.

RICHARDS, RALPH (BUD),
6413 Beech St, Bauxite, AR 72011, Phone: 501-602-5367, DoubleR042@aol.com; Web: SwampPoodleCreations.com
　　Specialties: Forges 55160, 1084, and 15N20 for Damascus. S30V, 440C, and others. Wood, mammoth, giraffe and mother of pearl handles.

RICHARDSON JR., PERCY,
1117 Kettler St., Navasota, TX 77868, Phone: 936-288-1690, Web: www.richardsonknives.com
　　Specialties: Working straight knives and folders. **Patterns:** Hunters, skinners, bowies, fighters and folders. **Technical:** Grinds 154CM, ATS-34, and D2. **Prices:** $175 - $750 some bowies to $1200. **Remarks:** Part time maker, first knife sold in 1990. Doing business as Richardsons Handmade Knives. **Mark:** Texas star with last name across it.

RICHERSON, RON,
P.O. Box 51, Greenburg, KY 42743, Phone: 270-405-0491, Fax: 270-299-2471, rricherson@windstream.net
　　Specialties: Collectible and functional fixed blades, locking liners, and autos of his design. **Technical:** Grinds ATS-34, S30V, S60V, CPM-154, D2, 440, high carbon steel, and his and others' Damascus. Prefers natural materials for handles and does both stock removal and forged work, some with embellishments. **Prices:** $160 to $850, some higher. **Remarks:** Full-time maker. Probationary member Knifemakers' Guild and apprentice member American Bladesmith Society. Made first knife in September 2006, sold first knife in December 2006. **Mark:** Name in oval with city and state. Also name in center of oval Green River Custom Knives.

RICKE, DAVE,
1209 Adams St, West Bend, WI 53090, Phone: 262-334-5739, R.L5710@sbcglobal.net
　　Specialties: Working knives; period pieces. **Patterns:** Hunters, boots, Bowies; locking folders and slip joints. **Technical:** Grinds ATS-34, A2, 440C and 154CM. **Prices:** $145 and up. **Remarks:** Full-time maker; first knife sold in 1976. Knifemakers Guild voting member. **Mark:** Last name.

RIDEN, DOUG,
12 Weeks Rd, Box 945, Eastford, CT 06242, Phone: 860-974-0518, Web: www.darkwaterforge.com
　　Specialties: Hard working, high performance knives. **Patterns:** Hunters, fighters, choppers, kitchen knives. **Technical:** Forged 5160, 1084, W2, L6. **Prices:** $100 to $600. **Remarks:** Full-time maker, first knife sold 2006.

RIDER, DAVID M,
PO Box 5946, Eugene, OR 97405-0911, Phone: 541-343-8747

RIEPE, RICHARD A,
17604 E 296 St, Harrisonville, MO 64701

RIETVELD, BERTIE,
PO Box 53, Magaliesburg 1791, SOUTH AFRICA, Phone: 2783 232 8766, bertie@rietveldknives.com; Web: www.rietveldknives.com
　　Specialties: Art daggers, Bolster lock folders, Persian designs, embraces elegant designs. **Patterns:** Mostly one-of-a-kind. **Technical:** Sole authorship, work only in own Damascus, gold inlay, blued stainless fittings. **Prices:** $500 - $8,000 **Remarks:** First knife made in 1979. Annual shows attended: ECCKS, Blade Show, Milan Show, South African Guild Show. **Marks:** Logo is elephant in half circle with name, enclosed in Stanhope lens

RIGNEY JR., WILLIE,
191 Colson Dr, Bronston, KY 42518, Phone: 606-679-4227
　　Specialties: High-tech period pieces and fancy working knives. **Patterns:** Fighters, boots, daggers and push knives. **Technical:** Grinds 440C and 154CM; buys Damascus. Most knives are embellished. **Prices:** $150 to $1500; some to $10,000. **Remarks:** Full-time maker; first knife sold in 1978. **Mark:** First initial, last name.

RINKES, SIEGFRIED,
Am Sportpl 2, D 91459, Markterlbach, GERMANY

RIZZI, RUSSELL J,
37 March Rd, Ashfield, MA 01330, Phone: 413-625-2842
　　Specialties: Fancy working and using straight knives and folders of his design or to customer specs. **Patterns:** Hunters, locking folders and fighters. **Technical:** Grinds 440C, D2 and commercial Damascus. **Prices:** $150 to $750; some to $2500. **Remarks:** Part-time maker; first knife sold in 1990. **Mark:** Last name, Ashfield, MA.

ROBBINS, BILL,
192 S. Fairview St, Globe, AZ 85501, Phone: 928-402-0052, billrknifemaker@aol.com
　　Specialties: Plain and fancy working straight knives. Makes to his designs and most anything you can draw. **Patterns:** Hunting knives, utility knives, and Bowies. **Technical:** Grinds ATS-34, 440C, tool steel, high carbon, buys Damascus. **Prices:** $70 to $450. **Remarks:** Part-time maker, first knife sold in 2001. **Mark:** Last name or desert scene with name.

ROBBINS, HOWARD P,
1310 E. 310th Rd., Flemington, MO 65650, Phone: 417-282-5055, ARobb1407@aol.com
Specialties: High-tech working knives with clean designs, some fancy. **Patterns:** Folders, hunters and camp knives. **Technical:** Grinds 440C. Heat-treats; likes mirror finishes. Offers leatherwork. **Prices:** $100 to $500; some to $1000. **Remarks:** Full-time maker; first knife sold in 1982. **Mark:** Name, city and state.

ROBERTS, CHUCK,
PO Box 7174, Golden, CO 80403, Phone: 303-642-2388, chuck@crobertsart.com; Web: www.crobertsart.com
Specialties: Price daggers, large Bowies, hand-rubbed satin finish. **Patterns:** Bowies and California knives. **Technical:** Grinds 5160 and ATS-34. Handles made of stag, ivory or mother-of-pearl. **Prices:** $1250. **Remarks:** Full-time maker. Company name is C. Roberts - Art that emulates the past. **Mark:** Last initial or last name.

ROBERTS, GEORGE A,
PO Box 31228, 211 Main St., Whitehorse, YT, CANADA Y1A 5P7, Phone: 867-667-7099, Fax: 867-667-7099, Web: www.yuk-biz.com/bandit blades
Specialties: Mastadon ivory, fossil walrus ivory handled knives, scrimshawed or carved. **Patterns:** Side lockers, fancy bird and trout knives, hunters, fillet blades. **Technical:** Grinds stainless Damascus, all surgical steels. **Prices:** Up to $3500 U.S. **Remarks:** Full-time maker; first knives sold in 1986. Doing business as Bandit Blades. Most recent works have gold nuggets in fossilized Mastadon ivory. Something new using mosaic pins in mokume bolster and in mosaic Damascus, it creates a new look. **Mark:** Bandit Yukon with pick and shovel crossed.

ROBERTS, JACK,
10811 Sagebluff Dr, Houston, TX 77089, Phone: 281-481-1784, jroberts59@houston.rr.com
Specialties: Hunting knives and folders, offers scrimshaw by wife Barbara. **Patterns:** Drop point hunters and LinerLock® folders. **Technical:** Grinds 440-C, offers file work, texturing, natural handle materials and Micarta. **Prices:** $200 to $800 some higher. **Remarks:** Part-time maker, sold first knife in 1965. **Mark:** Name, city, state.

ROBERTS, MICHAEL,
601 Oakwood Dr, Clinton, MS 39056, Phone: 601-540-6222, Fax: 601-213-4891
Specialties: Working and using knives in standard patterns and to customer specs. **Patterns:** Hunters, Bowies, tomahawks and fighters. **Technical:** Forges 5160, O1, 1095 and his own Damascus. Uses only natural handle materials. **Prices:** $145 to $500; some to $1100. **Remarks:** Part-time maker; first knife sold in 1988. **Mark:** Last name or first and last name in Celtic script.

ROBERTSON, LEO D,
3728 Pleasant Lake Dr, Indianapolis, IN 46227, Phone: 317-882-9899, ldr52@juno.com
Specialties: Hunting and folders. **Patterns:** Hunting, fillet, Bowie, utility, folders and tantos. **Technical:** Uses ATS-34, 154CM, 440C, 1095, D2 and Damascus steels. **Prices:** Fixed knives $75 to $350, folders $350 to $600. **Remarks:** Handles made with stag, wildwoods, laminates, mother-of-pearl. Made first knife in 1990. Member of American Bladesmith Society. **Mark:** Logo with full name in oval around logo.

ROBINSON, CALVIN,
5501 Twin Creek Circle, Pace, FL 32571, Phone: 850 572 1504, calvinshandmadeknives@yahoo.com
Specialties: Working knives of my own design. **Patterns:** Hunters, fishing, folding and kitchen and purse knives. **Technical:** Now using 13-C-26 stainless. **Prices:** $215.00 to $600.00. **Remarks:** Full-time maker. Probationary member of the Knifemaker's Guild. **Mark:** Calvin Robinson Pace, Florida.

ROBINSON, CHARLES (DICKIE),
PO Box 221, Vega, TX 79092, Phone: 806-676-6428, dickie@amaonline.com; Web: www.robinsonknives.com
Specialties: Classic and working/using knives. Does his own engraving. **Patterns:** Bowies, daggers, fighters, hunters and camp knives. **Technical:** Forges O1, 5160, 52100 and his own Damascus. **Prices:** $350 to $850; some to $5000. **Remarks:** Part-time maker; first knife sold in 1988. Doing business as Robinson Knives. ABS Master Smith. **Mark:** Robinson MS.

ROBINSON, CHUCK,
SEA ROBIN FORGE, 1423 Third Ave., Picayune, MS 39466, Phone: 601-798-0060, robi5515@bellsouth.net
Specialties: Deluxe period pieces and working / using knives of his design and to customer specs. **Patterns:** Bowies, fighters, hunters, utility knives and original designs. **Technical:** Forges own Damascus, 52100, O1, L6 and 1070 thru 1095. **Prices:** Start at $225. **Remarks:** First knife 1958. **Mark:** Fish logo, anchor and initials C.R.

ROBINSON III, REX R,
10531 Poe St, Leesburg, FL 34788, Phone: 352-787-4587
Specialties: One-of-a-kind high-art automatics of his design. **Patterns:** Automatics, liner locks and lock back folders. **Technical:** Uses tool steel and stainless Damascus and mokume; flat grinds. Hand carves folders. **Prices:** $1800 to $7500. **Remarks:** First knife sold in 1988. **Mark:** First name inside oval.

ROCHFORD, MICHAEL R,
PO Box 577, Dresser, WI 54009, Phone: 715-755-3520, mrrochford@centurytel.net
Specialties: Working straight knives and folders. Classic Bowies and Moran traditional. **Patterns:** Bowies, fighters, hunters: slip-joint, locking and liner locking folders. **Technical:** Grinds ATS-34, 440C, 154CM and D-2; forges W2, 5160, and his own Damascus. Offers metal and metal and leather sheaths. Filework and wire inlay. **Prices:** $150 to $1000; some to $2000. **Remarks:** Part-time maker; first knife sold in 1984. **Mark:** Name.

RODEBAUGH, JAMES L,
4875 County Rd, Carpenter, WY 82054

RODEWALD, GARY,
447 Grouse Ct, Hamilton, MT 59840, Phone: 406-363-2192
Specialties: Bowies of his design as inspired from historical pieces. **Patterns:** Hunters, Bowies and camp/combat. Forges 5160 1084 and his own Damascus of 1084, 15N20, field grade hunters AT-34-440C, 440V, and BG42. **Prices:** $200 to $1500. **Remarks:** Sole author on knives, sheaths done by saddle maker. **Mark:** Rodewald.

RODKEY, DAN,
18336 Ozark Dr, Hudson, FL 34667, Phone: 727-863-8264
Specialties: Traditional straight knives of his design and in standard patterns. **Patterns:** Boots, fighters and hunters. **Technical:** Grinds 440C, D2 and ATS-34. **Prices:** Start at $200. **Remarks:** Full-time maker; first knife sold in 1985. Doing business as Rodkey Knives. **Mark:** Etched logo on blade.

ROE JR., FRED D,
4005 Granada Dr, Huntsville, AL 35802, Phone: 205-881-6847
Specialties: Highly finished working knives of his design; period pieces. **Patterns:** Hunters, fighters and survival knives; specialty designs like diver's knives. **Technical:** Grinds 154CM, ATS-34 and Damascus. Field-tests all blades. **Prices:** $125 to $250; some to $2000. **Remarks:** Part-time maker; first knife sold in 1980. **Mark:** Last name.

ROGERS, RAY,
PO Box 126, Wauconda, WA 98859, Phone: 509-486-8069, knives @rayrogers.com; Web: www.rayrogers.com
Specialties: LinerLock® folders. Asian and European professional chef's knives. **Patterns:** Rayzor folders, chef's knives and cleavers of his own and traditional designs, drop point hunters and fillet knives. **Technical:** Stock removal S30V, 440, 1095, O1 Damascus and other steels. Does all own heat treating, clay tempering, some forging G-10, Micarta, carbon fiber on folders, stabilized burl woods on fixed blades. **Prices:** $200 to $450. **Remarks:** Knives are made one-at-a-time to the customer's order. Happy to consider customizing knife designs to suit your preferences and sometimes create entirely new knives when necessary. As a full-time knifemaker is willing to spend as much time as it takes (usually through email) discussing the options and refining details of a knife's design to insure that you get the knife you really want.

ROGERS, RICHARD,
PO Box 769, Magdalena, NM 87825, Phone: 575-838-7237, r.s.rogers@hotmail.com
Specialties: Sheffield-style folders and multi-blade folders. **Patterns:** Folders: various traditional patterns. One-of-a-kind fixed blades: Bowies, daggers, hunters, utility knives. **Technical:** Mainly uses ATS-34 and prefer natural handle materials. **Prices:** $400 and up. **Mark:** Last name.

ROGHMANS, MARK,
607 Virginia Ave, LaGrange, GA 30240, Phone: 706-885-1273
Specialties: Classic and traditional knives of his design. **Patterns:** Bowies, daggers and fighters. **Technical:** Grinds ATS-34, D2 and 440C. **Prices:** $250 to $500. **Remarks:** Part-time maker; first knife sold in 1984. Doing business as LaGrange Knife. **Mark:** Last name and/or LaGrange Knife.

ROHN, FRED,
7675 W Happy Hill Rd, Coeur d'Alene, ID 83814, Phone: 208-667-0774
Specialties: Hunters, boot knives, custom patterns. **Patterns:** Drop points, double edge, etc. **Technical:** Grinds 440 or 154CM. **Prices:** $85 and up. **Remarks:** Part-time maker. **Mark:** Logo on blade; serial numbered.

ROLLERT, STEVE,
PO Box 65, Keenesburg, CO 80643-0065, Phone: 303-732-4858, steve@doveknives.com; Web: www.doveknives.com
Specialties: Highly finished working knives. **Patterns:** Variety of straight knives; locking folders and slip-joints. **Technical:** Forges and grinds W2, 1095, ATS-34 and his pattern-welded, cable Damascus and nickel Damascus. **Prices:** $300 to $1000; some to $3000. **Remarks:** Full-time maker; first knife sold in 1980. Doing business as Dove Knives. **Mark:** Last name in script.

ROMEIS, GORDON,
1521 Coconut Dr., Fort Myers, FL 33901, Phone: 239-940-5060, gordonromeis@gmail.com Web: romeisknives.com
Specialties: Smaller using knives. **Patterns:** I have a number of standard designs that include both full tapered tangs and narrow tang knives. Custom designs are welcome. Many different types. No folders. **Technical:** My standard steel is 440C, but I will use most any steel requested by the customer. I also use quite a bit of Alabama Damascus steel made by Brad Vice. I use 416 stainless or brass for guards and fittings. Handle materials

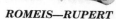

include Micarta, exotic wood, stag horn, or as requested. **Prices:** $165 for small guardless knives and up to $275 for larger full-tang knives. Fighters start at $500. **Remarks:** I am a part-time maker however I do try to keep waiting times to a minimum. **Mark:** Either my name, city, and state or simply ROMEIS depending on the knife.

RONZIO, N. JACK,
PO Box 248, Fruita, CO 81521, Phone: 970-858-0921

ROOT, GARY,
644 East 14th St, Erie, PA 16503, Phone: 814-459-0196
  Specialties: Damascus Bowies with hand carved eagles, hawks and snakes for handles. Few folders made. **Patterns:** Daggers, fighters, hunter/field knives. **Technical:** Using handforged Damascus from Ray Bybar Jr (M.S.) and Robert Eggerling. Grinds D2, 440C, 1095 and 5160. Some 5160 is hand forged. **Prices:** $80 to $300 some to $1000. **Remarks:** Full time maker, first knife sold in 1976. **Mark:** Name over Erie, PA.

ROSE, BOB,
PO BOX 126, Wagontown, PA 19376, Phone: 610-273-1151, medit8@ meditationsociety.com Web: www.bobroseknives.com
  Patterns: Bowies, fighters, drop point hunters, daggers, bird and trout, camp, and other fixed blade styles. **Technical:** Mostly using 1095 and damascus steel, desert ironwood and other top-of-the-line exotic woods as well as mammoth tooth. **Prices:** $49 - $300. **Remarks:** Been making and selling knives since 2004.

ROSE, DEREK W,
14 Willow Wood Rd, Gallipolis, OH 45631, Phone: 740-446-4627

ROSE II, DOUN T,
Ltc US Special Operations Command (ret), 1795/96 W Sharon Rd SW, Fife Lake, MI 49633, Phone: 231-645-1369, Web: www.epicureanclassic.com www.rosecutlery.com
  Specialties: Straight working, collector and presentation knives to a high level of fit and finish. Design in collaboration with customer. **Patterns:** Field knives, Scagel, Bowies, period pieces, axes and tomahawks, fishing and hunting spears. Fine cutlery under "Epicurean Classic" name. **Technical:** Forged and billet ground, high carbon and stainless steel appropriate to end use. Sourced from: Crucible, Frye, Admiral and Starret. Some period pieces from recovered stock. Makes own damascus and mokume gane. **Remarks:** Full-time maker, ABS since 2000, William Scagel Memorial Scholarship 2002, Bill Moran School of Blade Smithing 2003, Apprentice under Master Blacksmith Dan Nickels at Black Rock Forge current. **Mark:** Last name ROSE in block letters with five petal "wild rose" in place of O. Doing business as Rose Cutlery.

ROSENBAUGH, RON,
2806 Stonegate Dr, Crystal Lake, IL 60012, Phone: 815-477-0027, rgr@ rosenbaughcustomknives.com; Web: www.rosenbaughcustomknives.com
  Specialties: Fancy and plain working knives using own designs, collaborations, and traditional patterns. **Patterns:** Bird, trout, boots, hunters, fighters, some Bowies. **Technical:** Grinds high alloy stainless, tool steels, and Damascus; forges 1084,5160, 52100, and spring steels. **Prices:** $150 to $1000. **Remarks:** Part-time maker, first knife sold in 1004. **Mark:** Last name, logo, city.

ROSENFELD, BOB,
955 Freeman Johnson Rd, Hoschton, GA 30548, Phone: 770-867-2647, www.1bladesmith@msn.com
  Specialties: Fancy and embellished working/using straight knives of his design and in standard patterns. **Patterns:** Daggers, hunters and utility/ camp knives. **Technical:** Forges 52100, A203E, 1095 and L6 Damascus. Offers engraving. **Prices:** $125 to $650; some to $1000. **Remarks:** Full-time maker; first knife sold in 1984. Also makes folders; ABS Journeyman. **Mark:** Last name or full name, Knifemaker.

ROSS, D L,
27 Kinsman St, Dunedin, NEW ZEALAND, Phone: 64 3 464 0239, Fax: 64 3 464 0239
  Specialties: Working straight knives of his design. **Patterns:** Hunters, various others. **Technical:** Grinds 440C. **Prices:** $100 to $450; some to $700 NZ (not U.S. $). **Remarks:** Part-time maker; first knife sold in 1988. **Mark:** Dave Ross, Maker, city and country.

ROSS, GREGG,
4556 Wenhart Rd, Lake Worth, FL 33463, Phone: 407-439-4681
  Specialties: Working/using straight knives. **Patterns:** Bowies, hunters and utility/camp knives. **Technical:** Forges and grinds ATS-34, Damascus and cable Damascus. Uses decorative pins. **Prices:** $125 to $250; some to $400. **Remarks:** Part-time maker; first knife sold in 1992. **Mark:** Name, city and state.

ROSS, STEPHEN,
534 Remington Dr, Evanston, WY 82930, Phone: 307-789-7104
  Specialties: One-of-a-kind collector-grade classic and contemporary straight knives and folders of his design and to customer specs; some fantasy pieces. **Patterns:** Combat and survival knives, hunters, boots and folders. **Technical:** Grinds stainless; forges spring and tool steel. Engraves, scrimshaws. Makes leather sheaths. **Prices:** $160 to $3000. **Remarks:** Part-time-time maker; first knife sold in 1971. **Mark:** Last name in modified Roman; sometimes in script.

ROSS, TIM,
3239 Oliver Rd, Thunder Bay, Ont., CANADA P7G 1S9, Phone: 807-935-2667, Fax: 807-935-3179
  Specialties: Fixed blades, natural handle material. **Patterns:** Hunting, fishing, Bowies, fighters. **Technical:** 440C, D2, 52100, Cable, 5160, 1084, 66, W2. **Prices:** $150 to $750 some higher. **Remarks:** Forges and stock removal. **Mark:** Ross Custom Knives.

ROSSDEUTSCHER, ROBERT N,
133 S Vail Ave, Arlington Heights, IL 60005, Phone: 847-577-0404, Web: www. rnrknives.com
  Specialties: Frontier-style and historically inspired knives. **Patterns:** Trade knives, Bowies, camp knives and hunting knives, tomahawks and lances. **Technical:** Most knives are hand forged, a few are stock removal. **Prices:** $135 to $1500. **Remarks:** Journeyman Smith of the American Bladesmith Society. **Mark:** Back-to-back "R's", one upside down and backwards, one right side up and forward in an oval. Sometimes with name, town and state; depending on knife style.

ROTELLA, RICHARD A,
643 75th St, Niagara Falls, NY 14304
  Specialties: Working knives of his design. **Patterns:** Various fishing, hunting and utility knives; folders. **Technical:** Grinds ATS-34. Prefers hand-rubbed finishes. **Prices:** $65 to $450; some to $900. **Remarks:** Spare-time maker; first knife sold in 1977. Not taking orders at this time; only sells locally. **Mark:** Name and city in stylized waterfall logo.

ROULIN, CHARLES,
113 B Rt. de Soral, 1233 Geneva, SWITZERLAND, Phone: 022-757-4479, Fax: 079-218-9754, charles.roulin@bluewin.ch; Web: www.coutelier-roulin.com
  Specialties: Fancy high-art straight knives and folders of his design. **Patterns:** Bowies, locking folders, slip-joint folders and miniatures. **Technical:** Grinds 440C, ATS-34 and D2. Engraves; carves nature scenes and detailed animals in steel, ivory, on handles and blades. **Prices:** $500 to $3000; some to Euro: 14,600. **Remarks:** Full-time maker; first knife sold in 1988. **Mark:** Symbol of fish with name or name engraved.

ROWE, FRED,
BETHEL RIDGE FORGE, 3199 Roberts Rd, Amesville, OH 45711, Phone: 866-325-2164, fred.rowe@bethelridgeforge.com; Web: www.bethelridgeforge.com
  Specialties: Damascus and carbon steel sheath knives. **Patterns:** Bowies, hunters, fillet small kokris. **Technical:** His own Damascus, 52100, O1, L6, 1095 carbon steels, mosaics. **Prices:** $200 to $2000. **Remarks:** All blades are clay hardened. **Mark:** Bethel Ridge Forge.

ROYER, KYLE,
1962 State Route W, Mountain View, MO 65548, Phone: 417-934-6394, Fax: 417-247-5572, royerknifeworks@live.com Web: www.royerknifeworks.com
  Specialties: I currently specialize in fixed blades. **Technical:** I forge many different patterns of damascus using mostly 1080 and 15n20. **Remarks:** I am a full-time maker and nineteen years old (12-05-90). I received my ABS Journeyman Smith Stamp at the 2009 Blade Show in Atlanta.

ROZAS, CLARK D,
1436 W "G" St, Wilmington, CA 90744, Phone: 310-518-0488
  Specialties: Hand forged blades. **Patterns:** Pig stickers, toad stabbers, whackers, choppers. **Technical:** Damascus, 52100, 1095, 1084, 5160. **Prices:** $200 to $600. **Remarks:** A.B.S. member; part-time maker since 1995. **Mark:** Name over dagger.

RUA, GARY,
396 Snell Street, Fall River, MA 02721, Phone: 508-677-2664
  Specialties: Working straight knives of his design. 1800 to 1900 century standard patterns. **Patterns:** Bowies, hunters, fighters, and patch knives. **Technical:** Forges and grinds. Damascus, 5160, 1095, old files. Uses only natural handle material. **Prices:** $350 - $2000. **Remarks:** Part-time maker. (Harvest Moon Forge) **Mark:** Last name.

RUANA KNIFE WORKS,
Box 520, Bonner, MT 59823, Phone: 406-258-5368, Fax: 406-258-2895, info@ruanaknives.com; Web: www.ruanaknives.com
  Specialties: Working knives and period pieces. **Patterns:** Variety of straight knives. **Technical:** Forges 5160 chrome alloy for Bowies and 1095. **Prices:** $200 and up. **Remarks:** Full-time maker; first knife sold in 1938. Brand new non catalog knives available on ebay under seller name ruanaknives. For free catalog email regular mailing address to info@ruanaknives.com **Mark:** Name.

RUCKER, THOMAS,
194 Woodhaven Ct., Nacogdoches, TX 75965, Phone: 832-216-8122, admin@ knivesbythomas.com Web: www.knivesbythomas.com
  Specialties: Personal design and custom design. Hunting, tactical, folding knives, and cutlery. **Technical:** Design and grind ATS34, D2, O1, Damascus, and VG10. **Prices:** $150 - $5,000. **Remarks:** Full-time maker and custom scrimshaw and engraving done by wife, Debi Rucker. First knife done in 1969; first design sold in 1975 **Mark:** Etched logo and signature.

RUPERT, BOB,
301 Harshaville Rd, Clinton, PA 15026, Phone: 724-573-4569, rbrupert@aol.com
  Specialties: Wrought period pieces with natural elements. **Patterns:** Elegant straight blades, friction folders. **Technical:** Forges colonial 7; 1095; 5160; diffuse mokume-gane and Damascus. **Prices:** $150 to $1500; some higher. **Remarks:** Part-time maker; first knife sold in 1980. Evening hours studio since 1980. Likes simplicity that disassembles. **Mark:** R etched in Old English.

RUPLE, WILLIAM H,
201 Brian Dr., Pleasanton, TX 78064, Phone: 830-569-0007, bknives@devtex.net
    Specialties: Multi-blade folders, slip joints, some lock backs. **Patterns:** Like to reproduce old patterns. Offers filework and engraving. **Technical:** Grinds CPM-154 and other carbon and stainless steel and commercial Damascus. **Prices:** $950 to $2500. **Remarks:** Full-time maker; first knife sold in 1988. **Mark:** Ruple.

RUSS, RON,
5351 NE 160th Ave, Williston, FL 32696, Phone: 352-528-2603, RussRs@aol.com
    Specialties: Damascus and mokume. **Patterns:** Ladder, rain drop and butterfly. **Technical:** Most knives, including Damascus, are forged from 52100-E. **Prices:** $65 to $2500. **Mark:** Russ.

RUSSELL, MICK,
4 Rossini Rd, Pari Park, Port Elizabeth 6070, SOUTH AFRICA
    Specialties: Art knives. **Patterns:** Working and collectible bird, trout and hunting knives, defense knives and folders. **Technical:** Grinds D2, 440C, ATS-34 and Damascus. Offers mirror or satin finishes. **Prices:** Start at $100. **Remarks:** Full-time maker; first knife sold in 1986. **Mark:** Stylized rhino incorporating initials.

RUSSELL, TOM,
6500 New Liberty Rd, Jacksonville, AL 36265, Phone: 205-492-7866
    Specialties: Straight working knives of his design or to customer specs. **Patterns:** Hunters, folders, fighters, skinners, Bowies and utility knives. **Technical:** Grinds D2, 440C and ATS-34; offers filework. **Prices:** $75 to $225. **Remarks:** Part-time maker; first knife sold in 1987. Full-time tool and die maker. **Mark:** Last name with tulip stamp.

RUTH, MICHAEL G,
3101 New Boston Rd, Texarkana, TX 75501, Phone: 903-832-7166/cell:903-277-3663, Fax: 903-832-4710, mike@ruthknives.com; Web: www.ruthknives.com
    Specialties: Hunters, bowies & fighters. Damascus & carbon steel. **Prices:** $375 & up. **Mark:** Last name.

RYBAR JR., RAYMOND B,
2328 South Sunset Dr., Came Verde, AZ 86322, Phone: 928-567-6372, ray@rybarknives.com; Web: www.rybarknives.com
    Specialties: Straight knives or folders with customers name, logo, etc. in mosaic pattern. **Patterns:** Common patterns plus mosaics of all types. **Technical:** Forges own Damascus. Primary forging of self smelted steel - smelting classes. **Prices:** $200 to $1200; Bible blades to $10,000. **Remarks:** Master Smith (A.B.S.) Primary focus toward Biblicaly themed blades **Mark:** Rybar or stone church forge or Rev. 1:3 or R.B.R. between diamonds.

RYBERG, GOTE,
Faltgatan 2, S-562 00 Norrahammar, SWEDEN, Phone: 4636-61678

RYDBOM, JEFF,
PO Box 548, Annandale, MN 55302, Phone: 320-274-9639, jry1890@hotmail.com
    Specialties: Ring knives. **Patterns:** Hunters, fighters, Bowie and camp knives. **Technical:** Straight grinds O1, A2, 1566 and 5150 steels. **Prices:** $150 to $1000. **Remarks:** No pinning of guards or pommels. All silver brazed. **Mark:** Capital "C" with J R inside.

RYUICHI, KUKI,
504-7 Tokorozawa-Shinmachi, Tokorozawa-city, Saitama, JAPAN, Phone: 042-943-3451

RZEWNICKI, GERALD,
8833 S Massbach Rd, Elizabeth, IL 61028-9714, Phone: 815-598-3239

S

SAINDON, R BILL,
233 Rand Pond Rd, Goshen, NH 03752, Phone: 603-863-1874, dayskiev71@aol.com
    Specialties: Collector-quality folders of his design or to customer specs. **Patterns:** Latch release, LinerLock® and lockback folders. **Technical:** Offers limited amount of own Damascus; also uses Damas makers steel. Prefers natural handle material, gold and gems. **Prices:** $500 to $4000. **Remarks:** Full-time maker; first knife sold in 1981. Doing business as Daynia Forge. **Mark:** Sun logo or engraved surname.

SAKAKIBARA, MASAKI,
20-8 Sakuragaoka, 2-Chome Setagaya-ku, Tokyo 156-0054, JAPAN, Phone: 81-3-3420-0375

SAKMAR, MIKE,
903 S. Latson Rd. #257, Howell, MI 48843, Phone: 517-546-6388, Fax: 517-546-6399, sakmarent@yahoo.com; Web: www.sakmarenterprises.com
    Specialties: Mokume in various patterns and alloy combinations. **Patterns:** Bowies, fighters, hunters and integrals. **Technical:** Grinds ATS-34, Damascus and high-carbon tool steels. Uses mostly natural handle materials—elephant ivory, walrus ivory, stag, wildwood, oosic, etc. Makes mokume for resale. **Prices:** $250 to $2500; some to $4000. **Remarks:** Part-time maker; first knife sold in 1990. Supplier of mokume. **Mark:** Last name.

SALLEY, JOHN D,
3965 Frederick-Ginghamsburg Rd., Tipp City, OH 45371, Phone: 937-698-4588, Fax: 937-698-4131
    Specialties: Fancy working knives and art pieces. **Patterns:** Hunters, fighters, daggers and some swords. **Technical:** Grinds ATS-34, 12C27 and W2; buys Damascus. **Prices:** $85 to $1000; some to $6000. **Remarks:** Part-time maker; first knife sold in 1979. **Mark:** First initial, last name.

SAMPSON, LYNN,
381 Deakins Rd, Jonesborough, TN 37659, Phone: 423-348-8373
    Specialties: Highly finished working knives, mostly folders. **Patterns:** Locking folders, slip-joints, interframes and two-blades. **Technical:** Grinds D2, 440C and ATS-34; offers extensive filework. **Prices:** Start at $300. **Remarks:** Full-time maker; first knife sold in 1982. **Mark:** Name and city in logo.

SANDBERG, RONALD B,
24784 Shadowwood Ln, Brownstown, MI 48134-9560, Phone: 734-671-6866, msc2009@comcast.net
    Specialties: Good looking and functional hunting knives, filework, mixing of handle materials. **Patterns:** Hunters, skinners and Bowies. **Prices:** $120 and up. **Remarks:** Full lifetime workmanship guarantee. **Mark:** R.B. Sandberg

SANDERS, A.A.,
3850 72 Ave NE, Norman, OK 73071, Phone: 405-364-8660
    Specialties: Working straight knives and folders. **Patterns:** Hunters, fighters, daggers and Bowies. **Technical:** Forges his own Damascus; offers stock removal with ATS-34, 440C, A2, D2, O1, 5160 and 1095. **Prices:** $85 to $1500. **Remarks:** Full-time maker; first knife sold in 1985. Formerly known as Athern Forge. **Mark:** Name.

SANDERS, BILL,
335 Bauer Ave, PO Box 957, Mancos, CO 81328, Phone: 970-533-7223, Fax: 970-533-7390, billsand@frontier.net; Web: www.billsandershandmadeknives.com
    Specialties: Survival knives, working straight knives, some fancy and some fantasy, of his design. **Patterns:** Hunters, boots, utility knives, using belt knives. **Technical:** Grinds 440C, ATS-34 and commercial Damascus. Provides wide variety of handle materials. **Prices:** $170 to $800. **Remarks:** Full-time maker. Formerly of Timberline Knives. **Mark:** Name, city and state.

SANDERS, MICHAEL M,
PO Box 1106, Ponchatoula, LA 70454, Phone: 225-294-3601, sanders@bellsouth.net
    Specialties: Working straight knives and folders, some deluxe. **Patterns:** Hunters, fighters, Bowies, daggers, large folders and deluxe Damascus miniatures. **Technical:** Grinds O1, D2, 440C, ATS-34 and Damascus. **Prices:** $75 to $650; some higher. **Remarks:** Full-time maker; first knife sold in 1967. **Mark:** Name and state.

SANDOW, BRENT EDWARD,
50 O'Halloran Road, Howick, Manukau 2014, Auckland, New Zealand, Phone: 64 9 537 4166, Fax: 64 9 533 6655, knifebug@vodafone.co.nz
    Specialties: Tactical fixed blades, hunting, camp, Bowie. **Technical:** All blades made by stock removal method. **Prices:** From US $200 upward.

SANDOW, NORMAN E,
63 B Moore St, Howick, Auckland, NEW ZEALAND, Phone: 095328912, sanknife@ezysurf.co.nz
    Specialties: Quality LinerLock® folders. Working and fancy straight knives. Some one-of-a-kind. Embellishments available. **Patterns:** Most patterns, hunters, boot, bird and trout, etc., and to customer's specs. **Technical:** Predominate knife steel ATS-34. Also in use 12C27, D2 and Damascus. High class handle material used on both folders and straight knives. All blades made via the stock removal method. **Prices:** $350 to $2500. **Remarks:** Full-time maker. **Mark:** Norman E Sandow in semi-circular design.

SANDS, SCOTT,
2 Lindis Ln, New Brighton, Christchurch 9, NEW ZEALAND
    Specialties: Classic working and fantasy swords. **Patterns:** Fantasy, medieval, celtic, viking, katana, some daggers. **Technical:** Forges own Damascus; 1080 and L6; 5160 and L6; O1 and L6. All hand-polished, does own heat-treating, forges non-Damascus on request. **Prices:** $1500 to $15,000+. **Remarks:** Full-time maker; first blade sold in 1996. **Mark:** Stylized Moon.

SANFORD, DICK,
9 Satsop Court, Montesano, WA 98563, Phone: 360-249-5776, richardsanfo364@centurytel.net
    Remarks: Ten years experience hand forging knives

SANTIAGO, ABUD,
Av Gaona 3676 PB A, Buenos Aires 1416, ARGENTINA, Phone: 5411 4612 8396, info@phi-sabud.com; Web: www.phi-sabud.com/blades.html

SANTINI, TOM,
25358 Rose St., Chesterfield, MI 48051, Phone: 586-598-9471, tomsantiniknives@hotmail.com; Web: www.tomsantiniknives.com
    Specialties: working/using straight knives, tactical, and some slipjoints **Technical:** Grinds ATS-34, S-90-V, D2, and damascus. I handstitch my leather sheaths. **Prices:** $150 - $500. **Remarks:** Full-time maker, first knife sold in 2004. **Mark:** Full name.

SARGANIS, PAUL,
2215 Upper Applegate Rd, Jacksonville, OR 97530, Phone: 541-899-2831, paulsarganis@hotmail.com; Web: www.sarganis.50megs.com
Specialties: Hunters, folders, Bowies. **Technical:** Forges 5160, 1084. Grinds ATS-34 and 440C. **Prices:** $120 to $500. **Remarks:** Spare-time maker; first knife sold in 1987. **Mark:** Last name.

SASS, GARY N,
2048 Buckeye Dr, Sharpsville, PA 16150, Phone: 724-866-6165, gnsass@yahoo.com
Specialties: Working straight knives of his design or to customer specifications. **Patterns:** Hunters, fighters, utility knives, push daggers. **Technical:** Grinds 440C, ATS-34 and Damascus. Uses exotic wood, buffalo horn, warthog tusk and semi-precious stones. **Prices:** $50 to $250, some higher. **Remarks:** Part-time maker. First knife sold in 2003. **Mark:** Initials G.S. formed into a diamond shape or last name.

SAVIANO, JAMES,
124 Wallis St., Douglas, MA 01516, Phone: 508-476-7644, jimsaviano@gmail.com
Specialties: Straight knives. **Patterns:** Hunters, bowies, fighters, daggers, short swords. **Technical:** Hand-forged high-carbon and my own damascus steel. **Prices:** Starting at $300. **Remarks:** ABS mastersmith, maker since 2000, sole authorship. **Mark:** Last name or stylized JPS initials.

SAWBY, SCOTT,
480 Snowberry Ln, Sandpoint, ID 83864, Phone: 208-263-4171, scotmar@dishmail.net; Web: www.sawbycustomknives.com
Specialties: Folders, working and fancy. **Patterns:** Locking folders, patent locking systems and interframes. **Technical:** Grinds D2, 440C, CPM154, ATS-34, S30V, and Damascus. **Prices:** $700 to $3000. **Remarks:** Full-time maker; first knife sold in 1974. Engraving by wife Marian. **Mark:** Last name, city and state.

SCARROW, WIL,
c/o LandW Mail Service, PO Box 1036, Gold Hill, OR 97525, Phone: 541-855-1236, willsknife@earthlink.net
Specialties: Carving knives, also working straight knives in standard patterns or to customer specs. **Patterns:** Carving, fishing, hunting, skinning, utility, swords and Bowies. **Technical:** Forges and grinds: A2, L6, W1, D2, 5160, 1095, 440C, AEB-L, ATS-34 and others on request. Offers some filework. **Prices:** $105 to $850; some higher. Prices include sheath (carver's $40 and up). **Remarks:** Spare-time maker; first knife sold in 1983. Two to eight month construction time on custom orders. Doing business as Scarrow's Custom Stuff and Gold Hill Knife works (in Oregon). Carving knives available at Raven Dog Enterprises. Contact at Ravedog@aol.com. **Mark:** SC with arrow and year made.

SCHALLER, ANTHONY BRETT,
5609 Flint Ct. NW, Albuquerque, NM 87120, Phone: 505-899-0155, brett@schallerknives.com; Web: www.schallerknives.com
Specialties: Straight knives and locking-liner folders of his design and in standard patterns. **Patterns:** Boots, fighters, utility knives and folders. **Technical:** Grinds CPM154, S30V, and stainless Damascus. Offers filework, hand-rubbed finishes and full and narrow tangs. Prefers exotic woods or Micarta for handle materials, G-10 and carbon fiber to handle materials. **Prices:** $100 to $350; some to $500. **Remarks:** Part-time maker; first knife sold in 1990. **Mark:** A.B. Schaller - Albuquerque NM - handmade.

SCHEID, MAGGIE,
124 Van Stallen St, Rochester, NY 14621-3557
Specialties: Simple working straight knives. **Patterns:** Kitchen and utility knives; some miniatures. **Technical:** Forges 5160 high-carbon steel. **Prices:** $100 to $200. **Remarks:** Part-time maker; first knife sold in 1986. **Mark:** Full name.

SCHEMPP, ED,
PO Box 1181, Ephrata, WA 98823, Phone: 509-754-2963, Fax: 509-754-3212
Specialties: Mosaic Damascus and unique folder designs. **Patterns:** Primarily folders. **Technical:** Grinds CPM440V; forges many patterns of mosaic using powdered steel. **Prices:** $100 to $400; some to $2000. **Remarks:** Part-time maker; first knife sold in 1991. Doing business as Ed Schempp Knives. **Mark:** Ed Schempp Knives over five heads of wheat, city and state.

SCHEMPP, MARTIN,
PO Box 1181, 5430 Baird Springs Rd NW, Ephrata, WA 98823, Phone: 509-754-2963, Fax: 509-754-3212
Specialties: Fantasy and traditional straight knives of his design, to customer specs and in standard patterns; Paleolithic-styles. **Patterns:** Fighters and Paleolithic designs. **Technical:** Uses opal, Mexican rainbow and obsidian. Offers scrimshaw. **Prices:** $15 to $100; some to $250. **Remarks:** Spare-time maker; first knife sold in 1995. **Mark:** Initials and date.

SCHEPERS, GEORGE B,
PO Box 395, Shelton, NE 68876-0395
Specialties: Fancy period pieces of his design. **Patterns:** Bowies, swords, tomahawks; locking folders and miniatures. **Technical:** Grinds W1, W2 and his own Damascus; etches. **Prices:** $125 to $600; some higher. **Remarks:** Full-time maker; first knife sold in 1981. **Mark:** Schep.

SCHEURER, ALFREDO E FAES,
Av Rincon de los Arcos 104, Col Bosque Res del Sur, C.P. 16010, MEXICO, Phone: 5676 47 63
Specialties: Fancy and fantasy knives of his design. **Patterns:** Daggers. **Technical:** Grinds stainless steel; casts and grinds silver. Sets stones in silver. **Prices:** $2000 to $3000. **Remarks:** Spare-time maker; first knife sold in 1989. **Mark:** Symbol.

SCHILLING, ELLEN,
95 Line Rd, Hamilton Square, NJ 08690, Phone: 609-448-0483

SCHIPPNICK, JIM,
PO Box 326, Sanborn, NY 14132, Phone: 716-731-3715, ragnar@ragweedforge.com; Web: www.ragweedforge.com
Specialties: Nordic, early American, rustic. **Mark:** Runic R. **Remarks:** Also imports Nordic knives from Norway, Sweden and Finland.

SCHLUETER, DAVID,
2136 Cedar Gate Rd., Madison Heights, VA 24572, Phone: 434-384-8642, drschlueter@hotmail.com
Specialties: Japanese-style swords. **Patterns:** Larger blades. O-tanto to Tachi, with focus on less common shapes. **Technical:** Forges and grinds carbon steels, heat-treats and polishes own blades, makes all fittings, does own mounting and finishing. **Prices:** Start at $3000. **Remarks:** Sells fully mounted pieces only, doing business as Odd Frog Forge. **Mark:** Full name and date.

SCHMITZ, RAYMOND E,
PO Box 1787, Valley Center, CA 92082, Phone: 760-749-4318

SCHNEIDER, CRAIG M,
5380 N Amity Rd, Claremont, IL 62421, Phone: 217-377-5715, raephtownslam@att.blackberry.net
Specialties: Straight knives of his own design. **Patterns:** Bowies, hunters, tactical, bird & trout. **Technical:** Forged high-carbon steel and Damascus. Flat grind and differential heat treatment use a wide selection of handle, guard and bolster material, also offers leather sheaths. **Prices:** $125 to $3500. **Remarks:** Part-time maker; first knife sold in 1985. **Mark:** Stylized initials.

SCHNEIDER, HERMAN,
14084 Apple Valley Rd, Apple Valley, CA 92307, Phone: 760-946-9096
Specialties: Presentation pieces, Fighters, Hunters. **Prices:** Starting at $900. **Mark:** H.J. Schneider-Maker or maker's last name.

SCHNEIDER, KARL A,
209 N. Brownleaf Rd, Newark, DE 19713, Phone: 302-737-0277, dmatj@msn.com
Specialties: Traditional working and using straight knives of his design. **Patterns:** Hunters, kitchen and fillet knives. **Technical:** Grinds ATS-34, CM154, 52100, AUS8 - AUS6. Shapes handles to fit hands; uses Micarta, Pakkawood and exotic woods. Makes hand-stitched leather cases. **Prices:** $100 to $300. **Remarks:** Part-time maker; first knife sold in 1974. **Mark:** Name, address; also name in shape of fish.

SCHOEMAN, CORRIE,
Box 28596, Danhof 9310, SOUTH AFRICA, Phone: 027 51 4363528 Cell: 027 82-3750789, corries@intekom.co.za
Specialties: High-tech folders of his design or to customer's specs. **Patterns:** Linerlock folders and automatics. **Technical:** ATS-34, Damascus or stainless Damascus with titanium frames; prefers exotic materials for handles. **Prices:** $650 to $2000. **Remarks:** Full-time maker; first knife sold in 1984. All folders come with filed liners and back and jeweled inserts. **Mark:** Logo in knife shape engraved on inside of back bar.

SCHOENFELD, MATTHEW A,
RR #1, Galiano Island, B.C., CANADA V0N 1P0, Phone: 250-539-2806
Specialties: Working knives of his design. **Patterns:** Kitchen cutlery, camp knives, hunters. **Technical:** Grinds 440C. **Prices:** $85 to $500. **Remarks:** Part-time maker; first knife sold in 1978. **Mark:** Signature, Galiano Is. B.C., and date.

SCHOENINGH, MIKE,
49850 Miller Rd, North Powder, OR 97867, Phone: 541-856-3239

SCHOLL, TIM,
1389 Langdon Rd, Angier, NC 27501, Phone: 910-897-2051, tscholl@charter.net
Specialties: Fancy and working/using straight knives and folders of his design and to customer specs. **Patterns:** Bowies, hunters, tomahawks, daggers & fantasy knives. **Technical:** Forges high carbon and tool steel makes Damascus, grinds ATS-34 and D2 on request. **Prices:** $150 to $6000. **Remarks:** Part-time maker; first knife sold in 1990. Doing business as Tim Scholl Custom Knives. **Mark:** S pierced by arrow.

SCHRADER, ROBERT,
55532 Gross De, Bend, OR 97707, Phone: 541-598-7301
Specialties: Hunting, utility, Bowie. **Patterns:** Fixed blade. **Prices:** $150 to $600.

SCHRAP, ROBERT G,
CUSTOM LEATHER KNIFE SHEATH CO., 7024 W Wells St, Wauwatosa, WI 53213-3717, Phone: 414-771-6472, Fax: 414-479-9765, knifesheaths@aol.com; Web: www.customsheaths.com
Specialties: Leatherwork. **Prices:** $35 to $100. **Mark:** Schrap in oval.

SCHROEN—SFREDDO

SCHROEN, KARL,
4042 Bones Rd, Sebastopol, CA 95472, Phone: 707-823-4057, Fax: 707-823-2914, Web: http://users.ap.net/~schroen
 Specialties: Using knives made to fit. **Patterns:** Sgian dubhs, carving sets, wood-carving knives, fishing knives, kitchen knives and new cleaver design. **Technical:** Forges A2, ATS-34, D2 and L6 cruwear S30V S90V. **Prices:** $150 to $6000. **Remarks:** Full-time maker; first knife sold in 1968. Author of *The Hand Forged Knife*. **Mark:** Last name.

SCHUCHMANN, RICK,
3975 Hamblen Dr, Cincinnati, OH 45255, Phone: 513-553-4316
 Specialties: Replicas of antique and out-of-production Scagels and Randalls, primarily miniatures. **Patterns:** All sheath knives, mostly miniatures, hunting and fighting knives, some daggers and hatchets. **Technical:** Stock removal, 440C and O1 steel. Most knives are flat ground, some convex. **Prices:** $175 to $600 and custom to $4000. **Remarks:** Part-time maker, sold first knife in 1997. Knives on display in the Randall Museum. Sheaths are made exclusively at Sullivan's Holster Shop, Tampa, FL **Mark:** SCAR.

SCHULTZ, ROBERT W,
PO Box 70, Cocolalla, ID 83813-0070

SCHWARZER, LORA SUE,
119 Shoreside Trail, Crescent City, FL 32112, Phone: 386-698-2840, steveschwarzer@GBSO.net
 Specialties: Scagel style knives. **Patterns:** Hunters and miniatures **Technical:** Forges 1084 and Damascus. **Prices:** Start at $400. **Remarks:** Part-time maker; first knife sold in 1997. Journeyman Bladesmith, American Bladesmith Society. Now working with Steve Schwarzer on some projects. **Mark:** Full name - JS on reverse side.

SCHWARZER, STEPHEN,
119 Shoreside Trail, Crescent City, FL 32112, Phone: 386-698-2840, Fax: 386-698-2840, steveschwarzer@gbso.net; Web: www.steveschwarzer.com
 Specialties: Mosaic Damascus and picture mosaic in folding knives. All Japanese blades are finished working with Wally Hostetter considered the top Japanese lacquer specialist in the U.S.A. Also produces a line of carbon steel skinning knives at $300. **Patterns:** Folders, axes and buckskinner knives. **Technical:** Specializes in picture mosaic Damascus and powder metal mosaic work. Sole authorship; all work including carving done in-house. Most knives have file work and carving. Hand carved steel and precious metal guards. **Prices:** $1500 to $5000, some higher; carbon steel and primitive knives much less. **Remarks:** Full-time maker; first knife sold in 1976, considered by many to be one of the top mosaic Damascus specialists in the world. Mosaic Master level work. I am now working with Lora Schwarzer on some projects. **Mark:** Schwarzer + anvil.

SCIMIO, BILL,
4554 Creek Side Ln., Spruce Creek, PA 16683, Phone: 814-632-3751, sprucecreekforge@gmail.com Web: www.sprucecreekforge.com
 Specialties: Hand-forged primitive-style knives with curly maple, antler, bone and osage handles.

SCOFIELD, EVERETT,
2873 Glass Mill Rd, Chickamauga, GA 30707, Phone: 706-375-2790
 Specialties: Historic and fantasy miniatures. **Patterns:** All patterns. **Technical:** Uses only the finest tool steels and other materials. Uses only natural, precious and semi-precious materials. **Prices:** $100 to $1500. **Remarks:** Full-time maker; first knife sold in 1971. Doing business as Three Crowns Cutlery. **Mark:** Three Crowns logo.

SCORDIA, PAOLO,
Via Terralba 143, 00050 Torrimpietra, Roma, ITALY, Phone: 06-61697231, pands@mail.nexus.it; Web: www.scordia-knives.com
 Specialties: Working and fantasy knives of his own design. **Patterns:** Any pattern. **Technical:** Forges own Damascus, welds own mokume and grinds ATS-34, etc. use hardwoods and Micarta for handles, brass and nickel-silver for fittings. Makes sheaths. **Prices:** $100 to $1000. **Remarks:** Part-time maker; first knife sold in 1988. **Mark:** Initials with sun and moon logo.

SCOTT, AL,
2245 Harper Valley Rd, Harper, TX 78631, Phone: 830-928-1742, deadlybeauty@ctesc.net
 Specialties: High-art straight knives of his design. **Patterns:** Daggers, swords, early European, Middle East and Japanese knives. **Technical:** Uses ATS-34, 440C and Damascus. Hand engraves; does file work; cuts filigree in the blade; offers ivory carving and precious metal inlay. **Remarks:** Full-time maker; first knife sold in 1994. Doing business as Al Scott Maker of Fine Blade Art. **Mark:** Name engraved in Old English, sometime inlaid in 24K gold.

SCROGGS, JAMES A,
108 Murray Hill Dr, Warrensburg, MO 64093, Phone: 660-747-2568, jscroggsknives@embarqmail.com
 Specialties: Straight knives, prefers light weight. **Patterns:** Hunters, hideouts, and fighters. **Technical:** Grinds O1, 5160, plus experiments in steels. Uses high and low temperature of salt pots for heat treat. Prefers handles of walnut in English, bastonge, American black. Also uses myrtle, maple, Osage orange. **Prices:** $200 to $1000. **Remarks:** 1st knife sold in 1985. Part-time maker, no orders taken. **Mark:** SCROGGS in block or script.

SCULLEY, PETER E,
340 Sunset Dr, Rising Fawn, GA 30738, Phone: 706-398-0169

SEARS, MICK,
4473 Ernest Scott Rd., Kershaw, SC 29067, Phone: 803-475-4937
 Specialties: Scots and confederate reproductions; Bowies and fighters. **Patterns:** Bowies, fighters. **Technical:** Grinds 440C and 1095. **Prices:** $50 to $150; some to $300. **Remarks:** Full-time maker; first knife sold in 1975. Doing business as Mick's Custom Knives. **Mark:** First name.

SEIB, STEVE,
7914 Old State Road, Evansville, IN 47710, Phone: 812-867-2231, sseib@insightbb.com
 Specialties: Working straight knives. **Pattern:** Skinners, hunters, bowies and camp knives. **Technical:** Forges high-carbon and makes own damascus. **Remarks:** Part-time maker. ABS member. **Mark:** Last name.

SELENT, CHUCK,
PO Box 1207, Bonners Ferry, ID 83805-1207, Phone: 208-267-5807
 Specialties: Period, art and fantasy miniatures; exotics; one-of-a-kinds. **Patterns:** Swords, daggers and others. **Technical:** Works in Damascus, meteorite, 440C and tool steel. Offers scrimshaw. Offers his own casting and leatherwork; uses jewelry techniques. Makes display cases for miniatures. **Prices:** $75 to $400. **Remarks:** Part-time maker; first knife sold in 1990. **Mark:** Last name and bear paw print logo scrimshawed on handles or leatherwork.

SELF, ERNIE,
950 O'Neill Ranch Rd, Dripping Springs, TX 78620-9760, Phone: 512-940-7134, ernieself@hillcountrytx.net
 Specialties: Traditional and working straight knives and folders of his design and in standard patterns. **Patterns:** Hunters, locking folders and slipjoints. **Technical:** Grinds 440C, D2, 440V, ATS-34 and Damascus. Offers fancy filework. **Prices:** $250 to $1000; some to $2500. **Remarks:** Full-time maker; first knife sold in 1982. Also customizes Buck 110's and 112's folding hunters. **Mark:** In oval shape - Ernie Self Maker Dripping Springs TX.

SELLEVOLD, HARALD,
S Kleivesmau:2, PO Box 4134, N5835 Bergen, NORWAY, Phone: 47 55-310682, haraldsellevold@c2i.net; Web:knivmakeren.com
 Specialties: Norwegian-styles; collaborates with other Norse craftsmen. **Patterns:** Distinctive ferrules and other mild modifications of traditional patterns; Bowies and friction folders. **Technical:** Buys Damascus blades; blacksmiths his own blades. Semi-gemstones used in handles; gemstone inlay. **Prices:** $350 to $2000. **Remarks:** Full-time maker; first knife sold in 1980. **Mark:** Name and country in logo.

SELZAM, FRANK,
Martin Reinhard Str 23 97631, Bad Koenigshofen, GERMANY, Phone: 09761-5980, frankselzam.de
 Specialties: Hunters, working knives to customers specs, hand tooled and stitched leather sheaths large stock of wood and German stag horn. **Patterns:** Mostly own design. **Technical:** Forged blades, own Damascus, also stock removal stainless. **Prices:** $250 to $1500. **Remark:** First knife sold in 1978. **Mark:** Last name stamped.

SENTZ, MARK C,
4084 Baptist Rd, Taneytown, MD 21787, Phone: 410-756-2018
 Specialties: Fancy straight working knives of his design. **Patterns:** Hunters, fighters, folders and utility/camp knives. **Technical:** Forges 1085, 1095, 5160, 5155 and his Damascus. Most knives come with wood-lined leather sheath or wooden presentation sheath. **Prices:** Start at $275. **Remarks:** Full-time maker; first knife sold in 1989. Doing business as M. Charles Sentz Gunsmithing, Inc. **Mark:** Last name.

SERAFEN, STEVEN E,
24 Genesee St, New Berlin, NY 13411, Phone: 607-847-6903
 Specialties: Traditional working/using straight knives of his design and to customer specs. **Patterns:** Bowies, fighters, hunters. **Technical:** Grinds ATS-34, 440C, high-carbon steel. **Prices:** $175 to $600; some to $1200. **Remarks:** Part-time maker; first knife sold in 1990. **Mark:** First and middle initial, last name in script.

SERVEN, JIM,
PO Box 1, Fostoria, MI 48435, Phone: 517-795-2255
 Specialties: Highly finished unique folders. **Patterns:** Fancy working folders, axes, miniatures and razors; some straight knives. **Technical:** Grinds 440C; forges his own Damascus. **Prices:** $150 to $800; some to $1500. **Remarks:** Full-time maker; first knife sold in 1971. **Mark:** Name in map logo.

SEVEY CUSTOM KNIFE,
94595 Chandler Rd, Gold Beach, OR 97444, Phone: 541-247-2649, sevey@charter.net; Web: www.seveyknives.com
 Specialties: Fixed blade hunters. **Patterns:** Drop point, trailing paint, clip paint, full tang, hidden tang. **Technical:** D-2, and ATS-34 blades, stock removal. Heat treatment by Paul Bos. **Prices:** $225 and up depending on overall length and grip material. **Mark:** Sevey Custom Knife.

SFREDDO, RODRIGO MENEZES,
Rua 15 De Setembro 66, Centro Nova Petropolis RS, cep g5 150-000, BRAZIL 95150-000, Phone: 011-55-54-303-303-90, www.brazilianbladesmiths.com.br; www.sbccutelaria.org.br
 Specialties: Integrals, Bowies, hunters, dirks & swords. **Patterns:** Forges

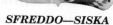

his own Damascus and 52100 steel. **Technical:** Specialized in integral knives and Damascus. **Prices:** From $350 and up. Most around $750 to $1000. **Remarks:** Considered by many to be the Brazil's best bladesmith. ABS SBC Member. **Mark:** S. Sfreddo on the left side of the blade.

SHADLEY, EUGENE W,
26315 Norway Dr, Bovey, MN 55709, Phone: 218-245-1639, Fax: call first, bses@uslink.net
Specialties: Gold frames are available on some models. **Patterns:** Whittlers, stockman, sowbelly, congress, trapper, etc. **Technical:** Grinds ATS-34, 416 frames. **Prices:** Starts at $600. **Remarks:** Full-time maker; first knife sold in 1985. Doing business as Shadley Knives. **Mark:** Last name.

SHADMOT, BOAZ,
MOSHAV PARAN D N, Arava, ISRAEL 86835, srb@arava.co.il

SHARRIGAN, MUDD,
111 Bradford Rd, Wiscasset, ME 04578-4457, Phone: 207-882-9820, Fax: 207-882-9835
Specialties: Custom designs; repair straight knives, custom leather sheaths. **Patterns:** Daggers, fighters, hunters, buckskinner, Indian crooked knives and seamen working knives; traditional Scandinavian-styles. **Technical:** Forges 1095, 52100, 5160, W2, O1. Laminates 1095 and mild steel. **Prices:** $50 to $325; some to $1200. **Remarks:** Full-time maker; first knife sold in 1982. **Mark:** First name and swallow tail carving.

SHAVER II, JAMES R,
1529 Spider Ridge Rd, Parkersburg, WV 26104, Phone: 304-422-2692, admin@spiderridgeforge.net Web:www.spiderridgeforge.net
Specialties: Hunting and working straight knives in carbon and Damascus steel. **Patterns:** Bowies and daggers in Damascus and carbon steels. **Technical:** Forges 5160 carbon and Damascus in O1 pure nickel 1018. **Prices:** $85 to $125; some to $750. Some to $1000 **Remarks:** Part-time maker; sold first knife in 1998. Believes in sole authorship. **Mark:** Last name.

SHEEHY, THOMAS J,
4131 NE 24th Ave, Portland, OR 97211-6411, Phone: 503-493-2843
Specialties: Hunting knives and ulus. **Patterns:** Own or customer designs. **Technical:** 1095/O1 and ATS-34 steel. **Prices:** $35 to $200. **Remarks:** Do own heat treating; forged or ground blades. **Mark:** Name.

SHEETS, STEVEN WILLIAM,
6 Stonehouse Rd, Mendham, NJ 07945, Phone: 201-543-5882

SHIFFER, STEVE,
PO Box 582, Leakesville, MS 39451, Phone: 601-394-4425, aiifish2@yahoo.com; Web: wwwchoctawplantationforge.com
Specialties: Bowies, fighters, hard use knives. **Patterns:** Fighters, hunters, combat/utility knives. Walker pattern LinerLock® folders. Allen pattern scale and bolster release autos. **Technical:** Most work forged, stainless stock removal. Makes own Damascus. O1 and 5160 most used also 1084, 440c, 154cm, s30v. **Prices:** $125 to $1000. **Remarks:** First knife sold in 2000, all heat treatment done by maker. Doing business as Choctaw Plantation Forge. **Mark:** Hot mark sunrise over creek.

SHINOSKY, ANDY,
3117 Meanderwood Dr, Canfield, OH 44406, Phone: 330-702-0299, andrew@shinosky.com; Web: www.shinosky.com
Specialties: Collectable folders and interframes. **Patterns:** Drop point, spear point, trailing point, daggers. **Technical:** Grinds ATS-34 and Damascus. Prefers natural handle materials. Most knives are engraved by Andy himself. **Prices:** Start at $800. **Remarks:** Part-time maker/engraver. First knife sold in 1992. **Mark:** Name.

SHIPLEY, STEVEN A,
800 Campbell Rd Ste 137, Richardson, TX 75081, Phone: 972-644-7981, Fax: 972-644-7985, steve@shipleysphotography
Specialties: Hunters, skinners and traditional straight knives. **Technical:** Hand grinds ATS-34, 440C and Damascus steels. Each knife is custom sheathed by his son, Dan. **Prices:** $175 to $2000. **Remarks:** Part-time maker; like smooth lines and unusual handle materials. **Mark:** S A Shipley.

SHOEMAKER, CARROLL,
380 Yellowtown Rd, Northup, OH 45658, Phone: 740-446-6695
Specialties: Working/using straight knives of his design. **Patterns:** Hunters, utility/camp and early American backwoodsmen knives. **Technical:** Grinds ATS-34; forges old files, O1 and 1095. Uses some Damascus; offers scrimshaw and engraving. **Prices:** $100 to $175; some to $350. **Remarks:** Spare-time maker; first knife sold in 1977. **Mark:** Name and city or connected initials.

SHOEMAKER, SCOTT,
316 S Main St, Miamisburg, OH 45342, Phone: 513-859-1935
Specialties: Twisted, wire-wrapped handles on swords, fighters and fantasy blades; new line of seven models with quick-draw, multi-carry Kydex sheaths. **Patterns:** Bowies, boots and one-of-a-kinds in his design or to customer specs. **Technical:** Grinds A6 and ATS-34; buys Damascus. Hand satin finish is standard. **Prices:** $100 to $1500; swords to $8000. **Remarks:** Part-time maker; first knife sold in 1984. **Mark:** Angel wings with last initial, or last name.

SHOGER, MARK O,
14780 SW Osprey Dr Suite 345, Beaverton, OR 97007, Phone: 503-579-2495, mosdds@msn.com
Specialties: Working and using straight knives and folders of his design; fancy and embellished knives. **Patterns:** Hunters, Bowies, daggers and folders. **Technical:** Forges O1, W2, 1084, 5160, 52100 and 1084/15n20 pattern weld. **Remarks:** Spare-time maker. **Mark:** Last name or stamped last initial over anvil.

SHORE, JOHN I,
2901 Sheldon Jackson St., Anchorage, AK 99508, Phone: 907-272-2253, akknife@acsalaska.net; Web: www.akknife.com
Specialties: Working straight knives, hatchets, and folders. **Patterns:** Hunters, skinners, Bowies, fighters, working using knives. **Technical:** Prefer using exotic steels, grinds most CPM's, Damasteel, RWL34, BG42, D2 and some ATS-34. Prefers exotic hardwoods, stabilized materials, Micarta, and pearl. **Prices:** Comparable to other top makers. **Remarks:** Full-time maker; first knife sold in 1985. Voting member Knifemakers Guild & Dertche Messermacker Guild. Doing business as Alaska Knifemaker. **Mark:** Name in script, Kenai, AK.

SHULL, JAMES,
5146 N US 231 W, Rensselaer, IN 47978, Phone: 219-866-0436, nbjs@netnitco.net Web: www.shullhandforgedknives.com
Specialties: Working knives of hunting, fillet, Bowie patterns. **Technical:** Forges or uses 1095, 5160, 52100 & O1. **Prices:** $100 to $300. **Remarks:** DBA Shull Handforged Knives. **Mark:** Last name in arc.

SIBRIAN, AARON,
4308 Dean Dr, Ventura, CA 93003, Phone: 805-642-6950
Specialties: Tough working knives of his design and in standard patterns. **Patterns:** Makes a "Viper utility"—a kukri derivative and a variety of straight using knives. **Technical:** Grinds 440C and ATS-34. Offers traditional Japanese blades; soft backs, hard edges, temper lines. **Prices:** $60 to $100; some to $250. **Remarks:** Spare-time maker; first knife sold in 1989. **Mark:** Initials in diagonal line.

SIMMONS, H R,
1100 Bay City Rd, Aurora, NC 27806, Phone: 252-322-5969
Specialties: Working/using straight knives of his design. **Patterns:** Fighters, hunters and utility/camp knives. **Technical:** Forges and grinds Damascus and L6; grinds ATS-34. **Prices:** $150 to $250; some to $400. **Remarks:** Part-time maker; first knife sold in 1987. Doing business as HRS Custom Knives, Royal Forge and Trading Company. **Mark:** Initials.

SIMONELLA, GIANLUIGI,
Via Battiferri 33, 33085 Maniago, ITALY, Phone: 01139-427-730350
Specialties: Traditional and classic folding and working/using knives of his design and to customer specs. **Patterns:** Bowies, fighters, hunters, utility/camp knives. **Technical:** Forges ATS-34, D2, 440C. **Prices:** $250 to $400; some to $1000. **Remarks:** Full-time maker; first knife sold in 1988. **Mark:** Wilson.

SIMS, BOB,
PO Box 772, Meridian, TX 76665, Phone: 254-435-6240
Specialties: Traditional working straight knives and folders in standard patterns. **Patterns:** Locking folders, slip-joint folders and hunters. **Technical:** Grinds D2, ATS-34 and O1. Offers filework on some knives. **Prices:** $150 to $275; some to $600. **Remarks:** Full-time maker; first knife sold in 1975. **Mark:** The division sign.

SINCLAIR, J E,
520 Francis Rd, Pittsburgh, PA 15239, Phone: 412-793-5778
Specialties: Fancy hunters and fighters, liner locking folders. **Patterns:** Fighters, hunters and folders. **Technical:** Flat-grinds and hollow grind, prefers hand rubbed satin finish. Uses natural handle materials. **Prices:** $185 to $800. **Remarks:** Part-time maker; first knife sold in 1995. **Mark:** First and middle initials, last name and maker.

SINYARD, CLESTON S,
27522 Burkhardt Dr, Elberta, AL 36530, Phone: 334-987-1361, nimoforge1@gulftel.com; Web: www.knifemakersguild
Specialties: Working straight knives and folders of his design. **Patterns:** Hunters, buckskinners, Bowies, daggers, fighters and all-Damascus folders. **Technical:** Makes Damascus from 440C, stainless steel, D2 and regular high-carbon steel; forges "forefinger pad" into hunters and skinners. **Prices:** In Damascus $450 to $1500; some $2500. **Remarks:** Full-time maker; first knife sold in 1980. Doing business as Nimo Forge. **Mark:** Last name, U.S.A. in anvil.

SISKA, JIM,
48 South Maple St, Westfield, MA 01085, Phone: 413-642-3059, siskaknives@comcast.net
Specialties: Traditional working straight knives, no folders. **Patterns:** Hunters, fighters, Bowies and one-of-a-kinds; folders. **Technical:** Grinds D2, A2, 54CM and ATS-34; buys Damascus. Likes exotic woods. **Prices:** $300 and up. **Remarks:** Part-time. **Mark:** Siska in Old English.

SJOSTRAND, KEVIN,
1541 S Cain St, Visalia, CA 93292, Phone: 559-625-5254
Specialties: Traditional and working/using straight knives and folders of his design or to customer specs. **Patterns:** Fixed blade hunters, Bowies, utility/camp knives. **Technical:** Grinds ATS-34, 440C and 1095. Prefers high polished blades and full tang. Natural and stabilized hardwoods, Micarta and stag handle material. **Prices:** $150 to $400. **Remarks:** Part-time maker; first knife sold in 1992. Doing business as Black Oak Blades. **Mark:** SJOSTRAND

SKIFF, STEVEN,
SKIFF MADE BLADES, PO Box 537, Broadalbin, NY 12025, Phone: 518-883-4875, skiffmadeblades @hotmail.com; Web: www.skiffmadeblades.com
Specialties: Custom using/collector grade straight blades and LinerLock® folders of maker's design or customer specifications. **Patterns:** Hunters, utility/camp knives, tactical/fancy art folders. **Prices:** Straight blades $225 and up. Folders $450 and up. **Technical:** Stock removal hollow ground ATS-34, 154 CM, S30V, and tool steel. Damascus-Devon Thomas, Robert Eggerling, Mike Norris and Delbert Ealy. Nickel silver and stainless in-house heat treating. Handle materials: man made and natural woods (stablilized). Horn shells sheaths for straight blades, sews own leather and uses sheaths by "Tree-Stump Leather." **Remarks:** First knife sold 1997. Started making folders in 2000. **Mark:** SKIFF on blade of straight blades and in inside of backspacer on folders.

SKOW, H.A. "TEX",
TEX KNIVES, 3534 Gravel Springs Rd, Senatobia, MS 38668, Phone: 662-301-1568, texknives@bellsouth.net; Web: www.texknives.com
Specialties: One-of-a-kind daggers, Bowies, boot knives and hunters. **Patterns:** Different Damascus patterns (by Bob Eggerling). **Technical:** 440C, 58, 60 Rockwell hardness. Engraving by Joe Mason. **Prices:** Negotiable. **Mark:** TEX.

SLEE, FRED,
9 John St, Morganville, NJ 07751, Phone: 732-591-9047
Specialties: Working straight knives, some fancy, to customer specs. **Patterns:** Hunters, fighters, fancy daggers and folders. **Technical:** Grinds D2, 440C and ATS-34. **Prices:** $285 to $1100. **Remarks:** Part-time maker; first knife sold in 1980. **Mark:** Letter "S" in Old English.

SLOAN, SHANE,
4226 FM 61, Newcastle, TX 76372, Phone: 940-846-3290
Specialties: Collector-grade straight knives and folders. **Patterns:** Uses stainless Damascus, ATS-34 and 12C27. Bowies, lockers, slip-joints, fancy folders, fighters and period pieces. **Technical:** Grinds D2 and ATS-34. Uses hand-rubbed satin finish. Prefers rare natural handle materials. **Prices:** $250 to $6500. **Remarks:** Full-time maker; first knife sold in 1985. **Mark:** Name and city.

SLOBODIAN, SCOTT,
4101 River Ridge Dr, PO Box 1498, San Andreas, CA 95249, Phone: 209-286-1980, Fax: 209-286-1982, scott@slobodianswords.com; Web: www.slobodianswords.com
Specialties: Japanese-style knives and swords, period pieces, fantasy pieces and miniatures. **Patterns:** Small kweikens, tantos, wakazashis, katanas, traditional samurai swords. **Technical:** Flat-grinds 1050, commercial Damascus. **Prices:** Prices start at $1500. **Remarks:** Full-time maker; first knife sold in 1987. **Mark:** Blade signed in Japanese characters and various scripts.

SMALE, CHARLES J,
509 Grove Ave, Waukegan, IL 60085, Phone: 847-244-8013

SMALL, ED,
Rt 1 Box 178-A, Keyser, WV 26726, Phone: 304-298-4254
Specialties: Working knives of his design; period pieces. **Patterns:** Hunters, daggers, buckskinners and camp knives; likes one-of-a-kinds. **Technical:** Forges and grinds W2, L6 and his own Damascus. **Prices:** $150 to $1500. **Remarks:** Full-time maker; first knife sold in 1978. Doing business as Iron Mountain Forge Works. **Mark:** Script initials connected.

SMART, STEVE,
907 Park Row Cir, McKinney, TX 75070-3847, Phone: 214-837-4216, Fax: 214-837-4111
Specialties: Working/using straight knives and folders of his design, to customer specs and in standard patterns. **Patterns:** Bowies, hunters, kitchen knives, locking folders, utility/camp, fishing and bird knives. **Technical:** Grinds ATS-34, D2, 440C and O1. Prefers mirror polish or satin finish; hollow-grinds all blades. All knives come with sheath. Offers some filework. **Prices:** $95 to $225; some to $500. **Remarks:** Spare-time maker; first knife sold in 1983. **Mark:** Name, Custom, city and state in oval.

SMIT, GLENN,
627 Cindy Ct, Aberdeen, MD 21001, Phone: 410-272-2959, wolfsknives@comcast.net
Specialties: Working and using straight and folding knives of his design or to customer specs. Customizes and repairs all types of cutlery. Exclusive maker of Dave Murphy Style knives. **Patterns:** Hunters, Bowies, daggers, fighters, utility/camp, folders, kitchen knives and miniatures, Murphy combat, C.H.A.I.K., Little 88 and Tiny 90-styles. **Technical:** Grinds 440C, ATS-34, O1, A2 also grinds 6AL4V titanium allox for blades. Reforges commercial Damascus and makes own Damascus, cast aluminum handles. **Prices:**

Miniatures start at $30; full-size knives start at $50. **Remarks:** Spare-time maker; first knife sold in 1986. Doing business as Wolf's Knives. **Mark:** G.P. SMIT, with year on reverse side, Wolf's Knives-Murphy's way with date.

SMITH, J D,
69 Highland, Roxbury, MA 02119, Phone: 617-989-0723, jdsmith02119@yahoo.com
Specialties: Fighters, Bowies, Persian, locking folders and swords. **Patterns:** Bowies, fighters and locking folders. **Technical:** Forges and grinds D2, his Damascus, O1, 52100 etc. and wootz-pattern hammer steel. **Prices:** $500 to $2000; some to $5000. **Remarks:** Full-time maker; first knife sold in 1987. Doing business as Hammersmith. **Mark:** Last initial alone or in cartouche.

SMITH, J.B.,
21 Copeland Rd., Perkinston, MS 39573, Phone: 228-380-1851
Specialties: Traditional working knives for the hunter and fisherman. **Patterns:** Hunters, Bowies, and fishing knives; copies of 1800 period knives. **Technical:** Grinds ATS-34, 440C. **Prices:** $100 to $800. **Remarks:** Full-time maker, first knife sold in 1972. **Mark:** J.B. Smith MAKER PERKINSTON, MS.

SMITH, JOHN M,
3450 E Beguelin Rd, Centralia, IL 62801, Phone: 618-249-6444, jknife@frontiernet.net
Specialties: Folders. **Patterns:** Folders. **Prices:** $250 to $2500. **Remarks:** First knife sold in 1980. Not taking orders at this time on fixed blade knives. Part-time maker. **Mark:** Etched signature or logo.

SMITH, JOHN W,
1322 Cow Branch Rd, West Liberty, KY 41472, Phone: 606-743-3599, jwsknive@mrtc.com; Web: www.jwsmithknives.com
Specialties: Fancy and working locking folders of his design or to customer specs. **Patterns:** Interframes, traditional and daggers. **Technical:** Grinds 530V and his own Damascus. Offers gold inlay, engraving with gold inlay, hand-fitted mosaic pearl inlay and filework. Prefers hand-rubbed finish. Pearl and ivory available. **Prices:** Utility pieces $375 to $650. Art knives $1200 to $10,000. **Remarks:** Full-time maker. **Mark:** Initials engraved inside diamond.

SMITH, JOSH,
Box 753, Frenchtown, MT 59834, Phone: 406-626-5775, joshsmithknives@gmail.com; Web: www.joshsmithknives.com
Specialties: Mosaic, Damascus, LinerLock® folders, automatics, Bowies, fighters, etc. **Patterns:** All kinds. **Technical:** Advanced Mosaic and Damascus. **Prices:** $450 and up. **Remarks:** A.B.S. Master Smith. **Mark:** Josh Smith with year (Josh10Smith).

SMITH, LENARD C,
PO Box D68, Valley Cottage, NY 10989, Phone: 914-268-7359

SMITH, MICHAEL J,
1418 Saddle Gold Ct, Brandon, FL 33511, Phone: 813-431-3790, smithknife@hotmail.com; Web: www.smithknife.com
Specialties: Fancy high art folders of his design. **Patterns:** Locking locks and automatics. **Technical:** Uses ATS-34, non-stainless and stainless Damascus; hand carves folders, prefers ivory and pearl. Hand-rubbed satin finish. Liners are 6AL4V titanium. **Prices:** $500 to $3000. **Remarks:** Full-time maker; first knife sold in 1989. **Mark:** Name, city, state.

SMITH, NEWMAN L.,
865 Glades Rd Shop #3, Gatlinburg, TN 37738, Phone: 423-436-3322, thesmithshop@aol.com; Web: www.thesmithsshop.com
Specialties: Collector-grade and working knives. **Patterns:** Hunters, slip-joint and lock-back folders, some miniatures. **Technical:** Grinds O1 and ATS-34; makes fancy sheaths. **Prices:** $165 to $750; some to $1000. **Remarks:** Full-time maker; first knife sold in 1984. Partners part-time to handle Damascus blades by Jeff Hurst; marks these with SH connected. **Mark:** First and middle initials, last name.

SMITH, RALPH L,
525 Groce Meadow Rd, Taylors, SC 29687, Phone: 864-444-0819, ralph_smith1@charter.net; Web: www.smithhandcraftedknives.com
Specialties: Working knives: straight and folding knives. Hunters, skinners, fighters, bird, boot, Bowie and kitchen knives. **Technical:** Concave Grind D2, ATS 34, 440C, steel hand finish or polished. **Prices:** $125 to $350 for standard models. **Remarks:** First knife sold in 1976. KMG member since 1981. SCAK founding member and past president. **Mark:** SMITH handcrafted knives in SC state outline.

SMITH, RAYMOND L,
217 Red Chalk Rd, Erin, NY 14838, Phone: 607-795-5257, Bladesmith@wildblue.net; Web: www.theanvilsedge.net
Specialties: Working/using straight knives and folders to customer specs and in standard patterns; period pieces. **Patterns:** Bowies, hunters, skipjoints. **Technical:** Forges 5160, 52100, 1018, 15N20, 1084, ATS 34. Damascus and wire cable Damascus. Filework. **Prices:** $125 to $1500; estimates for custom orders. **Remarks:** Full-time maker; first knife sold in 1991. ABS Master Smith. Doing business as The Anvils Edge. **Mark:** Ellipse with RL Smith, Erin NY MS in center.

SMITH, RICK,
BEAR BONE KNIVES, 1843 W Evans Creek Rd., Rogue River, OR 97537, Phone: 541-582-4144, BearBoneSmith@msn.com; Web: www.bearbone.com
Specialties: Classic, historical style Bowie knives, hunting knives and various contemporary knife styles. **Technical:** Blades are either forged or made by stock removal method depending on steel used. Also forge weld wire Damascus. Does own heat treating and tempering using digital even heat kiln. Stainless blades are sent out for cryogenic "freeze treat." Preferred steels are O1, tool, 5160, 1095, 1084, ATS-34, 154CM, 440C and various high carbon Damascus. **Prices:** $350 to $1500. Custom leather sheaths available for knives. **Remarks:** Full-time maker since 1997. Serial numbers no longer put on knives. Official business name is "Bear Bone Knives." **Mark:** Early maker's mark was "Bear Bone" over capital letters "RS" with downward arrow between letters and "Hand Made" underneath letters. Mark on small knives is 3/8 circle containing "RS" with downward arrow between letters. Current mark since 2003 is "R Bear Bone Smith" arching over image of coffin Bowie knife with two shooting stars and "Rogue River, Oregon" underneath.

SMITH, SHAWN,
2644 Gibson Ave, Clouis, CA 93611, Phone: 559-323-6234, kslc@sbcglobal.net
Specialties: Working and fancy straight knives. **Patterns:** Hunting, trout, fighters, skinners. **Technical:** Hollow grinds ATS-34, 154CM, A-2. **Prices:** $150.00 and up. **Remarks:** Part time maker. **Mark:** Shawn Smith hand-made.

SMITH JR., JAMES B "RED",
Rt 2 Box 1525, Morven, GA 31638, Phone: 912-775-2844
Specialties: Folders. **Patterns:** Rotating rear-lock folders. **Technical:** Grinds ATS-34, D2 and Vascomax 350. **Prices:** Start at $350. **Remarks:** Full-time maker; first knife sold in 1985. **Mark:** GA RED in cowboy hat.

SMOCK, TIMOTHY E,
1105 N Sherwood Dr, Marion, IN 46952, Phone: 765-664-0123

SMOKER, RAY,
113 Church Rd, Searcy, AR 72143, Phone: 501-796-2712
Specialties: Rugged, no nonsense working knives of his design only. **Patterns:** Hunters, skinners, utility/camp and flat-ground knives. **Technical:** Forges his own Damascus and 52100; makes sheaths. Uses improved multiple edge quench he developed. **Prices:** $450 and up; price includes sheath. **Remarks:** Semi-retired; first knife sold in 1992. **Mark:** Last name.

SNODY, MIKE,
135 Triple Creek Rd, Fredericksburg, TX 78624, Phone: 361-443-0161, info@snodyknives.com; Web: www.snodyknives.com
Specialties: High performance straight knives in traditional and Japanese-styles. **Patterns:** Skinners, hunters, tactical, Kwaiken and tantos. **Technical:** Grinds BG42, ATS-34, 440C and A2. Offers full or tapered tangs, upgraded handle materials such as fossil ivory, coral and exotic woods. Traditional diamond wrap over stingray on Japanese-style knives. Sheaths available in leather or Kydex. **Prices:** $100 to $1000. **Remarks:** Part-time maker; first knife sold in 1999. **Mark:** Name over knife maker.

SNOW, BILL,
4824 18th Ave, Columbus, GA 31904, Phone: 706-576-4390, tipikw@knology.net
Specialties: Traditional working/using straight knives and folders of his design and to customer specs. Offers engraving and scrimshaw. **Patterns:** Bowies, fighters, hunters and folders. **Technical:** Grinds ATS-34, 440V, 440C, 420V, CPM350, BG42, A2, D2, 5160, 52100 and O1; forges if needed. Cryogenically quenches all steels; inlaid handles; some integrals; leather or Kydex sheaths. **Prices:** $125 to $700; some to $3500. **Remarks:** Now also have 530V, 10V and 3V steels in use. Full-time maker; first knife sold in 1958. Doing business as Tipi Knife works. **Mark:** Old English scroll "S" inside a tipi.

SNYDER, MICHAEL TOM,
PO Box 522, Zionsville, IN 46077-0522, Phone: 317-873-6807, wildcatcreek@indy.pr.com

SOAPER, MAX H.,
2375 Zion Rd, Henderson, KY 42420, Phone: 270-827-8143
Specialties: Primitive Longhunter knives, scalpers, camp knives, cowboy Bowies, neck knives, working knives, period pieces from the 18th century. **Technical:** Forges 5160, 1084, 1095; all blades differentially heat treated. **Prices:** $80 to $500. **Remarks:** Part-time maker since 1989. **Mark:** Initials in script.

SOLOMON, MARVIN,
23750 Cold Springs Rd, Paron, AR 72122, Phone: 501-821-3170, Fax: 501-821-6541, mardot@swbell.net; Web: www.coldspringsforge.com
Specialties: Traditional working and using straight knives of his design and to customer specs, also lock back 7 LinerLock® folders. **Patterns:** Single blade folders. **Technical:** Forges 5160, 1095, O1 and random Damascus. **Prices:** $125 to $1000. **Remarks:** Part-time maker; first knife sold in 1990. Doing business as Cold Springs Forge. **Mark:** Last name.

SONNTAG, DOUGLAS W,
902 N 39th St, Nixa, MO 65714, Phone: 417-693-1640, Fax: 417-582-1392, dougsonntag@gmail.com
Specialties: Working knives; art knives. **Patterns:** Hunters, boots, straight working knives; Bowies, some folders, camp/axe sets. **Technical:** Grinds D2, ATS-34, forges own Damascus; does own heat treating. **Prices:** $225 and up. **Remarks:** Full-time maker; first knife sold in 1986. **Mark:** Etched name in arch.

SONTHEIMER, G DOUGLAS,
12604 Bridgeton Dr, Potomac, MD 20854, Phone: 301-948-5227
Specialties: Fixed blade knives. **Patterns:** Whitetail deer, backpackers, camp, claws, fillet, fighters. **Technical:** Hollow Grinds. **Price:** $500 and up. **Remarks:** Spare-time maker; first knife sold in 1976. **Mark:** LORD.

SOPPERA, ARTHUR,
"Pilatusblick", Oberer Schmidberg, CH-9631 Ulisbach, SWITZERLAND, Phone: 71-988 23 27, Fax: 71-988 47 57, doublelock@hotmail.com; Web: www.sopperaknifeart.ch
Specialties: High-art, high-tech knives of his design. **Patterns:** Locking folders, and fixed blade knives. **Technical:** Grinds ATS-34 and commercial Damascus. Folders have button lock of his own design; some are fancy folders in jeweler's fashion. Also makes jewelry with integrated small knives. **Prices:** $300 to $1500, some $2500 and higher. **Remarks:** Full-time maker; first knife sold in 1986. **Mark:** Stylized initials, name, country.

SORNBERGER, JIM,
25126 Overland Dr, Volcano, CA 95689, Phone: 209-295-7819
Specialties: Classic San Francisco-style knives. Collectible straight knives. **Patterns:** Forges 1095-1084/15W2. Makes own Damascus and powder metal. Fighters, daggers, Bowies; miniatures; hunters, custom canes, liner locks folders. **Technical:** Grinds 440C, 154CM and ATS-34; engraves, carves and embellishes. **Prices:** $500 to $20,000 in gold with gold quartz inlays. **Remarks:** Full-time maker; first knife sold in 1970. **Mark:** First initial, last name, city and state.

SOWELL, BILL,
100 Loraine Forest Ct, Macon, GA 31210, Phone: 478-994-9863, billsowell@reynoldscable.net
Specialties: Antique reproduction Bowies, forging Bowies, hunters, fighters, and most others. Also folders. **Technical:** Makes own Damascus, using 1084/15N20, also making own designs in powder metals, forges 5160-1095-1084, and other carbon steels, grinds ATS-34. **Prices:** Starting at $150 and up. **Remarks:** Part-time maker. Sold first knife in 1998. Does own leather work. **Mark:** Iron Horse Knives; Iron Horse Forge.

SPARKS, BERNARD,
PO Box 73, Dingle, ID 83233, Phone: 208-847-1883, dogknifeii@juno.com; Web: www.sparksknives.com
Specialties: Maker engraved, working and art knives. Straight knives and folders of his own design. **Patterns:** Locking inner-frame folders, hunters, fighters, one-of-a-kind art knives. **Technical:** Grinds 530V steel, 440-C, 154CM, ATS-34, D-2 and forges by special order; triple temper, cryogenic soak. Mirror or hand finish. New Liquid metal steel. **Prices:** $300 to $2000. **Remarks:** Full-time maker, first knife sold in 1967. **Mark:** Last name over state with a knife logo on each end of name. Prior 1980, stamp of last name.

SPENCER, KEITH,
PO Box 149, Chidlow Western Australia, AUSTRALIA 6556, Phone: 61 8 95727255, Fax: 61 8 95727266, spencer@knivesaustralia.com.au
Specialties: Survival & bushcraft bladeware. **Patterns:** Best known for Kakadu Bushcraft knife (since 1989). Leilira mini survival knife (since 1993). **Prices:** $100 to $400 AV. **Mark:** Spencer Australia.

SPICKLER, GREGORY NOBLE,
5614 Mose Cir, Sharpsburg, MD 21782, Phone: 301-432-2746

SPINALE, RICHARD,
4021 Canterbury Ct, Lorain, OH 44053, Phone: 440-282-1565
Specialties: High-art working knives of his design. **Patterns:** Hunters, fighters, daggers and locking folders. **Technical:** Grinds 440C, ATS-34 and 07; engraves. Offers gold bolsters and other deluxe treatments. **Prices:** $300 to $1000; some to $3000. **Remarks:** Spare-time maker; first knife sold in 1976. **Mark:** Name, address, year and model number.

SPIVEY, JEFFERSON,
9244 W Wilshire, Yukon, OK 73099, Phone: 405-721-4442
Specialties: The Saber tooth: a combination hatchet, saw and knife. **Patterns:** Built for the wilderness, all are one-of-a-kind. **Technical:** Grinds chromemoly steel. The saw tooth spine curves with a double row of biangular teeth. **Prices:** Start at $275. **Remarks:** First knife sold in 1977. As of September 2006 Spivey knives has resumed production of the sabertooth knife. **Mark:** Name and serial number.

SPRAGG, WAYNE E,
252 Oregon Ave, Lovell, WY 82431, Phone: 307-548-7212
Specialties: Working straight knives, some fancy. **Patterns:** Folders. **Technical:** Forges carbon steel and makes Damascus. **Prices:** $200 and up. **Remarks:** All stainless heat-treated by Paul Bos. Carbon steel in shop heat treat. **Mark:** Last name front side w/s initials on reverse side.

SPROKHOLT—STEKETEE

SPROKHOLT, ROB,
GATHERWOOD, Burgerweg5, Netherlands, Netherlands 1754KB Burgerbrug, Phone: 0031 6 51230225, Fax: 0031 84 2238446, info@gatherwood.nl; Web: www.gatherwood.nl
Specialties: One-of-a-kind knives. Top materials collector grade, made to use. **Patterns:** Outdoor knives (hunting, sailing, hiking), Bowies, man's surviving companions MSC, big tantos, folding knives. **Technical:** Handles mostly stabilized or oiled wood, ivory, Micarta, carbon fibre, G10. Stiff knives are full tang. Characteristic one row of massive silver pins or tubes. Folding knives have a LinerLock® with titanium or Damascus powdersteel liner thumb can have any stone you like. Stock removal grinder: flat or convex. Steel 440-C, RWL-34, ATS-34, PM damascener steel. **Prices:** Start at 320 euro. **Remarks:** Writer of the first Dutch knifemaking book, supply shop for knife enthusiastic. First knife sold in 2000. **Mark:** Gatherwood in an eclipse etched blade or stamped in an intarsia of silver in the spine.

ST. AMOUR, MURRAY,
RR 3, 222 Dicks Rd, Pembroke ON, CANADA K8A 6W4, Phone: 613-735-1061, knives@webhart.com; Web: www.stamourknives.com
Specialties: Working fixed blades. **Patterns:** Hunters, fish, fighters, Bowies and utility knives. **Technical:** Grinds ATS-34, 154CM, CPM-S-30-Y-60-Y-904 and Damascus. **Prices:** $75 and up. **Remarks:** Full-time maker; sold first knife in 1992. **Mark:** Last name over Canada.

ST. CLAIR, THOMAS K,
12608 Fingerboard Rd, Monrovia, MD 21770, Phone: 301-482-0264

ST. CYR, H RED,
1218 N Cary Ave, Wilmington, CA 90744, Phone: 310-518-9525

STAFFORD, RICHARD,
104 Marcia Ct, Warner Robins, GA 31088, Phone: 912-923-6372
Specialties: High-tech straight knives and some folders. **Patterns:** Hunters in several patterns, fighters, boots, camp knives, combat knives and period pieces. **Technical:** Grinds ATS-34 and 440C; satin finish is standard. **Prices:** Starting at $75. **Remarks:** Part-time maker; first knife sold in 1983. **Mark:** Last name.

STALCUP, EDDIE,
PO Box 2200, Gallup, NM 87305, Phone: 505-863-3107, sstalcup@cnetco.com
Specialties: Working and fancy hunters, bird and trout. Special custom orders. **Patterns:** Drop point hunters, locking liner and multi blade folders. **Technical:** ATS-34, 154 CM, 440C, CPM 154 and S30V. **Prices:** $150 to $1500. **Remarks:** Scrimshaw, exotic handle material, wet formed sheaths. Membership Arizona Knife Collectors Association. Southern California blades collectors & professional knife makers assoc. **Mark:** E.F. Stalcup, Gallup, NM.

STANCER, CHUCK,
62 Hidden Ranch Rd NW, Calgary, AB, CANADA T3A 5S5, Phone: 403-295-7370, stancerc@telusplanet.net
Specialties: Traditional and working straight knives. **Patterns:** Bowies, hunters and utility knives. **Technical:** Forges and grinds most steels. **Prices:** $175 and up. **Remarks:** Part-time maker. **Mark:** Last name.

STANFORD, PERRY,
405N Walnut #9, Broken Arrow, OK 74012, Phone: 918-251-7983 or 866-305-5690, stanfordoutdoors@valornet.com; Web: www.stanfordoutdoors.homestead.com
Specialties: Drop point, hunting and skinning knives, handmade sheaths. **Patterns:** Stright, hunting, and skinners. **Technical:** Grinds 440C, ATS-34 and Damascus. **Prices:** $65 to $275. **Remarks:** Part-time maker, first knife sold in 2007. Knifemaker supplier, manufacturer of paper sharpening systems. Doing business as Stanford Outdoors. **Mark:** Company name and nickname.

STANLEY, JOHN,
604 Elm St, Crossett, AR 71635, Phone: 970-304-3005
Specialties: Hand forged fixed blades with engraving and carving. **Patterns:** Scottish dirks, skeans and fantasy blades. **Technical:** Forge high-carbon steel, own Damascus. Prices $70 to $500. **Remarks:** All work is sole authorship. Offers engraving and carving services on other knives and handles. **Mark:** Varies.

STAPEL, CHUCK,
Box 1617, Glendale, CA 91209, Phone: 213-66-KNIFE, Fax: 213-669-1577, www.stapelknives.com
Specialties: Working knives of his design. **Patterns:** Variety of straight knives, tantos, hunters, folders and utility knives. **Technical:** Grinds D2, 440C and AEB-L. **Prices:** $185 to $12,000. **Remarks:** Full-time maker; first knife sold in 1974. **Mark:** Last name or last name, U.S.A.

STAPLETON, WILLIAM E,
BUFFALO 'B' FORGE, 5425 Country Ln, Merritt Island, FL 32953
Specialties: Classic and traditional knives of his design and customer spec. **Patterns:** Hunters and using knives. **Technical:** Forges, O1 and L6 Damascus, cable Damascus and 5160; stock removal on request. **Prices:** $150 to $1000. **Remarks:** Part-time maker, first knife sold 1990. Doing business as Buffalo "B" Forge. **Mark:** Anvil with S initial in center of anvil.

STECK, VAN R,
260 W Dogwood Ave, Orange City, FL 32763, Phone: 407-416-1723, van@thudknives.com
Specialties: Automatics, underlocks, and my own lock design for frame locks. **Patterns:** From miniatures to swords, Bowies and Asian influence on swords and spears, and tomahawks. **Technical:** Forged and stock removal. Temper lines on carbon blades. Favorite steels: 1080, 5160, 1095. forges damascus also. **Prices:** $75 to $750. **Remarks:** Free hand grinds, distal taper, hollow and chisel. Specialize in double-edged grinds. Voting member of the Knifemakers' Guild. **Mark:** GEISHA with sword & initials and T.H.U.D. knives.

STEFFEN, CHUCK,
504 Dogwood Ave NW, St. Michael, MN, Phone: 763-497-3615
Specialties: Custom hunting knives, fixed blades folders. Specializing in exotic materials. Damascus excellent fit form and finishes.

STEGALL, KEITH,
701 Outlet View Dr, Wasilla, AK 99654, Phone: 907-376-0703, kas5200@yahoo.com
Specialties: Traditional working straight knives. **Patterns:** Most patterns. **Technical:** Grinds 440C and 154CM. **Prices:** $100 to $300. **Remarks:** Spare-time maker; first knife sold in 1987. **Mark:** Name and state with anchor.

STEGNER, WILBUR G,
9242 173rd Ave SW, Rochester, WA 98579, Phone: 360-273-0937, wilbur@wgsk.net; Web: www.wgsk.net
Specialties: Working/using straight knives and folders of his design. **Patterns:** Hunters and locking folders. **Technical:** Grinds ATS-34 and other tool steels. Quenches, tempers and hardness tests each blade. **Prices:** $100 to $1000; some to $5000. **Remarks:** Full-time maker; first knife sold in 1979. Google search key words—"STEGNER KNIVES." **Mark:** First and middle initials, last name in bar over shield logo.

STEIER, DAVID,
7722 Zenith Way, Louisville, KY 40219, Web: www.steierknives.com
Specialties: Folding LinerLocks, Bowies, slip joints, lockbacks, and straight hunters. **Technical:** Stock removal blades of 440C, ATS-34, and Damascus from outside sources like Robert Eggerling and Mike Norris. **Prices:** $150 for straight hunters to $1400 for fully decked-out folders. **Remarks:** First knife sold in 1979. **Mark:** Last name STEIER.

STEIGER, MONTE L,
Box 186, Genesee, ID 83832, Phone: 208-285-1769, montesharon@genesee-id.com
Specialties: Traditional working/using straight knives of all designs. **Patterns:** Hunters, utility/camp knives, fillet and chefs. Carving sets and steak knives. **Technical:** Grinds 1095, O1, 440C, ATS-34. Handles of stacked leather, natural wood, Micarta or pakkawood. Each knife comes with right- or left-handed sheath. **Prices:** $110 to $600. **Remarks:** Spare-time maker; first knife sold in 1988. Retired librarian **Mark:** First initial, last name, city and state.

STEIGERWALT, KEN,
507 Savagehill Rd, Orangeville, PA 17859, Phone: 570-683-5156, Web: www.steigerwaltknives.com
Specialties: Carving on bolsters and handle material. **Patterns:** Folders, button locks and rear locks. **Technical:** Grinds ATS-34, 440C and commercial Damascus. Experiments with unique filework. **Prices:** $500 to $5000. **Remarks:** Full-time maker; first knife sold in 1981. **Mark:** Kasteigerwalt

STEINAU, JURGEN,
Julius-Hart Strasse 44, Berlin 0-1162, GERMANY, Phone: 372-6452512, Fax: 372-645-2512
Specialties: Fantasy and high-art straight knives of his design. **Patterns:** Boots, daggers and switch-blade folders. **Technical:** Grinds 440B, 2379 and X90 Cr.Mo.V. 78. **Prices:** $1500 to $2500; some to $3500. **Remarks:** Full-time maker; first knife sold in 1984. **Mark:** Symbol, plus year, month day and serial number.

STEINBERG, AL,
5244 Duenas, Laguna Woods, CA 92653, Phone: 949-951-2889, lagknife@fea.net
Specialties: Fancy working straight knives to customer specs. **Patterns:** Hunters, Bowies, fishing, camp knives, push knives and high end kitchen knives. **Technical:** Grinds O1, 440C and 154CM. **Prices:** $60 to $2500. **Remarks:** Full-time maker; first knife sold in 1972. **Mark:** Signature, city and state.

STEINBRECHER, MARK W,
1122 92nd Place, Pleasant Prairie, WI 53158-4939
Specialties: Working and fancy folders. **Patterns:** Daggers, pocket knives, fighters and gents of his own design or to customer specs. **Technical:** Hollow grinds ATS-34, O1 other makers Damascus. Uses natural handle materials: stag, ivories, mother-of-pearl. File work and some inlays. **Prices:** $500 to $1200, some to $2500. **Remarks:** Part-time maker, first folder sold in 1989. **Mark:** Name etched or handwritten on ATS-34; stamped on Damascus.

STEKETEE, CRAIG A,
871 NE US Hwy 60, Billings, MO 65610, Phone: 417-744-2770, stekknives04@yahoo.com
Specialties: Classic and working straight knives and swords of his design.

Patterns: Bowies, hunters, and Japanese-style swords. **Technical:** Forges his own Damascus; bronze, silver and Damascus fittings, offers filework. Prefers exotic and natural handle materials. **Prices:** $200 to $4000. **Remarks:** Full-time maker. **Mark:** STEK.

STEPHAN, DANIEL,
2201 S Miller Rd, Valrico, FL 33594, Phone: 727-580-8617, knifemaker@verizon.net
Specialties: Art knives, one-of-a-kind.

STERLING, MURRAY,
693 Round Peak Church Rd, Mount Airy, NC 27030, Phone: 336-352-5110, Fax: Fax: 336-352-5105, sterck@surry.net; Web: www.sterlingcustomknives.com
Specialties: Single and dual blade folders. Interframes and integral dovetail frames. **Technical:** Grinds ATS-34 or Damascus by Mike Norris and/or Devin Thomas. **Prices:** $300 and up. **Remarks:** Full-time maker; first knife sold in 1991. **Mark:** Last name stamped.

STERLING, THOMAS J,
ART KNIVES BY, 120 N Pheasant Run, Coupeville, WA 98239, Phone: 360-678-9269, Fax: 360-678-9269, netsuke@comcast.net; Web: www.bladegallery.com or www.sterlingsculptures.com
Specialties: Since 2003 Tom Sterling and Dr. J.P. Higgins have created a unique collaboration of one-of-a-kind, ultra-quality art knives with percussion or pressured flaked stone blades and creatively sculpted handles. Their knives are often highly influenced by the traditions of Japanese netsuke and unique fusions of cultures, reflecting stylistically integrated choices of exotic hardwoods, fossil ivories and semi-precious materials, contrasting inlays and polychromed and pyrographed details. **Prices:** $300 to $900. **Remarks:** Limited output ensures highest quality artwork and exceptional levels of craftsmanship. **Mark:** Signatures Sterling and Higgins.

STETTER, J. C.,
115 E College Blvd PMB 180, Roswell, NM 88201, Phone: 505-627-0978
Specialties: Fixed and folding. **Patterns:** Traditional and yours. **Technical:** Forged and ground of varied materials including his own pattern welded steel. **Prices:** Start at $250. **Remarks:** Full-time maker, first knife sold 1989. **Mark:** Currently "J.C. Stetter."

STEWART, EDWARD L,
4297 Audrain Rd 335, Mexico, MO 65265, Phone: 573-581-3883
Specialties: Fixed blades, working knives some art. **Patterns:** Hunters, Bowies, utility/camp knives. **Technical:** Forging 1095-W-2-I-6-52100 makes own Damascus. **Prices:** $85 to $500. **Remarks:** Part-time maker first knife sold in 1993. **Mark:** First and last initials-last name.

STEYN, PETER,
PO Box 76, Welkom 9460, Freestate, SOUTH AFRICA, Phone: 27573525201, Fax: 27573523566, Web:www.petersteynknives.com email:info@petersteynknives.com
Specialties: Fixed blade working knives of own design, tendency toward tactical creative & artistic styles all with hand stitched leather sheaths. **Patterns:**Hunters, skinners, fighters & wedge ground daggers. **Technical:** Grinds 12C27, D2, N690. Blades are bead-blasted in plain or camo patterns & own exclusive crator finish. Prefers synthetic handle materials also uses cocobolo & ironwood. **Prices:** $200-$600. **Remarks:**Full time maker, first knife sold 2005, member of South African Guild.**Mark:** Letter 'S' in shape of pyramid with full name above & 'Handcrafted' below.

STIDHAM, DANIEL,
3106 Mill Cr. Rd., Gallipolis, Ohio 45631, Phone: 740-446-1673
Remarks: Since 1961 I have made fixed blades. Folders since 1986. I also sell various knife brands.

STIMPS, JASON M,
374 S Shaffer St, Orange, CA 92866, Phone: 714-744-5866

STIPES, DWIGHT,
2651 SW Buena Vista Dr, Palm City, FL 34990, Phone: 772-597-0550, dwightstipes@adelphia.net
Specialties: Traditional and working straight knives in standard patterns. **Patterns:** Boots, Bowies, daggers, hunters and fighters. **Technical:** Grinds 440C, D2 and D3 tool steel. Handles of natural materials, animal, bone or horn. **Prices:** $75 to $150. **Remarks:** Full-time maker; first knife sold in 1972. **Mark:** Stipes.

STOCKWELL, WALTER,
368 San Carlos Ave, Redwood City, CA 94061, Phone: 650-363-6069, walter@stockwellknives.com; Web: www.stockwellknives.com
Specialties: Scottish dirks, sgian dubhs. **Patterns:** All knives one-of-a-kind. **Technical:** Grinds ATS-34, forges 5160, 52100, L6. **Prices:** $125 to $500. **Remarks:** Part-time maker since 1992; graduate of ABS bladesmithing school. **Mark:** Shooting star over "STOCKWELL." Pre-2000, "WKS."

STODDART, W B BILL,
2357 Mack Rd #105, Fairfield, OH 45014, Phone: 513-851-1543
Specialties: Sportsmen's working knives and multi-blade folders. **Patterns:** Hunters, camp and fish knives; multi-blade reproductions of old standards. **Technical:** Grinds A2, 440C and ATS-34; makes sheaths to match handle materials. **Prices:** $80 to $300; some to $850. **Remarks:** Part-time maker; first knife sold in 1976. **Mark:** Name, Cincinnati, state.

STOKES, ED,
22614 Cardinal Dr, Hockley, TX 77447, Phone: 713-351-1319
Specialties: Working straight knives and folders of all designs. **Patterns:** Boots, Bowies, daggers, fighters, hunters and miniatures. **Technical:** Grinds ATS-34, 440C and D2. Offers decorative butt caps, tapered spacers on handles and finger grooves, nickel-silver inlays, handmade sheaths. **Prices:** $185 to $290; some to $350. **Remarks:** Full-time maker; first knife sold in 1973. **Mark:** First and last name, Custom Knives with Apache logo.

STONE, JERRY,
PO Box 1027, Lytle, TX 78052, Phone: 830-709-3042
Specialties: Traditional working and using folders of his design and to customer specs; fancy knives. **Patterns:** Fighters, hunters, locking folders and slip joints. Also make automatics. **Technical:** Grinds 440C and ATS-34. Offers filework. **Prices:** $175 to $1000. **Remarks:** Full-time maker; first knife sold in 1973. **Mark:** Name over Texas star/town and state underneath.

STORCH, ED,
RR4 Mannville, Alberta T0B 2W0, CANADA, Phone: 780-763-2214, storchkn@agt.net; Web: www.storchknives.com
Specialties: Working knives, fancy fighting knives, kitchen cutlery and art knives. Knifemaking classes. **Patterns:** Working patterns, Bowies and folders. **Technical:** Forges his own Damascus. Grinds ATS-34. Builds friction folders. Salt heat treating. **Prices:** $45 to $750 (U.S.). **Remarks:** Part-time maker; first knife sold in 1984. Hosts annual Northwest Canadian Knifemakers Symposium; 60 to 80 knifemakers and families. **Mark:** Last name.

STORMER, BOB,
34354 Hwy E, Dixon, MO 65459, Phone: 636-734-2693, bs34354@gmail.com
Specialties: Straight knives, using collector grade. **Patterns:** Bowies, skinners, hunters, camp knives. **Technical:** Forges 5160, 1095. **Prices:** $200 to $500. **Remarks:** Part-time maker, ABS Journeyman Smith 2001. **Mark:** Setting sun/fall trees/initials.

STOUT, CHARLES,
RT3 178 Stout Rd, Gillham, AR 71841, Phone: 870-386-5521

STOUT, JOHNNY,
1205 Forest Trail, New Braunfels, TX 78132, Phone: 830-606-4067, johnny@stoutknives.com; Web: www.stoutknives.com
Specialties: Folders, some fixed blades. Working knives, some fancy. **Patterns:** Hunters, tactical, Bowies, automatics, liner locks and slip-joints. **Technical:** Grinds stainless and carbon steels; forges own Damascus. **Prices:** $450 to $895; some to $3500. **Remarks:** Full-time maker; first knife sold in 1983. Hosts semi-annual Guadalupe Forge Hammer-in and Knifemakers Rendezvous. **Mark:** Name and city in logo with serial number.

STOVER, HOWARD,
100 Palmetto Dr Apt 7, Pasadena, CA 91105, Phone: 765-452-3928

STOVER, TERRY "LEE",
1809 N 300 E, Kokomo, IN 46901, Phone: 765-452-3928
Specialties: Damascus folders with filework; Damascus Bowies of his design or to customer specs. **Patterns:** Lockback folders and Sheffield-style Bowies. **Technical:** Forges 1095, Damascus using O2, 203E or O2, pure nickel. Makes mokume. Uses only natural handle material. **Prices:** $300 to $1700; some to $2000. **Remarks:** Part-time maker; first knife sold in 1984. **Mark:** First and middle initials, last name in knife logo; Damascus blades marked in Old English.

STRAIGHT, KENNETH J,
11311 103 Lane N, Largo, FL 33773, Phone: 813-397-9817

STRANDE, POUL,
Soster Svenstrup Byvej 16, Dastrup 4130 Viby Sj., DENMARK, Phone: 46 19 43 05, Fax: 46 19 53 19, Web: www.poulstrande.com
Specialties: Classic fantasy working knives; Damasceret blade, Nikkel Damasceret blade, Lamineret: Lamineret blade with Nikkel. **Patterns:** Bowies, daggers, fighters, hunters and swords. **Technical:** Uses carbon steel and 15C20 steel. **Prices:** NA. **Remarks:** Full-time maker; first knife sold in 1985. **Mark:** First and last initials.

STRAUB, SALEM F.,
324 Cobey Creek Rd., Tonasket, WA 98855, Phone: 509-486-2627, vorpalforge@hotmail.com Web: www.prometheanknives.com
Specialties: Elegant working knives, fixed blade hunters, utility, skinning knives; liner locks. Makes own horsehide sheaths. **Patterns:** A wide range of syles, everything from the gentleman's pocket to the working kitchen, integrals, Bowies, folders, check out my website to see some of my work for ideas. **Technical:** Forges several carbon steels, 52100, W1, etc. Grinds stainless and makes/uses own damascus, cable, san mai, stadard patterns. Likes clay quenching, hamons, hand rubbed finishes. Flat, hollow, or convex grinds. Prefers synthetic handle materials. Hidden and full tapered tangs. **Prices:** $150 - $600, some higher. **Remarks:** Full-time maker. Doing what it takes to make your knife ordering and buying experience positive and enjoyable; striving to exceed expectations. All knives backed by lifetime guarantee. **Mark:** "Straub" stamp or "Promethean Knives" etched. Some older pieces stamped "Vorpal" though no longer using this mark. **Other:** Feel free to call or e-mail anytime. I love to talk knives.

STRICKLAND, DALE,
1440 E Thompson View, Monroe, UT 84754, Phone: 435-896-8362
Specialties: Traditional and working straight knives and folders of his design and to customer specs. **Patterns:** Hunters, folders, miniatures and utility knives. **Technical:** Grinds Damascus and 440C. **Prices:** $120 to $350; some to $500. **Remarks:** Part-time maker; first knife sold in 1991. **Mark:** Oval stamp of name, Maker.

STRIDER, MICK,
STRIDER KNIVES, 120 N Pacific Unit L-7, San Marcos, CA 92069, Phone: 760-471-8275, Fax: 503-218-7069, striderguys@striderknives.com; Web: www.striderknives.com

STRONG, SCOTT,
1599 Beaver Valley Rd, Beavercreek, OH 45434, Phone: 937-426-9290
Specialties: Working knives, some deluxe. **Patterns:** Hunters, fighters, survival and military-style knives, art knives. **Technical:** Forges and grinds O1, A2, D2, 440C and ATS-34. Uses no solder; most knives disassemble. **Prices:** $75 to $450; some to $1500. **Remarks:** Spare-time maker; first knife sold in 1983. **Mark:** Strong Knives.

STROYAN, ERIC,
Box 218, Dalton, PA 18414, Phone: 717-563-2603
Specialties: Classic and working/using straight knives and folders of his design. **Patterns:** Hunters, locking folders, slip-joints. **Technical:** Forges Damascus; grinds ATS-34, D2. **Prices:** $200 to $600; some to $2000. **Remarks:** Part-time maker; first knife sold in 1968. **Mark:** Signature or initials stamp.

STUART, MASON,
24 Beech Street, Mansfield, MA 02048, Phone: 508-339-8236, smasonknives@verizon.net
Specialties: Straight knives of his design, standard patterns. **Patterns:** Bowies, hunters, fighters and neck knives. **Technical:** Forges and grinds. Damascus, 5160, 1095, 1084, old files. Uses only natural handle material. **Prices:** $350 - 2,000. **Remarks:** Part-time maker. **Mark:** First initial and last name.

STUART, STEVE,
Box 168, Gores Landing, Ont., CANADA K0K 2E0, Phone: 905-440-6910, stevestuart@xplornet.com
Specialties: Straight knives. **Patterns:** Tantos, fighters, skinners, file and rasp knives. **Technical:** Uses 440C, CPM154, CPMS30V, Micarta and natural handle materials. **Prices:** $60 to $400. **Remarks:** Part-time maker. **Mark:** SS.

STYREFORS, MATTIAS,
Unbyn 23, SE-96193 Boden, SWEDEN, infor@styrefors.com
Specialties: Damascus and mosaic Damascus. Fixed blade Nordic hunters, folders and swords. **Technical:** Forges, shapes and grinds Damascus and mosaic Damascus from mostly UHB 15N20 and 20C with contrasts in nickel and 15N20. Hardness HR 58. **Prices:** $800 to $3000. **Remarks:** Full-time maker since 1999. International reputation for high end Damascus blades. Uses stabilized Arctic birch and willow burl, horn, fossils, exotic materials, and scrimshaw by Viveca Sahlin for knife handles. Hand tools and hand stitches leather sheaths in cow raw hide. Works in well equipped former military forgery in northern Sweden. **Mark:** MS.

SUEDMEIER, HARLAN,
762 N 60th Rd, Nebraska City, NE 68410, Phone: 402-873-4372
Patterns: Straight knives. **Technical:** Forging hi carbon Damascus. **Prices:** Starting at $175. **Mark:** First initials & last name.

SUGIHARA, KEIDOH,
4-16-1 Kamori-Cho, Kishiwada City, Osaka, F596-0042, JAPAN, Fax: 0724-44-2677
Specialties: High-tech working straight knives and folders of his design. **Patterns:** Bowies, hunters, fighters, fishing, boots, some pocket knives and liner-lock folders. **Technical:** Grinds ATS-34, COS-25, buys Damascus and high-carbon steels. Prices $60 to $4000. **Remarks:** Full-time maker, first knife in 1980. **Mark:** Initial logo with fish design.

SUGIYAMA, EDDY K,
2361 Nagayu, Naoirimachi Naoirigun, Ohita, JAPAN, Phone: 0974-75-2050
Specialties: One-of-a-kind, exotic-style knives. **Patterns:** Working, utility and miniatures. **Technical:** CT rind, ATS-34 and D2. **Prices:** $400 to $1200. **Remarks:** Full-time maker. **Mark:** Name or cedar mark.

SUMMERS, ARTHUR L,
1310 Hess Rd, Concord, NC 28025, Phone: 704-787-9275 Cell: 704-305-0735, arthursummers88@hotmail.com
Specialties: Drop points, clip points, straight blades. **Patterns:** Hunters, Bowies and personal knives. **Technical:** Grinds 440C, ATS-34, D2 and Damascus. **Prices:** $250 to $1000. **Remarks:** Full-time maker; first knife sold in 1987. **Mark:** Serial number is the date.

SUMMERS, DAN,
2675 NY Rt. 11, Whitney Pt., NY 13862, Phone: 607-692-2391, dansumm11@msn.com
Specialties: Period knives and tomahawks. **Technical:** All hand forging. **Prices:** Most $100 to $400.

SUMMERS, DENNIS K,
827 E. Cecil St, Springfield, OH 45503, Phone: 513-324-0624
Specialties: Working/using knives. **Patterns:** Fighters and personal knives. **Technical:** Grinds 440C, A2 and D2. Makes drop and clip point. **Prices:** $75 to $200. **Remarks:** Part-time maker; first knife sold in 1995. **Mark:** First and middle initials, last name, serial number.

SUNDERLAND, RICHARD,
Av Infraganti 23, Col Lazaro Cardenas, Puerto Escondido Oaxaca, MEXICO 71980, Phone: 011 52 94 582 1451, sunamerica@prodigy.net.mx7
Specialties: Personal and hunting knives with carved handles in oosic and ivory. **Patterns:** Hunters, Bowies, daggers, camp and personal knives. **Technical:** Grinds 440C, ATS-34 and O1. Handle materials of rosewoods, fossil mammoth ivory and oosic. **Prices:** $150 to $1000. **Remarks:** Part-time maker; first knife sold in 1983. Doing business as Sun Knife Co. **Mark:** SUN.

SUTTON, S RUSSELL,
4900 Cypress Shores Dr, New Bern, NC 28562, Phone: 252-637-3963, srsutton@suddenlink.net; Web: www.suttoncustomknives.com
Specialties: Straight knives and folders to customer specs and in standard patterns. **Patterns:** Boots, hunters, interframes, slip joints and locking liners. **Technical:** Grinds ATS-34, 440C and stainless Damascus. **Prices:** $220 to $950; some to $1250. **Remarks:** Full-time maker; first knife sold in 1992. **Mark:** Etched last name. **Other:** Engraved bolsters and guards available on some knives by maker.

SWEAZA, DENNIS,
4052 Hwy 321 E, Austin, AR 72007, Phone: 501-941-1886, knives4den@aol.com

SWEENEY, COLTIN D,
1216 S 3 St W, Missoula, MT 59801, Phone: 406-721-6782

SWYHART, ART,
509 Main St, PO Box 267, Klickitat, WA 98628, Phone: 509-369-3451, swyhart@gorge.net; Web: www.knifeoutlet.com/swyhart.htm
Specialties: Traditional working and using knives of his design. **Patterns:** Bowies, hunters and utility/camp knives. **Technical:** Forges 52100, 5160 and Damascus 1084 mixed with either 15N20 or O186. Blades differentially heat-treated with visible temper line. **Prices:** $75 to $250; some to $350. **Remarks:** Part-time maker; first knife sold in 1983. **Mark:** First name, last initial in script.

SYLVESTER, DAVID,
465 Sweede Rd., Compton, Quebec CANADA, Phone: 819-837-0304, david@swedevilleforge.com Web: swedevilleforge.com
Patterns: I hand forge all my knives and I like to make hunters and integrals and some Bowies and fighters. I work with W2, 1084, 1095, and my damascus. **Prices:** $200 - $1500. **Remarks:** Part-time maker. ABS Journeyman Smith. **Mark:** D.Sylvester

SYMONDS, ALBERTO E,
Rambla M Gandhi 485, Apt 901, Montevideo 11300, URUGUAY, Phone: 011 598 5608207, Fax: 011 598 2 7103201, albertosymonds@hotmail.com
Specialties: All kinds including puukos, nice sheaths, leather and wood. **Prices:** $300 to $2200. **Mark:** AESH and current year.

SYSLO, CHUCK,
3418 South 116 Ave, Omaha, NE 68144, Phone: 402-333-0647, ciscoknives@cox.net
Specialties: Hunters, working knives, daggers & misc. **Patterns:** Hunters, daggers and survival knives; locking folders. **Technical:** Flat-grinds D2, 440C and 154CM; hand polishes only. **Prices:** $250 to $1000; some to $3000. **Remarks:** Part-time maker; first knife sold in 1978. Uses many natural materials. **Mark:** CISCO in logo.

SZAREK, MARK G,
94 Oakwood Ave, Revere, MA 02151, Phone: 781-289-7102
Specialties: Classic period working and using straight knives and tools. **Patterns:** Hunting knives, American and Japanese woodworking tools. **Technical:** Forges 5160, 1050, Damascus; differentially hardens blades with fireclay. **Prices:** $50 to $750. **Remarks:** Part-time maker; first knife sold in 1989. Produces Japanese alloys for sword fittings and accessories. Custom builds knife presentation boxes and cabinets. **Mark:** Last name.

SZILASKI, JOSEPH,
52 Woods Dr, Pine Plains, NY 12567, Phone: 518-398-0309, Web: www.szilaski.com
Specialties: Straight knives, folders and tomahawks of his design, to customer specs and in standard patterns. Many pieces are one-of-a-kind. **Patterns:** Bowies, daggers, fighters, hunters, art knives and early American-styles. **Technical:** Forges A2, D2, O1 and Damascus. **Prices:** $450 to $4000; some to $10,000. **Remarks:** Full-time maker; first knife sold in 1990. ABS Master Smith and voting member KMG. **Mark:** Snake logo.

T

TABOR, TIM,
18925 Crooked Lane, Lutz, FL 33548, Phone: 813-948-6141, taborknives.com
Specialties: Fancy folders, Damascus Bowies and hunters. **Patterns:** My own design folders & customer requests. **Technical:** ATS-34, hand forged Damascus, 1084, 15N20 mosaic Damascus, 1095, 5160 high carbon

blades, flat grind, file work & jewel embellishments. **Prices:** $175 to $1500. **Remarks:** Part-time maker, sold first knife in 2003. **Mark:** Last name.

TAKACH, ANDREW,
1390 Fallen Timber Rd., Elizabeth, PA 15037, Phone: 724-691-2271, a-takach@takachforge.com; Web: www.takachforge.com
Specialties: One-of-a-kind fixed blade working knives (own design or customer's). Mostly all fileworked. **Patterns:** Hunters, skinners, caping, fighters, and designs of own style. **Technical:** Forges mostly 5160, 1090, 01, in a down pattern welded Damascus, nickle Damascus, and cable and various chain Damascus. Also do some San Mai. **Prices:** $100 to $350, some over $550. **Remarks:** Doing business as Takach Forge. First knife sold in 2004. **Mark:** Takach (stamped).

TAKAHASHI, MASAO,
39-3 Sekine-machi, Maebashi-shi, Gunma 371 0047, JAPAN, Phone: 81 27 234 2223, Fax: 81 27 234 2223
Specialties: Working straight knives. **Patterns:** Daggers, fighters, hunters, fishing knives, boots. **Technical:** Grinds ATS-34 and Damascus. **Prices:** $350 to $1000 and up. **Remarks:** Full-time maker; first knife sold in 1982. **Mark:** M. Takahashi.

TALLY, GRANT,
26961 James Ave, Flat Rock, MI 48134, Phone: 734-789-8961
Specialties: Straight knives and folders of his design. **Patterns:** Bowies, daggers, fighters. **Technical:** Grinds ATS-34, 440C and D2. Offers filework. **Prices:** $250 to $1000. **Remarks:** Part-time maker; first knife sold in 1985. Doing business as Tally Knives. **Mark:** Tally (last name).

TAMBOLI, MICHAEL,
12447 N 49 Ave, Glendale, AZ 85304, Phone: 602-978-4308, mnbtamboli@gmail.com
Specialties: Miniatures, some full size. **Patterns:** Miniature hunting knives to fantasy art knives. **Technical:** Grinds ATS-34 & Damascus. **Prices:** $75 to $500; some to $2000. **Remarks:** Full time maker; first knife sold in 1978. **Mark:** Initials, last name, last name city and state, MT Custom Knives or Mike Tamboli in Japanese script.

TASMAN, KERLEY,
9 Avignon Retreat, Pt Kennedy 6172, Western Australia, AUSTRALIA, Phone: 61 8 9593 0554, Fax: 61 8 9593 0554, taskerley@optusnet.com.au
Specialties: Knife/harness/sheath systems for elite military personnel and body guards. **Patterns:** Utility/tactical knives, hunters small game and presentation grade knives. **Technical:** ATS-34 and 440C, Damascus, flat and hollow grids. **Prices:** $200 to $1800 U.S. **Remarks:** Will take presentation grade commissions. Multi award winning maker and custom jeweler. **Mark:** Maker's initials.

TAYLOR, BILLY,
10 Temple Rd, Petal, MS 39465, Phone: 601-544-0041
Specialties: Straight knives of his design. **Patterns:** Bowies, skinners, hunters and utility knives. **Technical:** Flat-grinds 440C, ATS-34 and 154CM. **Prices:** $60 to $300. **Remarks:** Part-time maker; first knife sold in 1991. **Mark:** Full name, city and state.

TAYLOR, C GRAY,
560 Poteat Ln, Fall Branch, TN 37656, Phone: 423-348-8304, graysknives@aol.com or graysknives@hotmail.com; Web: www.cgraytaylor.net
Specialties: Traditonal multi-blade lobster folders, also art display Bowies and daggers. **Patterns:** Orange Blossom, sleeveboard and gunstocks. **Technical:** Grinds. **Prices:** Upscale. **Remarks:** Full-time maker; first knife sold in 1975. **Mark:** Name, city and state.

TAYLOR, DAVID,
113 Stewart Hill Dr, Rogersville, TN 37857, Phone: 423-921-0733, dtaylor0730@charter.net; Web: www.dtguitars.com
Patterns: Multi-blade folders, traditional patterns. **Technical:** Grinds ATS-34. **Prices:** $400 and up. **Remarks:** First sold knife in 1981 at age 14. Became a member of Knifemakers Guild at age 14. Made first folder in 1983. Full-time pastor of Baptist Church and part-time knifemaker.

TAYLOR, SHANE,
42 Broken Bow Ln, Miles City, MT 59301, Phone: 406-234-7175, shane@taylorknives.com; Web: www.taylorknives.com
Specialties: One-of-a-kind fancy Damascus straight knives and folders. **Patterns:** Bowies, folders and fighters. **Technical:** Forges own mosaic and pattern welded Damascus. **Prices:** $450 and up. **Remarks:** ABS Master Smith, full-time maker; first knife sold in 1982. **Mark:** First name.

TERAUCHI, TOSHIYUKI,
7649-13 219-11 Yoshida, Fujita-Cho Gobo-Shi, JAPAN

TERRILL, STEPHEN,
16357 Goat Ranch Rd, Springville, CA 93265, Phone: 559-539-3116, slterrill@yahoo.com
Specialties: Deluxe working straight knives and folders. **Patterns:** Fighters, tantos, boots, locking folders and axes; traditional oriental patterns. **Technical:** Forges 1095, 5160, Damascus, stock removal ATS-34. **Prices:** $300+. **Remarks:** Full-time maker; first knife sold in 1972. **Mark:** Name, city, state in logo.

TERZUOLA, ROBERT,
10121 Eagle Rock NE, Albuquerque, NM 87122, Phone: 505-473-1002, Fax: 505-438-8018, terzuola@earthlink.net
Specialties: Working folders of his design; period pieces. **Patterns:** High-tech utility, defense and gentleman's folders. **Technical:** Grinds CPM154, Damascus, and CPM S30V. Offers titanium, carbon fiber and G10 composite for side-lock folders and tactical folders. **Prices:** $550 to $2000. **Remarks:** Full-time maker; first knife sold in 1980. **Mark:** Mayan dragon head, name.

THAYER, DANNY O,
8908S 100W, Romney, IN 47981, Phone: 765-538-3105, dot61h@juno.com
Specialties: Hunters, fighters, Bowies. **Prices:** $250 and up.

THEIS, TERRY,
21452 FM 2093, Harper, TX 78631, Phone: 830-864-4438
Specialties: All European and American engraving styles. **Prices:** $200 to $2000. **Remarks:** Engraver only.

THEVENOT, JEAN-PAUL,
16 Rue De La Prefecture, Dijon, FRANCE 21000
Specialties: Traditional European knives and daggers. **Patterns:** Hunters, utility-camp knives, daggers, historical or modern style. **Technical:** Forges own Damascus, 5160, 1084. **Remarks:** Part-time maker. ABS Master Smith. **Mark:** Interlocked initials in square.

THIE, BRIAN,
13250 150th St, Burlington, IA 52601, Phone: 319-985-2276, bkthie@mepotelco.net; Web: www.mepotelco.net/web/tknives
Specialties: Working using knives from basic to fancy. **Patterns:** Hunters, fighters, camp and folders. **Technical:** Forges blades and own Damascus. **Prices:** $100 and up. **Remarks:** ABS Journeyman Smith, part-time maker. Sole author of blades including forging, heat treat, engraving and sheath making. **Mark:** Last name hand engraved into the blade, JS stamped into blade.

THILL, JIM,
10242 Bear Run, Missoula, MT 59803, Phone: 406-251-5475
Specialties: Traditional and working/using knives of his design. **Patterns:** Fighters, hunters and utility/camp knives. **Technical:** Grinds D2 and ATS-34; forges 10-95-85, 52100, 5160, 10 series, reg. Damascus-mosaic. Offers hand cut sheaths with rawhide lace. **Prices:** $145 to $350; some to $1250. **Remarks:** Full-time maker; first knife sold in 1962. **Mark:** Running bear in triangle.

THOMAS, DAVID E,
8502 Hwy 91, Lillian, AL 36549, Phone: 251-961-7574, redbluff@gulftel.com
Specialties: Bowies and hunters. **Technical:** Hand forged blades in 5160, 1095 and own Damascus. **Prices:** $400 and up. **Mark:** Stylized DT, maker's last name, serial number.

THOMAS, DEVIN,
PO Box 568, Panaca, NV 89042, Phone: 775-728-4363, hoss@devinthomas.com; Web: www.devinthomas.com
Specialties: Traditional straight knives and folders in standard patterns. **Patterns:** Bowies, fighters, hunters. **Technical:** Forges stainless Damascus, nickel and 1095. Uses, makes and sells mokume with brass, copper and nickel-silver. **Prices:** $300 to $1200. **Remarks:** Full-time maker; first knife sold in 1979. **Mark:** First and last name, city and state with anvil, or first name only.

THOMAS, KIM,
PO Box 531, Seville, OH 44273, Phone: 330-769-9906
Specialties: Fancy and traditional straight knives of his design and to customer specs; period pieces. **Patterns:** Boots, daggers, fighters, swords. **Technical:** Forges own Damascus from 5160, 1010 and nickel. **Prices:** $135 to $1500; some to $3000. **Remarks:** Part-time maker; first knife sold in 1986. Doing business as Thomas Iron Works. **Mark:** KT.

THOMAS, ROCKY,
1716 Waterside Blvd, Moncks Corner, SC 29461, Phone: 843-761-7761
Specialties: Traditional working knives in standard patterns. **Patterns:** Hunters and utility/camp knives. **Technical:** ATS-34 and commercial Damascus. **Prices:** $130 to $350. **Remarks:** Spare-time maker; first knife sold in 1986. **Mark:** First name in script and/or block.

THOMPSON, KENNETH,
4887 Glenwhite Dr, Duluth, GA 30136, Phone: 770-446-6730
Specialties: Traditional working and using knives of his design. **Patterns:** Hunters, Bowies and utility/camp knives. **Technical:** Forges 5168, O1, 1095 and 52100. **Prices:** $75 to $1500; some to $2500. **Remarks:** Part-time maker; first knife sold in 1990. **Mark:** P/W; or name, P/W, city and state.

THOMPSON, LEON,
45723 SW Saddleback Dr, Gaston, OR 97119, Phone: 503-357-2573
Specialties: Working knives. **Patterns:** Locking folders, slip-joints and liner locks. **Technical:** Grinds ATS-34, D2 and 440C. **Prices:** $200 to $600. **Remarks:** Full-time maker; first knife sold in 1976. **Mark:** First and middle initials, last name, city and state.

THOMPSON, LLOYD,
PO Box 1664, Pagosa Springs, CO 81147, Phone: 970-264-5837
Specialties: Working and collectible straight knives and folders of his design. Patterns: Straight blades, lock back folders and slip joint folders. Technical: Hollow-grinds ATS-34, D2 and O1. Uses sambar stag and exotic woods. Prices: $150 to upscale. Remarks: Full-time maker; first knife sold in 1985. Doing business as Trapper Creek Knife Co. Remarks: Offers three-day knife-making classes. Mark: Name.

THOMPSON, TOMMY,
4015 NE Hassalo, Portland, OR 97232-2607, Phone: 503-235-5762
Specialties: Fancy and working knives; mostly liner-lock folders. Patterns: Fighters, hunters and liner locks. Technical: Grinds D2, ATS-34, CPM440V and T15. Handles are either hardwood inlaid with wood banding and stone or shell, or made of agate, jasper, petrified woods, etc. Prices: $75 to $500; some to $1000. Remarks: Part-time maker; first knife sold in 1987. Doing business as Stone Birds. Knife making temporarily stopped due to family obligations. Mark: First and last name, city and state.

THOMSEN, LOYD W,
30173 Black Banks Rd, Oelrichs, SD 57763, Phone: 605-535-6162, loydt@yahoo.com; Web: horseheadcreekknives.com
Specialties: High-art and traditional working/using straight knives and presentation pieces of his design and to customer specs; period pieces. Hand carved animals in crown of stag on handles and carved display stands. Patterns: Bowies, hunters, daggers and utility/camp knives. Technical: Forges and grinds 1095HC, 1084, L6, 15N20, 440C stainless steel, nickel 200; special restoration process on period pieces. Makes sheaths. Uses natural materials for handles. Prices: $350 to $1000. Remarks: Full-time maker; first knife sold in 1995. Doing business as Horsehead Creek Knives. Mark: Initials and last name over a horse's head.

THORBURN, ANDRE E.,
P.O. Box 1748, Bela Bela, Warmbaths 0480, SOUTH AFRICA, Phone: 27-82-650-1441, thorburn@icon.co.za; Web: www.thorburnknives.com
Specialties: Working and fancy folders of own design to customer specs. Technical: Uses RWL34, 12C27, 19C27, D2, Carbon and stainless Damascus. Prices: Starting at $350. Remarks: Full-time maker since 1996, first knife sold in 1990. Member of American Knifemakers Guild and South African, Italian, and German guilds; chairman of Knifemakers Guild of South Africa. Mark: Initials and name in a double circle.

THOUROT, MICHAEL W,
T-814 Co Rd 11, Napoleon, OH 43545, Phone: 419-533-6832, Fax: 419-533-3516, mike2row@henry-net.com; Web: wwwsafariknives.com
Specialties: Working straight knives to customer specs. Designed two-handled skinning ax and limited edition engraved knife and art print set. Patterns: Fishing and fillet knives, Bowies, tantos and hunters. Technical: Grinds O1, D2, 440C and Damascus. Prices: $200 to $5000. Remarks: Part-time maker; first knife sold in 1968. Mark: Initials.

THUESEN, ED,
21211 Knolle Rd, Damon, TX 77430, Phone: 979-553-1211, Fax: 979-553-1211
Specialties: Working straight knives. Patterns: Hunters, fighters and survival knives. Technical: Grinds D2, 440C, ATS-34 and Vascowear. Prices: $150 to $275; some to $600. Remarks: Part-time maker; first knife sold in 1979. Runs knifemaker supply business. Mark: Last name in script.

TICHBOURNE, GEORGE,
7035 Maxwell Rd #5, Mississauga, Ont., CANADA L5S 1R5, Phone: 905-670-0200, sales @tichbourneknives.com; Web: www.tichbourneknives.com
Specialties: Traditional working and using knives as well as unique collectibles. Patterns: Bowies, hunters, outdoor, kitchen, integrals, art, military, Scottish dirks, folders, kosher knives. Technical: Stock removal 440C, Stellite 6K, stainless Damascus. Handle materials include mammoth, meteorite, mother-of-pearl, precious gems, mosiac, abalone, stag, Micarta, exotic high resin woods and corian scrimshawed by George. Leather sheaths are hand stitched and tooled by George as well as the silver adornments for the dirk sheaths. Prices: $60 up to $5000 U.S. Remarks: Full-time maker with his OWN STORE. First knife sold in 1990. Mark: Full name over maple leaf.

TIENSVOLD, ALAN L,
PO Box 355, Rushville, NE 69360, Phone: 308-327-2046
Specialties: Working knives, tomahawks and period pieces, high end Damascus knives. Patterns: Random, ladder, twist and many more. Technical: Hand forged blades, forges own Damascus. Prices: Working knives start at $300. Remarks: Received Journeyman rating with the ABS in 2002. Does own engraving and fine work. Mark: Tiensvold hand made U.S.A. on left side, JS on right.

TIENSVOLD, JASON,
PO Box 795, Rushville, NE 69360, Phone: 308-327-2046, ironprik@gpcom.net
Specialties: Working and using straight knives of his design; period pieces. Gentlemen folders, art folders. Single action automatics. Patterns: Hunters, skinners, Bowies, fighters, daggers, liner locks. Technical: Forges own Damascus using 15N20 and 1084, 1095, nickel, custom file work. Prices: $200 to $4000. Remarks: Full-time maker, first knife sold in 1994; doing business under Tiensvold Custom Knives. Mark: J. Tiensvold.

TIGHE, BRIAN,
12-111 Fourth Ave, Suite 376 Ridley Square, St. Catharines, Ont., CANADA L0S 1M0, Phone: 905-892-2734, Fax: 905-892-2734, Web: www.tigheknives.com
Specialties: High tech tactical folders. Patterns: Boots, daggers, locking and slip-joint folders. Technical: CPM 440V and CPM 420V. Prefers natural handle material inlay; hand finishes. Prices: $450 to $2000. Remarks: Part-time maker; first knife sold in 1989. Mark: Etched signature.

TILL, CALVIN E AND RUTH,
211 Chaping, Chadron, NE 69337
Specialties: Straight knives, hunters, Bowies; no folders Patterns: Training point, drop point hunters, Bowies. Technical: ATS-34 sub zero quench RC59, 61. Prices: $700 to $1200. Remarks: Sells only the absolute best knives they can make. Manufactures every part in their knives. Mark: RC Till. The R is for Ruth.

TILTON, JOHN,
24041 Hwy 383, Iowa, LA 70647, Phone: 337-582-6785, john@jetknives.com
Specialties: Bowies, camp knives, skinners and folders. Technical: All forged blades. Makes own Damascus. Prices: $150 and up. Remarks: ABS Journeyman Smith. Mark: Initials J.E.T.

TINDERA, GEORGE,
BURNING RIVER FORGE, 751 Hadcock Rd, Brunswick, OH 44212-2648, Phone: 330-220-6212
Specialties: Straight knives; his designs. Patterns: Personal knives; classic Bowies and fighters. Technical: Hand-forged high-carbon; his own cable and pattern welded Damascus. Prices: $125 to $600. Remarks: Spare-time maker; sold first knife in 1995. Natural handle materials.

TINGLE, DENNIS P,
19390 E Clinton Rd, Jackson, CA 95642, Phone: 209-223-4586, dtknives@earthlink.net
Specialties: Swords, fixed blades: small to medium, tomahawks. Technical: All blades forged. Remarks: ABS, JS. Mark: D. Tingle over JS.

TIPPETTS, COLTEN,
4068 W Miners Farm Dr, Hidden Springs, ID 83714, Phone: 208-229-7772, coltentippetts@gmail.com
Specialties: Fancy and working straight knives and fancy locking folders of his own design or to customer specifications. Patterns: Hunters and skinners, fighters and utility. Technical: Grinds BG-42, high-carbon 1095 and Damascus. Prices: $200 to $1000. Remarks: Part-time maker; first knife sold in 1996. Mark: Fused initials.

TKOMA, FLAVIO,
R Manoel Rainho Teixeira 108-Pres, Prudonte SP19031-220, BRAZIL, Phone: 0182-22-0115, fikoma@itelesonica.com.br
Specialties: Tactical fixed blade knives, LinerLock® folders and balisongs. Patterns: Utility and defense tactical knives built with hi-tech materials. Technical: Grinds S30V and Damasteel. Prices: $500 to $1000. Mark: Ikoma hand made beside Samurai

TODD, RICHARD C,
375th LN 46001, Chambersburg, IL 62323, Phone: 217-327-4380, ktodd45@yahoo.com
Specialties: Multi blade folders and silver sheaths. Patterns: Jewel setting and hand engraving. Mark: RT with letter R crossing the T or R Todd.

TOICH, NEVIO,
Via Pisacane 9, Rettorgole di Caldogna, Vincenza, ITALY 36030, Phone: 0444-985065, Fax: 0444-301254
Specialties: Working/using straight knives of his design or to customer specs. Patterns: Bowies, hunters, skinners and utility/camp knives. Technical: Grinds 440C, D2 and ATS-34. Hollow-grinds all blades and uses mirror polish. Offers hand-sewn sheaths. Uses wood and horn. Prices: $120 to $300; some to $450. Remarks: Spare-time maker; first knife sold in 1989. Doing business as Custom Toich. Mark: Initials and model number punched.

TOKAR, DANIEL,
Box 1776, Shepherdstown, WV 25443
Specialties: Working knives; period pieces. Patterns: Hunters, camp knives, buckskinners, axes, swords and battle gear. Technical: Forges L6, 1095 and his Damascus; makes mokume, Japanese alloys and bronze daggers; restores old edged weapons. Prices: $25 to $800; some to $3000. Remarks: Part-time maker; first knife sold in 1979. Doing business as The Willow Forge. Mark: Arrow over rune and date.

TOLLEFSON, BARRY A,
104 Sutter Pl, PO Box 4198, Tubac, AZ 85646, Phone: 520-398-9327
Specialties: Working straight knives, some fancy. Patterns: Hunters, skinners, fighters and camp knives. Technical: Grinds 440C, ATS-34 and D2. Likes mirror-finishes; offers some fancy filework. Handles made from elk, deer and exotic hardwoods. Prices: $75 to $300; some higher. Remarks: Part-time maker; first knife sold in 1990. Mark: Stylized initials.

TOMBERLIN, BRION R,
ANVIL TOP CUSTOM KNIVES, 825 W Timberdell, Norman, OK 73072, Phone: 405-202-6832, anviltopp@aol.com
Specialties: Hand forged blades, working pieces, standard classic patterns, some swords, and customer designs. Patterns: Bowies, hunters,

fighters, Persian and eastern-styles. Likes Japanese blades. **Technical:** Forge 1050, 1075, 1084, 1095, 5160, some forged stainless, also do some stock removal in stainless. Also makes own damascus. **Prices:** Start at $275 up to $2000 or higher for swords and custom pieces. **Remarks:** Part-time maker, Mastersmith America Bladesmith Society. Prefers natural handle materials, hand rubbed finishes. Likes temperlines. **Mark:** BRION with MS.

TOMES, P J,
594 High Peak Ln, Shipman, VA 22971, Phone: 434-263-8662, tomgsknives@juno.com; Web: www.tomesknives.com
Specialties: Scagel reproductions. **Patterns:** Front-lock folders. **Technical:** Forges 52100. **Prices:** $150 to $750. **Mark:** Last name, USA, MS, stamped in forged blades.

TOMEY, KATHLEEN,
146 Buford Pl, Macon, GA 31204, Phone: 478-746-8454, ktomey@tomeycustomknives.com; Web: www.tomeycustomknives.com
Specialties: Working hunters, skinners, daily users in fixed blades, plain and embellished. Tactical neck and belt carry. Japanese influenced. Bowies. **Technical:** Grinds O1, ATS-34, flat or hollow grind, filework, satin and mirror polish finishes. High quality leather sheaths with tooling. Kydex with tactical. **Prices:** $150 to $500. **Remarks:** Almost full-time maker. **Mark:** Last name in diamond.

TOMPKINS, DAN,
PO Box 398, Peotone, IL 60468, Phone: 708-258-3620
Specialties: Working knives, some deluxe, some folders. **Patterns:** Hunters, boots, daggers and push knives. **Technical:** Grinds D2, 440C, ATS-34 and 154CM. **Prices:** $85 to $150; some to $400. **Remarks:** Part-time maker; first knife sold in 1975. **Mark:** Last name, city, state.

TONER, ROGER,
531 Lightfoot Pl, Pickering, Ont., CANADA L1V 5Z8, Phone: 905-420-5555
Specialties: Exotic sword canes. **Patterns:** Bowies, daggers and fighters. **Technical:** Grinds 440C, D2 and Damascus. Scrimshaws and engraves. Silver cast pommels and guards in animal shapes; twisted silver wire inlays. Uses semi-precious stones. **Prices:** $200 to $2000; some to $3000. **Remarks:** Part-time maker; first knife sold in 1982. **Mark:** Last name.

TORGESON, SAMUEL L,
25 Alpine Ln, Sedona, AZ 86336-6809

TORRES, HENRY,
2329 Moody Ave., Clovis, CA 93619, Phone: 559-297-9154, Web: www.htknives.com
Specialties: Forged high-performance hunters and working knives, Bowies, and fighters. **Technical:** 52100 and 5160 and makes own Damascus. **Prices:** $350 to $3000. **Remarks:** Started forging in 2004. Has mastersmith with American Bladesmith Association.

TOSHIFUMI, KURAMOTO,
3435 Higashioda, Asakura-gun, Fukuoka, JAPAN, Phone: 0946-42-4470

TOWELL, DWIGHT L,
2375 Towell Rd, Midvale, ID 83645, Phone: 208-355-2419
Specialties: Solid, elegant working knives; art knives, high quality hand engraving and gold inlay. **Patterns:** Hunters, Bowies, daggers and folders. **Technical:** Grinds 154CM, ATS-34, 440C and other maker's Damascus. **Prices:** Upscale. **Remarks:** Full-time maker. First knife sold in 1970. Member of AKI. **Mark:** Towell, sometimes hand engraved.

TOWNSEND, ALLEN MARK,
6 Pine Trail, Texarkana, AR 71854, Phone: 870-772-8945

TOWNSLEY, RUSSELL,
PO BOX 185, Concord, AR 72523, Phone: 870-307-8069, townsley.jackie@yahoo.com
Specialties: Using knives of his own design. **Patterns:** Hunters, skinners, folders. **Technical:** Hollow grinds D2 and O1. Handle material - antler, tusk, bone, exotic woods. **Prices:** Prices start at $125. **Remarks:** Arkansas knifemakers association. Sold first knife in 2009. **Mark:** Circle T.

TRACE RINALDI CUSTOM BLADES,
28305 California Ave, Hemet, CA 92545, Phone: 951-926-5422, Trace@thrblades.com; Web: www.thrblades.com
Technical: Grinds S30V, 3V, A2 and talonite fixed blades. **Prices:** $300-$1000. **Remarks:** Tactical and utility for the most part. **Mark:** Diamond with THR inside.

TRACY, BUD,
495 Flanders Rd, Reno, NV 8951-4784

TREIBER, LEON,
PO Box 342, Ingram, TX 78025, Phone: 830-367-2246, treiberknives@hotmail.com; Web: www.treiberknives.com
Specialties: Folders of his design and to customer specs. **Patterns:** Fixed blades. **Technical:** Grinds CPM-T-440V, D2, 440C, Damascus, 420V and ATS-34. **Prices:** $350 to $3500. **Remarks:** Part-time maker; first knife sold in 1992. Doing business as Treiber Knives. **Mark:** First initial, last name, city, state.

TREML, GLENN,
RR #14 Site 12-10, Thunder Bay, Ont., CANADA P7B 5E5, Phone: 807-767-1977
Specialties: Working straight knives of his design and to customer specs.

Patterns: Hunters, kitchen knives and double-edged survival knives. **Technical:** Grinds 440C, ATS-34 and O1; stock removal method. Uses various woods and Micarta for handle material. **Prices:** $150 and up. **Mark:** Stamped last name.

TRINDLE, BARRY,
1660 Ironwood Trail, Earlham, IA 50072-8611, Phone: 515-462-1237
Specialties: Engraved folders. **Patterns:** Mostly small folders, classical-styles and pocket knives. **Technical:** 440 only. Engraves. Handles of wood or mineral material. **Prices:** Start at $1000. **Mark:** Name on tang.

TRISLER, KENNETH W,
6256 Federal 80, Rayville, LA 71269, Phone: 318-728-5541

TRITZ, JEAN JOSE,
Schopstrasse 23, 20255 Hamburg, GERMANY, Phone: 040-49 78 21
Specialties: Scandinavian knives, Japanese kitchen knives, friction folders, swords. **Patterns:** Puukkos, Tollekniven, Hocho, friction folders, swords. **Technical:** Forges tool steels, carbon steels, 52100 Damascus, mokume, San Maj. **Prices:** $200 to $2000; some higher. **Remarks:** Full-time maker; first knife sold in 1989. Does own leatherwork, prefers natural materials. Sole authorship. Speaks French, German, English, Norwegian. **Mark:** Initials in monogram.

TRUJILLO, ALBERT M B,
2035 Wasmer Cir, Bosque Farms, NM 87068, Phone: 505-869-0428, trujilloscutups@comcast.net
Specialties: Working/using straight knives of his design or to customer specs. **Patterns:** Hunters, skinners, fighters, working/using knives. File work offered. **Technical:** Grinds ATS-34, D2, 440C, S30V. Tapers tangs, all blades cryogenically treated. **Prices:** $75 to $500. **Remarks:** Part-time maker; first knife sold in 1997. **Mark:** First and last name under logo.

TRUJILLO, MIRANDA,
6366 Commerce Blvd, Rohnert Park, CA 94928
Specialties: Working/using straight knives of her design. **Patterns:** Hunters and utility/camp knives. **Technical:** Grinds ATS-34 and 440C. Sheaths are water resistant. **Prices:** $145 - $400; some to $600. **Remarks:** Spare-time maker; first knife sold in 1989. Doing business as Alaska Knife and Service Co. **Mark:** NA.

TRUNCALI, PETE,
2914 Anatole Court, Garland, TX 75043, Phone: 214-763-7127, truncaliknives@yahoo.com Web:www.truncaliknives.com
Specialties: Lockback folders, locking liner folders, automatics and fixed blades. Does business as Truncali Custom Knives.

TSCHAGER, REINHARD,
Piazza Parrocchia 7, I-39100 Bolzano, ITALY, Phone: 0471-970642, Fax: 0471-970642, goldtschager@dnet.it
Specialties: Classic, high-art, collector-grade straight knives of his design. **Patterns:** Jewel knife, daggers, and hunters. **Technical:** Grinds ATS-34, D2 and Damascus. Oval pins. Gold inlay. Offers engraving. **Prices:** $900 to $2000; some to $3000. **Remarks:** Spare-time maker; first knife sold in 1979. **Mark:** Gold inlay stamped with initials.

TUOMINEN, PEKKA,
Pohjois-Keiteleentie 20, 72930 Tossavanlahti, FINLAND, Phone: 358405167853, puukkopekka@luukku.com; Web: www.puukkopekka.com
Specialties: Puukko knives. **Patterns:** Puukkos, hunters, leukus, and folders. **Technical:** Forges silversteel, 1085, 52100, and makes own Damascus 15N20 and 1095. Grinds RWL-34 and ATS-34. **Prices:** Starting at $170. **Remarks:** Part-time maker. **Mark:** Name.

TURCOTTE, LARRY,
1707 Evergreen, Pampa, TX 79065, Phone: 806-665-9369, 806-669-0435
Specialties: Fancy and working/using knives of his design and to customer specs. **Patterns:** Hunters, kitchen knives, utility/camp knives. **Technical:** Grinds 440C, D2, ATS-34. Engraves, scrimshaws, silver inlays. **Prices:** $150 to $350; some to $1000. **Remarks:** Part-time maker; first knife sold in 1977. Doing business as Knives by Turcotte. **Mark:** Last name.

TURECEK, JIM,
12 Elliott Rd, Ansonia, CT 06401, Phone: 203-734-8406
Specialties: Exotic folders, art knives and some miniatures. **Patterns:** Trout and bird knives with split bamboo handles and one-of-a-kind folders. **Technical:** Grinds and forges stainless and carbon Damascus. **Prices:** $750 to $1500; some to $3000. **Remarks:** Full-time maker; first knife sold in 1983. **Mark:** Last initial in script, or last name.

TURNBULL, RALPH A,
14464 Linden Dr, Spring Hill, FL 34609, Phone: 352-688-7089, tbull2000@bellsouth.net; Web: www.turnbullknives.com
Specialties: Fancy folders. **Patterns:** Primarily gents pocket knives. **Technical:** Wire EDM work on bolsters. **Prices:** $300 and up. **Remarks:** Full-time maker; first knife sold in 1973. **Mark:** Signature or initials.

TURNER, KEVIN,
17 Hunt Ave, Montrose, NY 10548, Phone: 914-739-0535
Specialties: Working straight knives of his design and to customer specs; period pieces. **Patterns:** Daggers, fighters and utility knives. **Technical:** Forges 5160 and 52100. **Prices:** $90 to $500. **Remarks:** Part-time maker; first knife sold in 1991. **Mark:** Acid-etched signed last name and year.

TURNER, MIKE,
PO BOX 196, Williams, OR 97544, Phone: 541-846-0204, mike@turnerknives.com
Specialties: Forged and stock removed full tang, hidden and thru tang knives. **Patterns:** Hunters, fighters, Bowies, boot knives, skinners and kitchen knives. **Technical:** I make my own damascus. **Prices:** $200 - $1,000. **Remarks:** Part-time maker, sold my first knife in 2008, doing business as Mike Turner Custom Knives. **Mark:** Name, City, & State.

TYCER, ART,
117 Callaway Ln., Meridianville, AL 35759-1503, Phone: 256-829-1442
Specialties: Fancy working/using straight knives of his design, to customer specs and standard patterns. **Patterns:** Boots, Bowies, daggers, fighters, hunters, kitchen and utility knives. **Technical:** Grinds ATS-34, 440C and a variety of carbon steels. Uses exotic woods with spacer material, stag and water buffalo. Offers filework. **Prices:** $175 and up depending on size and embellishments or Damascus. **Remarks:** Now making folders (liner locks). Making and using his own Damascus and other Damascus also. Full-time maker. **Mark:** Flying "T" over first initial inside an oval.

TYRE, MICHAEL A,
1219 Easy St, Wickenburg, AZ 85390, Phone: 928-684-9601/602-377-8432, michaeltyre@msn.com
Specialties: Quality folding knives upscale gents folders one-of-a-kind collectable models. **Patterns:** Working fixed blades for hunting, kitchen and fancy Bowies. **Technical:** Grinds prefer hand rubbed satin finishes and use natural handle materials. **Prices:** $250 to $1300.

TYSER, ROSS,
1015 Hardee Court, Spartanburg, SC 29303, Phone: 864-585-7616
Specialties: Traditional working and using straight knives and folders of his design and in standard patterns. **Patterns:** Bowies, hunters and slip-joint folders. **Technical:** Grinds 440C and commercial Damascus. Mosaic pins; stone inlay. Does filework and scrimshaw. Offers engraving and cut-work and some inlay on sheaths. **Prices:** $45 to $125; some to $400. **Remarks:** Part-time maker; first knife sold in 1995. Doing business as RT Custom Knives. **Mark:** Stylized initials.

U

UCHIDA, CHIMATA,
977-2 Oaza Naga Shisui Ki, Kumamoto, JAPAN 861-1204

V

VAGNINO, MICHAEL,
PO Box 67, Visalia, CA 93279, Phone: 559-636-0501, mvknives@lightspeed.net; Web: www.mvknives.com
Specialties: Folders and straight knives, working and fancy. **Patterns:** Folders--locking liners, slip joints, lock backs, double and single action autos. Straight knives--hunters, Bowies, camp and kitchen. **Technical:** Forges 52100, W2, 15N20 and 1084. Grinds stainless. Makes own damascus and does engraving. **Prices:** $275 to $4000 and above. **Remarks:** Full-time maker, ABS Mastersmith. **Mark:** Logo, last name.

VAIL, DAVE,
554 Sloop Point Rd, Hampstead, NC 28443, Phone: 910-270-4456
Specialties: Working/using straight knives of his own design or to the customer's specs. **Patterns:** Hunters/skinners, camp/utility, fillet, Bowies. **Technical:** Grinds ATS-34, 440c, 154 CM and 1095 carbon steel. **Prices:** $90 to $450. **Remarks:** Part-time maker. Member of NC Custom Knifemakers Guild. **Mark:** Etched oval with "Dave Vail Hampstead NC" inside.

VALLOTTON, BUTCH and AREY,
621 Fawn Ridge Dr, Oakland, OR 97462, Phone: 541-459-2216, Fax: 541-459-7473
Specialties: Quick opening knives w/complicated mechanisms. **Patterns:** Tactical, fancy, working, and some art knives. **Technical:** Grinds all steels, uses others' Damascus. Uses Spectrum Metal. **Prices:** From $350 to $4500. **Remarks:** Full-time maker since 1984; first knife sold in 1981. Co/designer, Applegate Fairbarn folding w/Bill Harsey. **Mark:** Name w/viper head in the "V."

VALLOTTON, RAINY D,
1295 Wolf Valley Dr, Umpqua, OR 97486, Phone: 541-459-0465
Specialties: Folders, one-handed openers and art pieces. **Patterns:** All patterns. **Technical:** Stock removal all steels; uses titanium liners and bolsters; uses all finishes. **Prices:** $350 to $3500. **Remarks:** Full-time maker. **Mark:** Name.

VALLOTTON, SHAWN,
621 Fawn Ridge Dr, Oakland, OR 97462, Phone: 503-459-2216
Specialties: Left-hand knives. **Patterns:** All styles. **Technical:** Grinds 440C, ATS-34 and Damascus. Uses titanium. Prefers bead-blasted or anodized finishes. **Prices:** $250 to $1400. **Remarks:** Full-time maker. **Mark:** Name and specialty.

VALLOTTON, THOMAS,
621 Fawn Ridge Dr, Oakland, OR 97462, Phone: 541-459-2216
Specialties: Custom autos. **Patterns:** Tactical, fancy. **Technical:** File work, uses Damascus, uses Spectrum Metal. **Prices:** From $350 to $700. **Remarks:** Full-time maker. Maker of Protégé 3 canoe. **Mark:** T and a V mingled.

VALOIS, A. DANIEL,
3552 W Lizard Ck Rd, Lehighton, PA 18235, Phone: 717-386-3636
Specialties: Big working knives; various sized lock-back folders with new safety releases. **Patterns:** Fighters in survival packs, sturdy working knives, belt buckle knives, military-style knives, swords. **Technical:** Forges and grinds A2, O1 and 440C; likes full tangs. **Prices:** $65 to $240; some to $600. **Remarks:** Full-time maker; first knife sold in 1969. **Mark:** Anvil logo with last name inside.

VAN CLEVE, STEVE,
Box 372, Sutton, AK 99674, Phone: 907-745-3038

VAN DE MANAKKER, THIJS,
Koolweg 34, 5759 px Helenaveen, HOLLAND, Phone: 0493539369
Specialties: Classic high-art knives. **Patterns:** Swords, utility/camp knives and period pieces. **Technical:** Forges soft iron, carbon steel and Bloomery Iron. Makes own Damascus, Bloomery Iron and patterns. **Prices:** $20 to $2000; some higher. **Remarks:** Full-time maker; first knife sold in 1969. **Mark:** Stylized "V."

VAN DEN ELSEN, GERT,
Purcelldreef 83, 5012 AJ Tilburg, NETHERLANDS, Phone: 013-4563200, gvdelsen@home.nl
Specialties: Fancy, working/using, miniatures and integral straight knives of the maker's design or to customer specs. **Patterns:** Bowies, fighters, hunters and Japanese-style blades. **Technical:** Grinds ATS-34 and 440C; forges Damascus. Offers filework, differentially tempered blades and some mokume-gane fittings. **Prices:** $350 to $1000; some to $4000. **Remarks:** Part-time maker; first knife sold in 1982. Doing business as G-E Knives. **Mark:** Initials GE in lozenge shape.

VAN DER WESTHUIZEN, PETER,
PO Box 1698, Mossel Bay 6500, SOUTH AFRICA, Phone: 27 446952388, pietvdw@telkomsa.net
Specialties: Working knives, folders, daggers and art knives. **Patterns:** Hunters, skinners, bird, trout and sidelock folders. **Technical:** Sandvik, 12627. Damascus indigenous wood and ivory. **Prices:** From $450 to $5500. **Remarks:** First knife sold in 1987. Full-time since 1996. **Mark:** Initial & surname. Handmade RSA.

VAN DIJK, RICHARD,
76 Stepney Ave Rd 2, Harwood Dunedin, NEW ZEALAND, Phone: 0064-3-4780401, Web: www.hoihoknives.com
Specialties: Damascus, Fantasy knives, sgiandubhs, dirks, swords, and hunting knives. **Patterns:** Mostly one-ofs, anything from bird and trout to swords, no folders. **Technical:** Forges mainly own Damascus, some 5160, O1, 1095, L6. Prefers natural handle materials, over 35 years experience as goldsmith, handle fittings are often made from sterling silver and sometimes gold, manufactured to cap the handle, use gemstones if required. Makes own sheaths. **Prices:** $300 and up. **Remarks:** Full-time maker, first knife sold in 1980. Doing business as HOIHO KNIVES. **Mark:** Stylized initials RvD in triangle.

VAN EIZENGA, JERRY W,
14281 Cleveland, Nunica, MI 49448, Phone: 616-638-2275
Specialties: Hand forged blades, Scagel patterns and other styles. **Patterns:** Camp, hunting, bird, trout, folders, axes, miniatures. **Technical:** 5160, 52100, 1084. **Prices:** Start at $250. **Remarks:** Part-time maker, sole author of knife and sheath. First knife made 1970s. ABS member who believes in the beauty of simplicity. **Mark:** J.S. stamp.

VAN ELDIK, FRANS,
Ho Flaan 3, 3632BT Loenen, NETHERLANDS, Phone: 0031 294 233 095, Fax: 0031 294 233 095
Specialties: Fancy collector-grade straight knives and folders of his design. **Patterns:** Hunters, fighters, boots and folders. **Technical:** Forges and grinds D2, 154CM, ATS-34 and stainless Damascus. **Prices:** Start at $450. **Remarks:** Spare-time maker; first knife sold in 1979. Knifemaker 30 years, 25 year member of Knifemakers Guild. **Mark:** Lion with name and Amsterdam.

VAN HEERDEN, ANDRE,
P.O. Box 905-417, Garsfontein, Pretoria, SOUTH AFRICA 0042, Phone: 27 82 566 6030, andrevh@iafrica.com; Web: www.andrevanheerden.com
Specialties: Fancy and working folders of his design to customer specs. **Technical:** Grinds RWL34, 19C27, D2, carbon and stainless Damascus. **Prices:** Starting at $350. **Remarks:** Part-time maker, first knife sold in 2003. **Mark:** Initials and name in a double circle.

VAN REENEN, IAN,
6003 Harvard St, Amarillo, TX 79109, Phone: 806-236-8333, ianvanreenen@suddenlink.net Web:www.ianvanreenenknives.com
Specialties: Slipjoints, single and double blades. **Patterns:** Trappers, peanuts, saddle horn trappers. **Technical:** ATS-34 and CPM 154. **Prices:** $360 to $700. **Remarks:** Specializing in slipjoints. **Mark:** VAN REENEN and IVR with TEXAS underneath.

VAN RIJSWIJK, AAD,
AVR KNIVES, Werf Van Pronk 8, 3134 HE Vlaardingen, NETHERLANDS, Phone: +31 10 2343227, Fax: +31 10 2343648, info@avrknives.com; Web: www.avrknives.com
Specialties: High-art interframe folders of his design and in shaving sets. **Patterns:** Hunters and locking folders. **Technical:** Uses semi-precious

stones, mammoth, ivory, walrus ivory, iron wood. **Prices:** $550 to $3800. **Remarks:** Full-time maker; first knife sold in 1993. **Mark:** NA.

VANDERFORD, CARL G,
2290 Knob Creek Rd, Columbia, TN 38401, Phone: 931-381-1488
Specialties: Traditional working straight knives and folders of his design. **Patterns:** Hunters, Bowies and locking folders. **Technical:** Forges and grinds 440C, O1 and wire Damascus. **Prices:** $60 to $125. **Remarks:** Part-time maker; first knife sold in 1987. **Mark:** Last name.

VANDERKOLFF, STEPHEN,
5 Jonathan Crescent, Mildmay Ontario, CANADA N0g 2JO, Phone: 519-367-3401, steve@vanderkolffknives.com; Web: www.vanderkolffknives.com
Specialties: Fixed blades from gent's pocketknives and drop hunters to full sized Bowies and art knives. **Technical:** Primary blade steel 440C, Damasteel or custom made Damascus. All heat treat done by maker and all blades hardness tested. Handle material: stag, stabilized woods or MOP. **Prices:** $150 to $1200. **Remarks:** Started making knives in 1998 and sold first knife in 2000. Winner of the best of show art knife 2005 Wolverine Knife Show.

VANDEVENTER, TERRY L,
3274 Davis Rd, Terry, MS 39170-8719, Phone: 601-371-7414, tvandeventer@comcast.net
Specialties: Bowies, hunters, camp knives, friction folders. **Technical:** 1084, 1095, 15N20 and L6 steels. Damascus and mokume. Natural handle materials. **Prices:** $350 to $2500. **Remarks:** Sole author; makes everything here. First ABS MS from the state of Mississippi. **Mark:** T.L. Vandeventer (silhouette of snake underneath). MS on ricasso.

VANHOY, ED AND TANYA,
24255 N Fork River Rd, Abingdon, VA 24210, Phone: 276-944-4885, vanhoyknives@hughes.net
Specialties: Traditional and working/using straight knives of his design, make folders. **Patterns:** Fighters, straight knives, folders, hunters and art knives. **Technical:** Grinds ATS-34 and 440V; forges D2. Offers filework, engraves, acid etching, mosaic pins, decorative bolsters and custom fitted English bridle leather sheaths. **Prices:** $250 to $3000. **Remarks:** Full-time maker; first knife sold in 1977. Wife also engraves. Doing business as Van Hoy Custom Knives. **Mark:** Acid etched last name.

VARDAMAN, ROBERT,
2406 Mimosa Lane, Hattiesburg, MS 39402, Phone: 601-268-3889, rv7x@comcast.net
Specialties: Working straight knives of his design or to customer specs. **Patterns:** Bowies, hunters, skinners, utility and camp knives. **Technical:** Forges 52100, 5160, 1084 and 1095. Filework. **Prices:** $100 to $500. **Remarks:** Part-time maker. First knife sold in 2004. **Mark:** Last name, last name with Mississippi state logo.

VASQUEZ, JOHNNY DAVID,
1552 7th St, Wyandotte, MI 48192, Phone: 734-281-2455

VAUGHAN, IAN,
351 Doe Run Rd, Manheim, PA 17545-9368, Phone: 717-665-6949

VEIT, MICHAEL,
3289 E Fifth Rd, LaSalle, IL 61301, Phone: 815-223-3538, whitebear@starband.net
Specialties: Damascus folders. **Technical:** Engraver, sole author. **Prices:** $2500 to $6500. **Remarks:** Part-time maker; first knife sold in 1985. **Mark:** Name in script.

VELARDE, RICARDO,
7240 N Greenfield Dr, Park City, UT 84098, Phone: 435-901-1773, velardeknives.com
Specialties: Investment grade integrals and interframs. **Patterns:** Boots, fighters and hunters; hollow grind. **Technical:** BG on Integrals. **Prices:** $1450 to $5200. **Remarks:** First knife sold in 1992. **Mark:** First initial, last name on blade; city, state, U.S.A. at bottom of tang.

VELICK, SAMMY,
3457 Maplewood Ave, Los Angeles, CA 90066, Phone: 310-663-6170, metaltamer@gmail.com
Specialties: Working knives and art pieces. **Patterns:** Hunter, utility and fantasy. **Technical:** Stock removal and forges. **Prices:** $100 and up. **Mark:** Last name.

VENSILD, HENRIK,
Gl Estrup, Randersvei 4, DK-8963 Auning, DENMARK, Phone: +45 86 48 44 48
Specialties: Classic and traditional working and using knives of his design; Scandinavian influence. **Patterns:** Hunters and using knives. **Technical:** Forges Damascus. Hand makes handles, sheaths and blades. **Prices:** $350 to $1000. **Remarks:** Part-time maker; first knife sold in 1967. **Mark:** Initials.

VESTAL, CHARLES,
26662 Shortsville Rd., Abingdon, VA 24210, Phone: 276-492-3262, charles@vestalknives.com; Web: www.vestalknives.com
Specialties: Hunters and double ground fighters in traditional designs and own designs. **Technical:** Grinds CPM-154, ATS-134, 154-CM and other steels. **Prices:** $300 to $1000, some higher. **Remarks:** First knife sold in 1995.

VIALLON, HENRI,
Les Belins, 63300 Thiers, FRANCE, Phone: 04-73-80-24-03, Fax: 04 73-51-02-02
Specialties: Folders and complex Damascus **Patterns:** His draws. **Technical:** Forge. **Prices:** $1000 to $5000. **Mark:** H. Viallon.

VICKERS, DAVID,
11620 Kingford Dr., Montgomery, TX 77316, Phone: 936-537-4900, jdvickers@gmail.com
Specialties: Working/using blade knives especially for hunters. His design or to customer specs. **Patterns:** Hunters, skinners, camp/utility. **Technical:** Grinds ATS-34, 440C, and D-2. Uses stag, various woods, and micarta for handle material. Hand-stitched sheaths. **Remark:** Full-time maker. **Prices:** $125 - $350. **Mark:** VICKERS

VIELE, H J,
88 Lexington Ave, Westwood, NJ 07675, Phone: 201-666-2906, h.viele@verizon.net
Specialties: Folding knives of distinctive shapes. **Patterns:** High-tech folders and one-of-a-kind. **Technical:** Grinds ATS-34 and S30V. **Prices:** Start at $575. **Remarks:** Full-time maker; first knife sold in 1973. **Mark:** Japanese design for the god of war.

VIKING KNIVES (SEE JAMES THORLIEF ERIKSEN),

VILAR, RICARDO AUGUSTO FERREIRA,
Rua Alemada Dos Jasmins NO 243, Parque Petropolis, Mairipora Sao Paulo, BRAZIL 07600-000, Phone: 011-55-11-44-85-43-46, ricardovilar@ig.com.br.
Specialties: Traditional Brazilian-style working knives of the Sao Paulo state. **Patterns:** Fighters, hunters, utility, and camp knives, welcome customer design. Specialize in the "true" Brazilian camp knife "Soracabana." **Technical:** Forges only with sledge hammer to 100 percent shape in 5160 and 52100 and his own Damascus steels. Makes own sheaths in the "true" traditional "Paulista"-style of the state of Sao Paulo. **Remark:** Full-time maker. **Prices:** $250 to $600. Uses only natural handle materials. **Mark:** Special designed signature styled name R. Vilar.

VILLA, LUIZ,
R. Com. Miguel Calfat, 398 Itaim Bibi, Sao Paulo, SP-04537-081, BRAZIL, Phone: 011-8290649
Specialties: One-of-a-kind straight knives and jewel knives of all designs. **Patterns:** Bowies, hunters, utility/camp knives and jewel knives. **Technical:** Grinds D6, Damascus and 440C; forges 5160. Prefers natural handle material. **Prices:** $70 to $200. **Remarks:** Part-time maker; first knife sold in 1990. **Mark:** Last name and serial number.

VILLAR, RICARDO,
Al. dos Jasmins 243 Mairipora, S.P. 07600-000, BRAZIL, Phone: 011-4851649
Specialties: Straight working knives to customer specs. **Patterns:** Bowies, fighters and utility/camp knives. **Technical:** Grinds D6, ATS-34 and 440C stainless. **Prices:** $80 to $200. **Remarks:** Part-time maker; first knife sold in 1993. **Mark:** Percor over sword and circle.

VINING, BILL,
9 Penny Lane, Methuen, MA 01844, Phone: 978-688-4729, billv@medawebs.com; Web: www.medawebs.com/knives
Specialties Liner locking folders. Slip joints & lockbacks. **Patterns:** Likes to make patterns of his own design. **Technical:** S30V, 440C, ATS-34. Damascus from various makers. **Prices:** $450 and up. **Remarks:** Part-time maker. **Mark:** VINING or B. Vining.

VISTE, JAMES,
EDGE WISE FORGE, 13401 Mt Elliot, Detroit, MI 48212, Phone: 313-664-7455, grumblejunky@hotmail.com
Mark: EWF touch mark.

VISTNES, TOR,
N-6930 Svelgen, NORWAY, Phone: 047-57795572
Specialties: Traditional and working knives of his design. **Patterns:** Hunters and utility knives. **Technical:** Grinds Uddeholm Elmax. Handles made of rear burls of different Nordic stabilized woods. **Prices:** $300 to $1100. **Remarks:** Part-time maker; first knife sold in 1988. **Mark:** Etched name and deer head.

VITALE, MACE,
925 Rt 80, Guilford, CT 06437, Phone: 203-457-5591, Web: www.laurelrockforge.com
Specialties: Hand forged blades. **Patterns:** Hunters, utility, chef, Bowies and fighters. **Technical:** W2, 1095, 1084, L6. Hand forged and finished. **Prices:** $100 to $1000. **Remarks:** American Bladesmith Society, Journeyman Smith. Full-time maker; first knife sold 2001. **Mark:** MACE.

VOGT, DONALD J,
9007 Hogans Bend, Tampa, FL 33647, Phone: 813-973-3245, vogtknives@verizon.net
Specialties: Art knives, folders, automatics. **Technical:** Uses Damascus steels for blade and bolsters, filework, hand carving on blade bolsters and handles. Other materials used: jewels, gold, mother-of-pearl, gold-lip pearl, black-lip pearl, ivory. **Prices:** $4,000 to $10,000. **Remarks:** Part-time maker; first knife sold in 1997. **Mark:** Last name.

VOGT, PATRIK,
Kungsvagen 83, S-30270 Halmstad, SWEDEN, Phone: 46-35-30977
  Specialties: Working straight knives. **Patterns:** Bowies, hunters and fighters. **Technical:** Forges carbon steel and own Damascus. **Prices:** From $100. **Remarks:** Not currently making knives. **Mark:** Initials or last name.

VOORHIES, LES,
14511 Lk Mazaska Tr, Faribault, MN 55021, Phone: 507-332-0736, lesvor@msn.com; Web: www.lesvoorhiesknives.com
  Specialties: Steels. **Patterns:** Liner locks & autos. **Technical:** ATS-34 Damascus. **Prices:** $250 to $1200. **Mark:** L. Voorhies.

VOSS, BEN,
2212 Knox Rd. 1600 Rd. E, Victoria, IL 61485-9644, Phone: 309-879-2940
  Specialties: Fancy working knives of his design. **Patterns:** Bowies, fighters, hunters, boots and folders. **Technical:** Grinds 440C, ATS-34 and D2. **Prices:** $35 to $1200. **Remarks:** Part-time maker; first knife sold in 1986. **Mark:** Name, city and state.

VOTAW, DAVID P,
305 S State St, Pioneer, OH 43554, Phone: 419-737-2774
  Specialties: Working knives; period pieces. **Patterns:** Hunters, Bowies, camp knives, buckskinners and tomahawks. **Technical:** Grinds O1 and D2. **Prices:** $100 to $200; some to $500. **Remarks:** Part-time maker; took over for the late W.K. Kneubuhler. Doing business as W-K Knives. **Mark:** WK with V inside anvil.

W

WADA, YASUTAKA,
2-6-22 Fujinokidai, Nara City, Nara prefect 631-0044, JAPAN, Phone: 0742 46-0689
  Specialties: Fancy and embellished one-of-a-kind straight knives of his design. **Patterns:** Bowies, daggers and hunters. **Technical:** Grinds ATS-34. **Prices:** $400 to $2500; some higher. **Remarks:** Part-time maker; first knife sold in 1990. **Mark:** Owl eyes with initial and last name underneath or last name.

WAGAMAN, JOHN K,
107 E Railroad St, Selma, NC 27576, Phone: 919-965-9659, Fax: 919-965-9901
  Specialties: Fancy working knives. **Patterns:** Bowies, miniatures, hunters, fighters and boots. **Technical:** Grinds D2, 440C, 154CM and commercial Damascus; inlays mother-of-pearl. **Prices:** $110 to $2000. **Remarks:** Part-time maker; first knife sold in 1975. **Mark:** Last name.

WAITES, RICHARD L,
PO Box 188, Broomfield, CO 80038, Phone: 303-465-9970, Fax: 303-465-9971, dickknives@aol.com
  Specialties: Working fixed blade knives of all kinds including "paddle blade" skinners. Hand crafted sheaths, some upscale and unusual. **Technical:** Grinds 440C, ATS 34, D2. **Prices:** $100 to $500. **Remarks:** Part-time maker. First knife sold in 1998. Doing business as R.L. Waites Knives. **Mark:** Oval etch with first and middle initial and last name on top and city and state on bottom. Memberships; Professional Knifemakers Association and Rocky Mountain Blade Collectors Club.

WALKER, BILL,
431 Walker Rd, Stevensville, MD 21666, Phone: 410-643-5041

WALKER, DON,
2850 Halls Chapel Rd, Burnsville, NC 28714, Phone: 828-675-9716, dlwalkernc@aol.com

WALKER, JIM,
22 Walker Ln, Morrilton, AR 72110, Phone: 501-354-3175, jwalker46@att.net
  Specialties: Period pieces and working/using knives of his design and to customer specs. **Patterns:** Bowies, fighters, hunters, camp knives. **Technical:** Forges 5160, O1, L6, 52100, 1084, 1095. **Prices:** Start at $450. **Remarks:** Full-time maker; first knife sold in 1993. **Mark:** Three arrows with last name/MS.

WALKER, JOHN W,
10620 Moss Branch Rd, Bon Aqua, TN 37025, Phone: 931-670-4754
  Specialties: Straight knives, daggers and folders; sterling rings, 14K gold wire wrap; some stone setting. **Patterns:** Hunters, boot knives, others. **Technical:** Grinds 440C, ATS-34, L6, etc. Buys Damascus. **Prices:** $150 to $500 some to $1500. **Remarks:** Part-time maker; first knife sold in 1982. **Mark:** Hohenzollern Eagle with name, or last name.

WALKER, MICHAEL L,
925-A Paseo del, Pueblo Sur Taos, NM 87571, Phone: 505-751-3409, Fax: 505-751-3417, metalwerkr@msn.com
  Specialties: Innovative knife designs and locking systems; titanium and SS furniture and art. **Patterns:** Folders from utility grade to museum quality art; others upon request. **Technical:** State-of-the-art materials: titanium, stainless Damascus, gold, etc. **Prices:** $3500 and above. **Remarks:** Designer/MetalCrafts; full-time professional knifemaker since 1980; four U.S. patents; invented LinerLock® and was awarded registered U.S. trademark no. 1,585,333. **Mark:** Early mark MW, Walker's Lockers by M.L. Walker; current M.L. Walker or Michael Walker.

WALLINGFORD JR., CHARLES W,
9024 Old Union Rd, Union, KY 41091, Phone: 859-384-4141, Web: www.cwknives.com
  Specialties: 18th and 19th century styles, patch knives, rifleman knives. **Technical:** 1084 and 5160 forged blades. **Prices:** $125 to $300. **Mark:** CW.

WALTERS, A F,
PO Box 523, 275 Crawley Rd., TyTy, GA 31795, Phone: 229-528-6207
  Specialties: Working knives, some to customer specs. **Patterns:** Locking folders, straight hunters, fishing and survival knives. **Technical:** Grinds D2, 154CM and 13C26. **Prices:** Start at $200. **Remarks:** Part-time maker. Label: "The jewel knife." **Mark:** "J" in diamond and knife logo.

WARD, CHUCK,
PO Box 2272, 1010 E North St, Benton, AR 72018-2272, Phone: 501-778-4329, chuckbop@aol.com
  Specialties: Traditional working and using straight knives and folders of his design. **Technical:** Grinds 440C, D2, A2, ATS-34 and O1; uses natural and composite handle materials. **Prices:** $90 to $400, some higher. **Remarks:** Part-time maker; first knife sold in 1990. **Mark:** First initial, last name.

WARD, J J,
7501 S R 220, Waverly, OH 45690, Phone: 614-947-5328
  Specialties: Traditional and working/using straight knives and folders of his design. **Patterns:** Hunters and locking folders. **Technical:** Grinds ATS-34, 440C and Damascus. Offers handmade sheaths. **Prices:** $125 to $250; some to $500. **Remarks:** Spare-time maker; first knife sold in 1980. **Mark:** Etched name.

WARD, KEN,
1125 Lee Roze Ln, Grants Pass, OR 97527, Phone: 541-956-8864
  Specialties: Working knives, some to customer specs. **Patterns:** Straight, axes, Bowies, buckskinners and miniatures. **Technical:** Grinds ATS-34, Damascus. **Prices:** $100 to $700. **Remarks:** Part-time maker; first knife sold in 1977. **Mark:** Name.

WARD, RON,
1363 Nicholas Dr, Loveland, OH 45140, Phone: 513-722-0602
  Specialties: Classic working and using straight knives, fantasy knives. **Patterns:** Bowies, hunter, fighters, and utility/camp knives. **Technical:** Grinds 440C, 154CM, ATS-34, uses composite and natural handle materials. **Prices:** $50 to $750. **Remarks:** Part-time maker, first knife sold in 1992. Doing business as Ron Ward Blades. **Mark:** Ron Ward Blades, Loveland OH.

WARD, W C,
817 Glenn St, Clinton, TN 37716, Phone: 615-457-3568
  Specialties: Working straight knives; period pieces. **Patterns:** Hunters, Bowies, swords and kitchen cutlery. **Technical:** Grinds O1. **Prices:** $85 to $150; some to $500. **Remarks:** Part-time maker; first knife sold in 1969. He styled the Tennessee Knife Maker. **Mark:** TKM.

WARDELL, MICK,
20 Clovelly Rd, Bideford, N Devon EX39 3BU, ENGLAND, Phone: 01237 475312, wardellknives@hotmail.co.uk Web: www.wardellscustomknives.com
  Specialties: Folders of his design. **Patterns:** Locking and slip-joint folders, Bowies. **Technical:** Grinds stainless Damascus, S30V and RWL34. Heat-treats. **Prices:** $300 to $2500. **Remarks:** Full-time maker; first knife sold in 1986. **Mark:** M. Wardell - England.

WARDEN, ROY A,
275 Tanglewood Rd, Union, MO 63084, Phone: 314-583-8813, rwarden@yhti.net
  Specialties: Complex mosaic designs of "EDM wired figures" and "stack up" patterns and "lazer cut" and "torch cut" and "sawed" patterns combined. **Patterns:** Mostly "all mosaic" folders, automatics, fixed blades. **Technical:** Mosaic Damascus with all tool steel edges. **Prices:** $100 to $1000. **Remarks:** Part-time maker; first knife sold in 1987. **Mark:** WARDEN stamped or initials connected.

WARE, TOMMY,
158 Idlewilde, Onalaska, TX 77360, Phone: 936-646-4649
  Specialties: Traditional working and using straight knives, folders and automatics of his design and to customer specs. **Patterns:** Hunters, automatics and locking folders. **Technical:** Grinds ATS-34, 440C and D2. Offers engraving and scrimshaw. **Prices:** $425 to $650; some to $1500. **Remarks:** Full-time maker; first knife sold in 1990. Doing business as Wano Knives. **Mark:** Last name inside oval, business name above, city and state below, year on side.

WARREN, AL,
1423 Sante Fe Circle, Roseville, CA 95678, Phone: 916-784-3217/Cell phone 916-257-5904, Fax: 215-318-2945, al@warrenknives.com; Web: www.warrenknives.com
  Specialties: Working straight knives and folders, some fancy. **Patterns:** Hunters, Bowies, fillets, lockback, folders & multi blade. **Technical:** Grinds ATS-34 and S30V.440V. **Prices:** $135 to $3200. **Remarks:** Part-time maker; first knife sold in 1978. **Mark:** First and middle initials, last name.

WARREN, DANIEL,
571 Lovejoy Rd, Canton, NC 28716, Phone: 828-648-7351
Specialties: Using knives. **Patterns:** Drop point hunters. **Prices:** $200 to $500. **Mark:** Warren-Bethel NC.

WARREN (SEE DELLANA), DELLANA,

WASHBURN, ARTHUR D,
ADW CUSTOM KNIVES, 211 Hinman St / PO Box 625, Pioche, NV 89043, Phone: 775-962-5463, awashburn@adwcustomknives.com; Web: www.adwcustomknives.com
Specialties: Locking liner folders. **Patterns:** Slip joint folders (single and multiplied), lock-back folders, some fixed blades. Do own heat-treating; Rockwell test each blade. **Technical:** Carbon and stainless Damascus, some 1084, 1095, ATS-34, 154CM and S30V. Makes own two color Mokum. **Prices:** $200 to $1000 and up. **Remarks:** Sold first knife in 1997. Part-time maker. **Mark:** ADW enclosed in an oval or ADW.

WASHBURN JR., ROBERT LEE,
1162 West Diamond Valley Drive, St George, UT 847700, Phone: 435-619-4432, Fax: 435-574-8554, rlwashburn@excite.com; Web:www.washburnknives.com
Specialties: Hand-forged period, Bowies, tactical, boot and hunters. **Patterns:** Bowies, tantos, loot hunters, tactical and folders. **Prices:** $100 to $2500. **Remarks:** All hand forged. 52100 being his favorite steel. **Mark:** Washburn Knives W.

WATANABE, MELVIN,
1297 Kika St., Kailua, HI 96734, Phone: 808-261-2842, meltod808@yahoo.com
Specialties: Fancy folding knives. Some hunters. **Patterns:** Liner-locks and hunters. **Technical:** Grinds ATS-34, stainless Damascus. **Prices:** $350 and up. **Remarks:** Part-time maker, first knife sold in 1985. **Mark:** Name and state.

WATANABE, WAYNE,
PO Box 3563, Montebello, CA 90640, wwknives@gmail.com; Web: www.geocities.com/ww-knives
Specialties: Straight knives in Japanese-styles. One-of-a-kind designs; welcomes customer designs. **Patterns:** Tantos to katanas, Bowies. **Technical:** Flat grinds A2, O1 and ATS-34. Offers hand-rubbed finishes and wrapped handles. **Prices:** Start at $200. **Remarks:** Part-time maker. **Mark:** Name in characters with flower.

WATERS, GLENN,
11 Shinakawa Machi, Hirosaki City 036-8183, JAPAN, Phone: 172-33-8881, gwaters@luck.ocn.ne.jp; Web: www.glennwaters.com
Specialties: One-of-a-kind collector-grade highly embellished art knives. Folders, fixed blades, and automatics. **Patterns:** Locking liner folders, automatics and fixed art knives. **Technical:** Grinds blades from Damasteel, and selected Damascus makers, mostly stainless. Does own engraving, gold inlaying and stone setting, filework, and carving. Gold and Japanese precious metal fabrication. Prefers exotic material, high karat gold, silver, Shyaku Dou, Shibu Ichi Gin, precious gemstones. **Prices:** Upscale. **Remarks:** Designs and makes some-of-a-kind highly embellished art knives often with fully engraved handles and blades. A jeweler by trade for 20 years before starting to make knives. Full-time since 1999, first knife sold in 1994. **Mark:** Glenn Waters maker Japan, G. Waters or Glen in Japanese writing.

WATERS, HERMAN HAROLD,
2516 Regency, Magnolia, AR 71753, Phone: 870-234-5409

WATERS, LU,
2516 Regency, Magnolia, AR 71753, Phone: 870-234-5409

WATSON, BERT,
PO Box 26, Westminster, CO 80036-0026, Phone: 303-587-3064, watsonlock@aol.com
Specialties: Working/using straight knives of his design and to customer specs. **Patterns:** Hunters, utility/camp knives. **Technical:** Grinds O1, ATS-34, 440C, D2, A2 and others. **Prices:** $150 to $800. **Remarks:** Full-time maker. **Mark:** GTK and/or Bert.

WATSON, BILLY,
440 Forge Rd, Deatsville, AL 36022, Phone: 334-365-1482, billy@watsonknives.com; Web: www.watsonknives.com
Specialties: Working and using straight knives and folders of his design; period pieces. **Patterns:** Hunters, Bowies and utility/camp knives. **Technical:** Forges and grinds his own Damascus, 1095, 5160 and 52100. **Prices:** $40 to $1500. **Remarks:** Full-time maker; first knife sold in 1970. Doing business as Billy's Blacksmith Shop. **Mark:** Last name.

WATSON, DANIEL,
350 Jennifer Ln, Driftwood, TX 78619, Phone: 512-847-9679, info@angelsword.com; Web: http://www.angelsword.com
Specialties: One-of-a-kind knives and swords. **Patterns:** Hunters, daggers, swords. **Technical:** Hand-purify and carbonize his own high-carbon steel, pattern-welded Damascus, cable and carbon-induced crystalline Damascus. Teehno-Wootz™ Damascus steel, heat treats including cryogenic processing. European and Japanese tempering. **Prices:** $125 to $25,000. **Remarks:** Full-time maker; first knife sold in 1979. **Mark:** "Angel Sword" on forged pieces; "Bright Knight" for stock removal. Avatar on Techno-Wootz™ Damascus. Bumon on traditional Japanese blades.

WATSON, PETER,
66 Kielblock St, La Hoff 2570, SOUTH AFRICA, Phone: 018-84942
Specialties: Traditional working and using straight knives and folders of his design. **Patterns:** Hunters, locking folders and utility/camp knives. **Technical:** Sandvik and 440C. **Prices:** $120 to $250; some to $1500. **Remarks:** Part-time maker; first knife sold in 1989. **Mark:** Buffalo head with name.

WATSON, TOM,
1103 Brenau Terrace, Panama City, FL 32405, Phone: 850-785-9209, tom@tomwatsonknives.com; Web: www.tomwatsonknives.com
Specialties: Utility/tactical linerlocks. **Patterns:** Tactical and utility. **Technical:** Flat grinds satin finished D2 and Damascus. **Prices:** Starting at $375. **Remarks:** Full time maker. In business since 1978. **Mark:** Name and city.

WATTELET, MICHAEL A,
PO Box 649, 125 Front, Minocqua, WI 54548, Phone: 715-356-3069, redtroll@verizon.net
Specialties: Working and using straight knives of his design and to customer specs; fantasy knives. **Patterns:** Daggers, fighters and swords. **Technical:** Grinds 440C and L6; forges and grinds O1. Silversmith. **Prices:** $75 to $1000; some to $5000. **Remarks:** Full-time maker; first knife sold in 1966. Doing business as M and N Arts Ltd. **Mark:** First initial, last name.

WATTS, JOHNATHAN,
9560 S Hwy 36, Gatesville, TX 76528, Phone: 254-487-2866
Specialties: Traditional folders. **Patterns:** One and two blade folders in various blade shapes. **Technical:** Grinds ATS-34 and Damascus on request. **Prices:** $120 to $400. **Remarks:** Part-time maker; first knife sold in 1997. **Mark:** J Watts.

WATTS, WALLY,
9560 S Hwy 36, Gatesville, TX 76528, Phone: 254-223-9669
Specialties: Unique traditional folders of his design. **Patterns:** One- to five-blade folders and single-blade gents in various blade shapes. **Technical:** Grinds ATS-34; Damascus on request. **Prices:** $150 to $400. **Remarks:** Full-time maker; first knife sold in 1986. **Mark:** Last name.

WEBSTER, BILL,
58144 West Clear Lake Rd, Three Rivers, MI 49093, Phone: 269-244-2873, wswebster_5@msn.com Web: www.websterknifeworks.com
Specialties: Working and using straight knives, especially for hunters. His patterns are custom designed. **Patterns:** Hunters, skinners, camp knives, Bowies and daggers. **Technical:** Hand-filed blades made of D2 steel only, unless other steel is requested. Preferred handle material is stabilized and exotic wood and stag. Sheaths are made by Green River Leather in Kentucky. Hand-sewn sheaths by Bill Dehn in Three Rivers, MI. **Prices:** $75 to $500. **Remarks:** Part-time maker, first knife sold in 1978. **Mark:** Originally WEB stamped on blade, at present, Webster Knifeworks Three Rivers, MI laser etched on blade.

WEHNER, RUDY,
297 William Warren Rd, Collins, MS 39428, Phone: 601-765-4997
Specialties: Reproduction antique Bowies and contemporary Bowies in full and miniature. **Patterns:** Skinners, camp knives, fighters, axes and Bowies. **Technical:** Grinds 440C, ATS-34, 154CM and Damascus. **Prices:** $100 to $500; some to $850. **Remarks:** Full-time maker; first knife sold in 1975. **Mark:** Last name on Bowies and antiques; full name, city and state on skinners.

WEILAND JR., J REESE,
PO Box 2337, Riverview, FL 33568, Phone: 813-671-0661, RWPHIL413@earthlink.net; Web: www.rwcustomknive.som
Specialties: Hawk bills; tactical to fancy folders. **Patterns:** Hunters, tantos, Bowies, fantasy knives, spears and some swords. **Technical:** Grinds ATS-34, 154CM, 440C, D2, O1, A2, Damascus. Titanium hardware on locking liners and button locks. **Prices:** $150 to $4000. **Remarks:** Full-time maker, first knife sold in 1978. Knifemakers Guild member since 1988.

WEINAND, GEROME M,
14440 Harpers Bridge Rd, Missoula, MT 59808, Phone: 406-543-0845
Specialties: Working straight knives. **Patterns:** Bowies, fishing and camp knives, large special hunters. **Technical:** Grinds O1, 440C, ATS-34, 1084, L6, also stainless Damascus, Aebl and 304; makes all-tool steel Damascus; Dendritic D2 from powdered steel. Heat-treats. **Prices:** $30 to $100; some to $500. **Remarks:** Full-time maker; first knife sold in 1982. **Mark:** Last name.

WEINSTOCK, ROBERT,
PO Box 170028, San Francisco, CA 94117-0028, Phone: 415-731-5968, robertweinstock@att.net
Specialties: Folders, slip joins, lockbacks, autos. **Patterns:** Daggers, folders. **Technical:** Grinds A2, O1 and 440C. Chased and hand-carved blades and handles. Also using various Damascus steels from other makers. **Prices:** $3000 to 7000. **Remarks:** Full-time maker; first knife sold in 1994. **Mark:** Last name carved in steel.

WEISS, CHARLES L,
PO BOX 1037, Waddell, AZ 85355, Phone: 623-935-0924, weissknife@juno.com; Web: www.weissknives.com
Specialties: High-art straight knives and folders; deluxe period pieces. **Patterns:** Daggers, fighters, boots, push knives and miniatures. **Technical:** Grinds 440C, 154CM and ATS-34. **Prices:** $300 to $1200; some to $2000. **Remarks:** Full-time maker; first knife sold in 1975. **Mark:** Name and city.

WELLING, RONALD L,
15446 Lake Ave, Grand Haven, MI 49417, Phone: 616-846-2274
Specialties: Scagel knives of his design or to customer specs. **Patterns:** Hunters, camp knives, miniatures, bird, trout, folders, double edged, hatchets, skinners and some art pieces. **Technical:** Forges Damascus 1084 and 1095. Antler, ivory and horn. **Prices:** $250 to $3000. **Remarks:** Full-time maker. ABS Journeyman maker. **Mark:** First initials and or name and last name. City and state. Various scagel kris (1or 2).

WERTH, GEORGE W,
5223 Woodstock Rd, Poplar Grove, IL 61065, Phone: 815-544-4408
Specialties: Period pieces, some fancy. **Patterns:** Straight fighters, daggers and Bowies. **Technical:** Forges and grinds O1, 1095 and his Damascus, including mosaic patterns. **Prices:** $200 to $650; some higher. **Remarks:** Full-time maker. Doing business as Fox Valley Forge. **Mark:** Name in logo or initials connected.

WESCOTT, CODY,
5330 White Wing Rd, Las Cruces, NM 88012, Phone: 575-382-5008
Specialties: Fancy and presentation grade working knives. **Patterns:** Hunters, locking folders and Bowies. **Technical:** Hollow-grinds D2 and ATS-34; all knives file worked. Offers some engraving. Makes sheaths. **Prices:** $110 to $500; some to $1200. **Remarks:** Full-time maker; first knife sold in 1982. **Mark:** First initial, last name.

WEST, CHARLES A,
1315 S Pine St, Centralia, IL 62801, Phone: 618-532-2777
Specialties: Classic, fancy, high tech, period pieces, traditional and working/using straight knives and folders. **Technical:** Grinds ATS-34, O1 and Damascus. Prefers hot blued finishes. **Prices:** $100 to $1000; some to $2000. **Remarks:** Full-time maker; first knife sold in 1963. Doing business as West Custom Knives. **Mark:** Name or name, city and state.

WEST, PAT,
PO Box 9, Charlotte, TX 78011, Phone: 830-277-1290
Specialties: Classic working and using straight knives and folders. **Patterns:** Hunters, slip-joint folders. **Technical:** Grinds ATS-34, D2. Offers filework and decorates liners on folders. **Prices:** $400 to $700. **Remarks:** Spare-time maker; first knife sold in 1984. **Mark:** Name.

WESTBERG, LARRY,
305 S Western Hills Dr, Algona, IA 50511, Phone: 515-295-9276
Specialties: Traditional and working straight knives of his design and in standard patterns. **Patterns:** Bowies, hunters, fillets and folders. **Technical:** Grinds 440C, D2 and 1095. Heat-treats. Uses natural handle materials. **Prices:** $85 to $600; some to $1000. **Remarks:** Part-time maker; first knife sold in 1987. **Mark:** Last name-town and state.

WHEELER, GARY,
351 Old Hwy 48, Clarksville, TN 37040, Phone: 931-552-3092, LR22SHTR@charter.net
Specialties: Working to high end fixed blades. **Patterns:** Bowies, Hunters, combat knives, daggers and a few folders. **Technical:** Forges 5160, 1095, 52100 and his own Damascus. **Prices:** $125 to $2000. **Remarks:** Full-time maker since 2001, first knife sold in 1985 collaborates/works at B&W Blade Works. ABS Journeyman Smith 2008. **Mark:** Stamped last name.

WHEELER, ROBERT,
289 S Jefferson, Bradley, IL 60915, Phone: 815-932-5854, b2btaz@brmemc.net

WHETSELL, ALEX,
1600 Palmetto Tyrone Rd, Sharpsburg, GA 30277, Phone: 770-463-4881
Specialties: Knifekits.com, a source for fold locking liner type and straight knife kits. These kits are industry standard for folding knife kits. **Technical:** Many selections of colored G10 carbon fiber and wood handle material for kits, as well as bulk sizes for the custom knifemaker, heat treated folding knife pivots, screws, bushings, etc.

WHIPPLE, WESLEY A,
PO Box 2127, Kodiak, AK 99615, Phone: 907-486-6737, wildernessknife@yahoo.com
Specialties: Working straight knives, some fancy. **Patterns:** Hunters, Bowies, camp knives, fighters. **Technical:** Forges high-carbon steels, Damascus, offers relief carving and silver wire inlay checkering. **Prices:** $300 to $1400; some higher. **Remarks:** Full-time maker; first knife sold in 1989. A.K.A. Wilderness Knife and Forge. **Mark:** Last name/JS.

WHITE, BRYCE,
1415 W Col Glenn Rd, Little Rock, AR 72210, Phone: 501-821-2956
Specialties: Hunters, fighters, makes Damascus, file work, handmade only. **Technical:** L6, 1075, 1095, O1 steels used most. **Patterns:** Will do any pattern or use his own. **Prices:** $200 to $300. Sold first knife in 1995. **Mark:** White.

WHITE, DALE,
525 CR 212, Sweetwater, TX 79556, Phone: 325-798-4178, dalew@taylortel.net
Specialties: Working and using knives. **Patterns:** Hunters, skinners, utilities and Bowies. **Technical:** Grinds 440C, offers file work, fancy pins and scrimshaw by Sherry Sellers. **Prices:** From $45 to $300. **Remarks:** Sold first knife in 1975. **Mark:** Full name, city and state.

WHITE, GARRETT,
871 Sarijon Rd, Hartwell, GA 30643, Phone: 706-376-5944
Specialties: Gentlemen folders, fancy straight knives. **Patterns:** Locking liners and hunting fixed blades. **Technical:** Grinds 440C, S30V, and stainless Damascus. **Prices:** $150 to $1000. **Remarks:** Part-time maker. **Mark:** Name.

WHITE, GENE E,
9005 Ewing Dr, Bethesda, MD 20817-3357, Phone: 301-564-3164
Specialties: Small utility/gents knives. **Patterns:** Eight standard hunters; most other patterns on commission basis. Currently no swords, axes and fantasy knives. **Technical:** Stock removal 440C and D2; others on request. Mostly hollow grinds; some flat grinds. Prefers natural handle materials. Makes own sheaths. **Prices:** Start at $85. **Remarks:** Part-time maker; first knife sold in 1971. **Mark:** First and middle initials, last name.

WHITE, JOHN PAUL,
231 S Bayshore, Valparaiso, FL 32580, Phone: 850-729-9174, johnwhiteknives@gmail.com
Specialties: Forged hunters, fighters, traditional Bowies and personal carry knives with handles of natural materials and fittings with detailed file work. **Technical:** Forges carbon steel and own Damascus. **Prices:** $500 to $3500 **Remarks:** Master Smith, American Bladesmith Society. **Mark:** First initial, last name.

WHITE, LOU,
7385 Red Bud Rd NE, Ranger, GA 30734, Phone: 706-334-2273

WHITE, RICHARD T,
359 Carver St, Grosse Pointe Farms, MI 48236, Phone: 313-881-4690

WHITE, ROBERT J,
RR 1 641 Knox Rd 900 N, Gilson, IL 61436, Phone: 309-289-4487
Specialties: Working knives, some deluxe. **Patterns:** Bird and trout knives, hunters, survival knives and locking folders. **Technical:** Grinds A2, D2 and 440C; commercial Damascus. Heat-treats. **Prices:** $125 to $250; some to $600. **Remarks:** Full-time maker; first knife sold in 1976. **Mark:** Last name in script.

WHITE JR., ROBERT J BUTCH,
RR 1, Gilson, IL 61436, Phone: 309-289-4487
Specialties: Folders of all sizes. **Patterns:** Hunters, fighters, boots and folders. **Technical:** Forges Damascus; grinds tool and stainless steel. **Prices:** $500 to $1800. **Remarks:** Spare-time maker; first knife sold in 1980. **Mark:** Last name in block letters.

WHITENECT, JODY,
Elderbank, Halifax County, Nova Scotia, CANADA B0N 1K0, Phone: 902-384-2511
Specialties: Fancy and embellished working/using straight knives of his design and to customer specs. **Patterns:** Bowies, fighters and hunters. **Technical:** Forges 1095 and O1; forges and grinds ATS-34. Various filework on blades and bolsters. **Prices:** $200 to $400; some to $800. **Remarks:** Part-time maker; first knife sold in 1996. **Mark:** Longhorn stamp or engraved.

WHITESELL, J. DALE,
P.O. Box 455, Stover, MO 65078, Phone: 573-372-5182, dwknives@heroesonline.us Web: whitesell-knives.webs.com
Specialties: Fixed blade working knives, and some collector pieces. **Patterns:** Hunting and skinner knives and camp knives. **Technical:** Blades ground from O1, 1095, and 440C in hollow, flat and saber grinds. Wood, bone, deer antler, and G10 are basic handle materials. **Prices:** $100 to $250. **Remarks:** Part-time maker, first knife sold in 2003. Doing business as Dale's Knives. **Mark:** Whitesell on the left side of the blade.

WHITLEY, L WAYNE,
1675 Carrow Rd, Chocowinity, NC 27817-9495, Phone: 252-946-5648

WHITLEY, WELDON G,
4308 N Robin Ave, Odessa, TX 79764, Phone: 432-530-0448, Fax: 432-530-0048, wgwhitley@juno.com
Specialties: Working knives of his design or to customer specs. **Patterns:** Hunters, folders and various double-edged knives. **Technical:** Grinds 440C, 154CM and ATS-34. **Prices:** $150 to $1250. **Mark:** Name, address, road-runner logo.

WHITMAN, JIM,
21044 Salem St, Chugiak, AK 99567, Phone: 907-688-4575, Fax: 907-688-4278, Web: www.whitmanknives.com
Specialties: Working straight knives and folders; some art pieces. **Patterns:** Hunters, skinners, Bowies, camp knives, working fighters, swords and hatchets. **Technical:** Grinds AEB-L Swedish, 440C, 154CM, ATS-34, and Damascus in full convex. Prefers exotic hardwoods, natural and native handle materials: whale bone, antler, ivory and horn. **Prices:** Start at $150. **Remarks:** Full-time maker; first knife sold in 1983. **Mark:** Name, city, state.

WHITTAKER, ROBERT E,
PO Box 204, Mill Creek, PA 17060
Specialties: Using straight knives. Has a line of knives for buckskinners. **Patterns:** Hunters, skinners and Bowies. **Technical:** Grinds O1, A2 and D2. Offers filework. **Prices:** $35 to $100. **Remarks:** Part-time maker; first knife sold in 1980. **Mark:** Last initial or full initials.

WHITTAKER, WAYNE,
2900 Woodland Ct, Metamore, MI 48455, Phone: 810-797-5315, lindorwayne@yahoo.com
Specialties: Liner locks and autos. **Patterns:** Folders. **Technical:** Damascus, mammoth, ivory, and tooth. **Prices:** $500 to $1500. **Remarks:** Full-time maker. **Mark:** Inside of backbar.

WHITWORTH, KEN J,
41667 Tetley Ave, Sterling Heights, MI 48078, Phone: 313-739-5720
Specialties: Working straight knives and folders. **Patterns:** Locking folders, slip joints and boot knives. **Technical:** Grinds 440C, 154CM and D2. **Prices:** $100 to $225; some to $450. **Remarks:** Part-time maker; first knife sold in 1976. **Mark:** Last name.

WICKER, DONNIE R,
2544 E 40th Ct, Panama City, FL 32405, Phone: 904-785-9158
Specialties: Traditional working and using straight knives of his design or to customer specs. **Patterns:** Hunters, fighters and slip-joint folders. **Technical:** Grinds 440C, ATS-34, D2 and 154CM. Heat-treats and does hardness testing. **Prices:** $90 to $200; some to $400. **Remarks:** Part-time maker; first knife sold in 1975. **Mark:** First and middle initials, last name.

WIGGINS, HORACE,
203 Herndon Box 152, Mansfield, LA 71502, Phone: 318-872-4471
Specialties: Fancy working knives. **Patterns:** Straight and folding hunters. **Technical:** Grinds O1, D2 and 440C. **Prices:** $90 to $275. **Remarks:** Part-time maker; first knife sold in 1970. **Mark:** Name, city and state in diamond logo.

WILCHER, WENDELL L,
RR 6 Box 6573, Palestine, TX 75801, Phone: 903-549-2530
Specialties: Fantasy, miniatures and working/using straight knives and folders of his design and to customer specs. **Patterns:** Fighters, hunters, locking folders. **Technical:** Hand works (hand file and hand sand knives), not grind. **Prices:** $75 to $250; some to $600. **Remarks:** Part-time maker; first knife sold in 1987. **Mark:** Initials, year, serial number.

WILE, PETER,
RR 3, Bridgewater, Nova Scotia, CANADA B4V 2W2, Phone: 902-543-1373, peterwile@ns.sympatico.ca
Specialties: Collector-grade one-of-a-kind file-worked folders. **Patterns:** Folders or fixed blades of his design or to customers specs. **Technical:** Grinds ATS-34, carbon and stainless Damascus. Does intricate filework on blades, spines and liners. Carves. Prefers natural handle materials. Does own heat treating. **Prices:** $350 to $2000; some to $4000. **Remarks:** Part-time maker; sold first knife in 1985; doing business as Wile Knives. **Mark:** Wile.

WILKINS, MITCHELL,
15523 Rabon Chapel Rd, Montgomery, TX 77316, Phone: 936-588-2696, mwilkins@consolidated.net

WILLEY, WG,
14210 Sugar Hill Rd, Greenwood, DE 19950, Phone: 302-349-4070, Web: www.willeyknives.com
Specialties: Fancy working straight knives. **Patterns:** Small game knives, Bowies and throwing knives. **Technical:** Grinds 440C and 154CM. **Prices:** $350 to $600; some to $1500. **Remarks:** Part-time maker; first knife sold in 1975. Owns retail store. **Mark:** Last name inside map logo.

WILLIAMS, JASON L,
PO Box 67, Wyoming, RI 02898, Phone: 401-539-8353, Fax: 401-539-0252
Specialties: Fancy and high tech folders of his design, co-inventor of the Axis Lock. **Patterns:** Fighters, locking folders, automatics and fancy pocket knives. **Technical:** Forges Damascus and other steels by request. Uses exotic handle materials and precious metals. Offers inlaid spines and gemstone thumb knobs. **Prices:** $1000 and up. **Remarks:** Full-time maker; first knife sold in 1989. **Mark:** First and last initials on pivot.

WILLIAMS JR., RICHARD,
1440 Nancy Circle, Morristown, TN 37814, Phone: 615-581-0059
Specialties: Working and using straight knives of his design or to customer specs. **Patterns:** Hunters, dirks and utility/camp knives. **Technical:** Forges 5160 and uses file steel. Hand-finish is standard; offers filework. **Prices:** $80 to $180; some to $250. **Remarks:** Spare-time maker; first knife sold in 1985. **Mark:** Last initial or full initials.

WILLIAMSON, TONY,
Rt 3 Box 503, Siler City, NC 27344, Phone: 919-663-3551
Specialties: Flint knapping: knives made of obsidian flakes and flint with wood, antler or bone for handles. **Patterns:** Skinners, daggers and flake knives. **Technical:** Blades have width/thickness ratio of at least 4 to 1. Hafts with methods available to prehistoric man. **Prices:** $58 to $160. **Remarks:** Student of Errett Callahan. **Mark:** Initials and number code to identify year and number of knives made.

WILLIS, BILL,
RT 7 Box 7549, Ava, MO 65608, Phone: 417-683-4326
Specialties: Forged blades, Damascus and carbon steel. **Patterns:** Cable, random or ladder lamented. **Technical:** Professionally heat treated blades. **Prices:** $75 to $600. **Remarks:** Lifetime guarantee on all blades against breakage. All work done by maker; including leather work. **Mark:** WF.

WILLUMSEN, MIKKEL,
Nyrnberggade 23, 2300 Copenhagen S, Denmark, Phone: 4531176333, mw@willumsen-cph.com
Specialties: Folding knives, fixed blades, and balisongs. Also kitchen knives. **Patterns:** Primarily influenced by design that is function and quality based. Tactical style knives inspired by classical designs mixed with modern tactics. **Technical:** Uses CPM 154, RW 134, S30V, and carbon fiber titanium G10 for handles.

WILSON, CURTIS M,
PO Box 383, Burleson, TX 76097, Phone: 817-295-3732, cwknifeman2026@att.net; Web: www.cwilsonknives.com
Specialties: Traditional working/using knives, fixed blade, folders, slip joint, LinerLock® and lock back knives. Art knives, presentation grade Bowies, folder repair, heat treating services. Sub-zero quench. **Patterns:** Hunters, camp knives, military combat, single and multi-blade folders. Dr's knives large or small or custom design knives. **Technical:** Grinds ATS-34, 440C 52100, D2, S30V, CPM 154, mokume gane, engraves, scrimshaw, sheaths leather of kykex heat treating and file work. **Prices:** $150-750. **Remarks:** Part-time maker since 1984. Sold first knife in 1993. **Mark:** Curtis Wilson in ribbon or Curtis Wilson with hand made in a half moon.

WILSON, JAMES G,
PO Box 4024, Estes Park, CO 80517, Phone: 303-586-3944
Specialties: Bronze Age knives; Medieval and Scottish-styles; tomahawks. **Patterns:** Bronze knives, daggers, swords, spears and battle axes; 12-inch steel Misericorde daggers, sgian dubhs, "his and her" skinners, bird and fish knives, capers, boots and daggers. **Technical:** Casts bronze; grinds D2, 440C and ATS-34. **Prices:** $49 to $400; some to $1300. **Remarks:** Part-time maker; first knife sold in 1975. **Mark:** WilsonHawk.

WILSON, JON J,
1826 Ruby St, Johnstown, PA 15902, Phone: 814-266-6410
Specialties: Miniatures and full size. **Patterns:** Bowies, daggers and hunters. **Technical:** Grinds Damascus, 440C and O1. Scrimshaws and carves. **Prices:** $75 to $500; some higher. **Remarks:** Full-time maker; first knife sold in 1988. **Mark:** First and middle initials, last name.

WILSON, MIKE,
1416 McDonald Rd, Hayesville, NC 28904, Phone: 828-389-8145
Specialties: Fancy working and using straight knives of his design or to customer specs, folders. **Patterns:** Hunters, Bowies, utility knives, gut hooks, skinners, fighters and miniatures. **Technical:** Hollow grinds 440C, L6, O1 and D2. Mirror finishes are standard. Offers filework. **Prices:** $50 to $600. **Remarks:** Full-time maker; first knife sold in 1985. **Mark:** Last name.

WILSON, PHILIP C,
SEAMOUNT KNIFEWORKS, PO Box 846, Mountain Ranch, CA 95246, Phone: 209-754-1990, seamount@bigplanet.com; Web: www.seamountknifeworks.com
Specialties: Working knives; emphasis on salt water fillet knives and utility hunters of his design. **Patterns:** Fishing knives, hunters, utility knives. **Technical:** Grinds CPM S-30V, CPM10V, S-90V, CPMS110V, and CPM154. Heat-treats and Rockwell tests all blades. **Prices:** Start at $400. **Remarks:** First knife sold in 1985. Doing business as Sea-Mount Knife Works. **Mark:** Signature.

WILSON, RON,
2639 Greenwood Ave, Morro Bay, CA 93442, Phone: 805-772-3381
Specialties: Classic and fantasy straight knives of his design. **Patterns:** Daggers, fighters, swords and axes, mostly all miniatures. **Technical:** Forges and grinds Damascus and various tool steels; grinds meteorite. Uses gold, precious stones and exotic wood. **Prices:** Vary. **Remarks:** Part-time maker; first knives sold in 1995. **Mark:** Stamped first and last initials.

WILSON, RW,
PO Box 2012, Weirton, WV 26062, Phone: 304-723-2771, rwknives@comcast.net
Specialties: Working straight knives; period pieces. **Patterns:** Bowies, tomahawks and patch knives. **Technical:** Grinds 440C; scrimshaws. **Prices:** $85 to $175; some to $1000. **Remarks:** Part-time maker; first knife sold in 1966. Knifemaker supplier. Offers free knife-making lessons. **Mark:** Name in tomahawk.

WILSON, STAN,
8931 Pritcher Rd, Lithia, FL 33547, Phone: 727-461-1992, swilson@stanwilsonknives.com; Web: www.stanwilsonknives.com
Specialties: Fancy folders and automatics of his own design. **Patterns:** Locking liner folders, single and dual action autos, daggers. **Technical:** Stock removal, uses Damascus, stainless and high carbon steels, prefers ivory and pearl, Damascus with blued finishes and filework. **Prices:** $400 and up. **Remarks:** Member of Knifemakers Guild and Florida Knifemakers Association. Full-time maker will do custom orders. **Mark:** Name in script.

WILSON (SEE SIMONELLA, GIANLUIGI),

WINGO, GARY,
240 Ogeechee, Ramona, OK 74061, Phone: 918-536-1067, wingg_2000@yahoo.com; Web: www.geocities.com/wingg_2000/gary.html
Specialties: Folder specialist. Steel 44OC, D2, others on request. Handle bone-stag, others on request. **Patterns:** Trapper three-blade stockman, four-blade congress, single- and two-blade barlows. **Prices:** 150 to $400. **Mark:** First knife sold 1994. Steer head with Wingo Knives or Straight line Wingo Knives.

WINGO, PERRY,
22 55th St, Gulfport, MS 39507, Phone: 228-863-3193
Specialties: Traditional working straight knives. **Patterns:** Hunters, skinners, Bowies and fishing knives. **Technical:** Grinds 440C. **Prices:** $75 to $1000. **Remarks:** Full-time maker; first knife sold in 1988. **Mark:** Last name.

WINKLER, DANIEL,
PO Box 2166, Blowing Rock, NC 28605, Phone: 828-295-9156, danielwinkler@bellsouth.net; Web: www.winklerknives.com
Specialties: Forged cutlery styled in the tradition of an era past as well as producing a custom-made stock removal line. **Patterns:** Fixed blades, friction folders, lock back folders, and axes/tomahawks. **Technical:** Forges, grinds, and heat treats carbon steels, specialty steels, and his own Damascus steel. **Prices:** $350 to $4000+. **Remarks:** Full-time maker since 1988. Exclusively offers leatherwork by Karen Shook. ABS Master Smith; Knifemakers Guild voting member. **Mark:** Before 2008: initials connected. 2008 and after: hand forged marked Dwinkler; stock removal marked WinklerKnives II

WINN, TRAVIS A.,
558 E 3065 S, Salt Lake City, UT 84106, Phone: 801-467-5957
Specialties: Fancy working knives and knives to customer specs. **Patterns:** Hunters, fighters, boots, Bowies and fancy daggers, some miniatures, tantos and fantasy knives. **Technical:** Grinds D2 and 440C. Embellishes. **Prices:** $125 to $500; some higher. **Remarks:** Part-time maker; first knife sold in 1976. **Mark:** TRAV stylized.

WINSTON, DAVID,
1671 Red Holly St, Starkville, MS 39759, Phone: 601-323-1028
Specialties: Fancy and traditional knives of his design and to customer specs. **Patterns:** Bowies, daggers, hunters, boot knives and folders. **Technical:** Grinds 440C, ATS-34 and D2. Offers filework; heat-treats. **Prices:** $40 to $750; some higher. **Remarks:** Part-time maker; first knife sold in 1984. Offers lifetime sharpening for original owner. **Mark:** Last name.

WINTER, GEORGE,
5940 Martin Hwy, Union City, TN 38261

WIRTZ, ACHIM,
Mittelstrasse 58, Wuerselen, D-52146, GERMANY, Phone: 0049-2405-462-486, wootz@web.de
Specialties: Medieval, Scandinavian and Middle East-style knives. **Technical:** Forged blades only, Damascus steel, Wootz, Mokume. **Prices:** Start at $200. **Remarks:** Part-time maker. First knife sold in 1997. **Mark:** Stylized initials.

WISE, DONALD,
304 Bexhill Rd, St Leonardo-On-Sea, East Sussex, TN3 8AL, ENGLAND
Specialties: Fancy and embellished working straight knives to customer specs. **Patterns:** Hunters, Bowies and daggers. **Technical:** Grinds Sandvik 12C27, D2 D3 and O1. Scrimshaws. **Prices:** $110 to $300; some to $500. **Remarks:** Full-time maker; first knife sold in 1983. **Mark:** KNIFECRAFT.

WITSAMAN, EARL,
3957 Redwing Circle, Stow, OH 44224, Phone: 330-688-4208, eawits@aol.com; earlwitsaman.com
Specialties: Straight and fantasy miniatures. **Patterns:** Wide variety—Randalls to D-guard Bowies. **Technical:** Grinds O1, 440C and 300 stainless; buys Damascus; highly detailed work. **Prices:** $85 to $300. **Remarks:** Part-time maker; first knife sold in 1974. **Mark:** Initials.

WOLF, BILL,
4618 N 79th Ave, Phoenix, AZ 85033, Phone: 623-846-3585, Fax: 623-846-3585, wolfknives@yahoo.com
Specialties: Investor-grade folders and straight knives. **Patterns:** Lockback, slip joint and slide lock interframes. **Technical:** Grinds ATS-34 and 440C. **Prices:** $400 to $10,000. **Remarks:** Full-time maker; first knife sold in 1989. **Mark:** Name.

WOLF JR., WILLIAM LYNN,
4006 Frank Rd, Lagrange, TX 78945, Phone: 409-247-4626

WOOD, ALAN,
Greenfield Villa, Greenhead, Brampton CA8 7HH, ENGLAND, a.wood@knivesfreeserve.co.uk; Web: www.alanwoodknives.co.uk
Specialties: High-tech working straight knives of his design. **Patterns:** Hunters, utility/camp and bushcraft knives. **Technical:** Grinds 12C27, RWL-34, stainless Damascus and O1. Blades are cryogenic treated. **Prices:** $200 to $800; some to $750. **Remarks:** Full-time maker; first knife sold in 1979. Not currently taking orders. **Mark:** Full name with stag tree logo.

WOOD, LARRY B,
PO BOX 222, Jamesville, VA 23398-0222, Phone: 757-442-2660
Specialties: Fancy working knives of his design. **Patterns:** Hunters, buckskinners, Bowies, tomahawks, locking folders and Damascus miniatures. **Technical:** Forges 1095, file steel and his own Damascus. **Prices:** $125 to $500; some to $2000. **Remarks:** Full-time maker; first knife sold in 1974. Doing business as Wood's Metal Studios. **Mark:** Variations of last name, sometimes with blacksmith logo.

WOOD, OWEN DALE,
6492 Garrison St, Arvada, CO 80004-3157, Phone: 303-456-2748, wood.owen@gmail.com; Web: www.owenwoodcustomknives.com
Specialties: Folding knives and daggers. **Patterns:** Own Damascus, specialties in 456 composite blades. **Technical:** Materials: Damascus stainless steel, exotic metals, gold, rare handle materials. **Prices:** $1000 to $9000. **Remarks:** Folding knives in art deco and art noveau themes. Full-time maker from 1981. **Mark:** OWEN WOOD.

WOOD, WEBSTER,
22041 Shelton Trail, Atlanta, MI 49709, Phone: 989-785-2996, littlewolf@racc2000.com
Specialties: Works mainly in stainless; art knives, Bowies, hunters and folders. **Remarks:** Full-time maker; first knife sold in 1980. Retired guild member. All engraving done by maker. **Mark:** Initials inside shield and name.

WRIGHT, KEVIN,
671 Leland Valley Rd W, Quilcene, WA 98376-9517, Phone: 360-765-3589, kevinw@ptpc.com
Specialties: Fancy working or collector knives to customer specs. **Patterns:** Hunters, boots, buckskinners, miniatures. **Technical:** Forges and grinds L6, 1095, 440C and his own Damascus. **Prices:** $75 to $500; some to $2000. **Remarks:** Part-time maker; first knife sold in 1978. **Mark:** Last initial in anvil.

WRIGHT, L T,
1523 Pershing Ave, Steubenville, OH 43952, Phone: 740-282-4947, knifemkr@sbcglobal.net; Web: www.ltwrightknives.com
Specialties: Hunting and tactical knives. **Patterns:** Drop point hunters, bird, trout and tactical. **Technical:** Grinds D2, 440C and O1. **Remarks:** Full-time maker.

WRIGHT, RICHARD S,
PO Box 201, 111 Hilltop Dr, Carolina, RI 02812, Phone: 401-364-3579, rswswitchblades@hotmail.com; Web: www.richardswright.com
Specialties: Bolster release switchblades. **Patterns:** Folding fighters, gents pocket knives, one-of-a-kind high-grade automatics. **Technical:** Re-forges and grinds various makers Damascus. Uses a variety of tool steels. Uses natural handle material such as ivory and pearl, extensive file-work on most knives. **Prices:** $2000 and up. **Remarks:** Full-time knifemaker with background as a gunsmith. Made first folder in 1991. **Mark:** RSW on blade, all folders are serial numbered.

WRIGHT, TIMOTHY,
PO Box 3746, Sedona, AZ 86340, Phone: 928-282-4180
Specialties: High-tech folders and working knives. **Patterns:** Interframe locking folders, non-inlaid folders, straight hunters and kitchen knives. **Technical:** Grinds BG-42, AEB-L, K190 and Cowry X; works with new steels. All folders can disassemble and are furnished with tools. **Prices:** $150 to $1800; some to $3000. **Remarks:** Full-time maker; first knife sold in 1975. **Mark:** Last name and type of steel used.

WUERTZ, TRAVIS,
2487 E Hwy 287, Casa Grande, AZ 85222, Phone: 520-723-4432

WYATT, WILLIAM R,
Box 237, Rainelle, WV 25962, Phone: 304-438-5494
Specialties: Classic and working knives of all designs. **Patterns:** Hunters and utility knives. **Technical:** Forges and grinds saw blades, files and rasps. Prefers stag handles. **Prices:** $45 to $95; some to $350. **Remarks:** Part-time maker; first knife sold in 1990. **Mark:** Last name in star with knife logo.

Y

YASHINSKI, JOHN L,
207 N Platt, PO Box 1284, Red Lodge, MT 59068, Phone: 406-446-3916
Specialties: Native American Beaded sheathes. **Prices:** Vary.

YEATES, JOE A,
730 Saddlewood Circle, Spring, TX 77381, Phone: 281-367-2765, joeyeates291@cs.com; Web: www.yeatesBowies.com
Specialties: Bowies and period pieces. **Patterns:** Bowies, toothpicks and combat knives. **Technical:** Grinds 440C, D2 and ATS-34. **Prices:** $600 to $2500. **Remarks:** Full-time maker; first knife sold in 1975. **Mark:** Last initial within outline of Texas; or last initial.

YESKOO, RICHARD C,
76 Beekman Rd, Summit, NJ 07901

YORK, DAVID C,
PO Box 3166, Chino Valley, AZ 86323, Phone: 928-636-1709, dmatj@msn.com
Specialties: Working straight knives and folders. **Patterns:** Prefers small hunters and skinners; locking folders. **Technical:** Grinds D2. **Prices:** $75 to $300; some to $600. **Remarks:** Part-time maker; first knife sold in 1975. **Mark:** Last name.

YOSHIHARA, YOSHINDO,
8-17-11 Takasago Katsushi, Tokyo, JAPAN

YOSHIKAZU, KAMADA,
, 540-3 Kaisaki Niuta-cho, Tokushima, JAPAN, Phone: 0886-44-2319

YOSHIO, MAEDA,
, 3-12-11 Chuo-cho tamashima Kurashiki-city, Okayama, JAPAN, Phone: 086-525-2375

YOUNG, BUD,
Box 336, Port Hardy, BC, CANADA V0N 2P0, Phone: 250-949-6478
Specialties: Fixed blade, working knives, some fancy. **Patterns:** Drop-points to skinners. **Technical:** Hollow or flat grind, 5160, 440C, mostly ATS-34, satin finish. Using supplied damascus at times. **Prices:** $150 to $2000 CDN. **Remarks:** Spare-time maker; making knives since 1962; first knife sold in 1985. Not taking orders at this time, sell as produced. **Mark:** Name.

YOUNG, CLIFF,
Fuente De La Cibeles No 5, Atascadero, San Miguel De Allende, GTO., MEXICO, Phone: 37700, Fax: 011-52-415-2-57-11
Specialties: Working knives. **Patterns:** Hunters, fighters and fishing knives. **Technical:** Grinds all; offers D2, 440C and 154CM. **Prices:** Start at $250. **Remarks:** Part-time maker; first knife sold in 1980. **Mark:** Name.

YOUNG, ERROL,
4826 Storey Land, Alton, IL 62002, Phone: 618-466-4707
Specialties: Traditional working straight knives and folders. **Patterns:** Wide range, including tantos, Bowies, miniatures and multi-blade folders. **Technical:** Grinds D2, 440C and ATS-34. **Prices:** $75 to $650; some to $800. **Remarks:** Part-time maker; first knife sold in 1987. **Mark:** Last name with arrow.

YOUNG, GEORGE,
713 Pinoak Dr, Kokomo, IN 46901, Phone: 765-457-8893
Specialties: Fancy/embellished and traditional straight knives and folders of his design and to customer specs. **Patterns:** Hunters, fillet/camp knives and locking folders. **Technical:** Grinds 440C, CPM440V, and stellite 6K. Fancy ivory, black pearl and stag for handles. Filework: all stellite construction (6K and 25 alloys). Offers engraving. **Prices:** $350 to $750; some $1500 to $3000. **Remarks:** Full-time maker; first knife sold in 1954. Doing business as Young's Knives. **Mark:** Last name integral inside Bowie.

YOUNG, RAYMOND L,
CUTLER/BLADESMITH, 2922 Hwy 188E, Mt. Ida, AR 71957, Phone: 870-867-3947
Specialties: Cutler-Bladesmith, sharpening service. **Patterns:** Hunter, skinners, fighters, no guard, no ricasso, chef tools. **Technical:** Edge tempered 1095, 516C, mosaic handles, water buffalo and exotic woods. **Prices:** $100 and up. **Remarks:** Federal contractor since 1995. Surgical steel sharpening. **Mark:** R.

YURCO, MIKE,
PO Box 712, Canfield, OH 44406, Phone: 330-533-4928, shorinki@aol.com
Specialties: Working straight knives. **Patterns:** Hunters, utility knives, Bowies and fighters, push knives, claws and other hideouts. **Technical:** Grinds 440C, ATS-34 and 154CM; likes mirror and satin finishes. **Prices:** $20 to $500. **Remarks:** Part-time maker; first knife sold in 1983. **Mark:** Name, steel, serial number.

Z

ZACCAGNINO JR., DON,
2256 Bacom Point Rd, Pahokee, FL 33476-2622, Phone: 561-924-7032, zackknife@aol.com
Specialties: Working knives and some period pieces of their designs. **Patterns:** Heavy-duty hunters, axes and Bowies; a line of light-weight hunters, fillets and personal knives. **Technical:** Grinds 440C and 17-4 PH; highly finished in complex handle and blade treatments. **Prices:** $165 to $500; some to $2500. **Remarks:** Part-time maker; first knife sold in 1969 by Don Zaccagnino Sr. **Mark:** ZACK, city and state inside oval.

ZAHM, KURT,
488 Rio Casa, Indialantic, FL 32903, Phone: 407-777-4860
Specialties: Working straight knives of his design or to customer specs. **Patterns:** Daggers, fancy fighters, Bowies, hunters and utility knives. **Technical:** Grinds D2, 440C; likes filework. **Prices:** $75 to $1000. **Remarks:** Part-time maker; first knife sold in 1985. **Mark:** Last name.

ZAKABI, CARL S,
PO Box 893161, Mililani Town, HI 96789-0161, Phone: 808-626-2181
Specialties: User-grade straight knives of his design, cord wrapped and bare steel handles exclusively. **Patterns:** Fighters, hunters and utility/camp knives. **Technical:** Grinds 440C and ATS-34. **Prices:** $90 to $400. **Remarks:** Spare-time maker; first knife sold in 1988. Doing business as Zakabi's Knifeworks LLC. **Mark:** Last name and state inside a Hawaiian sharktooth dagger.

ZAKHAROV, GLADISTON,
Bairro Rio Comprido, Rio Comprido Jacarei, Jacaret SP, BRAZIL 12302-070, Phone: 55 12 3958 4021, Fax: 55 12 3958 4103, arkhip@terra.com.br; Web: www.arkhip.com.br
Specialties: Using straight knives of his design. **Patterns:** Hunters, kitchen, utility/camp and barbecue knives. **Technical:** Grinds his own "se-cret steel." **Prices:** $30 to $200. **Remarks:** Full-time maker. **Mark:** Arkhip Special Knives.

ZBORIL, TERRY,
5320 CR 130, Caldwell, TX 77836, Phone: 979-535-4157, terry.zboril@worldnet.att.net
Specialties: ABS Journeyman Smith.

ZEMBKO III, JOHN,
140 Wilks Pond Rd, Berlin, CT 06037, Phone: 860-828-3503, johnzembko@hotmail.com
Specialties: Working knives of his design or to customer specs. **Patterns:** Likes to use stabilized high-figured woods. **Technical:** Grinds ATS-34, A2, D2; forges O1, 1095; grinds Damasteel. **Prices:** $50 to $400; some higher. **Remarks:** First knife sold in 1987. **Mark:** Name.

ZEMITIS, JOE,
14 Currawong Rd, Cardiff Hts, 2285 Newcastle, AUSTRALIA, Phone: 0249549907, jjvzem@bigpond.com
Specialties: Traditional working straight knives. **Patterns:** Hunters, Bowies, tantos, fighters and camp knives. **Technical:** Grinds O1, D2, W2 and 440C; makes his own Damascus. Embellishes; offers engraving. **Prices:** $150 to $3000. **Remarks:** Full-time maker; first knife sold in 1983. **Mark:** First initial, last name and country, or last name.

ZIMA, MICHAEL F,
732 State St, Ft. Morgan, CO 80701, Phone: 970-867-6078, Web: http://www.zimaknives.com
Specialties: Working and collector quality straight knives and folders. **Patterns:** Hunters, lock backs, LinerLock®, slip joint and automatic folders. **Technical:** Grinds Damascus, 440C, ATS-34 and 154CM. **Prices:** $200 and up. **Remarks:** Full-time maker; first knife sold in 1982. **Mark:** Last name.

ZINKER, BRAD,
BZ KNIVES, 1591 NW 17 St, Homestead, FL 33030, Phone: 305-216-0404, bzknives@aol.com
Specialties: Fillets, folders and hunters. **Technical:** Uses ATS-34 and stainless Damascus. **Prices:** $200 to $600. **Remarks:** Voting member of Knifemakers Guild and Florida Knifemakers Association. **Mark:** Offset connected initials BZ.

ZIRBES, RICHARD,
Neustrasse 15, D-54526 Niederkail, GERMANY, Phone: 0049 6575 1371, r.zirbes@freenet.de Web: www.zirbes-knives.com www.zirbes-messer.de
Specialties: Fancy embellished knives with engraving and self-made scrimshaw (scrimshaw made by maker). High-tech working knives and high-tech hunters, boots, fighters and folders. All knives made by hand. **Patterns:** Boots, fighters, folders, hunters. **Technical:** Uses only the best steels for blade material like CPM-T 440V, CPM-T 420V, ATS-34, D2, C440, stainless Damascus or steel according to customer's desire. **Prices:** Working knives and hunters: $200 to $600. Fancy embellished knives with engraving and/or scrimshaw: $800 to $3000. **Remarks:** Part-time maker; first knife sold in 1991. Member of the German Knifemaker Guild. **Mark:** Zirbes or R. Zirbes.

ZOWADA, TIM,
4509 E Bear River Rd, Boyne Falls, MI 49713, Phone: 231-348-5446, knifeguy@nmo.net
Specialties: Working knives, some fancy. **Patterns:** Hunters, camp knives, boots, swords, fighters, tantos and locking folders. **Technical:** Forges O2, L6, W2 and his own Damascus. **Prices:** $150 to $1000; some to $5000. **Remarks:** Full-time maker; first knife sold in 1980.

ZSCHERNY, MICHAEL F,
1840 Rock Island Dr, Ely, IA 52227, Phone: 319-848-3629, zschernyknives@aol.com
Specialties: Quality folding knives. **Patterns:** Liner-lock and lock-back folders in titanium, working straight knives. **Technical:** Grinds ATS-34 and commercial Damascus, prefers natural materials such as pearls and ivory. **Prices:** Starting at $500. **Remarks:** Full-time maker, first knife sold in 1978. **Mark:** Last name, city and state; folders, last name with stars inside folding knife.

Carolina Custom Knives,
    See Tommy Mcnabb
Iron Wolf Forge, See Nelson Ken
Viking Knives (See James Thorlief
    Eriksen),
Warren (See Dellana), Dellana
Wilson (See Simonella, Gianluigi),

AK

Barlow, Jana Poirier	Anchorage
Brennan, Judson	Delta Junction
Breuer, Lonnie	Wasilla
Broome, Thomas A	Kenai
Cawthorne, Christopher A	Wrangell
Chamberlin, John A	Anchorage
Dempsey, Gordon S	N. Kenai
Dufour, Arthur J	Anchorage
England, Virgil	Anchorage
Flint, Robert	Anchorage
Gouker, Gary B	Sitka
Grebe, Gordon S	Anchor Point
Harvey, Mel	Nenana
Hibben, Westley G	Anchorage
Hook, Bob	North Pole
Kelsey, Nate	Anchorage
Knapp, Mark	Fairbanks
Lance, Bill	Eagle River
Malaby, Raymond J	Juneau
Mcfarlin, Eric E	Kodiak
Miller, Nate	Fairbanks
Miller, Ron	NORTH POLE
Miller, Terry	Healy
Mirabile, David	Juneau
Moore, Marve	Willow
Parrish Iii, Gordon A	North Pole
Shore, John I	Anchorage
Stegall, Keith	Wasilla
Van Cleve, Steve	Sutton
Whipple, Wesley A	Kodiak
Whitman, Jim	Chugiak

AL

Batson, James	Madison
Baxter, Dale	Trinity
Bell, Tony	Woodland
Bowles, Chris	Reform
Brend, Walter	Vinemont
Brothers, Dennis L.	Oneonta
Coffman, Danny	Jacksonville
Conn Jr., C T	Attalla
Daniels, Alex	Town Creek
Dark, Robert	Oxford
Di Marzo, Richard	Birmingham
Durham, Kenneth	Cherokee
Elrod, Roger R	Enterprise
Fogg, Don	Jasper
Gilbreath, Randall	Dora
Golden, Randy	Montgomery
Hammond, Jim	Arab
Howard, Durvyn M	Hokes Bluff
Howell, Len	Opelika
Howell, Ted	Wetumpka
Huckabee, Dale	Maylene
Hulsey, Hoyt	Attalla
Mccullough, Jerry	Georgiana
Militano, Tom	Jacksonville
Morris, C H	Frisco City
Pardue, Melvin M	Repton
Roe Jr., Fred D	Huntsville
Russell, Tom	Jacksonville
Sinyard, Cleston S	Elberta
Thomas, David E	Lillian
Tycer, Art	Meridianville
Watson, Billy	Deatsville

AR

Anders, David	Center Ridge
Ardwin, Corey	North Little Rock
Barnes Jr., Cecil C.	Center Ridge
Brown, Jim	Little Rock
Browning, Steven W	Benton
Bullard, Tom	Flippin
Cabe, Jerry (Buddy)	Hattieville
Cook, James R	Nashville
Copeland, Thom	Nashville
Cox, Larry	Murfreesboro
Crawford, Pat And Wes	West Memphis
Crowell, James L	Mtn. View
Dozier, Bob	Springdale
Duvall, Fred	Benton
Echols, Roger	Nashville
Edge, Tommy	Cash
Ferguson, Lee	Hindsville
Ferguson, Linda	Hindsville
Fisk, Jerry	Nashville
Fitch, John S	Clinton
Flournoy, Joe	El Dorado
Foster, Ronnie E	Morrilton
Foster, Timothy L	El Dorado
Frizzell, Ted	West Fork
Gadberry, Emmet	Hattieville
Greenaway, Don	Fayetteville
Herring, Morris	Dyer
Lawrence, Alton	De Queen
Livesay, Newt	Siloam Springs
Lunn, Gail	Mountain Home
Lunn, Larry A	Mountain Home
Lynch, Tad	Beene
Maringer, Tom	Springdale
Martin, Bruce E	Prescott
Martin, Hal W	Morrilton
Massey, Roger	Texarkana
Newton, Ron	London
O'Dell, Clyde	Camden
Olive, Michael E	Leslie
Passmore, Jimmy D	Hoxie
Perry, Jim	Hope
Perry, John	Mayflower
Peterson, Lloyd (Pete) C	Clinton
Polk, Clifton	Van Buren
Polk, Rusty	Van Buren
Red, Vernon	Conway
Rhea, Lin	Prattsville
Reeves, J.R.	Texarkana
Richards, Ralph (Bud)	Bauxite
Smoker, Ray	Searcy
Solomon, Marvin	Paron
Stanley, John	Crossett
Stout, Charles	Gillham
Sweaza, Dennis	Austin
Townsend, Allen Mark	Texarkana
Townsley, Russell	Concord
Walker, Jim	Morrilton
Ward, Chuck	Benton
Waters, Herman Harold	Magnolia
Waters, Lu	Magnolia
White, Bryce	Little Rock
Young, Raymond L	Mt. Ida

ARGENTINA

Ayarragaray, Cristian L.	
	(3100) Parana-Entre Rios
Bertolami, Juan Carlos	Neuquen
Gibert, Pedro	
Kehiayan, Alfredo CP B1623GXU Buenos Aires	
Rho, Nestor Lorenzo	Buenos Aires
Santiago, Abud	Buenos Aires 1416

AUSTRALIA

Bennett, Peter	Engadine N.S.W. 2233
Brodziak, David	Albany, Western Australia
Crawley, Bruce R	Croydon 3136 Victoria
Cross, Robert	Tamworth 2340, NSW
Del Raso, Peter	Mt. Waverly, Victoria, 3149
Gerner, Thomas	Western Australia
Giljevic, Branko	N.S.W.
Green, William (Bill)	View Bank Vic.
Harvey, Max	Perth 6155, Western Australia
Husiak, Myron	Victoria
Jones, John	Gympie, Queensland 4570
K B S, Knives	Vic 3450
Maisey, Alan	Vincentia 2540, NSW
Mcintyre, Shawn	Hawthorn East Victoria
Phillips, Alistair	ACT, 2914
Spencer, KeithChidlow	Western Australia
Tasman, Kerley	Western Australia
Zemitis, Joe	2285 Newcastle

AZ

Ammons, David C	Tucson
Bennett, Glen C	Tucson
Birdwell, Ira Lee	Congress
Boye, David	Dolan Springs
Bryan, Tom	Gilbert
Cheatham, Bill	Laveen
Choate, Milton	Somerton
Clark, R W	Surprise
Dawson, Lynn	Prescott Valley
Deubel, Chester J.	Tucson
Dodd, Robert F	Camp Verde
Fuegen, Larry	Prescott
Goo, Tai	Tucson
Hancock, Tim	Scottsdale
Hoel, Steve	Pine
Holder, D'Alton	Peoria
Hull, Michael J	Cottonwood
Karp, Bob	Phoenix
Kiley, Mike And Jandy	Chino Valley
Kopp, Todd M	Apache Jct.
Lampson, Frank G	Rimrock
Lee, Randy	St. Johns
Mcfall, Ken	Lakeside
Mcfarlin, J W	Lake Havasu City
Miller, Michael	Kingman
Mooney, Mike	Queen Creek
Newhall, Tom	Tucson
Purvis, Bob And Ellen	Tucson
Robbins, Bill	Globe
Rybar Jr., Raymond B	Came Verde
Tamboli, Michael	Glendale
Tollefson, Barry A	Tubac
Torgeson, Samuel L	Sedona
Tyre, Michael A	Wickenburg
Weiss, Charles L	Waddell
Wolf, Bill	Phoenix
Wright, Timothy	Sedona
Wuertz, Travis	Casa Grande
York, David C	Chino Valley

BELGIUM

Dox, Jan	B 2900 Schoten
Monteiro, Victor	1360 Maleves Ste Marie

BRAZIL

Bodolay, Antal	Belo Horizonte MG-31730-700
Bossaerts, Carl	14051-110, Ribeirao Preto, S.P.
Campos, Ivan	Tatui, SP

Dorneles, Luciano Oliverira
    Nova Petropolis, RS
Gaeta, Angelo   SP-17201-310
Gaeta, Roberto   Sao Paulo
Garcia, Mario Eiras   Sao Paulo
    SP-05516-070
Lala, Paulo Ricardo P And Lala, Roberto P.
    SP-19031-260
Neto Jr., Nelson And De Carvalho,
    Henrique M.   SP-12900-000
Paulo, Fernandes R   Sao Paulo
Petean, Francisco And Mauricio
    SP-16200-000
Ricardo Romano, Bernardes Itajuba MG
Sfreddo, Rodrigo Menezes
    cep g5 150-000
Tkoma, Flavio   Prudonte SP19031-220
Vilar, Ricardo Augusto Ferreira Mairipora
    Sao Paulo
Villa, Luiz   Sao Paulo, SP-04537-081
Villar, Ricardo   S.P. 07600-000
Zakharov, Gladiston   Jacaret SP

CA

Abegg, Arnie   Huntington Beach
Abernathy, Paul J   Eureka
Adkins, Richard L   Mission Viejo
Aldrete, Bob   Lomita
Athey, Steve   Riverside
Barnes, Gregory   Altadena
Barron, Brian   San Mateo
Benson, Don   Escalon
Berger, Max A.   Carmichael
Biggers, Gary   Ventura
Blum, Chuck   Brea
Bost, Roger E   Palos Verdes
Boyd, Francis   Berkeley
Brack, Douglas D   Ventura
Breshears, Clint   Manhattan Beach
Brooks, Buzz   Los Angles
Browne, Rick   Upland
Bruce, Richard L.   Yankee Hill
Brunetta, David   Laguna Beach
Butler, Bart   Ramona
Cabrera, Sergio B   Wilmington
Cantrell, Kitty D   Ramona
Caston, Darriel   Sacramento
Caswell, Joe   Newbury
Clinco, Marcus   Venice
Coffey, Bill   Clovis
Cohen, Terry A   Laytonville
Coleman, John A   Citrus Heights
Connolly, James   Oroville
Cucchiara, Matt   Fresno
Davis, Charlie   Santee
De Maria Jr., Angelo   Carmel Valley
Dion, Greg   Oxnard
Dixon Jr., Ira E   Ventura
Doolittle, Mike   Novato
Driscoll, Mark   La Mesa
Dwyer, Duane   San Marcos
Ellis, Dave/Abs Mastersmith   Vista
Ellis, William Dean   Sanger
Emerson, Ernest R   Torrance
English, Jim   Jamul
English, Jim   Jamul
Ernest, Phil (Pj)   Whittier
Essegian, Richard   Fresno
Felix, Alexander   Torrance
Ferguson, Jim   Temecula
Fisher, Theo (Ted)   Montague
Forrest, Brian   Descanso
Fraley, D B   Dixon
Fred, Reed Wyle   Sacramento
Freer, Ralph   Seal Beach
Fulton, Mickey   Willows

Girtner, Joe   Brea
Gofourth, Jim   Santa Paula
Guarnera, Anthony R   Quartzhill
Guidry, Bruce   Murrieta
Hall, Jeff   Los Alamitos
Hardy, Scott   Placerville
Harris, Jay   Redwood City
Harris, John   Riverside
Helton, Roy   San Diego
Herndon, Wm R "Bill"   Acton
Hink Iii, Les   Stockton
Hoy, Ken   North Fork
Humenick, Roy   Rescue
Iames, Gary   Tahoe
Jacks, Jim   Covina
Jackson, David   Lemoore
Jensen, John Lewis   Pasadena
Johnson, Randy   Turlock
Kazsuk, David   Perris
Kelly, Dave   Los Angeles
Keyes, Dan   Chino
Kilpatrick, Christian A   Citrus Hieghts
Koster, Steven C   Huntington Beach
Laner, Dean   Susanville
Larson, Richard   Turlock
Leland, Steve   Fairfax
Likarich, Steve   Colfax
Lockett, Sterling   Burbank
Loveless, R W   Riverside
Luchini, Bob   Palo Alto
Mackie, John   Whittier
Massey, Ron   Joshua Tree
Mata, Leonard   San Diego
Maxwell, Don   Clovis
Mcabee, William   Colfax
Mcclure, Michael   Menlo Park
Mcgrath, Patrick T   Westchester
Melin, Gordon C   La Mirada
Meloy, Sean   Lemon Grove
Montano, Gus A   San Diego
Morgan, Jeff   Santee
Moses, Steven   Santa Ana
Mutz, Jeff   Rancho Cucamonga
Naten, Greg   Bakersfield
Orton, Rich   Riverside
Osborne, Donald H   Clovis
Packard, Bob   Elverta
Palm, Rik   San Diego
Pendleton, Lloyd   Volcano
Perry, Chris   Fresno
Pfanenstiel, Dan   Modesto
Phillips, Randy   Ontario
Pitt, David F   Anderson
Posner, Barry E   N. Hollywood
Quesenberry, Mike   Blairsden
Randall, Patrick   Newbury Park
Rozas, Clark D   Wilmington
Schmitz, Raymond E   Valley Center
Schneider, Herman   Apple Valley
Schroen, Karl   Sebastopol
Sibrian, Aaron   Ventura
Sjostrand, Kevin   Visalia
Slobodian, Scott   San Andreas
Smith, Shawn   Clouis
Sornberger, Jim   Volcano
St. Cyr, H Red   Wilmington
Stapel, Chuck   Glendale
Steinberg, Al   Laguna Woods
Stimps, Jason M   Orange
Stockwell, Walter   Redwood City
Stover, Howard   Pasadena
Strider, Mick   San Marcos
Terrill, Stephen   Springville
Tingle, Dennis P   Jackson
Torres, Henry   Clovis
Trace Rinaldi Custom Blades,   Hemet
Trujillo, Miranda   Rohnert Park

Vagnino, Michael   Visalia
Velick, Sammy   Los Angeles
Warren, Al   Roseville
Watanabe, Wayne   Montebello
Weinstock, Robert   San Francisco
Wilson, Philip C   Mountain Ranch
Wilson, Ron   Morro Bay

CANADA

Arnold, Joe   London, Ont.
Beauchamp, Gaetan   Stoneham, PQ
Beets, Marty   Williams Lake, BC
Bell, Donald   Bedford, Nova Scotia
Berg, Lothar   Kitchener ON
Beshara, Brent (Besh)   Stayner, ON
Boos, Ralph   Edmonton, Alberta
Bourbeau, Jean Yves Ile Perrot, Quebec
Bradford, Garrick   Kitchener ON
Dallyn, Kelly   Calgary, AB
Debraga, Jose C Trois Rivieres, Quebec
Debraga, Jovan   Quebec
Deringer, Christoph   Cookshire, Quebec
Desaulniers, Alain   Cookshire, Quebec
Diotte, Jeff   LaSalle Ontario
Doiron, Donald   Messines, PQ
Doucette, R   Brantford, Ont.
Doussot, Laurent   St. Bruno, Quebec
Downie, James T   Port Franks, Ont.
Frigault, Rick   Niagara Falls, Ont.
Ganshorn, Cal Regina, Saskatchewan
Garvock, Mark W   Balderson, Ont.
Gilbert, Chantal   Quebec City Quebec
Haslinger, Thomas   Calgary, AB
Hayes, Wally   Essex, Ont.
Hindmarch, G   Carlyle SK S0C 0R0
Hofer, Louis   Rose Prairie, B.C.
Jobin, Jacques   Levis Quebec
Kaczor, Tom   Upper London, Ont.
Lambert, Kirby
    Regina Saskatchewan S4N X3
Langley, Mick   Qualicum Beach, B.C.
Lay, R J (Bob)   Logan Lake, B.C.
Leber, Heinz   Hudson's Hope, B.C.
Lightfoot, Greg   Kitscoty, AB
Linklater, Steve   Aurora, Ont.
Loerchner, Wolfgang   Bayfield, Ont.
Lyttle, Brian   High River, AB
Maneker, Kenneth Galiano Island, B.C.
Marzitelli, Peter   Langley, B.C.
Massey, Al Mount Uniacke, Nova Scotia
Mckenzie, David Brian Campbell River B
Miville-Deschenes, Alain
    Quebec
Niro, Frank   Blind Bay, B.C.
O'Hare, Sean   Grand Manan, NB
Olson, Rod   High River, AB
Painter, Tony   Whitehorse Yukon
Patrick, Bob   S. Surrey, B.C.
Pepiot, Stephan   Winnipeg, Man.
Piesner, Dean   Conestogo, Ont.
Roberts, George A   Whitehorse, YT
Ross, Tim   Thunder Bay, Ont.
Schoenfeld, Matthew A
    Galiano Island, B.C.
St. Amour, Murray   Pembroke ON
Stancer, Chuck   Calgary, AB
Storch, Ed   Alberta T0B 2W0
Stuart, Steve   Gores Landing, Ont.
Sylvester, David   Compton, Quebec
Tichbourne, George   Mississauga, Ont.
Tighe, Brian   St. Catharines, Ont.
Toner, Roger   Pickering, Ont.
Treml, Glenn   Thunder Bay, Ont.
Vanderkolff, Stephen   Mildmay Ontario
Whitenect, Jody   Nova Scotia
Wile, Peter Bridgewater, Nova Scotia
Young, Bud   Port Hardy, BC

CO

Anderson, Mark Alan	Denver
Anderson, Mel	Hotchkiss
Barrett, Cecil Terry	Colorado Springs
Booco, Gordon	Hayden
Brandon, Matthew	Denver
Brock, Kenneth L	Allenspark
Burrows, Chuck	Durango
Dannemann, Randy	Hotchkiss
Davis, Don	Loveland
Dawson, Barry	Durango
Delong, Dick	Aurora
Dennehy, Dan	Del Norte
Dennehy, John D	Wellington
Dill, Robert	Loveland
Fronefield, Daniel	Peyton
Hackney, Dana A.	Monument
High, Tom	Alamosa
Hockensmith, Dan	Carr
Hughes, Ed	Grand Junction
Irie, Michael L	Colorado Springs
Kitsmiller, Jerry	Montrose
Leck, Dal	Hayden
Magruder, Jason	Colorado Springs
Miller, Hanford J	Cowdrey
Miller, M A	Northglenn
Olson, Wayne C	Bailey
Ott, Fred	Durango
Owens, John	Nathrop
Rexford, Todd	Woodland Park
Roberts, Chuck	Golden
Rollert, Steve	Keenesburg
Ronzio, N. Jack	Fruita
Sanders, Bill	Mancos
Thompson, Lloyd	Pagosa Springs
Waites, Richard L	Broomfield
Watson, Bert	Westminster
Wilson, James G	Estes Park
Wood, Owen Dale	Arvada
Zima, Michael F	Ft. Morgan

CT

Barnes, William	Wallingford
Buebendorf, Robert E	Monroe
Chapo, William G	Wilton
Framski, Walter P	Prospect
Jean, Gerry	Manchester
Meyer, Christopher J	Tolland
Plunkett, Richard	West Cornwall
Putnam, Donald S	Wethersfield
Rainville, Richard	Salem
Riden, Doug	Eastford
Turecek, Jim	Ansonia
Vitale, Mace	Guilford
Zembko Iii, John	Berlin

DE

Antonio Jr., William J	Newark
Schneider, Karl A	Newark
Willey, Wg	Greenwood

DENMARK

Andersen, Henrik Lefolii	
	3480, Fredensborg
Anso, Jens	116, 8472 Sporup
Dyrnoe, Per	DK 3400 Hilleroed
Henriksen, Hans J	DK 3200 Helsinge
Strande, Poul	Dastrup 4130 Viby Sj.
Vensild, Henrik	DK-8963 Auning
Willumsen, Mikkel	

ENGLAND

Bailey, I.R.	Colkirk
Barker, Stuart	Oadby, Leicester
Boden, Harry	Derbyshire DE4 2AJ
Farid R, Mehr	Kent
Harrington, Roger	East Sussex
Jackson, Jim	
	Chapel Row Bucklebury RG7 6PU
Morris, Darrell Price	Devon
Orford, Ben	Worcestershire
Penfold, Mick Tremar, Cornwall PL14 5SJ	
Wardell, Mick	N Devon EX39 3BU
Wise, Donald	East Sussex, TN3 8AL
Wood, Alan	Brampton CA8 7HH

FINLAND

Tuominen, Pekka	72930 Tossavanlahti

FL

Adams, Les	Hialeah
Alexander, Oleg, Cossack Blades	
	Wellington
Anders, Jerome	Miramar
Angell, Jon	Hawthorne
Atkinson, Dick	Wausau
Bacon, David R.	Bradenton
Barry Iii, James J.	West Palm Beach
Bartrug, Hugh E.	St. Petersburg
Beers, Ray	Lake Wales
Benjamin Jr., George	Kissimmee
Birnbaum, Edwin	Miami
Blackwood, Neil	Lakeland
Bosworth, Dean	Key Largo
Bradley, John	Pomona Park
Bray Jr., W Lowell	New Port Richey
Brown, Harold E	Arcadia
Burris, Patrick R	Jacksonville
Butler, John	Havana
Chase, Alex	DeLand
Cole, Dave	Satellite Beach
D'Andrea, John	Citrus Springs
Davis Jr., Jim	Zephyrhills
Dietzel, Bill	Middleburg
Doggett, Bob	Brandon
Dotson, Tracy	Baker
Ellerbe, W B	Geneva
Ellis, Willy B	Palm Harbor
Enos Iii, Thomas M	Orlando
Ferrara, Thomas	Naples
Ferris, Bill	Palm Beach Garden
Fowler, Charles R	Ft McCoy
Gamble, Roger	Newberry
Gibson Sr., James Hoot	Bunnell
Goers, Bruce	Lakeland
Granger, Paul J	Largo
Greene, Steve	Kissimmee
Griffin Jr., Howard A	Davie
Grospitch, Ernie	Orlando
Harris, Ralph Dewey	Brandon
Heaney, John D	Haines City
Heitler, Henry	Tampa
Hodge Iii, John	Palatka
Humphreys, Joel	Lake Placid
Hunter, Richard D	Alachua
Hytovick, Joe "Hy"	Dunnellon
Jernigan, Steve	Milton
Johanning Custom Knives, Tom Sarasota	
Johnson, John R	Plant City
King, Bill	Tampa
Krapp, Denny	Apopka
Levengood, Bill	Tampa
Lewis, Mike	DeBary
Long, Glenn A	Dunnellon
Lovestrand, Schuyler	Vero Beach
Lozier, Don	Ocklawaha
Lyle Iii, Ernest L	Chiefland
Mandt, Joe	St. Petersburg
Mcdonald, Robert J	Loxahatchee
Mcgowan, Frank E	Sebring
Miller, Ronald T	Largo
Mink, Dan	Crystal Beach
Newton, Larry	Jacksonville
Ochs, Charles F	Largo
Owens, Donald	Melbourne
Parker, Cliff	Zephyrhills
Partridge, Jerry D.	DeFuniak Springs
Pendray, Alfred H	Williston
Piergallini, Daniel E	Plant City
Randall Made Knives,	Orlando
Reed, John M	Oak Hill
Robinson, Calvin	Pace
Robinson Iii, Rex R	Leesburg
Rodkey, Dan	Hudson
Romeis, Gordon	Fort Myers
Ross, Gregg	Lake Worth
Russ, Ron	Williston
Schwarzer, Lora Sue	Crescent City
Schwarzer, Stephen	Crescent City
Smith, Michael J	Brandon
Stapleton, William E	Merritt Island
Steck, Van R	Orange City
Stephan, Daniel	Valrico
Stipes, Dwight	Palm City
Straight, Kenneth J	Largo
Tabor, Tim	Lutz
Turnbull, Ralph A	Spring Hill
Vogt, Donald J	Tampa
Watson, Tom	Panama City
Weiland Jr., J Reese	Riverview
White, John Paul	Valparaiso
Wicker, Donnie R	Panama City
Wilson, Stan	Lithia
Zaccagnino Jr., Don	Pahokee
Zahm, Kurt	Indialantic
Zinker, Brad	Homestead

FRANCE

Bennica, Charles	
	34190 Moules et Baucels
Chauzy, Alain	21140 Seur-en-Auxios
Doursin, Gerard	Pernes les Fontaines
Graveline, Pascal And Isabelle	
	29350 Moelan-sur-Mer
Headrick, Gary	Juane Les Pins
Madrulli, Mme Joelle	Salon De Provence
Reverdy, Nicole And Pierre	
Thevenot, Jean-Paul	Dijon
Viallon, Henri	

GA

Arrowood, Dale	Sharpsburg
Ashworth, Boyd	Powder Springs
Barker, Robert G.	Bishop
Bentley, C L	Albany
Bish, Hal	Jonesboro
Black, Scott	Covington
Bradley, Dennis	Blairsville
Buckner, Jimmie H	Putney
Chamblin, Joel	Concord
Cole, Welborn I	Athens
Crockford, Jack	Chamblee
Davis, Steve	Powder Springs
Dempsey, David	Macon
Dunn, Charles K	Shiloh
Frost, Dewayne	Barnesville
Gaines, Buddy	Commerce
Glover, Warren D	Cleveland
Greene, David	Covington
Halligan, Ed	Sharpsburg
Hammond, Hank	Leesburg
Hardy, Douglas E	Franklin
Hawkins, Rade	Fayetteville

Hensley, Wayne — Conyers
Hinson And Son, R — Columbus
Hoffman, Kevin L — Savannah
Hossom, Jerry — Duluth
Jones, Franklin (Frank) W — Columbus
Kimsey, Kevin — Cartersville
King, Fred — Cartersville
Knott, Steve — Guyton
Landers, John — Newnan
Lonewolf, J Aguirre — Demorest
Mathews, Charlie And Harry — Statesboro
Mcgill, John — Blairsville
Mclendon, Hubert W — Waco
Mitchell, James A — Columbus
Moncus, Michael Steven — Smithville
Parks, John — Jefferson
Poole, Marvin O — Commerce
Powell, Robert Clark — Smarr
Prater, Mike — Flintstone
Price, Timmy — Blairsville
Pridgen Jr., Larry — Fitzgerald
Ragsdale, James D — Lithonia
Roghmans, Mark — LaGrange
Rosenfeld, Bob — Hoschton
Scofield, Everett — Chickamauga
Sculley, Peter E — Rising Fawn
Smith Jr., James B "Red" — Morven
Snow, Bill — Columbus
Sowell, Bill — Macon
Stafford, Richard — Warner Robins
Thompson, Kenneth — Duluth
Tomey, Kathleen — Macon
Walters, A F — TyTy
Whetsell, Alex — Sharpsburg
White, Garrett — Hartwell
White, Lou — Ranger

GERMANY

Balbach, Markus — 35789 Weilmunster-Laubuseschbach/Ts.
Becker, Franz — 84533, Marktl/Inn
Boehlke, Guenter — 56412 Grossholbach
Borger, Wolf — 76676 Graben-Neudorf
Dell, Wolfgang — D-73277 Owen-Teck
Drumm, Armin — D-89160 Dornstadt
Faust, Joachim — 95497 Goldkronach
Fruhmann, Ludwig — 84489 Burghausen
Greiss, Jockl — D 77773 Schenkenzell
Hehn, Richard Karl — 55444 Dorrebach
Herbst, Peter — 91207 Lauf a.d. Pegn.
Joehnk, Bernd — 24148 Kiel
Kressler, D F — D-28832 Achim
Neuhaeusler, Erwin — 86179 Augsburg
Rankl, Christian — 81476 Munchen
Rinkes, Siegfried — Markterlbach
Selzam, Frank — Bad Koenigshofen
Steinau, Jurgen — Berlin 0-1162
Tritz, Jean Jose — 20255 Hamburg
Wirtz, Achim — D-52146
Zirbes, Richard — D-54526 Niederkail

GREECE

Filippou, Ioannis-Minas — Athens 17122

HI

Evans, Vincent K And Grace — Keaau
Fujisaka, Stanley — Kaneohe
Gibo, George — Hilo
Lui, Ronald M — Honolulu
Mann, Tim — Honokaa
Matsuoka, Scot — Mililani
Mayo Jr., Tom — Waialua
Mitsuyuki, Ross — Honolulu
Onion, Kenneth J — Kaneohe

Ouye, Keith — Honolulu
Watanabe, Melvin — Kailua
Zakabi, Carl S — Mililani Town

HOLLAND

Van De Manakker, Thijs — 5759 px Helenaveen

IA

Brooker, Dennis — Chariton
Brower, Max — Boone
Clark, Howard F — Runnells
Cockerham, Lloyd — Denham Springs
Helscher, John W — Washington
Lainson, Tony — Council Bluffs
Lewis, Bill — Riverside
Mckiernan, Stan — Lamoni
Miller, James P — Fairbank
Thie, Brian — Burlington
Trindle, Barry — Earlham
Westberg, Larry — Algona
Zscherny, Michael — Ely

ID

Alderman, Robert — Sagle
Alverson, Tim (R.V.) — Moscow
Bloodworth Custom Knives, — Meridian
Burke, Bill — Boise
Eddy, Hugh E — Caldwell
Hawk, Grant And Gavin — Idaho City
Hogan, Thomas R — Boise
Horton, Scot — Buhl
Howe, Tori — Athol
Mann, Michael L — Spirit Lake
Metz, Greg T — Cascade
Patton, Dick And Rob — Nampa
Quarton, Barr — McCall
Reeve, Chris — Boise
Rohn, Fred — Coeur d'Alene
Sawby, Scott — Sandpoint
Schultz, Robert W — Cocolalla
Selent, Chuck — Bonners Ferry
Sparks, Bernard — Dingle
Steiger, Monte L — Genesee
Tippetts, Colten — Hidden Springs
Towell, Dwight L — Midvale

IL

Bloomer, Alan T — Maquon
Camerer, Craig — Chesterfield
Cook, Louise — Ozark
Cook, Mike — Ozark
Detmer, Phillip — Breese
Dicristofano, Anthony P — Northlake
Eaker, Allen L — Paris
Fiorini, Bill — Grayville
Hawes, Chuck — Weldon
Heath, William — Bondville
Hill, Rick — Maryville
Knuth, Joseph E — Rockford
Kovar, Eugene — Evergreen Park
Leone, Nick — Pontoon Beach
Markley, Ken — Sparta
Meier, Daryl — Carbondale
Myers, Paul — Wood River
Myers, Steve — Virginia
Nevling, Mark — Hume
Nowland, Rick — Waltonville
Pellegrin, Mike — Troy
Pritchard, Ron — Dixon
Rados, Jerry F — Grant Park
Rosenbaugh, Ron — Crystal Lake
Rossdeutscher, Robert N — Arlington Heights

Rzewnicki, Gerald — Elizabeth
Schneider, Craig M — Claremont
Smale, Charles J — Waukegan
Smith, John M — Centralia
Todd, Richard C — Chambersburg
Tompkins, Dan — Peotone
Veit, Michael — LaSalle
Voss, Ben — Victoria
Werth, George W — Poplar Grove
West, Charles A — Centralia
Wheeler, Robert — Bradley
White, Robert J — Gilson
White Jr., Robert J Butch — Gilson
Young, Errol — Alton

IN

Adkins, Larry — Indianapolis
Ball, Ken — Mooresville
Barkes, Terry — Edinburgh
Barrett, Rick L. (Toshi Hisa) — Goshen
Bose, Reese — Shelburn
Bose, Tony — Shelburn
Chaffee, Jeff L — Morris
Claiborne, Jeff — Franklin
Cramer, Brent — Wheatland
Crowl, Peter — Waterloo
Damlovac, Sava — Indianapolis
Darby, Jed — Greensburg
Fitzgerald, Dennis M — Fort Wayne
Fraps, John R — Indianpolis
Good, D.R. — Tipton
Hunt, Maurice — Brownsburg
Imel, Billy Mace — New Castle
Johnson, C E Gene — Chesterton
Kain, Charles — Indianapolis
Keeslar, Steven C — Hamilton
Keeton, William L — Laconia
Kinker, Mike — Greensburg
Mayville, Oscar L — Marengo
Minnick, Jim — Middletown
Oliver, Todd D — Spencer
Parsons, Michael R — Indianapolis
Patton, Phillip — Yoder
Quakenbush, Thomas C — Ft Wayne
Robertson, Leo D — Indianapolis
Seib, Steve — Evansville
Shull, James — Rensselaer
Smock, Timothy E — Marion
Snyder, Michael Tom — Zionsville
Stover, Terry "Lee" — Kokomo
Thayer, Danny O — Romney
Young, George — Kokomo

ISRAEL

Shadmot, Boaz — Arava

ITALY

Albericci, Emilio — 24100, Bergamo
Ameri, Mauro — 16010 Genova
Ballestra, Santino — 18039 Ventimiglia (IM)
Bertuzzi, Ettore — 24068 Seriate (Bergamo)
Bonassi, Franco — Pordenone 33170
Fogarizzu, Boiteddu — 07016 Pattada
Giagu, Salvatore And Deroma Maria Rosaria — 07016 Pattada (SS)
Pachi, Francesco — 17046 Sassello (SV)
Ramondetti, Sergio — 12013 CHIUSA DI PESIO (CN)
Riboni, Claudio — Truccazzano (MI)
Scordia, Paolo — Roma
Simonella, Gianluigi — 33085 Maniago
Toich, Nevio — Vincenza
Tschager, Reinhard — I-39100 Bolzano

JAPAN

Aida, Yoshihito	Itabashi-ku, Tokyo 175-0094
Ebisu, Hidesaku	Hiroshima City
Fujikawa, Shun	Osaka 597 0062
Fukuta, Tak	Seki-City, Gifu-Pref
Hara, Kouji	Gifu-Pref. 501-3922
Hirayama, Harumi	Saitama Pref. 335-0001
Hiroto, Fujihara	Hiroshima
Isao, Ohbuchi	Fukuoka
Ishihara, Hank	Chiba Pref.
Kagawa, Koichi	Kanagawa
Kanda, Michio	Yamaguchi 7460033
Kanki, Iwao	Hyogo
Kansei, Matsuno	Gitu-city
Kato, Shinichi	Moriyama-ku Nagoya
Katsumaro, Shishido	Hiroshima
Kawasaki, Akihisa	Kobe
Keisuke, Gotoh	Ohita
Koyama, Captain Bunshichi	Nagoya City 453-0817
Mae, Takao	Toyonaka, Osaka
Makoto, Kunitomo	Hiroshima
Matsuno, Kansei	Gifu-City 501-1168
Matsusaki, Takeshi	Nagasaki
Michinaka, Toshiaki	Tottori 680-0947
Micho, Kanda	Yamaguchi
Ryuichi, Kuki	Saitama
Sakakibara, Masaki	Tokyo 156-0054
Sugihara, Keidoh	Osaka, F596-0042
Sugiyama, Eddy K	Ohita
Takahashi, Masao	Gunma 371 0047
Terauchi, Toshiyuki	Fujita-Cho Gobo-Shi
Toshifumi, Kuramoto	Fukuoka
Uchida, Chimata	Kumamoto
Wada, Yasutaka	Nara prefect 631-0044
Waters, Glenn	Hirosaki City 036-8183
Yoshihara, Yoshindo	Tokyo
Yoshikazu, Kamada	Tokushima
Yoshio, Maeda	Okayama

KS

Bradburn, Gary	Wichita
Burrows, Stephen R	Humboldt
Chard, Gordon R	Iola
Courtney, Eldon	Wichita
Craig, Roger L	Topeka
Culver, Steve	Meriden
Darpinian, Dave	Olathe
Davison, Todd A.	Lyons
Dawkins, Dudley L	Topeka
Dick, Dan	Hutchinson
Dugger, Dave	Westwood
Hegwald, J L	Humboldt
Herman, Tim	Olathe
King, Jason M	St. George
King Jr., Harvey G	Alta Vista
Kraft, Steve	Abilene
Lamb, Curtis J	Ottawa
Magee, Jim	Salina
Petersen, Dan L	Auburn

KY

Adams, Jim	Scottsville
Addison, Kyle A	Hazel
Barbara Baskett Custom Knives,	Eastview
Barr, A.T.	Nicholasville
Baskett, Barbara	Eastview
Baskett, Lee Gene	Eastview
Baumgardner, Ed	Glendale
Bodner, Gerald "Jerry"	Louisville
Bybee, Barry J	Cadiz
Carson, Harold J "Kit"	Vine Grove

Coil, Jimmie J	Owensboro
Downing, Larry	Bremen
Dunn, Steve	Smiths Grove
Edwards, Mitch	Glasgow
Finch, Ricky D	West Liberty
Fister, Jim	Simpsonville
France, Dan	Cawood
Frederick, Aaron	West Liberty
Gevedon, Hanners (Hank)	Crab Orchard
Greco, John	Greensburg
Hibben, Daryl	LaGrange
Hibben, Gil	LaGrange
Hibben, Joleen	LaGrange
Hoke, Thomas M	LaGrange
Holbrook, H L	Sandy Hook
Howser, John C	Frankfort
Keeslar, Joseph F	Almo
Lott, Sherry	Greensburg
Miller, Don	Lexington
Pease, W D	Ewing
Pierce, Harold L	Louisville
Pulliam, Morris C	Shelbyville
Richerson, Ron	Greenburg
Rigney Jr., Willie	Bronston
Smith, John W	West Liberty
Soaper, Max H.	Henderson
Steier, David	Louisville
Wallingford Jr., Charles W	Union

LA

Barker, Reggie	Springhill
Blaum, Roy	Covington
Caldwell, Bill	West Monroe
Calvert Jr., Robert W (Bob)	Rayville
Capdepon, Randy	Carencro
Capdepon, Robert	Carencro
Chauvin, John	Scott
Culpepper, John	Monroe
Dake, C M	New Orleans
Dake, Mary H	New Orleans
Durio, Fred	Opelousas
Faucheaux, Howard J	Loreauville
Fontenot, Gerald J	Mamou
Gorenflo, James T (Jt)	Baton Rouge
Graves, Dan	Shreveport
Johnson, Gordon A.	Choudrant
Ki, Shiva	Baton Rouge
Laurent, Kermit	LaPlace
Leonard, Randy Joe	Sarepta
Mitchell, Max Dean And Ben	Leesville
Phillips, Dennis	Independence
Potier, Timothy F	Oberlin
Primos, Terry	Shreveport
Provenzano, Joseph D	Ponchatoula
Randall Jr., James W	Keithville
Randow, Ralph	Pineville
Reggio Jr., Sidney J	Sun
Sanders, Michael M	Ponchatoula
Tilton, John	Iowa
Trisler, Kenneth W	Rayville
Wiggins, Horace	Mansfield

MA

Dailey, G E	Seekonk
Dugdale, Daniel J.	Walpole
Entin, Robert	Boston
Gaudette, Linden L	Wilbraham
Gedraitis, Charles J	Holden
Grossman, Stewart	Clinton
Hinman, Theodore	Greenfield
Jarvis, Paul M	Cambridge
Khalsa, Jot Singh	Millis
Kubasek, John A	Easthampton
Lapen, Charles	W. Brookfield
Little, Larry	Spencer

Martin, Randall J	Bridgewater
Mcluin, Tom	Dracut
Moore, Michael Robert	Lowell
Rebello, Indian George	New Bedford
Reed, Dave	Brimfield
Rizzi, Russell J	Ashfield
Rua, Gary	Fall River
Saviano, James	Douglas
Siska, Jim	Westfield
Smith, J D	Roxbury
Stuart, Mason	Mansfield
Szarek, Mark G	Revere
Vining, Bill	Methuen

MD

Bagley, R. Keith	White Plains
Barnes, Aubrey G.	Hagerstown
Barnes, Gary L.	New Windsor
Beers, Ray	Monkton
Cohen, N J (Norm)	Baltimore
Dement, Larry	Prince Fredrick
Freiling, Albert J	Finksburg
Fuller, Jack A	New Market
Gossman, Scott	Forest Hill
Hart, Bill	Pasadena
Hendrickson, E Jay	Frederick
Hendrickson, Shawn	Knoxville
Hurt, William R	Frederick
Kreh, Lefty	"Cockeysville"
Kretsinger Jr., Philip W	Boonsboro
Mccarley, John	Taneytown
Mcgowan, Frank E	Sykesvile
Merchant, Ted	White Hall
Nicholson, R. Kent	Phoenix
Sentz, Mark C	Taneytown
Smit, Glenn	Aberdeen
Sontheimer, G Douglas	Potomac
Spickler, Gregory Noble	Sharpsburg
St. Clair, Thomas K	Monrovia
Walker, Bill	Stevensville
White, Gene E	Bethesda

ME

Ceprano, Peter J.	Auburn
Coombs Jr., Lamont	Bucksport
Courtois, Bryan	Saco
Gray, Daniel	Brownville
Hillman, Charles	Friendship
Leavitt Jr., Earl F	E. Boothbay
Oyster, Lowell R	Corinth
Sharrigan, Mudd	Wiscasset

MEXICO

Scheurer, Alfredo E Faes	C.P. 16010
Sunderland, Richard	Puerto Escondido Oaxaca
Young, Cliff	San Miguel De Allende, GTO.

MI

Ackerson, Robin E	Buchanan
Alcorn, Douglas A.	Chesaning
Andrews, Eric	Grand Ledge
Arms, Eric	Tustin
Behnke, William	Kingsley
Booth, Philip W	Ithaca
Buckbee, Donald M	Grayling
Canoy, Andrew B	Hubbard Lake
Carr, Tim	Muskegon
Carroll, Chad	Grant
Casey, Kevin	Hickory Corners
Cashen, Kevin R	Hubbardston
Cook, Mike A	Portland
Cousino, George	Onsted
Cowles, Don	Royal Oak

Dilluvio, Frank J — Warren
Ealy, Delbert — Indian River
Erickson, Walter E. — Atlanta
Gordon, Larry B — Farmington Hills
Gottage, Dante — Clinton Twp.
Gottage, Judy — Clinton Twp.
Harm, Paul W — Attica
Harrison, Brian — Cedarville
Hartman, Arlan (Lanny) — Baldwin
Hughes, Daryle — Nunica
Keranen, Paul — Ahmeek
Krause, Roy W — St. Clair Shores
Lankton, Scott — Ann Arbor
Leach, Mike J — Swartz Creek
Lucie, James R — Fruitport
Mankel, Kenneth — Cannonsburg
Marsh, Jeremy — Ada
Mills, Louis G — Ann Arbor
Morris, Michael S. — Yale
Noren, Douglas E — Springlake
Parker, Robert Nelson — Royal Oak
Repke, Mike — Bay City
Rose Ii, Doun T — Fife Lake
Sakmar, Mike — Howell
Sandberg, Ronald B — Brownstown
Santini, Tom — Chesterfield
Serven, Jim — Fostoria
Tally, Grant — Flat Rock
Van Eizenga, Jerry W — Nunica
Vasquez, Johnny David — Wyandotte
Viste, James — Detroit
Webster, Bill — Three Rivers
Welling, Ronald L — Grand Haven
White, Richard T — Grosse Pointe Farms
Whittaker, Wayne — Metamore
Whitworth, Ken J — Sterling Heights
Wood, Webster — Atlanta
Zowada, Tim — Boyne Falls

MN

Davis, Joel — Albert Lea
Goltz, Warren L — Ada
Hagen, Doc — Pelican Rapids
Hansen, Robert W — Cambridge
Johnson, R B — Clearwater
Knipschield, Terry — Rochester
Maines, Jay — Wyoming
Metsala, Anthony — Princeton
Mickley, Tracy — North Mankato
Rydbom, Jeff — Annandale
Shadley, Eugene W — Bovey
Steffen, Chuck — St. Michael
Voorhies, Les — Faribault

MO

Allred, Elvan — St. Charles
Andrews, Russ — Sugar Creek
Betancourt, Antonio L. — St. Louis
Braschler, Craig W. — Doniphan
Buxton, Bill — Kaiser
Chinnock, Daniel T. — Union
Cover, Raymond A — Festus
Cox, Colin J — Raymore
Davis, W C — El Dorado Springs
Dippold, Al — Perryville
Duncan, Ron — Cairo
Ehrenberger, Daniel Robert — Mexico
Engle, William — Boonville
Hanson Iii, Don L. — Success
Harris, Jeffery A — Chesterfield
Harrison, Jim (Seamus) — St. Louis
Jones, John A — Holden
Kinnikin, Todd — Pacific
Knickmeyer, Hank — Cedar Hill
Knickmeyer, Kurt — Cedar Hill

Martin, Tony — Arcadia
Mason, Bill — Excelsior Springs
Mccrackin, Kevin — House Spings
Mccrackin And Son, V J — House Springs
Miller, Bob — Oakville
Mosier, David — Independence
Mulkey, Gary — Branson
Muller, Jody — Goodson
Newcomb, Corbin — Moberly
Pryor, Stephen L — Boss
Ramsey, Richard A — Neosho
Rardon, A D — Polo
Rardon, Archie F — Polo
Riepe, Richard A — Harrisonville
Robbins, Howard P — Flemington
Royer, Kyle — Mountain View
Scroggs, James A — Warrensburg
Sonntag, Douglas W — Nixa
Steketee, Craig A — Billings
Stewart, Edward L — Mexico
Stormer, Bob — Dixon
Warden, Roy A — Union
Whitesell, J. Dale — Stover
Willis, Bill — Ava

MS

Black, Scott — Picayune
Boleware, David — Carson
Cohea, John M — Nettleton
Davis, Jesse W — Sarah
Dickerson, Gordon S — New Augusta
Evans, Bruce A — Booneville
Flynt, Robert G — Gulfport
Jones, Jack P. — Ripley
Lamey, Robert M — Biloxi
Lebatard, Paul M — Vancleave
May, Charles — Aberdeen
Mayo Jr., Homer — Biloxi
Nichols, Chad — Blue Springs
Pickett, Terrell — Lumberton
Roberts, Michael — Clinton
Robinson, Chuck — Picayune
Shiffer, Steve — Leakesville
Skow, H.A. "Tex" — Senatobia
Smith, J.B. — Perkinston
Taylor, Billy — Petal
Vandeventer, Terry L — Terry
Vardaman, Robert — Hattiesburg
Wehner, Rudy — Collins
Wingo, Perry — Gulfport
Winston, David — Starkville

MT

Barnes, Jack — Whitefish
Barnes, Wendell — Clinton
Barth, J.D. — Alberton
Beam, John R. — Kalispell
Beaty, Robert B. — Missoula
Bell, Don — Lincoln
Bizzell, Robert — Butte
Boxer, Bo — Whitefish
Brooks, Steve R — Walkerville
Caffrey, Edward J — Great Falls
Campbell, Doug — McLeod
Carlisle, Jeff — Simms
Christensen, Jon P — Stevensville
Colter, Wade — Colstrip
Conklin, George L — Ft. Benton
Crowder, Robert — Thompson Falls
Curtiss, Steve L — Eureka
Dunkerley, Rick — Lincoln
Eaton, Rick — Broadview
Ellefson, Joel — Manhattan
Fassio, Melvin G — Lolo
Forthofer, Pete — Whitefish

Fritz, Erik L — Forsyth
Gallagher, Barry — Lewistown
Harkins, J A — Conner
Hill, Howard E — Polson
Hintz, Gerald M — Helena
Hulett, Steve — West Yellowstone
Kajin, Al — Forsyth
Kauffman, Dave — Montana City
Kelly, Steven — Bigfork
Luman, James R — Anaconda
Mcguane Iv, Thomas F — Bozeman
Mckee, Neil — Stevensville
Moyer, Russ — Havre
Nedved, Dan — Kalispell
Parsons, Pete — Helena
Patrick, Willard C — Helena
Peele, Bryan — Thompson Falls
Peterson, Eldon G — Whitefish
Pursley, Aaron — Big Sandy
Rodewald, Gary — Hamilton
Ruana Knife Works, — Bonner
Smith, Josh — Frenchtown
Sweeney, Coltin D — Missoula
Taylor, Shane — Miles City
Thill, Jim — Missoula
Weinand, Gerome M — Missoula
Yashinski, John L — Red Lodge

NC

Baker, Herb — Eden
Barefoot, Joe W. — Wilmington
Best, Ron — Stokes
Bisher, William (Bill) — Denton
Britton, Tim — Bethania
Busfield, John — Roanoke Rapids
Daniel, Travis E — Chocowinity
Drew, Gerald — Mill Spring
Edwards, Fain E — Topton
Fox, Paul — Claremont
Gaddy, Gary Lee — Washington
Goode, Brian — Shelby
Greene, Chris — Shelby
Gross, W W — Archdale
Gurganus, Carol — Colerain
Gurganus, Melvin H — Colerain
Guthrie, George B — Bassemer City
Hazen, Mark — Charlotte
Kommer, Russ — Fargo
Laramie, Mark — Raeford
Livingston, Robert C — Murphy
Maynard, William N. — Fayetteville
Mclurkin, Andrew — Raleigh
Mcnabb, Tommy — Bethania
Mcrae, J Michael — Mint Hill
Parrish, Robert — Weaverville
Patrick, Chuck — Brasstown
Patrick, Peggy — Brasstown
Rapp, Steven J — Marshall
Scholl, Tim — Angier
Simmons, H R — Aurora
Sterling, Murray — Mount Airy
Summers, Arthur L — Concord
Sutton, S Russell — New Bern
Vail, Dave — Hampstead
Wagaman, John K — Selma
Walker, Don — Burnsville
Warren, Daniel — Canton
Whitley, L Wayne — Chocowinity
Williamson, Tony — Siler City
Wilson, Mike — Hayesville
Winkler, Daniel — Blowing Rock

ND

Pitman, David — Williston

NE

Archer, Ray And Terri	Omaha
Jokerst, Charles	Omaha
Marlowe, Charles	Omaha
Moore, Jon P	Aurora
Mosier, Joshua J	Deshler
Schepers, George B	Shelton
Suedmeier, Harlan	Nebraska City
Syslo, Chuck	Omaha
Tiensvold, Alan L	Rushville
Tiensvold, Jason	Rushville
Till, Calvin E And Ruth	Chadron

NETHERLANDS

Sprokholt, Rob	Netherlands
Van Den Elsen, Gert	5012 AJ Tilburg
Van Eldik, Frans	3632BT Loenen
Van Rijswijk, Aad	3134 HE Vlaardingen

NEW ZEALAND

Bassett, David J.	Glendene, Auckland 0645
Gunther, Eddie	2013 Auckland
Pennington, C A	Kainga Christchurch 8009
Reddiex, Bill	Palmerston North
Ross, D L	Dunedin
Sandow, Brent Edward	Auckland
Sandow, Norman E	Howick, Auckland
Sands, Scott	Christchurch 9
Van Dijk, Richard	Harwood Dunedin

NH

Carlson, Kelly	Antrim
Hill, Steve E	Goshen
Hitchmough, Howard	Peterborough
Hudson, C Robbin	Rummney
Macdonald, John	Raymond
Philippe, D A	Cornish
Saindon, R Bill	Goshen

NJ

Eden, Thomas	Cranbury
Grussenmeyer, Paul G	Cherry Hill
Kearney, Jarod	Bordentown
Licata, Steven	Boonton
Mccallen Jr., Howard H	So Seaside Park
Polkowski, Al	Chester
Pressburger, Ramon	Howell
Schilling, Ellen	Hamilton Square
Sheets, Steven William	Mendham
Slee, Fred	Morganville
Viele, H J	Westwood
Yeskoo, Richard C	Summit

NM

Black, Tom	Albuquerque
Burnley, Lucas	Albuquerque
Cherry, Frank J	Albuquerque
Cordova, Joseph G	Peralta
Cumming, Bob	Cedar Crest
Digangi, Joseph M	Santa Cruz
Duran, Jerry T	Albuquerque
Dyess, Eddie	Roswell
Fisher, Jay	Clovis
Goode, Bear	Navajo Dam
Gunter, Brad	Tijeras
Hartman, Tim	Albuquerque
Hethcoat, Don	Clovis
Hume, Don	Albuquerque
Kimberley, Richard L.	Santa Fe
Lewis, Tom R	Carlsbad

Lynn, Arthur	Galisteo
Macdonald, David	Los Lunas
Mcdonald, Robin J	Albuquerque
Meshejian, Mardi	Santa Fe
Pollock, Wallace J	Reserve
Rogers, Richard	Magdalena
Schaller, Anthony Brett	Albuquerque
Stalcup, Eddie	Gallup
Stetter, J. C.	Roswell
Terzuola, Robert	Albuquerque
Trujillo, Albert M B	Bosque Farms
Walker, Michael L	Pueblo Sur Taos
Wescott, Cody	Las Cruces

NORWAY

Bache-Wiig, Tom	Eivindvik
Sellevold, Harald	N5835 Bergen
Vistnes, Tor	

NV

Barnett, Van	Reno
Beasley, Geneo	Wadsworth
Cameron, Ron G	Logandale
Dellana,	Reno
George, Tom	Henderson
Hrisoulas, Jim	Henderson
Kreibich, Donald L.	Reno
Mount, Don	Las Vegas
Nishiuchi, Melvin S	Las Vegas
Thomas, Devin	Panaca
Tracy, Bud	Reno
Washburn, Arthur D	Pioche

NY

Baker, Wild Bill	Boiceville
Castellucio, Rich	Amsterdam
Cute, Thomas	Cortland
Davis, Barry L	Castleton
Farr, Dan	Rochester
Faust, Dick	Rochester
Hobart, Gene	Windsor
Isgro, Jeffery	West Babylon
Johnson, Mike	Orient
Johnston, Dr. Robt	Rochester
Levin, Jack	Brooklyn
Loos, Henry C	New Hyde Park
Ludwig, Richard O	Maspeth
Lupole, Jamie G	Kirkwood
Maragni, Dan	Georgetown
Mccornock, Craig	Willow
Meerdink, Kurt	Barryville
Page, Reginald	Groveland
Pattay, Rudy	Long Beach
Peterson, Karen	Brooklyn
Phillips, Scott C	Gouverneur
Rachlin, Leslie S	Elmira
Rappazzo, Richard	Cohoes
Rotella, Richard A	Niagara Falls
Scheid, Maggie	Rochester
Schippnick, Jim	Sanborn
Serafen, Steven E	New Berlin
Skiff, Steven	Broadalbin
Smith, Lenard C	Valley Cottage
Smith, Raymond L	Erin
Summers, Dan	Whitney Pt.
Szilaski, Joseph	Pine Plains
Turner, Kevin	Montrose

OH

Bailey, Ryan	Galena
Bendik, John	Olmsted Falls
Busse, Jerry	Wauseon
Collins, Lynn M	Elyria
Coppins, Daniel	Cambridge

Cottrill, James I	Columbus
Downing, Tom	Cuyahoga Falls
Downs, James F	Powell
Etzler, John	Grafton
Foster, R L (Bob)	Mansfield
Francis, John D	Ft. Loramie
Franklin, Mike	Aberdeen
Geisler, Gary R	Clarksville
Gittinger, Raymond	Tiffin
Glover, Ron	Mason
Greiner, Richard	Green Springs
Hinderer, Rick	Shreve
Hudson, Anthony B	Amanda
Humphrey, Lon	Newark
Imboden Ii, Howard L.	Dayton
Jones, Roger Mudbone	Waverly
Kiefer, Tony	Pataskala
Longworth, Dave	Neville
Loro, Gene	Crooksville
Maienknecht, Stanley	Sardis
Mcdonald, Rich	Columbiana
Mcgroder, Patrick J	Madison
Mercer, Mike	Lebanon
Messer, David T	Dayton
Morgan, Tom	Beloit
O'Machearley, Michael	Wilmington
Panak, Paul S	Kinsman
Potter, Billy	Dublin
Ralph, Darrel	Galena
Rose, Derek W	Gallipolis
Rowe, Fred	Amesville
Salley, John D	Tipp City
Schuchmann, Rick	Cincinnati
Shinosky, Andy	Canfield
Shoemaker, Carroll	Northup
Shoemaker, Scott	Miamisburg
Spinale, Richard	Lorain
Stoddart, W B Bill	Fairfield
Strong, Scott	Beavercreek
Summers, Dennis K	Springfield
Thomas, Kim	Seville
Thourot, Michael W	Napoleon
Tindera, George	Brunswick
Votaw, David P	Pioneer
Ward, J J	Waverly
Ward, Ron	Loveland
Witsaman, Earl	Stow
Wright, L T	Steubenville
Yurco, Mike	Canfield
Stidham, Daniel	Gallipolis

OK

Baker, Ray	Sapulpa
Burke, Dan	Edmond
Carrillo, Dwaine	Moore
Crenshaw, Al	Eufaula
Damasteel Stainless Damascus,	Norman
Darby, David T	Cookson
Dill, Dave	Bethany
Duff, Bill	Poteau
Englebretson, George	Oklahoma City
Gepner, Don	Norman
Giraffebone Inc.,	Norman
Heimdale, J E	Tulsa
Johns, Rob	Enid
Kennedy Jr., Bill	Yukon
Kirk, Ray	Tahlequah
Lairson Sr., Jerry	Ringold
Martin	
Martin, John Alexander	Okmulgee
Mcclure, Jerry	Norman
Menefee, Ricky Bob	Blawchard
Miller, Michael E	Chandler
Parsons, Larry	Mustang
Sanders, A.A.	Norman
Spivey, Jefferson	Yukon

Stanford, Perry — Broken Arrow
Tomberlin, Brion R — Norman
Wingo, Gary — Ramona

OR

Bell, Michael — Coquille
Bochman, Bruce — Grants Pass
Brandt, Martin W — Springfield
Buchanan, Thad — Prineville
Buchman, Bill — Bend
Buchner, Bill — Idleyld Park
Busch, Steve — Oakland
Cameron House, — Salem
Carter, Murray M — Vernonia
Clark, Nate — Yoncalla
Coon, Raymond C — Gresham
Crowner, Jeff — Cottage Grove
Davis, Terry — Sumpter
Dowell, T M — Bend
Frank, Heinrich H — Dallas
Gamble, Frank — Salem
Goddard, Wayne — Eugene
Harsey, William H — Creswell
Hilker, Thomas N — Williams
Horn, Jess — Eugene
Kelley, Gary — Aloha
Lake, Ron — Eugene
Little, Gary M — Broadbent
Martin, Gene — Williams
Martin, Walter E — Williams
Olson, Darrold E — Springfield
Richard, Raymond — Gresham
Richards, Chuck — Salem
Rider, David M — Eugene
Sarganis, Paul — Jacksonville
Scarrow, Wil — Gold Hill
Schoeningh, Mike — North Powder
Schrader, Robert — Bend
Sevey Custom Knife, — Gold Beach
Sheehy, Thomas J — Portland
Shoger, Mark O — Beaverton
Smith, Rick — Rogue River
Thompson, Leon — Gaston
Thompson, Tommy — Portland
Turner, Mike — Williams
Vallotton, Butch And Arey — Oakland
Vallotton, Rainy D — Umpqua
Vallotton, Shawn — Oakland
Vallotton, Thomas — Oakland
Ward, Ken — Grants Pass

PA

Anderson, Gary D — Spring Grove
Anderson, Tom — Manchester
Appleby, Robert — Shickshinny
Besedick, Frank E — Ruffsdale
Candrella, Joe — Warminster
Clark, D E (Lucky) — Johnstown
Corkum, Steve — Littlestown
Darby, Rick — Levittown
Derespina, Richard — Willow Grove
Evans, Ronald B — Middleton
Frey Jr., W Frederick — Milton
Godlesky, Bruce F. — Apollo
Goldberg, David — Ft Washington
Gottschalk, Gregory J — Carnegie
Harner, Lloyd R. "Butch" — Hanover
Heinz, John — Upper Black Eddy
Hudson, Rob — Northumberland
Johnson, John R — New Buffalo
Jones, Curtis J — Washington
Malloy, Joe — Freeland
Marlowe, Donald — Dover
Mensch, Larry C — Milton
Miller, Rick — Rockwood

Moore, Ted — Elizabethtown
Morett, Donald — Lancaster
Nealy, Bud — Stroudsburg
Neilson, J — Wyalusing
Nott, Ron P — Summerdale
Ogden, Bill — Avis
AVIS
Ortega, Ben M — Wyoming
Parker, J E — Clarion
Root, Gary — Erie
Rose, Bob — Wagontown
Rupert, Bob — Clinton
Sass, Gary N — Sharpsville
Scimio, Bill — Spruce Creek
Sinclair, J E — Pittsburgh
Steigerwalt, Ken — Orangeville
Stroyan, Eric — Dalton
Takach, Andrew — Elizabeth
Valois, A. Daniel — Lehighton
Vaughan, Ian — Manheim
Whittaker, Robert E — Mill Creek
Wilson, Jon J — Johnstown

RI

Bardsley, Norman P. — Pawtucket
Dickison, Scott S — Portsmouth
Jacques, Alex — Wakefield
Mchenry, William James — Wyoming
Olszewski, Stephen — Coventry
Williams, Jason L — Wyoming
Wright, Richard S — Carolina

RUSSIA

Kharlamov, Yuri — 300007

SC

Beatty, Gordon H. — Seneca
Branton, Robert — Awendaw
Cannady, Daniel L — Allendale
Cox, Sam — Gaffney
Denning, Geno — Gaston
Fecas, Stephen J — Anderson
Gainey, Hal — Greenwood
George, Harry — Aiken
Gregory, Michael — Belton
Hendrix, Jerry — Clinton
Hendrix, Wayne — Allendale
Hucks, Jerry — Moncks Corner
Kay, J Wallace — Liberty
Knight, Jason — Harleyville
Kreger, Thomas — Lugoff
Langley, Gene H — Florence
Lutz, Greg — Greenwood
Manley, David W — Central
Mcmanus, Danny — Taylors
Miles Jr., C R "Iron Doctor" — Lugoff
Montjoy, Claude — Clinton
Odom Jr., Victor L. — North
Page, Larry — Aiken
Parler, Thomas O — Charleston
Peagler, Russ — Moncks Corner
Perry, Johnny — Inman
Sears, Mick — Kershaw
Smith, Ralph L — Taylors
Thomas, Rocky — Moncks Corner
Tyser, Ross — Spartanburg

SD

Boley, Jamie — Parker
Boysen, Raymond A — Rapid Ciy
Ferrier, Gregory K — Rapid City
Thomsen, Loyd W — Oelrichs

SLOVAK REPUBLIC

Albert, Stefan — Filakovo 98604

SLOVAKIA

Bojtos, Arpad — 98403 Lucenec
Kovacik, Robert — 98401 Lucenec
Mojzis, Julius
Pulis, Vladimir — 96701 Kremnica

Slovensko (Slovakia)

Laoislav, Santa-Lasky — Okres Banska
Bystrica

SOUTH AFRICA

Arm-Ko Knives, — Marble Ray 4035 KZN
Baartman, George — Limpopo
Bauchop, Robert — Kwazulu-Natal 4278
Beukes, Tinus — Vereeniging 1939
Bezuidenhout, Buzz — Malvern, KZN
Boardman, Guy — New Germany 3619
Brown, Rob E — Port Elizabeth
Burger, Fred — Kwa-Zulu Natal
Burger, Tiaan — Riviera, Pretoria
Dickerson, Gavin — Petit 1512
Fellows, Mike — Mosselbay 6500
Grey, Piet — Naboomspruit 0560
Harvey, Heather — Belfast 1100
Harvey, Kevin — Belfast 1100
Herbst, Thinus — Karenpark 0118, Akasia
Horn, Des
Klaasee, Tinus — George 6530
Kojetin, W — Germiston 1401
Lagrange, Fanie — Table View 7441
Lancaster, C G — Free State
Liebenberg, Andre
— Bordeauxrandburg 2196
Mackrill, Stephen — JHB 2123
Mahomedy, A R — Marble Ray KZN, 4035
Nelson, Tom — Gauteng
Pienaar, Conrad — Bloemfontein 9300
Prinsloo, Theuns — Bethlehem, 9700
Rietveld, Bertie — Magaliesburg 1791
Russell, Mick — Port Elizabeth 6070
Schoeman, Corrie — Danhof 9310
Steyn, Peter — Freestate
Thorburn, Andre E.
— Bela Bela, Warmbaths 0480
Van Der Westhuizen, Peter
— Mossel Bay 6500
Van Heerden, Andre — Garsfontein, Pretoria
Watson, Peter — La Hoff 2570

South Australia

Edmonds, Warrick — Adelaide Hills

SWEDEN

Bergh, Roger — 91598 Bygdea
Billgren, Per
Eklund, Maihkel — S-820 41 Farila
Embretsen, Kaj — S-82830 Edsbyn
Hedlund, Anders — Brastad
Hogstrom, Anders T — Johanneshov
Johansson, Anders — S-772 40
Grangesberg
Lundstrom, Jan-Ake — 66010 Dals-Langed
Nilsson, Jonny Walker
— SE-933 33 Arvidsjaur
Nordell, Ingemar — 82041 Färila
Persson, Conny — 820 50 Loos
Ryberg, Gote — S-562 00 Norrahammar
Styrefors, Mattias
Vogt, Patrik — S-30270 Halmstad

SWITZERLAND

Roulin, Charles	1233 Geneva
Soppera, Arthur	CH-9631 Ulisbach

TN

Accawi, Fuad	Clinton
Bailey, Joseph D.	Nashville
Blanchard, G R (Gary)	Sevierville
Breed, Kim	Clarksville
Byrd, Wesley L	Evensville
Canter, Ronald E	Jackson
Casteel, Dianna	Monteagle
Casteel, Douglas	Monteagle
Claiborne, Ron	Knox
Clay, Wayne	Pelham
Conley, Bob	Jonesboro
Coogan, Robert	Smithville
Corby, Harold	Johnson City
Elder Jr., Perry B	Clarksville
Ewing, John H	Clinton
Harley, Larry W	Bristol
Harley, Richard	Bristol
Heflin, Christopher M	Nashville
Hughes, Dan	Spencer
Hurst, Jeff	Rutledge
Hutcheson, John	Chattanooga
Johnson, David A	Pleasant Shade
Johnson, Ryan M	Hixson
Kemp, Lawrence	Ooletwah
Largin,	Sevierville
Levine, Bob	Tullahoma
Marshall, Stephen R	Mt. Juliet
Mccarty, Harry	Blaine
Mcdonald, W J "Jerry"	Germantown
Moulton, Dusty	Loudon
Raley, R. Wayne	Collierville
Sampson, Lynn	Jonesborough
Smith, Newman L.	Gatlinburg
Taylor, C Gray	Fall Branch
Taylor, David	Rogersville
Vanderford, Carl G	Columbia
Walker, John W	Bon Aqua
Ward, W C	Clinton
Wheeler, Gary	Clarksville
Williams Jr., Richard	Morristown
Winter, George	Union City

TX

Adams, William D	Burton
Alexander, Eugene	Ganado
Allen, Mike "Whiskers"	Malakoff
Appleton, Ron	Bluff Dale
Ashby, Douglas	Dallas
Barnes, Jim	Christoval
Barnes, Marlen R.	Atlanta
Barr, Judson C.	Irving
Batts, Keith	Hooks
Blackwell, Zane	Eden
Blum, Kenneth	Brenham
Bradshaw, Bailey	Diana
Bratcher, Brett	Plantersville
Broadwell, David	Wichita Falls
Brooks, Michael	Lubbock
Budell, Michael	Brenham
Bullard, Randall	Canyon
Burden, James	Burkburnett
Callahan, F Terry	Boerne
Carey, Peter	Lago Vista
Carpenter, Ronald W	Jasper
Carter, Fred	Wichita Falls
Champion, Robert	Amarillo
Chase, John E	Aledo
Chew, Larry	Granbury
Churchman, T W (Tim)	Bandera
Cole, James M	Bartonville

Connor, John W	Odessa
Connor, Michael	Winters
Costa, Scott	Spicewood
Crain, Jack W	Granbury
Darcey, Chester L	College Station
Davidson, Larry	New Braunfels
Davis, Vernon M	Waco
Dean, Harvey J	Rockdale
Dietz, Howard	New Braunfels
Dominy, Chuck	Colleyville
Dyer, David	Granbury
Eldridge, Allan	Ft. Worth
Elishewitz, Allen	New Braunfels
Epting, Richard	College Station
Eriksen, James Thorlief	Garland
Evans, Carlton	Fort Davis
Fant Jr., George	Atlanta
Ferguson, Jim	San Angelo
Fortune Products, Inc.,	Marble Falls
Foster, Al	Magnolia
Foster, Norvell C	Marion
Fowler, Jerry	Hutto
Fritz, Jesse	Slaton
Fuller, Bruce A	Baytown
Gann, Tommy	Canton
Garner, Larry W	Tyler
George, Les	Corpus Christi
Graham, Gordon	New Boston
Green, Bill	Sachse
Griffin, Rendon And Mark	Houston
Guinn, Terry	Eastland
Halfrich, Jerry	San Marcos
Hamlet Jr., Johnny	Clute
Hand, Bill	Spearman
Hawkins, Buddy	Texarkana
Hayes, Scotty	Tesarkana
Haynes, Jerry	Gunter
Hays, Mark	Austin
Hemperley, Glen	Willis
Hicks, Gary	Tuscola
Howell, Jason G	Lake Jackson
Hudson, Robert	Humble
Hughes, Lawrence	Plainview
Jackson, Charlton R	San Antonio
Jaksik Jr., Michael	Fredericksburg
Johnson, Gorden W	Houston
Johnson, Ruffin	Houston
Keller, Bill	San Antonio
Kern, R W	San Antonio
Kious, Joe	Kerrville
Knipstein, R C (Joe)	Arlington
Ladd, Jim S	Deer Park
Ladd, Jimmie Lee	Deer Park
Lambert, Jarrell D	Granado
Laplante, Brett	McKinney
Lay, L J	Burkburnett
Lemcke, Jim L	Houston
Lennon, Dale	Alba
Lister Jr., Weldon E	Boerne
Lively, Tim And Marian	Marble Falls
Love, Ed	San Antonio
Lovett, Michael	Mound
Luchak, Bob	Channelview
Luckett, Bill	Weatherford
Marshall, Glenn	Mason
Martin, Michael W	Beckville
Mcconnell Jr., Loyd A	Marble Falls
Mellard, J R	Houston
Merz Iii, Robert L	Katy
Miller, R D	Dallas
Mitchell, Wm Dean	Warren
Moore, James B	Ft. Stockton
Neely, Greg	Bellaire
Nelson, Dr Carl	Texarkana
Nolen, Steve	Pottsboro
Odgen, Randy W	Houston
Ogletree Jr., Ben R	Livingston

Osborne, Warren	Waxahachie
Overeynder, T R	Arlington
Ownby, John C	Murphy
Pardue, Joe	Spurger
Patterson, Pat	Barksdale
Pierce, Randall	Arlington
Polzien, Don	Lubbock
Powell, James	Texarkana
Pugh, Jim	Azle
Ray, Alan W	Lovelady
Richardson Jr., Percy	Navasota
Roberts, Jack	Houston
Robinson, Charles (Dickie)	Vega
Rucker, Thomas	Nacogdoches
Ruple, William H	Pleasanton
Ruth, Michael G	Texarkana
Scott, Al	Harper
Self, Ernie	Dripping Springs
Shipley, Steven A	Richardson
Sims, Bob	Meridian
Sloan, Shane	Newcastle
Smart, Steve	McKinney
Snody, Mike	Fredericksburg
Stokes, Ed	Hockley
Stone, Jerry	Lytle
Stout, Johnny	New Braunfels
Theis, Terry	Harper
Thuesen, Ed	Damon
Treiber, Leon	Ingram
Truncali, Pete	Garland
Turcotte, Larry	Pampa
Van Reenen, Ian	Amarillo
Vickers, David	Montgomery
Ware, Tommy	Onalaska
Watson, Daniel	Driftwood
Watts, Johnathan	Gatesville
Watts, Wally	Gatesville
West, Pat	Charlotte
White, Dale	Sweetwater
Whitley, Weldon G	Odessa
Wilcher, Wendell L	Palestine
Wilkins, Mitchell	Montgomery
Wilson, Curtis M	Burleson
Wolf Jr., William Lynn	Lagrange
Yeates, Joe A	Spring
Zboril, Terry	Caldwell

UNITED ARAB EMIRATES

Kukulka, Wolfgang	Dubai

UNITED KINGDOM

Hague, Geoff	Quarley, SP11 8PX
Heasman, H G	Llandudno, N. Wales
Horne, Grace	Sheffield Britain
Maxen, Mick	"Hatfield, Herts"

URUGUAY

Gonzalez, Leonardo Williams	CP 20000
Symonds, Alberto E	Montevideo 11300

UT

Allred, Bruce F	Layton
Black, Earl	Salt Lake City
Ence, Jim	Richfield
Ennis, Ray	Ogden
Erickson, L.M.	Ogden
Hunter, Hyrum	Aurora
Johnson, Steven R	Manti
Lang, David	Kearns
Maxfield, Lynn	Layton
Nielson, Jeff V	Monroe
Nunn, Gregory	Castle Valley
Palmer, Taylor	Blanding
Peterson, Chris	Salina

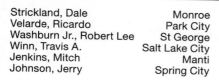

Strickland, Dale — Monroe
Velarde, Ricardo — Park City
Washburn Jr., Robert Lee — St George
Winn, Travis A. — Salt Lake City
Jenkins, Mitch — Manti
Johnson, Jerry — Spring City

VA

Apelt, Stacy E — Norfolk
Arbuckle, James M — Yorktown
Ball, Butch — Floyd
Ballew, Dale — Bowling Green
Batley, Mark S. — Wake
Batson, Richard G. — Rixeyville
Beverly Ii, Larry H — Spotsylvania
Catoe, David R — Norfolk
Chamberlain, Charles R — Barren Springs
Davidson, Edmund — Goshen
Douglas, John J — Lynch Station
Eaton, Frank L Jr — Stafford
Foster, Burt — Bristol
Frazier, Ron — Powhatan
Harris, Cass — Bluemont
Hedrick, Don — Newport News
Hendricks, Samuel J — Maurertown
Herb, Martin — Richmond
Holloway, Paul — Norfolk
Jones, Barry M And Phillip G — Danville
Jones, Enoch — Warrenton
Martin, Herb — Richmond
Mccoun, Mark — DeWitt
Metheny, H A "Whitey" — Spotsylvania
Mills, Michael — Colonial Beach
Murski, Ray — Reston
Norfleet, Ross W — Providence Forge
Parks, Blane C — Woodbridge
Pawlowski, John R — Newport News
Quattlebaum, Craig — Suffolk
Schlueter, David — Madison Heights
Tomes, P J — Shipman
Vanhoy, Ed And Tanya — Abingdon
Vestal, Charles — Abingdon
Wood, Larry B — Jamesville

VT

Haggerty, George S — Jacksonville
Kelso, Jim — Worcester

WA

Amoureux, A W — Northport
Begg, Todd M. — Spanaway
Ber, Dave — San Juan Island
Berglin, Bruce D — Mount Vernon
Boguszewski, Phil — Lakewood
Boyer, Mark — Bothell
Bromley, Peter — Spokane
Brothers, Robert L — Colville
Brown, Dennis G — Shoreline
Brunckhorst, Lyle — Bothell
Bump, Bruce D. — Walla Walla
Butler, John R — Shoreline
Campbell, Dick — Colville
Chamberlain, Jon A — E. Wenatchee
Conti, Jeffrey D — Bonney Lake
Conway, John — Kirkland
Crowthers, Mark F — Rolling Bay
D'Angelo, Laurence — Vancouver
Davis, John — Selah
Diskin, Matt — Freeland
Ferry, Tom — Auburn
Gray, Bob — Spokane
Greenfield, G O — Everett
Hansen, Lonnie — Spanaway
House, Gary — Ephrata

Hurst, Cole — E. Wenatchee
Keyes, Geoff P. — Duvall
Lisch, David K — Seattle
Norton, Don — Port Townsend
O'Malley, Daniel — Seattle
Padilla, Gary — Bellingham
Rader, Michael — Wilkeson
Rogers, Ray — Wauconda
Sanford, Dick — Montesano
Schempp, Ed — Ephrata
Schempp, Martin — Ephrata
Stegner, Wilbur G — Rochester
Sterling, Thomas J — Coupeville
Straub, Salem F. — Tonasket
Swyhart, Art — Klickitat
Wright, Kevin — Quilcene

Western Australia

Barnett, Bruce — Mundaring 6073

Western Cape

Naude, Louis — Cape Town

WI

Boyes, Tom — Addison
Brandsey, Edward P — Janesville
Bruner Jr., Fred Bruner Blades — Fall Creek
Carr, Joseph E. — Menomonee Falls
Coats, Ken — Stevens Point
Delarosa, Jim — Janesville
Genske, Jay — Fond du Lac
Haines, Jeff Haines Custom Knives — Wauzeka
Hembrook, Ron — Neosho
Johnson, Richard — Germantown
Kanter, Michael — New Berlin
Kohls, Jerry — Princeton
Kolitz, Robert — Beaver Dam
Lary, Ed — Mosinee
Lerch, Matthew — Sussex
Maestri, Peter A — Spring Green
Martin, Peter — Waterford
Millard, Fred G — Richland Center
Nelson, Ken — Pittsville
Niemuth, Troy — Sheboygan
Ponzio, Doug — Beloit
Revishvili, Zaza — Madison
Ricke, Dave — West Bend
Rochford, Michael R — Dresser
Schrap, Robert G — Wauwatosa
Steinbrecher, Mark W — Pleasant Prairie
Wattelet, Michael A — Minocqua

WV

Crist, Zoe — Marlinton
Derr, Herbert — St. Albans
Drost, Jason D — French Creek
Drost, Michael B — French Creek
Elliott, Jerry — Charleston
Jeffries, Robert W — Red House
Liegey, Kenneth R — Millwood
Maynard, Larry Joe — Crab Orchard
Morris, Eric — Beckley
Pickens, Selbert — Dunbar
Reynolds, Dave — Harrisville
Shaver Ii, James R — Parkersburg
Small, Ed — Keyser
Tokar, Daniel — Shepherdstown
Wilson, Rw — Weirton
Wyatt, William R — Rainelle

WY

Alexander, Darrel — Ten Sleep

Ankrom, W.E. — Cody
Banks, David L. — Riverton
Barry, Scott — Laramie
Bartlow, John — Sheridan
Bennett, Brett C — Cheyenne
Draper, Audra — Riverton
Draper, Mike — Riverton
Fowler, Ed A. — Riverton
Friedly, Dennis E — Cody
Justice, Shane — Sheridan
Kilby, Keith — Cody
Rexroat, Kirk — Wright
Reynolds, John C — Gillette
Rodebaugh, James L — Carpenter
Ross, Stephen — Evanston
Spragg, Wayne E — Lovell

ZIMBABWE

Burger, Pon — Bulawayo

Not all knifemakers are organization-types, but those listed here are in good standing with these organizations.

the knifemakers' guild

2010 membership

a Les Adams, Douglas A. Alcorn, Mike "Whiskers" Allen, W. E. Ankrom, Elvan Allred

b Robert K. Bagley, Santino e Arlete Ballestra, Norman P. Bardsley, A. T. Barr, James J. Barry, III, John Bartlow, Gene Baskett, Dawayne Batten, Ed Baumgardner, Ron Best, Gary Blanchard ,Michael S. Blue, Arpad Bojtos, Philip W. Booth, Tony Bose, Dennis Bradley, Gordon Gayle Bradley, Edward Brandsey, W. Lowell Bray, Jr., George Clint Breshears, Richard E. Browne, Fred Bruner, Jr., Jimmie H. Buckner, Patrick R. Burris, John Busfield, Barbara Baskett

c Ron G. Cameron, Harold J. "Kit" Carson, Michael Carter, Dianna Casteel, Douglas Casteel, William Chapo, Daniel Chinnock, Howard F. Clark, Wayne Clay, Kenneth R. Coats, Blackie Collins, Bob F. Conley, Gerald Corbit, George Cousino, Colin J. Cox, Pat Crawford, Kevin Casey

d Charles Dake, Alex K. Daniels, Jack Davenport, Edmund Davidson, John H Davis, William C. Davis, Dan Dennehy, Herbert K. Derr, William J. Dietzel, Frank Dilluvio, Mike Dilluvio, David Dodds, T. M. Dowell, Larry Downing, Tom Downing, James F. Downs, William Duff, Fred Durio, Will Dutton

e Jacob Elenbaas, Jim Elliott, William B. Ellis, William E. Engle, James T. Eriksen, Carlton R. Evans

f Stephen J. Fecas, Lee Ferguson, Linda Ferguson, Michael H. Franklin, John R Fraps, Ronald A. Frazier, Dennis E. Friedly, Stanley Fujisaka, Tak Fukuta, Bruce A. Fuller, Cliff Fendley, Robert G. Flynt

g Steve Gatlin, Warren Glover, Stefan Gobec, Richard R. Golden, Gregory J. Gottschalk ,Ernie Grospitch, Kenneth W. Guth

h Philip (Doc) L. Hagen, Gerald Halfrich, Jim Hammond, Don L Hanson III, Koji Hara, Ralph Dewey Harris, Rade Hawkins, Henry Heitler, Glenn Hemperley, Earl Jay Hendrickson, Wayne Hendrix, Wayne G. Hensley, Gil Hibben, R. Hinson, Steven W. Hoel, Kevin Hoffman, Desmond R. Horn, Jerry Hossom, Durvyn Howard, Rob Hudson, Roy Humenick, Joseph Hytovick, Marshall Chad Hall, Wesley G Hibben, Larry Hoststler

i Billy Mace Imel, Michael Irie

j James T. Jacks, Brad Johnson, Keith R. Johnson, Ronald B. Johnson, Steven R. Johnson, William "Bill" C. Johnson, Enoch D. Jones, Jerry L. Johnson, Jack Jones, Lonnie L Jones

k William L. Keeton, Bill Kennedy, Jr., Bill King, Harvey King, J. Kenneth King, Terry Knipschield

l Kermit Laurent, Paul M LeBetard, Gary E. LeBlanc, Tommy B. Lee, Kevin T. Lesswing, William L. Levengood, Yakov Levin, Bob Levine, Steve Linklater, Ken Linton, Wolfgang Loerchner, R. W. Loveless, Schuyler Lovestrand, Don Lozier, Bill Luckett, Gail Lunn, Larry Lunn, Ernest Lyle

m Stephen Mackrill, Joe Malloy, Tom Maringer, Herbert A. Martin, Charlie B. Mathews, Harry S. Mathews, Jerry McClure, Lloyd McConnell, Robert J. McDonald, W. J. McDonald, Frank McGowan, Mike Mercer, Ted Merchant, Robert L. Merz, III, Toshiaki Michinaka, James P. Miller, Stephen C. Miller, Dan Mink, James B. Moore, Jeff Morgan, C.H. & Jason Morris, Riccardo Mainolfi, Rick Menefee, Jerry Moen

n Bud Nealy, Corbin Newcomb, Larry Newton, Ross W Norfleet

o Clifford W. O'Dell, Charles F. Ochs, III, Ben R. Ogletree, Jr., Warren Osborne, T. R. Overeynder, John E. Owens, Clifford W. O'Dell, Sean O'Hare

p Larry Page, Cliff Parker, John R. Pawlowski, W. D. Pease, Alfred Pendray, John W. PerMar, Daniel Piergallini, Otakar Pok, Joseph R. Prince, Theunis C. Prinsloo, Jim Pugh, Morris C. Pulliam, Jerry Partridge, Flavio Poratelli, Larry Pridgen, Jr.

r James D. Ragsdale, Steven Rapp, John Reynolds, Ron F. Richard, Dave Ricke, Michael Rochford, A. G. Russell, Jason Rabuck, Joseph Calvin Robinson, Gordon Romeis

s Michael A. Sakmar, Hiroyuki Sakurai, Scott W. Sawby, Juergen Schanz, Maurice & Alan Schrock, Stephen Schwarzer, Mark C. Sentz, Yoshinori Seto, Eugene W. Shadley, James R. Shaver, II, John I Shore, R. J. Sims, Jim Siska, Steven C. Skiff, Scott Slobodian, Ralph Smith, Marvin Solomon, Arthur Soppera, Jim Sornberger, David Steier, Murray Sterling, Russ Sutton, Charles C. Syslo, John M. Stafford

t Timothy W. Tabor, Robert Terzuola, Leon Thompson, Michael A. Tison, Dan Tompkins, John Toner, Bobby L. Toole, Reinhard Tschager, Ralph Turnbull

v Aas van Rijswijk, Donald Vogt

w George A. Walker, Edward Wallace, Charles B. Ward, Dale E. Warther, Charles G. Weeber, John S. Weever, Weldon G. Whitley, Zachary Whitson, Wayne Whittaker, Donnie R. Wicker, RW Wilson, Stan Wilson, Daniel Winkler

y George L. Young, John Young, Mike Yurco

z Brad Zinker, Michael Zscherny

abs mastersmith listing

a   David Anders, Jerome Anders, Gary D. Anderson, E. R. Russ Andrews II

b   Gary Barnes, Aubrey G. Barnes Sr., James L. Batson, Bailey Bradshaw, Jimmie H. Buckner, Bruce D. Bump, Bill Burke, Bill Buxton

c   Ed Caffrey, Murray M. Carter, Kevin R. Cashen, Hsiang Lin (Jimmy) Chin, Jon Christensen, Howard F. Clark, Wade Colter, Michael Connor, James R. Cook, Joseph G. Cordova, Jim Crowell, Steve Culver

d   Sava Damlovac, Harvey J. Dean, Christoph Deringer, Bill Dietzel, Audra L. Draper, Rick Dunkerley, Steve Dunn, Kenneth Durham

e   Dave Ellis

f   Robert Thomas Ferry III, Jerry Fisk, John S. Fitch, Joe Flournoy, Don Fogg, Burt Foster, Ronnie E. Foster, Timothy L. Foster, Ed Fowler, Larry D. Fuegen, Bruce A. Fuller, Jack A. Fuller

g   Bert Gaston, Thomas Gerner, Wayne Goddard, Greg Gottschalk

h   Tim Hancock, Don .L Hanson III, Heather Harvey, Kevin Harvey, Wally Hayes, E. Jay Hendrickson, Don Hethcoat, John Horrigan, Rob Hudson

j   Jim L. Jackson

k   Joseph F. Keeslar, Keith Kilby, Ray Kirk, Hank Knickmeyer, Jason Knight, Bob Kramer, Phil Kretsinger

l   Jerry Lairson Sr., Mick Langley

m   J. Chris Marks, John Alexander Martin, Roger D. Massey, Victor J. McCrackin, Shawn McIntyre, Hanford J. Miller, Wm Dean Mitchell

n   Greg Neely, J. Neilson, Ron Newton, Douglas E. Noren

o   Charles F. Ochs III

p   Alfred Pendray, John L. Perry, Dan Petersen Ph.D., Timothy Potier

r   Michael Rader, J. W. Randall, Kirk Rexroat, Linden W. Rhea, Dickie Robinson, James L. Rodebaugh, Raymond B. Rybar Jr.

s   James P. Saviano, Stephen C. Schwarzer, Mark C. Sentz, Rodrigo Menezes Sfreddo, J. D. Smith, Josh Smith, Raymond L. Smith, Bill Sowell, H. Red St. Cyr, Charles Stout, Joseph Szilaski

t   Shane Taylor, Jean-paul Thevenot, Jason Tiensvold, Brion Tomberlin, P. J. Tomes, Henry Torres

v   Michael V. Vagnino Jr., Terry L. Vandeventer

w   James L. Walker, John White, Michael L. Williams, Daniel Winkler

miniature knifemaker's society

Paul Abernathy, Gerald Bodner, Fred Cadwell, Barry Carithers, Kenneth Corey, Don Cowles, David J. Davis, Allen Eldridge, Linda Ferguson, Buddy Gaines, Larry Greenburg, Tom & Gwenn Guinn, Karl Hallberg, Bob Hergert, Laura Holmes, Brian Jacobson, Gary Kelley, R. F. Koebeman, Sterling Kopke, Gary E. Lack, Les Levinson, Henry C. Loos, Howard Maxwell, Mal Mele, Ray Mende, Toshiaki Michinaka, Paul Myer, Noriaki Narushima, Carol A. Olmsted, Allen R. Olsen, Charles Ostendorf, David Perkins, John Rakusan, Mark Rogers, Mary Ann Schultz, Jack Taylor, Valentin V. Timofeyev, Mike Viehman, Michael A. Wattelet, Kenneth P. Whitchard Jr., James D. Whitehead, Steve Williams, Carol A. Winold, Earl and Sue Witsaman, John Yashinski

professional knifemaker's association

Mike Allen, James Agnew, Usef Arie, Ray Archer, Eddie J. Baca, John Bartlow, Donald Bell, Brett C. Bennett, Tom Black, James E. Bliss, Philip Booth, Douglas Brack, Kenneth L. Brock, Ron Burke, Lucas Burnley, Ward Byrd, Craig Camerer, Tim S. Cameron, Ken Cardwell, Rod S. Carter, Del Corsi, Roger L. Craig, Joel Davis, John D. Dennehy, Dan Dennehy, Chester Deubel, Audra L. Draper, Mike J. Draper, Jim English, Ray W. Ennis, James T. Eriksen, Kirby Evers, Lee Ferguson, John Fraps, Scott Gere, Bob Glassman, Sal Glesser, Marge Hartman, Mike Henry, Don Hethcoat, Gary Hicks, Guy E. Hielscher, Alan Hodges, Mike L. Irie, David Johansen, Donald Jones, Jack Jones, Jot Singh Khalsa, Harvey King, Steve Kraft, Jim R. Largent, Ken Linton, Mike A. Lundemann, Jim Magee, Daniel May, Jerry & Sandy McClure, Clayton Miller, Skip Miller, Mark S. Molnar, Tyree L. Montell, Mike Mooney, Gary Moore, Steve Nolen, Rick Nowland, Fred A. Ott, Rob Patton, Dick Patton, James L. Poplin, Bill Redd, Dennis Riley, Terry Roberts, Steve Rollert, Charles R. Sauer, Jerry Schroeder, James Scroggs, Pete Semich, Eddie F. Stalcup, Craig Steketee, J.C. Stetter, Troy Taylor, Robert Terzuola, Roy Thompson, Loyd W. Thomsen, Jim D. Thrash, Ed Thuesen, Dick Waites, Mark Waites, Bill Waldrup, Tommy Ware, David Wattenberg, Hans Weinmueller, Dan Westlind, Harold J. Wheeler, RW Wilson, Denise Wolford, Michael C. Young, Monte Zavatta, Michael F. Zima, Daniel F. Zvonek

state/regional associations

alaska interior knifemakers association
Frank Ownby, Fred DeCicco, Bob Hook, Jenny Day, Kent Setzer, Kevin Busk, Loren Wellnite, Mark Knapp, Matthew Hanson, Mel Harvey, Nate Miller, Richard Kacsur, Ron Miller, Terry Miller, Bob LaFrance, Randy Olsen

alaska knifemakers association
A.W. Amoureux, John Arnold, Bud Aufdermauer, Robert Ball, J.D. Biggs, Lonnie Breuer, Tom Broome, Mark Bucholz, Irvin Campbell, Virgil Campbell, Raymond Cannon, Christopher Cawthorne, John Chamberlin, Bill Chatwood, George Cubic, Bob Cunningham, Gordon S. Dempsey, J.L. Devoll, James Dick, Art Dufour, Alan Eaker, Norm Grant, Gordon Grebe, Dave Highers, Alex Hunt, Dwight Jenkins, Hank Kubaiko, Bill Lance, Bob Levine, Michael Miller, John Palowski, Gordon Parrish, Mark W. Phillips, Frank Pratt, Guy Recknagle, Ron Robertson, Steve Robertson, Red Rowell, Dave Smith, Roger E. Smith, Gary R. Stafford, Keith Stegall, Wilbur Stegner, Norm Story, Robert D. Shaw, Thomas Trujillo, Ulys Whalen, Jim Whitman, Bob Willis

arizona knifemakers association
D. "Butch" Beaver, Bill Cheatham, Dan Dagget, Tom Edwards, Anthony Goddard, Steve Hoel, Ken McFall, Milford Oliver, Jerry Poletis, Merle Poteet, Mike Quinn, Elmer Sams, Jim Sornberger, Glen Stockton, Bruce Thompson, Sandy Tudor, Charles Weiss

arkansas knifemakers association
Mike Allen, David Anders, Robert Ball, Reggie Barker, James Batson, Twin Blades, Craig Braschler, Kim and Gary Breed, Wheeler, Tim Britton, Benoni Bullard, Bill Buxton, J.R. Cook, Gary Crowder, James Crowell, Steve Culver, Jesse Davis, Jim Downie, Bill Duff, Fred Durio, Rodger Echols, Shawn Ellis, Lee Ferguson, Linda Ferguson, Jerry Fisk, Joe Flournoy, Ronnie Foster, James Glisson, Gordon Graham, Bob Ham, Douglas and Gail Hardy, Gary Hicks, Alan Hutchinson, Jack Jones, Lacy Key, Harvey King, Ray Kirk, Bill Kirkes, Jim Krause, Jerry Lairson, Ken Linton, Bill Luckett, Tad Lynch, Jim Magee, Roger Massey, Jerry McClure, Rusty McDonald, W.J. McDonald, Don McIntosh, Tony Metsala, Bill Miller, Skip Miller, Ronnie Mobbs, Sidney Moon, Gary Mulkey, Keith Murr, Steve Myers, Mark Nevling, Allen Newberry, Corbin Newcomb, Ron Newton, Chad Nichols, John Perry, Paul Piccola, Rusty Polk, Bill Post, J.W. Randall, Vernon Red, Lin Rhea, Ralph Richards, Ron Richerson, Bobby Rico, Dennis Riley, T.C. Roberts, Kenny Rowe, Kyle Royer, Mike Ruth, James Scroggs, Richard Self, Tex Skow, Mike Snider, Marvin Snider, Marvin Snider,

Marvin Solomon, Craig Steketee, Ed Sticker, Charles Stout, Jeff Stover, Tim Tabor, Brian Thie, Brion Tomberlin, Russell Townsley, Leon Treiber, Pete Truncali, Terry Vandeventer, Charles Vestal, Jim Walker, John White, Mike Williams

australian knifemakers guild inc.
Peter Bald, Col Barn, Bruce Barnett, Denis Barrett, Alistair Bastian, David Brodziak, Stuart Burdett, Jim Deering, Peter Del Raso, Michael Fechner, Keith Fludder, John Foxwell, Thomas Gerner, Branko Giljevic, Stephen Gregory-Jones, Peter Gordon, Barry Gunston, Mal Hannan, Rod Harris, Glenn Henke, Matt James, Peter Kenney, Joe Kiss, Robert Klitscher, Maurie McCarthy, Shawn McIntyre, John McLarty, Ray Mende, Richard Moase, Adam Parker, Jeff Peck, Mike Petersen, Alistair Phillps, Mick Ramage, Wayne Saunders, Murray Shanaughan, Andre Smith, Jim Steele, Rod Stines, Doug Timbs, Stewart Townsend, Hardy Wangermann, Brendan Ware, Ross Yeats

california knifemakers association
Stewart Anderson, Elmer Art, Anton Bosch, Roger Bost, Clint Breshears, Christian Bryant, Mike Butcher, Joe Caswell, Marcus Clinco, Clow Richard, Mike Desensi, Parker Dunbar, Frank Dunkin, Vern Edler III, Stephanie Engnath, Robert Ewing, Chad Fehmie, Alex Felix, Jim Ferguson, Bob Fitlin, Brian Forrest, Dave Gibson, Joe Girtner, Jerry Goettig, Jeanette Gonzales, Russ Green, Tim Harbert, John Harris, Wm. R. 'Bill' Herndon, Neal A. Hodges, Jerid Johnson, Lawrence Johnson, David Kahn, David Kazsuk, Paul Kelso, Steve Koster, Robert Liguori, Harold Locke, R.W. Loveless, Gerald Lundgren, Gordon Melin, Jim Merritt, Russ Moody, Gerald Morgan, Mike Murphy, Tim Musselman, Jeff Mutz, Aram Nigoghossian, Bruce Oakley, Rich Orton, Barry E. Posner, Pat Randall, E. J. Robison, Valente Rosas, Clark Rozas, H. J. Schneider, Red St. Cyr, Chris Stanko, Bill Stroman, Tyrone Swader, Reinhardt Swanson, Tony Swatton, Billy Traylor, Trugrit, Larry White, Stephen A. Williams

canadian knifemakers guild
Joe Arnold, John Benoit, Andre Benoit, Paul Bold, Guillaume Cote, Christoph Deringer, Alain Desaulniers, Sylvain Dion, Jim Downie, Eric Elson, Paul-Aime Fortier, Rick Frigault, Thomas Haslinger, Paul H. Johnston, Kirby Lambert, Greg Lightfoot, Steve Linklater, Wolfgang Loerchner, Brian Lyttle, David MacDonald, Antoine Marcal, James McGowan, Edward McRae, Mike Mossington, William Nease, Simone Raimondi, George Roberts, Paul Savage, Murray St. Amour, Stephen Stuart, David Sylvester, Brian Tighe, Stephen Vanderkolff, Craig Wheatley, Peter Wile, Elizabeth Loerchner, Fred Thynne, Rick Todd

florida knifemaker's association
Dick Atkinson, Barney Barnett, James J. Barry III, Dawayne Batten, Howard Bishop, Andy Blackton, Dennis Blaine, Dennis Blankenhem, Dr. Stephen A. Bloom, Dean Bosworth, John Boyce, Bill Brantley, W. Lowell Bray Jr., Patrick Burris, Norman J. Caesar, Steve Christian, Mark Clark, Lowell Cobb, William Cody, David Cole, Steve Corn, David Cross, Jack Davenport, Kevin Davey, J.D. Davis, Kenny Davis, Ralph D'Elia, Bob Doggett, Jim Elliot, William Ellis, Tom M. Enos, Jon Feazell, Mike Fisher, Todd Fisher, Roger Gamble, James "Hoot" Gibson, Pedro Gonzalez, Ernie Grospitch, Fred Harrington, Dewey Harris, Henry Heitler, Kevin Hoffman, Edward O. Holloway, Stewart Holloway, Joe Hytovick, Tom Johanning, Raymond C. Johnson II, Richard Johnson, Roy Kelleher, Paul S. Kent, Bill King, F.D. Kingery, John E. Klingensmith, William S. Letcher, Bill Levengood, Glenn Long, Gail Lunn, Larry Lunn, Ernie Lyle, Bob Mancuso, Joe Mandt, Kevin A. Manley, Michael Matthews, Jim McNeil, Faustina Mead, Steve Miller, Dan Mink, Steven Morefield, Martin L. "Les" Murphy, Gary Nelson, Larry Newton, Toby Nipper, Praddep Singh Parihar, Cliff Parker, Larry Patterson, Dan Piergallini, Martin Prudente, Bud Pruitt, John "Mickey" Reed, Terry Lee Renner, Roberto Sanchez, Rusty Sauls, Dennis J. Savage, David Semones, Ann Sheffield, Brad Shepherd, Bill Simons, Stephen J. Smith, Kent Swicegood, Tim Tabor, Michael Tison, Ralph Turnbull, Louis M. Vallet, Donald Vogt, Reese Weiland Jr., Travis Williamson, Stan Wilson, Denny & Maggie Young, Brad Zinker

georgia custom knifemakers' guild
Don R. Adams, Doug Adams, Dennis Bradley, Aaron Brewer, Mike Brown, Robert Busbee, Henry Cambron, Jim Collins, John Costa, Jerry Costin, Scott Davidson, Charles K. Dunn, Will Dutton, Emory Fennell, Stephan Fowler, Dean Gates, Warren Glover, George Hancox,

Rade Hawkins, Wayne Hensley, Ronald Hewitt, Kevin Hoffman, Frank Jones, Davin Kates, Dan Masson, Charlie Mathews, Harry Mathews, Leroy Mathews, David McNeal, Dan Mink, James Mitchell, Ralph Mitchell, Sandy Morrisey, Jerry Partridge, Wes Peterson, James Poplin, Joan Poythress, Carey Quinn, Jim Ragsdale, Carl Rechsteiner, David Roberts, Andrew Roy, Joe Sangster, Jamey Saunders, Craig Schneeberger, Randy Scott, Ken Simmons, Nelson Simmons, Jim Small, Bill Snow, Don Tommey, Alex Whetsel, Mike Wilson, Patrick & Hillary Wilson, Robert A. Wright

knife group association of oklahoma
Mike "Whiskers" Allen, Ed Allgood, David Anders, Rocky Anderson, Tony and Ramona Baker, Jerry Barlow, Troy Brown, Dan Burke, Tom Buchanan, F. L. Clowdus Bill Coye, Gary Crowder, Steve Culver, Marc Cullip, David Darby, Voyne Davis, Dan Dick, Dave Dill, Lynn Drury, Bill Duff, Beau Erwin, David Etchieson, Harry Fentress, Lee Ferguson, Linda Ferguson, Daniel Fulk, Gary Gloden, Steve Hansen, Paul Happy, Calvin Harkins, Ron Hebb, Billy Helton, Ed Hites, Tim Johnston, Les Jones, Jim Keen, Bill Kennedy, Stew Killiam, Barbara Kirk, Ray Kirk, Nicholas Knack, Jerry Lairson, Sr., Al Lawrence, Ken Linton, Ron Lucus, Aidan Martin, Barbara Martin, Duncan Martin, John Martin, Jerry McClure, Sandy McClure, Rick Menefee, Ben Midgley, Michael E. Miller, Roy Miller, Ray Milligan, Duane Morganflash, Gary Mulkey, Jerald Nickels, Jerry Parkhurst, Chris Parson, Larry Parsons, Jerry Paul, Larry Paulen, Paul Piccola, Cliff Polk, Roland Quimby, Ron Reeves, Lin Rhea, Mike Ruth, Dan Schneringer, Terry Schreiner, Allen Shafer, Shawn Shropshire, Randell Sinnett, Clifford Smith, Jeremy Steely, Doug Sonntag, Perry Stanford, Mike Stegall, Gary Steinmetz, Mike Stott, Dud Hart Thomas, Brian Tomberlin, Tom Upton, Chuck Ward, Brett Wheat-Simms, Jesse Webb, Rob Weber, Joe Wheeler, Bill Wiggins, Joe Wilkie, Gary Wingo, Daniel Zvonek

knifemakers' guild of southern africa
Jeff Angelo, John Arnold, George Baartman, Francois Basson, Rob Bauchop, George Beechey, Arno Bernard, Buzz Bezuidenhout, Harucus Blomerus, Chris Booysen, Thinus Bothma, Ian Bottomley, Peet Bronkhorst, Rob Brown, Fred Burger, Sharon Burger, Trevor Burger, William Burger, Brian Coetzee, Larry Connelly, Andre de Beer, André de Villiers, Melodie de Witt, Gavin Dickerson, Roy Dunseith, Mike Fellows, Leigh Fogarty, Werner Fourie, Andrew Frankland, Brian Geyer, Ettoré Gianferrari, Dale Goldschmidt, Stan Gordon, Nick Grabe, John Grey, Piet Gray, Heather Harvey, Kevin Harvey, Dries Hattingh, Gawie Herbst, Thinus Herbst, Greg Hesslewood, Des Horn, Nkosi Jubane, Billy Kojetin, Mark Kretschmer, Steven Lewis, Garry Lombard, Steve Lombard, Ken Madden, Abdur-Rasheed Mahomedy, Peter Mason, Edward Mitchell, George Muller, Günther Muller, Tom Nelson, Andries Olivier, Jan Olivier, Christo Oosthuizen, Cedric Pannell, Willie Paulsen, Nico Pelzer, Conrad Pienaar, David Pienaar, Jan Potgieter, Lourens Prinsloo, Theuns Prinsloo, Hilton Purvis, Derek Rausch, Chris Reeve, Bertie Rietveld, Melinda Rietveld, Dean Riley, John Robertson, Corrie Schoeman, Eddie Scott, Harvey Silk, Mike Skellern, Toi Skellern, Carel Smith, Ken Smythe, Graham Sparks, Peter Steyn, André Thorburn, Hennie Van Brakel, Fanie Van Der Linde, Johan van der Merwe, Van van der Merwe, Marius Van der Vyver, Louis Van der Walt, Cor Van Ellinckhuijzen, Andre van Heerden, Danie Van Wyk, Ben Venter, Willie Venter, Gert Vermaak, René Vermeulen, Erich Vosloo, Desmond, Waldeck, Albie Wantenaar, Henning Wilkinson, John Wilmot, Wollie Wolfaardt, Owen Wood

midwest knifemakers association
E.R. Andrews III, Frank Berlin, Charles Bolton, Tony Cates, Mike Chesterman, Ron Duncan, Larry Duvall, Bobby Eades, Jackie Emanuel, James Haynes, John Jones, Mickey Koval, Ron Lichlyter, George Martoncik, Gene Millard, William Miller, Corbin Newcomb, Chris Owen, A.D. Rardon, Archie Rardon, Max Smith, Ed Stewart, Charles Syslo, Melvin Williams

montana knifemaker's association
Peter C. Albert, Chet Allinson, Marvin Allinson, Tim & Sharyl Alverson, Bill Amoureux, Jan Anderson, Wendell Barnes, Jim & Kay Barth, Bob & Marian Beaty, Don Bell, Brett Bennett, Robert Bizzell, BladeGallery, Paul Bos, Daryl & Anna May Boyd, Chuck Bragg, Frederick Branch, Peter Bromley, Bruce Brown, Emil Bucharksky, Bruce & Kay Bump, Bill Burke, Alpha Knife Supply Bybee, Ed Caffrey, Jim & Kate Carroll, Murray Carter, Jon & Brenda Christensen, Norm Cotterman, Seith Coughlin, Bob Crowder, Mike Dalimata, John Davis, Maria

DesJardins, Rich & Jacque Duxbury, Dan Erickson, Mel & Darlene Fassio, E.V. Ford, Eric Fritz, Dana & Sandy Hackney, Doc & Lil Hagen, Gary & Betsy Hannon, Eli Hansen, J.A. Harkins, Tedd Harris, Sam & Joy Hensen, Loren Higgins, Mickey Hines, Gerald & Pamela Hintz, Gary House, Tori Howe, Kevin Hutchins, Al Inman, Frank & Shelley Jacobs, Karl Jermunson, Keith Johnson, Don Kaschmitter, Steven Kelly, Dan & Penny Kendrick, Monte Koppes, Donald Kreuger, David Lisch, James Luman, Robert Martin, Max McCarter, Neil McKee, Larry McLaughlin, Mac & Nancy McLaughlin, Phillip Moen, Gerald Morgan, Randy Morgan, Dan & Andrea Nedved, Daniel O'Malley, Joe Olson, Collin Paterson, Willard & Mark Patrick, Jeffrey & Tyler Pearson, Brian Pender, James Poling, Chance & Kerri Priest, Richard Prusz, Greg Rabatin, Jim Raymond, Jim Rayner, Darren Reeves, John Reynolds, Ryan Robison, Gary Rodewald, Buster Ross, Ruana Knifeworks, Charles Sauer, Dean Schroeder, Michael Sheperes, Mike Smith, Gordon St. Clair, Terry Steigers, George Stemple, Dan & Judy Stucky, Art & Linda Swyhart, Jim Thill, Cary Thomas, James & Tammy Venne, Bill & Lori Waldrup, Jonathan & Doris Walther, Kenneth Ward, Michael Wattelet, Darlene Weinand, Gerome & Darlene Weinand, Daniel & Donna Westlind, Matt & Michelle Whitmus, Dave Wilkes, Mike & Sean Young

national independent cutlery association
Ron & Patsy Beck, Bob Bennett, Dave Bishop, Steve Corn, Dave Harvey, C.J. McKay, Mike Murray, Gary Parker, Rachel Schindler, Joe Tarbell

new england bladesmiths guild
Phillip Baldwin, Gary Barnes, Paul Champagne, Jimmy Fikes, Don Fogg, Larry Fuegen, Rob Hudson, Midk Langley, Louis Mills, Dan Maragni, Jim Schmidt, Wayne Valachovic and Tim Zowada

north carolina custom knifemakers' guild
Dr. James Batson, Tom Beverly, Wayne Bernauer, William "Bill" Bisher, Mark Cary, Ray Clontz, Travis Daniel, Jim Decoster, David Driggs, Ronald Fisher, Ed Halligan, Robert Ham, Koji Hara, John Hege, Curtis Iovito, Tommy Johnson, Barry and Phillip Jones, Frank Joyce, Guy Junkins, Bobby Keller, Tony Kelly, Robert Knight, Gib Kohr, Eric Luther, Aubrey McDonald, Tommy McNabb, Arthur McNeil, William Morris, Van Royce Morton, Victor Odom, Jr., Charles Ostendorf, Paul Ondic, Cory Owens, James Poplin, Murphy Ragsdale, Bruce Ryan, Joel Sandifer, Tim Scholl, Danks Seel, Andy Sharpe, Harland and Karen Simmons, Johnnie Sorrell, Chuck Staples, Jr., Arthur Summers, Russ Sutton, Eddie Swing, David Vail

ohio knifemakers association
Raymond Babcock, Van Barnett, Harold A. Collins, Larry Detty, Tom Downing, Jim Downs, Patty Ferrier, Jeff Flannery, James Fray, Bob Foster, Raymond Guess, Scott Hamrie, Rick Hinderer, Curtis Hurley, Ed Kalfayan, Michael Koval, Judy Koval, Larry Lunn, Stanley Maienknecht, Dave Marlott, Mike Mercer, David Morton, Patrick McGroder, Charles Pratt, Darrel Ralph, Roy Roddy, Carroll Shoemaker, John Smith, Clifton Smith, Art Summers, Jan Summers, Donald Tess, Dale Warther, John Wallingford, Earl Witsaman, Joanne Yurco, Mike Yurco

saskatchewan knifemakers guild
Vern Alton, Al Bakke, Marty Beets, Clarence Broeksma, Irv Brunas, Emil Bucharsky, Jim Clow, Murray Cook, Bob Crowder, Herb Davison, Ray Dilling, Kevin Donald, Brian Drayton, Dallas Dreger, Ray Fehler, Cal Ganshorn, Dale Garling, Wayne Hamilton, Robert Hazell, Bryan Hebb, Garth Hindmarch, John Hopkins, Cliff Kaufmann, Doug Kirkness, Donald Kreuger, Paul Laronge, Pat Macnamara, David McLellan, Ed McRae, Len Meeres, Arnold Miller, Robert Minnes, Ron Nelson, Morris Nesdole, Blaine Parry, Greg Penner, Barry Popick, Jim Quickfall, Ryan Reich, Rob Ridley, Marilyn Ridley, Robert Robson, Carl Sali, Eugene Schreiner, Kim Senft, Don Spasoff, Anthony Wachowicz, Ken Watt, Andy Weeks, Trevor Whitfield, David Wilkes, Merle Williams

south carolina association of knifemakers
Douglas Bailey, Ken Black, Bobby Branton, Richard Bridwell, Gordo Brooks, Dan Cannady, Rodger Cassey, John Conn, Allen Corbet, Bill Dauksch, Geno Denning, Charlie Douan, Gene Ellison, Eddy

Elsmore, Robbie Estabrook Jr., Lewis Fowler, Jim Frazier, Tally Grant, Jerry Hendrix, Wayne Hendrix, Johnny Johnson, Lonnie Jones, John Keaton, Jason Knight, Col. Thomas Kreger, Gene Langley, Tommy Lee, David Manley, Bill Massey, C.R. Miles, Gene Miller, Claude Montjoy, Patrick Morgan, Barry Meyers, Paul Nystrom Jr., Lee O'Quinn, Victor Odom Jr., Larry Page, James Rabb, Ricky Rankin, Rick Rockwood, John Sarratt, Gene Scaffe, Mick Sears, Ralph Smith, David Stroud, Rocky Thomas, Allen Timmons, Justin Walker, Mickey Walker, Woody Walker, Syd Willis Jr.

tennessee knifemakers association
John Bartlow, Doug Casteel, Harold Crisp, Larry Harley, John W. Walker, Harold Woodward, Harold Wright

texas knifemakers & collectors association
Doug Arnew, Doug Ashby, Ed Barker, George Blackburn, Zane Blackwell, Garrett Blackwell, David Blair, Gayle Bradley, Craig Brewer, Nathan Burgess, Stanley Buzek, Dennis Clark, Dwain Coats, Emil Colmenares, Stewart Crawford, Chester Darcey, Wesley Davis, Rorick Davis, Brian Davis, Harvey Dean, James Drouillard II, Stan Edge, Carlton Evans, Jesse Everett Jr., Sammy Fischer, Christopher Flo, Norvell Foster, Theodore Friesenhahn, Glenn Hemperley, Roy Hinds, Darrel Holmquist, Mark Hornung, Karl Jakubik, Mickey Kaehr, Bill Keller, David Kinn, Greg Ledet, Jim Lemcke, Ken Linton, Michael LoGiudice, Paul Long, Eliot Maldonado, Glenn Marshall, Newton Martin, Riley Martin, Bob Merz, Jerry Moen, Don Morrow, Ted Munson, Clifford O'Dell, Tom Overeynder, John Ownby, Ronnie Packard, Glenn Parks, Pat Patterson, Garrett Patterson, Troy Patterson, Steven Patterson, William Petersen III, Jeff Petzke, Paul Piccola, Bill and Pat Post, Gary Powell, Rusty Preston, Martin Rizo, Thomas Rucker, Bill Ruple, Merle Rush, James Schiller, Dwight Schoneweis, Richard Self, Kirby Simmons, Adam Starr, Linda Stone, Wayne Stone, Johnny Stout, Katie Stout, Luke Swenson, Leon Treiber, Larry Turcotte, Charles Turnage, Jimmy Vasquez, David Vickers, Austin Walter, John Walts, Chuck Ward, Bruce Weber, John Weever, Harold Wheeler, Marvin Winn, John Wootters

The firms listed here are special in the sense that they make or market special kinds of knives made in facilities they own or control either in the U.S. or overseas. Or they are special because they make knives of unique design or function. The second phone number listed is the fax number.

sporting cutlers

A.G. RUSSELL KNIVES INC
2900 S. 26th St
Rogers, AR 72758-8571
800-255-9034 or 479-631-0130;
fax 479-631-8493
ag@agrussell.com; www.agrussell.com
The oldest knife mail-order company, highest quality. Free catalog available. In these catalogs you will find the newest and the best. If you like knives, this catalog is a must

AL MAR KNIVES
PO Box 2295
Tualatin, OR 97062-2295
503-670-9080; 503-639-4789
www.almarknives.com
Featuring our Ultralight™ series of knives. Sere 2000™ Shrike, Sere™, Operator™, Nomad™ and Ultraligh series™

ANZA KNIVES
C Davis
Dept BL 12 PO Box 710806
Santee, CA 92072-0806
619-561-9445; 619-390-6283
sales@anzaknives.com;
www.anzaknives.com

B&D TRADING CO.
3935 Fair Hill Rd
Fair Oaks, CA 95628

BARTEAUX MACHETES, INC.
1916 SE 50th St
Portland, OR 97215
503-233-5880
barteaux@machete.com; www.machete.com
Manufacture of machetes, saws, garden tools

**BEAR & SON CUTLERY
(FORMERLY BEAR MGC CUTLERY)**
PO Box 600
5111 Berwyn Rd Suite 110
College Park, MD 20740 USA
800-338-6799; 301-486-0901
www.knifecenter.com
Folding pocket knives, fixed blades, specialty products

BECK'S CUTLERY & SPECIALTIES
McGregor Village Center
107 Edinburgh South Dr
Cary, NC 27511
919-460-0203; 919-460-7772
beckscutlery@mindspring.com;
www.beckscutlery.com

BENCHMADE KNIFE CO. INC.
300 Beavercreek Rd
Oregon City, OR 97045
800-800-7427
info@benchmade.com;
www.benchmade.com
Sports, utility, law enforcement, military, gift and semi custom

BERETTA U.S.A. CORP.
17601 Beretta Dr
Accokeek, MD 20607
800-636-3420 Customer Service
www.berettausa.com
Full range of hunting & specialty knives

BEST KNIVES / GT KNIVES
PO Box 151048
Fort Myers, FL 33914
800-956-5696; fax 941-240-1756
info@bestknives.com;
www.bestknives.com/gtknives.com
Law enforcement & military automatic knives

BLACKJACK KNIVES
PO Box 3
Greenville, WV 24945
304-832-6878; Fax 304-832-6550
knifeware@verizon.net;
www.knifeware.com

BLUE GRASS CUTLERY CORP.
20 E Seventh St PO Box 156
Manchester, OH 45144
937-549-2602; 937-549-2709 or 2603
sales @bluegrasscutlery.com;
www.bluegrasscutlery.com
Manufacturer of Winchester Knives, John Primble Knives and many contract lines

BOB'S TRADING POST
308 N Main St
Hutchinson, KS 67501
620-669-9441
www.gunshopfinder.com
Tad custom knives with Reichert custom sheaths one at a time, one-of-a-kind

BOKER USA INC
1550 Balsam St
Lakewood, CO 80214-5917
303-462-0662; 303-462-0668
sales@bokerusa.com; www.bokerusa.com
Wide range of fixed blade and folding knives for hunting, military, tactical and general use

BROWNING
One Browning Place
Morgan, UT 84050
800-333-3504; Customer Service:
801-876-2711 or 800-333-3288
www.browning.com
Outdoor hunting & shooting products

BUCK KNIVES INC.
660 S Lochsa St
Post Falls, ID 83854-5200
800-326-2825; Fax: 208-262-0555
www.buckknives.com
Sports cutlery

BULLDOG BRAND KNIVES
6715 Heritage Business Ct
Chattanooga, TN 37421
423-894-5102; 423-892-9165
Fixed blade and folding knives for hunting and general use

BUSSE COMBAT KNIFE CO.
11651 Co Rd 12
Wauseon, OH 43567
419-923-6471; 419-923-2337
www.bussecombat.com
Simple & very strong straight knife designs for tactical & expedition use

CAMILLUS CUTLERY CO.
54 W Main St.
Camillus, NY 13031
315-672-8111; 315-672-8832
customerservice@camilluscknives.com

CAS IBERIA INC.
650 Industrial Blvd
Sale Creek, TN 37373
423-332-4700
www.cashanwei.com
Extensive variety of fixed-blade and folding knives for hunting, diving, camping, military and general use. Japanese swords and European knives.

CASE CUTLERY
W R & Sons
PO Box 4000
Owens Way
Bradford, PA 16701
800-523-6350; Fax: 814-368-1736
consumer-relations@wrcase.com
www.wrcase.com
Folding pocket knives

CHICAGO CUTLERY CO.
5500 Pearl St.
Rosemont, IL 60018
847-678-8600
www.chicagocutlery.com
Sport & utility knives.

CHRIS REEVE KNIVES
2949 S. Victory View Way
Boise, ID 83709-2946
208-375-0367; Fax: 208-375-0368
crknifo@chrisreeve.com;
www.chrisreeve.com
Makers of the award winning Yarborough/ Green Beret Knife; the One Piece Range; and the Sebenza and Mnandi folding knives

COAST CUTLERY CO
PO Box 5821
Portland, OR 97288
800-426-5858
www.coastcutlery.com
Variety of fixed-blade and folding knives and multi-tools for hunting, camping and general use

COLD STEEL INC
3036-A Seaborg Ave.
Ventura, CA 93003
800-255-4716 or 805-650-8481
customerservice@coldsteel.com;
www.coldsteel.com
Wide variety of folding lockbacks and fixed-blade hunting, fishing and neck knives, as well as bowies, kukris, tantos, throwing knives, kitchen knives and swords

COLONIAL KNIFE COMPANY DIVISION OF COLONIAL CUTLERY INTERNATIONAL
PO Box 960
North Scituate, RI 02857
866-421-6500; Fax: 401-737-0054
colonialcutlery@aol.com;
www.colonialcutlery@aol.com or
www.colonialknifecompany.com
Collectors edition specialty knives. Special promotions. Old cutler, barion, trappers, military knives. Industrial knives-electrician.

COLUMBIA RIVER KNIFE & TOOL
18348 SW 126th Place
Tualatin, OR 97026
800-891-3100; 503-685-5015
info@crkt.com; www.crkt.com
Complete line of sport, work and tactical knives

CONDOR™ TOOL & KNIFE
Rick Jones, Natl. Sales Manager
6309 Marina Dr
Orlando, FL 32819
407-876-0886
rtj@earthlink.net

CRAWFORD KNIVES, LLC
205 N Center Drive
West Memphis, AR 72301
870-732-2452
www.crawfordknives.com
Folding knives for tactical and general use

CUT CO. CORPORATION
1116 E State St
Olean, NY 14760
716-372-3111; 716-373-6155
www.cutco.com
Household cutlery / sport knives

DAVID BOYE KNIVES
PO Box 1238
Dolan Springs, AZ 86441-1238
800-853-1617 or 928-767-4273
boye@ctaz.com; www.boyeknives.com
Boye Dendritic Cobalt boat knives

DUNN KNIVES
Steve Greene
PO Box 204; 5830 NW Carlson Rd
Rossville KS 66533
800-245-6483
steve.greene@dunnknives.com;
www.dunnknives.com
Custom knives

EMERSON KNIVES, INC.
PO Box 4180
Torrance, CA 90510-4180
310-212-7455; Fax: 310-212-7289
www.emersonknives.com
Hard use tactical knives; folding & fixed blades

EXTREMA RATIO SAS
Mauro Chiostri/Maurizio Castrati
Via Tourcoing 40/p
59100 Prato
ITALY
0039 0574 584639; Fax: 0039 0574 581312
info@extremaratio.com
Tactical/military knives and sheaths, blades and sheaths to customers specs

FALLKNIVEN AB
Havrevägen 10
S-961 42 Boden
SWEDEN
46-921 544 22; Fax: 46-921 544 33
info@fallkniven.se; www.fallkniven.com
High quality stainless knives

FROST CUTLERY CO
PO Box 22636
Chattanooga, Tn 37422
800-251-7768; Fax: 423-894-9576
www.frostcutleryco.com
Wide range of fixed-blade and folding knives with a multitude of handle materials

GATCO SHARPENERS
PO Box 600
Getzville, NY 14068
716-877-2200; Fax: 716-877-2591
gatco@buffnet.net;
www.gatcosharpeners.com
Precision sharpening systems, diamond sharpening systems, ceramic sharpening systems, carbide sharpening systems, natural Arkansas stones

GERBER LEGENDARY BLADES
14200 SW 72nd Ave
Portland, OR 97224
503-639-6161; Fax: 503-684-7008
www.gerberblades.com
Knives, multi-tools, axes, saws, outdoor products

GROHMANN KNIVES LTD.
PO Box 40
116 Water St
Pictou, Nova Scotia B0K 1H0
CANADA
888-756-4837; Fax: 902-485-5872
www.grohmannknives.com
Fixed-blade belt knives for hunting and fishing, folding pocketknives for hunting and general use. Household cutlery.

H&B FORGE CO.
235 Geisinger Rd
Shiloh, OH 44878
419-895-1856
hbforge@direcway.com; www.hbforge.com
Special order hawks, camp stoves, fireplace accessories, muzzleloading accroutements

HISTORIC EDGED WEAPONRY
1021 Saddlebrook Dr
Hendersonville, NC 28739
828-692-0323; 828-692-0600
histwpn@bellsouth.net
Antique knives from around the world; importer of puukko and other knives from Norway, Sweden, Finland and Lapland; also edged weaponry book "Travels for Daggers" by Eiler R. Cook

JOY ENTERPRISES-FURY CUTLERY
Port Commerce Center III
1862 M.L. King Jr. Blvd
Riviera Beach, FL 33404
800-500-3879; Fax: 561-863-3277
mail@joyenterprises.com;
www.joyenterprises.com;
www.furycutlery.com
Fury™ Mustang™ extensive variety of fixed-blade and folding knives for hunting, fishing, diving, camping, military and general use; novelty key-ring knives. Muela Sporting Knives. KA-BAR KNIVES INC. Fury Tactical, Muela of Spain, Mustang Outdoor Adventure

KA-BAR KNIVES INC
200 Homer St
Olean, NY 14760
800-282-0130; Fax: 716-790-7188
info@ka-bar.com; www.ka-bar.com

KATZ KNIVES, INC.
10924 Mukilteo Speedway #287
Mukilteo, WA 98275
480-786-9334; 480-786-9338
katzkn@aol.com; www.katzknives.com

KELLAM KNIVES CO.
902 S Dixie Hwy
Lantana, FL 33462
800-390-6918; Fax: 561-588-3186
info@kellamknives.com;
www.kellamknives.com
Largest selection of Finnish knives; handmade & production

KERSHAW/KAI CUTLERY CO.
7939 SW Burns Way
Wilsonville, OR 97070

KLOTZLI (MESSER KLOTZLI)
Hohengasse 3 CH 3400
Burgdorf
SWITZERLAND
(34) 422-23 78; Fax: (34) 422-76 93
info@klotzli.com; www.klotzli.com
High-tech folding knives for tactical and general use

KNIFEWARE INC
PO Box 3
Greenville, WV 24945
304-832-6878; Fax: 304-832-6550
knifeware@verizon.net; www.knifeware.com
Blackjack and Big Country Cross reference Big Country Knives see Knifeware Inc.

KNIGHTS EDGE LTD.
5696 N Northwest Highway
Chicago, IL 60646-6136
773-775-3888; Fax: 773-775-3339
sales@knightsedge.com;
www.knightsedge.com
Medieval weaponry, swords, suits of armor, katanas, daggers

KNIVES OF ALASKA, INC.
Charles or Jody Allen
3100 Airport Dr
Denison, TX 75020
800-572-0980; 903-786-7371
info@knivesofalaska.com;
www.knivesofalaska.com
High quality hunting & outdoorsmen's knives

KNIVES OF ALASKA, INC.
Charles or Jody Allen
3100 Airport Dr
Denison, TX 75020
800-572-0980; 903-786-7371
info@knivesofalaska.com;
www.knivesofalaska.com
High quality hunting & outdoorsmen's knives

KNIVES PLUS
2467 40 West
Amarillo, TX 79109
800-687-6202
www.knivesplus.com
Retail cutlery and cutlery accessories since 1987; free catalog available

LAKOTA (BRUNTON CO.)
620 E Monroe Ave
Riverton, WY 82501
307-856-6559
AUS 8-A high-carbon stainless steel blades

LEATHERMAN TOOL GROUP, INC.
PO Box 20595
Portland, OR 97294-059 0595 5
800-847-8665; Fax: 503-253-7830
mktg@leatherman.com;
www.leatherman.com
Multi-tools

LONE WOLF KNIVES
Doug Hutchens, Marketing Manager
9373 SW Barber Street, Suite A
Wilsonville, OR 97070
503-431-6777
customerservice@lonewolfknives.com;
www.lonewolfknives.com

LONE STAR WHOLESALE
P.O. Box 587
Amarillo, TX 79105
806-356-9540; Fax 806-359-1603
knivesplus@knivesplus.com
Great prices, dealers only, most major brands

MARBLE'S OUTDOORS
420 Industrial Park
Gladstone, MI 49837
906-428-3710; Fax: 906-428-3711
info@marblescutlery.com;
www.marblesoutdoors.com

MASTER CUTLERY INC
701 Penhorn Ave
Secaucus, NJ 07094
888-271-7229; Fax: 201-271-7666
www.mastercutlery.com
Largest variety in the knife industry

MASTERS OF DEFENSE KNIFE CO.
   (BLACKHAWK PRODUCTS GROUP)
4850 Brookside Court
Norfolk, VA 23502
800-694-5263; 888-830-2013
cs@blackhawk.com; www.modknives.com
Fixed-blade and folding knives for tactical and general use

MCCANN INDUSTRIES
132 S 162nd PO Box 641
Spanaway, WA 98387
253-537-6919; Fax: 253-537-6993
mccann.machine@worldnet.att.net;
www.mccannindustries.com

MEYERCO MANUFACTURING
4481 Exchange Service Dr
Dallas, TX 75236
214-467-8949; 214-467-9241
www.meyercousa.com
Folding tactical,rescue and speed-assisted pocketknives; fixed-blade hunting and fishing designs; multi-function camping tools and machetes

MICROTECH KNIVES
300 Chestnut Street Ext.
Bradford, PA 16701
814-363-9260; Fax: 814-363-9284
mssweeney@microtechknives.com;
www.microtechknives.com
Manufacturers of the highest quality production knives

MORTY THE KNIFE MAN, INC.
80 Smith St
Farmingdale, NY 11735
631-249-2072
clkiff@mtkm.com;
www.mortytheknifeman.com

MUSEUM REPLICAS LTD.
P.O. Box 840
2147 Gees Mill Rd
Conyers, GA 30012
800-883-8838; Fax: 770-388-0246
www.museumreplicas.com
Historically accurate & battle-ready swords & daggers

MYERCHIN, INC.
14765 Nova Scotia Dr
Fontana, CA 92336
909-463-6741; 909-463-6751
myerchin@myerchin.com;
www.myerchin.com
Rigging/ Police knives

NATIONAL KNIFE DISTRIBUTORS
125 Depot St
Forest City, NC 28043
800-447-4342; 828-245-5121
nkdi@nkdi.com; www.nkdi.com
Benchmark pocketknives from Solingen, Germany

NORMARK CORP.
10395 Yellow Circle Dr
Minnetonka, MN 55343-9101
800-874-4451; 612-933-0046
www.rapala.com
Hunting knives, game shears and skinning ax

ONTARIO KNIFE CO.
PO Box 145
Franklinville, NY 14737
800-222-5233; 800-299-2618
sales@ontarioknife.com;
www.ontarioknife.com
Fixed blades, tactical folders, military & hunting knives, machetes

OUTDOOR EDGE CUTLERY CORP.
4699 Nautilus Ct. S #503
Boulder, CO 80301
800-447-3343; 303-530-7667
info@outdooredge.com;
www.outdooredge.com

PILTDOWN PRODUCTIONS
Errett Callahan
2 Fredonia Ave
Lynchburg, VA 24503
434-528-3444
www.errettcallahan.com

QUEEN CUTLERY COMPANY
PO Box 500
Franklinville, NY 14737
800-222-5233; 800-299-2618
sales@ontarioknife.com;
www.queencutlery.com
Pocket knives, collectibles, Schatt & Morgan, Robeson, club knives

QUIKUT
118 East Douglas Road
Walnut Ridge, AR 72476
800-338-7012; Fax: 870-886-9162
www.quikut.com

RANDALL MADE KNIVES
4857 South Orange Blossom Trail
Orlando, FL 32839
407-855-8075; Fax: 407-855-9054
grandall@randallknives.com;
www.randallknives.com
Handmade fixed-blade knives for hunting, fishing, diving, military and general use

REMINGTON ARMS CO., INC.
PO Box 700
870 Remington Drive
Madison, NC 27025-0700
800-243-9700; Fax: 336-548-7801
www.remington.com

SANTA FE STONEWORKS
3790 Cerrillos Rd.
Santa Fe, NM 87507
800-257-7625; Fax: 505-471-0036
knives@rt66.com;
www.santafestoneworks.com
Gem stone handles

SARCO CUTLERY LLC
449 Lane Dr
Florence AL 35630
256-766-8099
www.sarcoknives.com
Etching and engraving services, club knives, etc. New knives, antique-collectible knives

SOG SPECIALTY KNIVES & TOOLS, INC.
6521 212th St SW
Lynnwood, WA 98036
425-771-6230; Fax: 425-771-7689
info@sogknives.com; www.sogknives.com
SOG assisted technology, Arc-Lock, folding knives, specialized fixed blades, multi-tools

SPYDERCO, INC.
820 Spyderco Way
Golden, CO 80403
800-525-7770; 303-278-2229
sales@spyderco.com;
www.spyderco.com
Knives and sharpeners

SWISS ARMY BRANDS INC.
Service Center
65 Trap Falls Road
Shelton, CT 06484
800-442-2706; Fax: 800-243-4006
www.swissarmy.com
Folding multi-blade designs and multi-tools for hunting, fishing, camping, hiking, golfing and general use. One of the original brands (Victorinox) of Swiss Army Knives

TAYLOR BRANDS LLC
1043 Fordtown Road
Kingsport, TN 37663
800-251-0254; Fax: 423-247-5371
info@taylorbrandsllc.com;
www.taylorbrands.com
Fixed-blade and folding knives for tactical, rescue, hunting and general use. Also provides etching, engraving, scrimshaw services.

TIGERSHARP TECHNOLOGIES
1002 N Central Expwy Suite 499
Richardson TX 75080
888-711-8437; Fax: 972-907-0716
www.tigersharp.com

TIMBERLINE KNIVES
PO Box 600
Getzville, NY 14068-0600
800-548-7427; Fax: 716-877-2591
www.timberlineknives.com
High technology production knives for professionals, sporting, tradesmen & kitchen use

TINIVES
1725 Smith Rd
Fortson, GA 31808
888-537-9991; 706-322-9892
info@tinives.com; www.tinives.com
High-tech folding knives for tactical, law enforcement and general use

TRU-BALANCE KNIFE CO.
6869 Lake Bluff Dr
Comstock Park, MI 49321
(616) 647-1215

TURNER, P.J., KNIFE MFG., INC.
P.O. Box 1549
164 Allred Rd
Afton, WY 83110
307-885-0611
pjtkm@silverstar.com;
www2.silverstar.com/turnermfg

UTICA CUTLERY CO
820 Noyes St
PO Box 10527
Utica, NY 13503-1527
800-879-2526; Fax: 315-733-6602
info@uticacutlery.com; www.uticacutlery.com
Wide range of folding and fixed-blade designs, multi-tools and steak knives

WARNER, KEN
PO Box 3
Greenville, WV 24945
304-832-6878; 304-832-6550
www.knifeware.com

WENGER NORTH AMERICA
15 Corporate Dr
Orangeburg, NY 10962
800-267-3577 or 800-447-7422
www.wengerna.com
One of the official makers of folding multi-blade Swiss Army knives

WILD BOAR BLADES / KOPROMED USA
1701 Broadway PMB 282
Vancouver, WA 98663
360-735-0570; Fax: 360-735-0390
info@wildboarblades.com;
wildboarblades@aol.com;
www.wildboarblade.com
Wild Boar Blades is pleased to carry a full line of Kopromed knives and kitchenware imported from Poland

WORLD CLASS EXHIBITION KNIVES
Cary Desmon
941-504-2279
www.withoutequal.com
Carries an extensive line of Pius Lang knives

WILLIAM HENRY FINE KNIVES
3200 NE Rivergate St
McMinnville, OR 97128
888-563-4500; Fax: 503-434-9704
www.williamhenryknives.com
Semi-custom folding knives for hunting and general use; some limited editions

WUU JAU CO. INC
2600 S Kelly Ave
Edmond, OK 73013
800-722-5760; Fax: 877-256-4337
mail@wuujau.com; www.wuujau.com
Wide variety of imported fixed-blade and folding knives for hunting, fishing, camping, and general use. Wholesale to knife dealers only

WYOMING KNIFE CORP.
101 Commerce Dr
Ft. Collins, CO 80524
970-224-3454; Fax: 970-226-0778
wyoknife@hotmail.com;
www.wyomingknife.com

XIKAR INC
PO Box 025757
Kansas City MO 64102
888-676-7380; 816-474-7555
info@xikar.com; www.xikar.com
Gentlemen's cutlery and accessories

importers

A.G. RUSSELL KNIVES INC
2900 S. 26th St.
Rogers, AR 72758-8571
800-255-9034 or 479-631-0130;
fax 479-631-8493
ag@agrussell.com; www.agrussell.com
The oldest knife mail-order company, highest quality. Free catalog available. In these catalogs you will find the newest and the best. If you like knives, this catalog is a must. Celebrating over 40 years in the industry

ADAMS INTERNATIONAL KNIFEWORKS
8710 Rosewood Hills
Edwardsville, IL 62025
Importers & foreign cutlers

AITOR-BERRIZARGO S.L.
P.I. Eitua PO Box 26
48240 Berriz Vizcaya
SPAIN
946826599; 94602250226
info@aitor.com; www.aitor.com
Sporting knives

ATLANTA CUTLERY CORP.
P.O.Box 839
Conyers, Ga 30012
800-883-0300; Fax: 770-388-0246
custserve@atlantacutlery.com;
www.atlantacutlery.com
Exotic knives from around the world

BAILEY'S
PO Box 550
Laytonville, CA 95454
800-322-4539; 707-984-8115
baileys@baileys-online.com;
www.baileys-online.com

BELTRAME, FRANCESCO
Fratelli Beltrame F&C snc Via dei Fabbri
15/B-33085 MANIAGO (PN)
ITALY
39 0427 701859
www.italianstiletto.com

BOKER USA, INC.
1550 Balsam St
Lakewood, CO 80214-5917
303-462-0662; 303-462-0668
sales@bokerusa.com; www.bokerusa.com
Ceramic blades

CAMPOS, IVAN DE ALMEIDA
R. Stelio M. Loureiro, 205
Centro, Tatui
BRAZIL
00-55-15-33056867
www.ivancampos.com

C.A.S. IBERIA, INC.
650 Industrial Blvd
Sale Creek, TN 37373
423-332-4700; 423-332-7248
info@casiberia.com; www.casiberia.com

CAS/HANWEI, MUELA
Catoctin Cutlery
PO Box 188
Smithsburg, MD 21783

CLASSIC INDUSTRIES
1325 Howard Ave, Suite 408
Burlingame, CA 94010

COAST CUTLERY CO.
8033 NE Holman St.
Portland, OR 97218
800-426-5858
staff@coastcutlery.com;
www.coastcutlery.com

COLUMBIA PRODUCTS CO.
PO Box 1333
Sialkot 51310
PAKISTAN

COLUMBIA PRODUCTS INT'L
PO Box 8243
New York, NY 10116-8243
201-854-3054; Fax: 201-854-7058
nycolumbia@aol.com;
http://www.columbiaproducts.homestead.com/cat.html
Pocket, hunting knives and swords of all kinds

COMPASS INDUSTRIES, INC.
104 E. 25th St
New York, NY 10010
800-221-9904; Fax: 212-353-0826
jeff@compassindustries.com;
www.compassindustries.com
Imported pocket knives

CONAZ COLTELLERIE
Dei F.Lli Consigli-Scarperia
Via G. Giordani, 20
50038 Scarperia (Firenze)
ITALY
36 55 846187; 39 55 846603
conaz@dada.it; www.consigliscarpeia.com
Handicraft workmanship of knives of the ancient Italian tradition. Historical and collection knives

CONSOLIDATED CUTLERY CO., INC.
696 NW Sharpe St
Port St. Lucie, FL 34983
772-878-6139

CRAZY CROW TRADING POST
PO Box 847
Pottsboro, TX 75076
800-786-6210; Fax: 903-786-9059
info@crazycrow.com; www.crazycrow.com
Solingen blades, knife making parts & supplies

DER FLEISSIGEN BEAVER
(The Busy Beaver)
Harvey Silk
PO Box 1166
64343 Griesheim
GERMANY
49 61552231; 49 6155 2433
Der.Biber@t-online.de
Retail custom knives. Knife shows in Germany & UK

EXTREMA RATIO SAS
Mauro Chiostri; Mavrizio Castrati
Via Tourcoing 40/p
59100 Prato (PO)
ITALY
0039 0574 58 4639; 0039 0574 581312
info@extremarazio.com;
www.extremaratio.com
Tactical & military knives manufacturing

FALLKNIVEN AB
Havrevagen 10
S-96142 Boden
SWEDEN
46 92154422; 46 92154433
info@fallkniven.se
www.fallkniven.com
High quality knives

FREDIANI COLTELLI FINLANDESI
Via Lago Maggiore 41
I-21038 Leggiuno
ITALY

GIESSER MESSERFABRIK GMBH, JOHANNES
Raiffeisenstr 15
D-71349 Winnenden
GERMANY
49-7195-1808-29
info@giesser.de; www.giesser.de
Professional butchers and chef's knives

HIMALAYAN IMPORTS
3495 Lakeside Dr
Reno, NV 89509
775-825-2279
unclebill@himalayan-imports.com; www.
himilayan-imports.com

IVAN DE ALMEIDA CAMPOS-KNIFE DEALER
R. Xi De Agosto
107, Centro, Tatui, Sp 18270
BRAZIL
55-15-251-8092; 55-15-251-4896
campos@bitweb.com.br
Custom knives from all Brazilian knifemakers

JOY ENTERPRISES
1862 M.L. King Blvd
Riviera Beach, FL 33404
800-500-3879; 561-863-3277
mail@joyenterprises.com;
www.joyenterprises.com
Fury™, Mustang™, Hawg Knives, Muela

KELLAM KNIVES CO.
902 S Dixie Hwy
Lantana, FL 33462
800-390-6918; 561-588-3186
info@kellamknives.com;
www.kellamknives.com
Knives from Finland; own line of knives

KNIFE IMPORTERS, INC.
11307 Conroy Ln
Manchaca, TX 78652
512-282-6860, Fax: 512-282-7504
Wholesale only

KNIGHTS EDGE
5696 N Northwest Hwy
Chicago, IL 60646
773-775-3888; 773-775-3339
www.knightsedge.com
Exclusive designers of our Rittersteel, Stagesteel and Valiant Arms and knightedge lines of weapon

LEISURE PRODUCTS CORP.
PO Box 1171
Sialkot-51310
PAKISTAN

L. C. RISTINEN
Suomi Shop
17533 Co Hwy 38
Frazee MN 56544
218-538-6633; 218-538-6633
icrist@wcta.net
Scandinavian cutlery custom antique, books and reindeer antler

LINDER, CARL NACHF.
Erholungstr. 10
D-42699 Solingen
GERMANY
212 33 0 856; Fax: 212 33 71 04
info@linder.de; www.linder.de

MARTTIINI KNIVES
PO Box 44 (Marttiinintie 3)
96101 Rovaniemi
FINLAND

MATTHEWS CUTLERY
4401 Sentry Dr, Suite K
Tucker, GA 30084-6561
770-939-6915

MESSER KLÖTZLI
PO Box 104
Hohengasse 3, Ch-3402 Burgdorf
SWITZERLAND
034 422 2378; 034 422 7693
info@klotzli.com; www.klotzli.com

MURAKAMI, ICHIRO
Knife Collectors Assn. Japan
Tokuda Nishi 4 Chome, 76 Banchi, Ginancho
Hashimagun, Gifu
JAPAN
81 58 274 1960; 81 58 273 7369
www.gix.orjp/~n-resin/

MUSEUM REPLICAS LIMITED
2147 Gees Mill Rd
Conyers, GA 30012
800-883-8838
www.museumreplicas.com

NICHOLS CO.
Pomfret Rd
South Pomfret, VT 05067
Import & distribute knives from EKA (Sweden), Helle (Norway), Brusletto (Norway), Roselli (Finland). Also market Zippo products, Snow, Nealley axes and hatchets and snow & Neally axes

NORMARK CORP.
Craig Weber
10395 Yellow Circle Dr
Minnetonka, MN 55343

PRODUCTORS AITOR, S.A.
Izelaieta 17
48260 Ermua
SPAIN
943-170850; 943-170001
info@aitor.com
Sporting knives

PROFESSIONAL CUTLERY SERVICES
9712 Washburn Rd
Downey, CA 90241
562-803-8778; 562-803-4261
Wholesale only. Full service distributor of domestic & imported brand name cutlery. Exclusive U.S. importer for both Marto Swords and Battle Ready Valiant Armory edged weapons

SCANDIA INTERNATIONAL INC.
5475 W Inscription Canyon Dr
Prescott, AZ 86305
928-442-0140; Fax: 928-442-0342
mora@cableone.net; www.frosts-scandia.com
Frosts knives of Sweden

STAR SALES CO., INC.
1803 N. Central St
Knoxville, TN 37917
800-745-6433; Fax: 865-524-4889
www.starknives.com

SVORD KNIVES
Smith Rd., RD 2
Waiuku, South Auckland
NEW ZEALAND
64 9 2358846; Fax: 64 9 2356483
www.svord.com

SWISS ARMY BRANDS LTD.
The Forschner Group, Inc.
One Research Drive
Shelton, CT 06484
203-929-6391; 203-929-3786
www.swissarmy.com

TAYLOR BRANDS, LLC
1043 Fordtown Road
Kingsport, TN 37663
800-251-0254; Fax: 423-247-5371
info@taylorbrandsllc.com;
www.taylorbrands.com
Fixed-blade and folding knives for tactical, rescue, hunting and general use. Also provides etching, engraving, scrimshaw services.

UNITED CUTLERY CORP.
1425 United Blvd
Sevierville, TN 37876
865-428-2532; 865-428-2267
order@unitedcutlery.com;
www.unitedcutlery.com
Harley-Davidson ® Colt ® , Stanley ®, U21 ®, Rigid Knives ®, Outdoor Life ®, Ford ®, hunting, camping, fishing, collectible & fantasy knives

UNIVERSAL AGENCIES INC
4690 S Old Peachtree Rd, Suite C
Norcross, GA 30071-1517
678-969-9147; Fax: 678-969-9169
info@knifecupplies.com;
www.knifesupplies.com;
www.thunderforged.com; www.uai.org
*Serving the cutlery industry with the finest
selection of India Stag, Buffalo Horn,
Thurnderforged ™ Damascus. Mother of Pearl,
Knife Kits and more*

VALOR CORP.
1001 Sawgrass Corp Pkwy
Sunrise, FL 33323
800-899-8256; Fax: 954-377-4941
www.valorcorp.com
Wide variety of imported & domestic knives

WENGER N. A.
15 Corporate Dr
Orangeburg, NY 10962
800-431-2996
www.wengerna.com
Swiss Army ™ Knives

WILD BOAR BLADES
1701 Broadway, Suite 282
Vancouver, WA 98663
888-476-4400; 360-735-0390
usakopro@aol.com;
www.wildboarblades.com
*Carries a full line of Kopromed knives and
kitchenware imported from Poland*

WORLD CLASS EXHIBITION KNIVES
Cary Desmon
941-504-2279
www.withoutequal.com
Carries an extensive line of Pius Lang knives

ZWILLING J.A. HENCKELS USA
171 Saw Mill River Rd
Hawthorne, NY 10532
800-777-4308; Fax: 914-747-1850
info@jahenckels.com;
www.jahenckels.com
*Kitchen cutlery, scissors, gadgets, flatware and
cookware*

knife making supplies

AFRICAN IMPORT CO.
Alan Zanotti
22 Goodwin Rd
Plymouth, MA 02360
508-746-8552; 508-746-0404
africanimport@aol.com
Ivory

AMERICAN SIEPMANN CORP.
65 Pixley Industrial Parkway
Rochester, NY 14624
800-724-0919; Fax: 585-247-1883
www.siepmann.com
*CNC blade grinding equipment, grinding
wheels, production blade grinding services.
Sharpening stones and sharpening equipment*

ANKROM EXOTICS
Pat Ankrom
22900 HWY 5
Centerville, IA 52544
641-436-0235
ankromexotics@hotmail.com
www.ankromexotics.com
*Stabilized handle material; Exotic burls
and hardwoods from around the world;
Stabilizing services available*

ATLANTA CUTLERY CORP.
P.O.Box 839
Conyers, Ga 30012
800-883-0300; Fax: 770-388-0246
custserve@atlantacutlery.com;
www.atlantacutlery.com

BATAVIA ENGINEERING
PO Box 53
Magaliesburg, 1791
SOUTH AFRICA
27-14-5771294
bertie@batavia.co.za; www.batavia.co.za
*Contact wheels for belt grinders and surface
grinders; damascus and mokume*

BLADEMAKER, THE
Gary Kelley
17485 SW Phesant Ln
Beaverton, OR 97006
503-649-7867
garykelly@theblademaker.com;
www.theblademaker.com
*Period knife and hawk blades for hobbyists
& re-enactors and in dendritic D2 steel.
"Ferroulithic" steel-stone spear point, blades
and arrowheads*

BOONE TRADING CO., INC.
PO Box 669
562 Coyote Rd
Brinnon, WA 98320
800-423-1945; Fax: 360-796-4511
www.boonetrading.com
Ivory of all types, bone, horns

BORGER, WOLF
Benzstrasse 8
76676 Graben-Neudorf
GERMANY
wolf@messerschmied.de;
www.messerschmied.de

BOYE KNIVES
PO Box 1238
Dolan Springs, AZ 86441-1238
800-853-1617; 928-767-4273
info@boyeknives.com;
www.boyeknives.com
Dendritic steel and Dendritic cobalt

BRONK'S KNIFEWORKS
Lyle Brunckhorst
Country Village
23706 7th Ave SE, Suite B
Bothell, WA 98021
425-402-3484
bronks@bronksknifeworks.com;
www.bronksknifeworks.com
Damascus steel

CRAZY CROW TRADING POST
PO Box 847
Pottsboro, TX 75076
800-786-6210; Fax: 903-786-9059
info@crazycrow.com; www.crazycrow.com
Solingen blades, knife making parts & supplies

CULPEPPER & CO.
Joe Culpepper
P.O. Box 690
8285 Georgia Rd.
Otto, NC 28763
828-524-6842; Fax: 828-369-7809
culpepperandco@verizon.net
www.knifehandles.com http://www.
knifehandles.com
www.stingrayproducts.com <http://www.
stingrayproducts.com>
*Mother of pearl, bone, abalone, stingray,
dyed stag, blacklip, ram's horn, mammoth
ivory, coral, scrimshaw*

CUSTOM FURNACES
PO Box 353
Randvaal, 1873
SOUTH AFRICA
27 16 365-5723; 27 16 365-5738
johnlee@custom.co.za
Furnaces for hardening & tempering of knives

DAMASCUS-USA CHARLTON LTD.
149 Deans Farm Rd
Tyner, NC 27980-9607
252-221-2010
rcharlton@damascususa.com;
www.damascususa.com

DAN'S WHETSTONE CO., INC.
418 Hilltop Rd
Pearcy, AR 71964
501-767-1616; 501-767-9598
questions@danswhetstone.com;
www.danswhetstone.com
Natural abrasive Arkansas stone products

**DIAMOND MACHINING TECHNOLOGY,
INC. DMT**
85 Hayes Memorial Dr
Marlborough, MA 01752
800-666-4DMT
dmtsharp@dmtsharp.com;
www.dmtsharp.com
*Knife and tool sharpeners-diamond, ceramic
and easy edge guided sharpening kits*

DIGEM DIAMOND SUPPLIERS
7303 East Earll Drive
Scottsdale, Arizona 85251
602-620-3999
eglasser@cox.net
*#1 international diamond tool provider. Every
diamond tool you will ever need 1/16th of an
inch to 11'x9'. BURRS, CORE DRILLS, SAW
BLADES, MILLING SHAPES, AND WHEELS*

DIXIE GUN WORKS, INC.
PO Box 130
Union City, TN 38281
800-238-6785; Fax: 731-885-0440
www.dixiegunworks.com
Knife and knifemaking supplies

EZE-LAP DIAMOND PRODUCTS
3572 Arrowhead Dr
Carson City, NV 89706
800-843-4815; Fax: 775-888-9555
sales@eze-lap.com; www.eze-lap.com
Diamond coated sharpening tools

FLITZ INTERNATIONAL, LTD.
821 Mohr Ave
Waterford, WI 53185
800-558-8611; Fax: 262-534-2991
info@flitz.com; www.flitz.com
Metal polish, buffing pads, wax

FORTUNE PRODUCTS, INC.
205 Hickory Creek Rd
Marble Falls, TX 78654-3357
830-693-6111; Fax: 830-693-6394
www.accusharp.com
AccuSharp knife sharpeners

GALLERY HARDWOODS
Larry Davis
Acworth, GA
www.galleryhardwoods.com
Stabilized exotic burls and woods

GILMER WOOD CO.
2211 NW St Helens Rd
Portland, OR 97210
503-274-1271; Fax: 503-274-9839
www.gilmerwood.com

GREEN RIVER LEATHER, INC.
1100 Legion Park Rd.
Greensburg, KY 42743
270-932-2212; Fax: 270-299-2471
sherrylott@alltel.net;
www.greenriverleather.com
Complete line of veg tan and exotic leathers, shethmaking hardware, thread, dyes, finishes, etc.

GRS CORP.
D.J. Glaser
PO Box 1153
Emporia, KS 66801
800-835-3519; Fax: 620-343-9640
glendo@glendo.com; www.glendo.com
Engraving, equipment, tool sharpener, books/ videos

HALPERN TITANIUM INC.
Les and Marianne Halpern
PO Box 214
4 Springfield St
Three Rivers, MA 01080
888-283-8627; Fax: 413-289-2372
info@halperntitanium.com;
www.halperntitanium.com
Titanium, carbon fiber, G-10, fasteners; CNC milling

HAWKINS KNIVE MAKING SUPPLIES
110 Buckeye Rd
Fayetteville, GA 30214
770-964-1177; Fax: 770-306-2877
Sales@hawkinsknifemakingsupplies.com
www.HawkinsKnifeMakingSupllies.com
All styles

HILTARY-USGRC
6060 East Thomas Road
Scottsdale, AZ 85251
Office: 480-945-0700
Fax: 480-945-3333
usgrc@cox.net
Gibeon Meteorite, Recon Gems, Diamond cutting tools, Exotic natural minerals, garaffe bone. Atomic absorbtion/ spectographic analyst, precisious metal

HOUSE OF TOOLS LTD.
#54-5329 72 Ave. S.E.
Calgary, Alberta
CANADA T2C 4X
403-640-4594; Fax: 403-451-7006

INDIAN JEWELERS SUPPLY CO.
Mail Order: 601 E Coal Ave
Gallup, NM 87301-6005
2105 San Mateo Blvd NE
Albuquerque, NM 87110-5148
505-722-4451; 505-265-3701
orders@ijsinc.com; www.ijsinc.com
Handle materials, tools, metals

INTERAMCO INC.
5210 Exchange Dr
Flint, MI 48507
810-732-8181; 810-732-6116
solutions@interamco.com
Knife grinding and polishing

JANTZ SUPPLY / KOVAL KNIVES
PO Box 584
309 West Main
Davis, OK 73030
800-351-8900; 580-369-2316
jantz@brightok.net; www.knifemaking.com
Pre shaped blades, kit knives, complete knifemaking supply line

JOHNSON, R.B.
I.B.S. Int'l. Folder Supplies
Box 11
Clearwater, MN 55320
320-558-6128; 320-558-6128
Threaded pivot pins, screws, taps, etc.

JOHNSON WOOD PRODUCTS
34897 Crystal Rd
Strawberry Point, IA 52076
563-933-6504

K&G FINISHING SUPPLIES
1972 Forest Ave
Lakeside, AZ 85929
800-972-1192; 928-537-8877
csinfo@knifeandgun.com;
www.knifeandgun.com
Full service supplies

KOWAK IVORY
Roland and Kathy Quimby
(April-Sept): PO Box 350
Ester, AK 99725
907-479-9335
(Oct-March)
PO Box 693
Bristow, OK 74010
918-367-2684
sales@kowakivory.com;
www.kowakivory.com
Fossil ivories

LITTLE GIANT POWER HAMMER
Harlan "Sid" Suedmeier
420 4th Corso
Nebraska City, NE 68410
402-873-6603
www.littlegianthammer.com
Rebuilds hammers and supplies parts

LIVESAY, NEWT
3306 S Dogwood St
Siloam Springs, AR 72761
479-549-3356; 479-549-3357
Combat utility knives, titanium knives, sportsmen knives, custom made orders taken on knives and after market Kydex© sheaths for commercial or custom cutlery

LOHMAN CO., FRED
3405 NE Broadway
Portland, OR 97232
503-282-4567; Fax: 503-287-2678
lohman@katana4u.com;
www.japanese-swords.com

M MILLER ORIGINALS
Michael Miller
2960 E Carver Ave
Kingman AZ 86401
928-757-1359
mike@milleroriginals.com;
www.mmilleroriginals.com
Supplies stabilized juniper burl blocks and scales

MARKING METHODS, INC.
Sales
301 S. Raymond Ave
Alhambra, CA 91803-1531
626-282-8823; Fax: 626-576-7564
experts@markingmethods.com;
www.markingmethods.com
Knife etching equipment & service

MASECRAFT SUPPLY CO.
254 Amity St
Meriden, CT 06450
800-682-5489; Fax: 203-238-2373
info@masecraftsupply.com;
www.masecraftsupply.com
Natural & specialty synthetic handle materials & more

MEIER STEEL
Daryl Meier
75 Forge Rd
Carbondale, IL 62903
618-549-3234; Fax: 618-549-6239
www.meiersteel.com

NICO, BERNARD
PO Box 5151
Nelspruit 1200
SOUTH AFRICA
011-2713-7440099; 011-2713-7440099
bernardn@iafrica.com

NORRIS, MIKE
Rt 2 Box 242A
Tollesboro, KY 41189
606-798-1217
Damascus steel

NORTHCOAST KNIVES
17407 Puritas Ave
Cleveland, Ohio 44135
www.NorthCoastKnives.com
Tutorials and step-by-step projects. Entry level knifemaking supplies.

OSO FAMOSO
PO Box 654
Ben Lomond, CA 95005
831-336-2343
oso@osofamoso.com;
www.osofamoso.com
Mammoth ivory bark

OZARK KNIFE & GUN
3165 S Campbell Ave
Springfield, MO 65807
417-886-CUTT; 417-887-2635
danhoneycutt@sbcglobal.net
28 years in the cutlery business, Missouri's oldest cutlery firm

PARAGON INDUSTRIES, INC. L. P.
2011 South Town East Blvd
Mesquite, TX 75149-1122
800-876-4328; Fax: 972-222-0646
info@paragonweb.com;
www.paragonweb.com
Heat treating furnaces for knifemakers

POPLIN, JAMES / POP'S KNIVES & SUPPLIES
103 Oak St
Washington, GA 30673
706-678-5408; Fax: 706-678-5409
www.popsknifesupplies.com

PUGH, JIM
PO Box 711
917 Carpenter
Azle, TX 76020
817-444-2679; Fax: 817-444-5455
Rosewood and ebony Micarta blocks, rivets for Kydex sheaths, 0-80 screws for folders

RADOS, JERRY
7523E 5000 N. Rd
Grant Park, IL 60940
815-405-5061
jerry@radosknives.com;
www.radosknives.com
Damascus steel

REACTIVE METALS STUDIO, INC.
PO Box 890
Clarksdale, AZ 86324
800-876-3434; 928-634-3434; Fax: 928-634-6734
info@reactivemetals.com; www.reactivemetals.com

R. FIELDS ANCIENT IVORY
Donald Fields
790 Tamerlane St
Deltona, FL 32725
386-532-9070
donaldfields@aol.com
Selling ancient ivories; Mammoth, fossil & walrus

RICK FRIGAULT CUSTOM KNIVES
3584 Rapidsview Dr
Niagara Falls, Ontario
CANADA L2G 6C4
905-295-6695
zipcases@zipcases.com;
www.zipcases.com
Selling padded zippered knife pouches with an option to personalize the outside with the marker, purveyor, stores-address, phone number, email web-site or any other information needed. Available in black cordura, mossy oak camo in sizes 4"x2" to 20"x4.5"

RIVERSIDE MACHINE
201 W Stillwell
DeQueen, AR 71832
870-642-7643; Fax: 870-642-4023
uncleal@riversidemachine.net
www.riversidemachine.net

ROCKY MOUNTAIN KNIVES
George L. Conklin
PO Box 902, 615 Franklin
Ft. Benton, MT 59442
406-622-3268; Fax: 406-622-3410
bbgrus@ttc-cmc.net
Working knives

RUMMELL, HANK
10 Paradise Lane
Warwick, NY 10990
845-469-9172
hank@newyorkcustomknives.com;
www.newyorkcustomknives.com

SAKMAR, MIKE
1451 Clovelly Ave
Rochester, MI 48307
248-852-6775; Fax: 248-852-8544
mikesakmar@yahoo.com
Mokume bar stock. Retail & wholesale

SANDPAPER, INC. OF ILLINOIS
P.O. Box 2579
Glen Ellyn, IL 60138
630-629-3320; Fax: 630-629-3324
sandinc@aol.com; www.sandpaperinc.com
Abrasive belts, rolls, sheets & discs

SCHEP'S FORGE
PO Box 395
Shelton, NE 68876-0395

SENTRY SOLUTIONS LTD.
PO Box 214
Wilton, NH 03086
800-546-8049; Fax: 603-654-3003
info@sentrysolutions.com;
www.sentrysolutions.com
Knife care products

SHEFFIELD KNIFEMAKERS SUPPLY, INC.
PO Box 741107
Orange City, FL 32774
386-775-6453
email@sheffieldsupply.com;
www.sheffieldsupply.com

SHINING WAVE METALS
PO Box 563
Snohomish, WA 98291
425-334-5569
info@shiningwave.com;
www.shiningwave.com
A full line of mokume-gane in precious and non-precious metals for knifemakers, jewelers and other artists

SMITH ABRASIVES, INC. / SMITH WHETSTONE, INC.
1700 Sleepy Valley Rd
Hot Springs, AR 71901
www.smithabrasives.com

SMOLEN FORGE, INC.
Nick Smolen
S1735 Vang Rd
Westby, WI 54667
608-634-3569; Fax: 608-634-3869
smoforge@mwt.net;
www.smolenforge.com
Damascus billets & blanks, Mokume gane billets

SOSTER SVENSTRUP BYVEJ 16
Søster Svenstrup Byvej 16
4130 Viby Sjælland
Denmark
45 46 19 43 05; Fax: 45 46 19 53 19
www.poulstrande.com

STAMASCUS KNIFEWORKS INC.
Ed VanHoy
24255 N Fork River Rd
Abingdon, VA 24210
276-944-4885; Fax: 276-944-3187
stamascus@hughes.net;
www.stamascus-knive-works.com
Blade steels

STOVER, JEFF
PO Box 43
Torrance, CA 90507
310-532-2166
edgedealer1@yahoo.com;
www.edgedealer.com
Fine custom knives, top makers

TEXAS KNIFEMAKERS SUPPLY
10649 Haddington Suite 180
Houston TX 77043
713-461-8632; Fax: 713-461-8221
sales@texasknife.com;
www.texasknife.com
Working straight knives. Hunters including upswept skinners and custom walking sticks

TRU-GRIT, INC.
760 E Francis Unit N
Ontario, CA 91761
909-923-4116; Fax: 909-923-9932
www.trugrit.com
The latest in Norton and 3/M ceramic grinding belts. Also Super Flex, Trizact, Norax and Micron belts to 3000 grit. All of the popular belt grinders. Buffers and variable speed motors. ATS-34, 440C, BG-42, CPM S-30V, 416 and Damascus steel

UNIVERSAL AGENCIES INC
4690 S Old Peachtree Rd, Suite C
Norcross, GA 30071-1517
678-969-9147; Fax: 678-969-9169
info@knifecupplies.com;
www.knifesupplies.com;
www.thunderforged.com; www.uai.org
Serving the cutlery industry with the finest selection of India Stag, Buffalo Horn, Thurnderforged ™ Damascus. Mother of Pearl, Knife Kits and more

WASHITA MOUNTAIN WHETSTONE CO.
PO Box 20378
Hot Springs, AR 71903-0378
501-525-3914; Fax: 501-525-0816
wmw@hsnp

WEILAND, J. REESE
PO Box 2337
Riverview, FL 33568
813-671-0661; 727-595-0378
rwphil413@earthlink.net
Folders, straight knives, etc.

WILD WOODS
Jim Fray
9608 Monclova Rd
Monclova, OH 43542
419-866-0435

WILSON, R.W.
PO Box 2012
113 Kent Way
Weirton, WV 26062
304-723-2771

WOOD CARVERS SUPPLY, INC.
PO Box 7500-K
Englewood, FL 34223
800-284-6229; 941-460-0123
info@woodcarverssupply.com;
www.woodcarverssupply.com
Over 2,000 unique wood carving tools

WOOD LAB
Michael Balaskovitz
P.O. Box 222
Hudsonville, MI 49426
616-322-5846
michael@woodlab.biz;
www.woodlab.biz
Acrylic stabilizing services and materials

WOOD STABILIZING SPECIALISTS INT'L, LLC
2940 Fayette Ave
Ionia, IA 50645
800-301-9774; 641-435-4746
mike@stabilizedwood.com;
www.stabilizedwood.com
Processor of acrylic impregnated materials

ZOWADA CUSTOM KNIVES
Tim Zowada
4509 E. Bear River Rd
Boyne Falls, MI 49713
231-348-5416
tim@tzknives.com; www.tzknives.com
Damascus, pocket knives, swords, Lower case gothic tz logo

mail order sales

A.G. RUSSELL KNIVES INC
2900 S. 26th St
Rogers, AR 72758-8571
800-255-9034 or 479-631-0130;
fax 479-631-8493
ag@agrussell.com; www.agrussell.com
The oldest knife mail-order company, highest quality. Free catalog available. In these catalogs you will find the newest and the best. If you like knives, this catalog is a must

ARIZONA CUSTOM KNIVES
Julie Hyman
2225 A1A South
Suite B-5
St. Augustine, FL 32080
904-826-4178
sharptalk@arizonacustomknifes.com;
www.arizonacustomknives.com
Color catalog $5 U.S. / $7 Foreign

ARTISAN KNIVES
Ty Young
575 Targhee Twn Rd
Alta, WY 83414
304-353-8111
ty@artisanknives.com;
www.artisanknives.com
Feature master artisan knives and makers in a unique "coffee table book" style format

ATLANTA CUTLERY CORP.
P.O.Box 839
Conyers, Ga 30012
800-883-0300; Fax: 770-388-0246
custserve@atlantacutlery.com;
www.atlantacutlery.com

ATLANTIC BLADESMITHS/PETER STEBBINS
50 Mill Rd
Littleton, MA 01460
978-952-6448
Sell, trade, buy; carefully selected handcrafted, benchmade and factory knives

BALLARD CUTLERY
1495 Brummel Ave.
Elk Grove Village, IL 60007
847-228-0070

BECK'S CUTLERY SPECIALTIES
107 S Edinburgh Dr
Cary, NC 27511
919-460-0203; Fax: 919-460-7772
beckscutlery@mindspring.com;
www.beckscutlery.com
Knives

BLADEGALLERY, INC. / EPICUREAN EDGE, THE
107 Central Way
Kirkland, WA 98033
425-889-5980; Fax: 425-889-5981
info@bladegallery.com;
www.bladegallery.com
Bladegallery.com specializes in hand-made one-of-a-kind knives from around the world. We have an emphasis on forged knives and high-end gentlemen's folders

BLUE RIDGE KNIVES
166 Adwolfe Rd
Marion, VA 24354
276-783-6143; 276-783-9298
onestop@blueridgeknives.com;
www.blueridgeknives.com
Wholesale distributor of knives

BOB NEAL CUSTOM KNIVES
PO Box 20923
Atlanta, GA 30320
770-914-7794
bob@bobnealcustomknives.com;
www.bobnealcustomknives.com
Exclusive limited edition custom knives-sets & single

BOB'S TRADING POST
308 N Main St
Hutchinson, KS 67501
620-669-9441
bobstradingpost@cox.net;
www.gunshopfinder.com
Tad custom knives with reichert custom sheaths one at a time, one of a kind

BOONE TRADING CO., INC.
PO Box 669
562 Coyote Rd
Brinnon, WA 98320
800-423-1945; Fax: 360-796-4511
www.boonetrading.com
Ivory of all types, bone, horns

CARMEL CUTLERY
Dolores & 6th
PO Box 1346
Carmel, CA 93921
831-624-6699; 831-624-6780
ccutlery@ix.netcom.com;
www.carmelcutlery.com
Quality custom and a variety of production pocket knives, swords; kitchen cutlery; personal grooming items

CUSTOM KNIFE CONSIGNMENT
PO Box 20923
Atlanta, GA 30320
770-914-7794; 770-914-7796
bob@customknifeconsignment.com; www. customknifeconsignment.com
We sell your knives

CUTLERY SHOPPE
3956 E Vantage Pointe Ln
Meridian, ID 83642-7268
800-231-1272; Fax: 208-884-4433
order@cutleryshoppe.com;
www.cutleryshoppe.com
Discount pricing on top quality brands

CUTTING EDGE, THE
2900 South 26th St
Rogers, AR 72758-8571
800-255-9034; Fax: 479-631-8493
ce_info@cuttingedge.com;
www.cuttingedge.com
After-market knives since 1968. They offer about 1,000 individual knives for sale each month. Subscription by first class mail, in U.S. $20 per year, Canada or Mexico by air mail, $25 per year. All overseas by air mail, $40 per year. The oldest and the most experienced in the business of buying and selling knives. They buy collections of any size, take knives on consignment. Every month there are 4-8 pages in color featuring the work of top makers

DENTON, J.W.
102 N. Main St
Hiawassee, GA 30546
706-896-2292
jwdenton@alltel.net
Loveless knives

DUNN KNIVES INC.
PO Box 204
5830 NW Carlson Rd
Rossville, KS 66533
800-245-6483
steve.greene@dunnknives.com;
www.dunnknives.com

FAZALARE, ROY
PO Box 7062
Thousand Oaks, CA 91359
805-496-2002 after 7pm
ourfaz@aol.com
Handmade multiblades; older case; Fight'n Rooster; Bulldog brand & Cripple Creek

FROST CUTLERY CO.
PO Box 22636
Chattanooga, TN 37422
800-251-7768; Fax: 423-894-9576
www.frostcutlery.com

GENUINE ISSUE INC.
949 Middle Country Rd
Selden, NY 11784
631-696-3802; 631-696-3803
gicutlery@aol.com
Antique knives, swords

GEORGE TICHBOURNE CUSTOM KNIVES
7035 Maxwell Rd #5
Mississauga, Ontario L5S 1R5
CANADA
905-670-0200
sales@tichbourneknives.com;
www.tichbourneknives.com
Canadian custom knifemaker has full retail knife store

GODWIN, INC. G. GEDNEY
PO Box 100
Valley Forge, PA 19481
610-783-0670; Fax: 610-783-6083
sales@gggodwin.com;
www.gggodwin.com
18th century reproductions

GOLCZEWS KNIVES
Larry Golczewski, dba New Jersey Knifer
30 Quigley Rd.
Hewitt, NJ 07421
973-728-2386
Medium- to high-priced custom and handmade knives, some production if made in USA, Japan, Germany, or Italy. Practical to tactical. Consignments welcome. Also buy, design, and appraise.

GRAZYNA SHAW/QUINTESSENTIAL CUTLERY
715 Bluff St.
Clearwater, MN 55320
201-655-4411; Fax: 320-558-6128; www. quintcut.com
Specializing in investment-grade custom knives and early makers

GUILD KNIVES
Donald Guild
320 Paani Place 1A
Paia, HI 96779
808-877-3109
don@guildknives.com;
www.guildknives.com
Purveyor of custom art knives

HOUSE OF TOOLS LTD.
#136, 8228 Macleod Tr. SE
Calgary, Alberta, Canada
T2H 2B8

JENCO SALES, INC. / KNIFE IMPORTERS, INC. / WHITE LIGHTNING
PO Box 1000
11307 Conroy Ln
Manchaca, TX 78652
303-444-2882
kris@finishlineusa.com
www.whitelightningco.com
Wholesale only

KELLAM KNIVES CO.
902 S Dixie Hwy
Lantana, FL 33462
800-390-6918; 561-588-3186
info@kellamknives.com;
www.kellamknives.com
Largest selection of Finnish knives; own line of folders and fixed blades

KNIFEART.COM
13301 Pompano Dr
Little Rock AR 72211
501-221-1319; Fax: 501-221-2695
www.knifeart.com
Large internet seller of custom knives & upscale production knives

KNIFEPURVEYOR.COM LLC
646-872-0476
mdonato@knifepurveyor.com; www.knifepurveyor.com
Owned and operated by Michael A. Donato (full-time knife purveyor since 2002). We buy, sell, trade, and consign fine custom knives. We also specialize in buying and selling valuable collections of fine custom knives. Our goal is to make every transaction a memorable one.

KNIVES PLUS
2467 I 40 West
Amarillo, TX 79109
800-687-6202
salessupport@knivesplus.com; www.knivesplus.com
Retail cutlery and cutlery accessories since 1987

KRIS CUTLERY
2314 Monte Verde Dr
Pinole, CA 94564
510-758-9912 Fax: 510-223-8968
kriscutlery@aol.com; www.kriscutlery.com
Japanese, medieval, Chinese & Philippine

LONE STAR WHOLESALE
2407 W Interstate 40
Amarillo, TX 79109
806-356-9540
Wholesale only; major brands and accessories

MATTHEWS CUTLERY
4401 Sentry Dr
Tucker, GA 30084-6561
770-939-6915

MOORE CUTLERY
PO Box 633
Lockport, IL 60441
708-301-4201
www.knives.cx
Owned & operated by Gary Moore since 1991 (a full-time dealer). Purveyor of high quality custom & production knives

MORTY THE KNIFE MAN, INC.
4 Manorhaven Blvd
Pt Washington, NY 11050
516-767-2357; 516-767-7058

MUSEUM REPLICAS LIMITED
2147 Gees Mill Rd
Conyers, GA 30012
800-883-8838
www.museumreplicas.com
Historically accurate and battle ready swords & daggers

NORDIC KNIVES
1634-C Copenhagen Drive
Solvang, CA 93463
805-688-3612; Fax: 805-688-1635
info@nordicknives.com;
www.nordicknives.com
Custom and Randall knives

PARKERS' KNIFE COLLECTOR SERVICE
6715 Heritage Business Court
Chattanooga, TN 37422
615-892-0448; Fax: 615-892-9165

PLAZA CUTLERY, INC.
3333 S. Bristol St., Suite 2060
South Coast Plaza
Costa Mesa, CA 92626
866-827-5292; 714-549-3932
dan@plazacutlery.com;
www.plazacutlery.com
Largest selection of knives on the west coast. Custom makers from beginners to the best. All customs, William Henry, Strider, Reeves, Randalls & others available online by phone

RANDALL KNIFE SOCIETY
PO Box 158
Meadows of Dan, VA 24120
276-952-2500
payrks@gate.net;
www.randallknifesociety.com
Randall, Loveless, Scagel, moran, antique pocket knives

ROBERTSON'S CUSTOM CUTLERY
4960 Sussex Dr
Evans, GA 30809
706-650-0252; 706-860-1623
rccedge@csranet.com; www.robertsoncustomcutlery.com
World class custom knives, Vanguard knives-Limited exclusive design

SMOKY MOUNTAIN KNIFE WORKS, INC.
2320 Winfield Dunn Pkwy
PO Box 4430
Sevierville, TN 37864
800-251-9306; 865-453-5871
info@smkw.com; www.eknifeworks.com
The world's largest knife showplace, catalog and website

VOYLES, BRUCE
PO Box 22007
Chattanooga, TN 37422
423-238-6753; Fax: 423-238-3960
bruce@jbrucevoyles.com;
www.jbrucevoyles.com
Knives, knife auctions

knife services

appraisers

Levine, Bernard, P.O. Box 2404, Eugene, OR, 97402, 541-484-0294, brlevine@ix.netcom.com

Russell, A.G., Knives Inc, 2900 S. 26th St., Rogers, AR 72758-8571, phone 800-255-9034 or 479-631-0130, fax 479-631-8493, ag@agrussell.com, www.agrussell.com

Vallini, Massimo, Via G. Bruno 7, 20154 Milano, ITALY, 02-33614751, massimo_vallini@yahoo.it, Knife expert

custom grinders

McGowan Manufacturing Company, 4854 N Shamrock Pl #100, Tucson, AZ, 85705, 800-342-4810, 520-219-0884, info@mcgowanmfg.com, www.mcgowanmfg.com, Knife sharpeners, hunting axes

Peele, Bryan, The Elk Rack, 215 Ferry St. P.O. Box 1363, Thompson Falls, MT, 59873

Schlott, Harald, Zingster Str. 26, 13051 Berlin, GERMANY, 049 030 9293346, harald.schlott@T-online.de, Custom grinder, custom handle artisan, display case/box maker, etcher, scrimshander

Wilson, R.W., P.O. Box 2012, Weirton, WV, 26062

custom handles

Cooper, Jim, 1221 Cook St, Ramona, CA, 92065-3214, 760-789-1097, (760) 788-7992, jamcooper@aol.com

Burrows, Chuck, dba Wild Rose Trading Co, 289 Laposta Canyon Rd, Durango, CO, 81303, 970-259-8396, chuck@wrtcleather.com, www.wrtcleather.com

Fields, Donald, 790 Tamerlane St, Deltona, FL, 32725, 386-532-9070, donaldfields@aol.com, Selling ancient ivories; mammoth & fossil walrus

Grussenmeyer, Paul G., 310 Kresson Rd, Cherry Hill, NJ, 08034, 856-428-1088, 856-428-8997, pgrussentne@comcast.net, www.pgcarvings.com

Holland, Dennis K., 4908-17th Pl., Lubbock, TX, 79416

Imboden II, Howard L., hi II Originals, 620 Deauville Dr., Dayton, OH, 45429

Kelso, Jim, 577 Collar Hill Rd, Worcester, VT, 05682, 802-229-4254, (802) 223-0595

Knack, Gary, 309 Wightman, Ashland, OR, 97520

Marlatt, David, 67622 Oldham Rd., Cambridge, OH, 43725, 740-432-7549

Mead, Dennis, 2250 E. Mercury St., Inverness, FL, 34453-0514

Myers, Ron, 6202 Marglenn Ave., Baltimore, MD, 21206, 410-866-6914

Saggio, Joe, 1450 Broadview Ave. #12, Columbus, OH, 43212, jvsag@webtv.net, www.j.v.saggio@worldnet.att.net, Handle Carver

Schlott, Harald, Zingster Str. 26, 13051 Berlin, GERMANY, 049 030 9293346, harald.schlott@T-online.de, Custom grinder, custom handle artisan, display case/box maker, etcher, scrimshander

Snell, Barry A., 4801 96th St. N., St. Petersburg, FL, 33708-3740

Vallotton, A., 621 Fawn Ridge Dr., Oakland, OR, 97462

Watson, Silvia, 350 Jennifer Lane, Driftwood, TX, 78619

Wilderness Forge, 315 North 100 East, Kanab, UT, 84741, 435-644-3674, bhatting@xpressweb.com

Williams, Gary, (GARBO), PO Box 210, Glendale, KY, 42740-2010

display cases and boxes

Bill's Custom Cases, P O Box 603, Montague, CA, 96064, 530-459-5968, billscustomcases@earthlink.net

Brooker, Dennis, Rt. 1, Box 12A, Derby, IA, 50068

Chas Clements' Custom Leathercraft, Chas, 1741 Dallas St., Aurora, CO, 80010-2018, 303-364-0403, GRYPHONS@HOME.NET, Display case/box maker, Leatherworker, Knife appraiser

Freund, Steve, Tomway LLC, 1646 Tichenor Court, Atlanta, GA, 30338, 770-393-8349, steve@tomway.com, www.tomway.com

Gimbert, Nelson, P.O. Box 787, Clemmons, NC, 27012

McLean, Lawrence, 12344 Meritage Ct, Rancho Cucamonga, CA, 91739, 714-848-5779, lmclean@charter.net

Miller, Michael K., M&M Kustom Krafts, 28510 Santiam Highway, Sweet Home, OR, 97386

Miller, Robert, P.O. Box 2722, Ormond Beach, FL, 32176

Retichek, Joseph L., W9377 Co. TK. D, Beaver Dam, WI, 53916

Robbins, Wayne, 11520 Inverway, Belvidere, IL, 61008

S&D Enterprises, 20 East Seventh St, Manchester, OH, 45144, 937-549-2602, 937-549-2602, sales@s-denterprises.com, www.s-denterprises.com, Display case/ box maker. Manufacturer of aluminum display, chipboard type displays, wood displays. Silk screening or acid etching for logos on product

Schlott, Harald, Zingster Str. 26, 13051 Berlin, GERMANY, 049 030 9293346, harald.schlott@T-online.de, Custom grinder, custom handle artisan, display case/box maker, etcher, scrimshander

engravers

Adlam, Tim, 1705 Witzel Ave., Oshkosh, WI, 54902, 920-235-4589, www.adlamngraving.com

Alfano, Sam, 36180 Henry Gaines Rd., Pearl River, LA, 70452

Allard, Gary, 2395 Battlefield Rd., Fishers Hill, VA, 22626

Alpen, Ralph, 7 Bentley Rd., West Grove, PA, 19390, 610-869-7141

Baron, David, Baron Technology Inc., 62 Spring Hill Rd., Trumbull, CT, 06611, 203-452-0515, bti@baronengraving.com, www.baronengraving.com, Polishing, plating, inlays, artwork

Bates, Billy, 2302 Winthrop Dr. SW, Decatur, AL, 35603, bbrn@aol.com, www.angelfire.com/al/billybates

Bettenhausen, Merle L., 17358 Ottawa, Tinley Park, IL, 60477

Blair, Jim, PO Box 64, 59 Mesa Verde, Glenrock, WY, 82637, 307-436-8115, jblairengrav@msn.com

Bonshire, Benita, 1121 Burlington, Muncie, IN, 47302

Boster, A.D., 3000 Clarks Bridge Rd Lot 42, Gainesville, GA, 30501, 770-532-0958

Brooker, Dennis B., Rt. 1 Box 12A, Derby, IA, 50068

Churchill, Winston G., RFD Box 29B, Proctorsville, VT, 05153

Collins, Michael, Rt. 3075, Batesville Rd., Woodstock, GA, 30188

Cupp, Alana, PO Box 207, Annabella, UT, 84711

Dashwood, Jim, 255 Barkham Rd., Wokingham, Berkshire RG11 4BY, ENGLAND

Dean, Bruce, 13 Tressider Ave., Haberfield, N.S.W. 2045, Sydney, AUSTRALIA, 02 97977608

DeLorge, Ed, 6734 W Main St, Houma, LA, 70360, 504-223-0206

Dickson, John W., PO Box 49914, Sarasota, FL, 34230

Dolbare, Elizabeth, PO Box 502, Dubois, WY, 82513-0502

Downing, Jim, PO Box 4224, Springfield, MO, 65808, 417-865-5953, www.thegunengraver.com, Scrimshander

Duarte, Carlos, 108 Church St., Rossville, CA, 95678

Dubben, Michael, 414 S. Fares Ave., Evansville, IN, 47714

Dubber, Michael W., 8205 Heather Pl, Evansville, IN, 47710-4919

Eklund, Maihkel, Föne 1111, S-82041 Färila, SWEDEN, www.art-knives.com

Eldridge, Allan, 1424 Kansas Lane, Gallatin, TN, 37066

Ellis, Willy B, Willy B's Customs by William B Ellis, 4941 Cardinal Trail, Palm Harbor, FL, 34683, 727-942-6420, www.willyb.com

Engel, Terry (Flowers), PO Box 96, Midland, OR, 97634

Flannery Engraving Co., Jeff, 11034 Riddles Run Rd., Union, KY, 41091, engraving@fuse.net, http://home.fuse.net/ engraving/

Foster, Norvell, Foster Enterprises, PO Box 200343, San Antonio, TX, 78220

Fountain Products, 492 Prospect Ave., West Springfield, MA, 01089

Gipe, Sandi, Rt. 2, Box 1090A, Kendrick, ID, 83537

Glimm, Jerome C., 19 S. Maryland, Conrad, MT, 59425

Gournet, Geoffroy, 820 Paxinosa Ave., Easton, PA, 18042, 610-559-0710, www.geoffroygournet.com

Halloran, Tim 316 Fence line Dr. Blue Grass, IA 52726 563-381-5202

Harrington, Fred A., Winter: 3725 Citrus, Summer: 2107 W Frances Rd Mt Morris MI 48458-8215, St. James City, FL, 33956, Winter: 239-283-0721 Summer: 810-686-3008

Henderson, Fred D., 569 Santa Barbara Dr., Forest Park, GA, 30297, 770-968-4866

Hendricks, Frank, 396 Bluff Trail, Dripping Springs, TX, 78620, 512-858-7828

Holder, Pat, 7148 W. Country Gables Dr., Peoria, AZ, 85381

Ingle, Ralph W., 151 Callan Dr., Rossville, GA, 30741, 706-858-0641, riengraver@aol.com, Photographer

Johns, Bill, 1716 8th St, Cody, WY, 82414, 307-587-5090

Kelly, Lance, 1723 Willow Oak Dr., Edgewater, FL, 32132

Kelso, Jim, 577 Coller Hill Rd, Worcester, VT, 05682

Koevenig, Eugene and Eve, Koevenig's Engraving Service, Rabbit Gulch, Box 55, Hill City, SD, 57745-0055

Kostelnik, Joe and Patty, RD #4, Box 323, Greensburg, PA, 15601

Kudlas, John M., 55280 Silverwolf Dr, Barnes, WI, 54873, 715-795-2031, jkudlas@cheqnet.net, Engraver, scrimshander

Limings Jr., Harry, 959 County Rd. 170, Marengo, OH, 43334-9625

Lindsay, Steve, 3714 West Cedar Hills Drive, Kearney, NE, 68847

Lyttle, Brian, Box 5697, High River AB CANADA, T1V 1M7

Lytton, Simon M., 19 Pinewood Gardens, Hemel Hempstead, Herts. HP1 1TN, ENGLAND

Mason, Joe, 146 Value Rd, Brandon, MS, 39042, 601-824-9867, www.joemasonengraving.com

McCombs, Leo, 1862 White Cemetery Rd., Patriot, OH, 45658

McDonald, Dennis, 8359 Brady St., Peosta, IA, 52068

McKenzie, Lynton, 6940 N Alvernon Way, Tucson, AZ, 85718

McLean, Lawrence, 12344 Meritage Ct, Rancho Cucamonga, CA, 91739, 714-848-5779, lmclean@charter.net

Meyer, Chris, 39 Bergen Ave., Wantage, NJ, 07461, 973-875-6299

Minnick, Joyce, 144 N. 7th St., Middletown, IN, 47356

Morgan, Tandie, P.O. Box 693, 30700 Hwy. 97, Nucla, CO, 81424

Morton, David A., 1110 W. 21st St., Lorain, OH, 44052

Moulton, Dusty, 135 Hillview Ln, Loudon, TN, 37774, 865-408-9779

Muller, Jody & Pat, PO Box 35, Pittsburg, MO, 65724, 417-852-4306/417-752-3260, mullerforge@hotmail.com, www.mullerforge.com

Nelida, Toniutti, via G. Pasconi 29/c, Maniago 33085 (PN), ITALY

Nilsson, Jonny Walker, Tingsstigen 11, SE-933 33 Arvidsjaur, SWEDEN, +(46) 960-13048, 0960.13048@telia.com, www.jwnknives.com

Nott, Ron, Box 281, Summerdale, PA, 17093

Parsons, Michael R., McKee Knives, 7042 McFarland Rd, Indianapolis, IN, 46227, 317-784-7943

Patterson, W.H., P.O. Drawer DK, College Station, TX, 77841

Peri, Valerio, Via Meucci 12, Gardone V.T. 25063, ITALY

Pilkington Jr., Scott, P.O. Box 97, Monteagle, TN, 37356, 931-924-3400, scott@pilkguns.com, www.pilkguns.com

Poag, James, RR1, Box 212A, Grayville, IL, 62844

Potts, Wayne, 1580 Meade St Apt A, Denver, CO, 80204

Rabeno, Martin, Spook Hollow Trading Co, 530 Eagle Pass, Durango, CO, 81301

Raftis, Andrew, 2743 N. Sheffield, Chicago, IL, 60614

Roberts, J.J., 7808 Lake Dr., Manassas, VA, 20111, 703-330-0448, jjrengraver@aol.com, www.angelfire.com/va2/ engraver

Robidoux, Roland J., DMR Fine Engraving, 25 N. Federal Hwy.

Studio 5, Dania, FL, 33004

Rosser, Bob, Hand Engraving, 2809 Crescent Ave Ste 20, Homewood, AL, 35209-2526, www.hand-engravers.com

Rudolph, Gil, 20922 Oak Pass Ave, Tehachapi, CA, 93561, 661-822-4949, www.gtraks@csurfers.net

Rundell, Joe, 6198 W. Frances Rd., Clio, MI, 48420

Schickl, L., Ottingweg 497, A-5580 Tamsweg, AUSTRIA, 0043 6474 8583, Scrimshander

Schlott, Harald, Zingster Str. 26, 13051 Berlin, GERMANY, 049 030 9293346, 049 030 9293346, harald.schlott@T-online. de, www.gravur-kunst-atelier.de.vu, Custom grinder, custom handle artisan, display case/box maker, etcher, scrimshander

Schönert, Elke, 18 Lansdowne Pl., Central, Port Elizabeth, SOUTH AFRICA

Shaw, Bruce, P.O. Box 545, Pacific Grove, CA, 93950, 831-646-1937, 831-644-0941

Shostle, Ben, 1121 Burlington, Muncie, IN, 47302

Slobodian, Barbara, 4101 River Ridge Dr., PO Box 1498, San Andreas, CA 95249, 209-286-1980, fax 209-286-1982, barbara@dancethetide.com. Specializes in Japanese-style engraving.

Smith, Ron, 5869 Straley, Ft. Worth, TX, 76114

Smitty's Engraving, 21320 Pioneer Circle, Hurrah, OK, 73045, 405-454-6968, smittys.engraving@prodigy.net, www.smittys-engraving.us

Spode, Peter, Tresaith Newland, Malvern, Worcestershire WR13 5AY, ENGLAND

Swartley, Robert D., 2800 Pine St., Napa, CA, 94558

Takeuchi, Shigetoshi, 21-14-1-Chome kamimuneoka Shiki shi, 353 Saitama, JAPAN

Theis, Terry, 21452 FM 2093, Harper, TX, 78631, 830-864-4438

Valade, Robert B., 931 3rd Ave., Seaside, OR, 97138, 503-738-7672, (503) 738-7672

Waldrop, Mark, 14562 SE 1st Ave. Rd., Summerfield, FL, 34491

Warenski, Julie, 590 East 500 N., Richfield, UT, 84701, 435-896-5319, julie@warenskiknives.com, www.warenskiknives.com

Warren, Kenneth W., P.O. Box 2842, Wenatchee, WA, 98807-2842, 509-663-6123, (509) 663-6123

Whitehead, James 2175 South Willow Ave. Space 22 Fresno, CA 93725 559-412-4374 jdwmks@yahoo.com

Whitmore, Jerry, 1740 Churchill Dr., Oakland, OR, 97462

Winn, Travis A., 558 E. 3065 S., Salt Lake City, UT, 84106

Wood, Mel, P.O. Box 1255, Sierra Vista, AZ, 85636

Zietz, Dennis, 5906 40th Ave., Kenosha, WI, 53144

Zima, Russ, 7291 Ruth Way, Denver, CO, 80221, 303-657-9378, www.rzengraving.com

etchers

Baron Technology Inc., David Baron, 62 Spring Hill Rd., Trumbull, CT, 06611

Fountain Products, 492 Prospect Ave., West Springfield, MA, 01089

Hayes, Dolores, P.O. Box 41405, Los Angeles, CA, 90041

Holland, Dennis, 4908 17th Pl., Lubbock, TX, 79416

Kelso, Jim, 577 Collar Hill Rd, Worcester, VT, 05682

Larstein, Francine, FRANCINE ETCHINGS & ETCHED KNIVES, 368 White Rd, Watsonville, CA, 95076, 800-557-1525/831-426-6046, 831-684-1949, francine@francinetchings.com, www.boyeknivesgallery.com

Lefaucheux, Jean-Victor, Saint-Denis-Le-Ferment, 27140 Gisors, FRANCE

Mead, Faustina L., 2550 E. Mercury St., Inverness, FL, 34453-0514, 352-344-4751, scrimsha@infionline.net, www.scrimshaw-by-faustina.com

Myers, Ron, 6202 Marglenn Ave., Baltimore, MD, 21206, (acid) etcher

Nilsson, Jonny Walker, Tingsstigen 11, SE-933 33 Arvidsjaur, SWEDEN, +(46) 960-13048, 0960.13048@telia.com, www.jwnknives.com

Schlott, Harald, Zingster Str. 26, 13051 Berlin, GERMANY, 049

030 9293346, harald.schlott@T-online.de, Custom grinder, custom handle artisan, display case/box maker, etcher, scrimshander
Vallotton, A., Northwest Knife Supply, 621 Fawn Ridge Dr., Oakland, OR, 97462
Watson, Silvia, 350 Jennifer Lane, Driftwood, TX, 78619

heat treaters

Bay State Metal Treating Co., 6 Jefferson Ave., Woburn, MA, 01801
Bos Heat Treating, Paul, Shop: 1900 Weld Blvd., El Cajon, CA, 92020, 619-562-2370 / 619-445-4740 Home, PaulBos@BuckKnives.com
Holt, B.R., 1238 Birchwood Drive, Sunnyvale, CA, 94089
Kazou, Okaysu, 12-2 1 Chome Higashi, Ueno, Taito-Ku, Tokyo, JAPAN, 81-33834-2323, 81-33831-3012
Metal Treating Bodycote Inc., 710 Burns St., Cincinnati, OH, 45204
O&W Heat Treat Inc., One Bidwell Rd., South Windsor, CT, 06074, 860-528-9239, (860) 291-9939, owht1@aol.com
Progressive Heat Treating Co., 2802 Charles City Rd, Richmond, VA, 23231, 804-545-0010, 804-545-0012
Texas Heat Treating Inc., 303 Texas Ave., Round Rock, TX, 78664
Texas Knifemakers Supply, 10649 Haddington, Suite 180, Houston, TX, 77043
Tinker Shop, The, 1120 Helen, Deer Park, TX, 77536
Valley Metal Treating Inc., 355 S. East End Ave., Pomona, CA, 91766
Wilderness Forge, 315 North 100 East, Kanab, UT, 84741, 435-644-3674, bhatting@xpressweb.com
Wilson, R.W., P.O. Box 2012, Weirton, WV, 26062

leather workers

Abramson, David, 116 Baker Ave, Wharton, NJ, 07885, lifter4him1@aol.com, www.liftersleather.com
Bruner, Rick, 7756 Aster Lane, Jenison, MI, 49428, 616-457-0403
Burrows, Chuck, dba Wild Rose Trading Co, 289 Laposta Canyon Rd, Durango, CO, 81303, 970-259-8396, chuck@wrtcleather.com
Clements' Custom Leathercraft, Chas, 1741 Dallas St., Aurora, CO, 80010-2018
Cole, Dave, 620 Poinsetta Dr., Satellite Beach, FL 32937, 321-773-1687, www.dcknivesandleather.blademakers.com. Custom sheath services.
Cooper, Harold, 136 Winding Way, Frankfort, KY, 40601
Cooper, Jim, 1221 Cook St, Ramona, CA, 92065-3214, 760-789-1097, 760-788-7992, jamcooper@aol.com
Cow Catcher Leatherworks, 3006 Industrial Dr, Raleigh, NC, 27609
Cubic, George, GC Custom Leather Co., 10561 E. Deerfield Pl., Tucson, AZ, 85749, 520-760-0695, gcubic@aol.com
Dawkins, Dudley, 221 N. Broadmoor Ave, Topeka, KS, 66606-1254, 785-235-3871, dawkind@sbcglobal.net, ABS member/ knifemaker forges straight knives
Evans, Scott V, Edge Works Mfg, 1171 Halltown Rd, Jacksonville, NC, 28546, 910-455-9834, (910) 346-5660, edgeworks@coastalnet.com, www.tacticalholsters.com
Genske, Jay, 283 Doty St, Fond du Lac, WI, 54935, 920-921-8019/Cell Phone 920-579-0144, jaygenske@hotmail.com, Custom Grinder, Custom Handle Artisan
Hawk, Ken, Rt. 1, Box 770, Ceres, VA, 24318-9630
Homyk, David N., 8047 Carriage Ln., Wichita Falls, TX, 76306
John's Custom Leather, John R. Stumpf, 523 S. Liberty St, Blairsville, PA, 15717, 724-459-6802, 724-459-5996
Kelley, Jo Ann, 52 Mourning Dove Dr., Watertown, WI 53094, 920-206-0807, ladybug@ticon.net, www.hembrookcustomknives.com. Custom leather knife sheaths $40 to $100; making sheaths since 2002.

Kravitt, Chris, HC 31 Box 6484, Rt 200, Ellsworth, ME, 04605-9805, 207-584-3000, 207-584-3000, sheathmkr@aol.com, www.treestumpleather.com, Reference: Tree Stump Leather
Larson, Richard, 549 E. Hawkeye, Turlock, CA, 95380
Layton, Jim, 2710 Gilbert Avenue, Portsmouth, OH, 45662
Lee, Randy, P.O. Box 1873, 270 N 9th West, St. Johns, AZ, 85936, 928-337-2594, 928-337-5002, randylee@randyleeknives.com, info@randyleeknives.com, Custom knifemaker; www.randyleeknives.com
Long, Paul, 108 Briarwood Ln W, Kerrville, TX, 78028, 830-367-5536, PFL@cebridge.net
Lott, Sherry, 1100 Legion Park Rd., Greenburg, KY 42743, phone 270-932-2212, fax 270-299-2471, sherrylott@alltel.net
Mason, Arne, 258 Wimer St., Ashland, OR, 97520, 541-482-2260, (541) 482-7785, www.arnemason.com
McGowan, Liz, 12629 Howard Lodge Dr., Winter Add-2023 Robin Ct Sebring FL 33870, Sykesville, MD, 21784, 410-489-4323
Metheny, H.A. "Whitey", 7750 Waterford Dr., Spotsylvania, VA, 22553, 540-582-3228 Cell 540-542-1440, 540-582-3095, nametheny@aol.com, www.methenyknives.com
Miller, Michael K., 28510 Santiam Highway, Sweet Home, OR, 97386
Mobley, Martha, 240 Alapaha River Road, Chula, GA, 31733
Morrissey, Martin, 4578 Stephens Rd., Blairsville, GA, 30512
Niedenthal, John Andre, Beadwork & Buckskin, Studio 3955 NW 103 Dr., Coral Springs, FL, 33065-1551, 954-345-0447, a_niedenthal@hotmail.com
Neilson, Tess, RR2 Box 16, Wyalusing, PA, 18853, 570-746-4944, www.mountainhollow.net, Doing business as Neilson's Mountain Hollow
Parsons, Larry, 1038 W. Kyle, Mustang, OK 73064 405-376-9408 s.m.parsons@sbcglobal.net
Parsons, Michael R., McKee Knives, 7042 McFarland Rd, Indianapolis, IN, 46227, 317-784-7943
Poag, James H., RR #1 Box 212A, Grayville, IL, 62844
Red's Custom Leather, Ed Todd, 9 Woodlawn Rd., Putnam Valley, NY, 10579, 845-528-3783
Rowe, Kenny, 3219 Hwy 29 South, Hope, AR, 71801, 870-777-8216, 870-777-0935, rowesleather@yahoo.com, www.knifeart.com or www.theedgeequipment.com
Schrap, Robert G., 7024 W. Wells St., Wauwatosa, WI, 53213-3717, 414-771-6472, (414) 479-9765, knifesheaths@aol.com, www.customsheaths.com
Strahin, Robert, 401 Center St., Elkins, WV, 26241, *Custom Knife Sheaths
Tierney, Mike, 447 Rivercrest Dr., Woodstock ON CANADA, N4S 5W5
Turner, Kevin, 17 Hunt Ave., Montrose, NY, 10548
Velasquez, Gil, 7120 Madera Dr., Goleta, CA, 93117
Walker, John, 17 Laber Circle, Little Rock, AR, 72210, 501-455-0239, john.walker@afbic.com
Watson, Bill, #1 Presidio, Wimberly, TX, 78676
Whinnery, Walt, 1947 Meadow Creek Dr., Louisville, KY, 40218
Williams, Sherman A., 1709 Wallace St., Simi Valley, CA, 93065

miscellaneous

Hendryx Design, Scott, 5997 Smokey Way, Boise, ID, 83714, 208-377-8044, www.shdsheaths@msn.com
Kydex Sheath Maker
Robertson, Kathy, Impress by Design, PO Box 1367, Evans, GA, 30809-1367, 706-650-0982, (706) 860-1623, impressbydesign@comcast.net, Advertising/graphic designer
Strahin, Robert, 401 Center St., Elkins, WV, 26241, 304-636-0128, rstrahin@copper.net, *Custom Knife Sheaths

photographers

Alfano, Sam, 36180 Henery Gaines Rd., Pearl River, LA, 70452
Allen, John, Studio One, 3823 Pleasant Valley Blvd., Rockford, IL, 61114

Balance Digital, Rob Szajkowski, 261 Riverview Way, Oceanside, CA 92057, 760-815-6131, rob@balancedigital.com, www.balancedigital.com

Bilal, Mustafa, Turk's Head Productions, 908 NW 50th St., Seattle, WA, 98107-3634, 206-782-4164, (206) 783-5677, mustafa@turkshead.com, www.turkshead.com, Graphic design, marketing & advertising

Bogaerts, Jan, Regenweg 14, 5757 Pl., Liessel, HOLLAND

Box Photography, Doug, 1804 W Main St, Brenham, TX, 77833-3420

Brown, Tom, 6048 Grants Ferry Rd., Brandon, MS, 39042-8136

Butman, Steve, P.O. Box 5106, Abilene, TX, 79608

Calidonna, Greg, 205 Helmwood Dr., Elizabethtown, KY, 42701

Campbell, Jim, 7935 Ranch Rd., Port Richey, FL, 34668

Cooper, Jim, Sharpbycoop.com photography, 9 Mathew Court, Norwalk, CT, 06851, jcooper@sharpbycoop.com, www.sharpbycoop.com

Courtice, Bill, P.O. Box 1776, Duarte, CA, 91010-4776

Crosby, Doug, RFD 1, Box 1111, Stockton Springs, ME, 04981

Danko, Michael, 3030 Jane Street, Pittsburgh, PA, 15203

Davis, Marshall B., P.O. Box 3048, Austin, TX, 78764

Earley, Don, 1241 Ft. Bragg Rd., Fayetteville, NC, 28305

Ehrlich, Linn M., 1850 N Clark St #1008, Chicago, IL, 60614, 312-209-2107

Etzler, John, 11200 N. Island Rd., Grafton, OH, 44044

Fahrner, Dave, 1623 Arnold St., Pittsburgh, PA, 15205

Faul, Jan W., 903 Girard St. NE, Rr. Washington, DC, 20017

Fedorak, Allan, 28 W. Nicola St., Amloops BC CANADA, V2C 1J6

Fox, Daniel, Lumina Studios, 6773 Industrial Parkway, Cleveland, OH, 44070, 440-734-2118, (440) 734-3542, lumina@en.com

Freiberg, Charley, PO Box 42, Elkins, NH, 03233, 603-526-2767, charleyfreiberg@tos.net

Gardner, Chuck, 116 Quincy Ave., Oak Ridge, TN, 37830

Gawryla, Don, 1105 Greenlawn Dr., Pittsburgh, PA, 15220

Goffe Photographic Associates, 3108 Monte Vista Blvd., NE, Albuquerque, NM, 87106

Graham, James, 7434 E Northwest Hwy, Dallas, TX, 75231, 214-341-5138, jamie@jamiephoto.com, www.jamiephoto.com, Product photographer

Graley, Gary W., RR2 Box 556, Gillett, PA, 16925

Griggs, Dennis, 118 Pleasant Pt Rd, Topsham, ME, 04086, 207-725-5689

Hanusin, John, Reames-Hanusin Studio, PO Box 931, Northbrook, IL, 60065 0931

Hardy, Scott, 639 Myrtle Ave., Placerville, CA, 95667

Hodge, Tom, 7175 S US Hwy 1 Lot 36, Titusville, FL, 32780-8172, 321-267-7989, egdoht@hotmail.com

Holter, Wayne V., 125 Lakin Ave., Boonsboro, MD, 21713, 301-416-2855, mackwayne@hotmail.com

Hopkins, David W, Hopkins Photography inc, 201 S Jefferson, Iola, KS, 66749, 620-365-7443, nhoppy@netks.net

Kerns, Bob, 18723 Birdseye Dr., Germantown, MD, 20874

LaFleur, Gordon, 111 Hirst, Box 1209, Parksville BC CANADA, V0R 270

Lear, Dale, 6544 Cora Mill Rd, Gallipolis, OH, 45631, 740-245-5482, dalelear@yahoo.com, Ebay Sales

LeBlanc, Paul, No. 3 Meadowbrook Cir., Melissa, TX, 75454

Lester, Dean, 2801 Junipero Ave Suite 212, Long Beach, CA, 90806-2140

Leviton, David A., A Studio on the Move, P.O. Box 2871, Silverdale, WA, 98383, 360-697-3452

Long, Gary W., 3556 Miller's Crossroad Rd., Hillsboro, TN, 37342

Long, Jerry, 402 E. Gladden Dr., Farmington, NM, 87401

Lum, Billy, 16307 Evening Star Ct., Crosby, TX, 77532

McCollum, Tom, P.O. Box 933, Lilburn, GA, 30226

Mitch Lum Website and Photography, 22115 NW Imbrie Dr. #298, Hillsboro, OR 97124, mitch@mitchlum.com, www.mitchlum.com, 206-356-6813

Moake, Jim, 18 Council Ave., Aurora, IL, 60504

Moya Inc., 4212 S. Dixie Hwy., West Palm Beach, FL, 33405

Norman's Studio, 322 S. 2nd St., Vivian, LA, 71082

Owens, William T., Box 99, Williamsburg, WV, 24991

Palmer Studio, 2008 Airport Blvd., Mobile, AL, 36606

Payne, Robert G., P.O. Box 141471, Austin, TX, 78714

Pigott, John, 9095 Woodprint LN, Mason, OH, 45040

Point Seven, 6450 Weatherfield Ct., Unit 2A, Maumee, OH, 43537, 419-243-8880, 877-787-3836, www.pointsevenstudios.com

Professional Medica Concepts, Patricia Mitchell, P.O. Box 0002, Warren, TX, 77664, 409-547-2213, pm0909@wt.net

Rasmussen, Eric L., 1121 Eliason, Brigham City, UT, 84302

Rhoades, Cynthia J., Box 195, Clearmont, WY, 82835

Rice, Tim, PO Box 663, Whitefish, MT, 59937

Richardson, Kerry, 2520 Mimosa St., Santa Rosa, CA, 95405, 707-575-1875, kerry@sonic.net, www.sonic.net/~kerry

Ross, Bill, 28364 S. Western Ave. Suite 464, Rancho Palos Verdes, CA, 90275

Rubicam, Stephen, 14 Atlantic Ave., Boothbay Harbor, ME, 04538-1202

Rush, John D., 2313 Maysel, Bloomington, IL, 61701

Schreiber, Roger, 429 Boren Ave. N., Seattle, WA, 98109

Semmer, Charles, 7885 Cyd Dr., Denver, CO, 80221

Silver Images Photography, 2412 N Keystone, Flagstaff, AZ, 86004

Slobodian, Scott, 4101 River Ridge Dr., P.O. Box 1498, San Andreas, CA, 95249, 209-286-1980, (209) 286-1982, www.slobodianswords.com

Smith, Earl W., 5121 Southminster Rd., Columbus, OH, 43221

Smith, Randall, 1720 Oneco Ave., Winter Park, FL, 32789

Storm Photo, 334 Wall St., Kingston, NY, 12401

Surles, Mark, P.O. Box 147, Falcon, NC, 28342

Third Eye Photos, 140 E. Sixth Ave., Helena, MT, 59601

Thurber, David, P.O. Box 1006, Visalia, CA, 93279

Tighe, Brian, RR 1, Ridgeville ON CANADA, L0S 1M0, 905-892-2734, www.tigheknives.com

Towell, Steven L., 3720 N.W. 32nd Ave., Camas, WA, 98607, 360-834-9049, sltowell@netscape.net

Valley Photo, 2100 Arizona Ave., Yuma, AZ, 85364

Verno Studio, Jay, 3030 Jane Street, Pittsburgh, PA, 15203

Ward, Chuck, 1010 E North St, PO Box 2272, Benton, AR, 72018, 501-778-4329, chuckbop@aol.com

Weyer International, 2740 Nebraska Ave., Toledo, OH, 43607, 800-448-8424, (419) 534-2697, law-weyerinternational@msn.com, Books

Wise, Harriet, 242 Dill Ave., Frederick, MD, 21701

Worley, Holly, Worley Photography, 6360 W David Dr, Littleton, CO, 80128-5708, 303-257-8091, 720-981-2800, hsworley@aol.com, Products, Digital & Film

scrimshanders

Adlam, Tim, 1705 Witzel Ave., Oshkosh, WI, 54902, 920-235-4589, www.adlamngraving.com

Alpen, Ralph, 7 Bentley Rd., West Grove, PA, 19390, 610-869-7141

Anderson, Terry Jack, 10076 Birnamwoods Way, Riverton, UT, 84065-9073

Bailey, Mary W., 3213 Jonesboro Dr., Nashville, TN, 37214, mbscrim@aol.com, www.members.aol.com/mbscrim/ scrim.html

Baker, Duane, 2145 Alum Creek Dr., Cambridge Park Apt. #10, Columbus, OH, 43207

Barrows, Miles, 524 Parsons Ave., Chillicothe, OH, 45601

Brady, Sandra, P.O. Box 104, Monclova, OH, 43542, 419-866-0435, (419) 867-0656, sandyscrim@hotmail.com, www.knifeshows.com

Beauchamp, Gaetan, 125 de la Riviere, Stoneham, PQ, G0A 4P0, CANADA, 418-848-1914, (418) 848-6859, knives@gbeauchamp.ca, www.beauchamp.cjb.net

Bellet, Connie, PO Box 151, Palermo, ME, 04354 0151, 207-993-2327, phwhitehawk@gwl.net

Benade, Lynn, 2610 Buckhurst Dr, Beachwood, OH, 44122, 216-464-0777, llbnc17@aol.com

Bonshire, Benita, 1121 Burlington Dr., Muncie, IN, 47302

Boone Trading Co. Inc., P.O. Box 669, Brinnon, WA, 98320, 800-423-1945, ww.boonetrading.com

Bryan, Bob, 1120 Oak Hill Rd., Carthage, MO, 64836

Burger, Sharon, Cluster Box 1625, Forest Hills/KLOOF 3624, KZN, South Africa, cell: +27 83 7891675, tel/fax: +27 31 7621349, scribble@iafrica.com, www.kgsa.co.za/members/sharonburger

Byrne, Mary Gregg, 1018 15th St., Bellingham, WA, 98225-6604

Cable, Jerry, 332 Main St., Mt. Pleasant, PA, 15666

Caudill, Lyle, 7626 Lyons Rd., Georgetown, OH, 45121

Cole, Gary, PO Box 668, Naalehu, HI, 96772, 808-929-9775, 808-929-7371, www.community.webshots.com/album/11836830uqyeejirsz

Collins, Michael, Rt. 3075, Batesville Rd., Woodstock, GA, 30188

Conover, Juanita Rae, P.O. Box 70442, Eugene, OR, 97401, 541-747-1726 or 543-4851, juanitaraeconover@yahoo.com

Courtnage, Elaine, Box 473, Big Sandy, MT, 59520

Cover Jr., Raymond A., Rt. 1, Box 194, Mineral Point, MO, 63660

Cox, J. Andy, 116 Robin Hood Lane, Gaffney, SC, 29340

Dietrich, Roni, Wild Horse Studio, 1257 Cottage Dr, Harrisburg, PA, 17112, 717-469-0587, ronimd@aol

DiMarzo, Richard, 2357 Center Place, Birmingham, AL, 35205

Dolbare, Elizabeth, PO Box 502, Dubois, WY, 82513-0502

Eklund, Maihkel, Föne 1111, S-82041 Färila, SWEDEN, +46 6512 4192, maihkel.eklund@swipnet.se, www.art-knives.com

Eldridge, Allan, 1424 Kansas Lane, Gallatin, TN, 37066

Ellis, Willy b, Willy B's Customs by William B Ellis, 4941 Cardinal Trail, Palm Harbor, FL, 34683, 727-942-6420, www.willyb.com

Fisk, Dale, Box 252, Council, ID, 83612, dafisk@ctcweb.net

Foster Enterprises, Norvell Foster, P.O. Box 200343, San Antonio, TX, 78220

Fountain Products, 492 Prospect Ave., West Springfield, MA, 01089

Gill, Scott, 925 N. Armstrong St., Kokomo, IN, 46901

Halligan, Ed, 14 Meadow Way, Sharpsburg, GA, 30277, ehkiss@bellsouth.net

Hands, Barry Lee, 26192 East Shore Route, Bigfork, MT, 59911

Hargraves Sr., Charles, RR 3 Bancroft, Ontario CANADA, K0L 1C0

Harless, Star, c/o Arrow Forge, P.O. Box 845, Stoneville, NC, 27048-0845

Harrington, Fred A., Summer: 2107 W Frances Rd, Mt Morris MI 48458 8215, Winter: 3725 Citrus, St. James City, FL, 33956, Winter 239-283-0721, Summer 810-686-3008

Hergert, Bob, 12 Geer Circle, Port Orford, OR, 97465, 541-332-3010, hergert@harborside.com, www.scrimshander.com

Hielscher, Vickie, 6550 Otoe Rd, P.O. Box 992, Alliance, NE, 69301, 308-762-4318, g-hielsc@bbcwb.net

High, Tom, 5474 S. 112.8 Rd., Alamosa, CO, 81101, 719-589-2108, scrimshaw@vanion.com, www.rockymountainscrimshaw.com, Wildlife Artist

Himmelheber, David R., 11289 40th St. N., Royal Palm Beach, FL, 33411

Holland, Dennis K., 4908-17th Place, Lubbock, TX, 79416

Hutchings, Rick "Hutch", 3007 Coffe Tree Ct, Crestwood, KY, 40014, 502-241-2871, baron1@bellsouth.net

Imboden II, Howard L., 620 Deauville Dr., Dayton, OH, 45429, 937-439-1536, Guards by the "Last Wax Technic"

Johnson, Corinne, W3565 Lockington, Mindora, WI, 54644

Johnston, Kathy, W. 1134 Providence, Spokane, WA, 99205

Karst Stone, Linda, 903 Tanglewood Ln, Kerrville, TX, 78028-2945, 830-896-4678, 830-257-6117, karstone@ktc.com

Kelso, Jim, 577 Coller Hill Rd, Worcester, VT, 05682

Kirk, Susan B., 1340 Freeland Rd., Merrill, MI, 48637

Koevenig, Eugene and Eve, Koevenig's Engraving Service, Rabbit Gulch, Box 55, Hill City, SD, 57745-0055

Kostelnik, Joe and Patty, RD #4, Box 323, Greensburg, PA, 15601

Lemen, Pam, 3434 N. Iroquois Ave., Tucson, AZ, 85705

Martin, Diane, 28220 N. Lake Dr., Waterford, WI, 53185

McDonald, René Cosimini-, 14730 61 Court N., Loxahatchee, FL, 33470

McFadden, Berni, 2547 E Dalton Ave, Dalton Gardens, ID, 83815-9631

McGowan, Frank, 12629 Howard Lodge Dr., Winter Add-2023 Robin Ct Sebring FL 33870, Sykesville, MD, 21784, 863-385-1296

McGrath, Gayle, PMB 232 15201 N Cleveland Ave, N Ft Myers, FL, 33903

McLaran, Lou, 603 Powers St., Waco, TX, 76705

McWilliams, Carole, P.O. Box 693, Bayfield, CO, 81122

Mead, Faustina L., 2550 E. Mercury St., Inverness, FL, 34453-0514, 352-344-4751, scrimsha@infionline.net, www.scrimshaw-by-faustina.com

Mitchell, James, 1026 7th Ave., Columbus, GA, 31901

Moore, James B., 1707 N. Gillis, Stockton, TX, 79735

Ochonicky, Michelle "Mike", Stone Hollow Studio, 31 High Trail, Eureka, MO, 63025, 636-938-9570, www.bestofmissourihands.com

Ochs, Belle, 124 Emerald Lane, Largo, FL, 33771, 727-530-3826, chuckandbelle@juno.com, www.oxforge.com

Pachi, Mirella, Via Pometta 1, 17046 Sassello (SV), ITALY, 019 720086, WWW.PACHI-KNIVES.COM

Parish, Vaughn, 103 Cross St., Monaca, PA, 15061

Peterson, Lou, 514 S. Jackson St., Gardner, IL, 60424

Poag, James H., RR #1 Box 212A, Grayville, IL, 62844

Polk, Trena, 4625 Webber Creek Rd., Van Buren, AR, 72956

Purvis, Hilton, P.O. Box 371, Noordhoek, 7979, SOUTH AFFRIC, 27 21 789 1114, hiltonp@telkomsa.net, www.kgsa.co.za/member/hiltonpurvis

Ramsey, Richard, 8525 Trout Farm Rd, Neosho, MO, 64850

Ristinen, Lori, 14256 County Hwy 45, Menahga, MN, 56464, 218-538-6608, lori@loriristinen.com, www.loriristinen.com

Roberts, J.J., 7808 Lake Dr., Manassas, VA, 22111, 703-330-0448, jjrengraver@aol.com, www.angelfire.com/va2/ engraver

Rudolph, Gil, 20922 Oak Pass Ave, Tehachapi, CA, 93561, 661-822-4949, www.gtraks@csurfers.net

Rundell, Joe, 6198 W. Frances Rd., Clio, MI, 48420

Saggio, Joe, 1450 Broadview Ave. #12, Columbus, OH, 43212, 614-481-1967, jvsaggio@earthlink.net, www.j.v.saggio@worldnet.att.net

Sahlin, Viveca, Konstvaktarevagem 9, S-772 40 Grangesberg, SWEDEN, 46 240 23204, www.scrimart.use

Satre, Robert, 518 3rd Ave. NW, Weyburn SK CANADA, S4H 1R1

Schlott, Harald, Zingster Str. 26, 13051 Berlin, 929 33 46, GERMANY, 049 030 9293346, 049 030 9293346, harald.schlott@t-online.de, www.gravur-kunst-atelier.de.vu

Schulenburg, E.W., 25 North Hill St., Carrollton, GA, 30117

Schwallie, Patricia, 4614 Old Spartanburg Rd. Apt. 47, Taylors, SC, 29687

Selent, Chuck, P.O. Box 1207, Bonners Ferry, ID, 83805

Semich, Alice, 10037 Roanoke Dr., Murfreesboro, TN, 37129

Shostle, Ben, 1121 Burlington, Muncie, IN, 47302

Smith, Peggy, 676 Glades Rd., #3, Gatlinburg, TN, 37738

Smith, Ron, 5869 Straley, Ft. Worth, TX, 76114

Stahl, John, Images In Ivory, 2049 Windsor Rd., Baldwin, NY, 11510, 516-223-5007, imivory@msn.com, www.imagesinivory.org

Steigerwalt, Jim, RD#3, Sunbury, PA, 17801

Stuart, Stephen, 15815 Acorn Circle, Tavares, FL, 32778, 352-343-8423, (352) 343-8916, inkscratch@aol.com

Talley, Mary Austin, 2499 Countrywood Parkway, Memphis, TN, 38016, matalley@midsouth.rr.com

Thompson, Larry D., 23040 Ave. 197, Strathmore, CA, 93267

Toniutti, Nelida, Via G. Pascoli, 33085 Maniago-PN, ITALY

Trout, Lauria Lovestrand, 1555 Delaney Dr, No. 1723, Talahassee, FL, 32309, 850-893-8836, mayalaurie@aol.com

Tucker, Steve, 3518 W. Linwood, Turlock, CA, 95380

Tyser, Ross, 1015 Hardee Court, Spartanburg, SC, 29303

Velasquez, Gil, Art of Scrimshaw, 7120 Madera Dr., Goleta, CA, 93117

Wilderness Forge, 475 NE Smith Rock Way, Terrebonne, OR, 97760, bhatting@xpressweb.com

Williams, Gary, PO Box 210, Glendale, KY, 42740, 270-369-6752, garywilliam@alltel.net

Winn, Travis A., 558 E. 3065 S., Salt Lake City, UT, 84106

Young, Mary, 4826 Storeyland Dr., Alton, IL, 62002

organizations

AMERICAN BLADESMITH SOCIETY
c/o Jan DuBois; PO Box 1481; Cypress, TX 77410-1481; 281-225-9159; Web: www.americanbladesmith.com

AMERICAN KNIFE & TOOL INSTITUTE***
David Kowalski, Comm. Coordinator, AKTI; DEPT BL2, PO Box 432, Iola, WI 54945-0432;715-445-3781; Web: communications@akti.org; www. akti.org

AMERICAN KNIFE THROWERS ALLIANCE
c/o Bobby Branton; 4976 Seewee Rd; Awendaw, SC 29429; www.AKTA-USA.com

ARIZONA KNIFE COLLECTOR'S ASSOCIATION
c/o D'Alton Holder, President, 7148 W. Country Gables Dr., Peoria, AZ 85381; Web: www.akca.net

ART KNIFE COLLECTOR'S ASSOCIATION
c/o Mitch Weiss, Pres.; 2211 Lee Road, Suite 104; Winter Park, FL 32789

BAY AREA KNIFE COLLECTOR'S ASSOCIATION
Doug Isaacson, B.A.K.C.A. Membership, 36774 Magnolia, Newark, CA 94560; Web: www.bakca.org

ARKANSAS KNIFEMAKERS ASSOCIATION
David Etchieson, 60 Wendy Cove, Conway, AR 72032; Web: www.arkansasknifemakers.com

AUSTRALASIAN KNIFE COLLECTORS
PO BOX 149 CHIDLOW 6556 WESTERN AUSTRALIA TEL: (08) 9572 7255; FAX: (08) 9572 7266. International Inquiries: TEL: + 61 8 9572 7255; FAX: + 61 8 9572 7266, akc@knivesaustralia.com.au

CALIFORNIA KNIFEMAKERS ASSOCIATION
c/o Clint Breshears, Membership Chairman; 1261 Keats St; Manhattan Beach CA 90266; 310-372-0739; breshears@mindspring.com
Dedicated to teaching and improving knifemaking

CANADIAN KNIFEMAKERS GUILD
c/o Peter Wile; RR # 3; Bridgewater N.S. CANADA B4V 2W2; 902-543-1373; www.ckg.org

CUSTOM KNIFE COLLECTORS ASSOCIATION
c/o Jim Treacy, PO Box 5893, Glen Allen, VA 23058-5893; E-mail: customknifecollectorsassociation@yahoo.com; Web: www.customknifecollectorsassociation.com
The purpose of the CKCA is to recognize and promote the artistic significance of handmade knives, to advnace their collection and conservation, and to support the creative expression of those who make them. Open to collectors, makers purveyors, and other collectors. Has members from eight countries. Produced a calednar which features custom knives either owned or made by CKCA members.

CUTTING EDGE, THE
1920 N 26th St, Lowell, AR 72745; 479-631-0055; 479-636-4618; ce-info@cuttingedge.com
After-market knives since 1968. We offer about 1,000 individual knives each month. The oldest and the most experienced in the business of buying and selling knives. We buy collections of any size, take knives on consignment or we will trade. Web: www.cuttingedge.com

FLORIDA KNIFEMAKERS ASSOCIATION
c/o President, Dan Mink, PO Box 861, Crystal beach, Florida, 34681 (727) 786 5408; Web: www.floridaknifemakers.org

JAPANESE SWORD SOCIETY OF THE U.S.
PO Box 712; Breckenridge, TX 76424

KNIFE COLLECTORS CLUB INC, THE
1920 N 26th St; Lowell AR 72745; 479-631-0130; 479-631-8493; ag@agrussell.com; Web:www.club@k-c-c.com
The oldest and largest association of knife collectors. Issues limited edition knives, both handmade and highest quality production, in very limited numbers. The very earliest was the CM-1, Kentucky Rifle

KNIFE WORLD
PO Box 3395; Knoxville, TN 37927; 800-828-7751; 865-397-1955; 865-397-1969; knifepub@knifeworld.com
Publisher of monthly magazine for knife enthusiasts and world's largest knife/cutlery bookseller. Web: www.knifeworld.com

KNIFEMAKERS GUILD
c/o Beverly Imel, Knifemakers Guild, Box 922, New Castle, IN 47362; (765) 529-1651; Web: www.knifemakersguild.com

KNIFEMAKERS GUILD OF SOUTHERN AFRICA, THE
c/o Carel Smith; PO Box 1744; Delmars 2210; SOUTH AFRICA; carelsmith@therugby.co.za; Web:www.kgsa.co.za

KNIVES ILLUSTRATED
265 S. Anita Dr., Ste. 120; Orange, CA 92868; 714-939-9991; 714-939-9909; knivesillustrated@yahoo.com; Web:www.knivesillustrated.com
All encompassing publication focusing on factory knives, new handmades, shows and industry news, plus knifemaker features, new products, and travel pieces

MONTANA KNIFEMAKERS' ASSOCIATION, THE
14440 Harpers Bridge Rd; Missoula, MT 59808; 406-543-0845
Annual book of custom knife makers' works and directory of knife making supplies; $19.99

NATIONAL KNIFE COLLECTORS ASSOCIATION
PO Box 21070; Chattanooga, TN 37424; 423-892-5007; 423-899-9456; info@nationalknife.org; Web: www.nationalknife.org

NEO-TRIBAL METALSMITHS
PO Box 44095; Tucson, AZ 85773-4095; Web: www.neo-tribalmetalsmiths.com

NEW ENGLAND CUSTOM KNIFE ASSOCIATION
George R. Rebello, President; 686 Main Rd; Brownville, ME 04414; Web: www.knivesby.com/necka.html

NORTH CAROLINA CUSTOM KNIFEMAKERS GUILD
c/o 2112 Windy Woods Drive, Raleigh, NC 27607 (919) 834-4693; Web: www.nckniveguild.org

NORTH STAR BLADE COLLECTORS
PO Box 20523, Bloomington, MN 55420

OHIO KNIFEMAKERS ASSOCIATION
c/o Jerry Smith, Anvils and Ink Studios, P.O. Box 7887, Columbus, Ohio 43229-7887; Web: www.geocities.com/ohioknives/

OREGON KNIFE COLLECTORS ASSOCIATION
Web: www.oregonknifeclub.org

RANDALL KNIFE SOCIETY
PO Box 158, Meadows of Dan, VA 24120 email: payrks@gate.net; Web: www.randallknifesociety.com

ROCKY MOUNTAIN BLADE COLLECTORS ASSOCIATION
Mike Moss. Pres., P.O. Box 324, Westminster, CO 80036

RESOURCE GUIDE AND NEWSLETTER / AUTOMATIC KNIVES
2269 Chestnut St., Suite 212; San Francisco, CA 94123; 415-731-0210; Web: www.thenewsletter.com

SOUTH CAROLINA ASSOCIATION OF KNIFEMAKERS
c/o Victor Odom, Jr., Post Office Box 572, North, SC 29112 (803) 247-5614; Web: www.scak.org

SOUTHERN CALIFORNIA BLADES
SC Blades, PO Box 1140, Lomita, CA 90717; Web: www.scblades.com

TEXAS KNIFEMAKERS & COLLECTORS ASSOCIATION
2254 Fritz Allen Street, Fort Worth, Texas 76114; Web: www.tkca.org

TACTICAL KNIVES
Harris Publications; 1115 Broadway; New York, NY 10010; Web: www.tacticalknives.com

TRIBAL NOW!
Neo-Tribal Metalsmiths; PO Box 44095; Tucson, AZ 85733-4095; Web: www.neo-tribalmetalsmiths.com

WEYER INTERNATIONAL BOOK DIVISION
2740 Nebraska Ave; Toledo, OH 43607-3245; Web: www.weyerinternational.com

publications

BLADE
700 E. State St., Iola, WI 54990-0001; 715-445-2214; Web: www.blademag.com
The world's No. 1 knife magazine

CUTLERY NEWS JOURNAL (BLOG)
www.cutlerynewsjournal.blog
Covers significant happenings from the world of knife collecting, in addition to editorials, trends, events, auctions, shows, cutlery history, and reviews

KNIFE WORLD
PO Box 3395, Knoxville, TN 37927; www.knifeworld.com

KNIVES ILLUSTRATED
265 S. Anita Dr., Ste. 120, Orange, CA 92868; 714-939-9991; knivesillustrated@yahoo.com; Web: www.knivesillustrated.com
All encompassing publication focusing on factory knives, new handmades, shows and industry news

RESOURCE GUIDE AND NEWSLETTER / AUTOMATIC KNIVES
2269 Chestnut St., Suite 212, San Francisco, CA 94123; 415-731-0210; Web: www.thenewsletter.com

TACTICAL KNIVES
Harris Publications, 1115 Broadway, New York, NY 10010; Web: www.tacticalknives.com

WEYER INTERNATIONAL BOOK DIVISION
2740 Nebraska Ave., Toledo, OH 43607-3245